WILLS, TRUSTS, AND ESTATES

Examples and Explanations

WILLS, TRUSTS, AND ESTATES

Examples and Explanations

Gerry W. Beyer

Professor of Law
St. Mary's University School of Law

ASPEN LAW & BUSINESS
A Division of Aspen Publishers, Inc.
Gaithersburg   New York

Permissions
Aspen Law & Business
1185 Avenue of the Americas
New York, NY 10036

Printed in the United States of America

ISBN 0-7355-0061-4

2 3 4 5 6 7 8 9 0

Library of Congress Cataloging-in-Publication Data

Beyer, Gerry W.
  Wills, trusts, and estates: examples and explanations / Gerry W. Beyer.
    p.   cm.
  Includes bibliographical references and index.
  ISBN 0-7355-0061-4 (alk. paper)
  1. Wills—United States—Outlines, syllabi, etc. 2. Trusts and trustees—United States—Outlines, syllabi, etc. 3. Estate planning—United States—Outlines, syllabi, etc. I. Title.
KF755.Z9B49 1999
346.7305—dc21   98-55960
                                                                CIP

About Aspen Law & Business
Legal Education Division

In 1996, Aspen Law & Business welcomed the Law School Division of Little, Brown and Company into its growing business — already established as a leading provider of practical information to legal practitioners.

Acquiring much more than a prestigious collection of educational publications by the country's foremost authors, Aspen Law & Business inherited the long-standing Little, Brown tradition of excellence — born over 150 years ago. As one of America's oldest and most venerable publishing houses, Little, Brown and Company commenced in a world of change and challenge, innovation and growth. Sharing that same spirit, Aspen Law & Business has dedicated itself to continuing and strengthening the integrity begun so many years ago.

ASPEN LAW & BUSINESS
A Division of Aspen Publishers, Inc.
A Wolters Kluwer Company

Summary of Contents

Contents

Contents

Contents

Contents

Permissions
Aspen Law & Business
1185 Avenue of the Americas
New York, NY 10036

Printed in the United States of America

ISBN 0-7355-0061-4

2 3 4 5 6 7 8 9 0

Library of Congress Cataloging-in-Publication Data

Beyer, Gerry W.
    Wills, trusts, and estates: examples and explanations / Gerry W. Beyer.
        p.   cm.
    Includes bibliographical references and index.
    ISBN 0-7355-0061-4 (alk. paper)
    1. Wills—United States—Outlines, syllabi, etc. 2. Trusts and trustees—United States—Outlines, syllabi, etc. 3. Estate planning—United States—Outlines, syllabi, etc. I. Title.
KF755.Z9B49 1999
346.7305—dc21   98-55960
                                                                            CIP

Part Five
TRUSTS   297

Chapter 18. Introduction to Trusts   299

Chapter 19. Trust Creation   307

Contents

Contents

Contents

Preface

Wills, Trusts, and Estates: Examples and Explanations covers intestate succession, wills, trusts, estate administration, nonprobate assets, wealth transfer taxation, disability and death planning, and malpractice and professional responsibility. I designed this book to augment Wills, Trusts, and Estates and related courses that expose students to estate planning, decedents' estates, and trusts. This book also provides essential background and review material for students taking advanced courses in estate planning and wealth transfer taxation. The discussion, along with the examples and explanations, covers both the theoretical and practical applications of the legal concepts.

I have attempted to present the material in a lively, lucid, and conversational style to grab and hold your interest. Sections begin typically with a discussion of the applicable concept (including policies and basic "rules") followed by a series of examples (hypothetical questions) accompanied by explanations (answers). I am confident that this "learning-by-doing" approach will enable you to master the concepts and enjoy yourself in the process. The exercises in this book also let you evaluate how well you can apply what you have learned.

Working through problems is one of the best ways to understand intestacy, wills, and trusts concepts. For example, it is one thing to learn about per stirpes, per capita, per capita by representation, and per capita at each generation in the abstract but the differences really strike home only when you see the tremendous impact they can make on an heir's inheritance depending on which view is adopted by local law. Likewise, full appreciation of concepts such as exoneration, ademption, abatement, and lapse cannot be achieved until you see their effect on the distribution of a testator's estate.

Practical suggestions are liberally sprinkled throughout the book. You will also find sample will and trust provisions. These features should help you to appreciate the "real world" application of your law school course and help motivate you to study. Wills, trusts, and estates is the only subject that will apply to all of your clients eventually. As Shakespeare wrote in *King Henry IV,* "death . . . is certain to all, all shall die." You can appreciate the value of being able to draft wills and trusts which avert legal problems and help alleviate some of the emotional stress and financial costs surrounding this undeniable and inescapable fact.

Organization and Scope of This Book

Part One focuses on intestate succession. Issues relating to the distribution schemes for property are covered first, followed by how different types of persons (e.g., adopted children and children born out of wedlock) fit into these schemes. Part One ends with a discussion of assorted intestate succession issues such as advancements and disclaimers.

Part Two is the book's comprehensive coverage of wills. The first chapter details the requirements of a valid will followed by chapters exploring changes in the testator's circumstances, will revocation, will interpretation and construction, and will contests.

Part Three presents an overview of estate administration. As the details of administration are heavily dependent on local law, this section is relatively brief and highlights the typical procedure and the issues that frequently arise.

Part Four deals with nonprobate transfers such as inter vivos gifts, joint tenancies, multiple-party accounts, life insurance, and annuities. These assets must be removed from the decedent's holdings at death before applying the terms of the applicable intestacy statute or will to determine the property's new owner.

Part Five examines trusts beginning with reasons people use trusts, trust creation issues, trust administration matters, and trust enforcement methods. Subsequent chapters discuss the related topics of resulting and constructive trusts.

Part Six covers other estate planning concerns. This part includes discussions of (1) the basics of federal gift and estate taxation to familiarize you with fundamental concepts such as the annual exclusion, unified credit, marital deduction, and by-pass planning; (2) methods available to plan for a person's property management and health care decisions upon disability, as well as the death event itself, including durable powers of attorney, living wills, anatomical gift documents, and instruments to control the final disposition of the body; and (3) a discussion of negligent will and trust drafting and a review of the most common ethical concerns that arise in a wills, estates, and trusts practice.

How to Use This Book

Wills, Trusts, and Estates: Examples and Explanations is designed to be used in three ways:

Read in the order presented. You may study the material in the order presented. This order is designed to trace the traditional organization of wills, trusts, and estates casebooks and law school courses. An alternative approach, gaining in popularity, is to cover the nonprobate assets discussed in Part Four first, because these assets are removed from a decedent's estate before the rules of intestate succession or the terms of the decedent's will are applied.

Read in the order covered by your professor. You may read the material in the order covered by your professor in class. Using the Table of Contents as a guide, you should have no difficulty correlating your professor's syllabus with the relevant chapters of this book.

Use as a reference tool. You may use the book to assist your study on an issue-by-issue basis. Consult the comprehensive Index to quickly locate the material relevant to your inquiry.

Recommendations and Advice

Probate law is very dependent on state law. A will valid in one state may be totally ineffectual in another. If you already know the state in which you intend to practice, you may want to obtain a copy of your state's probate code and see how the examples discussed in this book would be resolved under your state's law. You will then be in a better position to give advice to your future clients. In addition, you will have an easier time preparing for and taking the bar exam because the bar examiners of almost every state regularly test on wills, estates, and trusts.

Many professors teaching wills and trusts require their students to purchase a copy of the Uniform Probate Code so that they have a common statute to examine. To aid in this process, this book makes frequent reference to the relevant UPC provisions from the Official 1993 Text. Please note, however, that this book is not designed to provide a comprehensive review of probate law as set forth in the UPC because only about fifteen states have enacted some version of the UPC.

Although the basic law of wills, trusts, and estates is relatively static, significant developments frequently occur. If you would like a free e-mail update containing recent developments, please direct your request to me at gbeyer@alvin.stmarytx.edu. In addition, if you detect any problems with this book or have suggestions for future editions, I would greatly appreciate your sharing them with me.

Good luck in your course and in your legal career.

St. Mary's University   GERRY W. BEYER
February 1999

Acknowledgments

The author wishes to thank the following individuals for their assistance in the preparation of this book.

Aspen Law & Business Personnel: Jessica Barmack, Teresa Chimienti, Sandy Doherty, Joan Horan, Megan A. Hughes.

Attorneys & Professors: Professor Mark Cochran (St. Mary's University); Professor Aloysius A. Leopold (St. Mary's University); Lee C. Schwemer, Esq. (Fort Worth, Texas).

Student Assistants: Kimberly D. Brooks (Southern Methodist University); Stacey Cunningham (Southern Methodist University); Kyle Dundon (Southern Methodist University); Ellen M. Ferris (Southern Methodist University); Andrew Gilbert (St. Mary's University); John T. Hubert (St. Mary's University); Kimberly M. Isaacs (St. Mary's University); Jennifer Jeffress (Southern Methodist University); Heather Y. Kaufman (Southern Methodist University); Stephen Kennedy (St. Mary's University); James G. M. Lenschau (Southern Methodist University); Jana Maeda (Southern Methodist University); Alexandria Hien Nguyen (Southern Methodist University); David Ovard (Southern Methodist University); Michael K. Pinkus (Southern Methodist University); Paul K. Roberts (St. Mary's University); Lynne M. Thomas (St. Mary's University); Ryan Kellus Turner (Southern Methodist University); Coby Waddill (St. Mary's University).

WILLS, TRUSTS, AND ESTATES

Examples and Explanations

1

Introduction and Overview

§1.1 Brief History of Property Transference When Owner Dies

Possessions. Property ownership. Think about all the things you own: clothes, a car, jewelry, a television, a computer, a stereo system, a home, and even this book. Barring bankruptcy, excessive spending habits, natural disasters, thievery, or large expenses such as those associated with a long-term illness, you will continue to accumulate possessions and will own more property as you grow older. When the inevitable comes and you are metabolically challenged, who will take over as the new owner of what you have left behind?

Early in the history of mankind, owning property was not a concern. Ancient peoples were nomadic and thus real property ownership was not an issue. There was just personal property such as clothes, weapons, farm implements, food preparation equipment, and perhaps some jewelry or other ornamentation. Where did this stuff go when the owner died? Before organized civilizations developed, the first person who picked up a deceased person's property after the person died would become the new owner. Just as they do today, some people died at the hands of the person who wanted to be the owner of their property. As people banded together in groups for camaraderie and survival, they needed to develop rules for the transmission of property upon death. An uncontrolled scramble for a decedent's property would not be conducive to harmonious living.

In many of these early cultures, the family ownership model of personal property prevailed. When a person died, there was no need for a formal

1

transfer of property because the property belonged to the family, rather than the deceased individual. As civilizations developed, however, many recognized individual property ownership and thus more sophisticated methods for handling the transfer of ownership became necessary.

Some societies sidestepped the property transfer issue by including the deceased person's property in the decedent's place of burial, be it a simple burial mound or a sophisticated tomb such as a pyramid. This procedure allowed the decedent to take the property with him or her to an after-life existence or use it upon returning to this world. Although the burying of property with a deceased person is now viewed as an inefficient use of resources, many cultures still include some of a decedent's property with the decedent. For example, people following western religions are often buried in favorite clothes or jewelry, and Native American ceremonies may include the burial of certain personal items with the deceased.

Most cultures eventually had to decide who among the survivors should have ownership of a decedent's property. Accordingly, either by custom or through more formal mechanisms, societies devised a fixed set of rules to control property transference. These rules typically stressed the importance of family relationships, but the way in which family relationships were determined varied tremendously among different societies. For example, some determined relationships through the mother's side of the family while others stressed the father's side. Rules often varied depending on the age or sex of the surviving family members. The rules were typically rigid and did not allow for alteration due to the circumstances or the desires of the decedent. These rules evolved into what we now call *intestate succession* or *descent and distribution*.

Societies also developed methods for a person to issue instructions while alive that would specify the new owners of the person's property upon death. This power of testation has a basis in Egyptian society perhaps as long ago as 2900 B.C. Greek and Roman civilizations had extensive rules regarding wills; you can even find translations of wills of people such as Aristotle and Plato. The development of wills at common law began in the Anglo-Saxon era, grew after the Norman Conquest of 1066 A.D., and was formally codified in 1540 in the English Statute of Wills, the precursor to the modern law of wills.

§1.2 Basic Terminology Used in This Book

Before continuing, we must have a common basis of communication. To do this, you need to be familiar with some basic terminology. This section contains lists of the fundamental terms used in this book for intestate succession, wills, and trusts along with some general terms. As you proceed through the book, you will learn scores of additional terms and nuances to the definitions provided here. This section will give you a foundation on which to base the rest of our discussion. If you are interested in the meaning of a term not defined in this section, need additional information, or have difficulty finding a term because the terms in these subsections are in a pedagogical rather than alphabetical order, check the index in the back of this book for the appropriate page references.

§1.2.1 *Intestate Succession Terms*

Intestate Succession; Intestacy; Descent and Distribution. Passage of property when the decedent dies without a valid will.

Descent. Succession to real property. (Please do not spell this term "d-i-s-s-e-n-t.") Compare *Distribution*.

Distribution. Succession to personal property. Compare *Descent*.

Intestate. Dying without a will. The term also refers to the person who dies intestate. Compare *Testator*.

Heir. A person entitled to take under intestate succession laws. Remember, you have no heirs because you are alive. You may be an heir (i.e., inherit from a person who dies intestate), but you cannot have heirs. The persons who would be your heirs if you were to die intestate are often called your *presumptive heirs* or your *heirs apparent*. At old common law, heirs referred to people who took land while the term *next of kin* referred to people who took personal property. (Please do not refer to persons who take under a will as heirs.) Compare *Beneficiary* as defined in §1.2.2, below.

Ancestor. A person related to the decedent in an ascending lineal line, e.g., parents and grandparents. Compare *Descendant* and *Collateral Relative*.

Descendant. A person related to the decedent in a descending lineal line, e.g., children and grandchildren. (Although this term may be spelled "d-e-s-c-e-n-d-*e*-n-t," this is not its usual spelling in a probate context.) Compare *Ancestor* and *Collateral Relative*.

Collateral Relative. A person related to the decedent but not in a lineal line, e.g., siblings, nieces and nephews, aunts and uncles, and cousins. Compare *Ancestor* and *Descendant*. If the collateral relative is a descendant of the decedent's parents, the relative is a *first line collateral* (e.g., siblings, nieces and nephews). If the collateral relative is a descendant of the decedent's grandparents, other than the decedent's parents and their descendants, the relative is a *second line collateral* (e.g., aunts, uncles, and cousins). The chart below should help place family relationships into perspective. The names given to relatives in the chart are based on the way you would refer to these individuals.

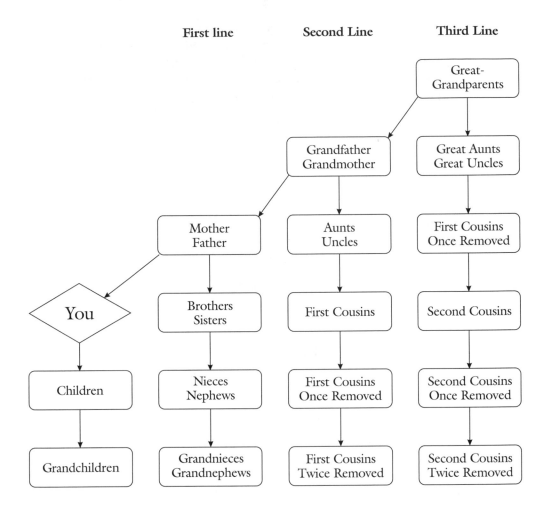

Consanguineous Relationship. A biological or blood relationship. Compare *Affinity Relationship*.

Affinity Relationship. A relationship by marriage, i.e., relatives people usually refer to as their "in-laws." Compare *Consanguineous Relationship*.

§1.2.2 Wills Terms

Testate Succession. The passage of property under the decedent's will.

Will. A written document or oral declaration directing who will own the decedent's property upon the decedent's death. At common law, a will disposed of real property and a *testament* disposed of personal property. This distinction is rarely made today.

Codicil. A type of will that merely amends an already existing will.

Testator; Testatrix. A person who dies with a valid will. Traditionally, the term *testator* refers to a male and the term *testatrix* refers to a female. In modern usage, *testator* refers to any person who dies with a valid will, regardless of sex. Compare *Intestate.*

Devise. A gift of real property in a will. (Please do not spell this term "d-e-v-i-c-e.") The person who receives the devise is called the *devisee.*

Bequest. A gift of personal property in a will. See *Legacy.*

Legacy. A gift of money in a will. The person who receives the legacy is called the *legatee.* A legacy is a type of bequest.

Beneficiary. Generic term for a person who receives property under a will regardless of whether it is real or personal property. Compare *Heir.* Also compare *Beneficiary* as defined in §1.2.3, below.

§1.2.3 Trusts Terms

Trust. A property conveyance whereby the owner divides title to the property into legal and equitable interests and imposes fiduciary duties on the holder of the legal title to deal with the property for the benefit of the holder of the equitable title.

Settlor. The person who creates a trust by making the property transfer which divides title and imposes duties. The settlor may also be called the *trustor,* the *grantor,* or the *donor.*

Beneficiary. The person who receives the equitable title to trust property and hence the right to benefit from that property according to the settlor's instructions. The beneficiary may also be called the *cestui que trust,* the *donee,* or the *grantee.*

Trustee. The person who holds the legal title to trust property and has the fiduciary duty to manage that property according to the settlor's instructions and applicable trust law.

Principal. The property conveyed in trust form. The principal is also referred to as the trust *corpus, estate,* or *res.* (Please do not spell this term "p-r-i-n-c-i-p-l-e.")

Income. The profits or other earnings made by property after it is conveyed in trust form (e.g., the interest on a certificate of deposit or the rent collected from real property).

§1.2.4 *General Terms*

Administration. Process of collecting and managing all of a decedent's property so that the decedent's creditors are paid to the fullest extent allowed by law and the remaining property, if any, is turned over to the heirs or beneficiaries.

Administrator. Person in charge of administering the estate of an intestate decedent. Compare *Executor.* See *Personal Representative.*

Executor. Person in charge of administering the estate of a testate decedent. Compare *Administrator.* See *Personal Representative.*

Personal Representative. Generic term for the person in charge of administering the estate of a decedent. Compare *Administrator* and *Executor.*

Probate. In a broad sense, probate refers to the entire process of administering a decedent's estate. In a narrow sense, probate means to prove a document or declaration to be the decedent's valid will.

Probate Asset. An asset of a decedent that passes either under intestate succession or through a will.

Non-Probate Asset. An asset of a decedent that passes via a manner other than under intestate succession or through a will. Typical non-probate arrangements include joint tenancies with rights of survivorship and contracts that provide for the payment of benefits upon death to designated persons such as life insurance, retirement plans, and accounts with financial institutions (e.g., joint accounts with survivorship rights and pay on death accounts). Part Four of this book provides a comprehensive coverage of these assets.

§1.3 Determination of Applicable Law

§1.3.1 *Generally*

State law, rather than federal law, governs property succession at death, trusts, disability planning techniques, and other estate planning matters. Except for Louisiana, whose law is based on the Roman civil law system that still prevails in continental European countries and in nations with a Roman-based system such as Mexico, the estate planning laws used in all other states originated with the English Common Law. Because of this shared ancestry, the general concepts and policies of probate and trust law are relatively similar among the states. The details, however, may differ widely resulting in intestate distributions, determinations of will or trust validity, and constructions and interpretations that are highly dependent on each state's particular law. Thus,

you must always be certain to check the law of the relevant state to resolve any probate related issue. Relying on a "general" principle can lead to disastrous results for your client and a call to your malpractice carrier.

Each state has a set of statutes, usually called a *Probate Code,* which sets forth the state's intestate distribution scheme, the requirements of a valid will, rules of construction and interpretation, and the methods of estate administration. Approximately fifteen states have adopted one of the many versions of the Uniform Probate Code (UPC) and many other states have enacted one or more provisions on an ad hoc basis. A small but growing number of states have comprehensive trust statutes. The National Commissioners on Uniform State Laws is in the process of drafting a Uniform Trust Act. Some other areas of estate planning law are highly codified while others are still based on common law concepts.

§1.3.2 Ownership and Marital Rights

If the decedent was married at the time of death, it is crucial to determine which property the decedent owned at death and which property actually belongs to the surviving spouse. Only the deceased spouse's property will pass through intestacy or be controlled by the deceased spouse's will.

You must determine what type of marital property system governs the parties and their property. Two types of marital property systems are used in the United States: *common law* and *community property.* Under a common law system, each spouse owns his or her entire income as well as any property brought into the marriage or acquired during the marriage by gift. Under a community property system, each spouse owns any property brought into the marriage or acquired during the marriage by gift, but only one-half of his or her income; the other half of the income vests in the other spouse as soon as it is earned. Although only nine states use the community property system (Arizona, California, Idaho, Louisiana, New Mexico, Nevada, Texas, and Washington along with Wisconsin due to its adoption of the Uniform Marital Property Act), these states account for over 25 percent of the population of the United States.

If the spouses have lived in more than one type of marital property jurisdiction during the marriage, you must determine whether a spouse's earnings (and, consequently, any property purchased with those earnings) belongs solely to the spouse who earned the money or whether it is co-owned. The general rule is that the ownership of the earnings is governed by the law of the spouse's domicile at the time the property was acquired. Marital title does not change as the couple moves from one type of marital property state to another.

Example 1-1. Marital Rights

Wife earned $100,000 while domiciled in a common law marital property state and placed it into a certificate of deposit (CD-1). Husband and Wife then moved to a community property marital property state. Wife earned an additional $100,000 and placed it into another certificate of deposit (CD-2). To what property is Wife entitled; that is, what property may Wife dispose of by her will?

Explanation

Wife owns at least $150,000 and may dispose of that money by her will. Wife owns the $100,000 earned in the separate property state and placed into CD-1. The fact that she later moved to a community property state does not matter; ownership of the property does not change. Wife is also entitled to all of the interest CD-1 earned while Wife lived in the separate property state. Depending on the particular law of the community property state, she may or may not be entitled to the interest on CD-1 that accrues after the move. Wife only owns 50 percent of CD-2 because she earned the money placed in this CD while domiciled in a community property state, which treats income as if earned equally by each spouse. Wife is also entitled to half of the interest on CD-2.

§1.3.3 Real vs. Personal Property

Issues regarding the transfer of real property at death are governed by the law of the state in which the land is located. On the other hand, the law of the decedent's domicile at the time of death governs personal property matters. Thus, you may need to apply the probate law of several states to determine the proper distribution of a decedent's estate.

§1.4 The "Big Picture"

We are conceived without property. During our lifetimes, we acquire property from a variety of sources. Some property we dispose of while alive and other property we retain until we die. Our goal is to learn the legal methods for property transfer focusing on gratuitous transfers, i.e., transfers in which we receive nothing of monetary value in return, although we may receive appreciation, affection, and kind words.

The following diagram provides the "big picture" and places property acquisition and disposition into perspective.

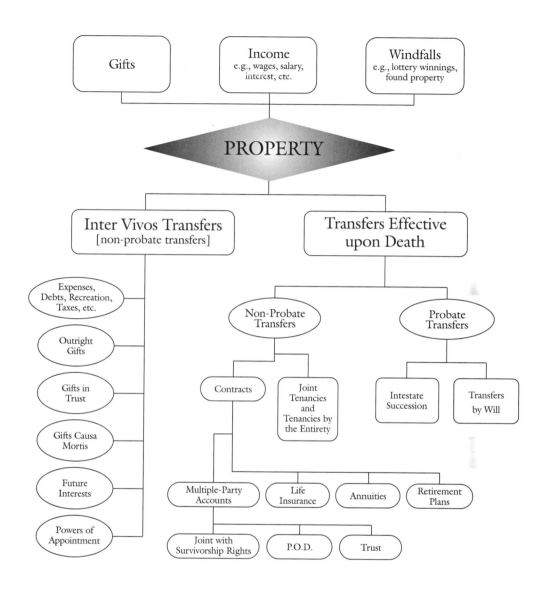

Gifts

Income
e.g., wages, salary,
interest, etc.

Windfalls
e.g., lottery winnings,
found property

PROPERTY

Inter Vivos Transfers
[non-probate transfers]

Transfers Effective
upon Death

Expenses,
Debts, Recreation,
Taxes, etc.

Outright
Gifts

Gifts in
Trust

Gifts Causa
Mortis

Future
Interests

Powers of
Appointment

Non-Probate
Transfers

Probate
Transfers

Contracts

Joint
Tenancies
and
Tenancies by
the Entirety

Intestate
Succession

Transfers
by Will

Multiple-Party
Accounts

Life
Insurance

Annuities

Retirement
Plans

Joint with
Survivorship Rights

P.O.D.

Trust

Part One

INTESTATE SUCCESSION

2

Descent and Distribution

The new owner of a person's property upon death depends on two main factors — first, the type of asset and second, whether the decedent made a valid will. Certain property, commonly referred to as *nonprobate assets*, is controlled by the terms of the property arrangement itself such as land held in joint tenancy with survivorship rights and contractual arrangements that specify the at-death owner such as life insurance and pay on death accounts at banks, savings and loan associations, and other financial institutions. Part Four of this book provides a comprehensive review of these assets. The passage of the remaining property, the *probate estate*, depends on whether the decedent died after executing a valid will that disposed of all of the decedent's probate property.

In Part One, we will examine what happens when a person dies without a valid will or dies with a valid will that does not encompass all of the person's probate estate. When this happens, the person's probate property that is not covered by a valid will is distributed through a process called *intestate succession*. A person may die totally intestate, that is, *intestate as to the person*, if the person did not leave any type of valid will. A person may also die partially intestate, that is, *intestate as to property*, if the person's valid will fails to dispose of all of the person's probate estate.

Please review the terminology and relationship chart in §1.2.1 before proceeding with this chapter.

§2.1 Reasons Most Individuals Die Intestate

The ability to specify the new owners of property upon death is an important and powerful privilege that each state grants to its citizens. Although you

13

are taking a course that focuses on wills and their importance, the odds are that you do not have one. And you would be in good company. Many famous and wealthy people have died intestate including President Abraham Lincoln and Texas billionaire Howard Hughes. Surveys reveal that between 60-75 percent of Americans die intestate. Intestacy causes the decedent's property to pass to those individuals whom the state government in its infinite (?) wisdom believes the decedent would have wanted to receive the probate estate when the decedent died. None of the decedent's family members or friends are allowed to present evidence to show that the decedent actually wanted property to pass to them or to a charity. A question you may now logically ask is why would so many people not take full advantage of their ability to write a will?

§2.1.1 *Lack of Property*

One of the most commonly cited reasons people do not have wills is that they own very little property. Because you may be borrowing mass quantities of money to attend law school, you could fall into this category, that is, "Why should I bother with a will when I don't have property?" There are, however, very important reasons for everyone, even persons with limited estates, to have an effective will. Here are some of the reasons. (1) In some states, the right of the surviving spouse to deal with household items and other property may be subject to the claims of the children if there is no will. (2) The surviving parent of a minor child has the ability to nominate a guardian for the child's person and property in the parent's will. This is better than forcing the court to make the selection because the court may choose a person the parent would not have wanted to control the child's personal or financial affairs. (3) Just because the estate is small now does not mean it will not be large at the time the individual actually dies. A person could win the lottery or a mail order sweepstakes, inherit a hefty sum of money under intestacy, be a significant will beneficiary, or land a high-paying job. Additionally, the person could die in a manner that gives the person's estate a winnable survival action against the individual or business that contributed to the death, such as a drunk driver or the manufacturer of a defective vehicle.

§2.1.2 *Unaware of Importance*

Many people are naive about the critical importance of having a will. They simply wander through life without giving thought to what happens to their property upon death. Perhaps worse, other individuals have serious misconceptions about at-death property distribution. If you want to have some fun, go ask ten "regular" folks who they believe would receive their property if they were to go to their final reward (or punishment) without a will. You may get a good laugh followed by the sobering realization that most people do not have a clue.

§2.1.3 Indifference

Apathy is a contributing factor to why some people do not prepare a will. As the cliché goes, "You can't take it with you," and thus some people simply do not care.

§2.1.4 Cost

An attorney-drafted will requires a person to spend money that the person might rather spend on the necessities of life or recreation. Many people cannot afford even the "bargain" wills some attorneys offer, and people with sufficient resources to incur the cost may have "better" things to do with their money. Seeking economical wills, some individuals use self-help will kits and computer programs that are available in bookstores and advertised in magazines, mail order catalogs, and late night television infomercials. Although the wisdom of using such do-it-yourself techniques is beyond the scope of our discussion, you may want to give some thought to the ramifications that may follow from their use. In addition, you should be aware that the unauthorized practice of law committees of some state bar associations attempt to enjoin the sale of these publications to non-lawyers with varying degrees of success.

§2.1.5 Time and Effort

Even for simple estates, the will preparation process requires a significant investment of time. Here is a typical scenario. The client has an initial meeting with you. As you start to gather the information you need to write the will, you will often discover that the client has not given thought to all aspects of property disposition (e.g., secondary recipients if the primary beneficiaries die before the client) or may need to supply you with additional documentation (e.g., adoption decrees, divorce papers, property appraisals, etc.). Thus, after the client leaves, the client must both ponder various aspects of the estate plan and gather material for your review. The client then gets this information to your office in person or by mail, telephone, e-mail, or fax. You then conduct a second formal meeting, review a rough draft of the will, and engage in a more detailed discussion of options. In a straightforward situation, this may be when the client signs the will. In many cases, however, one or more additional meetings are necessary. If you consider the client's time spent on preparing, traveling, waiting, and meeting, you can appreciate that will preparation requires clients to sacrifice sizable blocks of time and expend considerable effort.

§2.1.6 *Complexity*

Wills may become extremely complex, especially if the estate is large enough to trigger tax consequences. It is probably safe to say that most potential testators do not view complexity as a stimulating challenge. Rather, complexity tends to dampen any enthusiasm that may exist about executing a will.

§2.1.7 *Admission of Mortality*

In the past, many people believed that they would not live long after executing a will, even if they were then in good health. For many, this belief persists today. Because "personal death is a thought modern [individuals] will do almost anything to avoid,"[1] people procrastinate (usually indefinitely) the preparation of a will as a conscious or unconscious defense against admitting their own mortality.

§2.1.8 *Reluctance to Reveal Private Facts*

To prepare a good will, you must inquire into your client's personal and private matters. For example, you need to know about children born out of wedlock, the value of property, medical conditions, and family situations. Your client may not want to open his or her private life for your inspection.

§2.2 Historical Development of Descent and Distribution

Early in the evolution of civilization, societies developed customs and laws to control the transmission of a person's property after death. Our modern intestacy laws are traced originally to the Anglo-Saxons. The Norman Con-

---

1. Thomas Shaffer, *The "Estate Planning" Counselor and Values Destroyed by Death,* 55 Iowa L. Rev. 376, 377 (1969).

quest of 1066 A.D. played a significant role in the development of these rules. William the Conqueror was irritated that English landowners refused to recognize his right to the English Crown after his victory. Accordingly, William took ownership of all land by force and instituted the Norman form of feudalism. Under this system, the Crown was the true owner of all real property with others holding the property in a hierarchical scheme under which lower ranked holders owed various financial and service-oriented duties to higher ranked holders.

As a result, real property became the most essential element in the political, economic, and social structure of the Middle Ages. The Crown and its tough royal courts controlled the *descent* of real property. The basic features of descent included the following rules. (1) Male heirs inherited real property to the exclusion of female heirs unless no male heir existed. The reason underlying this discriminatory preference for male over female heirs was based on the feudal incidents of ownership. One of the primary duties of lower ranked holders of property was to provide military service to higher ranked holders. Under the then-existing social climate, women were deemed unable to perform these services and thus were not able to inherit realty if a male heir existed. (2) If two or more males were equally related to the decedent, the oldest male would inherit all of the land to the total exclusion of the younger males. This is the rule of *primogeniture*. Primogeniture was applied because the Crown thought it was too impractical to divide the duty to provide military services as well as to subdivide the property. (3) If there were no male heirs and several female heirs, each female heir shared equally.

Before the industrial revolution, personal property was of lesser importance. There were no machines or corporate securities to worry about. Instead, most chattels were of relatively little value, such as clothing, furniture, jewelry, and livestock. Thus, the Crown permitted the church and its courts to govern the *distribution* of personal property. The ecclesiastical courts based distribution on canon law, which had its foundation in Roman law. In general, personal property was distributed equally among equally related heirs. There was no preference for male heirs and the ages of the heirs were irrelevant.

After centuries of movement toward a unified system, the English Parliament passed the Administration of Estates Act in 1925, which abolished primogeniture and the preference for male heirs and provided uniform rules for all types of property. Most intestacy statutes in the United States, including the Uniform Probate Code, make no distinction based on the age and sex of the heirs nor between the descent of real property and the distribution of personal property. However, some state statutes retain this latter common law principle and provide different intestacy schemes for real and personal property.

§2.3 Surviving Spouse

§2.3.1 *Protection at Common Law—Real Property*

At common law, the surviving spouse of an intestate decedent was not an heir and thus was not entitled to receive any of the deceased spouse's land. The tremendous importance of real property, coupled with the prevailing attitude that blood relationships were of the utmost importance, meant that a non-blood relative, such as a surviving spouse, could never be an heir to land. Instead, the common law protected spouses by giving each spouse a marital estate in the lands of the other. These estates were inchoate while both were alive. When the first spouse died, the surviving spouse would come into enjoyment of the property covered by the marital estate.

§2.3.1.1 Dower Rights of Widow

Upon surviving her husband, a widow was entitled to a life estate in one-third of the real property that her husband owned at any time during the marriage, even if he did not own the property at the time of his death. Although the widow's right was relatively small, that is, only a life estate and then only in one-third of the realty, it was a strong interest. The husband could not unilaterally deprive his wife of her dower rights merely by transferring the land inter vivosly or by a will. The grantee or devisee would take the land subject to the wife's dower rights unless she expressly waived her rights.

§2.3.1.2 Curtesy Rights of Widower

A surviving husband was entitled to a life estate in all of his wife's real property. However, the husband had to satisfy an important condition before claiming this right. A widower received curtesy rights only if he had fathered a child with his now-deceased wife. Note that the husband had this right even if no child survived his wife.

§2.3.2 *Protection at Common Law—Personal Property*

Because of the lesser role personal property played in the Middle Ages, a spouse was allowed to receive an outright interest in the other spouse's personal property. A husband did not need to wait until his wife died to receive his rights because a husband gained ownership of all of his wife's personal property immediately upon marriage. A wife, on the other hand, had to survive her husband to receive her share. The size of this share often depended on whether her husband left any surviving descendants. For example, under the Statute of Distribution of 1670, a widow received one-half of her husband's personalty if there were no surviving descendants but only one-third if at least one descendant survived.

§2.3.3 Modern Law

Most jurisdictions have abolished the common law marital estates of dower and curtesy. Even in those few jurisdictions that have retained these concepts, there is no distinction between the rights that a widow or widower may claim. Instead, most states include the surviving spouse as an heir under their intestacy statutes.

The methods used by states to compute the intestate share that a surviving spouse may claim vary tremendously among the jurisdictions. Statutes may take several factors into consideration such as the existence and number of surviving children and, in the case of no children or their descendants, the existence of other close relatives.

As modern statutes evolve, legislatures have been increasing the size of the surviving spouse's share, especially if the deceased spouse does not have surviving descendants who are not also descendants of the surviving spouse. This movement is the result of empirical studies that show married individuals who do not have children from other partners tend to prefer each other to their children as the primary beneficiaries of their wills.

UPC §2-102 is reproduced below as an example of how modern statutes determine the surviving spouse's share.

> The intestate share of a decedent's surviving spouse is:
> (1) the entire intestate estate if:
> (i) no descendant or parent of the decedent survives the decedent; or
> (ii) all of the decedent's surviving descendants are also descendants of the surviving spouse and there is no other descendant of the surviving spouse who survives the decedent;
> (2) the first [$200,000], plus three-fourths of any balance of the intestate estate, if no descendant of the decedent survives the decedent, but a parent of the decedent survives the decedent;
> (3) the first [$150,000], plus one-half of any balance of the intestate estate, if all of the decedent's surviving descendants are also descendants of the surviving spouse and the surviving spouse has one or more surviving descendants who are not descendants of the decedent;
> (4) the first [$100,000], plus one-half of any balance of the intestate estate, if one or more of the decedent's surviving descendants are not descendants of the surviving spouse.

§2.3.4 *Community Property Jurisdictions*

In community property jurisdictions, the surviving spouse retains one-half of the community property; that is, the portion of the community that already belongs to the surviving spouse by virtue of the property's community characterization. Depending on state law and factors such as the number of descendants and their relationship to the surviving spouse, the surviving spouse may inherit some or all of the deceased spouse's community property. The surviving spouse may also be entitled to a portion of the deceased spouse's separate property. Depending on the state, the intestacy scheme for separate property could be the same or considerably different from the intestacy statutes applicable to community property.

§2.4   Descendants

Intestacy statutes almost universally give descendants all of an intestate decedent's probate assets that do not pass to the surviving spouse. Thus, if the intestate was single at the time of death, the intestate's descendants take the entire probate estate. If the intestate was married, the descendants receive whatever is left, if anything, after removing the share for the surviving spouse. If the intestate has no surviving descendants and no surviving spouse, then any remaining property is divided among ancestors and collateral relatives as discussed in §2.5.

§2.4.1 *Basic Procedure for Determining Shares of Descendants*

Now that we know that the intestate's descendants take whatever probate property that does not pass to the surviving spouse, we need to determine how to divide this property if there is more than one surviving descendant. The division of property is very simple if all of the intestate's children are alive. Each child receives an equal share. This is called a *per capita* distribution. But, if some of the intestate's children predeceased the intestate after having children of their own who outlive the intestate, the division may start to get complicated because there are at least three methods of dividing property between descendants when different generations are involved.

§2.4.1.1   Step One—Identify Intestate's Children

The first step is to ascertain the identity of all of the intestate's children. (We will learn later whether to include children born after the intestate's death, children whom the intestate adopted, or the intestate's children who were born out of wedlock. See §§3.1 to 3.3.) Note that these children may not have both parents in common; that is, they may be half-siblings.

§2.4.1.2 Step Two—Determine If Any Predeceased Child Left a Descendant Who Outlived Intestate

The second step is to determine if any of the intestate's children predeceased the intestate leaving at least one descendant who survived the intestate. For example, (1) Daughter died before Intestate, (2) Daughter was survived by her child, Granddaughter, and (3) Granddaughter outlived Intestate.

If none of an intestate's children predeceased the intestate or if none of the intestate's predeceased children left descendants who survived the intestate, then you simply divide the distributable estate into as many equal shares as there are surviving children and give each child one share. As mentioned above, this is a per capita distribution. Descendants of living descendants are not included in the distribution because a younger generation descendant cannot inherit from an ancestor if an older generation descendant is still alive. Thus, you cannot inherit from your maternal grandparents if your mother is alive.

If one or more of the intestate's children predeceased the intestate leaving at least one descendant who survives the intestate, continue with Step Three.

§2.4.1.3 Step Three—Ascertain State's Method of Handling Multi-Generation Succession

The third and final step is to determine the method used by your state to determine the shares of descendants when they are not all of the first generation. This can arise either if (1) all descendants belong to a more distant generation (e.g., they are the intestate's grandchildren), or (2) the descendants are from different generations (e.g., children and grandchildren). The three most common methods used in the United States are discussed below.

§2.4.2 *Per Stirpes (by Right of Representation)*

A *per stirpes* distribution literally means one that determines takers by the roots or stocks. (There are several ways to pronounce "stirpes"; the one I like best is "stir-peas" but your professor may like another and, of course, you should use that one!) Thus, younger generation descendants divide the share the older generation descendant would have received had that older generation descendant survived the intestate. In effect, these younger generation descendants "represent," that is, stand in the shoes of, the older generation. The intestate's estate is divided into shares with one share being created for each surviving child and for each deceased child who left descendants who survive the intestate. Each surviving child receives one share and the share of each deceased child passes to that child's descendants.

Example 2-1. Per Stirpes — Children and Grandchildren

Intestate had three children, Son One, Son Two, and Daughter. Son One predeceased Intestate survived by two children of his own, Arthur and Brenda, both of whom survive Intestate. Son Two also predeceased Intestate but Son Two had no surviving descendants. How would Intestate's property be distributed applying a per stirpes distribution?

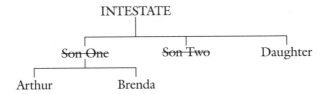

Explanation

Daughter receives one-half, Arthur receives one quarter, and Brenda receives one-quarter. If Son One had survived, Son One would have received one-half of the estate. This one-half is divided equally between Son One's descendants, Arthur and Brenda, with each getting one-quarter of Intestate's estate (one-half each of Son One's one-half). No share is created for Son Two because Son Two was not survived by a descendant and thus Son Two has no one to represent him.

Example 2-2. Per Stirpes — Grandchildren

Using the same basic facts as in Example 2-1, assume that Daughter also predeceased Intestate and was survived by her only child, Charles. Charles survived Intestate. How would Intestate's property be distributed applying a per stirpes distribution?

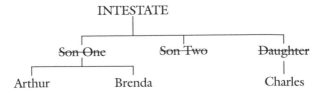

Explanation

Arthur receives one-quarter, Brenda receives one-quarter, and Charles receives one-half. Arthur and Brenda would each still receive 25 percent as in Example 2-2, and Charles, as Daughter's only descendant, would take the share Daughter would have received if she had survived Intestate, i.e., 50 percent. Although all takers are of the same generation (Arthur, Brenda, and Charles are all Intestate's grandchildren), they do not receive equal shares.

A per stirpes approach stresses blood line over degree of relationship and may cause equally related individuals to be treated differently as in Example 2-2. The seeming unfairness of this result has led to the unpopularity of this "strict," "classic," "English," or "pure" per stirpes approach. (Note that the term "per stirpes" is sometimes imprudently used in a broad sense to refer to any type of distribution scheme under which the descendants of a deceased heir receive the deceased heir's share.)

§2.4.3 *Per Capita with Representation*

The per capita with representation approach operates in many aspects like the per stirpes approach with one major difference. Instead of using the intestate's children as the "root" of the distribution, the nearest generation with descendants who survive the intestate is used. Thus, if all takers are of the same generation, they take per capita (equal shares). Only if takers are of different generations is the share of the younger generation descendants based on the share that the older generation descendant would have received had the older generation descendant survived the intestate.

Example 2-3. Per Capita with Representation — Children and Grandchildren

Intestate had two children, Son and Daughter. Son predeceased Intestate survived by two children of his own, Arthur and Brenda, both of whom survived Intestate. How would Intestate's property be distributed applying a per capita with representation distribution?

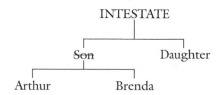

Explanation

Daughter receives one-half, Arthur receives one-quarter, and Brenda receives one-quarter. Although this is the same answer as under a per stirpes distribution, the reasoning is significantly different. The key issue is to determine at what level Intestate's estate is initially broken into shares. Under per stirpes, the level of children is always used because it is the first level below that of Intestate. However, under per capita with representation, shares are divided at the children level because it is the first level with members who outlived Intestate. It is only a coincidence that the result is the same in this example under both per stirpes and per capita with representation.

Example 2-4. Per Capita with Representation — Grandchildren

Using the same facts as in Example 2-3, assume that Daughter also predeceased Intestate survived by her only child, Charles, who survived Intestate. How would Intestate's property be distributed applying a per capita with representation distribution?

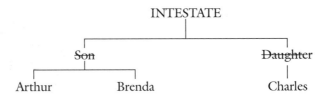

Explanation

Arthur receives one-third, Brenda receives one-third, and Charles receives one-third. Because the level of grandchildren is the nearest generation to Intestate with survivors, it is the root generation. All members of this generation are alive and thus they take equal shares. Notice that this result is considerably different from the per stirpes approach as discussed in the Explanation to Example 2-2, which made the initial division into shares at the children level even though no members of that level outlived Intestate.

The per capita with representation approach is regarded as being fairer to both the intestate and the heirs than per stirpes. A per capita with representation result is more likely to be in harmony with the intestate's presumed intent than a per stirpes one because of the equal treatment accorded each heir when all heirs are related to the intestate in the same manner. Accordingly, this approach is used by a majority of jurisdictions. (As mentioned earlier, per capita with representation is often imprecisely referred to as per stirpes or by the moniker "modern per stirpes.") Per capita with representation, however, still does not treat all equally related persons the same as illustrated in Example 2-5.

Example 2-5. Per Capita with Representation — Children and Grandchildren from Multiple Predeceased Children

Intestate had four children, Arthur, Brenda, Charles, and Doris. Both Arthur and Brenda died before Intestate. Arthur was survived by one child, Edward, and Brenda was survived by two children, Fran and George. How would Intestate's property be distributed using a per capita with representation distribution?

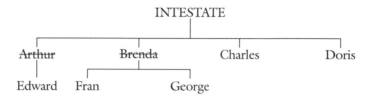

Explanation

Charles receives one-quarter, Doris receives one-quarter, Edward receives one-quarter, Fran receives one-eighth, and George receives one-eighth. Intestate's property is divided into shares at the first generation with survivors, that is, children. The initial division is into quarters — one share for each of the surviving children and one share for each of the deceased children who left surviving descendants. Charles and Doris as surviving children will each receive one of the quarters. Edward takes all of Arthur's share because Edward is Arthur's only child. Fran and George divide Brenda's share equally. Although Edward, Fran, and George are equally related to Intestate as grandchildren, they take different shares because their parents did not have equal numbers of children who outlived Intestate.

§2.4.4 Per Capita at Each Generation

The newest approach and the one contained in U.P.C. §2-106 is called per capita at each generation. Under this approach, equality among like-related persons is achieved. The basic plan begins as with per capita with representation but once the division into shares is done at the first generation with survivors, the shares created on behalf of the deceased members of that generation are combined and then distributed per capita among the younger generation heirs.

Example 2-6. Per Capita at Each Generation — Children and Grandchildren from Multiple Predeceased Children

Intestate had four children, Arthur, Brenda, Charles, and Doris. Both Arthur and Brenda died before Intestate. Arthur was survived by one child, Edward, and Brenda was survived by two children, Fran and George. How would Intestate's property be distributed using a per capita at each generation distribution? [Note: These are the same facts as Example 2-5.]

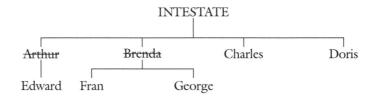

Explanation

Charles receives one-quarter, Doris receives one-quarter, Edward receives one-sixth, Fran receives one-sixth, and George receives one-sixth. Intestate's property is divided into shares at the first generation with survivors, that is, children. The initial division is into quarters — one share for each of the surviving children and one share for each of the deceased children who left surviving descendants. Charles and Doris as surviving children will each receive one of the quarters. The shares created on behalf of the predeceased children, Arthur and Brenda, are pooled and then divided evenly among their children, Intestate's grandchildren. The two shares created for the descendants of Arthur and Brenda total one-half of the estate. There are three descendants, each of whom is equally related to Intestate. Thus, each descendent takes one-third of one-half of the estate, or one-sixth. Under this form of distribution, all equally related heirs receive the same portion of Intestate's estate (each child receives one-quarter and each grandchild receives one-sixth).

§2.4.5 Distribution Exercises

Example 2-7. Compare and Contrast Per Stirpes, Per Capita with Representation, and Per Capita at Each Generation

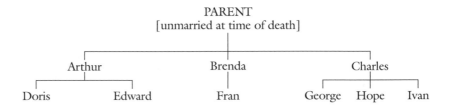

How would Parent's estate be distributed under each of the following scenarios? For each scenario, provide answers under the following approaches: (1) per stirpes, (2) per capita with representation, and (3) per capita at each generation.

Example 2-7a. Parent is deceased

Explanation

Arthur, Brenda, and Charles each inherit one-third of Parent's estate. Because all of Parent's children are still alive, the result is the same regardless of which distribution approach you apply. The first generation is the same as the first generation with survivors. The differences among the various approaches impact the distribution only if the intestate has predeceased children with descendants who outlive the intestate.

Example 2-7b. Arthur died first, followed by Parent

Explanation

Under all three types of distribution schemes, Brenda receives one-third, Charles receives one-third, Doris receives one-sixth, and Edward receives one-sixth. Why is the answer the same regardless of the method?

The per stirpes approach divides Parent's estate into equal parts at the first generation. One share is created for each child who survives and one for each predeceased child who left surviving descendants. Thus, there are a total of three shares. One share goes to each of the surviving children so Brenda and Charles get their one-third each. The remaining one-third is divided between Arthur's descendants and thus Doris and Edward each receive one-half of one-third, or one-sixth.

Applying per capita with representation, we divide into shares at the first generation with survivors, which in this case is the first generation (Parent's children). Thus, the computation is the same as per stirpes.

A per capita at each generation computation does not affect the distribution because descendants of only one predeceased older generation person are taking. For per capita at each generation to yield a different result, we must have descendants of two or more predeceased older generation descendants who did not leave equal numbers of descendants. The next part of this example illustrates this difference.

Example 2-7c. Arthur and Brenda died first, followed by Parent

Explanation

Per stirpes and per capita with representation yield the same result. We divide the estate into three shares, give one to Charles as the only surviving child, divide Arthur's share between Doris and Edward with each taking one-sixth of the total estate, and give Brenda's one-third share to Brenda's only descendant, Fran.

However, the result is considerably different applying per capita at each generation. We again divide the estate into three shares and give one to Charles as the only surviving child. However, the remaining two-thirds is now given in equal shares to Doris, Edward, and Fran. Thus, each gets one-third of two-thirds, i.e., two-ninths, of Parent's estate.

Example 2-7d. Arthur, Brenda, and Charles died first, followed by Parent

Explanation

There is again a difference based on the method used, but this time the per stirpes method causes the different result, with per capita with representation and per capita at each generation yielding the same distribution. With per stirpes, we continue to divide Parent's estate into three shares despite the fact that there are no survivors in the first generation. Thus, Arthur's one-third passes in equal shares to Doris and Edward (one-sixth each), Brenda's one-third passes to Fran, and Charles's one-third passes to George, Hope, and Ivan (one-ninth each).

Under both per capita with representation and per capita at each generation, we divide into shares beginning with the first generation in which there are survivors. Because all members of the second generation are alive (or if any had died, they did not leave surviving descendants), we simply give each of the six grandchildren a one-sixth share.

Example 2-8. Predeceased Child without Descendants

Parent had three children, Arthur, Brenda, and Charles. Charles predeceased Parent but was survived by Spouse. Charles had no descendants. How would you distribute Parent's estate?

Explanation

Parent's estate would pass 50 percent each to Arthur and Brenda. No share is set aside for Charles because Charles did not have any descendants who survived Parent. Spouse has no claim to the property because Spouse, Parent's child-in-law, is not a descendant of Parent.

Example 2-9. Statutory Language

Study the following two statutes and decide what type of distribution scheme each one adopts.

   a. The estate is divided into as many equal shares as there are (i) surviving descendants in the generation nearest to the decedent which contains one or more surviving descendants and (ii) deceased descendants in the same generation who left surviving descendants, if any. Each surviving descendant in the nearest generation is allocated one share. The remaining shares, if any, are combined and then divided in the same manner among the surviving descendants of the deceased descendants as if the surviving descendants who were allocated a share and their surviving descendants had predeceased the decedent.

b. When the intestate's descendants standing in the first or same degree alone come into the distribution upon intestacy, they shall take per capita, namely by persons; and, when a part of them being dead and a part living, the descendants of those dead shall have right to distribution upon intestacy, such descendants shall inherit only such portion of said property as the parent through whom they inherit would be entitled to if alive.

Explanation

a. This language is adapted from U.P.C. §2-106 and reflects a per capita at each generation approach.

b. This language is adapted from Tex. Prob. Code Ann. §43 (Vernon Supp. 1998) and describes a per capita with representation scheme. (The statute is actually labeled inartfully as "per stirpes.")

§2.5 Ancestors and Collaterals

If none of the intestate's descendants survive, the intestate's ancestors and collaterals will inherit the balance of the intestate's probate property that does not pass to the intestate's surviving spouse. Under the law of all states, descendants are preferred to ancestors and collaterals even if one of these individuals, such as a parent, is more closely related than a descendant, such as a grandchild.

§2.5.1 Parents and First-Line Collaterals

§2.5.1.1 Both Parents Survive Intestate

Under all modern intestacy statutes, an intestate's parents divide the intestate's probate estate that does not pass to the surviving spouse if the intestate died without surviving descendants.

§2.5.1.2 One Parent and at Least One Sibling (or Descendant of Sibling) Survive Intestate

Example 2-10. Intestate Survived by One Parent and Siblings

Intestate dies survived by Mother, Brother, and Sister. How is Intestate's estate distributed?

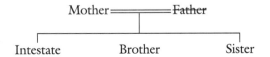

Explanation

Jurisdictions are divided on the appropriate resolution of this situation. Some statutes mandate that Mother would inherit the entire estate as the surviving parent. This is the approach adopted by U.P.C. §2-103. On the other hand, some states provide for the deceased parent's share to pass to Intestate's siblings. Under this type of statute, Mother would take one-half of the estate with Brother and Sister each taking one-quarter.

§2.5.1.3 No Parent and at Least One Sibling (or Descendant of Sibling) Survive Intestate

Jurisdictions are in agreement that if the intestate dies without a surviving descendant or parent, the balance of the probate estate not passing to the surviving spouse passes to the siblings or their descendants. If one or more siblings die before the intestate, the distribution among their descendants, the intestate's nieces and nephews, will depend on whether that jurisdiction uses per stirpes, per capita with representation, or per capita at each generation.

§2.5.2 *Grandparents, Second-Line Collaterals, and More Distant Relatives*

If the intestate dies without a surviving descendant, a parent, or a first-line collateral relative, the intestate's property not passing to the surviving spouse passes to grandparents, second-line collaterals, and perhaps to more distant relatives. Jurisdictions typically adopt one of two main methods for determining the intestate's heirs in this situation: a parentelic system or a degree-of-relationship approach. In addition, many states develop their own distribution schemes by combining various aspects of these systems to achieve the inheritance plan legislators deem appropriate.

Locating second-line or more distant relatives may be difficult. Many businesses specialize in tracking down heirs, often for a fee based on the size of the anticipated inheritance.

§2.5.2.1 Parentelic Systems

Parentelic systems search on each side of the family until an ancestor, or a descendant of an ancestor, is found. The intestate's probate estate not passing to the surviving spouse is divided into two halves. These halves are often referred to as *moieties* (pronounced "moy-ih-tease"). One of these portions passes to the intestate's maternal grandparents and the other portion to the paternal grandparents. If all four grandparents are alive, each would receive one-quarter of the estate. If one grandparent is already deceased, that grandparent's share will either pass to the surviving grandparent on the same side of the family or pass to the deceased grandparent's children and their descendants, that is, the intestate's aunts, uncles, and cousins. If both grandparents on the same side of the family are deceased, the entire moiety passes to the intestate's aunts and uncles and their descendants in that family line. If none of these descendants survive, that portion of the estate is divided among the great-grandparents in a similar manner. This process continues until an heir is located. If no heir is found on one side of the family, then both moieties are usually combined and inherited by the heirs on the side of the family where survivors were located.

Some modern parentelic statutes, such as U.P.C. §2-103, do not permit the indefinite tracing of heirs. Because remote relatives usually do not have an emotional or financial interest in the intestate, legislatures may decide that these *laughing heirs* (heirs who laugh all the way to the bank rather than grieve for the intestate) are not worthy of taking. Accordingly, if no heir is found at a certain statutorily defined level, no further search for heirs is conducted and the property escheats to the state government, as discussed in §2.6. Under U.P.C. §2-103, this is the level of grandparents and their descendants.

Example 2-11. Parentelic Inheritance

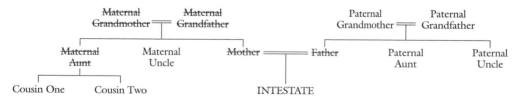

How would Intestate's estate be distributed under a parentelic system?

Explanation

Because Intestate is not survived by a spouse, a descendant, or a parent, Intestate's entire estate passes to grandparents and second-line collaterals. The estate is initially divided in half with one-half passing to each side of Intestate's family. Because both of Intestate's paternal grandparents are still alive, each of them receive equal portions of this share or one-quarter each of Intestate's estate. The half passing to the maternal side of Intestate's family passes to second-line collateral relatives because both maternal grandparents are deceased. The maternal grandparent's moiety is divided at the level of aunts and uncles with one share created for each survivor and one share for each predeceased member who left surviving descendants. Thus, there are a total of two shares, each of which represents one-quarter of Intestate's estate. Maternal Uncle as a survivor takes one of the quarter shares and Maternal Aunt's share is divided between Cousin One and Cousin Two with each receiving one-eighth. Note that under these facts, the result is the same regardless of whether the jurisdiction uses per stirpes, per capita with representation, or per capita at each generation because the first relevant generation (aunts and uncles) is the same as the first generation with survivors (Maternal Uncle) and only one member of this generation has predeceased Intestate (Maternal Aunt).

§2.5.2.2   Degree-of-Relationship Systems

Degree-of-relationship systems determine heirs by counting the degrees of kinship between the intestate and the heir and then awarding the probate estate to the nearest next of kin. Jurisdictions adopting degree-of-relationship systems use one of two basic methods to determine the closest heir.

§2.5.2.2.1   Civil Law System

The most common method used for determining degrees of relationship is the civil law method. The status of each potential heir is determined by counting the number of steps between the intestate and the potential heir as you pass through the common ancestor of both. The total is the degree of relationship. The potential heir with the smallest number inherits the estate. If several heirs are equally related, some jurisdictions follow a *parentelic preference* rule by giving priority to the heirs who have the nearest common ancestor to the intestate.

Example 2-12.   Civil Law Degrees of Relationship

Who is entitled to inherit Intestate's estate under a civil law degree of relationship statute?

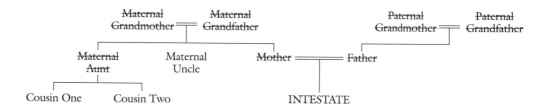

Explanation

Maternal Uncle inherits Intestate's entire estate. There are three potential heirs, Maternal Uncle, Cousin One, and Cousin Two. Maternal Uncle is three degrees removed from Intestate, that is, one step from Intestate to Mother, one step from Mother to Maternal Grandmother or Maternal Grandfather (the common ancestor), and one step from the maternal grandparent to Maternal Uncle. Both cousins, however, are related by four degrees because there is an additional step from Maternal Aunt down to the cousins. Thus, the cousins are more distantly related than Maternal Uncle and would not inherit.

§2.5.2.2.2 Canon Law System

The canon law system developed in the church courts to determine how near a relative an individual could marry. A few states have also applied this method to determine degrees of relationship for inheritance purposes. Under a canon law system, you begin by counting the number of steps from the intestate to the common ancestor of the intestate and the potential heir. Then count the number of steps from the common ancestor to the potential heir. But instead of adding these numbers together to determine the degree of relationship as with the civil law method, the degree of relationship is the larger of the two numbers. The heirs with the smallest numbers inherit the intestate's estate.

Example 2-13. Canon Law Degrees of Relationship

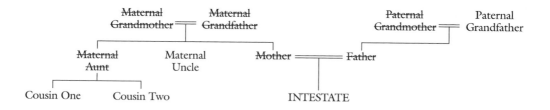

Who is entitled to inherit Intestate's estate under a canon law degree of relationship statute? [Note: These are the same facts as Example 2-12.]

Explanation

Cousin One, Cousin Two, and Maternal Uncle are equally related to Intestate and thus able to inherit. There are two steps between Intestate and the maternal grandparents and one step between these grandparents and Maternal Uncle. The longer of the legs has two steps and thus the degree or relationship is two. There are two steps between Intestate and the maternal grandparents and two steps between these grandparents and the cousins. Both legs are the same length so the degree of relationship is two, the same as Maternal Uncle.

§2.6   Escheat

If the intestate dies without an heir who is entitled to take under the jurisdiction's intestacy statutes, the intestate's property estate reverts to the state government through the escheat process.

Example 2-14.   Escheat

Intestate died domiciled in State A. In addition to property located in State A, Intestate owned real property in State B as well as a large bank account in State C. Under the applicable intestacy statutes of States A, B, and C, all of Intestate's property escheats. Which state government is entitled to Intestate's property?

Explanation

Real property escheats to the state government of the state in which the real property is located. Thus, State A will receive the realty, if any, in State A and State B will receive the realty located in State B. Jurisdictions take various approaches with regard to the escheat of personal property. Some states follow the general choice of law rule that personal property is governed by the law of the intestate's domicile at time of death. Many, however, follow a different rule when escheat is involved and hold that the state in which the property is actually located has a priority claim to the property. Consequently, State C is the most likely recipient of the bank account although it is possible that State A, as Intestate's domicile, could make a superior claim.

3
Treatment of Certain Categories of Potential Heirs

Ascertaining the identity of the intestate's heirs often involves more than simply figuring out the family tree. A wide variety of factors can affect whether a certain person who is biologically otherwise entitled to inherit can actually succeed in claiming a share as the intestate's heir. In addition, an individual who is not biologically related to the intestate may, under certain circumstances, be able to inherit as an heir. This chapter discusses the treatment of these types of individuals.

§3.1 Posthumous or Afterborn Heirs

A posthumous or afterborn heir is an heir conceived while the intestate is alive but who is not born until after the intestate's death. At common law, a posthumous heir was treated as "in being" and capable of inheriting from the time of conception if the heir was thereafter born alive. This common law rule has gained widespread acceptance in the United States. See UPC §2-108.

Some state statutes make a distinction based on the relationship between the intestate and the posthumous heir. For example, if the posthumous heir is a descendant of the intestate, the posthumous heir has inheritance rights. Thus, if the father dies before his child is born or if a mother is declared dead but sustained on artificial life support until her child can be delivered, the child inherits. However, if the posthumous heir is a more distant relative, the heir does not inherit. For example, assume that an intestate died without a surviving spouse, descendants, or parents. As a result, all property would pass to the siblings. If the intestate had a brother and a sister, but the brother predeceased survived by his pregnant wife (intestate's sister-in-law) who gives birth to the intestate's niece or nephew after the intestate's death, the intestate's entire estate would pass to the sister; the afterborn niece or nephew would not inherit.

§3.2   Adopted Individuals

The ability of a person to adopt a non-biologically related person and cause that person to be treated as a biologically related child was recognized thousands of years ago by societies such as the ancient Greeks, Romans, and Egyptians. However, the concept of adoption was beyond the grasp of common law attorneys and courts. The idea that a person could have "parents" other than the biological mother and biological father was unthinkable. In fact, English law did not recognize adoption until 1926. Accordingly, modern law relating to adoption developed in the United States with Vermont and Texas taking the lead when their legislatures enacted adoption statutes in 1850.

§3.2.1   *Inheritance Rights of Adopted Children*

§3.2.1.1   From and through Adoptive Parents

Example 3-1.   Inheritance from Adoptive Parents

Mother and Father had one child, Barney. Mother and Father subsequently adopted Arthur. Mother died intestate survived only by Arthur and Barney. Who is entitled to claim her estate?

Explanation

Most, if not all, jurisdictions provide that an adopted individual is treated as a biological child of the adoptive parents. The adopted child is inserted into the adoptive parents' family trees. Thus, Arthur will inherit from his adoptive mother just like Barney, the biological child.

Example 3-2.   Inheritance through Adoptive Parents

Mother and Father had one child, Barney. Mother and Father subsequently adopted Arthur. Father died with a valid will leaving his entire estate to Mother. Later, Grandmother (Father's mother) died intestate. Who is entitled to represent Father and take the share Father would have received had he outlived his mother?

Explanation

Both Arthur and Barney will share the portion of Grandmother's estate that Father would have inherited had he survived. An adopted child inherits through the adoptive parents and their relatives. In addition, the adopted child's descendants represent the adopted child in the inheritance scheme upon the adopted child's death. See U.P.C. §2-114(b).

§3.2.1.2 From and through Biological Parents

Example 3-3. Inheritance from Biological Parents

Mother and Father had one child, Barney. Mother and Father subsequently adopted Arthur. Arthur's Biological Mother died intestate survived by her two children, Arthur and Nancy. Who is entitled to share in Biological Mother's estate?

Explanation

Jurisdictions disagree as to whether an adopted child like Arthur retains the right to inherit from and through the biological parents. Some states provide that an adopted child is no longer in the biological parents' family trees and thus the adopted child does not inherit from any biological ancestors or collateral relatives. This rule is usually adjusted if the child is adopted by the spouse of a biological parent so the child does not lose inheritance rights from either biological parent. See U.P.C. §2-114(b).

Other states permit the adopted child to continue to inherit from and through the biological parents. In these jurisdictions, an adopted child may have as many as four parents from whom to inherit: adoptive mother, adoptive father, biological mother, and biological father. Some of these states allow the parties to the adoption to alter this rule by expressly eliminating the adopted child's ability to inherit from and through the biological parents by the terms of the adoption decree.

§3.2.2 *Inheritance Rights of Adoptive Parents*

Example 3-4. Inheritance by Adoptive Parents

Mother and Father had one child, Barney. Mother and Father subsequently adopted Arthur. Arthur died intestate survived by Mother, Father, and Barney. Who is entitled to Arthur's estate?

Explanation

Mother and Father will divide Arthur's estate. The prevailing view is that the adoptive parents and their kin will inherit from and through the adopted child as if the adopted child were their biological child. Thus, if the adopted child dies without a surviving spouse and descendants, the adopted child's probate estate passes to the adoptive parents or, if they are deceased, to the siblings by adoption, grandparents by adoption, aunts and uncles by adoption, and so forth.

§3.2.3 *Inheritance Rights of Biological Parents*

Example 3-5. Inheritance by Biological Parents

Mother and Father had one child, Barney. Mother and Father subsequently adopted Arthur. Arthur died intestate survived only by Barney and Biological Father. Who is entitled to Arthur's estate?

Explanation

Barney will receive all of Arthur's property. Adoption cuts off the ability of the biological parents and their kin to inherit from or through the biological parents. Thus, if the adopted child dies without a surviving spouse and descendants, the adoptive parents and their kin take as heirs, not the biological parents and their kin.

§3.2.4 *Adoption by Estoppel/Equitable Adoption*

Adoption by estoppel, also called *equitable adoption,* occurs when a "parent" acts as though the "parent" has adopted the "child" even though a formal court-approved adoption never occurred. The courts in states that recognize this type of relationship examine a host of surrounding factors in making a determination that an adoption by estoppel occurred including whether the "parent" breached an agreement to adopt, made a good-faith attempt to adopt that failed for some reason, or held the "child" out as actually having been adopted. This type of conduct acts to estop the "parent" from claiming that the adoption did not occur. Thus, when the "parent" dies, the adopted by estoppel child is entitled to share in the estate just as if an adoption had actually occurred.

In many states, the result is different if the adopted by estoppel child dies. The adoptive by estoppel parents and their kin are often prohibited from inheriting from or through the adopted by estoppel child. The courts explain that it is the parents' fault that a formal adoption did not take place and thus the equities are not in their favor. As a result, the child's biological kin are the child's heirs.

§3.2.5 *Adult Adoption*

Most states make no distinction based on the age of the child at the time of the adoption. However, some states restrict inheritance rights if the adopted individual was an adult and had not lived with the adoptive parents while still a minor. The rules may also be different based on whether the adopted person is mentally challenged; that is, the adoption of a mentally challenged adult may create inheritance rights while the adoption of other adults would not.

Adult adoption between non-marital partners has gained popularity in recent years. Non-marital partners adopt each other to create an inheritance relationship between them. Thus, if one partner dies without a valid will, the surviving partner can inherit as a child, often the sole heir. Although the partners could achieve the same result by using simple wills, the adoption technique may be used instead because biological relatives of non-marital partners often contest the will of the deceased partner if it makes the other partner a significant beneficiary of the estate. These relatives have a greater chance of setting aside the will, for example, on the basis of undue influence, than they do a court-approved adoption.

§3.3 Non-Marital Children

At common law, a child born outside of a valid marriage was considered as having no parents (*filius nullius*). Thus, a non-marital child did not inherit from or through the child's biological mother or father. Likewise, the biological parents could not inherit from or through the child. However, the non-marital child did retain the right to inherit from the child's spouse and descendants. If the child died intestate with neither a surviving spouse nor descendants, the child's property escheated to the government.

This harsh treatment of non-marital children, formerly referred to by pejorative terms such as "illegitimate children" or "bastards," has been greatly alleviated under modern law. In the 1977 United States Supreme Court case of *Trimble v. Gordon*, 430 U.S. 726 (1977), the Court held that marital and non-marital children must be treated the same when determining heirs under intestacy statutes. The Court held that discriminating against non-marital children was a violation of the equal protection clause of the Fourteenth Amendment.

One year later, the Supreme Court retreated from its broad holding in

Trimble. In the five-four decision of *Lalli v. Lalli,* 439 U.S. 259 (1978), the Court held that a state may have legitimate reasons to apply a more demanding standard for non-marital children to inherit from their fathers than from their mothers. The Court cited several justifications for this unequal treatment including the more efficient and orderly administration of estates, the avoidance of spurious claims, the maintenance of the finality of judgments, and the inability of the purported father to contest the child's paternity allegations.

In response to these cases, states have expanded the ability of non-marital children to inherit, either by enacting their own statutes or by adopting the Uniform Parentage Act. Most, if not all, jurisdictions permit the non-marital child to inherit from and through the biological mother (and vice versa) without any difference in the amount of maternity proof from that which a marital child is required to produce. On the other hand, many states impose higher standards on a non-marital child to inherit from the father, especially if the father did not recognize or take other steps to make paternity clear during the child's lifetime. Examples of the type of proof required by these statutes include the subsequent marriage of the biological parents, the child living with the father coupled with the father holding out the child as a biological child, a court decree of paternity, and the father consenting to being named as the father on the child's birth certificate.

Many states also permit the non-marital child to prove paternity after the purported father has died. In an attempt to limit the number of false claims, these states typically impose a higher standard of proof of paternity in post-death actions. For example, there may need to be clear and convincing evidence of paternity. DNA evidence is especially helpful in making these determinations.

§3.4 Children from Alternative Reproduction Technologies

Modern medical technology permits children to be born via reproduction techniques that involve more than the traditional two people. Examples of these methodologies include (1) *artificial insemination* (donated semen artificially introduced into the mother's vagina or uterus), (2) *in vitro fertilization* (donated egg and donated semen combined in a laboratory with the resulting embryo transferred to a donee), (3) *gamete intrafallopian transfer* (donated egg and donated sperm combined in a donee's fallopian tube), and (4) *embryo lavage and transfer* (fertilized egg removed from the donor and transferred to the donee's uterus).

Several options exist regarding the parentage of children born as a result of these techniques. The father could be (1) the supplier of the genetic material (sperm), (2) the husband of the supplier of the female genetic material (egg), or (3) the husband of the woman who gestates the child. Likewise, the mother could be (1) the supplier of the female genetic material, (2) the wife of the man who supplies the male genetic material, or (3) the woman who gestates the child even though this woman did not supply any genetic material (a surrogate mother).

Jurisdictions have taken a variety of approaches to deal with these matters. Because artificial insemination is a relatively old technique that has successfully been practiced on humans since 1770, many states have statutes directly on point. Most of these statutes provide that the sperm donor is not the father. The father is typically the husband of the woman who receives the donated sperm. There is less uniformity with the other techniques resulting from their newness and the social and political issues they raise. Some states use these statutes to legislate family values by providing for parentage resolutions only in cases where the donee is married and both husband and wife consent.

Most of the existing legislation is not extensive or is designed to address issues of child support rather than inheritance rights. The Uniform Status of Children of Assisted Conception Act attempts to cover these issues in a comprehensive manner.

§3.5 Stepchildren

A *stepchild* is a child of a person's spouse who is not a biological or adopted child of the person. Generally, stepchildren may not inherit from their stepparents.

Example 3-6. Stepchildren

Marsha and Fred were married in 1990 and they had one child, Chris. After divorcing in 1995, Marsha married Henry. Henry wanted to adopt Chris but Fred refused to consent. If Henry dies intestate, may Chris inherit? Does it matter how old Chris is when Henry dies?

Explanation

In the vast majority of states, Chris would not be an heir because Chris is neither Henry's biological nor adopted child. Chris may argue that he is an equitably adopted child, as discussed in §3.2.4 above, but that argument is weak because Henry did not fail to do something that would trigger an equitable estoppel remedy. However, in a few states, such as California, a stepchild may inherit from a stepparent if the relationship began while the stepchild was a minor, continued during their joint lifetimes, and there is clear and convincing evidence that the stepparent would have adopted the person but for some legal barrier such as, in this example, Fred's refusal to consent. If Henry dies after Chris reaches the age of majority, Henry's other heirs may claim that Chris cannot inherit because the legal barrier did not exist when Henry died. Chris was an adult and could have consented to the adoption; Fred's approval was no longer required.

§3.6   Half-Blooded Collateral Heirs

The term *half-blood* refers to collateral relatives who share only one common ancestor. For example, a brother and sister who have the same mother but different fathers would be half-siblings. On the other hand, if the brother and sister have the same parents, they would be related by *whole-blood* because they share the same common ancestors. When collateral relatives (as contrasted with ancestors or descendants) are among the potential heirs, you must determine the relevance of being related by the half-blood.

At common law, half-blooded heirs could not inherit real property from a half-blooded intestate although they were entitled to inherit personal property. This strict rule with its emphasis on blood relationships has been modified by the states. States adopt one of three modern approaches: (1) The majority of states have totally eliminated the distinction between half- and whole-blooded relatives in determining inheritance rights. Thus, half-blooded collaterals inherit just as if they were of the whole-blood. See U.P.C. §2-107. (2) Some states adopt the Scottish rule, which provides that half-blooded collaterals receive half shares. (3) A few states permit half-blooded collateral heirs to inherit only if there is no whole-blooded heir of the same degree.

Example 3-7.   Half-Blooded Heirs

Barbara was married to John and they had two children, Art and Brenda. Art is married and has two children, Emily and Fred. Brenda is also married and has one daughter, Grace. Barbara divorced John and married Ray. Barbara and Ray had two children, Chad and Dennis.

Example 3-7a.   What is the relationship between Art and Ray?

Explanation

Art and Ray are related as stepfather and stepson. They are related by affinity only, not by blood.

Example 3-7b. What is the relationship between Brenda and Chad?

Explanation

Brenda and Chad are half-siblings because they share only one common ancestor (Barbara). Brenda is Chad's half-sister and Chad is Brenda's half-brother.

Example 3-7c. What is the relationship between Emily and Chad?

Explanation

Emily is Chad's half-niece and Chad is Emily's half-uncle.

Example 3-7d. Chad's parents, Barbara and Ray, die and then Chad dies intestate. How should Chad's estate be distributed?

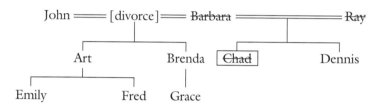

Explanation

The most likely outcome is that Art, Brenda, and Dennis would share equally in Chad's estate with each taking one-third. The fact that Art and Brenda are only half related to Chad is irrelevant in the majority of jurisdictions. In states following the Scottish rule, Dennis would receive one-half and Art and Brenda would each receive one-quarter. To give each whole-blooded heir a share twice as big as each half-blooded relative, Chad's estate would be divided in shares with two shares being created for each whole-blooded relative and one share for each half-blooded relative. Because there is one whole-blooded sibling (creating two shares) and two half-blooded siblings (creating one share each), a total of four shares would be created. Dennis would then get two of them (one-half of Chad's estate) and Art and Brenda would each receive one share (one-quarter each of Chad's estate). In states following the priority for whole-blooded rule, Dennis would receive Chad's entire estate because he is the only whole-blooded heir.

§3.7 Non-United States Citizens

At common law, a noncitizen could not acquire or transmit real property through intestacy. This rule made sense because the landowner owed duties to the Crown which would be difficult to enforce if the landowner was not a citizen. On the other hand, noncitizens from friendly countries could both acquire and transmit personal property through intestacy.

Under modern law, noncitizens are treated no differently than citizens when it comes to inheritance rights. See UPC §2-111. Note, however, that during the World Wars, the United States government restricted the inheritance rights of citizens of enemy nations.

§3.8   Unworthy Heirs

§3.8.1   Forfeiture

At common law, a person who was convicted of a felony forfeited all of the person's property to the government so there was no property for the person's heirs to inherit. Although most states have abolished forfeiture for most felonies, it is occasionally retained as a remedy for specific crimes. For example, under federal law, a person convicted of certain drug offenses forfeits a portion of the person's property to the government.[1]

§3.8.2   Civil Death

Under the law of some states, persons who are convicted of certain serious crimes, especially if the sentence is for life, are treated as being civilly dead. A civilly dead person may lose a variety of rights such as the ability to contract, the right to vote, and the right to maintain a lawsuit. The issue that then arises is whether the person's property passes to the heirs as if the person had actually died. The prevailing view, either by statute or judicial decision, is that civil death does not have this effect; property passes to a person's heirs only upon a biological death. The policy behind this result is that it would be inequitable to deprive the person of property because the conviction could be subsequently overturned or the person could be pardoned or receive a commuted sentence. In such a case, the person's civil rights would be immediately returned, but the heirs may no longer be able to return the "inherited" property or its proceeds.

§3.8.3   Corruption of the Blood

At common law, a person could not inherit land if the person was convicted or imprisoned for certain offenses, especially treason and other capital of-

---

1. 21 U.S.C.A. §853 (West Supp. 1996).

fenses. The English parliament abolished corruption of the blood by the mid-1800s and the concept never gained popularity in the United States. Accordingly, an imprisoned person, even one on death row, may inherit property. As discussed in the next section, the result is quite different if the person is convicted for murdering the person from whom the property is being inherited.

§3.8.4 Heir Killing Intestate

Two public policies must be balanced when deciding whether an heir who kills the intestate may inherit from the intestate. First, the heir should not be rewarded for causing the intestate's death. Second, an heir should not be deprived of an inheritance without just cause. Thus, courts and legislatures carefully examine the particular type of killing performed by the heir.

§3.8.4.1 Murder

At common law, an individual convicted of murder forfeited all property to the Crown and thus could not benefit by inheriting from the victim. See §3.8.1, above. Most states, however, abolished forfeiture by constitutional or statutory provisions early in their history. Thus, for many years American courts permitted murderers to inherit from their victims. Despite the obvious inequity of this result, the courts held that they were without the power or authority to alter the statutorily mandated intestate distribution plan by creating an exception for murderers.

To prevent murderers from benefiting from their evil acts, most state legislatures have enacted statutes prohibiting murderers from inheriting. These provisions are often referred to as *slayer's statutes*. For example, UPC §2-803 provides that "[a]n individual who feloniously and intentionally kills the decedent" may not claim inheritance rights. The intestate's estate passes as if the murderer disclaimed the inheritance, that is, as if the murderer predeceased the intestate. See §4.4, below.

In many of the states without statutes on point, courts impose a constructive trust on the murderer. As discussed in Chapter 23, below, a constructive trust is an equitable remedy courts impose on unworthy individuals to prevent unjust enrichment. Thus, legal title to the intestate's property passes to the heir even though the heir murdered the intestate. However, the heir is deemed to be a constructive trustee because of the unconscionable means the heir used to acquire the property and thus cannot retain legal title. The constructive trust arises in favor of the intestate's heirs, exclusive of the murderer.

Example 3-8. Heir Murders Intestate — No Criminal Conviction

Father, Daughter, and Son intentionally killed Mother to accelerate their inheritances. Grief-stricken by his conduct, Father committed suicide shortly after Mother died. The police gathered evidence against Daughter without a valid search warrant and thus the court acquitted Daughter of the murder. The district attorney was unable to gather conclusive evidence against Son and decided not to prosecute. May Father, Daughter, or Son inherit from Mother?

Explanation

Because no heir was convicted of a crime, the ability of each to inherit is uncertain. Under many slayer's statutes, a criminal conviction is a prerequisite to disqualification. However, some modern statutes, such as UPC §2-803, are designed to cover these situations. The heir does not have to be convicted to be prevented from taking as long as "under the preponderance of evidence standard, the individual would be found criminally accountable for the felonious and intentional killing of the decedent." If no statute applies, the court may nonetheless impose a constructive trust.

Example 3-9. Heir Murders Intestate — Voluntary Euthanasia

Husband was in agonizing pain because of a terminal illness. Husband begged to be put out of his misery. In response to Husband's pleas, Wife killed Husband. May Wife inherit?

Explanation

No state authorizes voluntary euthanasia, that is, the killing of someone upon that person's request for the humanitarian purpose of alleviating suffering. Almost all courts hold that the motives of the murderer are irrelevant. Thus, it is likely that Wife could not inherit.

§3.8.4.2 Voluntary Manslaughter

Voluntary manslaughter involves an intentional and unlawful killing that the killer performed with the intent of causing death, but the killing was the result of sudden passion or great provocation. For example, Wife returns home early from a business trip only to find Husband in bed with another woman. In a fit of rage, Wife kills Husband. Many, but not all, courts would prevent Wife from inheriting from Husband because Wife did have the intent to kill and should not benefit from her evil intent.

§3.8.4.3 Involuntary Manslaughter

If the killer unlawfully caused the death of the intestate but had no intention to take the deceased's life, the vast majority of courts permit the killer to inherit. For example, Husband got liquored up after work and in a drunken stupor ran over and killed Wife while pulling into the driveway of their home. It would serve no social purpose to deprive Husband of the inheritance because Husband, although acting recklessly and negligently, did not intend for Wife to die.

§3.8.4.4 Non-Criminal Killings

If the killing was non-criminal, the heir usually retains the ability to inherit. Examples of non-criminal killings include (1) the heir kills the intestate totally by accident (that is, not with an intent to kill and not through the heir's recklessness or negligence), (2) the killing is in self-defense, or (3) the heir was insane at the time of the killing.

§3.8.5 Suicide

The property of a person who committed suicide was subject to special rules at common law. If the intestate committed suicide to avoid punishment after committing a felony, the intestate's heirs took nothing. Instead, the real property escheated and personal property was forfeited. However, if the intestate committed suicide because of pain or exhaustion from living, only personal property was forfeited and real property still descended to the heirs.

American jurisdictions have abolished this common law rule. Many states have statutes that provide for the property of a person who commits suicide to pass just as if the death were caused by some other means.

§3.8.6 Parent's Failure to Support Child

Some jurisdictions do not allow a biological parent or the parent's kin to inherit from or through a child unless the parent can prove that the parent "deserves" to inherit. For example, U.P.C. §2-114(c) permits inheritance only if the parent (1) has openly treated the child as belonging to the parent, and (2) has not refused to support the child.

Example 3-10. Failure to Support Child

Child lived with Mother from birth until age eighteen. During this time, Mother provided all of Child's support. Upon reaching eighteen, Child married and lived with Spouse until getting divorced at age thirty. The divorce was very difficult on Child and Child asked Mother for support assistance. Mother refused. Many years later and after accumulating a sizable estate, Child died intestate without a surviving spouse or descendants. May Mother inherit from Child?

Explanation

In the majority of jurisdictions, Mother may inherit. If, however, the state has a statute such as U.P.C. §2-114(c) discussed above, Mother's inheritance rights are problematic. The express language of the statute provides that inheritance is precluded if the biological parent refused to support the child, which is exactly what Mother did in this example. However, the commentary to the UPC indicates that a parent's refusal to provide support during a time when the parent has no legal obligation to support the child, as in this example where Child was an adult at the time of Mother's refusal, would not impair the parent's inheritance rights.

§3.8.7 *Adultery*

At common law under the Statute of Westminster II (1285), a wife who left her husband and then entered an adulterous relationship was barred from receiving her dower interest unless her husband forgave her and allowed her to return home. However, if the wife stayed at home with her husband while committing adultery, she retained her dower rights. Remnants of this common law rule, expanded to limit the rights of either spouse who commits adultery, have been retained and codified in several states. For example, a Kentucky statute provides that "[if] either spouse voluntarily leaves the other and lives in adultery, the offending party forfeits all right and interest in and to the property and estate of the other, unless they afterward become reconciled and live together as husband and wife."[2]

---

2. Ky. Rev. Stat. Ann. §392.090(2) (Michie 1984).

4

Other Intestate Succession Issues

This chapter reviews a variety of additional factors that may affect whether an heir receives an intestate share and, if so, the size of that share.

§4.1 Ancestral Property

The common law policy of keeping real property in the blood line of the original owner led to the development of the principle of *ancestral property*. This doctrine applied if an individual inherited real property and then died intestate without surviving descendants or first line collateral relatives. Under this doctrine, real property inherited from the intestate's paternal side of the family would pass to the paternal collateral relatives and property inherited from the maternal side would pass to the maternal collateral relatives. The doctrine of ancestral property has never been applied to personal property.

Example 4-1. Ancestral Property

Upon the death of Paternal Grandfather, Intestate inherited Blackacre. Intestate died without surviving descendants or first line collaterals. Intestate was survived by two paternal aunts and one maternal uncle. Applying the doctrine of ancestral property, who inherits Blackacre?

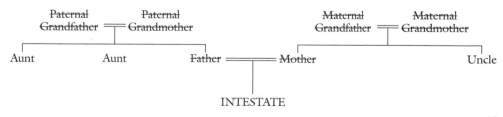

Explanation

Applying the doctrine of ancestral property, the paternal aunts would receive Blackacre to the exclusion of the maternal uncle.

Almost all states and the UPC have rejected the doctrine of ancestral property. Under modern law, an intestate decedent is treated as the original purchaser of all property the intestate owns at time of death.

§4.2   Advancements

An *advancement* is a special type of inter vivos gift. The advancer (donor) anticipates dying intestate and the advancee (donee) is an individual who is likely to be one of the advancer's heirs. Although the gift is irrevocable and unconditional, the advancer intends the advancement to be an early distribution from the advancer's estate. Thus, the advancee's share of the advancer's estate is reduced to compensate for the advancement.

When the advancer dies intestate, the advanced property is treated as if it were still in the advancer's probate estate when computing the size of the intestate shares. Thus, the advancee receives a smaller share in the estate because the advancee already has part of the advancer's estate, that is, the advancement. This equalization process is referred to as *going into hotchpot*.

Example 4-2.   Advancements — Basic Hotchpot

Intestate had three children, Arthur, Brenda, and Charles. Intestate made a $100,000 advancement to Arthur. Intestate died with a distributable probate estate of $500,000. What is the proper distribution of Intestate's estate?

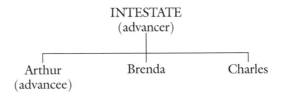

Explanation

Arthur receives $100,000, Brenda receives $200,000, and Charles receives $200,000. Because the $100,000 gift to Arthur was an advancement, that amount is treated as if it were still in Intestate's estate. Thus, Intestate's estate is distributed as if it contained $600,000. Intestate had three children and thus each child is entitled to a per capita share of $200,000. Because Arthur has already received $100,000 by way of the advancement, he is entitled only to an additional $100,000 from Intestate's estate. Brenda and Charles each receive their share from Intestate's estate. The hotchpot process ensures that each child receives an equal share from Intestate accounting for both inter vivos and at-death transfers.

Example 4-3. Advancements — Advancement Disproportionately Large

Intestate had three children, Arthur, Brenda, and Charles. Intestate made a $100,000 advancement to Arthur. Intestate died with a distributable probate estate of $50,000. What is the proper distribution of Intestate's estate?

Explanation

Arthur receives none of Intestate's estate, Brenda receives $25,000 and Charles receives $25,000. Like other inter vivos gifts, advancements are irrevocable. Thus, Arthur is under no obligation to actually return the advanced amount to Intestate's estate. Arthur is not indebted for the advanced amount. Instead, Arthur simply does not share in Intestate's estate because he has already received property in excess of the share to which he would be entitled under a hotchpot computation. Thus, Intestate's entire estate is distributed to Brenda and Charles.

Example 4-4. Advancements — Value of Advanced Property

Intestate had three children, Arthur, Brenda, and Charles. Intestate advanced two assets to Arthur, a house worth $100,000 at the time of the advancement and a car worth $30,000 at the time of the advancement. Intestate died with a distributable probate estate of $500,000. At the time of Intestate's death, the house had appreciated to $300,000 and the car had depreciated to $1,000. What is the proper distribution of Intestate's estate?

Explanation

Arthur receives $80,000, Brenda receives $210,000, and Charles receives $210,000. Advancements are typically valued as of the date of the advancement. See UPC §2-104(b). Thus, subsequent appreciation and depreciation of advanced property is ignored when going into hotchpot. The house valued at $100,000 and the car valued at $30,000 come into hotchpot. The value of the hotchpot, that is, advancements plus Intestate's estate, is $630,000. Each of the three children is entitled to $210,000. Because Arthur already received advancements valued at $130,000, he receives only $80,000 from the estate. Brenda and Charles each receive a full $210,000 share because neither of them had received an advancement.

Example 4-5. Advancements — Proof

Intestate had three children, Arthur, Brenda, and Charles. Intestate made an inter vivos gift of $100,000 to Arthur. Intestate died with a distributable probate estate of $500,000. What is the proper distribution of Intestate's estate?

Explanation

The key issue in this example is whether Intestate's $100,000 gift to Arthur is an advancement. At common law, inter vivos transfers to children were presumed to be advancements. Under modern law, the heirs who wish to establish an advancement have the burden of proof to show that the intestate decedent intended the gift to be an advancement. In some states, the non-advancee heirs may use any type of evidence to establish the advancement nature of the transfer. However, most states require written documentation. For example, UPC §2-109(a) requires a writing clearly indicating the advancement nature of the inter vivos gift that is executed either (1) by the advancer contemporaneously with the transfer, or (2) by the advancee at any time.

Example 4-6. Advancements — Advancee Predeceases Advancer

Intestate had three children, Arthur, Brenda, and Charles. Intestate made a $100,000 advancement to Arthur. Arthur died survived by his two children, Sam and Susan. Subsequently, Intestate died with a distributable probate estate of $500,000. What is the proper distribution of Intestate's estate?

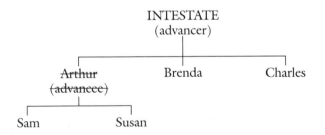

Explanation

The answer to this example turns on whether an advancement is taken into account when the advancee predeceases the advancer and the advancee's heirs are taking by representation from the advancer's estate. Jurisdictions vary in the resolution of this issue. The modern view adopted by UPC §2-109(c) is that the advancement is not considered and hotchpot does not occur unless the advancer specified in writing that the advancement is to be brought into hotchpot even if the advancee predeceases the advancer. Accordingly, Brenda and Charles would each receive one-third of Intestate's probate estate (approximately $166,666) while Sam and Susan would each receive one-sixth (approximately $83,333). The policy behind this approach is that the advancee's heirs may not have received the advanced property or its value from the advancee's estate. On the other hand, some states would nonetheless place the advancement in hotchpot so Brenda and Charles would receive $200,000 each with Sam and Susan receiving $50,000 each.

Example 4-7. Advancements — Nondescendant Advancees

Intestate had two siblings, Brother and Sister. Intestate made a $100,000 advancement to Brother. Intestate died survived by Brother and Sister, his only heirs. Intestate's distributable probate estate is valued at $500,000. What is the proper distribution of Intestate's estate?

Explanation

Jurisdictions are divided regarding whether hotchpot would be necessary in this case. Many states require the hotchpot process only for advancements to children and other descendants. Other states require hotchpot in any situation where an heir receives an advancement. See UPC §2-109.

Example 4-8. Advancements — Partial Intestacy

Intestate had three children, Arthur, Brenda, and Charles. Intestate made a $100,000 advancement to Arthur. Intestate's valid will gave his house, valued at $250,000, to Charles. Intestate's will had no residual clause and thus the remainder of his probate estate valued at $500,000 passes by intestate succession. What is the proper distribution of Intestate's estate?

Explanation

Jurisdictions vary as to whether an advancee must go into hotchpot if the advancer dies partially intestate, instead of totally intestate. Some states ignore advancements in partial intestacy situations figuring that the advancer took the advancement into consideration when the advancer prepared the will. On the other hand, many jurisdictions require hotchpot in the partial intestacy context. See UPC §2-109(a).

§4.3 Survival

To be an heir, an individual must outlive the intestate. Property cannot pass to a decedent because a decedent lacks the capacity to take and hold title. At common law and under the 1953 version of the Uniform Simultaneous

Death Act, an heir needed to survive the intestate for only a mere instant to be entitled to inherit. This rule led to many proof problems as family members tried to prove that one person outlived the other or vice versa. Some of these cases read like horror novels as the courts evaluate evidence of which person twitched, gurgled, or gasped longer.

Most jurisdictions now impose a survival period; that is, the heir must outlive the intestate by a statutorily mandated length of time before being entitled to inherit. Under the 1991 version of the Uniform Simultaneous Death Act and UPC §2-104, the heir must outlive the intestate by 120 hours (five days). If an heir survives the intestate but dies prior to the expiration of the survival period, the intestate's property passes as if the heir had actually predeceased the intestate.

Example 4-9. Survival — Distribution of Property

Intestate died on May 1, survived by Son and Daughter. Overcome by grief, Son committed suicide on May 4, survived by Spouse, Grandson, and Granddaughter. Son died with a valid will leaving his entire estate to Spouse. Intestate's distributable probate estate is valued at $100,000. What is the proper distribution of Intestate's estate assuming the jurisdiction has a 120-hour survival requirement?

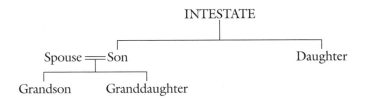

Explanation

Daughter receives $50,000, Grandson receives $25,000, and Granddaughter receives $25,000. Because Son did not survive by 120 hours, Son is treated as if he had predeceased Intestate. None of Intestate's property is in Son's estate so Spouse has no claim to Intestate's property. Instead, the $50,000 that Son would have received had he outlived Intestate by 120 hours passes as if Son had died first. Thus, Son's two children take by representation with each receiving $25,000.

Example 4-10. Survival — Evidence

Intestate and Heir were hiking in the Rocky Mountains during January. A blizzard hit and they were stranded. Two weeks after their expected return, both Intestate and Heir were found dead. Because their bodies were preserved by the cold, forensic examiners were unable to determine with certainty who lived longer or by how long. However, the experts opined that Heir survived Intestate because Heir was younger and in better physical condition. Heir is Intestate's only child. Heir's valid will leaves Heir's entire estate to Charity. What is the proper distribution of Intestate's estate?

Explanation

Intestate's other relatives (e.g., parents and siblings) will argue that Heir did not survive. On the other hand, Charity will assert that Heir survived causing Intestate's property to pass to Heir so that Charity is entitled to the property under Heir's will. Jurisdictions vary regarding the level of proof necessary to show that a person survived. For example, under the pre-1991 Uniform Simultaneous Death Act, Heir would not be deemed to have survived unless there was "sufficient" evidence to the contrary. It is arguable whether the experts' opinions would meet this standard. However, the standard is higher in the current version of this act, which requires "clear and convincing evidence" of the survival. Under this standard, Heir will probably be deemed to have not survived Intestate.

Example 4-11. Survival — Escheat

Intestate died on May 1. Heir died on May 4. Heir was Intestate's last surviving heir. Thus, if Heir does not inherit, Intestate's property will escheat. Heir's will leaves the entire estate to Charity. Who is entitled to Intestate's property in a jurisdiction with a 120-hour survival requirement?

Explanation

Although Heir did not outlive Intestate by the required 120 hours, most statutes provide that the survival period does not apply if escheat would result. See UPC §2-104. Accordingly, Heir is entitled to inherit and Charity receives Intestate's property as the sole beneficiary of Heir's will.

Example 4-12. Survival — Ethical Considerations

Two brothers, Brian and Terry, were in an automobile accident. Brian's will provides that his entire estate passes to Terry, or if Terry has predeceased, to his friend, Arthur. Terry has no will and only one heir, his daughter, Victoria. Brian died immediately; 110 hours have passed and the doctor is considering pronouncing Terry dead and removing the life support equipment. The equipment could keep Terry "alive" for at least another ten hours. Victoria and Arthur are at the hospital. Assuming that a 120-hour survival period applies, what does each person want and why? Whose request should the doctor honor?

Explanation

Victoria wants Terry kept alive beyond the 120 hours. Terry could then take under Brian's will and upon Terry's death, Victoria would receive the property through intestacy. On the other hand, Arthur wants Terry to die before the 120-hour period expires so Terry will be treated as predeceasing Brian. The property would then pass to Arthur under Brian's will. There is no easy answer to the doctor's dilemma, which involves ethical questions from both legal and medical perspectives.

§4.4   Disclaimers

At common law, an heir had no choice but to accept property passing from an intestate decedent. Someone always had to be responsible for performing the feudal obligations that accompanied land ownership. Under modern law, an heir may disclaim or renounce the heir's share in the estate of an intestate decedent. See UPC §2-801 and the Uniform Disclaimer of Property Interests Act.

§4.4.1   *Reasons Heir May Disclaim*

In the normal course of events, heirs do not disclaim their inheritances. Most people like the idea of getting something for free. However, there are many good reasons why an heir may desire to forgo the offered bounty. Four of the most common reasons are discussed below.

First, the property may be undesirable or accompanied by an onerous burden. For example, the property could be littered with leaky barrels of toxic chemical waste, be subject to back taxes exceeding the value of the land, or be of the "white elephant" variety; that is, junk the heir simply does not want and that has no significant resale value.

Second, the heir may believe that it is wrong to benefit from the death of another and refuse the property on moral or religious grounds.

Third, an heir who is in debt may disclaim the property to prevent the property from being taken by the heir's creditors. Jurisdictions are divided on whether this use of a disclaimer operates as a fraudulent conveyance that the aggrieved creditor may set aside. See UPC §2-801(d) which adopts a nonfraudulent conveyance approach.

Fourth, the heir may disclaim to reduce the heir's transfer tax burden. If a disclaimer meets the requirements of a *qualified disclaimer* under IRC

§2518, then the heir is treated as if the heir never owned the property. Thus, the heir is not considered to have made a gift when the property passes to another person and the property is not part of the heir's estate.

Example 4-13. Disclaimers — Tax Benefits

Grandfather died intestate. Daughter is entitled to $1,000,000 under the applicable intestate succession statute. Daughter is very wealthy on her own and does not need the money. However, Daughter's only child, Grandson, a recent law school graduate, is in need of money to open his own office. Why might Daughter want to consider making a qualified disclaimer of all or a portion of her inheritance?

Explanation

If Daughter were to accept the inheritance and then give the money to Grandson, the transfer would subject Daughter to federal gift tax. If Daughter were to accept the inheritance and die before making the gift, Daughter's estate would incur estate tax liability on the money. If Daughter were to accept the inheritance and distribute it to Grandson as he needed it, Daughter would also be subject to income tax on the income earned by the money she still retained. However, if Daughter properly disclaims her inheritance, she will be treated as never owning the property and will successfully avoid these adverse tax consequences.

§4.4.2 Requirements of a Disclaimer

State and federal law impose a host of formalities on disclaimers. State law requirements are often very similar to those imposed by federal law but significant differences may exist. A disclaiming heir must be certain to meet federal requirements if tax reduction is the goal motivating the disclaimer. Compliance with state law mandates would not be sufficient.

The most common requirements for a valid disclaimer are listed below:

1. The disclaimer must be memorialized in a writing that is signed by the disclaiming heir.
2. The disclaimer document must be timely filed with the proper authorities. Federal law requires the disclaimer to be filed within nine months of the intestate's death. The time period could expire even before the heir knows about the inheritance. However, some states soften the rule by requiring the disclaimer to be filed within nine months of when the heir learns of the inheritance or expand the time for future interests allowing the disclaimer within nine

months of when a future interest becomes indefeasibly vested. See UPC §2-801(b). Some states do not even impose a time restriction.

3. A copy of the disclaimer instrument usually must be delivered to the administrator so the administrator knows not to deliver estate property to the heir.

4. Disclaimers are irrevocable. Thus, once an heir disclaims, the heir cannot regain the property by revoking the disclaimer, even if the attempted revocation comes within the nine-month period. Likewise, courts do not allow disclaimers to be undone because the disclaiming heir misunderstood the effect of the disclaimer.

5. Partial disclaimers are allowed. Thus, the heir can elect to retain the desirable property and disclaim the rest.

6. If the heir has accepted the property or any of its benefits, it is too late for the heir to disclaim even if any applicable time period has not yet elapsed. Acceptance is manifested by any affirmative act consistent with ownership of the interest in the property, such as using the property or the interest in the property, accepting dividends, interest, or rents from the property, or directing others to act with respect to the property. See Treas. Reg. §25.2518-2(d)(1).

7. The disclaimer must be unconditional. In other words, the heir cannot receive something in exchange for making the disclaimer.

§4.4.3 Distribution of Disclaimed Property

Disclaimed property typically passes as if the disclaiming heir predeceased the intestate. See UPC §2-801(d). The heir cannot direct in any manner the distribution of the disclaimed property.

Example 4-14. Disclaimers — Distribution of Disclaimed Property

Intestate had two children, Son and Daughter. Son predeceased Intestate survived by his only child, Arthur. Daughter properly executed a disclaimer. Daughter has two children, Brenda and Charles. Intestate's distributable probate estate is valued at $100,000. What is the proper distribution of Intestate's estate assuming the state has a per capita with representation descent and distribution statute?

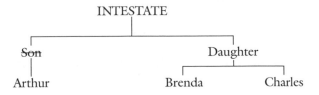

Explanation

Under the generally accepted application of disclaimer laws, Arthur receives $50,000, Brenda receives $25,000, and Charles receives $25,000. If Daughter had not executed the disclaimer, Daughter would have received $50,000 and Arthur, representing Son, would have received $50,000. Although Daughter executed a valid disclaimer, only the property subject to the disclaimer passes as if Daughter predeceased Intestate. Thus, $50,000 passes as if Daughter died first and was survived by Brenda and Charles. Under the law of most states and UPC §2-801, Brenda and Charles will be unable to claim a per capita share in Intestate's entire estate, which would have entitled each grandchild to $33,333. In other words, Brenda and Charles cannot treat Daughter as if she predeceased Intestate with respect to the entire estate and trigger a different type of distribution. Only the disclaimed property passes to alternate heirs. An argument may be made under some disclaimer statutes that Daughter's one-half interest is now divided among Arthur, Brenda, and Charles because if Daughter had actually predeceased, all three would have shared in the $50,000. This interpretation of treating Daughter as predeceasing is not usually followed. When a disclaiming heir has descendants, the courts do not permit one heir (Daughter) to disclaim and thereby manipulate the shares of the other heirs (Arthur); the disclaimer simply makes other more distantly related relatives of Intestate into heirs (Brenda and Charles), and they take the disclaimed property.

§4.5 Assignment or Release of Expectancy to Inherit

What may an individual do with the individual's hope of being an heir upon the death of another person who is still alive? Because a living person has no heirs, an heir apparent does not have an interest that rises to the level of being property. Instead, the hopeful heir's interest is a mere expectancy. The person whom the heir apparent hopes will die intestate may prevent the expectation from being fulfilled by taking a variety of steps such as writing a will, selling the property, or making a gift of the property. Accordingly, an heir apparent has nothing to transfer.

The heir apparent, however, may agree (1) to transfer the inheritance once received, or (2) not to claim a future inheritance. As long as the agreement meets all the requirements of a contract (e.g., offer, acceptance, and consideration), most courts will enforce the agreement if the heir apparent fails to perform upon the intestate's death. A few courts, however, will not enforce these contracts on the ground that they give the other party to the contract an incentive to cause the premature death of the anticipated intestate.

Example 4-15. Contract to Transfer Expectancy

Client explains that he was approached by Kevin, the only child of Parent. Kevin estimated that Parent's estate is worth $500,000. Kevin assured Client that Parent has not executed a will. Parent is not in good health and Kevin thinks Parent will die within six to twelve months. Kevin is in need of ready cash and is willing to execute a contract in which he promises to convey to Client everything he inherits from Parent if Client transfers $100,000 to him immediately. How do you advise Client assuming you are in a jurisdiction that enforces this type of contract?

Explanation

Client should be extremely cautious about entering into this contract because the risk is extremely high. For example, Parent could execute a will leaving Parent's estate to charity or Kevin could predecease Parent. In these cases, Client would receive nothing under the contract. Similarly, Parent could exhaust the estate paying for medical care or other expenses.

Example 4-16. Release of Expectancy

Client explains that he was approached by Parent. Parent's estate is worth $500,000 and Parent wants the bulk of the estate to pass to Preferred Child, Client's only sibling. Parent offered Client $100,000 in cash if Child executes a contract releasing all claims to Parent's intestate estate. How do you advise Client assuming you are in a jurisdiction that enforces this type of contract?

Explanation

Client may be well-advised to execute the contract. Client would then receive a certain $100,000 although giving up whatever other rights Client may have in Parent's estate. If Client does not agree, Parent could simply make a will leaving everything to Preferred Child. Unless Client successfully contested the will, Client would receive nothing from Parent.

In many jurisdictions, Parent runs the risk that Client may die first and be survived by descendants who outlive Parent. These descendants would take from Parent's estate by representation. The contract between Parent and Client would not prevent Client's descendants from receiving their intestate shares because they were not parties to the contract. On the other hand, in some states, Client's release acts to bind Client's descendants.

§4.6 Equitable Conversion

Equitable conversion is the process by which real property is treated as personal property or personal property is treated as real property. This result is based on the equitable principle that equity regards as done that which in fairness and good conscience ought to be done. Assume that Intestate and Purchaser entered into a contract to sell real property but Intestate died before performing that contract, that is, before the closing. Because this contract is specifically enforceable, equitable conversion occurs. Intestate is treated as owning personal property (the right to the sales proceeds) at death and Purchaser is deemed to own real property (the specifically enforceable right to demand the transfer of the real property).

Equitable conversion may be important in an intestacy context if the state makes a distinction between the descent of real property and the distribution of personal property. If Intestate dies prior to executing the contract, the property passes to the heirs entitled to realty but if the Intestate dies after signing the contract, the property passes as personalty to the next of kin.

§4.7 Liability for Debts of Predeceased Intermediary

Heirs are entitled to their full inheritances without reduction for debts owed by a predeceased intermediary. It does not matter that the predeceased intermediary owed the debt to the intestate or to third parties. As stated by UPC §2-110, "[a] debt owed to a decedent is not charged against the intestate share of any individual except the debtor. If the debtor fails to survive the decedent, the debt is not taken into account in computing the intestate share of the debtor's descendants."

Example 4-17. Liability for Debts of Predeceased Intermediary

When Son died, Son's estate was insolvent and two debts remained unpaid. The first debt was a $100,000 loan Son owed to Intestate, his mother. The second debt was to Visa for $13,452 in unpaid credit card charges. Subsequently, Intestate died survived by Daughter and Grandson (Son's child). What are the ramifications of Son's two unpaid debts?

Explanation

Property passes directly from Intestate to the heirs (Grandson and Daughter). The property is not used to satisfy debts of Son because Grandson's inheritance does not pass through the estate of the deceased intermediary (Son). Thus, Grandson's share is not reduced and Daughter's share is not increased to compensate for the loan Intestate made to Son, which had not been repaid. Likewise, VISA may not claim any of the property passing to Grandson to satisfy Son's debt.

§4.8   Heir Designation

A few states permit a person to designate a person to take as an heir in a nontestamentary document. No biological or family relationship is needed between the designating person and the heir. A designated heir will then take either in place of or in addition to other heirs. A designated heir typically inherits as a child.

§4.9   Choice of Law

The descent of real property is governed by the law of the situs of the real property. The distribution of personal property is governed by the law of the intestate's domicile at the time of death. Thus, the intestacy statutes of several states may apply to the same intestate's estate. The type of intestate distribution and the ways in which certain categories of potential heirs, such as adopted children and non-marital children, are treated may vary greatly among these different states.

Part Two

WILLS

5

Requirements for a Valid Will

The only way for a person to avoid having the probate estate pass to heirs under the law of intestate succession is to execute a valid will. A person has, however, no right to make a will. The United States Supreme Court confirmed that "[r]ights of succession to the property of a deceased . . . are of statutory creation, and the dead hand rules succession only by sufferance. Nothing in the Federal Constitution forbids the legislature of a state to limit, condition, or even abolish the power of testamentary disposition over property within its jurisdiction."[1]

Although not required to do so, all state legislatures have granted their citizens the privilege of designating the recipients of their property upon death. A state legislature could take away this privilege at any time. Of course, any legislator who voted to curtail the ability of a person to execute a will would be highly unlikely to be reelected!

Because the ability to execute a will is a privilege, a will typically has no effect unless the testator has precisely followed all the requirements. Most states demand strict compliance with the requirements discussed in this chapter; one trivial deviation may cause the entire will to fail. A few states, however, have adopted the *substantial compliance* standard of UPC §2-503, which grants the court a *dispensing power* to excuse a harmless error if there is clear and convincing evidence that the testator intended the document to be a will.

Many states have a *savings statute*, which permits a will that does not meet the requirements of a valid will under local law to nonetheless be

---

1. Irving Trust Co. v. Day, 314 U.S. 556, 562 (1942).

effective under certain circumstances. For example, UPC §2-506 provides that a testator's written will is valid, even though it does not satisfy the normal requirements, if it "complies with the law at the time of execution of the place where the will is executed, or of the law of the place where at the time of execution or at the time of death the testator is domiciled, has a place of abode, or is a national."

This chapter details the four main requirements of a valid will: (1) legal capacity, (2) testamentary capacity, (3) testamentary intent, and (4) formalities. Whenever you are asked to determine if a document purporting to be a will is valid, you must begin your analysis by ascertaining whether the testator satisfied each of these four requirements.

§5.1   Legal Capacity

A person must possess a certain status to be able to make a testamentary disposition of property. At common law and early in the history of the United States, a wide variety of classes of individuals were denied the privilege of making a will. For example, married women, aliens, convicts, and Native Americans were deemed to lack the legal capacity to execute wills merely because of their supposedly inferior status. Although modern law has removed most class-related restrictions, a person still must possess the appropriate legal status to make a will. This section discusses ways in which a person may acquire legal capacity.

§5.1.1 Age

The 1540 Statute of Wills neglected to state the minimum age a person must attain before being able to devise real property. The English Parliament quickly corrected this oversight by specifying the age of twenty-one. Until the Wills Act of 1837, men over fourteen and women over twelve could make bequests of personal property under the rules of the ecclesiastical courts. The Wills Act of 1837 established the minimum age of twenty-one for all types of testamentary dispositions of property without regard to the sex of the property owner.

Every state today grants a person the legal capacity to execute a will upon reaching a statutorily specified age. The most common age and the age adopted by UPC §2-501 is eighteen. A few states grant a person legal capacity at younger ages such as fourteen or sixteen. No state has different ages based on the sex of the testator or on the type of property being transferred.

Example 5-1. Legal Capacity—Age

Teresa followed the appropriate state law procedure to obtain a court decree removing all the disabilities of minority. Thereafter, Teresa executed a will while only seventeen years old. If state law requires a testator to be at least eighteen years of age, is Teresa's will valid?

Explanation

Most jurisdictions interpret the age of legal capacity as relating to biological age, not legal or mental age. Just as Teresa would be unable to vote, purchase intoxicating beverages, or own firearms, she could not execute a valid will because she is not at least eighteen years old. Note, however, that a few states do permit emancipated minors to execute wills.

§5.1.2 *Marital Status*

Several states permit a person below the statutorily mandated age to execute a will if the person is legally married. The policy supporting this deviation from the normal rule is that a person with the maturity to enter into a marriage and to assume the responsibilities inherent in such a relationship needs the ability to control the disposition of the person's property upon death to fulfill responsibilities to the spouse and any children.

Example 5-2. Legal Capacity—Marital Status

Harold and Wilma were validly married in a state which permits a married individual under eighteen years of age to execute a will. The marriage ended in divorce when Harold was seventeen years old. After the divorce but before reaching age eighteen, Harold wrote his will. Is this will valid?

Explanation

The answer depends on the exact language of the relevant state statute. Most states that permit married minors to execute wills provide that once legal capacity is achieved through the marriage, the capacity continues thereafter even if a divorce predates the person's eighteenth birthday. Thus, there is a strong probability that Harold's will is valid if state law authorizes a married minor to execute a will.

§5.1.3 *Military Service*

A few states provide that a person in military service may execute a will even if the person is under the normal minimum age for legal capacity. The reasoning behind this variation of the normal rule is that a person mature enough to die for his or her country certainly is old enough to execute a will.

§5.2 Testamentary Capacity (Sound Mind)

The second requirement for a valid will is that the testator must have had testamentary capacity at the time the testator executed the will. State legislatures rarely detail how a person achieves testamentary capacity other than to state that a testator must be of "sound mind." See UPC §2-501. Thus, courts have had the responsibility of defining the elements of testamentary capacity. Although courts vary in how they determine the soundness of a person's mind, it is typical for testamentary capacity to encompass the four elements discussed in this section; that is, that the testator (1) comprehended the action being taken and its effect, (2) knew the nature and extent of the testator's property, (3) recognized the natural objects of the testator's bounty, and (4) simultaneously held the first three elements in the testator's mind long enough to make a reasoned judgment regarding property disposition.

§5.2.1 *Elements of Testamentary Capacity*

§5.2.1.1 Comprehend Action and Its Effect

A testator must understand what the testator is doing and its effect. Thus, the testator must appreciate that the testator is making arrangements regarding who becomes the new owner of the testator's property upon the testator's death.

Example 5-3. Testamentary Capacity — Knowledge of Legal Term "Will"

Tommy signed a document reading, "When I die, I want my mother to have all my property." The document meets all the formalities for a valid will. If asked to identify this document, Tommy would say, "These are my death instructions." If asked to define "will," Tommy would say, "Will is a friend of mine who lives down the road." Does Tommy have a valid will?

Explanation

Yes, Tommy's will is valid. Tommy needs to understand the nature and effect of the instrument. Tommy understands that the instrument determines the identity of the person who will own his property upon his death. It is not necessary for Tommy to know that the legal name for the document is a will. Likewise, it would not matter if Tommy would mischaracterize the document by calling it a deed, power of attorney, or contract.

§5.2.1.2 Know Nature and Extent of Property

The testator must know, or be able to understand, the general nature and extent of the testator's property. However, the testator does not need to be able to provide a precise accounting of each asset the testator owns and its value.

Example 5-4. Testamentary Capacity — Extent of Property

After Toni's death, facts come to light revealing that Toni did not realize that her estate was worth approximately $1,000,000 more than she had thought when she wrote her will. How does this fact impact Toni's testamentary capacity?

Explanation

To resolve this question, you need to know the actual size of Toni's estate. The bigger the difference between the actual size and the perceived size, the more likely testamentary capacity was lacking. For example, if Toni thought her estate was worth $10, a court could decide she lacked capacity. However, if she could have comprehended the vastness of her estate if someone had brought it to her attention, courts would be reluctant to hold that Toni lacked testamentary capacity even though she wrote the will under a significant misconception. The issue is easy to resolve if, for example, she had thought that her estate was worth $55,000,000. The misunderstanding is small in percentage terms and it is clear that Toni could appreciate the significance of a large estate. Thus, a court would be very likely to hold that this error did not detract from Toni's testamentary capacity.

§5.2.1.3 Recognize Natural Objects of Bounty

The testator must know, or be able to understand, the individuals who would "naturally" benefit from the testator's death. Thus, a testator needs to know the identity of the testator's presumptive heirs, such as a spouse, children, parents, grandchildren, and siblings. Remember, of course, that a testator has no obligation to leave any property to these individuals. Merely because a disposition seems unfair or unnatural does not mean the testator lacked capacity.

Example 5-5. Testamentary Capacity — Natural Objects of Bounty

Grandmother decided to write a will leaving all her property to her grandchildren. When she executed her will, she believed she had twenty grandchildren but could only remember the names of eighteen. In reality, she had twenty-one grandchildren. Is Grandmother's will valid?

Explanation

Most courts would hold that Grandmother had testamentary capacity. Merely because she miscounted her grandchildren and could not remember all of their names is insufficient to deprive Grandmother of testamentary capacity unless she could not have understood such information had it been presented to her.

§5.2.1.4 Simultaneously Hold Elements in Mind and Make Reasonable Judgment

The fourth and final element of testamentary capacity requires the testator to hold the first three elements in the testator's mind simultaneously and for a long enough time to perceive their relationship to each other and to make a reasonable judgment. Thus, a testator would lack capacity if the testator could comprehend financial matters regarding the testator's property on even-numbered days, but could only appreciate personal and family matters, such as the identity of family members, on odd-numbered days.

§5.2.2 *Temporal Nature of Testamentary Capacity*

The testator must have testamentary capacity at the time the testator executes the will. The fact that the testator lacked capacity moments before or moments after will execution does not prevent a court from finding the existence of testamentary capacity.

Example 5-6. Testamentary Capacity — Adjudication of Incompetency and Lucid Intervals

Charlie was adjudicated incompetent. He later wrote an otherwise valid will and died. Could Charlie have testamentary capacity so that the will may be given effect?

Explanation

Charlie is presumed to lack capacity after there is an adjudication of incompetency. However, this presumption may be rebutted by evidence showing that Charlie was in a *lucid interval* at the time of will execution. In other words, the beneficiaries may be able to show that Charlie met the requirements of testamentary capacity when he executed the will despite the fact that he is usually reality challenged.

Example 5-7. Testamentary Capacity — Sane Individuals

Timothy is an extremely intelligent and sane person. However, he wrote a will while under the influence of recreational pharmaceuticals. Is the will valid?

Explanation

A sane individual may lack testamentary capacity. The person may be under the influence of intoxicating substances or disoriented because of a recent accident or medical procedure. Thus, a court may decide that Timothy's will is invalid because at the time he executed the will he was under the influence of drugs, which prevented him from meeting the requirements of testamentary capacity.

§5.2.3 *Testamentary Capacity Compared to Other Types of Capacity*

Testamentary capacity is a relatively low standard when compared to other capacities such as contractual capacity or the capacity to transact business. The ability of a person to perform the unilateral act of making a will normally requires less mind power than the bilateral acts of negotiating a contract and conducting business.

Example 5-8. Testamentary Capacity — Mentally Challenged Testator

Forrest is a slow learner and has attended special classes during his entire educational process. He works in a sheltered workshop environment and lives in a group home. Forrest inherited some property from his parents. May Forrest make a will disposing of this property to his siblings and friends?

Explanation

Many courts permit mentally challenged individuals to execute wills provided they have testamentary capacity. If Forrest understands that a will controls where his property goes upon death, knows the nature of the property, and recognizes his family members, the will is likely to be valid. Inquiry would, however, need to be made into the nature of Forrest's estate. The complexity of the estate may be such that Forrest lacks the ability to understand its nature and extent. Likewise, if the terms of the will were complex, for example, creating trusts and a variety of future interests that raise Rule against Perpetuities issues, the court could easily find that the will is too complicated to reflect Forrest's intent. (But, of course, wills of competent individuals often contain provisions they do not fully understand.)

§5.2.4 Aging Process

A natural accompaniment of the aging process is a decline in mental ability. In the absence of a disabling disease such as Alzheimer's, this process is relatively gradual and nonuniform in its effect. You may know a person who is eighty or more years old who is completely "with it" and thus has capacity. You may also know someone age sixty or younger whose capacity is already in doubt. It is very difficult to determine when, if ever, an individual loses testamentary capacity because of the aging process. All other factors being equal, wills made by older testators have a greater chance of being contested than those of younger individuals.

§5.2.5 Individuals with Questionable Capacity

One of the most difficult issues you may confront in practice is how to handle a client who asks you to prepare a will if you personally believe that this client lacks testamentary capacity. Model Rule of Professional Conduct 1.14 provides the following guidance:

> (a) When a client's ability to make adequately considered decisions in connection with the representation is impaired, . . . the lawyer shall, as far as reasonably possible, maintain a normal client-lawyer relationship with the client.
> (b) A lawyer may seek the appointment of a guardian or take other protective action with respect to a client only when the lawyer reasonably believes that the client cannot adequately act in the client's own interest.

The American College of Trust and Estate Counsel interprets this rule as meaning that

> [t]he lawyer generally should not prepare a will . . . for a client who the lawyer reasonably believes lacks the requisite capacity. On the other hand, because of the importance of testamentary freedom, the lawyer

may properly assist clients whose testamentary capacity appears to be borderline. In any case the lawyer should take steps to preserve evidence regarding the client's testamentary capacity.[2]

Example 5-9. Testamentary Capacity—Client with Questionable Capacity[3]

Dorothy disinherited her niece, Dolores, in a will made shortly before Dorothy's death. Dolores sued both the beneficiary of the new will and the lawyer who prepared it charging that the attorney should have known of Dorothy's alleged lack of testamentary capacity. Is Dorothy's attorney liable to Dolores?

Explanation

Courts are reluctant to hold attorneys liable in this type of case. An attorney is generally not required to investigate the client's condition and the attorney may rely on the attorney's own judgment regarding the client's capacity or lack thereof. The primary duty of the attorney was to Dorothy. This duty was fulfilled if the attorney reasonably and in good faith was convinced of Dorothy's testamentary capacity through the attorney's observations and experiences. An attorney does not have the authority to assume the role of a court and make a determination of testamentary capacity.

§5.2.6 *Demonstrating Lack of Capacity*

Individuals attempting to show that a testator lacked testamentary capacity use a wide array of evidence to make their point. Contestants introduce both expert and lay testimony. The exact method for having this evidence admitted depends on the applicable evidence rules. Any action a testator takes that is even slightly unusual or out of the ordinary may be asserted as evidence of lack of capacity.

Example 5-10. Testamentary Capacity—Demonstrating Lack of Testamentary Capacity[4]

A witness testified that Callie "had been rocking along drinking too much, eating too little." The evidence also revealed that at a Christmas party one

---

2. ACTEC Commentaries on the Model Rules of Professional Conduct Rule 1.14, at 133 (2d ed. 1995).

3. This example is based on *Gonsalves v. Alameda County Superior Court*, 24 Cal. Rptr. 2d 52 (Cal. Ct. App. 1993).

4. This example is based on *Warren v. Harnett*, 561 S.W.2d 860 (Tex. Civ. App. — Dallas 1977, writ ref'd n.r.e.).

year before Callie executed her will, she had a cocktail. A handwriting expert testified that Callie's handwriting demonstrated that she was an alcoholic and thus lacked testamentary capacity. Is this evidence sufficient to support a finding of lack of capacity?

Explanation

Courts are reluctant to set aside wills for lack of testamentary capacity, especially on weak grounds such as these. The conduct is very remote to Callie's execution of the will. The ability of a handwriting expert to determine capacity by merely studying handwriting samples is not widely recognized. Note, however, that in close cases juries may be prone to find lack of testamentary capacity if the will disinherits close relatives, such as a spouse or children, in favor of distant relatives, friends, or charities.

§5.3 Testamentary Intent

The third element of a valid will is that the will must reflect the testator's testamentary intent or *animus testandi*. The testator must intend that the very instrument the testator executed will serve as the testator's will; that is, the document that states the testamentary desires to be effective upon death.

Example 5-11. Testamentary Intent — Letter of Instruction

Florence executed a valid will in 1996. In 1998, she wrote, signed, and mailed a letter to her attorney containing the following language:

> I have been sick and unable to come to your office. I would like to make the following changes to my will. I no longer want to leave my car to my son, Sam. Instead, I want my daughter, Dawn, to receive it. In addition, I no longer want to leave $20,000 to Yvette Marcus. Please leave this sum to Henry Perez.

The attorney prepared a new will according to these instructions. However, Florence died without ever executing the new will. Are the changes as specified in the letter effective?

Explanation

The changes are not effective; Sam still receives the car and Yvette receives the money. Florence did not intend the letter to her attorney to be a testamentary disposition of property. Instead, it was merely a letter of instruction stating changes Florence would like to make to her will. Because testamentary intent is lacking, the letter cannot act as a codicil to Florence's will. If Florence's letter had instead contained language such as "I hereby make the following changes to my will," it is very likely that a court would find that the letter was testamentary in character.

Example 5-12. Testamentary Intent — Sham Will

As part of the hazing process when Ernie was being initiated into a legal fraternity, he was locked into a room until he wrote his will. Because Ernie had taken a course in wills he knew what to do and quickly complied. Although Ernie was married, he named his mother as the recipient of all of his property. Ten years later, Ernie died survived by his wife and his mother. Will Ernie's mother receive his entire estate?

Explanation

The court could decide either way under these facts. The court will examine all the surrounding circumstances to decide whether Ernie had testamentary intent with respect to this document. The will was written as part of an initiation ceremony and thus may have been executed without the necessary intent. Ernie may have cared only about the big party afterwards and wrote the will merely to comply with the rules of his fraternity. Also, the most logical beneficiary of his estate, his wife, was omitted. On the other hand, Ernie had a decade in which to revoke the will or to write a new will. In addition, Ernie may have good reasons for leaving his property to his mother rather than his wife. For example, his wife could be wealthy and Ernie's mother may be needy.

Example 5-13. Testamentary Intent — Specimen Will

Upon Zena's death, a document purporting to be her will is found. The will is handwritten in pencil on a yellow pad. There are numerous mark outs, insertions, and interlineations. Subsequent pages of the yellow pad contain handwritten letters to business associates with notations to Zena's secretary regarding when the letters are needed, the names of the individuals to receive copies, filing instructions, and related matters. Do the first pages of the yellow pad reflect Zena's testamentary intent?

Explanation

As with Example 5-12, above, a court could decide either way in this case after it examines extrinsic evidence and the surrounding circumstances. The instrument has the "look" of a rough draft. It is in pencil, on a yellow pad along with other draft documents, and contains many marks indicating changes. The court could easily decide that this is a specimen will intended merely as a rough draft, sample, or a guide that Zena was going to use to prepare her actual will at some later time. On the other hand, the court could decide that Zena meant this instrument to operate temporarily as her will until she had the time to prepare a formal instrument.

§5.4 Formalities

The final requirement of a valid will is for the will and the testator to comply with certain formalities as mandated by state statute. As discussed earlier in the introductory text to this chapter, most states require exact compliance with these basic formalities. The courts do not excuse minor errors even if they are harmless and the testator's intent for the document to serve as a will is clear. Although the basic requirements are relatively uniform among the states, there are considerable differences based both on state law and the type of will involved; that is, whether the will is attested (witnessed), holographic (handwritten by testator), or nuncupative (oral). This section details these formalities and the policies behind them.

§5.4.1 *Purposes*[5]

The formalities of wills serve four basic purposes. The first function of the formalities is to make sure the testator intended to make an at-death distribution of property. In other words, the formalities make certain the testator acted with deliberation and was not merely hypothesizing about what the testator might like to have done with the testator's property upon death. This is often called the *ritual* or *cautionary* function.

The second or *evidentiary* function of will formalities is to create reliable evidence of the testator's intent. This evidence reduces the chance for perjury and forgery and thus increases the likelihood that the court is carrying out the testator's actual wishes.

The third function is called the *protective* function. Formalities make it more difficult for an evil person to exert undue influence over the testator. A will execution ceremony takes place in the presence of several individuals who may be able to detect if any untoward influence is being brought to bear on the testator.

The fourth function is to increase the confidence of the testator that the testator's desires will actually be carried out upon death. Compliance

---

5. See Ashbel G. Gulliver & Catherine J. Tilson, *Classification of Gratuitous Transfers,* 51 Yale L.J. 1 (1941) & John H. Langbein, *Substantial Compliance with the Wills Act,* 88 Harv. L. Rev. 489 (1975).

with technical requirements makes the entire procedure seem more "legal" and thus reassures the testator that the will is valid. In addition, the uniformity that formalities create makes it easier for the court system to cope with wills. This function is called the *channeling* function.

§5.4.2 Attested Wills

Attested wills, that is, wills that are witnessed, are the most common type of will. An attested will must be (1) in writing, (2) signed by the testator, and (3) witnessed. Despite relative uniformity among the states regarding these formalities, the specifics are often significantly different.

§5.4.2.1 In Writing

An attested will must be in writing. Statutes generally do not specify with what or on what the will must be written. See UPC §2-502(a)(1). Accordingly, a wide variety of unusual wills have found their way into the courts; for example, written on a nurse's petticoat, inscribed on a bed post, scratched into the paint of a tractor fender, written on the bottom of a chest of drawers, and etched on an empty egg shell. Although wills on unusual surfaces and marked with untraditional implements may be legally permitted, wills should be prepared with conventional materials such as 8½" × 11" paper and nonerasable ink.

Example 5-14. Writing — Videotape

Steven made a videotape recording during which he carefully recited the names of the individuals and charities he wanted to receive his property upon his death. Steven also expressly stated that he intended the videotape to serve as his last will. Does this videotape satisfy the writing requirement?

Explanation

Under current law, it is unlikely that a phonograph record, motion picture film, audiotape, videotape, computer floppy disk or hard drive, or CD-ROM/DVD-ROM disk would satisfy the writing requirement for a will. In other contexts, the term "writing" is often defined as any "printing, typewriting or any other intentional reduction to tangible form." UCC §1-201(46). The major obstacle in trying to fit a videotape or other magnetic/optical medium within this type of definition stems from the deep-seated historical use of the word "writing" as referring to something that can be comprehended by the human eye without the intervention of mechanical or electronic devices. Of course, it is possible that the law could change to accommodate modern technology. A strong policy argument may be made in favor of new methods of evidencing wills because the purpose of requiring a will to be in writing is to provide a permanent and reliable record of the testator's intent and some types of modern media, such as a videotape, are more difficult to alter than a written document.

Example 5-15. Writing—Language

Nguyen wrote his will entirely in Chinese. Does this will satisfy the writing requirement?

Explanation

There is no requirement regarding the language in which a person's will must be written. Thus, Nguyen's will would satisfy the writing requirement. The main difficulty with a foreign language will is the interpretation of its contents. Portions of Nguyen's will may be translated differently by different people. In addition, there is always the danger of "losing something in the translation," especially with languages from different language groups or if technical matters, such as taxes, are involved. If, however, the will is prepared in English and Nguyen is not literate in English, problems of testamentary intent arise because evidence would be needed that Nguyen knew the contents of the English document and intended those contents to guide the disposition of his property. Perhaps Nguyen could approve a Chinese translation of the will but problems may arise if there are discrepancies between the English and Chinese versions.

Example 5-16. Writing—Secret Code

James wrote his will using a secret code that he had created. Does this will satisfy the writing requirement?

Explanation

Wills written in a secret code, shorthand, or otherwise encrypted satisfy the writing requirement. The key issue is one of decoding. As long as there is solid evidence of the key to the code, most courts would have little difficulty giving effect to the provisions of James's will.

§5.4.2.2 Signed by Testator

The original Statute of Wills did not require the testator to sign the will. The Statute of Frauds added the signature requirement in 1677 and it has been retained by all states for attested wills. See UPC §2-502(a)(1). The signature formality serves two main functions. First, it connects the will with the testator so there is some assurance that the testator actually approved the instrument. Second, the testator's signature gives the document an aura of finality, that is, that the testator was finished with the instrument and that it reflects the testator's final, rather than tentative or preliminary, wishes.

§5.4.2.2.1 Defined

Courts and legislatures broadly define "signature" to encompass any symbol the testator executes or adopts with *animus signandi,* that is, with present intent to authenticate the will. Thus, initials, first names, nicknames, statements of family relationship (e.g., "Mother," "Uncle Bud"), illegible writing, typed names, rubber-stamped names, and fingerprints may qualify as signatures as long as the testators who used them had the proper intent.

Example 5-17. Testator's Signature by Mark

The Artist (formerly known as Prince) decided to execute a will. He drew the unique symbol he created to represent himself at the end of the will. Does this mark operate as his signature?

Explanation

Courts have consistently recognized signatures by mark, whether the mark is a simple "X" or a sophisticated symbol such as the one used by the Artist (formerly known as Prince). When a testator signs by mark, it is good practice to write the testator's name near the mark, indicate that the testator's signature was by way of mark, and list the names of the persons who observed the testator making the mark.

§5.4.2.2.2 Proxy Signature

Most states permit the testator's signature to be affixed to the will by another person. A proxy signature, also called a signature *per alium,* must meet statutory requirements, which typically include two main components. First, the proxy must sign in the testator's presence; second, the proxy must sign at the testator's direction. See UPC §2-502(a)(2). Some states require the proxy's own signature to appear on the will as well. Even if the proxy's signature is not required, it is good practice to obtain it.

Example 5-18. Testator's Signature by Proxy — Testator's Ability

Cindy is literate and without physical challenge. Nonetheless, Cindy directs Stewart to sign her name to her will in her presence. Has this will been properly signed?

Explanation

The testator need not be physically or educationally unable to sign before a proxy may sign the testator's name. Thus, it is highly likely that a court would find that Cindy's signature appears on the will because it was made under her direction and in her presence.

Example 5-19.   Testator's Signature by Proxy — In Testator's Presence

Arthur spent weeks drafting a complicated will for Maria, one of his most wealthy and influential clients. Arthur received a telephone call from Maria on the Concorde to Europe. She explained she was running behind schedule and was not able to make it to Arthur's office to sign the will as she had planned. She then stated, "I hereby direct you to sign my will for me." Arthur complied. Is Maria's will valid?

Explanation

Courts typically hold that the testator need not actually see the proxy make the signature. Instead, the testator must be in a position where the testator could see or make use of the testator's other senses to determine what is happening. Maria's will is unlikely to be valid because Maria could not see or use her other senses to determine whether Arthur actually signed the appropriate document. It is an open question whether the presence test would be satisfied if Arthur signed Maria's will during a video-teleconference.

§5.4.2.2.3   Location of Signature

The original Statute of Frauds and the law of most states today do not mandate the location in which the testator's signature must appear. See UPC §2-502. Thus, the testator's signature may appear at the top, in the body, in the margin, or at the end of the will. However, some states follow the lead of the 1837 Wills Act and require that wills be subscribed or signed at the end or *foot* of the instrument.

Example 5-20.   Location of Testator's Signature — Physical v. Logical End

Mindy wrote a three-page will. After proofreading it carefully, she noticed that she had inadvertently left out the last provision of the will. Because there was no room to insert this provision on the last page of her will, she inserted it at the bottom of page one. Mindy then signed the will at the bottom of page three. If Mindy lives in a state that requires wills to be signed at the end, is her signature in the correct location?

Explanation

The key issue is the type of "end" to which the statute refers. Does it mean the "physical" end (end of page three) or the logical end, that is, after the last provision in the order the provisions should be read (end of page one)? Courts have decided both ways.

Example 5-21. Location of Testator's Signature — Blank Spaces

Nancy signed her will at the bottom of the last page of her six-page will. However, the last page of her will had only a few lines of text. Thus, there is approximately five inches of blank space between the last line of text and her signature. If Nancy lives in a state that requires wills to be signed at the end, is her signature in the correct location?

Explanation

Courts are unlikely to take the requirement that a will be signed at the end so literally as to cause Nancy's will to fail because of the five inches of blank space. Nonetheless, leaving blank spaces is unwise because such conduct makes it easier for evil persons to insert language in their favor.

§5.4.2.2.4 Testimonium Clause

The testator's signature may appear on the instrument without any type of formal provision preceding the signature. To add greater formality to the instrument, it is common practice for the testator to sign beneath a brief testimonium clause that declares the instrument to be a will and states the date of will execution.

Sample Testimonium Clause

I hereby sign my name to this my last will [in blue ink], consisting of this and the [number] preceding pages (each of which I am initialing and/or signing for the purpose of identification), all in the presence of the two persons who have at my request and in my presence acted as witnesses on this the [day] day of [month], [year], at [city], [state].

_____
[Testator]

§5.4.2.3 Attested by Witnesses

§5.4.2.3.1 Number

Originally the Statute of Frauds required an attested will to have three or four witnesses. The Wills Act of 1837 reduced the number of witnesses to two. Although practically all states and UPC §2-502(a)(3) require two witnesses, at least one state still requires three. Some practitioners in two-witness states routinely have extra witnesses just in case the will needs to be probated in a three-witness state or additional testimony is needed to prove what occurred during the will execution ceremony.

§5.4.2.3.2 Legal Capacity

Most states do not limit the legal capacity of a person to be a witness because of the person's age. See UPC §2-505(a). Thus, a person may serve as a witness even if the person is under eighteen years old. Some states do, however, impose minimum ages on witnesses, such as fourteen or eighteen. At common law, persons convicted of infamous crimes, such as felonies and treason, could not be witnesses. The modern trend is to remove this type of status disqualification.

§5.4.2.3.3 Attestation Capacity

Witnesses must be "competent" or "credible" at the time they attested to the will. See UPC §2-505(a). The prevailing view is that witnesses must be capable of giving testimony in court. Thus, they must understand the significance of an oath to tell the truth and be able to distinguish between fact and fiction.

§5.4.2.3.4 Attestation Intent

The witnesses must have *animus attestandi;* that is, they must intend to give validity to the document as an act of the testator.

Example 5-22. Publication

Vance called two of his assistants into his office. He told them that he needed them to witness his signing of an important document. Vance signed the document and then had both of the assistants do likewise. Can this document operate as Vance's will even though the witnesses did not know the nature of the document that they witnessed?

Explanation

In most states and under UPC §2-502(a), there is no requirement that a testator *publish* the will to the witnesses, that is, tell the witnesses that the document they are witnessing is a will. Thus, Vance's will is likely to be deemed as properly witnessed. There are, however, a significant number of states that require publication. In these states, the witnesses must know that they are witnessing a will. The testator should tell the witnesses, "This is my will," show them the top of the first page of the document, or take some other step to make certain the witnesses are aware of the nature of the document. Even in the states that require publication, the witnesses do not need to know the contents of the will.

§5.4.2.3.5 Temporal Order

The testator should sign the will prior to the attestation of the witnesses.

Example 5-23. Temporal Order of Testator's Signature and Attestation

Attorney, Testator, Witness One, and Witness Two were sitting around a conference table. Attorney handed the will to Witness One. Witness One attested and passed the will down to Testator who then signed the will. Testator gave the will to Witness Two who attested before returning the will to Attorney. Is Testator's will properly attested?

Explanation

States follow different views regarding the order of the testator's signature and the witnesses' attestation. Some states adopt the *English* or *strict view,* which requires the testator to sign prior to the attestation. On the other hand, most states follow the *American* or *continuous transaction approach.* Under this view, as long as the testator signs and the witnesses attest at approximately the same time as part of a continuous transaction, the execution/attestation is considered effective. A third approach is taken by UPC §2-502(a)(3), which requires that the attestation occurred within a reasonable time after either (1) the witness observed the testator sign the will (English view), (2) the testator acknowledged his or her signature on the will (English view), or (3) the testator acknowledged the will (quasi-American view; first, the testator acknowledged the will, second, the witnesses attested, and third, the testator signed).

§5.4.2.3.6 By Mark

Jurisdictions are divided regarding whether the witnesses may attest by mark. Some states and UPC §2-502(a)(3) provide that the witnesses "sign" the will. As discussed in §5.4.2.2, above, the term "signed" typically refers to any mark made with present intent to authenticate the will. On the other hand, some states require that the witnesses actually write "their names." A stricter rule for witnesses vis-à-vis testators may be justified because there is virtually an unlimited number of potential witnesses and it should not be difficult for a testator to locate two people who can write their names. On the other hand, it would be unfair to force a prospective testator to become literate or be miraculously cured just to execute a will.

§5.4.2.3.7 By Proxy

Jurisdictions are also divided with respect to the validity of a witness attesting by proxy. Some states permit the practice while others require witnesses to attest in their own handwriting. The same policy discussion in §5.4.2.3.6, above, also applies here.

§5.4.2.3.8 Location

Witnesses should attest at the end of the will following the testator's signature. Whether deviations from this procedure are fatal to the validity of a will is a matter of disagreement among the states. Some states, especially those with statutes requiring the witnesses to "subscribe," require that the witnesses attest at the end of the will, beneath the testator's signature. On the other hand, many states take a more liberal approach and permit the attestation to appear anywhere on the will.

§5.4.2.3.9 Presence — Testator Signing in Witnesses' Presence

Good practice mandates that the testator sign the will in the presence of the witnesses. However, many states do not impose this requirement. The testator may simply acknowledge the testator's signature to the witnesses. See UPC §2-502(a)(3). This acknowledgment can be by express words such as, "This is my signature" or "I signed this already," or by some gesture which carries the appropriate message, for example, pointing to the signature, nodding, and giving a thumbs-up sign.

§5.4.2.3.10 Presence — Witnesses Attesting in Testator's Presence

Consistent with the Statute of Frauds requirement dating from 1676, the vast majority of states require the witnesses to attest in the presence of the testator. This requirement helps ensure that the witnesses attest the testator's actual will and not some other instrument that was either accidentally or intentionally substituted. A few jurisdictions, however, have followed the lead of UPC §2-502(a) by eliminating this requirement. In these states, it is possible for the witnesses to attest even after the testator has died as long as the attestation occurs within a reasonable time after the testator signed the will or acknowledged the will or the signature to the witnesses.

Example 5-24. Witnesses Attesting in Testator's Presence

Just as Witness One was attesting Testator's will, Testator's nose began to itch. Testator got out a handkerchief and politely turned his head and sneezed. During the time his head was turned, Witness One attested. Witness Two was slow to get to the conference room so Attorney grabbed the will, flew out of the room leaving Testator behind, and ran down the hallway to find Witness Two. Attorney found Witness Two and had him attest right then and there. Are these attestations valid in a jurisdiction that requires the attestation to take place in the testator's presence?

Explanation

The attestation by Witness One is likely to be effective. The testator does not actually need to see the witnesses attest. Compliance with such a requirement would be extremely difficult to prove and would prevent visually impaired individuals from executing wills. The most widely accepted approach is *conscious presence*. Under this rule, an attestation is proper if the testator was able to see it from the testator's actual position or from a slightly altered position if the testator has the power to make the alteration without assistance. Because Testator could easily turn Testator's head without assistance and then watch Witness One attest, the attestation would be effective. A few states adopt a relatively tough *line of sight* rule meaning that the testator needs to have been in a position where the testator could have seen the attestation if the testator were looking. Under this approach, the attestation by Witness One may not have been effective because Testator was looking in a different direction.

Witness Two's attestation is ineffective. Testator did not see Witness Two attest, was not in line of sight when Witness Two attested, and Witness Two was not in Testator's conscious presence because Testator would have needed to get up, walk to the door of the conference room, and walk down the hallway before being in a position to see the attestation. This type of change of position is too great to be considered a "slight" alteration.

§5.4.2.3.11   Presence—Witnesses Attesting in Each Other's Presence

The 1837 Wills Act required the witnesses to be present at the same time when the testator signed or acknowledged the will. Although some states have retained this requirement, most states do not require the witnesses to be together either (1) when the testator signs or acknowledges the will, or (2) when the witnesses attest to the will.

§5.4.2.3.12   Interested Witnesses

An interested witness is a witness who stands to benefit if the testator's will is valid. The most common type of interest is being a beneficiary under the will. The testimony of an interested witness about the attestation is suspect because the witness has a motive to lie. Below are some of the potential ramifications of having an interested person serve as a necessary witness to the will.

1.   Entire will is void. This was the original common law rule unless there was a supernumerary (extra) witness to validate the will. The witness/beneficiary was deemed totally incompetent to testify

about the will because the witness lacked competency at the time of the witnessing.

2. Gift to the witness is void. The witness forfeits any benefit under the will and is thus made disinterested and capable of giving testimony about the will. A statutory provision providing this result is often called a *purging* statute.

3. Gift to the witness is void unless the witness is also an heir in which case the witness can receive the gift provided it does not exceed the share of the testator's estate the witness would take under intestate succession. With regard to the smaller of the gift under the will or the intestate share, the witness has no motive to lie because the witness will receive that amount regardless of the validity of the will.

4. Gift to the witness is void unless a disinterested person (either another witness or a third party who was present) can corroborate the testimony of the witness.

5. The gift to the witness is presumed to be the result of fraud or undue influence. However, the witness may bring forth evidence to rebut this presumption and, if successful, take under the will.

6. No effect, and thus the beneficiary takes the property exactly as the testator specified in the will. This is the approach adopted by UPC §2-505(b).

Example 5-25. Executor as Witness

One of the witnesses to Testator's will is the executor named in the will. The will provides that the executor is entitled to reasonable compensation for administering the estate. Is the executor an interested witness?

Explanation

Most jurisdictions would hold that the executor is not an interested witness. Although the executor stands to benefit financially from serving as the personal representative of the estate, the executor must perform services in a competent manner to be entitled to the money. This type of conflict of interest is usually considered too small to deem the witness interested.

Example 5-26. Relative of Beneficiary as Witness

Testator's will leaves the entire estate to his grandchildren. The witnesses to the will were one of Testator's children and the spouse of one of the grandchildren. Are these witnesses interested?

Explanation

Among states that limit the ability of an interested person to be a witness, there is considerable diversity with regard to how an interested person is determined. Both of these witnesses appear to have strong motives to lie and thus their gifts may be invalid. Nonetheless, many purging statutes are not broad enough to cover the situation where the actual beneficiary is not the witness.

§5.4.2.3.13   Attestation Clause

An attestation clause is a provision of a will that recites that the testator duly executed the will. The attestation clause is found after the testator's signature. Although no state requires that a will contain an attestation clause, wills traditionally contain them. The use of attestation clauses is partly a matter of tradition, but they may have a practical use as well. In many states, attestation clauses raise a strong presumption in favor of the matters stated therein.

Sample Attestation Clause

The foregoing instrument consisting of this and the [number] preceding pages was signed, published, and declared by [Client] to be [his] [her] last will. We now, at [his] [her] request, in [his] [her] presence, subscribe our names [in blue ink] as witnesses this the [day] day of [month], [year]. For identification, we have each initialed or signed the [number] preceding pages of this will.

_____	_____
[Witness One]	[Witness Two]
_____	_____
[Address]	[Address]
_____	_____
Social Security Number	Social Security Number

§5.4.2.3.14   Recommended Witnesses[6]

Little thought is usually given to the selection of witnesses. Typically, witnesses are individuals who merely by chance are available at the time of document execution; for example, secretaries, paralegals, law clerks, and delivery persons. In most cases, this practice is not harmful because a self-proving affidavit (as discussed in §5.4.2.4, below) eliminates the necessity for

---

6. This section is adapted from Gerry W. Beyer, *Drafting in Contemplation of Will Contests*, Prac. Law., Jan. 1992, at 61.

finding the witnesses to a will and the vast majority of wills are uncontested. The situation is considerably different, however, if a contest arises and the testimony of the witnesses regarding capacity or the details of the execution ceremony is crucial. Below are some of the factors that impact the selection of witnesses.

(1) Witnesses Familiar with Testator. "The jury is likely to give little weight to the testimony of a witness who never saw the testator before or after the execution of the will, and whose opportunity to form a conclusion was limited to the single brief occasion."[7] Accordingly, if you anticipate a will contest, it is prudent to select witnesses previously acquainted with the testator, such as personal friends, co-workers, and business associates. These people are more likely to remember the ceremony and provide testimony about how the testator acted at the relevant time. In addition, they can compare the testator's conduct at the ceremony with how the testator acted at a time when the contestants concede that the testator had capacity.

The witnesses should not be will beneficiaries, heirs, or other relatives of the testator either by consanguinity or affinity, creditors, or anyone else with a financial interest in the estate.

Considerable debate exists regarding the wisdom of having health care providers serve as witnesses or attend the will execution ceremony. The doctors and nurses who care for the testator appear well-qualified to testify about the testator's condition. During cross-examination, however, details about the testator's illness may come out that would not otherwise have been discovered. This additional information may prove sufficient to sway the fact-finder to conclude the testator lacked capacity. The danger is heightened if the doctor is a psychiatrist.

(2) Supernumerary Witnesses. Although attested wills in most states require only two witnesses, extra witnesses may be advisable if a contest is likely. The additional witnesses provide a greater pool of individuals who may be alive, available, and able to recollect the ceremony and the testator's condition.

(3) Youthful and Healthy Witnesses. Witnesses should be relatively young and in good health. The use of healthy witnesses who are younger than the testator increases the likelihood that the witnesses will be available (alive and competent) to testify if a will contest arises.

(4) Traceable Witnesses. The proponent of a will who is charged with locating attesting witnesses to counter a will contest is often faced with a

---

7. M. K. Woodward & Ernest E. Smith, III, *Probate and Decedents' Estates* §336, at 278 (17 Tex. Prac. 1971).

difficult task. Witnesses may move out of the city, state, or country. In addition, witnesses may change their names. For example, a female witness may marry and adopt her husband's name, a married female may divorce and retake her maiden name, or a witness may enter the federal witness relocation program and assume a new identity. To increase the chance of locating crucial witnesses, select witnesses who appear easy to trace; for example, individuals with close family, friendship, business, educational, or political ties with the local community. To assist in the location process, the witnesses should write their social security numbers on the will. Note, however, that some witnesses may balk at the prospect of placing their numbers on documents likely to become public record in the future.

(5) Witnesses Who Would Favorably Impress the Court and Jury. Carefully evaluate the personal characteristics of the witnesses. The witnesses should be people who would make a good impression on the court and jury by both words and demeanor.

§5.4.2.4 Self-Proving Affidavit

A self-proving affidavit is a notarized statement by the testator and the witnesses affirming under oath that all the requirements of a valid will have been satisfied. Practically all states permit this affidavit to substitute for the in-court testimony of the witnesses when the testator's will is probated. In addition, the affidavit raises a presumption that the matters stated therein are true. Thus, the existence of a self-proving affidavit makes probating the will easier, faster, and more economical.

Self-proving affidavits may require the testator or the witnesses to swear to facts or events that are not necessary for a valid will. For example, self-proving affidavits typically state that the testator published the document as the testator's will.

Example 5-27. Self-Proving Affidavit — Contesting Will

Testator's heirs believe that Testator lacked testamentary capacity and was subject to undue influence when Testator executed a will that omitted them as beneficiaries. The named beneficiaries point to the self-proving affidavit and claim that the affidavit precludes the contest. Are these beneficiaries right?

Explanation

A self-proving affidavit is a conclusory and self-serving document. Thus, it does not make the will better, stronger, or more resilient to contest; it merely makes it easier to probate. Thus, the heirs may contest the will despite the self-proving affidavit.

Example 5-28.   Self-Proving Affidavit — Changing the Will

Testator executed a self-proved will. Later, Testator revoked the will with a will that did not contain a self-proving affidavit. Is the revocation effective?

Explanation

The revocation is effective. The existence of a self-proving affidavit does not in any way alter the ability of a testator to revoke or amend a will. Subsequent instruments do not need to be self-proved.

Example 5-29.   Self-Proving Affidavit — Time

Larry executed his will in 1990. Larry's attorney, Albert, was not well versed in estate planning and thus neglected to have Larry sign a self-proving affidavit. Albert then attended some continuing legal education courses and realized his mistake. Larry is still Albert's client with regard to other matters and the two witnesses still work in Albert's office. Must Larry execute a new will or could Larry and the witnesses execute a self-proving affidavit at this late date?

Explanation

Most self-proving statutes do not require the testator and the witnesses to complete the affidavit at the time of will execution. Thus, Larry and the witnesses could now execute the self-proving affidavit. Of course, Albert should carefully review the will for other errors and for changes that may be necessary because of a change in Larry's situation or applicable laws.

Jurisdictions vary as to whether the self-proving affidavit is a separate document executed after the will (two sets of signatures) or whether it can be incorporated into the will substituting for the testimonium and attestation clauses (one set of signatures). Some states follow the lead of UPC §2-504 and permit both methods.

Sample Self-Proving Affidavit — Incorporated into Will[8]

I, _____, the testator, sign my name to this instrument this _____ day of _____, _____, and being first duly sworn, do hereby declare to the undersigned authority that I sign and execute this instrument as my will and that I sign it willingly (or willingly direct another to sign for me), that I execute it as my free and voluntary act for the purposes therein expressed, and that I am eighteen years of age or older, of sound mind, and under no constraint or undue influence.

_____
[Testator]

---

8. The provision is based on UPC §2-504(a).

We, _____, _____, the witnesses, sign our names to this instrument, being first duly sworn, and do hereby declare to the undersigned authority that the testator signs and executes this instrument as [his] [her] will and that [he] [she] signs it willingly (or willingly directs another to sign for [him] [her]), and that each of us, in the presence and hearing of the testator, hereby signs this will as witness to the testator's signing, and that to the best of our knowledge the testator is eighteen years of age or older, of sound mind, and under no constraint or undue influence.

_____   _____
[Witness]   [Witness]

The State of _____
County of _____

Subscribed, sworn to and acknowledged before me by _____ the testator, and subscribed and sworn to before me by _____ and _____, witnesses, this _____ day of _____, _____.

   (Seal)   (Signed) _____

                 _____
                 (Official capacity of officer)

Sample Self-Proving Affidavit — Separate Document[9]

The State of _____
County of _____

We, _____, _____, and _____, the testator and the witnesses, respectively, whose names are signed to the attached or foregoing instrument, being first duly sworn, do hereby declare to the undersigned authority that the testator signed and executed the instrument as the testator's will and that [he] [she] had signed willingly (or willingly directed another to sign for [him] [her]), and that [he] [she] executed it as [his] [her] free and voluntary act for the purposes therein expressed, and that each of the witnesses, in the presence and hearing of the testator, signed the will as witness and that to the best of [his] [her] knowledge the testator was at that time eighteen years of age or older, of sound mind, and under no constraint or undue influence.

                                 _____
                                 [Testator]

_____   _____
[Witness]   [Witness]

_____

9. The provision is based on UPC §2-504(b).

Subscribed, sworn to and acknowledged before me by _____, the testator, and subscribed and sworn to before me by _____, and _____, witnesses, this _____ day of _____, _____.

(Seal)   (Signed) _____
                                          _____
                                          (Official capacity of officer)

Example 5-30. Self-Proving Affidavit — Signatures on Affidavit Operating to Bootstrap Invalid Will

Testator signed the will and the self-proving affidavit. However, the witnesses signed only the self-proving affidavit. Is the will valid or did Testator die intestate?

Explanation

Jurisdictions have followed a variety of approaches when signatures of the testator or witnesses are missing from the will but appear on the self-proving affidavit. A few states take a strict approach. Courts in these jurisdictions view the self-proving affidavit as a separate and discrete document. The affidavit cannot save an instrument that does not meet the requirements of a will, such as the lack of the testator's signature or the witnesses' attestation. In fact, the witnesses who signed the affidavit are actually guilty of the crime of perjury because they swore under oath that they had signed the will when in reality they had not. Advocates of this approach claim that it lessens the chance for fraud. For example, an evil person could remove the self-proving affidavit from the testator's genuine will and attach it to the end of a fraudulent will containing provisions in favor of the evil person.

Most states, either by case law or by statute, take a more accommodating view and permit the signatures on the self-proving affidavit to bootstrap the otherwise invalid will. See UPC §2-504(c). Proponents of this approach claim that in most cases the error is a mere oversight and that strict compliance with the usual rules would unjustifiably defeat the testator's intent. To reduce the chance of fraud feared by proponents of the strict view, some states require the witnesses to testify in court despite the existence of the affidavit.

§5.4.2.5 Will Execution Ceremony[10]

One of the most crucial stages of a testator's estate plan is the will execution ceremony — the point at which the testator memorializes desires regarding at-death distribution of property. Unfortunately, attorneys may handle this

---

10. This section is adapted from Gerry W. Beyer, *Drafting in Contemplation of Will Contests,* Prac. Law., Jan. 1992, at 61, 67-72.

key event in a casual or sloppy fashion. There are even reports of attorneys mailing or hand-delivering unsigned wills to clients along with will execution instructions. Some attorneys may allow law clerks or paralegals to supervise a will execution ceremony. This practice is questionable not only because it raises the likelihood of error, but because the delegation of responsibility may be considered a violation of professional conduct rules proscribing the aiding of a non-lawyer in the practice of law.

An unprofessional or unsupervised ceremony may provide the necessary ammunition for a will contestant to successfully challenge a will. This section suggests a comprehensive step-by-step format for a proper will execution ceremony. Although the procedure meets or exceeds the requirements of most common law states, you must adapt this format to the statutory and case law of the state in which the testator is executing the will.

§5.4.2.5.1 Before the Ceremony

The following four steps will help impress on the testator the seriousness of the upcoming execution ceremony and give you another opportunity to check for potential problems.

(1) Proofread the Will. Before the testator arrives for the will execution ceremony, you should carefully proofread the will for errors such as misspellings, omissions, erasures, transposed paragraphs, and overstrikes. To reduce the number of inadvertent errors, another attorney should review the will. Correct all errors and create a new original without interlineations, markouts, erasures, or correction fluid smears.

(2) Ensure Internal Integration. You should inspect the will to ensure that the will fits together as a unified document. Methods of internal integration are discussed in §9.2.2, below.

(3) Review Will with Testator. The testator needs to review the final draft of the will to confirm that the testator understands the will and that it comports with the testator's intent. The testator should have adequate time to read the will to confirm that corrections to prior drafts have been made and to determine that no unauthorized provisions have inadvertently crept into the will.

(4) Explain Ceremony to Client. You should explain the mechanics of the will execution ceremony to the testator in language the testator understands. Avoid legal jargon because the testator may be too embarrassed to admit a lack of understanding.

§5.4.2.5.2 The Ceremony

A carefully scripted execution ceremony can help ensure that a testator's will is valid and thus prevent a contest.

(1) Select Appropriate Location. The will execution ceremony should take place in pleasant surroundings. A conference room works well, as does a large office with appropriate tables and chairs. The testator should be comfortable and at ease. A relaxed testator is more likely to present a better image to the witnesses.

(2) Avoid Interruptions. The ceremony should be free of interruptions. Thus, secretaries should hold all telephone calls and receive instructions not to interfere with the ceremony. Once the ceremony begins, no one should enter or leave the room until the ceremony is completed. Interruptions disrupt the flow of the ceremony and may cause the supervising attorney to inadvertently omit a key element.

(3) Gather Participants. You should gather the testator, the disinterested witnesses, and a notary at the appropriate location. As a precaution against claims of overreaching and undue influence, no one else should be present under normal circumstances.

(4) Seat Participants Strategically. The participants should be positioned so each can easily observe and hear the others. You need to sit near the participants to make certain the proper pages are signed in the correct places.

(5) Make General Introductions. You should introduce all participants to each other. Although it may be advisable to use witnesses already known to the client, it is a common practice for attorneys to recruit anyone who is around to serve as the witnesses. See §5.4.2.3.14, above. Accordingly, it is important to impress the identity of the testator on the witnesses so they will be able to remember the ceremony should their testimony later be needed.

(6) Explain Ceremony. You should explain that the will execution ceremony is about to commence and its importance. Although most states do not require publication, it is useful for the witnesses to know the document is a will should their testimony later be needed. In addition, publication may be required for the self-proving affidavit.

(7) Establish Testamentary Capacity. If you anticipate a will contest, it is especially important to establish each element of testamentary capacity during the ceremony. Engage the testator in a discussion covering the elements of testamentary capacity. See §5.2, above.

(8) Establish Testamentary Intent. You should direct questions to the testator in substantially the following form to demonstrate testamentary intent.

- [Testator's name], is this your will?
- Have you carefully read this will and do you understand it?
- Do you wish to make any additions, deletions, corrections, or other changes to your will?
- Does this will dispose of your property at your death in accordance with your desires?
- Do you request [witnesses' names] to witness the execution of your will?

(9) Conduct Will Execution. The following steps should be followed when the testator executes the will:

- All writing on the will should be in blue ink to make an obvious distinction between the original and a photocopy. The will's testimonium and attestation clauses should indicate that the testator and witnesses used blue ink.
- The testator initials each page of the will, except the last page, at the bottom or in the margin to reduce later claims of page substitution.
- The testator completes the testimonium clause by filling in the date and the location of the ceremony.
- The testator signs the will at the end. The testator should sign as the testator usually does when executing legal documents to prevent a contest based on forgery.
- Pay close attention to make certain everything is written in the proper locations.
- The witnesses should watch the testator sign the will so that they can testify to the signing.

(10) Conduct Witness Attestation. The following procedure should be used for the witnesses' attestation:

- One of the witnesses reads the attestation clause aloud to help impress the will execution ceremony on the minds of the witnesses.
- Each witness initials every page, except the page with the attestation clause, at the bottom or in the margin. This helps reduce claims of page substitution.
- One of the witnesses dates the attestation clause to provide additional evidence of when the execution occurred.
- Each witness signs the attestation clause and includes the witness's address and social security number. This information will be helpful should it later become necessary to locate the witnesses.
- You should carefully watch to make certain everything is written in the proper locations.
- The testator observes the witnesses signing the will.
- The witnesses should observe each other signing the will.

(11) Complete a Self-Proving Affidavit. If state law permits a will to be self-proved, complete the appropriate affidavit. Depending on the jurisdiction, another set of signatures from the testator and the witnesses may be necessary. See §5.4.2.3.14, above. The completion of the self-proving affidavit should include the following steps:

- You should explain the purpose and effect of the self-proving affidavit.
- The notary takes the oath of the testator and witnesses.
- The notary asks the testator and witnesses to swear to or affirm the items that state law requires. You should prepare a list of questions for the notary to ask the testator and witnesses modeled after the language of the affidavit that is normally found in a statutory form. This serves to impress the ceremony on the witnesses better than if they are merely asked to read and sign the affidavit.
- The testator and witnesses sign the affidavit.
- The notary signs the affidavit and affixes the appropriate seal or stamp.
- If required by state law, the notary records the ceremony in the notary's record book.

(12) Conclude Ceremony. If other estate planning documents, such as an inter vivos trust, living will, anatomical gift card, self-declaration of guardian, or durable power of attorney are needed in the estate plan, it is convenient to execute them at the same time because these other documents often require witnesses, notarization, or self-proving affidavits.

§5.4.2.5.3   After the Ceremony

As soon as the ceremony ends, take a few additional steps to make sure that the testator understands what just happened and to protect the newly executed will.

(1) Confirm Testator's Intent. You should talk with the testator to confirm that the testator understood the execution ceremony and does not have second thoughts about the disposition plan.

(2) Make Copies of Will. Photocopy the executed will for the attorney's file and make any copies that the testator may desire.

(3) Discuss Safekeeping of Original Will. The testator must determine the proper custodian for the original will. It is important to store the original will in a secure location where it may be readily found after the testator's death. Thus, some testators elect to keep the will at home or in a safe deposit box, while others prefer the drafting attorney to retain the will. In the normal situation, an attorney should refrain from offering to retain the original will because the original is then less accessible to the testator. Consequently, the testator may feel pressured to hire the attorney to make changes and the beneficiaries may feel obligated to retain the attorney to probate the will. Some courts hold that an attorney may keep the original will only if the testator makes a specific unsolicited request.

If a will contest is likely, however, it may be dangerous to permit the testator to retain the will because the will then stands a greater chance of being located and destroyed or altered by the unhappy heirs. You may need to urge the testator to find a safe storage place that is not accessible to the heirs, either now or after death, but yet a location where the will may be quickly found upon the testator's death.

(4) Provide Testator with Post-Will Instructions. You should provide the testator with a list of post-will instructions covering at least the following matters:

- The testator's need to reconsider the will should the testator's circumstances change because of births, adoptions, deaths, divorces, marriages, change in feelings toward beneficiaries and heirs, significant changes in size or composition of estate, change in state of domicile, etc.
- An explanation that mark-outs, interlineations, and other informal changes are usually insufficient to change the will. See §8.2.2, below.
- Instructions regarding safekeeping of the original will.
- A statement that the will must be reviewed if relevant state or federal tax laws change.

§5.4.3 Holographic Wills

A *holographic* or *olographic* will is prepared in the testator's own handwriting. In approximately one-half of the states, holographic wills are exempted from the attestation requirement. See UPC §2-502(b). This special treatment is justified by the aura of validity that surrounds a handwritten document because of the reduced chance of forgery and enhanced assurance of authenticity resulting from the large sample of the testator's writing. On the other hand, the balance of the states treat handwritten wills no differently from any other type of written will. For the remainder of the discussion in this section, please assume that you are in a jurisdiction that permits nonattested holographic wills.

Example 5-31. Holographic Wills — Typed or Computer Printed

Bill sat at the keyboard of his computer and inputted his entire will. He then printed the resulting document and signed it. Is this a holographic will?

Explanation

A typed or computer printed will is not holographic. To be holographic, the testator must hold a writing instrument and make marks on a writing surface that can then be read.

Example 5-32.   Holographic Wills—Written by Mouth or Foot

Christopher is physically challenged and thus cannot grasp a writing implement by hand. However, Chris is very skilled at writing both by holding a pen in his mouth and grasping a pen with his toes. May Chris make a holographic will?

Explanation

Most statutes authorizing holographic wills mandate that the will be in the testators "handwriting" rather than requiring the testator merely to "write" the will. See UPC §2-502(b). The result in Christopher's situation will depend on how strictly a court elects to interpret the statutory requirement. The policies supporting special treatment for a will written by hand are certainly just as applicable to a will written by mouth or foot.

§5.4.3.1   Requirements

In most states, holographic wills do not need to satisfy additional requirements. See UPC §2-502(b). Thus, as long as the testator signs the self-written instrument, it will satisfy the necessary formalities. However, some states require holographic wills to meet extra requirements. Common additional elements include a statement in the will of the date of execution and finding the will among the testator's valuable papers. A few states make it more difficult to use holographic wills such as by requiring three people to testify that the will is actually in the testator's handwriting, limiting the value of property the testator can dispose of with the will, or permitting them only under special circumstances such as by a person serving in the military outside of the United States.

§5.4.3.2   Extent of Holographic Material

Jurisdictions follow one of three main approaches with respect to the amount of nonholographic material a will may contain and still be valid without proper attestation. The strictest courts follow the *intent* view. Under this approach, if the testator intended any nonholographic material to be part of the will, the will is nonholographic even if the nonholographic material is not necessary to an understanding of the will. The prevailing approach is the *surplusage* view, which permits nonholographic material to be ignored if doing so does not alter the testator's dispositive arrangements. The most modern view, which is adopted by UPC §2-502(b), is the *material provision* approach, which deems a will to be holographic merely if the most important words are in the testator's handwriting.

Example 5-33. Holographic Wills — On Letterhead

While on vacation, Kendra decided to write her will. She opened the desk drawer in her hotel room, took out a piece of stationery containing the hotel's name, address, and telephone number, and wrote her will. Is this a holographic will?

Explanation

Under all three approaches, Kendra's will qualifies as holographic. She did not intend the letterhead to be part of her will, the language of the letterhead is surplusage, and all material provisions of the will are in her own handwriting.

Example 5-34. Holographic Will — Surplus Language

When Kendra from the above example returned home, she realized that her writing was somewhat sloppy. She then placed the will in her typewriter and typed out some of the messiest words immediately below the handwritten words. She also typed the following message, "Mom, I love you." Is this a holographic will?

Explanation

Kendra meant for the typed material to be part of her will and thus a court following the intent view could decide that the will was nonholographic. Jurisdictions applying the surplusage or material provision views would find the will holographic. The nonholographic language can be ignored without causing any change to Kendra's dispositive plans and the material provisions are in Kendra's own writing.

Example 5-35. Holographic Wills — Printed Will Forms

Kendra later decided that her will looked confusing so she tore it up and went to the local bookstore to find some will forms. She found a nice-looking form, purchased it, and brought it home. Kendra then filled out the blanks in the will inserting items such as her name, address, property given, and names of beneficiaries. For example, she inserted her name in the clause reading, "I, _____, being of sound mind hereby revoke all prior wills and declare this instrument to be my last will," and in the spaces in the sentence reading, "I leave _____ to _____," she inserted the figure $25,000 and her mother's name. Is this a holographic will?

Explanation

Kendra intended the nonholographic language of the form to be part of her will and thus a court in an intent jurisdiction would not consider the will holographic. Courts using the surplusage view are also unlikely to consider Kendra's will holographic because the nonholographic material ties the handwritten material together. Without the pre-printed language, all that remains is a disconnected list of names and property. A jurisdiction following the material provision approach could deem the will holographic because the material provisions, that is, the names of the beneficiaries and the identification of the items given, are in Kendra's own handwriting. UPC §2-502(c) even permits nonholographic language to be used to establish Kendra's testamentary intent.

§5.4.3.3   Uses of Holographic Wills

Holographic wills tend to be written by non-legally trained individuals who prepare homemade estate plans without professional advice. Accordingly, holographic wills frequently cause litigation because of the interpretation and construction problems that result.

Despite the problems with holographic wills, they have several important uses.

(1) Emergencies. Holographic wills are useful when there is no time to prepare a more formal instrument. Testators can prepare them quickly, perhaps receiving assistance from an attorney either in person or over the telephone.

(2) Privacy. A testator who desires extreme privacy may wish to use a holographic will. Holographic wills eliminate the risk that a witness might discover the nature or contents of the document.

(3) Interim Will. When a client hires an attorney to prepare an estate plan, it may take weeks or months before the client executes all the necessary documents. If the beneficiaries under the client's current will or the potential heirs under intestacy are not to the client's liking, it is prudent practice for the client to execute an interim will in case the client dies before executing the final documents. A holographic will, especially if the attorney helps by dictating it, may be useful in this type of temporary arrangement.

(4) Entertainment. Holographic wills provide some levity in an otherwise morbid area. The will of Rosa Doyle-Nolan is a good example.

> When—I pass—Out. see that. I. Am buried—Either next to Tony—on that side—Or—put me Over on the—Other side— Give me plenty of room: See that My grave is Marked by a Single Marker and be shure—that "I get plenty of room When—I am buried—dont Crowd me—in a "Small space—please—I —likewise—Request—that you—too have a "lot in this Family spot I ask you—to use special Care In selecting A Lawyer—to attend to This Will—"Dont get some <u>Grafter</u> (as most of them are: Who will rob you Out of your Eye—teenth—"And then pretend "they are your <u>Friend</u>" A Lawyer—Is more deadlier than a Rattlesnake—So—look—Out.[11]

§5.4.4 *Nuncupative Wills*

A *nuncupative* will is an oral or spoken will. The common law had a long history of recognizing nuncupative wills for personal property. Beginning with the Statute of Frauds of 1677, however, legislatures have increased the number of restrictions and conditions on their use. The Wills Act of 1837 eliminated oral wills except for soldiers and sailors. See §5.4.5, below.

Courts and legislatures in the United States do not favor nuncupative wills because of the difficulty of proof and potential for fraud. Thus, many states and the UPC no longer recognize oral wills. Nonetheless, a substantial number of jurisdictions still permit nuncupative wills under limited circumstances.

Below is a list of the types of restrictions a state may impose on the validity of a nuncupative will. Several states impose two or more of these types of limitations.

(1) Types of property covered—e.g., no disposition of real property.

(2) Amount of property — e.g., $30.00 or $1,000; in some states, the testator may make larger gifts if there are a specified number of witnesses.

(3) Condition of testator — e.g., *in extremis* (overtaken by sudden and violent sickness) or death from an injury that the testator suffered on the same day the testator spoke the testamentary words.

(4) Location of speaking will—e.g., the testator must speak the testamentary words at (a) home, (b) a place where the testator resided for ten days or more before speaking the words, or (c) if the testator became ill while away from home, the testator spoke the words before returning home.

---

11. Kramer v. Crout, 279 S.W.2d 932, 934-935 (Tex. Civ. App.—Waco 1955, writ ref'd n.r.e.).

(5) *Rogatio testium* — The testator may need to make a request that the witnesses bear witness that the spoken words constitute the testator's will. It may not be enough for the testator to say, "I want [name of beneficiary] to receive [item given] when I die."

(6) **Number of witnesses** — e.g., three, even if only two are needed for written wills.

(7) **Proof** — e.g., if the will is not probated within six months after the testator made the will, proof is needed that someone wrote down the substance of the will within six days from when the testator spoke the testamentary words.

(8) **Notice** — Better quality of notice to testator's heirs than is required to probate a written will may be required; e.g., personal service rather than posting or publication.

Attorneys rarely use nuncupative wills. Only in the cases of dire emergency or necessity would you recommend an oral will.

§5.4.5 *Soldiers' and Seamen's Wills*

Through the history of both the civil and common law, governments have made exceptions for wills written by soldiers in actual military service and sailors at sea. A significant number of states still permit military personnel and mariners to make wills that do not comply with the normal requirements either by being oral or unattested. Commonly imposed restrictions include limiting these wills to personal property and/or to property of some relatively small value (e.g., $1,000). Many states also impose requirements similar to those for nuncupative wills discussed in §5.4.4, above.

§5.4.6 *Statutory Wills*[12]

In the mid-1980s, the state legislatures of California, Maine, Michigan, and Wisconsin took a bold step to increase the number of people who execute wills by enacting fill-in-the-blank will forms designed to be completed without legal assistance. England had pioneered statutory wills in the 1920s, followed by the National Conference of Commissioners on Uniform State Laws when they approved the Uniform Statutory Will Act in 1984. However, the use of a fill-in-the-blank format was a dramatic departure from these

---

12. Portions of this section are adapted from Gerry W. Beyer, *Statutory Fill-in-the-Blank Will Forms*, Prob. & Prop., Nov./Dec. 1996, at 26.

earlier models, which merely provided provisions testators could incorporate into their wills by reference.

Although tremendous variation exists among the fill-in will forms, they follow the same basic format. The forms are prefaced by general estate planning information, instructions, and warnings that legal advice may be necessary. The wills themselves begin with the traditional language identifying the testator, declaring the instrument to be a will, and revoking prior wills. The dispositive provisions of the fill-in forms show great diversity. Some forms provide the user with many opportunities to make specific gifts of real or personal property as well as cash legacies while others restrict the user to relatively few options. The forms are quite uniform in mandating that all personal and household items not specifically gifted pass to the surviving spouse or, if no surviving spouse, to the testator's surviving children. The forms provide the user with a limited number of choices for the distribution of the remainder of the estate. The forms also contain provisions regarding estate administration matters and conclude with testimonium and attestation provisions. In Wisconsin, testators even have the option to create a testamentary trust for the surviving spouse and children.

Example 5-36. Statutory Wills

You have just been hired as a consultant to your state's governor. The legislature passed enabling legislation for statutory wills. What arguments, both pro and con, would you urge the governor to consider in deciding whether to sign or veto this bill?

Explanation

The ramifications of a statutory fill-in-the-blank will should be viewed from two perspectives: first, the nonlegal community and second, the legal community.

The potential benefits of statutory wills for the nonlegal community include: (1) increased use of wills to effectuate intent; (2) lowering of estate planning costs; (3) reduction in time and effort needed to create and update a will; (4) enhanced awareness by citizens of their ability to execute wills and their importance; (5) improvement of a client's emotional and psychological conditions; (6) reduction in family conflict; (7) education of the public; (8) expanded access to the legal system; (9) decreased reliance on commercialized self-help estate planning publications; and (10) conservation of resources. The negative results of statutory wills may include: (1) lack of individualization; (2) improper completion; (3) failure to comprehend the form and its effect; (4) encouragement of evil conduct; (5) lack of comprehensive estate plan; (6) increased legal expense for survivors; and (7) decreased quality of legal services.

The potential benefits of statutory wills on the legal community include: (1) enhanced image of legal profession; (2) improved quality of services and decreased malpractice risk; (3) abatement of court congestion; and (4) increased estate planning business. The ostensible disadvantages of statutory fill-in forms on the legal community include: (1) loss of estate planning business; (2) violation of obligation to public; (3) increase in unnecessary probate litigation; (4) encouragement of self-professed experts; and (5) damage to the image of the legal profession.

6

Changing Circumstances after Will Execution— Property

The property of a testator is not frozen when the testator executes a will. The composition and value of the estate are in constant flux. Likewise, the identity of the individuals the testator wishes to benefit can change due to births, adoptions, deaths, marriages, and divorces. All of these changes in circumstance can have a profound effect on the testator's intent, an existing will, and the distribution of property upon death both under the will and due to the application of legal rules.

States have developed a sophisticated set of rules to deal with changed circumstances. The general approach is for the legislature or the courts to create relatively rigid presumptions based on what they believe testators, in general, would have wanted had the testators thought about these issues. Courts then apply the presumptions to determine the appropriate distribution of property. Some of these rules are relatively uniform among the states while others are 180 degrees apart.

To avoid the application of these presumptions, a testator should include express provisions in the will dealing with each of these issues. A testator who provides specific instructions for how to handle circumstance changes empowers the court to carry out the testator's actual intention, rather than a presumed intent as determined by statutory or case law.

In this chapter, we will discuss changes that occur to the testator's property. In Chapter 7, our focus shifts to changes that occur to beneficiaries and family members.

§6.1   Classification of Testamentary Gifts

Gifts in a will can be broadly classified based on the type of property the testator is giving away. A *devise* is a gift of real property and a *bequest* is a gift of personal property. Many state statutes and courts do not define or use these terms in their technical sense, but rather use them interchangeably. Because the application of certain rules still depends on the nature of the gifted property, we will continue to give the terms "devise" and "bequest" their technical or common law meanings.

§6.1.1   *Specific Gifts*

A *specific gift* is identified in the will in sufficient detail so it is clear which exact assets from the testator's estate the beneficiary is entitled to receive. A specific gift may be described in two ways. The gift may be so precisely described that the property to which it refers may be determined at the time the testator executes the will. Examples of these types of gifts include, "I leave the gold pocket watch I inherited from my grandfather which has the initials JDE engraved on the back to [name of beneficiary]," "I leave my Toshiba notebook computer Model 780DVD serial number PJ472828125 to [name of beneficiary]," and "I leave my certificate of deposit number 57387AF43 in Octopus National Bank to [name of beneficiary]."

Alternatively, a specific gift may be described in broad terms so that the property to which it refers cannot be ascertained until the testator dies. This type of specific gift is often referred to as a *specific gift of a general nature*. For example, "I leave all my jewelry to [name of beneficiary]," "I leave my computer to [name of beneficiary]," and "I leave all my certificates of deposit to [name of beneficiary]." The beneficiaries of these gifts do not know which exact items they will receive until the testator actually dies. The beneficiaries will receive whatever jewelry, computer, or certificates of deposit the testator owns at the time of death, regardless of what the testator owned when the testator executed the will.

§6.1.2   *General Gifts*

A gift is deemed *general* when it is insufficiently described to be specific. In other words, the exact property to which the gift refers cannot be determined when the testator executed the will nor upon the testator's death. The most common type of general gift is the *legacy*. A legacy is a gift of money such as, "I leave $25,000 to [name of beneficiary]." Other examples of general gifts include "I give 50 shares of Aspen Publishers, Inc. stock to [name of beneficiary]" and "I give a computer to [name of beneficiary]." These are general gifts because they contain no indication that the gift is of property the testator actually owned; that is, they do not use ownership language such as "my stock" or "my computer" and they do not specifically indicate which shares of stock or which computer is the subject of the gift.

§6.1.3 Demonstrative Gifts

A *demonstrative gift* shares some of the qualities of both specific and general gifts. "I leave $50,000 from my account #45839820 at Octopus National Bank to [name of beneficiary]" is a typical demonstrative gift. This demonstrative legacy sounds like a general gift because it refers to a sum of money but yet appears specific because it designates a specific fund that can be ascertained with certainty. If the designated source is insufficient, the gift is payable from the general assets of the testator's estate. Demonstrative gifts are not very common.

§6.1.4 Residuary Gifts

The term *residuary gift* refers to the property remaining after all specific, general, and demonstrative gifts are satisfied. Testators use residuary gifts in two main ways. The property governed by the residual clause could be the items the testator neglected to give away using other types of gifts. In other words, the beneficiary of the residuary gift gets the overlooked, unimportant, and low-value property. On the other hand, the residuary gift could be the most important gift in the will. The testator could use specific, general, and demonstrative gifts to dispose of heirloom items and make nominal gifts leaving the bulk of the estate to pass through the residuary clause.

§6.1.5 Type of Beneficiary

Testamentary gifts may also be classified based on the recipient of the property rather than the type of property. This classification is quite simple —a gift is either private or charitable. A *private gift* is a gift to an individual for that person's enjoyment. A *charitable gift* benefits society because the testator directs the gift towards the relief of poverty, advancement of education, support of religion, promotion of health, or encouragement of governmental or municipal purposes, such as parks and museums. If litigation regarding a charitable gift occurs, many states require a state official, such as the attorney general, to receive notice of the lawsuit. The attorney general then has the right to intervene in the action to protect the interests of the charity.

§6.2 Ademption by Extinction

Ademption refers to the failure of a specific gift because the property is not in the testator's estate when the testator dies. The asset could have been sold, given away, consumed, stolen, or destroyed.

Most jurisdictions apply a very rigid rule, often called the *identity theory* or *Lord Thurlow's Rule*. If the exact item the testator attempted to give away in the will is not in the testator's estate, the gift adeems and the beneficiary receives nothing. No evidence that the testator intended ademption to occur is required. Likewise, the beneficiary does not receive the value of the attempted gift, may not demand that the executor obtain the item for the beneficiary, and cannot trace into the proceeds of the asset.

A minority of states have departed from the traditional rule to avoid the harsh results that sometimes occur under the identity rule. These jurisdictions have adopted rules which attempt to preserve specific gifts under a variety of circumstances. *Intent view* jurisdictions may allow tracing and may even permit the beneficiary to receive the value of the missing property. See UPC §2-606, which imposes a presumption that the testator did not want the gift to adeem and provides alternate gifts under a wide variety of circumstances.

To avoid ademption problems and to make certain the courts follow the testator's wishes, each specific gift should contain an express statement of the testator's intent should the gifted property not be in the estate. The testator should either (1) provide a substitute gift (e.g., another specific gift or a sum of money), or (2) state that the beneficiary receives nothing if the exact item is not part of the estate.

Sample Ademption Provision

I leave my [precisely described item] to [Beneficiary]. If [item] is not in my estate, [ademption instructions].

Example 6-1. Ademption — Stolen Bequest

Testator left his 1974 AMC Gremlin automobile to his son, Sam, and his 1975 Ford Pinto to his daughter, Doris. Shortly before Testator's death, a thief stole the Gremlin and the police have been unable to recover it. To what are Sam and Doris entitled?

Explanation

The Gremlin was not in Testator's estate and thus Sam's gift adeemed. Under the law of states following the identity view, Sam is out of luck. However, in jurisdictions adopting the intent view, Sam has several possible claims. Sam would be entitled to any unpaid insurance proceeds for the loss of the Gremlin. In addition, some states would permit Sam to receive the value of the Gremlin from the estate because it appeared that Testator was attempting to treat the two children equally and thus Testator did not intend the unfortuitous event to alter the distribution of Testator's estate.

Example 6-2. Ademption — Proceeds of Adeemed Property

Testator's will devised his house to Harold. Shortly before Testator's death, Testator sold the house on credit and received a promissory note from the buyer. To what is Harold entitled?

Explanation

Under the majority rule, Harold's gift adeems because Testator did not own the house when he died. Harold would not be able to trace into the promissory note constituting the proceeds of the sale. However, in a state that adopts the intent view, a court is very likely to permit Harold to claim the promissory note.

Example 6-3. Ademption — Substitute Property

Testator's will devised his "home, together with all the contents therein, located at #19 Holly Ridge" to Bertha. At the time of Testator's death, Testator no longer owned this home because he sold it to buy another home down the street at #28 Holly Ridge. To what is Bertha entitled?

Explanation

In identity view states, Bertha receives nothing. The gift totally adeems because the property devised, i.e., the home at #19 Holly Ridge, was not in Testator's estate at the time of death. In intent view states, on the other hand, Bertha stands an excellent chance of receiving the #28 Holly Ridge house as Testator acquired it as a replacement for the specifically devised house.

Example 6-4. Ademption — Change in Form

Testator owned a parcel of real property as tenants in common with two other individuals. Testator executed a will leaving Testator's undivided one-third interest in this property to Alice. Several years later, Testator partitioned the property so that when Testator died, he was the sole owner of a distinct part of the original property. To what is Alice entitled?

Explanation

Alice is entitled to Testator's remaining interest in the property. The change to the property was merely one of form, not substance, and thus ademption would not occur even in states following the identity approach.

Example 6-5. Ademption — Partial or Pro Tanto

Testator left a 1,000 acre ranch to Chris. To fund a European vacation, Testator sold 250 acres and spent all the proceeds. To what is Chris entitled?

Explanation

Partial or *pro tanto* ademption occurred. However, Chris remains entitled to the 750 acres which remain. Even in intent view jurisdictions, it is unlikely that Chris could obtain the value of the 250 acres. Testator's deliberate act of selling this property reflected Testator's intent for partial ademption to occur.

Example 6-6. Ademption — Corporate Stock

Testator's will contains the following dispositive provision:

> I leave 100 shares of Aspen Publishing, Inc. stock to Alice.
>
> I leave my 100 shares of Oak Publishing, Inc. stock to Oscar.
>
> I leave stock certificate #539283 of Maple Publishing, Inc. stock to Mary.

When Testator dies, Testator does not own any of the stocks listed in the will. To what are these beneficiaries entitled?

Explanation

The traditional analysis of an ademption question begins with a determination of the nature of the gift. Remember, ademption only applies to specific gifts. The gift to Alice is most likely a general bequest. The gift does not refer to any particular property of Testator, either at the time of will execution or at the time of death. Thus, it is analogous to a gift of money so Alice will receive the value of the stock from Testator's estate. Most courts would consider both Oscar's and Mary's gifts to be specific. Oscar's gift contains *words of possession,* i.e., "*my* 100 shares." Words of possession are references to the testator's ownership of the bequeathed item. Mary's gift contains *words of identification,* i.e., "stock certificate #539283." Words of identification also operate to reference the testator's ownership of the item. Thus, gifts containing words of possession or words of identification stand a good chance of being classified as specific and thus subject to ademption if the property is not in the testator's estate at the time of death.

Example 6-7. Ademption — Sale by Guardian

Testator was declared mentally incompetent and the court appointed a guardian to manage Testator's property. To raise money to pay expenses, the guardian sold Testator's valuable comic book collection. Testator's will specifically bequeathed that collection to Testator's best friend, Pat. To what is Pat entitled?

Explanation

In most states, even those following the identity approach, Pat would be entitled to the value of the collection. Ademption is unlikely to occur when there is a sale by a guardian under circumstances where a testator has no capacity or opportunity to adjust the testamentary disposition. Thus, if Testator recovered and died ten years thereafter, the likelihood of ademption occurring increases significantly. Many states would apply a similar rule if the testator loses real property to the government via eminent domain. The beneficiary stands a good chance of receiving any unpaid condemnation award.

§6.3 Ademption by Satisfaction

Satisfaction is the failure of a testamentary gift because the testator has already transferred the property to the beneficiary between the time of will execution and time of death. At common law, the doctrine applied only to gifts of personal property while the modern trend is to permit gifts of real property to be satisfied as well. Satisfaction is analogous to the advancement concept that applies in the context of intestate succession. See §4.2, above.

Example 6-8. Satisfaction — Specific Gifts

Testator's will specifically bequeathed his engraved gold watch to Brenda. After executing the will, Testator gave Brenda the watch as a holiday present. Brenda treasured the watch until she needed money at which point she sold the watch to an antique store. Testator noticed the watch on display at the store and purchased the watch. Will Brenda receive the watch upon Testator's death?

Explanation

Satisfaction does not usually apply to specific gifts. If Testator had died after giving Brenda the watch but before she sold it, the watch would not be in Testator's estate and thus the gift would have adeemed by extinction. See §6.2, above. However, in this case, Testator reacquired the watch and it was actually in Testator's estate so the gift would not adeem by extinction. However, many courts would hold that satisfaction occurred by concluding that Testator's intent was for the inter vivos gift to be in place of the testamentary gift. Brenda should not be able to benefit twice from the same gift. She could have assured herself of owning the watch merely by retaining possession of it.

Example 6-9.   Satisfaction — *Ejusdem Generis*

Assume that Testator from the above example did not give Brenda the watch but instead made another type of inter vivos transfer, such as an outright gift of money, or named Brenda as a beneficiary of Testator's life insurance policy. Could these gifts trigger satisfaction?

Explanation

Common law courts applied the doctrine of *ejusdem generis*. Under this doctrine, the character of the testamentary gift and the inter vivos gift had to be the same before satisfaction took place. A watch is not the same type of gift as cash, either outright or via life insurance proceeds, and thus satisfaction would not have occurred. However, some modern statutes reject this doctrine and testamentary gifts may be satisfied by a wide variety of inter vivos transfers.

Example 6-10.   Satisfaction — General Gifts

Testator's will contained a $100,000 legacy for each of his grandchildren with the residuary passing to Charity. After one of the grandchildren enrolled in an expensive private law school, Testator paid $75,000 in tuition and living expenses. To how much is this grandchild entitled upon Testator's death?

Explanation

Satisfaction issues arise frequently with general gifts, especially legacies. Charity will argue that the $75,000 paid to or for the benefit of the grandchild acted as a partial satisfaction of the legacy and thus this grandchild should receive only $25,000 from the estate. On the other hand, the grandchild will argue that Testator intended the legacy to be in addition to the inter vivos gifts. As discussed below, the resolution of this issue depends on how Charity is required to prove a satisfaction under the applicable state law.

Courts must determine whether the testator intended an inter vivos transfer to cause the satisfaction of a testamentary gift. Common law courts applied a rebuttable presumption in this endeavor. Satisfaction had to be proven unless the beneficiary was the testator's child, or someone over whom the testator was in the position of a parent, in which case satisfaction was presumed. Most states no longer follow this presumption and instead require that extrinsic evidence prove that the testator intended for the inter vivos gift to be a satisfaction in all cases.

The modern trend is to restrict the types of evidence that may be used to prove a satisfaction. For example, UPC §2-609 requires either (a) a writing signed by the testator or the beneficiary declaring the gift to be a satisfaction, or (b) express directions in the will providing for the deduction of inter vivos gifts from testamentary ones.

To avoid confusion, many wills contain express language addressing satisfaction issues.

Sample Anti-Satisfaction Provision

No gift of any kind that I make under this will shall be considered either fully or partially satisfied by any inter vivos gift that I hereafter make.

Example 6-11.   Satisfaction — Gift to Nonbeneficiary

Testator's will contains a gift of $100,000 to Vicky. To take advantage of the annual gift tax exclusion (see §24.1.4.1, below), Testator made $10,000 gifts to Vicky and Vicky's husband. Testator signed a document indicating that both gifts were in partial satisfaction of Vicky's legacy. Is Vicky's gift partially satisfied by the gift to a nonbeneficiary, that is, her husband?

Explanation

At common law, the gift to Vicky's husband would not partially satisfy Vicky's legacy. However, some jurisdictions no longer require that the inter vivos gift be made to the legatee to operate as a satisfaction. In states such as these, Vicky is entitled to a legacy of only $80,000 because both the gift to her and her husband are considered. See UPC §2-609.

§6.4   Changes in Value

§6.4.1   *Appreciation and Depreciation*

The change in value of specifically gifted property between the time of will execution and time of death is not considered when distributing the testator's property. The beneficiary of a specific gift receives that item, regardless of any changes to its value. If the testator is not content with this result, express directions to the contrary must be included in the will.

Example 6-12.   Appreciation and Depreciation

Testator died survived by his two sons, John and Bobby. Testator's will left $100,000 to John and a parcel of undeveloped land to Bobby. At the time Testator executed the will, this land was valued at approximately $100,000. When Testator died, however, this land had appreciated to $500,000 due to its location near a growing city. How should Testator's estate be distributed?

Explanation

Testator's estate will be distributed exactly as provided in the will. Despite Testator's likely intent to treat each child equally, John will receive only $100,000 (which now has less buying power than when Testator executed the will due to inflation) while Bobby gets the land regardless of its current value. If the land had instead plummeted in value to $5,000, the result would be the same. Thus, the beneficiaries of specific gifts bear the burden of depreciation and reap the benefits of appreciation.

§6.4.2   *Corporate Securities*

Gifts of corporate securities are commonly the subject of dispute because of the tremendous variety of changes that may occur to them between will execution and death. If the change is merely one of form, the beneficiary stands a good chance of taking the securities resulting from the change. However, if the change is one of substance, the beneficiary will usually not benefit from the newly acquired securities. Many states codify the applicable rules. See UPC §2-605.

Example 6-13.   Changes in Value — Cash Dividend

Testator owned 100 shares of ABC Corporation stock and 50 shares of XYZ Corporation stock. Testator's will left the ABC Corporation stock to Willie, the XYZ Corporation stock to Yvonne, and the rest of the estate to Ethyl. On March 1, ABC stated that anyone owning stock as of March 15 would get a cash dividend of $1.00 per share. Also on March 1, XYZ Corporation decided that anyone owning stock as of March 20 would get a cash dividend of $1.00 per share. Testator died on March 18. Who is entitled to these cash dividends?

Explanation

Cash dividends belong to the person who owns the stock on the *record date,* that is, the date on which a person must be a stockholder of record to be entitled to the dividend. As of March 15, Testator owned the ABC stock. Thus, when Testator died, the right to receive the dividend was part of Testator's residual estate to which Ethyl is entitled. As of March 18, Yvonne owned the XYZ stock. Title to the stock vested in Yvonne the moment Testator died. Thus, Yvonne will receive the dividend on the XYZ stock because she was the owner on the record date of March 20. Note that the dates on which these corporations actually pay the dividends are not relevant to determining the person who is entitled to receive those dividends.

Example 6-14.   Changes in Value — Stock Dividends and Stock Splits

Testator owned 100 shares of XYZ Corporation stock. Testator's will provided, "I leave my 100 shares of XYZ Corporation stock to Yvonne." After Testator executed the will, XYZ Corporation declared a stock dividend and a stock split so that by the time Testator died, Testator owned 250 shares of XYZ Corporation stock. To how many shares is Yvonne entitled?

Explanation

Stock dividends and stock splits are changes in substance, not form. After a dividend or split, the shareholder owns a greater number of shares but still owns the same percentage of the corporation. Thus, Yvonne has an excellent chance of receiving all 250 shares rather than just the 100 shares bequeathed to her in the will. If the gift were general rather than specific (e.g., "I leave 100 shares of XYZ Corporation stock to Yvonne") or if Testator did not actually own any shares of XYZ Corporation stock at the time Testator executed the will, the likelihood of Yvonne getting all 250 shares declines significantly. Under these circumstances, courts would probably award Yvonne only the number of shares of XYZ Corporation stock that Testator indicated in the will.

Example 6-15. Changes in Value — Mergers

Testator owned 100 shares of XYZ Corporation stock. Testator's will provided, "I leave my 100 shares of XYZ Corporation stock to Yvonne." After Testator executed the will, XYZ Corporation merged with ABC Corporation. Shareholders of XYZ Corporation received two shares of ABC for each share of XYZ they owned. Thus, Testator died owning no shares in XYZ Corporation and owning 200 shares in ABC Corporation. To what, if anything, is Yvonne entitled?

Explanation

The merger did not change the substance of Testator's investment, just its form. Thus, most courts would give Yvonne the 200 shares in ABC Corporation which Testator owned at the time of death despite no provision in the will bequeathing those shares to her.

Example 6-16. Changes in Value — Dividend Reinvestment

Testator owned 100 shares of XYZ Corporation stock. Testator's will provided, "I leave my 100 shares of XYZ Corporation stock to Yvonne." After Testator executed the will, Testator entered into a dividend reinvestment agreement with XYZ Corporation. Instead of receiving cash dividends, XYZ Corporation took that money and purchased additional shares of XYZ stock for Testator. Thus, at the time of Testator's death, Testator owned 150 shares. To how many shares is Yvonne entitled?

Explanation

Traditionally, shares acquired via a dividend reinvestment program constitute a change in substance. Not all shareholders enter into these agreements. The new shares actually increase the Testator's percentage of ownership of XYZ Corporation. Thus, Yvonne may only be entitled to the 100 shares left to her in the will. However, some modern statutes would give Yvonne the additional 50 shares as well. See UPC §2-605.

§6.4.3 Interest on Legacies

Interest, if any, earned by a legacy prior to the testator's death does not pass to the legatee as it is not part of the money that the testator is actually giving. Assume that Testator's 1960 will provides, "I leave $10,000 to Kenny." If Testator dies in 2000, Kenny is entitled only to $10,000. No adjustments are made for the interest or other profits Testator made with the $10,000, nor for the tremendous decrease in purchasing power caused by inflation.

At common law, unpaid legacies began to earn interest starting one year after the testator's death. Many modern statutes, such as UPC §3-904, change this rule and delay the running of interest by providing that interest does not begin to accrue until one year after the appointment of a personal representative. The rate of this interest is typically the judgment or legal rate in effect in that jurisdiction.

§6.5   Exoneration

Specifically devised or bequeathed property is often subject to encumbrances. Real property may be burdened by a mortgage or deed of trust, and the testator may have used personal property as collateral under a security agreement governed by Article 9 of the Uniform Commercial Code. Does the beneficiary of encumbered specific gifts take them free from the liens or does the beneficiary take subject to the liens receiving only the testator's equity in the property?

At common law, *exoneration* was presumed. A testator presumably would not have wanted to burden the recipient of a gift with a debt and thus there was, in effect, an implied gift of sufficient money to pay off the debt. Because of the potential of exoneration causing tremendous disruption of the testator's intent, many states and UPC §2-607 reverse the common law presumption by providing that exoneration occurs only if there is express language requiring it in the will.

Example 6-17. Exoneration

Testator had two children. Testator's will left a home worth $200,000 to Son and the rest of the estate to Daughter. The home was subject to a $100,000 mortgage and the value of the residuary was approximately $100,000. What is the proper distribution of Testator's estate?

Explanation

In the absence of express language in the will, the correct distribution of Testator's estate depends on the state law presumption regarding exoneration and whether there is any admissible evidence of Testator's intent to rebut that presumption. If exoneration is presumed and there is insufficient evidence to rebut this presumption, Son would receive the home unburdened by the mortgage while Daughter would receive nothing because the residuary would be exhausted by exonerating the home. Perhaps the terms of the will can be used to show that Testator was attempting to create an even division of the estate between Son and Daughter. If exoneration is not presumed, then Son would receive the home subject to the mortgage and Daughter would take the residue. Only if the will specifically provides otherwise, would Son receive more than Testator's equity in the home.

Exoneration Provisions

[if no exoneration desired] All specific gifts made in this will pass subject to any mortgage, security interest, or other lien existing at the date of my death without right of exoneration.

[if exoneration desired] If [any specific gift made in this will] [the gift made in Article ___ of this will] is subject to a mortgage, security interest, or other lien, I direct that my executor pay the debt from other property of my estate which is not specifically given.

§6.6   Abatement

A testator may attempt to give away more property in the testator's will than the testator is actually able to give. This could occur because the testator misjudged the value of the testator's estate. Just because a testator leaves a $500,000 legacy in the testator's will does not mean the testator actually has that money to give. The testator may also not have accounted for all of the testator's debts, including funeral and burial costs and expenses of last illness. In most situations, the claims of creditors have priority over assertions to property by beneficiaries.

Abatement is the reduction or elimination of a testamentary gift to pay an obligation of the estate or a testamentary gift of a higher priority. Most states, either by judicial decision or through legislation, have established an abatement order. The usual abatement order is set forth below:

1. Property passing via intestate succession (that is, the testator died partially intestate).
2. Residuary gifts.
3. General gifts.
4. Specific gifts.

Consequently, a beneficiary of a specific gift stands a much greater chance of actually receiving the gift than a residuary beneficiary. Some jurisdictions retain the common law rule of requiring personal property in each category to be exhausted before real property from that category may be used. Other states no longer make a distinction between real and personal property. See UPC §3-902. Within a category, abatement is pro rata so that each gift is reduced by the same percentage. A few jurisdictions give certain types of gifts top priority; that is, they are the last to abate, regardless of the classification of the gift. The most common gift given this super-priority is a gift to a spouse.

Example 6-18. Abatement

Ken's will contains the following dispositive language:

> I leave my gold watch to Randy.
>
> I leave $10,000 to Jeff.
>
> I leave $5,000 to Karla.
>
> I leave the remainder of my estate to Alvera.

Ken's estate consists of $20,000 in cash and the gold watch with a fair market value of $25,000. There are $12,500 worth of debts, funeral expenses, administration expenses, etc. What is the proper distribution of Ken's estate?

Explanation

If Ken's estate were not responsible for any obligations, Randy would receive the gold watch, Jeff $10,000, Karla $5,000, and Alvera $5,000 (the residual estate consisting of the balance of the cash after paying the legacies to Jeff and Karla). Because Ken's estate is subject to $12,500 worth of debts, they must be paid before making distributions to the beneficiaries. The first gift to abate is the residual gift to Alvera. Thus, the $5,000 she would have received is used to reduce the debts. Her gift totally abates. Because $7,500 still needs to be paid, we look to the next category of gifts, the general gifts. There are $15,000 total of general gifts. After the balance of the claims are paid, only $7,500 remains for distribution. Abatement within a classification of gifts is pro rata. The ratio between the amount available ($7,500) and the amount originally given ($15,000) is 1 to 2. Thus, each legatee receives one-half or 50 percent of the amount to which each was originally entitled; Jeff receives $5,000 and Karla receives $2,500. The specific gift to Randy is untouched because there was sufficient property in lower ranked gifts to pay all of the claims. If the estate obligations exceeded $20,000, Randy could pay the balance of those obligations himself and then receive the watch. Otherwise, the executor would sell the watch and give Randy whatever proceeds remained after satisfying the creditors.

A testator may not be satisfied with the usual abatement order. Perhaps the testator is more concerned that a legatee receive the cash gift than for the beneficiary of a specific gift to receive an automobile. If this is the case, the testator must include express language in the will indicating the desired abatement order.

Sample Abatement Provision

I direct that the gifts made in this will abate in the following order: [order].

§6.7 Tax Apportionment

The testator's estate may be subject to a tax on the privilege of making gratuitous transfers upon the testator's death. See Chapter 24. What testamentary gifts bear the burden of these tax obligations? Some states do not have any special rules for tax liabilities. In other words, gifts abate to pay tax liabilities just like they do to pay other claims against the estate. See §6.6, above. On the other hand, an increasing number of states have enacted tax apportionment statutes so that the amount of each gift is reduced by the amount of estate tax attributable to the transfer. See UPC §3-916 and the Uniform Estate Tax Apportionment Act. In effect, each transfer is reduced by its fair share of the tax rather than being subsidized by lower ranking gifts. Tax apportionment prevents the residual gift, which is often the most important gift in the will, from bearing the entire estate tax burden in addition to all of the other claims against the estate.

State and federal governments include many nonprobate transfers in a testator's taxable estate. Tax apportionment statutes often cover these nonprobate assets as well as testamentary transfers. Federal law mandates that life insurance beneficiaries and recipients under powers of appointment shoulder their fair share of transfer taxes. See I.R.C. §§2206 & 2207. State statutes commonly extend apportionment to other transfers, such as multiple-party bank accounts, survivorship rights, and trusts over which the testator held the power of revocation. Some states that do not apportion tax among testamentary gifts nonetheless apportion taxes with regard to nonprobate transfers.

Apportionment statutes are designed to carry out the testator's presumed intent. Legislatures believe that most testators would want each transfer, be it probate or nonprobate, to be responsible for its own tax. If the testator does not agree, the testator may provide otherwise in the will and those instructions will prevail over the apportionment statute.

7

Changing Circumstances after Will Execution— Persons

Continuing the discussion of Chapter 6 on changes to circumstances involving the testator's property, this chapter focuses on changes that occur to the testator's beneficiaries and family members.

§7.1 Marriage of Testator

§7.1.1 Common Law Marital Property States

§7.1.1.1 Historical Background

At common law, the mere fact that a male testator got married after executing his will had no effect on the disposition of property under his premarriage will unless a child was born to the marriage. However, the marriage did give rise to the wife's dower rights, that is, a life estate in one-third of all real property that her husband owned at any time during the marriage. See §2.3.1.1, above.

On the other hand, the valid will of a single woman was revoked upon her marriage at common law. This automatic revocation was based on the common law view that marriage removed a woman's legal capacity to execute a will or revoke a previously existing will. Because the wife could not revise her will to take her new family into account, the courts thought it inappropriate to force the wife to stick with the terms of the premarriage will and thus deemed her will revoked upon her marriage.

§7.1.1.2 Modern Law — The Forced or Elective Share

Under modern law, the effect of marriage on a will written before marriage no longer depends on the sex of the testator. While the laws of a few states deem a premarriage will totally ineffective upon marriage causing the deceased spouse's entire probate estate to pass under intestacy, most states revoke only a portion of the will, and then only if the will does not provide the surviving spouse with a sufficient amount of property. To protect a surviving spouse from being disinherited or receiving a relatively small share of the deceased spouse's estate, the surviving spouse is given the right to a *forced* or *elective* share of the deceased spouse's estate. This share is in lieu of the benefits, if any, provided to the surviving spouse in the deceased spouse's will. The surviving spouse is entitled to this statutory amount regardless of the deceased spouse's intent as documented in the will.

A surviving spouse must evaluate whether to take the share the deceased spouse intended the surviving spouse to receive under the will or to disregard that intent and choose the statutory share. Surviving spouses generally select the option giving the spouse the greater share of the deceased spouse's estate. The surviving spouse must be certain to make the election within the period of time specified in the appropriate statute. See UPC §2-211 (later of (1) nine months after the deceased spouse's death, or (2) six months after the deceased spouse's will was admitted to probate). The surviving spouse loses the right to a forced share once this period expires.

The method used to compute the surviving spouse's forced share varies tremendously among the states. Below are some commonly used schemes.

- A fixed percentage of the net probate estate, e.g., one-third.
- Fixed percentages of the net probate estate depending on the number of children, with the surviving spouse receiving a smaller percentage if the deceased spouse had children, e.g., one-half if no children, one-third if children.
- A minimum dollar amount plus a fixed percentage of any additional property in the net probate estate, e.g., the first $100,000 plus one-third of any excess.
- Variable percentages depending on the length of the marriage, e.g., UPC §2-202, which begins at 3 percent for a marriage lasting one to two years and increases to 50 percent for marriages of fifteen or more years.

Many statutes apply the elective share formula on an *augmented estate,* rather than the net probate estate. See UPC §§2-201 through 2-214. The augmented estate may contain the value of nonprobate assets such as the deceased spouse's share of jointly held property passing because of rights of survivorship and life insurance proceeds that are not payable to the surviving spouse. Under the law of a few states, even some property the deceased spouse gave away while alive is treated as part of the augmented estate when computing the forced share. The augmented estate concept prevents the deceased spouse from reducing the surviving spouse's elective share by using probate avoidance techniques to dispose of the property. If the surviving spouse received the benefit of a nonprobate transfer, however, some statutes require these amounts to offset the forced share.

Example 7-1. Marriage of Testator — Payment of Forced Share

Husband's will provides, "I leave my car to Arthur, I leave $95,000 to Brenda, and I leave the rest of my estate to Wife." Husband's distributable estate consists of the car valued at $5,000 and $70,000 in cash. Wife received $500,000 because she was named as the beneficiary of Husband's life insurance policy. Assume that the state has an elective share provision entitling a surviving spouse to one-third of the deceased spouse's net probate estate. What is the proper distribution of Husband's estate?

Explanation

The possibility of Wife making a claim for her forced share is high because Wife will receive nothing under the will due to the nonexistence of a residuary estate. Most states would permit Wife to claim a forced share even though she received a significant amount as a result of a nonprobate transfer, such as the life insurance. The value of Husband's net probate estate is $75,000 and thus Wife takes $25,000. Although states vary, most states apportion the forced share among all remaining will beneficiaries rather than having the forced share paid according to the normal abatement order. See §6.6, above. The value of the car ($5,000) is added to the remaining cash ($45,000) yielding a total value of $50,000 available for distribution to the will beneficiaries. The ratio of available value ($50,000) to value given ($100,000, that is, car valued at $5,000 plus $95,000 legacy) is 1 to 2. Thus, each beneficiary receives one-half or 50 percent of what the beneficiary would have received had there been no reduction for the forced share. Arthur must pay $2,500 for the car or else the executor will sell the car and give Arthur the proceeds that remain after contributing $2,500 towards the forced share. Brenda will receive $47,500.

Example 7-2. Marriage of Testator — Waiver of Forced Share

Testator and First Spouse were married in 1950 and subsequently had three children. First Spouse died in 1995. Testator married Second Spouse in 1997. Testator's will provides that all of Testator's property passes to the three children. Testator wants to prevent Second Spouse from claiming a forced share in Testator's estate. How should Testator proceed?

Explanation

Some jurisdictions may permit a spouse to waive the spouse's right to a forced share in a written agreement signed either before (*antenuptial*) or during (*postnuptial*) the marriage. See UPC §2-213. However, both case and statutory law reflect a public policy against the enforceability of such a waiver. For example, courts may ignore a waiver if the surviving spouse did not receive full disclosure of the deceased spouse's finances prior to signing the waiver or if the court believes the waiver is unconscionable. Thus, Testator should present Spouse Two with a detailed accounting of all of Testator's property prior to having Spouse Two sign the waiver. To increase the likelihood of the agreement's validity, Spouse Two should be represented by an independent attorney.

§7.1.2 *Community Property Marital Property States*

Under the law of community property states, such as Arizona, California, Idaho, Louisiana, Nevada, New Mexico, Texas, Washington, and Wisconsin,[1] spouses own undivided interests in the property they acquire from earnings during marriage. Thus, the marriage of a testator typically has no impact on the property disposition provided for in a premarriage will. The surviving spouse does not need a forced share to be protected from disinheritance because the surviving spouse already owns one-half of the community property; the deceased spouse's will may not dispose of the surviving spouse's share of community without the survivor's consent. See §11.4, below.

§7.1.3 *Change in Domicile*

The general rule in the United States is that the ownership of earnings between spouses is governed by the law of the spouse's domicile at the time the property was acquired. Marital rights in property do not change as the

---

1. Wisconsin originally had a common law marital property system but abandoned it when it adopted a statutory community property type system.

couple moves from one type of marital property state to another. See §1.3.2, above. This rule has the potential for causing a significant problem as demonstrated by the next example.

Example 7-3. Marriage of Testator — Change in Domicile

Husband and Wife lived in a separate property marital property jurisdiction for forty years. Wife was the primary wage earner. When Wife retired, the couple moved to a community property jurisdiction. Shortly thereafter, Wife died. Wife's will leaves the bulk of her estate to the children and grandchildren. What is the proper distribution of Wife's estate?

Explanation

Because Wife earned the money in a common law marital property state, it remained her separate property when she moved to the community property state. Consequently, all property traceable to her earnings belongs solely to her unless she transferred an interest in that property to Husband. While living in the common law state, Husband was protected from being disinherited because of his right to a forced share. However, at the time of death, the couple lived in a community property state that probably does not have a forced share statute. Thus, Husband is out of luck because Husband cannot avail himself of a forced share statute and there is little or no community property for him to claim. This example highlights the importance of careful planning for married couples when they move between the different types of states. This situation occurs with some frequency as people move from the northern states, which are predominately common law, to the southwestern states, which follow the community property system.

Note that an opposite type of move may result in a windfall to the surviving spouse. Assume in the above example that the couple originally lived in a community property state. Thus, Husband owned one-half of all Wife's earnings. Upon Wife's death in the common law state, Husband may claim the one-half of the property that is his by virtue of it being acquired in a community property state before they moved to the common law state as well as a forced share of her probate estate composed of her share of the former community property as well as her separate property.

§7.2 Divorce of Testator

Divorce was not a common occurrence in the early history of England or the United States. Thus, there is little common law addressing the ramifications of a divorce on a will executed during marriage that made a gift to a person who is now an ex-spouse. Early decisions usually held that the divorce had no effect on the will. The courts realized that a testator probably did not intend for the property to pass to an ex-spouse but felt that they had no legal basis for voiding the gift.

Most states now have statutes providing that upon divorce, all provisions of a will executed during marriage in favor of an ex-spouse are void. The balance of the will remains effective as written. See UPC §2-804. Thus, the ex-spouse would not be able to take as a beneficiary or serve in a fiduciary capacity such as the executor of the will, the guardian of any minor children, or the trustee of a testamentary trust. If the spouses remarry each other and remain married until the first spouse dies, the will typically remains effective as originally written. Some states also permit a will to include a provision validating a gift in favor of a spouse regardless of whether the spouses are married or divorced at the time of the testator's death.

Example 7-4. Divorce of Testator — Distribution of Property

While married, Testator executed a will containing the following dispositive language: "I leave my entire estate to Spouse. If Spouse does not survive me, I leave my entire estate to Mother." Testator and Spouse were divorced. Testator died survived by Spouse, Mother, and two children. What is the proper distribution of Testator's estate?

Explanation

The gift to Spouse is void because of the divorce. By statute or case law, most states treat Spouse as legally predeceasing Testator even though Spouse biologically survived. Thus, Mother is entitled to Testator's estate under the terms of the will.

Example 7-5. Divorce of Testator — Gifts to Other Ex-Relatives

While married, Testator executed a will containing the following dispositive language: "I leave my car to Father-in-Law. I leave $45,000 to Sarah, my stepdaughter. I leave the remainder of my estate to Spouse. If Spouse does not survive me, I leave the remainder of my estate to Mother." Testator and Spouse were divorced. Testator died survived by Spouse, Father-in-Law, Sarah, Mother, and two children. What is the proper distribution of Testator's estate?

Explanation

The gift to Spouse is void because of the divorce and thus Mother will take Testator's residuary estate. But what about the gifts to the other ex-relatives?

Most state statutes are not broad enough to void gifts to other ex-relatives and thus Father-in-Law and Sarah, the stepchild, stand a good chance of receiving their gifts. Some modern statutes, however, are more comprehensive and will void gifts to individuals who are no longer related to Testator because of the divorce. See UPC §2-804.

Example 7-6. Divorce of Testator — Marital Problems

While married, Testator executed a will containing the following dispositive language: "I leave my entire estate to Spouse. If Spouse does not survive me, I leave my entire estate to Mother." Spouse filed for divorce and the couple separated. On the day before the divorce hearing, Testator died survived by Spouse, Mother, and two children. What is the proper distribution of Testator's estate?

Explanation

The vast majority of statutes void provisions in favor of a spouse only upon a final divorce. Merely filing for divorce, living apart, or otherwise separating is typically not enough to trigger the voiding statute. Thus, Spouse is still entitled to Testator's entire estate. If you become a family law practitioner, you must keep this in mind. A client going through a divorce probably no longer wants the soon-to-be ex-spouse to benefit from the client's death. Thus, estate planning is a fundamental component of a family law practice. However, a person with marital problems is typically more concerned with child custody and the property settlement than with the disposition of property upon death and the naming of fiduciaries. This problem may be partially alleviated by including a will provision such as the following.

Sample Divorce Provision
If I am divorced from [Spouse] or if a divorce action is pending at the time of my death, all provisions in this will in favor of [Spouse] are to be given no effect. For purposes of this will, [Spouse] will then be treated as if [Spouse] predeceased me.

Example 7-7. Divorce of Testator — Post-Divorce Will

Testator was divorced in 1990. Testator, still deeply in love with Ex-Spouse, wrote a will in 1995 containing the following dispositive language: "I leave my entire estate to Ex-Spouse. If Ex-Spouse does not survive me, I leave my entire estate to Mother." Testator died in 1998 survived by Ex-Spouse, Mother, and two children. What is the proper distribution of Testator's estate?

Explanation

Ex-Spouse is entitled to Testator's entire estate. The automatic voiding of gifts to ex-spouses does not apply if the testator executes the will after the divorce. Testator clearly intended Ex-Spouse to receive the property even though their marriage had ended in divorce.

§7.3   Pretermitted Heirs

Parents have no obligation to provide testamentary gifts for their children under the law of common law jurisdictions. Thus, a parent may intentionally disinherit one or more of the parent's children. To protect a child from an accidental or inadvertent disinheritance, state legislatures have enacted statutes which may provide a forced share of the parent's estate for a *pretermitted* (omitted) child under certain circumstances.

§7.3.1   Defined

The determination of whether a person qualifies as a pretermitted heir varies among the states and raises some important issues.

Example 7-8.   Pretermitted Heirs — When Born

Testator had two children, Alice and Bruce, when Testator executed a will in 1990. In 1995, Testator had a third child, Cecilia. The dispositive language of Testator's will states, "I leave one-half of my estate to Alice. I leave the remaining half of my estate to my best friend, Victor." Upon Testator's death, may Bruce and Cecilia receive a portion of Testator's estate as pretermitted children?

Explanation

Although both Bruce and Cecilia are not provided for in Testator's will, there is a significant difference between their two situations. Bruce was born before Testator executed the will while Cecilia was born thereafter. The public policy of providing a forced share for Cecilia is stronger than that for Bruce. Testator probably omitted Bruce from the will on purpose; it is unlikely Testator forgot about Bruce's existence because he was alive when Testator executed the will. On the other hand, Cecilia did not yet exist. It is arguable that had Testator thought about Testator's will and the fact that it did not provide for Cecelia, Testator would have amended Testator's will to provide for her.

Consequently, under the law of most states, a child must be born or adopted after the Testator executed the will to receive a forced share as a pretermitted child. See UPC §2-302. In a few states, however, even an omitted child who was born before the parent executed the will can claim a forced share.

Example 7-9. Pretermitted Heirs — Children of Deceased Children

Testator's 1960 will provides, "I leave all my property to my best friend, Florence." In 1962, Testator's only child, Christy, is born. In 1995, Christy gave birth to John. Christy died in 1997. Testator died in 1999 without ever changing the 1960 will. Does John qualify as a pretermitted heir?

Explanation

Some states provide a forced share for descendants of a pretermitted child who predeceases the testator, that is, the testator's grandchildren. Thus, in these states, John would qualify as a pretermitted heir. In many states, however, forced shares are created only for pretermitted children, not for other heirs such as grandchildren. See UPC §2-302.

Example 7-10. Pretermitted Heirs — Mistaken Belief of Death

Testator's only child, Rambo, was a member of one of the elite branches of the United States special forces. Testator was informed that Rambo was killed during a classified and extremely dangerous mission. Testator then wrote a will leaving all of the property to various family members and friends. After Testator's death, Rambo shows up to everyone's amazement with fascinating tales of his escape from a heavily fortified foreign prison. May Rambo share in Testator's estate?

Explanation

Rambo will be able to share in states that broadly define pretermitted children to include all children who are omitted from a will, not just after-borns or after-adopteds. Even in some states that limit pretermitted child status to those born or adopted after will execution, Rambo may have a claim. For example, UPC §2-302(c) states that if the testator fails to provide for a living child solely because the testator thought that the child was dead, the child is entitled to a pretermitted child share.

§7.3.2 *Excluded Situations*

The goal of pretermitted child statutes is to carry out a testator's presumed intent, not to provide a share for a child whom the testator did not wish to name as a beneficiary. Thus, state statutes typically enumerate one or more situations in which a pretermitted child may not claim a forced share. Common excluded situations include the following:

- **Testator's will actually provides for the pretermitted child, such as by the testator's inclusion of a class gift to children.** Although the identities of the pretermitted children were unknown, it is clear that the testator anticipated the possibility of having additional children and made a provision that encompassed them. However, if the amount of the gift is nominal, some courts may hold that the gift does not actually provide for the pretermitted child.
- **Testator provided for the pretermitted child by way of a nonprobate transfer.** Some states prevent the pretermitted child from claiming a share of the testator's estate if the child is already benefiting from the testator's death, such as by being a beneficiary of a life insurance policy or taking under a pay on death bank account. The larger the nonprobate transfer, the more likely the testator intended the transfer to be in lieu of a testamentary gift.
- **Extrinsic evidence demonstrates the testator's intent to exclude pretermitted children.** Some jurisdictions have *Massachusetts-type* statutes, which allow the use of extrinsic evidence to show the testator's intent. For example, evidence that the testator and the pretermitted child have not spoken in thirty years may be enough to prove that the testator intentionally omitted that child.
- **Testator's will demonstrates an intent for pretermitted children not to share in the testator's estate.** Some states have *Missouri-type* statutes, which require the evidence of the testator's intent to exclude a pretermitted child to be contained in the will. In other words, extrinsic evidence is not admissible to show the testator's intent. In this type of jurisdiction, a testator who does not wish pretermitted children to share in the estate may include a provision such as, "I intentionally make no provision for any child who may be born to me or adopted by me after I execute this will." This type of provision is often found in the wills of male testators who want to prevent claims by afterborn children of whose existence they might be unaware either because they fear fictitious claims of afterborn status (especially if the testator is famous) or because the testator anticipates engaging in irresponsible sexual behavior.
- **Testator's entire estate is left to the pretermitted child's other parent.** This exclusion is based on the presumption that the child's

surviving parent is likely to take care of the child, if the child is a minor, or, if the child is an adult, to leave property to the child in the surviving parent's will.

§7.3.3 Determination of Share

Jurisdictions use a variety of methods to determine the share of a pretermitted child. Traditionally, the pretermitted child receives the share the child would have received if the testator had died intestate. Some states still follow the common law view that if a testator executes a will and then marries and has a child, the entire will is revoked so that the testator's entire estate passes by intestacy. Modern statutes are not so extreme and often do not base the pretermitted child's share on the size of the testator's probate estate. For example, some states give the pretermitted child an intestate share only of the property that does not pass to the child's other parent. If the testator's will leaves property to some of the testator's children, some states limit the pretermitted child to an intestate share based solely on gifts made to these children. This restriction prevents the pretermitted child from receiving a larger share of the estate than the children, as a class, who were actually provided for in the will.

§7.4 Death of Beneficiary—Lapse

§7.4.1 Situations Causing Lapse

Deceased individuals cannot take and hold title to property. Accordingly, a testamentary gift intended for a beneficiary who died before the testator will not take effect; that is, the gift *lapses*. Lapse may also occur if a beneficiary biologically outlives the testator but is legally treated as predeceasing the testator. For example, the beneficiary may disclaim the gift (see §11.5, below) or fail to satisfy the survival period imposed by the will or state law (see §7.6, below). If the beneficiary was already deceased when the testator executed the will, the gift was at common law deemed a *void gift*. Under modern law, however, there are few distinctions drawn based on whether the beneficiary died before or after will execution.

§7.4.2 Distribution of Lapsed Gifts—Generally

Courts follow a relatively uniform analysis to determine the proper recipients of lapsed property. The courts begin by ascertaining the testator's intent as reflected by the express terms of the will. If the will provides a substitute taker in the event of lapse, that alternate beneficiary will receive the gift. Testators should provide at least one contingent beneficiary for each testamentary gift.

Sample Clause to Prevent Lapse

I leave my [item] to [Beneficiary]. If [Beneficiary] does not survive me, I leave my [item] to [Alternate Beneficiary].

If the testator neglected to provide an alternate beneficiary, courts examine the applicable state law to see if the legislature provided a method for determining the recipients of lapsed gifts. This type of provision is called an *anti-lapse statute* and is discussed in §7.4.3, below.

If the gift is not saved by an anti-lapse statute, the lapsed property passes through the residuary clause of the will. If there is no residuary clause or if the residuary gift is the one that is lapsing, courts distribute the property according to intestate succession.

§7.4.3 Anti-Lapse Statutes

Anti-lapse statutes prevent lapse by providing substitute beneficiaries for the lapsed gift. The goal of these statutes is to provide a distribution that the testator would have preferred over the property passing under the residuary clause or via intestacy. These statutes operate on the presumption that if the testator had anticipated that the beneficiary would die first, the testator would have supplied an alternate gift to the descendants of the predeceased beneficiary who survive the testator. The manner of distribution among these descendants may be per stirpes, per capita with representation, or per capita at each generation depending on the jurisdiction. See §2.4, above.

The situations that trigger the application of an anti-lapse statute vary among the states. Some statutes are narrow and save gifts made to only a limited number of the testator's predeceased relatives such as descendants (children, grandchildren, etc.) or descendants of the testator's parents (brothers, sisters, nieces, nephews, etc.). Other anti-lapse statutes are broader. For example, UPC §2-603 saves gifts made to grandparents or descendants of grandparents (aunts, uncles, cousins, siblings, nieces, nephews, etc.). A few states have wide-sweeping anti-lapse statutes that save lapsed gifts in all cases where the predeceased beneficiary left descendants who survived the testator, even if there is no familial relationship between the testator and the beneficiary.

Most states apply anti-lapse statutes to class gifts, as well as to gifts to individuals. Thus, if a will provides, "I leave all my property to my children," the children of any predeceased child will take the predeceased child's share. However, if the predeceased child died before the testator executed the will, many states would not permit this predeceased child's descendants to take because the class never included the predeceased child.

Example 7-11. Anti-Lapse Statute — Generally

Testator's 1990 will provides a legacy of $50,000 for Elliott, Testator's uncle. The residuary of the estate passes to the American Red Cross. Elliott died in 1995 survived by two children, Art and Bob. Testator died in 1998 survived by Art and Bob. What is the proper distribution of Testator's estate?

Explanation

Testator's gift to Elliott lapses because Elliott did not survive Testator. Because Testator neglected to provide an alternate beneficiary, the court will examine the applicable anti-lapse statute. If the statute is narrow and thus not applicable to gifts to uncles (descendants of grandparents), the American Red Cross will receive the legacy as part of the residue. Cousins Art and Bob would be out of luck. However, if the gift is within the scope of the anti-lapse statute, Elliott's descendants will be substituted and consequently Art and Bob would each receive $25,000.

Example 7-12. Anti-Lapse Statute — Language to Avoid Application

Testator's 1990 will contains the following dispositive provision: "I leave $20,000 to my sister, Mary. If Mary predeceases me, I leave this legacy to my friend, Sarah. I leave the rest of my estate to my surviving children." Mary died in 1995. Testator had two children, Son and Daughter. Son died in 1996. Testator died in 1998 survived by Mary's three children, Sarah, Son's two children, and Daughter. What is the proper distribution of Testator's estate?

Explanation

Sarah will receive the $20,000 legacy. Even if the applicable anti-lapse statute applies to gifts to siblings, Testator's naming of an alternate beneficiary supercedes the anti-lapse statute. If, however, Sarah had also predeceased Testator, then Mary's children are the likely recipients of the legacy because the will would not name a substitute beneficiary capable of taking. Now, let's look at the residuary gift. Jurisdictions vary widely regarding whether language merely requiring a beneficiary to survive is sufficient to trump the anti-lapse statute. For example, some states have statutes expressly stating that gifts to "surviving children" mean that a child must survive to take and that the anti-lapse statute does not apply. In this case, Daughter would take the entire residuary estate. On the other hand, other states and UPC §2-603(b)(3) provide that the anti-lapse statute applies despite a testator's use of express survivorship language. Under this approach, Daughter would receive one-half of the residuary and Son's two children would divide the remaining half. Thus, if a testator really means to prevent the application of the anti-lapse statute, the testator should use language such as, "To my surviving children and not to the descendants of any of my children who do not survive me. It is my intent that no anti-lapse statute apply to this gift."

§7.4.4 *Partial Lapse in Residuary Clause*

Example 7-13. Partial Lapse in Residuary Clause

Testator's 1990 will contains the following dispositive provision: "I leave the residuary of my estate to my best friends, Barry and Mandy." Mandy died in 1995 survived by her two children. Testator died in 1998 survived by Barry, Mandy's two children, and Testator's only child, Carmen. What is the proper disposition of Testator's estate?

Explanation

Testator neglected to provide a substitute beneficiary. Testator did not indicate a replacement beneficiary for Mandy, nor did Testator include survivorship language, that is, a clause providing that the residuary passes to the survivor of Barry and Mandy should one of them die before Testator. Thus, the courts will look to the state's anti-lapse statute. If the statute is broad enough to cover gifts to nonrelatives, Mandy's two children would take in her place and each would receive 25 percent of the residue.

Courts typically adopt one of two approaches if the anti-lapse statute does not save a residuary gift to multiple beneficiaries. The traditional or orthodox view is that the lapsed gift passes via intestacy. Thus, Carmen would receive 50 percent of the residuary. This view is based on the assertion that one cannot have a residue of a residue and reflects the policy of courts not creating dispositive provisions, such as by reading survivorship language into a residuary gift, when there is no verified basis that Testator would have wanted such language included. The modern approach is for the court to prevent partial intestacy, a condition that the testator obviously did not want to occur because of the inclusion of a residuary clause, by pretending that the residuary clause contains survivorship language. If the court adopts this view, Barry would take Testator's entire residuary estate. The modern approach is being adopted by an increasing number of jurisdictions. Some state legislatures have even codified this approach. See UPC §2-603.

§7.5 Failure of Charitable Gift — Cy Pres

A charitable gift may fail because (a) the indicated charity no longer exists when the testator dies, or (b) the specified charitable purpose is illegal, impossible to fulfill, or has already been fulfilled. If the will indicates the appropriate distribution of property under these circumstances, the court will carry out those directions. However, if the testator neglected to detail the testator's intent, the court must decide between (a) letting the gift fail and the property passing to other beneficiaries or to heirs via intestacy, or (b) applying the *cy pres* doctrine to preserve the gift.

Cy pres is a doctrine of equitable approximation. The court attempts to find a charitable beneficiary or charitable purpose that is sufficiently similar to what the testator provided in the will so the court can reasonably conclude that the property is being used in a manner consistent with the testator's intent. Thus, the court must determine that the testator had a *general charitable intent*, that is, an intent to be charitable that is broader than the intent that cannot now be carried out. Because of the public policy favoring charitable gifts, courts are prone to find that the testator had general charitable intent. The fact that the testator left the property to charity is a good indication that the testator preferred charity over family members. If the court does not apply cy pres, the failed gift is likely to pass to family members under other provisions of the will or via intestacy.

Example 7-14. Cy Pres

Testator executed a will in 1930 leaving Testator's entire estate for the development of a polio vaccine. Testator has now died and a polio vaccine already exists. Claims to the estate are now being made by Testator's children as well as a variety of charities. How should a court proceed in determining the appropriate distribution of Testator's estate?

Explanation

Because the will does not provide an alternate charitable purpose, the court must decide between permitting Testator's children to take the property under intestacy or applying the cy pres doctrine and substituting another charity. Assuming Testator's estate is large enough, it is likely that a great number of charities will petition the court. Each will claim that its charitable purpose is the closest to Testator's charitable intent. The AIDS Foundation may claim that Testator wanted to assist the most devastating disease facing Americans and thus just as polio was feared in the 1930s, AIDS is feared today. A charity dealing with childhood leukemia may claim that its purpose is closer because Testator selected a disease that primarily affected children.

Charities focusing on other childhood diseases, such as muscular dystrophy or cerebral palsy, will claim that they are even closer to Testator's intent because like polio, these diseases affect the muscular system. An international polio organization could come forward and explain that it needs the money to distribute polio vaccines in underdeveloped nations and that its purpose is thus the closest to Testator's intent because it deals with the exact disease Testator wanted to eliminate.

In the process of selecting the appropriate charity or charities, the court may examine a wide array of extrinsic evidence to discover Testator's probable intent. For example, the court would find it significant if Testator had a child afflicted with polio.

§7.6 Survival

At common law and under the 1953 version of the Uniform Simultaneous Death Act, a beneficiary needed to outlive the testator for only a mere instant to take under the will. As discussed in §4.3, above, with regard to the survival requirement for heirs, this rule often caused litigation over who survived whom when the deaths of the testator and beneficiary occurred close together in an automobile accident, airplane crash, tornado, or other unfortunate event.

Most jurisdictions now impose a survival period by statute. Thus, a beneficiary must not only outlive the testator, but must also outlive by the statutorily specified period of time. Under the 1991 version of the Uniform Simultaneous Death Act and UPC §2-702, the beneficiary must survive by at least 120 hours (five days). If the beneficiary survives the testator but dies prior to the expiration of the survival period, the gift passes as if the beneficiary had actually died prior to the testator.

Example 7-15. Survival — Distribution of Property

Testator's will contained the following dispositive provisions: "I leave my diamond ring to Heidi. I leave the rest of my estate to Charity." Testator died on September 1 and Heidi died on September 4 survived by her two children. What is the proper distribution of Testator's estate assuming the applicable state law imposes a 120 hour survival requirement?

Explanation

Although Heidi biologically survived Testator, she did not legally survive because she died before the survival period elapsed. Thus, the diamond ring passes as if Heidi had predeceased Testator. We must then examine the state's anti-lapse statute to see if it may be used to save Heidi's gift. See §7.4, above.

If the anti-lapse statute applies, Heidi's two children will receive the ring as tenants in common. If the anti-lapse statute is inapplicable, the ring falls into the residue and passes to Charity.

Example 7-16. Survival — Alteration of Survival Period

Testator's will contains the following dispositive language: "I leave my gold watch to William, if he survives me. I leave my house to Homer, if he survives me by 30 days. I leave the rest of my estate to Charity." Testator died on January 1, William died on January 3, and Homer died on January 20. What is the proper distribution of Testator's estate assuming state law imposes a 120-hour survival requirement and that the anti-lapse statute does not apply to any of these gifts?

Explanation

Testators may lengthen or shorten the survival period by express provision in the will. Thus, the key issue is whether Testator's language is sufficient to alter the statutory period. With regard to Homer's gift, the result is clear. Testator specifically required Homer to survive by thirty days and he did not. Homer's gift lapses despite his surviving by the statutory 120 hours and consequently Charity receives the house. The result with regard to William is less clear. Did Testator's use of the phrase "if he survives me" reduce the survival period to a mere instant, or did it function only as a restatement of the statutory rule? Survival statutes vary on the resolution of this issue with some providing that any mention of survival trumps the survival statute while others require the testator to provide an express survival period to supplant the statutory period.

Please review §4.3, above, dealing with the survival of heirs. Most of the discussion and examples in that section are relevant in the testate context as well.

8

Revocation of Wills

The testator may change or revoke the will at any time with or without a reason. A will is an *ambulatory* instrument; that is, it walks with the testator during life but has no legal effect until the testator's death. As long as the testator has mental capacity, the testator has full authority to change or revoke the will. Only upon the testator's death does the will become irrevocable.

As is the case with will creation, the only ways to revoke a will are set forth by state law. Failure to revoke in a manner allowed by law will make the attempted revocation ineffective regardless of the testator's intent. This chapter begins by reviewing the three main categories of revocation: (1) revocation by operation of law; that is, partial or total revocation triggered automatically by certain events, (2) revocation by physical act as a result of the application of some type of violence to the will, and (3) revocation by a subsequent writing such as a new will or codicil. Discussions of other issues relevant to revocation round out the rest of this chapter.

§8.1 Revocation by Operation of Law

Certain events or circumstances may trigger a revocation by operation of law. Normally, this type of revocation occurs automatically to carry out a presumed intent of the testator. In other words, the law assumes these occurrences would cause most testators to make corresponding changes to their wills. If one or more of these events occurs and the testator does not adjust the testator's will thereafter, the law operates to revoke part or all of the will on the assumption that the testator would no longer have wanted the will to take effect as written. In most revocation by operation of law situations, extrinsic evidence may not be used to show that the testator actually would not have wanted the will or portions thereof changed or revoked.

§8.1.1 *Marriage of Testator*

Oftentimes a testator will write a will before marriage and then not make appropriate changes to the will to account for the spouse. To protect a spouse from being disinherited or receiving only a nominal share of the deceased spouse's estate, most states permit the surviving spouse to claim a specified share of the deceased spouse's estate regardless of the terms of the will. The details of how a marriage operates to revoke the deceased spouse's desires as documented in the will are discussed in §7.1, above.

§8.1.2 *Divorce of Testator*

The desire of a testator to leave property to a spouse is usually significantly diminished upon divorce. Thus, statutes in most states provide that all provisions in favor of the former spouse that are contained in a will executed during marriage are void. See §7.2, above, for a complete discussion of the effect of divorce on the testator's will.

§8.1.3 *Pretermitted Heirs*

If a testator does not provide for one of the testator's children in a will, there is a possibility that the exclusion was accidental, especially if the testator executed the will prior to the child's birth or adoption. Consequently, state legislatures have enacted statutes that may provide a forced share of the parent's estate for the omitted child. The ability of pretermitted heirs to share in the estate despite their omission from the will is analyzed in §7.3, above.

§8.1.4 *Death of Beneficiary*

A gift to a beneficiary who predeceases the testator is automatically revoked because property can be transferred only to people who are alive. In some situations, however, state statutes will prevent the gift from lapsing by substituting other individuals as the beneficiaries of the gift. The treatment of lapsed gifts is reviewed in §7.4, above.

§8.1.5 *Beneficiary Killed Testator*

A beneficiary cannot accelerate the receipt of property under a testator's will by murdering the testator. If a beneficiary murders the testator, the beneficiary will be precluded from taking a beneficial interest in the property either by statute or through the imposition of a constructive trust to prevent unjust enrichment. See UPC §2-803. The material dealing with an heir killing the intestate in §3.8.4, above, is applicable in the testate context as well.

§8.1.6 Alienation

If the testator makes an inter vivos transfer of an item subject to a specific devise or bequest in the testator's will, that gift is revoked by operation of law. The inter vivos transfer prevails over the attempted testamentary transfer because a will has no effect until death. For a complete discussion of the ramifications of the testator alienating a specific gift, see the discussion of ademption in §§6.2 and 6.3, above.

§8.1.7 Elapse of Time

Example 8-1. Revocation by Operation of Law — Elapse of Time

Testator executed a will in 1960 that stated, "I leave $50,000 to Daughter, $50,000 to Son, and the rest of my estate to Spouse." When Testator signed this will, his estate was valued at $120,000. At the time of Testator's death, Testator's estate was valued at over $10,000,000. What is the proper distribution of Testator's estate?

Explanation

Testator's estate will be distributed exactly as specified in the will. The common law never adopted the old Roman law that provided that wills were automatically revoked ten years after execution. It is evident that Testator intended the children to receive the bulk of the estate. However, the fact that Testator's will is approximately forty years old is irrelevant, even when coupled with the tremendous change in value of Testator's estate, which will cause the children to receive relatively insignificant amounts. Son and Daughter would not be able to introduce extrinsic evidence to show that Testator still intended them to be the primary beneficiaries of the estate.

§8.1.8   *Change in Feelings toward Beneficiary*

Example 8-2. Revocation by Operation of Law — Change in Feelings toward Beneficiary

Testator's 1980 will provides, "I leave my entire estate equally to my two children, Son and Daughter." Daughter ran away from home in 1984 and has had no contact with Testator since that time. Upon Testator's death, what is the proper distribution of Testator's estate?

Explanation

Testator's estate will be distributed exactly as provided in the will. The fact that Testator's feelings toward Daughter at the time of death may have been tremendously different from those Testator had when Testator executed the will is irrelevant. Son would have little, if any, success getting the court to consider evidence of the deteriorated relationship between Testator and Daughter.

§8.2   Revocation by Physical Act

The testator may revoke a will by destroying it or otherwise physically performing some act upon the will which manifests the testator's intent that the will is not to be used to determine the at-death disposition of the testator's property. A mere physical destruction of the will, however, is not enough to trigger a revocation. Each of the requirements discussed in §8.2.1, below, must be satisfied for an effective revocation by physical act.

At first glance, this method of revocation appears to be quite simple. If the testator no longer likes the will, the testator can just destroy it. However, revocation by physical act can be extremely ambiguous. After the testator dies, courts may have great difficulty determining who actually did the physical act, when it was done, and why. Courts admit a wide array of extrinsic evidence to ascertain these crucial facts. To avoid the confusion often caused by physical act revocations, prudent testators do not rely on this type of revocation but instead couple a revocation by physical act with a revocation by subsequent writing as discussed in §8.3, below.

§8.2.1   *Requirements*

This section discusses the four basic requirements for a valid revocation by physical act: (1) capacity to revoke, (2) intent to revoke, (3) a satisfactory physical act performed on the will, and (4) the simultaneous existence of the first three prerequisites.

§8.2.1.1 Capacity

Example 8-3. Revocation by Physical Act—Capacity—Incompetency

Testator executed a valid will in 1990. In 1998, Testator was adjudicated incompetent. In 1999, Testator physically destroyed the will. Is this revocation effective?

Explanation

If Testator lacked mental capacity when the Testator destroyed the will in 1999, no revocation occurred. An adjudication of incompetency raises a presumption of lack of capacity but the heirs may rebut this presumption by showing that Testator destroyed the will during a lucid interval. The discussion of testamentary capacity in §5.2, above, also applies to the capacity to revoke.

Example 8-4. Revocation by Physical Act—Capacity—Duress

Testator's only heir apparent withheld food, drink, and medicine from Testator, who was physically disabled, until Testator destroyed the will which named Testator's nurse as the primary beneficiary. Is this revocation effective?

Explanation

Although Testator had the mental capacity to revoke the will, the heir's conduct constitutes duress that vitiates that capacity. Assuming Testator's nurse can prove what happened, the will would take effect as written despite its physical destruction. Revocations induced by undue influence or fraud would likewise be ineffective.

§8.2.1.2 Intent

Example 8-5. Revocation by Physical Act—Intent

After years of sloppy living, Testator decided to organize everything in Testator's home and throw away anything unnecessary. In Testator's haste to become neat, Testator inadvertently tossed the will into the burning fireplace along with love letters from Testator's former romantic interests. Is this revocation effective?

Explanation

Testator did not revoke the will because Testator lacked the intent, the *animus revocandi*, to do so. The will remains effective as originally written.

§8.2.1.3 Physical Act

State statutes use various terms to describe the physical act necessary to effectuate a revocation. For example, many states have statutes based on the 1676 Statute of Frauds, which indicated that burning, canceling (effacing the will such as by drawing lines through its provisions), tearing, and obliterating would revoke the will. UPC §2-507 also adds destroying to the list. Some statutes use fewer words but they are typically interpreted as covering approximately the same type of acts. But if the physical act is not within the scope of the statute, the physical act will not cause a revocation.

Example 8-6. Revocation by Physical Act—Types of Acts

Which of the following acts would be sufficient to revoke a will?

Example 8-6a. Testator cuts or tears the will into four pieces.

Explanation

Tearing up the will is a sufficient physical act.

Example 8-6b. Testator draws large dark lines through Testator's signature.

Explanation

Drawing lines through the signature is usually considered a sufficient physical act. This act cancels the will by removing one of the requirements of a valid will, that is, the testator's signature.

Example 8-6c. Testator burns the will so that only a pile of ashes remain.

Explanation

Burning up the will is a sufficient physical act.

Example 8-6d. Testator burns the will so that the edges of the pages are singed but the will is otherwise intact and legible.

Explanation

Jurisdictions vary as to whether a physical act, such as a burn, tear, or cancellation, must actually touch the words on the will. The modern trend, as reflected in UPC §2-507(a)(2), is that these acts operate to revoke even if the burn, tear, or cancellation fails to touch the words on the will.

Example 8-6e. Testator writes the word "void" or "cancelled" on top of the dispositive provisions.

Explanation

Writing revocation terms on top of dispositive provisions is usually a sufficient cancelation to cause revocation. If these words are merely written in the margin of the will, however, many states would not consider it a sufficient act to trigger a revocation. Just as in the burning situation, some recent statutes permit revocation even though the canceling words do not touch the terms of the will.

Example 8-7. Revocation by Physical Act—Act Performed by Proxy

Testator called Attorney on the telephone and stated, "I direct you to tear up my will, shred it, and then burn the pieces. I intend to revoke my will." Attorney complied. Has Testator's will been revoked?

Explanation

Most states permit the testator to designate a proxy to perform the actual revoking physical act on the will. Just as with proxy signatures of the testator's name (see §5.4.2.2.2, above), most states require the proxy to act not only at the testator's direction, but also in the testator's conscious presence. See UPC §2-507(a)(2). Because Attorney was not in Testator's presence when the physical acts occurred, the revocation is ineffective. A few states also require the proxy revocation to be witnessed.

§8.2.1.4 Concurrence of Capacity, Intent, and Physical Act

The testator must intend to revoke the will and perform the necessary physical act while having the requisite capacity. If these three elements do not simultaneously exist, the revocation is ineffective.

Example 8-8. Revocation by Physical Act—Concurrence of Elements—Unilateral Mistake

Husband and Wife executed reciprocal wills naming each other as the primary beneficiary. Contemplating divorce, Husband took what he thought was his will and ran it through his paper shredder. Husband told Wife as well as his friends that he had destroyed his will. In reality, however, he had actually shredded Wife's will by mistake. The stress of the divorce proceedings induced a fatal heart attack and Husband died still married to Wife. Is Husband's will still effective?

Explanation

Despite Husband's clear intent, he did not actually perform a revoking act on his will. Thus, the will remains effective as written. The courts have no authority to revoke a will for a testator who does not comply with the requirements of a valid revocation by making such a unilateral mistake. Additionally, Wife's will is not revoked because she did not have the intent to revoke at the time the physical act occurred.

Example 8-9. Revocation by Physical Act—Concurrence of Elements—Mistake Induced by Fraud

Wife placed her will on her desk and called Husband into the room. Wife explained that she was filing for divorce and was going to shred the will, which named Husband as her primary beneficiary. At that moment, the door bell rang and Wife went to answer it. In the few moments that passed, Husband removed Wife's will from the envelope and carefully substituted an equal number of pages. He then placed her will in his pocket and waited for her to return. They continued their conversation. After reconciliation failed, Wife took the envelope and ran it through her shredder. Wife died prior to the finalization of the divorce. Is Wife's will still effective?

Explanation

Wife's will was not revoked because no revocatory act was performed on the will. Wife's mistaken belief that she had revoked her will, however, was induced by Husband's fraudulent conduct. Thus, the court could decide to impose a constructive trust. Legal title would still pass to Husband under the unrevoked will. However, due to his unconscionable and fraudulent conduct, the court could prevent him from retaining the beneficial title to the property and that title would then pass to her heirs. See Chapter 23, below, for a discussion of constructive trusts.

§8.2.2 Partial Revocation

Jurisdictions have adopted different approaches regarding the ability of a testator to revoke portions of the will, as contrasted to the entire will, by physical acts such as interlineations (words added to the existing text), strike-outs (text marked out but still readable), and obliterations (text marked out and no longer readable). Strong policy arguments are made on both sides of this issue.

The traditional approach to this issue is that these types of alterations are ineffective and the will is given effect in its prechanged form. Although the testator's intent may be frustrated in some cases, the potential for fraud in other cases is too great. Permitting this type of revocation would open the door to evil beneficiaries marking up the will to alter the disposition in their favor. (But, of course, all states permit total revocation by physical act, which could induce an evil heir to destroy the entire will.) In addition, partial revocation would permit the testator to enlarge gifts without observing the formalities required for a valid will. For example, if marking out a $40,000 legacy revoked the gift, the residuary beneficiary would consequently receive a larger gift. However, this new $40,000 gift would not comply with will formalities.

Partial revocations are permitted under the modern approach for several reasons. First, the court's goal is to carry out the testator's intent. Because testators typically believe these types of changes are effective, many jurisdictions permit a will to be partially revoked by physical act. See UPC §2-507. Secondly, jurisdictions have realized that the possibility for fraudulent partial alterations is just as great as the possibility for fraudulent destruction of the entire will.

Example 8-10. Revocation by Physical Act — Partial Revocation

Testator's will made two legacies. The first legacy was for $40,000 to Alice. The dispositive language in the will for this gift has a heavy dark line drawn through it and there is a preponderance of evidence showing that Testator made the mark with the intent to revoke the gift. The second legacy was for $20,000 to Bob. The number $20,000 is crossed out and $50,000 is written above it. There is a preponderance of the evidence showing that Testator made this change intending to increase the size of Bob's gift. What is the proper distribution of Testator's estate?

Explanation

In a jurisdiction that does not permit partial revocation by physical act, the will would be probated as originally written. Thus, Alice would receive $40,000 and Bob would take $20,000. If the state recognizes partial revocation by physical act, Alice's gift would be revoked. Bob could not take the $50,000 because it is not a revocation but rather an increase that did not comply with the required formalities. Although Bob's original gift of $20,000 is marked out, many courts would still allow Bob to receive the legacy by applying the doctrine of dependent relative revocation as discussed in §8.6, below. Although the revocation of Alice's legacy increases the residuary estate by $40,000, this type of increase is nonetheless effective because it is an automatic result of the revocation rather than an attempt at a direct enlargement as was the case with Bob's gift.

If Testator's will is holographic and the applicable law recognizes holographic wills without the necessity of witnesses, there is an enhanced chance the court would recognize acts of partial revocation as well as changes that increase the gifts of beneficiaries. These handwritten notations could be considered both as a revocation by subsequent instrument and as a codicil.

§8.3   Revocation by Subsequent Writing

The most predictable and reliable method to revoke a will is for the testator to execute a subsequent writing that satisfies all of the requirements of a valid will. This writing may be (1) a new will, (2) an amendment to the existing will, that is, a codicil, or (3) a document that revokes the prior will but does not contain replacement dispositive provisions. The subsequent writing may revoke the entire will or only the provisions specified by the testator. This section discusses the two methods of revocation by subsequent writing: the express revocation and the revocation by inconsistency.

§8.3.1   *Express Revocation*

A prior will or any provision thereof may be expressly revoked by the subsequent writing. See UPC §2-507(a)(1). This is the preferred method because it clearly shows what the testator intended to do. It is common practice for testators to include an express revocation provision at the beginning of a will in the introductory or *exordium* provision.

Sample Exordium Provision

I, [Testator], a resident of [City], [State], [County], declare that this is my last will and I revoke all prior wills and codicils. My social security number is [social security number].

Example 8-11.   Revocation by Subsequent Writing — Express

Upon Testator's death, two wills are found. One will expressly revokes all other wills and leaves Testator's entire estate to Spouse. The other will expressly revokes all other wills and leaves Testator's entire estate to Children. What is the proper distribution of Testator's estate?

Explanation

If both wills contain the date of execution or if that date can be ascertained from extrinsic evidence, Testator's estate will pass under the more current will, that is, the one executed closer to the time of Testator's death. That document would reflect the Testator's most recent intent. However, if one or both wills are undated and there is no evidence as to which will the Testator executed first, most courts would hold that neither will could be given effect because of the court's inability to determine Testator's intent. In such a case, Testator would die intestate.

§8.3.2   Revocation by Inconsistency

If the provisions of several testamentary documents conflict, the provision in the instrument the testator executed closest to the time of death controls as to the inconsistencies. Any portion of the will that is not inconsistent with the subsequent writings would ordinarily remain effective.

Example 8-12.   Revocation by Subsequent Writing — By Inconsistency

Testator's 1995 will bequeathed a diamond ring to Arthur and everything else to Bill. In 1998, Testator executed a valid codicil that bequeathed that same ring to Cindy and a computer to Doris. The codicil does not contain any language expressly revoking the 1995 will. What is the proper distribution of Testator's estate?

Explanation

The 1998 codicil bequeathed the diamond ring to Cindy and thus revoked the gift to Arthur by inconsistency. The codicil also revoked a portion of Bill's gift by inconsistency because the computer now passes to Doris rather than being included in the residuary estate. The balance of Testator's estate passes to Bill under the original will because the codicil did not change the residuary beneficiary. Testator's intent for the codicil to supplement rather than revoke the 1995 will is evidenced by the fact that the second instrument did not make a total disposition of Testator's estate. If the codicil had also included a residuary clause naming a different beneficiary, the codicil would have totally revoked the original will. See UPC §2-507 (b)-(c).

§8.3.3 New Will or Codicil?

Example 8-13. Revocation by Subsequent Writing—New Will or Codicil?

Assume that you drafted Testator's will in 1997. In 1999, Testator contacts you about making several minor changes to the will. Testator wants to add a specific devise of Testator's new house and wants to increase a legacy to Testator's niece by $10,000. Should you prepare an entirely new will or just a codicil?

Explanation

In the past, it was not uncommon for a testator to die with a will and multiple codicils. In many cases, this led to difficulties construing the testamentary instruments together, especially if the codicils had inconsistent provisions. Attorneys and testators tolerated this situation because of the problems associated with preparing a new will. A new will would greatly increase the cost of making the changes as well as the opportunity for error as a secretary retyped the original will and made the appropriate updates. In today's modern practice where wills are retained in a computer readable format, it is a simple matter to make a testator's changes and print a brand new will without significant cost or risk of error. Consequently, if changes to a will are necessary, you should seriously consider preparing a new will, rather than a codicil, for Testator.

§8.4   Presumptions

The proponent of a will, that is, the individual who wants that will to be valid, must prove that the will is indeed the testator's final expression of testamentary desires. Said another way, the proponent must prove the testator did not revoke the will. This burden may be relatively easy or difficult because courts indulge in various presumptions based on the particular circumstances surrounding the will. The two most common of these presumptions are discussed in this section.

§8.4.1 The Presumption of Nonrevocation

A will proponent who can present the original will to the court has a good chance of benefiting from a *presumption of continuity* that the testator died without revoking the will. To use this presumption, both the source of the will and the will itself must be free of suspicion. Typically, the will must be found either (1) in the possession of the individual to whom the testator delivered the will, such as the testator's attorney, the executor, a family member, or friend, or (2) among the testator's valuable papers in a place the testator kept such documents, such as a safe deposit box, shoe box, or filing cabinet. In addition, there must be no doubt about the authenticity of the document itself. For example, the instrument should not have large erasure marks, torn pages taped back together, or a signature page that looks like it originally came from another instrument.

§8.4.2   *The Presumption of Revocation*

A will proponent who cannot produce the original will is usually confronted with a presumption of revocation. If the testator had possession of the will or ready access to it because, for example, the will was stored in the testator's safe deposit box, failure of the proponent to produce the will raises the presumption that the testator destroyed it with the intent to revoke.

The proponent has a heavy burden to rebut this presumption and show that the will was inadvertently destroyed. Perhaps the will was destroyed in a natural disaster such as a flood, hurricane, tornado, or earthquake. Or, maybe it was destroyed by accident such as in a fire or automobile accident. Many states have *lost will statutes* that detail how the proponent must overcome the presumption. Typically, the proponent must prove why the original cannot be produced by any reasonable means and prove the contents of the will. Some statutes are very strict in how the contents must be proved. In some states, the contents must be proved by one or more individuals who read the will or heard it read to them; a mere copy of the will would be insufficient. Other states require proof of additional facts such as the existence of the will at the time of the testator's death or that it was destroyed by someone before that time without the testator's proper authorization.

Example 8-14.   Presumption of Revocation—Lost Wills

Testator did not have a safe deposit box and thus kept all of Testator's important papers, including the will, in a wooden filing cabinet in Testator's home. The same fire that killed Testator destroyed the filing cabinet and the will. A few days before the fire, Testator showed two of Testator's friends a large envelope marked "My Will" and said, "Here's where I keep my will. Now you will know where to find it when I die. I have also sent a copy of the will to Erin, the executor of my will." Is Testator's will entitled to probate?

Explanation

The court will begin with the presumption that Testator revoked the will because the original cannot be found. However, the evidence seems to show that Testator had a will and that it was stored in the home destroyed by the fire. Erin, the executor, also has a copy of the will. Testator's intent to have this instrument act as a will seems clear. Nonetheless, the evidentiary requirements many jurisdictions impose may prevent this will from being probated. The friends did not see the terms of the will and cannot testify regarding its contents. In addition, Testator could have revoked the will in the time between showing it to the friends and the destruction by the fire. Erin only has a copy and has not read the original. Many states do not permit a copy to serve as the only proof of the will's terms. Unless the attorney who drafted the will or the secretary who typed it remembers its provisions, the terms of the will may go unproven. Thus, despite Testator's intent, many jurisdictions may treat Testator as dying intestate even though there is no evidence that Testator destroyed the will with the intent to revoke it.

§8.5   Revival

Revival refers to the reinstatement of a will that the testator has already revoked. A testator could trigger revival by simply reexecuting the old will or by including an express statement in a new will that the old will is to be effective. The most common revival scenario is demonstrated in the following example.

Example 8-15.   Revival

Testator executed Will One in 1990. This will left Testator's entire estate to Mother. In 1994, Testator executed Will Two, which left Testator's entire estate to Friend. Will Two contained a clause that expressly revoked Will One. Testator physically destroyed Will Two in 1998 intending to revoke it. Testator died in 1999 survived by Mother, Friend, and Testator's only child, Daughter. Who is entitled to Testator's estate?

Explanation

This is the typical fact pattern that raises a revival issue; that is, what is the effect upon a prior will of the revocation of a later will that revoked the prior will? Courts have developed three basic approaches to handling this situation. Under the common law which followed a revival approach, Mother would take Testator's estate under Will One. This approach focuses on the principle that a will has no effect until the testator's death. Because Testator revoked

Will Two, the provision in Will Two revoking Will One never took effect. Thus, Will One revives. Only a few states still follow this common law approach.

Most states follow a no revival approach. Under this view, Will Two is perceived as two legal documents in one — a revocation instrument and a dispositive instrument. The revocation part of Will Two is treated as being immediately effective. Thus, the moment Will Two was properly executed, Will One was revoked just as if Testator had physically destroyed it. The dispositive part of Will Two would not take effect until Testator's death. Because Testator revoked Will Two, its provisions cannot govern Testator's estate. Thus, Testator died intestate and Daughter will inherit Testator's entire estate.

The modern approach adopted by UPC §2-509 is a compromise between the first two views. Under this approach, the court attempts to ascertain what Testator intended at the time Testator revoked Will Two. In other words, did Testator intend that the revocation of Will Two reinstate or revive Will One? The court would examine evidence such as the circumstances surrounding the revocation of Will One and any written or oral statements Testator may have made regarding Testator's belief that Will One was to be effective.

§8.6 Conditional Revocation

§8.6.1 Express Condition

A testator may execute a revoking instrument and expressly condition the revocation on the occurrence or nonoccurrence of a stated event or condition. For example, the testator could write, "I revoke my May 1, 1995 will if I am not married at the time of my death," or "I revoke my November 4, 1996 will if a Democrat is president of the United States at the time of my death." Express conditional revocations are quite rare. They are used only occasionally when necessary to carry out the wishes of a testator with relatively unusual needs.

§8.6.2 Implied Condition—Dependent Relative Revocation

Implied conditional revocation, commonly called *dependent relative revocation*, is a legal doctrine used to impose a condition on the testator's act of revoking a will. The testator does not expressly state the condition but because of compelling facts, the court determines that if the testator had been asked about what the testator would have wanted under these facts, the testator would have made the revocation conditional. (You may like to think of this as a Romeo and Juliet revocation. Just like the testator's intent to revoke, Romeo's intent to kill himself was conditioned on Juliet being dead. If Romeo knew that Juliet were actually alive, he would not have committed suicide. If the testator knew the true legal ramifications of what the testator was doing, the testator would not have revoked the will.) Using this doctrine, the court may ignore an otherwise valid revocation and permit the testator to die testate in situations where the court believes the testator would have preferred the revoked instrument to dispose of the testator's property rather than for the testator's estate to pass by intestacy or under a different will.

Example 8-16. Dependent Relative Revocation — Alternative Disposition

Testator executed valid Will One. This will left all of Testator's estate to Friend. On May 1, 1998, Testator tore up Will One and executed Will Two. This will made a $40,000 gift to Nephew and left the rest of Testator's estate to Friend. Will Two is not valid because of a glitch with the execution formalities. What is the proper distribution of Testator's estate assuming Testator is survived by Friend, Nephew, and Testator's only child, Son?

Explanation

Will Two cannot take effect because it does not meet the requirements of a valid will. Despite Testator's clear intent, the court would be unable to remedy the situation unless it is in one of the very few jurisdictions that have adopted the substantial compliance rule giving the court a dispensing power to fix trivial errors. See Chapter 5, above. At first glance, it would thus seem that Testator died intestate and Son would inherit Testator's entire estate. However, there is a good chance the court would apply the doctrine of dependent relative revocation. This doctrine would imply a condition on Testator's revocation of Will One; that is, Testator revoked Will One on the condition that Will Two was valid. Because Will Two is not valid, the condition was not satisfied and thus the revocation of Will One is ineffective. Accordingly, Testator's estate passes under the terms of Will One. Note that some jurisdictions restrict the application of dependent relative revocation to situations where Will One is revoked by physical act, as in this example. These courts will not apply the doctrine if the revocation was by a written instrument. The policy underlying the distinction is that physical act revocations are ambiguous and thus there is more leeway for a court to search for a presumed intent than if the revocation is in a clear unambiguous writing whose meaning can be determined without resorting to extrinsic evidence.

In applying the doctrine, the courts look closely at what the testator intended; that is, would the testator rather have the first will or die intestate.

To make this determination, the courts examine the dispositions made in the two instruments. In Example 8-16, the dispositions are quite similar, only differing with regard to the $40,000 legacy. Thus, it is reasonable to assume that Testator would rather have the entire estate pass to Friend under Will One than to Son via intestacy. However, if Will Two had read, "I leave $40,000 to Nephew and the remainder of my estate to Son," a court is likely to conclude that Testator meant to revoke the gift to Friend regardless of the effectiveness of Will Two. The disposition plans of the two instruments are so far apart that it would not be appropriate to assume that Testator would have preferred Will One to intestacy.

Example 8-17. Dependent Relative Revocation — Revival Remedy

Testator's 1990 will left Testator's entire estate to Friend. The relationship between Testator and Friend deteriorated. Testator then wrote a new will in 1995 that provided, "I hereby revoke all prior wills. I leave half my estate to Friend and half to Sister." In recent years, the relationship between Friend and Testator improved so much that Testator tore up the 1995 will and told Friend that Friend was once again the sole beneficiary of Testator's estate. Testator died survived by Friend, Sister, and Testator's only child, Daughter. What is the proper distribution of Testator's estate?

Explanation

This example raises both revival and dependent relative revocation issues. If Testator is in a jurisdiction that recognizes revival or takes the testator's intent into consideration, Friend may still be able to take under the original will. See §8.5, above. However, if Testator is in a state which does not recognize revival, the destruction of the 1995 will would normally mean that Testator died intestate and Daughter would inherit the entire estate. However, the court may be willing to use the doctrine of dependent relative revocation. Testator's revocation of the 1995 will was based on a mistaken belief that the 1990 will would be revived. Testator would rather have the estate disposed of by the 1995 will which leaves Friend half of Testator's estate than die intestate in which case Friend would receive nothing.

Example 8-18. Dependent Relative Revocation — Recited Mistake of Fact

Testator executed Will One leaving half of Testator's estate to Son and half to Cousin. Testator learned that the plane on which Cousin was traveling crashed and that out of the 235 passengers on board only one survived. Testator then executed Will Two, which stated, "Now that Cousin has died,

I leave the half of my estate I was going to leave to Cousin to Nephew."
Testator died before learning that Cousin was the one passenger who survived. What is the proper distribution of Testator's estate?

Explanation

Some courts will also apply the doctrine of dependent relative revocation to a simple mistake of fact if the second will describes the mistake. The court could conclude that Testator's change in disposition was impliedly conditioned on Cousin being deceased and thus permit Cousin to take. However, if Will Two did not describe the mistake, Cousin probably would not be able to take because there would be insufficient evidence of why Testator made the change. Perhaps Testator was planning on changing the beneficiary even before the plane crash.

Example 8-19. Dependent Relative Revocation — Partial Revocation by Physical Act

Among other dispositive provisions, Testator's will contained a $100,000 legacy to Friend. Testator crossed out the $100,000 and wrote $250,000 above it. To how much is Friend entitled?

Explanation

If Testator is in a jurisdiction that does not recognize partial revocation by physical act, Testator's mark-out and addition are ignored and Friend takes $100,000. If the state recognizes partial revocation by physical act, Testator's act of crossing out the $100,000 gift is an effective revocation. However, even in those states, specific gifts and legacies cannot be increased by these types of markings. Thus, it would appear that Friend's gift is revoked and that the new gift is ineffective for failing to comply with the requirements of a valid will. This result is not likely to occur because the court will apply dependent relative revocation. Testator would not have revoked the $100,000 gift if Testator knew the $250,000 legacy would be invalid. This partial revocation was conditioned on the effectiveness of the larger gift. Because the larger gift is ineffective, the revocation fails and Friend takes the $100,000. See also Example 8-10, above.

Example 8-20. Dependent Relative Revocation — Ineffective Revocation

Testator executed Will One in 1990 leaving the entire estate to Friend. In 1995, Testator executed Will Two, which provided, "I hereby revoke my 1990 will. I leave half of my estate to Friend and half to Brother." Will Two is invalid under state law. Testator died survived by Friend, Brother, and Testator's only child, Son. What is the proper distribution of Testator's estate?

Explanation

Neither dependent relative revocation nor revival are involved in this example. Instead, this is a simple ineffective revocation by subsequent writing case. Will Two is invalid. Thus, neither its revocation nor dispositive language is effective. Will One remains and Friend takes Testator's entire estate.

§8.7 Multiple Originals

A testator may legally execute several copies of the same will but it is not prudent to do so. Each copy that contains the testator's signature and any required attestation is considered an original even if the text is photocopied or a carbon copy. Unlike contracts, where executing multiple originals is a wise and accepted practice, the testator should execute only one copy of the will. As the following example demonstrates, problems arise if all of the originals cannot be found after the testator's death.

Example 8-21. Multiple Originals

On May 1, 1995, Testator executed two copies of Testator's will. Each copy was properly attested. Testator placed one copy in Testator's safe deposit box and one copy in a filing cabinet in Testator's office. Upon Testator's death, only the copy in the safe deposit box was located. Does Testator's property pass according to the terms of the will or did Testator die intestate?

Explanation

Testator's situation triggers two conflicting presumptions. Finding the will in the safe deposit box raises the presumption of nonrevocation. See §8.4.1, above. However, failure to produce the original kept in the filing cabinet raises the presumption that Testator destroyed the will with revocatory intent. See §8.4.2, above. Most courts confronted with this dilemma hold that the revocation of one original acts as the revocation of all originals. Thus, absent other evidence, Testator died intestate. However, many courts allow extrinsic evidence to alter this result. For example, there may be evidence that someone other than Testator had access to the filing cabinet and had a motive to destroy the will, or Testator may have realized that Testator can have only one "last" will and thus destroyed the filing cabinet copy to avoid confusion.

9

Interpretation and Construction

Regardless of how carefully testators select the language used in their wills, all wills must be interpreted and construed to some extent before their terms can be carried out. Even a gift as simple as, "I leave my ring to Frank" triggers a potentially lengthy process of determining what physical item of property the testator referred to as "my ring" and which individual the testator meant by "Frank." The more precise the testator is, the less interpretation and construction needed. Thus, if the gift reads, "I leave my diamond engagement ring I received from John Smith, my late husband, to my nephew, Frank Smith" there is a reduced need for the court to construe or interpret the will because the identities of the bequeathed item and the beneficiary are easier for the court to ascertain.

Technically, interpretation and construction are quite different. *Interpretation* refers to the process of determining the testator's actual intent from the language of the will and permissible extrinsic evidence. On the other hand, *construction* is an attempt to assign a meaning to a will provision when the testator's actual intent cannot be fully ascertained; that is, the court's attempt at interpretation failed. When a court construes a will, the court is making its best guess as to what the testator intended. The distinction between interpretation and construction is not usually made by the courts and thus the terms are typically used interchangeably. Unless the context requires a precise differentiation, the terms are used synonymously in this chapter.

Construction issues may arise prior to a will's admission to probate. For example, did the testator intend an unwitnessed instrument to be a holographic will or did the testator mean to revoke a will when the testator destroyed it? In most cases, however, construction issues do not arise until after the will is probated. They are then raised either by the beneficiaries who stand to gain under differing constructions or by the executor who wants to take the correct action and avoid liability for improper administration.

In seeking the testator's intent, a court starts by examining the exact language contained in the will. If this language resolves the issue, the court carries out the testator's intent even if it is unusual or nontraditional. Only if the testator's desires violate the law or public policy may the court ignore the testator's express desires. If the language contained within the four corners of the will fails to resolve the issue, the court will examine extrinsic evidence. The nature of the extrinsic evidence the court examines depends on the issue confronting the court and the applicable rules of evidence. If admissible extrinsic evidence does not enlighten the court about the testator's intent, either because the testator did not express or document the intent or because the testator never even thought about the issue, the court has various construction rules at its disposal. The court applies these rules to presume an intent based on what the court believes the testator would have wanted had the testator pondered the issue.

This chapter focuses on a variety of special situations where interpretation and construction are needed such as when a will contains ambiguous provisions or makes class gifts. In addition to these and other special cases discussed in this chapter, courts apply many maxims of construction in their attempt to determine the testator's actual or probable intent. A few of these rules are listed below:

- The fact that the testator executed a will, especially if it contains a residuary clause, demonstrates an intent not to die intestate.
- If several provisions of a will conflict, the provision located nearest the end of the will takes precedence.
- A will is construed as a whole and not from isolated parts out of context.
- If a will is subject to two constructions and there is no evidence for preferring one over the other, the construction that treats individuals who are equally related to the testator in the most similar manner is preferred.
- A statement in a will explaining the reason the testator is making a will is merely a statement of inducement and does not make the will conditioned on the testator's death being caused by the stated reason.
- Legal terms in a will are given their specialized meanings unless there is evidence that the testator, especially if the testator was not an attorney, used the terms in a different manner.
- Nonlegal terms in a will are given their plain and ordinary meanings.

§9.1 Ambiguity

Ambiguity is one of the most common will interpretation issues. The court begins by examining the purportedly ambiguous provision. If the court finds as a matter of law that it is not ambiguous, the court simply resolves the issue. If the court finds as a matter of law that the provision is ambiguous, the facts necessary to resolve that ambiguity are determined by the appropriate fact-finder, be it the judge or a jury. Of course, judges may differ regarding whether particular language is or is not ambiguous. The way in which ambiguities are resolved often depends on the type of ambiguity involved; that is, is the ambiguity (1) patent, (2) latent, or (3) not readily apparent.

§9.1.1 Patent (Obvious) Ambiguity

A will provision that is unclear on its face and does not convey a sensible meaning to the reader is considered *patently ambiguous*.

Example 9-1. Patent Ambiguity — Strangely Described Item

Testator's will contains the following dispositive provision, "I leave my Zipvert to Daughter and the rest of my estate to Son." What is the proper distribution of Testator's estate?

Explanation

Testator's will contains a patent ambiguity; the word "Zipvert" does not make sense. At common law, many courts would not permit the use of extrinsic evidence to reveal the item to which Testator was referring. These courts simply held that the gift failed because it was not described with sufficient clarity. Most modern courts, however, would permit extrinsic evidence to resolve the patent ambiguity. Thus, if Testator's friends and family knew that Testator called Testator's car by this unusual name, the court may allow Daughter to receive the car.

Example 9-2. Patent Ambiguity — Secret Code

Testator's will contains the following legacy, "I leave &%,))).)) United States dollars to Friend. I leave the rest of my estate to Daughter." What is the proper distribution of Testator's estate?

Explanation

The legacy to Friend is patently ambiguous because the amount of money is represented by symbols instead of numerals. As in Example 9-1, the common law courts were reluctant to admit extrinsic evidence to ascertain the amount of the legacy while modern courts are usually willing to consider outside evidence. Perhaps Friend could show that Testator always used a keyboard-shift code when writing amounts of money as a privacy and security measure and thus be able to decipher the symbols into their numerical equivalent by typing them on a keyboard without first depressing the shift key. The court may then permit Friend to take the $75,000 legacy as Testator intended.

Example 9-3. Patent Ambiguity — Blank Spaces

Testator's will contains the following language, "I leave my car to Son. I leave my computer to _____. I leave the rest of my estate to Daughter." What is the proper distribution of Testator's estate?

Explanation

Testator's failure to state the name of the beneficiary of the computer and inclusion of a blank line makes this bequest patently ambiguous. Both common law and modern courts would not permit extrinsic evidence to resolve this problem. Courts are unwilling to write will provisions for a testator. Thus, the court would very likely reject even strong and uncontroverted evidence that Testator intended a particular person to receive the computer. The computer would pass through the residuary clause to Daughter.

§9.1.2 Latent (Hidden) Ambiguity

A will provision is *latently ambiguous* if it conveys a sensible meaning on its face but cannot be carried out without further clarification. In other words, a proofreader would say the provision is fine but when the executor tries to do what it says, the executor discovers it is impossible to comply.

Example 9-4. Latent Ambiguity — Beneficiary Misdescription[1]

Among other provisions, Testator's will provides, "I leave $10,000 to each of David, Alvin, and Alma all of whom are children of my sister Annie."

---

1. Adapted from the facts of Hultquist v. Ring, 301 S.W.2d 303 (Tex. Civ. App. — Galveston 1957, writ ref'd n.r.e.).

Annie had three children, David, Alvin, and Elmer. Alma was the name of Testator's other sister. What is the proper distribution of Testator's estate?

Explanation

Nothing looks unusual from the mere reading of the dispositive provision. However, this provision cannot be carried out as written because the will contains a latent ambiguity. Alma is described as being a niece when she is really a sister. Elmer is not included in the will, but he is Annie's third child. Courts will look at extrinsic evidence to resolve the ambiguity. In the case from which this example was adapted, the court permitted Elmer to take the legacy for several reasons. Testator had poor eyesight and had not read the will. Instead, other people read it to him and there was a substantial vocal similarity between the two names, especially in Testator's native language (Swedish). In addition, the evidence showed that Testator really liked Elmer but had not spoken to Alma for thirty-five years.

Example 9-5. Latent Ambiguity — Property Misdescription

Testator's will contains the following devise, "I leave my house located at 1017 Main Street to Daughter. I leave the rest of my estate to Son." Testator owned a house at 1019 Main Street both at the time of will execution and at the time of death. Testator never owned the house at 1017 Main Street. What is the proper distribution of Testator's estate?

Explanation

Testator's will contains a *latent ambiguity*. The devise makes perfect sense on its face but questions arise when trying to carry out Testator's wishes. Courts generally apply the principle of *falsa demonstratio non nocet,* which states that a gift does not fail merely because the description of the property is not precisely correct. Testator was clearly referring to the house at 1019 Main Street and thus Daughter will receive this property. Courts will apply the same principle to misspellings in a beneficiary's name such as where the will refers to Tony Smith as "Toni Smith."

Example 9-6. Latent Ambiguity — Specific Bequest of General Nature

Testator's will provides, "I leave my car to Son. I leave the rest of my estate to Daughter." Testator died owning two cars. What is the proper distribution of Testator's estate?

Explanation

If Testator died owning only one car, no problem would arise. In this case, however, the bequest of the car is latently ambiguous because Testator died owning two cars and the will gives no indication of the car to which Testator was referring. The court would need to examine extrinsic evidence. Most courts are willing to consider evidence of the surrounding circumstances but balk at listening to evidence of what the testator said. Thus, evidence that Testator still owns the car Testator owned at the time of will execution would be very helpful to show Testator's intent for Son to receive that particular car. However, fewer courts would be impressed with evidence that Testator consistently told someone which car Testator planned for Son to receive. The court would have a very difficult time if Testator owned neither car when Testator executed the will, Testator never told anyone about Testator's wishes, and the two cars are of significantly different value.

§9.1.3 *No Apparent Ambiguity*

A *no apparent ambiguity* situation arises when the will provision is neither latently nor patently ambiguous but yet someone wants to introduce extrinsic evidence that the testator did not mean for the will to say what it appears to say.

Example 9-7. No Apparent Ambiguity

Testator's will provides, "I leave all my personal property to Niece." Testator's estate consists of $50,000 and a house. Testator was survived by Niece and Testator's only child, Daughter. What is the proper distribution of Testator's estate?

Explanation

The will does not appear ambiguous. Niece would receive the $50,000 and the house would pass by intestacy to Daughter. What would happen if Niece came to court arguing that Testator meant to include real property in the gift to her? Niece could claim, for example, the Testator was not a lawyer and did not really understand the difference between personal and real property. Niece may argue that Testator used the term "personal" to distinguish property Testator owned from property owned by someone else.

Jurisdictions are sharply divided on this issue. Traditionally, courts follow the *plain meaning rule*, also called the *single plain meaning rule*. Under this approach, extrinsic evidence cannot be used to disturb the clear meaning of the will. This rule enhances predictability for both the testator and the testator's attorney. A testator can rest assured that the words chosen will take effect as written. Otherwise, the testator could make a gift of "$10,000 to Mother" and then have Mother claim that the gift should be of some higher amount such as $100,000 and Father claim that the legacy was actually meant for him.

Other jurisdictions adopt a more liberal rule that permits the use of extrinsic evidence. These courts hold that the evidence is significant and assists the court to carry out the testator's intent. Although this approach makes it more difficult for the testator to be certain that the will is not tampered with or misconstrued after the testator's death, it operates to carry out the testator's intent when it is clear the will does not say what the testator meant it to say. Courts do keep a tight rein on these situations and generally allow the extrinsic evidence to alter the will's clear meaning only when the will was not professionally prepared and the evidence is very strong that carrying out the exact terms of the will would frustrate the testator's intent.

§9.2   Integration

§9.2.1   *External Integration*

External integration refers to the process of establishing the testator's will by piecing together all of the testator's wills, codicils, and other testamentary instruments. The more instruments that exist, the more difficult this process becomes. Prudent testators can easily avoid external integration problems. For example, all testamentary instruments should state the date of execution so the temporal order of the documents is easy to determine, a testator should execute an entirely new will rather than use a codicil, and a will revoked by a subsequent writing should also be revoked by physical act unless the testator is saving the old will for possible use as an unrevoked prior will should the new will be deemed invalid.

§9.2.2   *Internal Integration*

Only those pages of the will present at the time the testator executed the will are entitled to probate. *Internal integration* is the process of making certain the testator's will contains no fewer and no more pages than it did when the testator executed it. Testators may use many techniques, such as those listed below, to assure the continuity of the instrument and the inter-relationship among all its pages.

- The testator and the witnesses initial each page.
- All handwriting on the will is in a color of ink other than black so the difference between the original and a photocopy is readily discernable. The testimonium and attestation clauses should specifically state the

color of ink the testator and the witnesses used to sign the will. Some law firms include special chemical markers in their inks so the will can easily be traced. In addition, some individuals actually have their DNA mixed with the ink to enhance the likelihood of a positive identification.

- All pages are securely fastened together. Once the pages are connected, they should not be disconnected. Courts have considered multiple staple holes in a document to be evidence of improper page substitution.
- The will is numbered using *ex toto* pagination, that is, by using the "page [current page number] of [total number of pages]" format.
- All pages are the same type of paper and uniform in size and color.
- The will is prepared with a consistent typeface scheme. For example, suspicions of page substitution are likely to arise if one page is printed in Arial while all of the other pages are in Times New Roman. Some law firms use custom designed fonts that include unique characteristics visible under high magnification.
- The same toner cartridge, type of ink, or ribbon is used for all of the pages of the will.
- Blank space is avoided. If the testator needs to conclude a provision before the end of the page, some indication of that fact should be included in the will. For example, language such as the following could be included immediately after the text on the "short" page: "Article IV(C) ends here; Article V begins on the next page. The space below is intentionally left blank."
- The testator does not conclude each page with the end of a sentence. To avoid having a *loose-leaf will* that makes it easy for pages to be removed and inserted, the testator should have sentences that begin on one page and are carried over to the following page.

§9.3   Incorporation by Reference

Incorporation by reference is a method for treating a document as testamentary in character even though that document is not physically part of the testator's will. If the testator successfully incorporates a document by reference into the will, the will is treated as if the terms of the incorporated document are actually contained in the will. Although the incorporated document is not really part of the will, this doctrine creates the legal fiction that the will contains an exact copy of the incorporated document. Practically all states and UPC §2-510 recognize the doctrine of incorporation by reference.

§9.3.1 Requirements

Three requirements must be satisfied before a writing may be successfully incorporated by reference.

1. **Intent.** The testator must have the intent to incorporate the writing.
2. **In Existence.** The writing the testator wishes to incorporate must have been in existence when the testator executed the will.
3. **Identification.** The testator must identify the writing to be incorporated in the will with sufficient specificity so that no other document could reasonably be referred to by that description.

Example 9-8. Incorporation by Reference — In Existence

Testator's 1998 will contains the following dispositive provision.

> I leave all artwork listed on the April 23, 1990 appraisal done by Lloyds of London which I keep in a file marked "Artwork" to Son. I leave all the coins listed in a notebook labeled "Coins for Daughter" which I now keep in my top dresser drawer to Daughter. I leave all books listed in a notebook labeled "Books for Nephew" to Nephew. I leave the rest of my estate to Charity.

What is the appropriate distribution of Testator's estate?

Explanation

The distribution of Testator's estate depends on the effectiveness of the three attempted incorporations by reference. Testator's intent to incorporate each of the documents seems clear. Likewise, the descriptions appear adequate. For the purpose of this discussion, assume that all three documents are found exactly as Testator indicated. Thus, the remaining issue with regard to the effectiveness of each incorporation is whether the document was in existence at the time Testator executed the will. The basis of this requirement is that the law does not authorize a testator to create a power to dispose of property in the future by executing a document that does not comply with the requirements of a will.

The Lloyds of London appraisal was dated many years prior to the will and thus it satisfies the in existence requirement. Son will receive the artwork listed on the appraisal despite the fact that the appraisal was not executed with the formalities necessary for a valid will.

The notebook containing the list of coins for Daughter appears to have been in existence at the time Testator executed the will. The will indicates that Testator presently keeps the notebook in the dresser drawer. This is not, however, the end of our analysis. Testator may have added coins to the list after Testator executed the will or may have even torn up the original list and substituted a new one. Neither of these actions would change the terms of the incorporated list. The terms of any incorporated document are frozen at the time the testator executes the will. Subsequent changes to the document, or even its total destruction, do not change the terms of the "legal photocopy" of that document, which the testator inserted into the will at the date of will execution. Thus, extrinsic evidence would be needed to ascertain the contents of the list as of the date of will execution. Daughter would receive all the coins contained on the list as of that date and Charity would receive any unlisted coins.

Testator's will does not indicate that the list of books for Nephew existed when Testator executed the will. We do not know if Testator was referring to a list that Testator had already written or one that Testator intended to write at some later date. Traditionally, the failure to refer to the document as being in existence was fatal to the incorporation, even if the document had already been prepared. However, the widely accepted modern view is that the testator does not have to declare that the document exists in the will. Thus, the court would consult extrinsic evidence to determine if the list were in existence when Testator executed the will. Whichever books were on that list at the time of will execution would pass to Nephew and Charity would receive all the after-listed books.

Example 9-9. Incorporation by Reference — Adequate Identification

Testator's will contains the following dispositive provision: "I leave all the baseball cards listed on the attached page, which is hereby incorporated by reference into my will, to Friend." Is this language sufficient to cause an incorporation by reference?

Explanation

The key issue in this example is whether the document Testator wants to incorporate is adequately identified. Most courts would hold that this description is too vague because the document referred to could change merely by altering its physical connection to the will. The terms of an incorporated document remain static and do not change merely because of a change in the original document's location. Accordingly, the gift to Friend is likely to fail.

§9.3.2 *Validity of Incorporated Writing*

An incorporated writing does not have to be legally effective or valid. The writing merely needs to be in existence at the time the testator executed the will and adequately described therein. Thus, the incorporated writing does not need to be signed, witnessed, notarized, or effective for any purpose.

Example 9-10. Incorporation by Reference—Validity of Incorporated Document

Testator was adjudicated incompetent in 1994. In 1996, Son held a large caliber handgun to Testator's head and forced Testator to write the following document.

> Oct. 31, 1996. All my cars. All my clothes. My collection of pet rocks. My computer. All my stock in Aspen Publishing.

Son then forged Testator's name to this document. In 1998, Testator regained full capacity. Testator and Son entered counseling, resolved their problems, and became good friends. Testator then wrote a will which contains the following provision: "I leave Son all the property listed on a note dated Oct. 31, 1996. This note is inside of my Bible that I keep in my nightstand." Will Son receive the property listed on the October 31, 1996 note assuming the note is found as indicated?

Explanation

Testator successfully incorporated the October 31, 1996 list. Testator intended to do so, the list was in existence, and it appears to be adequately identified. It does not matter that the document contains a forged signature and was written by Testator when Testator was both incompetent and under duress. When Testator executed the will, Testator was competent and not under duress. As long as the will is otherwise valid, Son will receive the property on the list.

§9.3.3 Republication

Republication refers to the process of treating an old will as if it were executed at a later date. A simple but rarely used method of republication is for the testator to reexecute the same document and, if necessary, have a new attestation. The most common type of republication is where the testator executes a codicil to an existing will. The codicil incorporates by reference the terms of the original will that are not inconsistent with the codicil. These two documents are then treated as one will with the date of execution being the date the testator executed the codicil. Thus, it is on the date of codicil execution that all of the requirements of a valid will must be satisfied and that date is used to determine the proper law to apply and the effect of changed circumstances.

Example 9-11. Republication — Changed Circumstances

Testator executed a will in 1990 leaving the entire estate to various charities. In 1994 and 1998, Testator had two children, Son and Daughter. In 1999, Testator executed a codicil to the 1990 will changing one of the charitable beneficiaries. Upon Testator's death, will Son and Daughter succeed in obtaining a portion of their parent's estate as pretermitted children?

Explanation

The 1999 codicil acts to republish the 1990 will except for the inconsistent portions. Thus, Testator's entire will, both the new provisions and the incorporated provisions, are treated as being executed in 1999. In states where a child must be born or adopted after will execution to be considered pretermitted, Son and Daughter would have no claim because they were born prior to the execution of the 1999 codicil. See §7.3, above, for a discussion of pretermitted heirs. This same analysis would be used for other types of changes in circumstances that occur between the date of will execution and date of codicil execution such as marriage, divorce, change in composition of estate, and death of a beneficiary. In the usual case, these changes are ignored if they occurred prior to the execution of the codicil even if the codicil does not reflect the new circumstances.

Example 9-12. Republication — Codicil Bootstrapping Invalid Will

Testator executed a lengthy will in 1995. This will is invalid because only one witness attested the will while state law requires two witnesses. Testator signed a valid codicil to this will in 1998, which changed the name of the alternate executor. Does Testator's estate pass under the terms of the 1995 document or under intestacy?

Explanation

The 1998 codicil incorporated the 1995 document by reference and acted to republish it. The court treats the 1995 document, except for its provision naming the alternate executor, as if it were actually reprinted in the 1998 codicil. Consequently, Testator's property would pass to the beneficiaries named in the 1995 document. This example demonstrates how a valid codicil may be used to bootstrap the terms of an invalid will. Note that the reason for the invalidity of the 1995 document is irrelevant. The same result would be reached if the will were invalid due to lack of legal capacity, testamentary capacity, testamentary intent, proper formalities, or because it was executed while Testator was subject to undue influence, duress, or fraud.

In jurisdictions that recognize the validity of holographic wills without witnesses, the holographic nature of the invalid will and the valid codicil may be relevant. Assume that Testator's 1995 document is not holographic and that the 1998 codicil is holographic and unwitnessed. When the holographic codicil incorporates the nonholographic will, the codicil loses its holographic character. Legally, the codicil is treated as if Testator placed an exact copy of the will in the codicil. Accordingly, some courts hold the codicil cannot save the invalid will because if the terms of the will were treated as being in the codicil, the codicil would be invalid due to the nonholographic material. Only the terms of the codicil that can stand on their own would be admitted to probate. In this example, the only item in the codicil was a change to the alternate executor. Consequently, Testator's property would pass by intestacy. This relatively strict rule prevents an individual from validating a non-holographic will by simply signing a handwritten note on the back page of the will such as, "This is a codicil to my will. I hereby affirm all of the terms of that will." On the other hand, some courts ignore the problem because they do not believe this type of conduct is against public policy. In these jurisdictions, a holographic codicil may republish a nonholographic will.

§9.4 Facts of Independent Significance

The doctrine of *facts of independent significance* permits the use of facts and circumstances outside of the will to impact the property disposition the testator made in the will. This doctrine, sometimes referred to as *acts* or *events of independent significance* as well as the *doctrine of nontestamentary acts,* is widely accepted both at common law and under modern law. See UPC §2-512. These facts and circumstances have testamentary effect despite not being contained in an actual testamentary instrument.

Example 9-13. Facts of Independent Significance — Specific Gift of a General Nature

Testator's will provides, "I leave my car to Son. I leave the rest of my estate to Daughter." At the time of will execution, Testator owned a 1974 AMC Gremlin. Shortly before Testator's death, Testator realized that the Gremlin had little value and that Son was not going to be pleased with the bequest. Testator traded in the Gremlin for a brand new top-of-the-line Jaguar and paid the difference in cash. What is the proper distribution of Testator's estate?

Explanation

Testator's action of trading in the Gremlin and buying the Jaguar made a tremendous difference in the values of both the specific and residual gifts. Testator manipulated Testator's property with the intent of changing the disposition of Testator's property upon death without complying with the requirements for a valid codicil. Nonetheless, Son will take the Jaguar and Daughter will receive the diminished residual estate because the car qualifies as a fact of independent significance. The car has legal reasons for existing other than for the disposition of property at death — for example, to serve as a means of transportation.

Example 9-14.   Facts of Independent Significance — Identity of Beneficiary

Testator's will provides, "I leave my entire estate to my spouse at the time of my death. If I am unmarried at the time of my death, I leave my entire estate to Charity." Testator was not married at the time Testator executed the will and remained so until Testator was diagnosed with a terminal disease. Testator decided that Testator wanted the estate to pass to Friend and thus Testator married this person, not because Testator really wanted to be married, but primarily to make Friend the beneficiary of Testator's estate. What is the proper distribution of Testator's estate?

Explanation

Friend will receive Testator's entire estate although Testator married Friend to permit Friend to take under Testator's estate. Through an action taken outside of the formalities of a will, Testator deprived Charity of the entire estate. Nonetheless, courts consider the identity of an individual referred to by a gift to a spouse, or other individual designated by position such as "my housekeeper" or "my attorney," to be a fact of independent significance. Some courts will even extend this analysis to ascertain the identity of a beneficiary who is named in some other document (for example, "I leave my estate to the remainder beneficiary named in my spouse's will").

Example 9-15.   Facts of Independent Significance — Class Gifts

Testator's will provides, "I leave all my property to my children." When Testator executed the will, Testator had one child. In the years since will execution, Testator's estate grew substantially. Testator decided that leaving all this property to one person would be excessive and thus decided to have additional children to reduce the size of the estate that Testator's first child would receive. What is the proper distribution of Testator's estate?

Explanation

Testator consciously decided to have additional children to reduce the testamentary gift to Testator's first child. Despite this motivation behind Testator's acts, all of Testator's children will share in the estate. Courts view the identity of class members as a fact of independent significance even if the testator can manipulate the membership in the class such as by having children, as in this example, or by hiring or firing individuals in a gift to "my employees."

Example 9-16. Facts of Independent Significance — Contents — Time of Determination

Testator's will provides, "I leave the contents of my safe deposit box #774 at Octopus National Bank to Son. I leave the contents of my safe deposit box #775 at Octopus National Bank to Daughter. I leave the remainder of my estate to Charity." Every Wednesday around noon, Testator went to ONB and rearranged cash, rare coins, stamps, and jewelry between the two boxes based on how kindly Son and Daughter had treated Testator during the prior week. How will the court determine the extent of the gifts to Son and Daughter?

Explanation

The composition of gifts of the contents of items such as a safe deposit box, cedar chest, desk, automobile, or home are based on the contents at the time of the testator's death unless the will expressly provides otherwise. Thus, Son and Daughter will receive whatever the safe deposit boxes contain when Testator dies. Although testators can constantly change the at-death disposition of property without complying with the formalities of a will by altering the contents, courts treat these containers as facts of independent significance.

Example 9-17. Facts of Independent Significance — Contents — Property Included

Testator's will provides, "I leave the contents of my home to Son. I leave my home and the rest of my estate to Daughter." Upon Testator's death, the home contains various pieces of furniture, stock certificates in Aspen Publishing, $55,000 in cash, and assorted personal effects. In addition, there are two cars in the garage. What is the proper distribution of Testator's estate?

Explanation

Courts are frequently confronted with defining the scope of property that falls within the term "contents." There is basic agreement that furniture, money, and personal effects are contents and thus Son will receive these items. Intangible property, such as the stock certificates, raises problems because a stock certificate is merely evidence of ownership, not the item itself.

Similar problems would arise if checkbooks and certificates of deposit are found in the house. Accordingly, Daughter stands a good chance of receiving the Aspen stock. A physical inspection of the property is needed to determine whether the cars qualify as contents. If the garage is attached and an integral part of the house so that the cars are actually inside the home, the cars are more likely to be contents and pass to Son. But, if they are in a detached garage, a court could easily find that they are not contents and permit Daughter to take them as part of the residuary estate. Some jurisdictions have statutes that provide a default definition of "contents." These statutes usually limit contents to tangible personal property, exclude intangible items, and provide that items represented by a certificate of title, such as motor vehicles, are not transferred merely because the certificate of title is inside the gifted item.

Example 9-18. Facts of Independent Significance — Property Disposition Note

Testator's will provides, "I leave to each of my three children an amount which I will write on a piece of paper and staple, paper clip, or otherwise attach to this will. I leave the rest of my estate to Charity." When Testator died, a writing is found with the will listing the children and corresponding legacies. What is the proper distribution of Testator's estate?

Explanation

The attached writing has no legal effect. Thus, Charity receives Testator's entire estate. Testator's act of writing on the note the amount each child should receive is not an act of independent significance because the note has no significance other than to dispose of property upon death. In addition, the note cannot be incorporated by reference into the will because the note was not in existence at the time Testator executed the will. See §9.3, above. If, however, the writing is entirely in Testator's own handwriting and Testator signed it, it may operate as a holographic will in jurisdictions that eliminate the attestation requirement for this type of will. See §5.4.3, above.

§9.5 Tangible Personal Property Document

A limited number of states and UPC §2-513 authorize a testator to use a separate writing to dispose of tangible personal property even though that writing (a) does not meet the requirements of a will and thus could not be probated as a testamentary instrument, (b) was not in existence at the date of will execution and thus could not be incorporated by reference (see §9.3, above), and (c) exists for no reason other than to dispose of property at death and thus could not be a fact of independent significance (see §9.4, above).

The testator must comply with some relatively easy requirements to use this technique. Generally, the will must expressly refer to the list, the testator must sign the list, and the list must describe the items and the recipients with reasonable certainty. The type of property the testator can dispose of with this instrument is usually limited to tangible personal property that is not already specifically gifted in the will. Thus, the list could not be used to make cash legacies, bequests of corporate securities, or devises of real property. The list may be prepared before or after the testator executes the will and the testator may alter the list at any time.

Proponents of this technique recognize that it is a tremendous departure from established law. However, they believe that the risks of fraud and misuse are counterbalanced by the potential of enhancing the law's ability to assist the testator in accomplishing the testator's desires. This technique permits the testator to control the disposition of a portion of the testator's estate without having to endure the expense and inconvenience of (1) initially providing a lengthy list of specific gifts to the drafting attorney, and (2) later needing to execute a codicil or new will to make changes to that list. In addition, these gifts are usually not of great monetary value. Instead, the gifts are of jewelry, photograph albums, videotapes, books, furniture, and other items the testator wants to transfer primarily for sentimental or emotional reasons.

§9.6   Pour-Over Provisions

A clause in a will making a gift to an inter vivos trust is called a *pour-over provision*. Pour-over provisions are very common because a testator may wish to obtain the benefits of a trust but not want to create the trust in the testator's will. Reasons a testator may prefer the pour-over technique include (1) an inter vivos trust is easier to amend than a will, (2) an inter vivos trust can serve as a receptacle for a variety of other assets, such as life insurance proceeds and annuity payments, to provide a unified disposition of the testator's property, and (3) the testator may pour-over into a trust created by someone else, such as a spouse. For benefits of a trust in general, see §18.2, below.

Sample Pour-Over Provision
I leave the remainder of my estate in trust to the trustee of the Testator's Children Support Trust that I created on July 10, 1995.

Originally at common law, the courts did not give effect to pour-over provisions. A disposition of property at death had to be governed by a testamentary document, not by an inter vivos one. As the concept of incorporation by reference became widely accepted, pour-over provisions fared much better. See §9.3, above. The courts treated the will as incorporating the terms of the trust instrument by reference. The will did not actually make a gift to an existing trust, but because the terms of the trust were deemed to be in the will, the gift was legally treated as passing under a testamentary trust. Although this was a great improvement in the law, application of incorporation by reference theory to pour-over wills often caused problems, as demonstrated by the following example.

Example 9-19. Pour-Over Provision — Incorporation by Reference

Testator created the Testator's Family Support Trust in 1990. The sole beneficiary of this trust was Son. In 1993, Testator executed a will that contained the following dispositive provision: "I leave one-half of my estate in trust to the trustee of the Testator's Family Support Trust. I leave one-half of my estate in trust to the trustee of the Testator's Favorite Charity Trust." In 1998, Testator added Daughter as a beneficiary of the Testator's Family Support Trust and created the Testator's Favorite Charity Trust. Testator died in 1999. What is the proper distribution of Testator's estate assuming Testator lives in a jurisdiction that uses incorporation by reference to validate pour-over provisions?

Explanation

Testator incorporated the terms of the Testator Family Support Trust as of the date Testator executed the will in 1990. At that time, the trust named Son as the sole beneficiary. Thus, one-half of Testator's estate passes into a trust with Son as the sole beneficiary. Remember, the terms of an incorporated by reference document are frozen at the date of will execution. Even if Testator had revoked the Testator Family Support Trust, one-half of Testator's estate would still pass under the terms of that trust. The remaining half of Testator's estate passes by intestacy, not under the terms of the Testator's Favorite Charity Trust. The document creating this trust was not in existence in 1993 and thus could not be incorporated by reference. The fact that the document existed when Testator died is irrelevant.

In more recent times, the courts began to treat inter vivos trusts as facts of independent significance; that is, the trusts exist apart from their ability to transfer property upon a person's death. See §9.4, above. Thus, a pour-over provision actually causes property to pass to the existing inter vivos trust, not through a new testamentary trust as under incorporation by reference. In effect, the trust is like an individual; the property passes to that entity as the entity exists at the date of the testator's death.

Example 9-20.   Pour-Over Provisions — Facts of Independent Significance

How would the facts of Example 9-19 come out in a jurisdiction that uses facts of independent significance to support pour-over provisions?

Explanation

One-half of Testator's estate would pass to Testator's Family Support Trust for the benefit of both Son and Daughter. The terms of the trust are not frozen as of the date of will execution as under incorporation by reference. Instead, subsequent changes to the trust affect how the testamentary transfer is handled. The other half of Testator's estate passes to the Testator's Favorite Charity Trust. It does not matter that the trust did not exist when Testator executed the will as long as it was in existence when Testator died.

States no longer rely on the doctrines of incorporation by reference or facts of independent significance to support pour-over provisions. Instead, practically all jurisdictions have adopted one of the two versions of the Uniform Testamentary Additions to Trust Act. Both versions combine aspects of the two underlying doctrines. The 1960 formulation permits property to pour-over from a will to an inter vivos trust that was created before or concurrently with the execution of the will. The property that pours over is governed by the terms of the trust in effect at the time of the testator's death. The 1991 revision, which is also found in UPC §2-511, no longer requires the trust to be in existence when the testator executes the will. In fact, the initial funding of the trust can come from the property that pours over. In addition, this property is governed by current terms of the trust, not those in effect when the testator dies. Thus, if a testator leaves property to a trust created by someone else who is still alive, the potential exists for that person to make amendments to the trust after the testator's death that may change the identity of the beneficiaries and how the trust property is spent or managed.

Example 9-21.   Pour-Over Provisions — Unfunded Trust

Testator's 1990 will provides, "I leave $100,000 to the Testator's Family Support Trust. I leave the remainder of my estate to Charity." In 1995, Testator prepared the appropriate documents to create the Testator's Family Support Trust. However, Testator never transferred any property to the trust. What is the proper distribution of Testator's estate?

Explanation

The outcome is problematic in jurisdictions that use the original version of the Uniform Testamentary Additions to Trusts Act. This Act requires the trust to be in existence at the date of will execution. Testator had not even written the trust instrument when Testator executed the will. Even though Testator's situation does not fall under the Act, could traditional approaches be used to validate the arrangement? Incorporation by reference would be no help because the trust document was not in existence when Testator executed the will. Application of the doctrine of facts of independent significance would also not save Testator's arrangement because the trust itself did not exist before the Testator died. Although the physical document existed, the trust was unfunded, that is, it had no property, and a trust does not exist without property and consequently could not be a fact of independent significance. See §19.6, below. Consequently, under the 1960 version of the Act, Charity would receive Testator's entire estate. However, under the revised version of the Uniform Act, the $100,000 would be used to create Testator's Family Support Trust. The 1991 Act no longer requires that the trust be funded prior to the testator's death as long as the trust is adequately identified and set forth in a written instrument.

Example 9-22. Pour-Over Provisions — After-Death Amendments

Testator's spouse created a valid inter vivos trust for the benefit of their children. Testator's will left Testator's entire estate to this trust. After Testator's death, the spouse amended the trust removing the children as beneficiaries and substituting the spouse's new romantic partner. Do the children have any legal basis to complain?

Explanation

Under the 1960 version of the Act, the property pouring over is governed by the terms of the trust as they exist on the date of Testator's death. Thus, the children could make certain the property traceable to Testator's estate remained in the trust solely for their benefit. However, the revised Act provides that the poured over property is governed by all amendments made to the trust, even those made after Testator's death. In these jurisdictions, the children would be out of luck.

§9.7   Precatory Language

The testator's instructions in a will regarding property disposition must be mandatory to be enforceable. Courts normally consider precatory language such as "I wish," "I recommend," or "I suggest" as merely suggestive and not binding on the beneficiary. Although the beneficiary may have a moral responsibility to comply with the testator's intent, precatory requests do not impose legally enforceable responsibilities. Of course, if it is clear that the testator intended to impose a mandatory restriction, the court may give effect to the limitation. In addition, precatory language directed towards estate administration matters has a greater chance of being followed than precatory property disposition instructions.

Example 9-23. Precatory Language — Dispositive Provisions

Testator's will contains the following provision: "I leave $50,000 to Son with the hope that he will use the money for his children's education. I leave the rest of my estate to Octopus National Bank and it is my wish that ONB use the property for my children and, upon the death of my last child, to turn the remaining funds over to Charity." After grieving over Testator's death, Son took an around the world cruise and spent the entire legacy. Do Son's children have any claim against their father? Is ONB obligated to use the remainder of the estate as provided in the will?

Explanation

The provision expressing Testator's "hope" that Son would use the money for his children's education is precatory. Testator's legacy to Son is absolute and unrestricted. Thus, Son's children have no claim against Son. The remainder gift is also limited by precatory language. However, it is extremely unlikely that Testator intended to make a gift of the remainder of the estate to ONB and thus there is a strong likelihood that the court would require ONB to honor the restrictions on the gift despite it being couched in precatory terms.

Example 9-24. Precatory Language — Administrative Matters

Testator's will contains the following provision, "I name Lara Croft as executor of my will. I would like my executor to serve without bond." Does this provision waive bond for Lara?

Explanation

Although Testator used the precatory phrase "I would like," many courts will nonetheless give effect to this language. Courts are more willing to follow precatory language regarding administrative matters because giving effect to the language does not impact a person's property rights.

Testators should not include precatory language in a will. If a testator wishes to express nonmandatory wishes or give advice to beneficiaries, the testator should prepare a separate nontestamentary document. Some testators may prefer to make audio- or videotapes of their recommendations.

§9.8   Class Gifts

§9.8.1 Defined

A *class gift* is one in which the testator designates a group of beneficiaries by a generic reference rather than by their individual names. The most common type of class gift in a will is to "children." Other examples of class references include "grandchildren," "siblings," "nieces and nephews," and "employees."

Example 9-25.   Class Gifts — Determining Class Nature of Gift

Testator's will includes the following gift, "I leave the remainder of my estate to my sisters, Alice and Elizabeth." Is this a class gift to Testator's sisters or is it a gift to the two named individuals?

Explanation

Most courts hold that a gift that includes both a class designation and individual names is a gift to the named individuals. The specific listing of beneficiaries governs over the general use of a class reference. The testator is deemed to have used the class language to describe the named beneficiaries rather than to create a gift to all individuals who fit the description. Thus, Testator's other sisters will not share in the residuary gift.

§9.8.2 Time At Which Class Membership Determined

If the testator indicated the time at which class membership is to be determined, that time will be used. Thus, if the testator devised a house to "my spouse for life and then to my children who are alive at the time of my spouse's death," the determination of which children receive the house will be made upon the death of the spouse. The heirs or beneficiaries of any child who survives the testator but fails to outlive the spouse would have no claim to the house.

   If the testator fails to state the time at which the class closes, most courts determine class membership at the earliest of the following two events: (a) the *natural closing* of the class; that is, when it is impossible for additional individuals to join the class, and (b) the time determined by the *rule of convenience;* that is, the time when any existing member of the class is first entitled to demand distribution. Permitting a class to close via the rule of convenience prior to the natural closing of the class is justified on the basis of the extreme difficulty in distributing property to the class members who are entitled thereto and yet imposing on them the risk that a portion of their title might be divested at some undetermined future time if additional class members are born or otherwise enter the class.

Example 9-26.   Class Gifts — Determination of Class Members — Time

Testator's will contains the following gift, "I leave the remainder of my estate to the children of my best friend, Nathan." When Testator executed the will, Nathan had two children, Adam and Bonnie. After Testator executed the will but prior to Testator's death, Nathan had a third child, Chuck, and Bonnie was killed in an automobile accident. After Testator's death, Nathan had a fourth child, Donald. Nathan, Adam, Chuck, and Donald survive Testator. Who is entitled to share in the residuary of Testator's estate assuming the anti-lapse statute does not apply to this gift? (For a discussion of the possible application of anti-lapse statutes to class gifts, see §7.4.3, above.)

Time	Adam	Bonnie	Chuck	Donald
Will execution	X	X		
After will execution		dies	X	
When Testator dies				
After Testator dies				X

Explanation

Because Testator failed to state the time at which the recipients of the class gift to Nathan's children are to be determined, the court will look to the earliest of the times determined by the natural closing of the class and the rule of convenience. The class has not yet naturally closed because Nathan is alive and can have additional children. (Courts usually follow a presumption that a person can have children as long as the person is alive even though the person may be biologically incapable of reproduction.) Consequently, the courts will use the rule of convenience to determine class membership. The date that the first member of the class is entitled to distribution is the date of Testator's death. Thus, the residuary estate will be divided between Adam and Chuck. Bonnie died prior to the time of determining class membership and Donald was born thereafter and thus neither is included in the class.

§9.8.3 Types of Individuals Included in Classes

The types of individuals entitled to qualify as class members is an often litigated issue. Assume that a gift is made to your "children." Does this gift include individuals you adopt while they are minors, individuals you adopt after they become adults, or children born outside of a marriage? What if the gift was made instead to your "issue" or to your "bodily heirs"?

Historically, courts presumed that a testator intended to include adopted individuals in a class gift to the testator's own children. However, if the class gift was to someone else's children, courts typically followed the *stranger-to-the-adoption rule,* which raised a presumption that the testator did not intend to include the adopted individuals. These presumptions could be rebutted by evidence of the testator's intent to the contrary. For example, the testator may have known that the other person could not have biological children and the testator may have had a close relationship with that person's adopted children.

Modern courts and statutes have been very inclusive in determining class membership. For example, UPC §2-705(a) provides that adopted individuals and persons born outside of marriage are included in class gifts. However, under UPC §2-705(b) and (c), these individuals usually need to have lived in the parent's household when they were minors. Courts in some states have even included adopted individuals in classes traditionally reserved only for biological relatives such as "issue" and "bodily issue."

Example 9-27. Class Gifts — Determination of Class Members — Adopted Away Individuals

When Testator was very young, Testator had a child who was immediately adopted. Years later, Testator got married and had two children. After Testator's spouse died, Testator wrote a will which provides, "I leave all my property to my children." Testator died survived by all three children. Who is entitled to share in Testator's estate?

Explanation

Jurisdictions are divided on the issue of whether an individual who is adopted out of the family is still included in a class gift made by a member of the biological family. Some courts totally remove an adopted individual from the biological family and insert the person in the adoptive family. On the other hand, some states presume that the adopted individual remains in the biological family as well as being added to the adoptive family.

To resolve class gift issues, the testator should carefully explain the categories of individuals the testator wishes to encompass within a class gift.

For example, a class gift to children should address adopted-in minors, adopted-in adults, adopted-out individuals, and children born out of wedlock. Courts are extremely willing to follow the testator's intent as expressed in the will even if that intent is contrary to normal construction rules.

§9.9 Dead Person's Statute

Courts normally seek whatever evidence is helpful when they interpret and construe wills. However, this ability may be restricted by state evidentiary rules, especially *dead person's statutes* (formerly referred to as "dead man's statutes"). These statutes limit the admissibility of evidence of what the testator did or said if the testimony is being offered by a party to the action. The policy supporting this limitation is that the testator is deceased and thus cannot rebut the statements made by a party who is obviously biased. Under older formulations of the rule, a party could not testify about any transaction or communication with the decedent. Consequently, family members and friends who were named beneficiaries as well as parties to an interpretation action could not explain what they saw the testator do or what they heard the testator say. Modern rules allow most, if not all, of this testimony to be admitted. The fact-finder is then free to determine what weight to give the evidence based on the credibility of the witnesses.

10

Will Contests

An individual may have a strong motivation to have a testator's will deemed invalid and ineffective to dispose of the testator's property. First, this person could be an heir who would receive less under the will than under intestacy. Or, second, this person could be a beneficiary of a prior will who would receive a smaller gift under the more recent will. Such disgruntled individuals may attempt to contest the testator's will on one or more of the grounds discussed in this chapter.

Example 10-1. Standing to Contest

Father's will left the entire estate to Daughter. Son, Father's only other heir, was satisfied with this arrangement because he had received all of his mother's estate when she died several years earlier. Son's child, Grandchild, was very upset that Son was excluded and Friend thought the will was grossly unfair. As a result, Grandchild and Friend filed to contest the will. Do they have standing to maintain this action?

Explanation

A person must have a pecuniary interest to maintain a will contest action; mere expectancies or moral interests are insufficient. Although Grandchild may stand to gain if Son took part of Father's estate, either through inter vivos gifts, Son's will, or via intestacy, these eventualities are too speculative to give Grandchild standing. Friend lacks even a remote pecuniary interest and thus has no standing.

   If possible, the contestant should file the contest before the proponent is successful in having the will admitted to probate because the proponent typically has the burden to prove that the document is the testator's valid will. Once the court admits the will to probate, the contestant must prove that the will is invalid. Most will contests occur after the will is admitted to probate despite the procedural advantage of contesting a will prior to its admission. The contesting party often does not yet know the ramifications of the will and consequently may not have gathered the evidence needed to make a successful attack on the will. Other jurisdictions follow rules that are not based on the time of the contest. For example, UPC §3-407 provides that (a) the proponents of a will have the burden of establishing prima facie proof of due execution, and (b) the contestants have the burden of establishing lack of testamentary intent, lack of capacity, undue influence, fraud, duress, mistake, or revocation.

The contestant must be certain to bring the action within the time established by the applicable statute of limitations. For example, UPC §3-108(a)(3) requires the contest to be commenced within the later of (a) twelve months from the date the will is informally probated, or (b) three years after the decedent's death. Some states base the statute of limitations on the grounds for the contest with longer periods applying to reasons that the contestant could not readily ascertain, such as forgery or fraud. Of course, if the contestant is a minor or an incompetent person, there is a strong likelihood that state law will toll the running of limitations until the disability no longer exists. If the contestant permits limitations to expire, the contest will fail regardless of the evidence the contestant might be able to produce.

§10.1   Failure to Satisfy Requirements of a Valid Will

Contestants often attack a will on the ground that it does not initially meet the requirements of a valid will. Thus, the contestant may allege that (1) the testator lacked legal capacity, (2) the testator did not have testamentary capacity, (3) the testator did not execute the document with testamentary intent, or (4) the document and its execution did not comply with the requisite formalities. Review Chapter 5, above.

§10.2   Insane Delusions

§10.2.1 Defined

A testator's perception of reality may be so distorted that the testator's will is ineffective even though the testator knows that the testator is making a will, understands that a will disposes of the testator's property upon the testator's death, appreciates the nature and extent of the testator's property, and recognizes the natural objects of the testator's bounty. A testator suffering from an insane delusion may even be able to enter into contracts and handle complex business transactions with aplomb. An *insane delusion* exists when the testator's mind is so warped by a false and unfounded belief that the testator cannot make a rational disposition of the testator's property.

Although courts define insane delusion or mental derangement in a variety of ways, these definitions usually encompass two main components. First, the testator believes that something is true when in reality it is false. Second, this misbelief is irrational, that is, there is no credible evidence to support the testator's version of reality. The misconception of fact or untraditional mental attitude typically stems from an organic brain defect or from some functional disorder of the mind. Courts warn that a precise definition is not possible and stress that the determination of whether the testator was suffering from an insane delusion depends in each case on the exact facts and circumstances involved.

Courts are careful to make the distinction between an insane delusion that invalidates a will and a mere false belief. A testator who is suffering from an insane delusion will not change the testator's belief even when confronted with evidence to the contrary. Instead, the testator continues to insist on the correctness of the belief despite the conflicting evidence, regardless of how strong or incontrovertible. However, a testator operating under a false belief will change the testator's opinion once presented with convincing evidence demonstrating that the belief is incorrect.

Example 10-2. Insane Delusion — Mere False Belief

Testator's 1990 will divided Testator's estate evenly between Son and Daughter. While Testator was grocery shopping, Testator overhead a conversation in which one of the participants said she had heard that Son was "a dope fiend." Without doing any investigation, Testator immediately changed the will to exclude Son and leave everything to Daughter. After Testator's death, may Son prove that he has never used illegal drugs and that Testator was operating under an insane delusion and thus void the new will and take half of Testator's estate under the 1990 will?

Explanation

Son is probably out of luck. Testator indeed had a misbelief and was unreasonable in accepting such rank hearsay as fact without checking into the truthfulness of the slanderous rumor. However, Testator's false belief and quick-to-jump-to-the-worst-conclusion attitude is not enough to invalidate the will on the basis of insane delusion. If Testator had been confronted with facts showing Son's abstinence from drugs, Testator would have changed Testator's belief. See also the discussion of mistake in the inducement discussed in §10.6.3, below.

Example 10-3. Insane Delusion — Actual Insane Delusion

Testator's 1990 will divided Testator's estate evenly between Son and Daughter. Son suffered from a rare disease and died an agonizing death. Testator was overwrought with grief and began to believe the CIA was testing biological warfare weapons on Son which had caused Son's death. Testator was certain that Daughter and the hospital were cooperating with the CIA in exchange for large cash payments. Testator hired a private investigator, Rockford, to research the situation. Rockford's written report showed that none of Testator's suspicions had even a shred of evidence to support them. Testator ignored this report and concluded that the CIA must have bought off Rockford as well. Consequently, Testator changed the will and left everything to Friend. May Daughter contest this will on the ground that Testator was suffering from an insane delusion?

Explanation

Daughter is likely to succeed. Testator's belief was false, there was no evidence to support it, and Testator even ignored evidence showing that Testator's belief was not true. As with most insane delusion cases, however, the court can never be absolutely sure that a testator's belief is actually false. There is always a possibility that a testator's outrageous belief is true. For example, in years past, everyone "knew" that the earth was flat and was situated in the center of the solar system.

§10.2.2 Nexus between Delusion and Will

At common law, no nexus was required between the insane delusion and the will because a mind that was unsound on one subject was considered contaminated to the point that the testator's entire mind was unfit to create a valid property disposition. Under modern law, however, a connection must exist between the testator's insane delusion and the property disposition in the will before the court may invalidate the will. Just because the testator suffered from an insane delusion does not mean the terms of the will were affected by that delusion. "A [person] may believe [him/herself] to be the supreme ruler of the universe and nevertheless make a perfectly sensible disposition of . . . property, and the courts will sustain it when it appears that [the] mania did not dictate its provisions."[1]

Example 10-4.   Insane Delusion — Lack of Nexus

Testator believed that alien beings from outer space live among us disguised as humans. Testator even made a list of all the people Testator met whom Testator suspected as being extraterrestrial. Testator was afraid of being kidnapped and killed by these aliens and thus made a will leaving all of Testator's property to Testator's spouse and children. May this will be valid despite Testator's beliefs?

Explanation

The will is likely to be valid because Testator's delusion did not influence the property disposition in Testator's will. The identity of the beneficiaries and the extent of the property left to them was not affected by the delusion. To invalidate a will, the contestant must show that the insane delusion triggered the testator to execute a will containing terms it would not have contained but for the delusion.

Example 10-5.   Insane Delusion — Existence of Nexus

After Testator from Example 10-4 executed the will, Testator came home from work one day and noticed something peculiar about Testator's spouse. Testator needed only a few moments to detect the telltale signs of alien inhabitation. The next day, Testator changed Testator's will to disinherit the spouse and leave everything to the children. May Testator's spouse successfully contest this new will on the basis of insane delusion?

Explanation

Testator's spouse stands an excellent chance of setting aside Testator's new will on the ground of insane delusion. Testator's misbelief that the spouse was an alien is directly connected to the spouse's omission as a beneficiary under the new will.

Example 10-6.   Insane Delusion — Religion Based

Testator belonged to an organized religion whose members strongly believe in reincarnation. Testator hired a psychic to determine the identity of the

---

1. Fraser v. Jennison, 3 N.W. 882, 900 (Mich. 1879).

person in whom Testator would be reincarnated. Testator then executed a will leaving this person Testator's entire estate. May Testator's heirs successfully contest this will?

Explanation

Testator's belief influenced the disposition of Testator's property; the nexus between the belief and the will exists. However, Testator's belief was a spiritual or religious one. Religious beliefs are commonly accepted as a matter of faith rather than because of facts that can be empirically proved true or false. Accordingly, courts are more lenient with regard to religious-based beliefs, even if they are out of the mainstream of Western religions, than with other types of beliefs. Thus, a court would have a relatively difficult time concluding that the will is invalid because of Testator's belief.

§10.3   Undue Influence

§10.3.1 Defined

A testator who is *unduly influenced* has testamentary capacity but that capacity is subjected to and controlled by an evil individual. Although courts define undue influence in a variety of ways, these definitions typically encompass three elements. First, the person must actually exert an influence over the testator that is undue. Merely pleading with the testator or badgering the testator to make a will in a certain way is not enough. Second, the influence must turn the testator into a marionette; that is, the influence needs to be so strong that it subverts and overpowers the testator's mind at the time the testator executes the will. Third, the influence must cause the testator to execute a will that the testator would not have signed but for the undue influence. As a result of the influence, the will reflects the wishes of the influencer, not the testator.

Example 10-7.   Undue Influence — Mere Influence

Testator's 1985 will left Testator's estate equally to Son and Daughter. Testator showed a copy of the will to Testator's children thinking they would be pleased with the fairness of the disposition. However, Son believed that he deserved more than Daughter because Son and Testator had a much closer relationship than Daughter and Testator. Son spent the next ten years pleading with Testator to give him a greater portion of the estate. Son spent more time with Testator, took Testator on trips, and bought Testator presents, even when it was not a holiday occasion. In 1995, Testator executed a new will leaving 75 percent of the estate to Son and 25 percent to Daughter. What are Daughter's chances of setting aside the 1995 will on the basis of undue influence?

Explanation

Daughter will have a difficult time convincing a court that Testator was unduly influenced. Son definitely exerted influence over Testator and that influence caused Testator to write a will Testator would not have written but for the Son's actions. However, the influence does not appear to cross the line from mere influence to undue influence. Even if Testator had changed the will to leave everything to Son, Daughter would still have a tough time of proving undue influence despite the seeming unfairness of the will.

Example 10-8. Undue Influence—Subversion of Testator's Mind

Testator's 1985 will left Testator's estate equally to Son and Daughter. In 1990, Testator was in a serious accident and was confined to a nursing home. Nurse realized that Testator was wealthy and began a campaign to break up Testator's relationships with Testator's children. Nurse destroyed all letters and packages from Son and Daughter. If they telephoned, Nurse made certain the calls were not forwarded to Testator's room. Nurse also placed an outgoing call blocking device on Testator's phone so when Testator called the children, Testator always received a busy signal. Nurse spent an inordinate amount of time with Testator and took every opportunity to magnify the distance that was growing between Testator and the children. At first, Testator made excuses for the children but in time, Testator began to think that the children no longer cared. Nurse took great pains to describe Nurse's troubled life and miserable existence. Nurse also spent time boosting Testator's ego by telling Testator how smart, kind, understanding, and brave Testator was in the face of Testator's medical problems and desertion by Son and Daughter. Testator executed a new will leaving Testator's entire estate to Nurse. What are Son and Daughter's chances of setting aside this new will on the basis of undue influence?

Explanation

Son and Daughter have a good chance of showing that Nurse exerted undue influence over Testator. Nurse's entire course of conduct was designed to overpower Testator's mind and manipulate Testator's thoughts and actions. Nurse was successful and Testator executed a will that Testator would not have executed but for the influence. Consequently, the new will is ineffective and Testator's estate passes under the 1985 will. Note that Nurse's conduct may also make Testator's will subject to contest on the basis of fraud. See §10.5, below.

§10.3.2 Demonstrating Undue Influence

§10.3.2.1 Direct Evidence

An evil individual does not normally exert undue influence in front of witnesses. Instead, undue influence is performed in private so that the only witnesses are the testator and the influencer. When the time comes to contest the will, the testator is deceased and thus cannot testify and the influencer will lie. It is unrealistic to think that a person evil enough to exert undue influence would be afraid of a perjury charge for giving false testimony under oath and thus confess to exerting undue influence under cross-examination. Accordingly, direct evidence of undue influence is rarely available.

§10.3.2.2 Circumstantial Evidence

Courts examine a wide array of circumstantial evidence to determine whether the testator was subject to undue influence. The relevant extrinsic evidence can usually be placed into one of the six major categories listed below. As courts examine this extrinsic evidence, they are very careful to distinguish between situations where a person did not exert undue influence, although the person had the opportunity and was in a position to easily do so, from situations where the influence was actually exerted. Merely because the contestant brings forth circumstantial evidence from all the categories is no guarantee that the court will find that undue influence was exerted. Of course, the more extrinsic evidence that exists, the greater the chance that the court will determine that the testator was subject to undue influence.

(1) **Motive.** The person exerting undue influence does not have to be a beneficiary of the will. Of course, most individuals who exert undue influence do so to take under the will. Thus, a person named as a beneficiary under the testator's will had a greater motive to have exerted undue influence than someone who is not a beneficiary unless, of course, that person is acting on behalf of the beneficiary. The existence of the beneficiary's motive may be easier to show if the testator had executed an earlier will in which this person received a smaller share or was entirely excluded.

(2) **Untraditional Disposition.** The testator's disinheritance of close family members, such as a spouse and descendants, in favor of distant relatives, friends, or a charity serves as evidence of undue influence. The weight of this type of evidence is enhanced if the testator revoked a will making a traditional

disposition shortly before executing the will, especially if the testator died shortly thereafter.

(3) Opportunity and Access. An individual intending to unduly influence a testator usually wants access to the testator. It is easier to influence someone with whom you are in close physical proximity than a person located a distance away. For example, a child would have an easier time exerting undue influence over a parent who lives in the child's home than over a parent who lives a thousand miles away.

(4) Relationship between Testator and Alleged Undue Influencer. A contestant will have an easier time showing undue influence if the testator and the alleged influencer shared a confidential relationship. In some situations, the existence of a confidential relationship may even trigger a presumption of undue influence requiring the alleged influencer to prove otherwise. Courts sweep a wide variety of social, moral, and personal relationships within the coverage of confidential ones, not just those of a fiduciary character. Thus, a contestant may be able to show that the testator and the testator's family member or friend were in a non-arm's length type of relationship.

(5) Susceptibility and Ability to Resist. The courts look to the physical and mental condition of the testator to see how easy it would be for the alleged influencer to exert the undue influence. Factors the courts consider include the testator's age, health, intelligence, and business experience. Some people are easily swayed because of their trusting nature or their physical or psychological dependence on the influencer. On the other hand, some individuals are stubborn, making it very difficult to force them into doing something they really do not want to do.

(6) Connection between Will and Alleged Undue Influencer. The closer the connection between the will itself and the alleged undue influencer, the greater the likelihood of the court finding undue influence. For example, undue influence is more likely if the influencer suggested that the testator needed a will, wrote the will, and was physically present when the testator executed the will.

§10.3.3 Attorney as Will Drafter and Beneficiary

§10.3.3.1 Loss of Gift

Many states have a presumption, either by statute or judicial decision, that the testator was unduly influenced to execute the will if the drafting attorney is named as a beneficiary. Some states go even further and completely void the gift regardless of the evidence the attorney may be able to produce showing that the attorney did not exert undue influence and that the testator really wanted the attorney to be a beneficiary because, for example, they were best friends for fifty years. However, these states often have an exception that operates if the testator and the beneficiary are very closely related permitting, for example, a child to write a parent's will even though the child is named as a beneficiary.

§10.3.3.2   Loss of Law License

Model Rule of Professional Conduct 1.8(c) ("the Rule") provides that "[a] lawyer shall not prepare an instrument giving the lawyer or a person related to the lawyer as parent, child, sibling, or spouse any substantial gift from a client, including a testamentary gift, except where the client is related to the donee." Making a gift in violation of this rule does not make the gift void although, as discussed in §10.3.3.1, it may raise a presumption of undue influence. Instead, violation of this rule is grounds for the appropriate disciplinary authority to sanction the attorney by imposing a penalty any-where from a private reprimand all the way to disbarment, depending on the egregiousness of the case. To mitigate the harshness of this rule when a client really wants to leave property to the drafting attorney, some states provide special procedures to permit this type of gift if the will receives an inde-pendent review.

Example 10-9.   Undue Influence — Attorney as Drafter — Gift to Relative

As soon as you are sworn into your state's bar, Client asks you to prepare a will that leaves $50,000 to your nephew. May you ethically prepare this will?

Explanation

The Rule prohibits you from drafting a will that names you or certain closely related individuals as beneficiaries. However, the Rule is quite narrow be-cause it only restricts gifts to your spouse, parents, children, and siblings. Despite the obvious bias towards your nephew, the gift would not be within the scope of the Rule. Nonetheless, it is not a wise idea to prepare the will because of the likelihood of a contest by Client's heirs that you exerted undue influence. Note that many other close relatives are outside of the Rule's exclusion such as grandchildren, aunts and uncles, cousins, and in-laws.

Example 10-10.   Undue Influence—Attorney as Drafter—Testator Related to Donee

After watching you get sworn into your state's bar, your proud parent requests that you write a will that names you as one of the beneficiaries. May you ethically prepare this will?

Explanation

Although the will names you as a beneficiary, you could nonetheless prepare the will because the Rule makes an exception if the client (your parent) is related to the donee (you). However, from a practical standpoint, you should not prepare the will if you are receiving a disportionately large share of your parent's estate. If you receive more than your intestate share or more than your siblings, you should decline to write the will to avoid claims of undue influence.

Example 10-11.   Undue Influence—Attorney as Drafter—Substantiality of Gift

Shortly after receiving your law license, Friend wants you to write the Friend's will. Friend indicates that Friend wishes to name you as the beneficiary of a baseball card collection that you have admired for many years. The collection is currently valued at $10,000. May you ethically prepare this will?

Explanation

The Rule permits you to draft a will naming yourself as a beneficiary if the gift is not substantial. However, the Rule provides no guidance with regard to how the substantiality of a gift should be determined. Does it depend on the size of Friend's estate or your estate? For example, if Friend is a multi-millionaire, a gift valued at $10,000 is insignificant but if you are struggling financially, the gift could be very substantial to you. On the other hand, if Friend is economically disadvantaged, this gift could be the bulk of Friend's estate but merely a token amount from your perspective if you are wealthy. To avoid problems, you should simply not draft the will. If the value of the collection is very small with regard to both the size of your estate and the size of Friend's estate and you and Friend have had a long relationship, you could prepare the will with a modicum of safety.

§10.3.4 *Mortmain Statutes and Charitable Gifts*

Many states limited testamentary gifts to charity based on the 1736 Statute of Mortmain.[2] Mortmain statutes operated in a variety of ways. Typical restrictions included limiting a testamentary gift to a certain portion of the testator's estate or requiring the testator to survive by a certain period of time after executing a will containing a charitable gift. These statutes were based on the assumption that charitable gifts, especially those made near death, may have been induced by a member of the clergy promising a happy afterlife in exchange for a sizable testamentary gift. Mortmain statutes thus operated to prevent a testator from being unwisely generous to the detriment of the testator's family regardless of the testator's motivation for making the gift.

The number of states with mortmain statutes is rapidly decreasing. Many states have repealed their statutes and courts in other jurisdictions have deemed them unconstitutional as violating the Equal Protection Clause of the Fourteenth Amendment. For example, assume that a state statute invalidated gifts to charity made within five days of the testator's death. A court is likely to deem this statute both overbroad and underinclusive. True, it would void a deathbed gift made to a religious organization preying on the testator's fear of a fiery afterlife but it would also invalidate a charitable gift by a testator who was killed in an automobile accident two days after executing the will. The statute's protection would be imperfect because it would let stand a deathbed gift made under pressure if the testator lived at least five days. Consequently, most courts now rely on traditional undue influence analysis to determine the validity of deathbed gifts to religious organizations and other charities.

§10.4 Duress

Duress is very similar to undue influence as discussed in §10.3, above. The elements of duress and the methods of proof are virtually identical. The key difference is that duress connotes the direct use of violence, threats of brutality to the testator or testator's family, or the withholding of food or medicine to force the testator into submission whereas undue influence is more cerebral in character. In other words, an undue influencer messes with the testator's mind while a person exerting duress threatens physical harm.

Example 10-12. Duress

Testator's 1990 will divided Testator's estate equally between Son and Daughter. Testator was in a serious accident and was placed on a ventilator

---

2. 9 Geo. 2, ch. 36 (1736).

in the hospital. Daughter came to visit with a new will naming Daughter as the sole beneficiary of the estate. Testator refused to sign so Daughter grabbed Testator's air hose and began to squeeze. After a few moments, Testator began to gasp for air and agreed to sign the new will. May Son set aside this new will on the basis of duress?

Explanation

Assuming Son can prove these facts, Son should have no difficulty setting aside the new will because of duress.

§10.5   Fraud

§10.5.1   Defined

The definition of fraud applied in a will contest action is fundamentally the same as in a tort or contract context. The four basic elements of fraud are listed below:

(1) False Representation. Someone must have made a false representation to the testator.

(2) Knowledge of Falsity. The individual making the false representation must have known the statement was false. In other words, the liar must have intended to deceive the testator. See the discussion of mistake in §10.6, below, to see how the courts handle innocent misrepresentations.

(3) Reasonably Believed. The testator must have reasonably believed the false statement. Thus, if a reasonable person would not have believed the misrepresentation, fraud could not be established.

(4) Causation. The false representation must cause the testator to execute a will the testator would not have signed but for the misrepresentation.

Example 10-13.   Fraud — Basic Elements

Son told Testator that he had studied ancient books and had become a warlock. Son then warned Testator that he would turn Testator into a toad if Testator did not execute a will leaving Son all of Testator's property. Testator immediately wrote the desired will. Would Testator's other children be able to set aside this will on the basis of fraud?

Explanation

Son made a false representation of his ability to turn Testator into a toad. Son probably knew that he lacked this ability. The statement certainly caused Testator to execute a will he would not have signed but for the false statement. However, courts are unlikely to find fraud because a reasonable person would not believe Son had the ability to turn Testator into a toad. Note that if Testator was susceptible to superstitious beliefs or followed a religion that believed in human-animal transformation, it may be possible to argue that Son's threat constituted undue influence. See §10.3, above.

§10.5.2 Fraud in the Execution

Fraud in the execution, also called *fraud in the factum,* refers to a type of fraud by which the testator is deceived as to either (1) the identity of the instrument the testator signed, or (2) the contents of the will. The fraud prevented the testator from knowing the true nature of the document being signed, either that it was a will in the first place, or, even if the testator knew the testator was signing a will, the provisions of that will.

Example 10-14. Fraud in the Execution — Identity of Instrument

Barnabus approached Ray Charles, a visually challenged performer, after a concert and asked for an autograph. Although unable to see, Ray had no difficulty signing what he thought was an autograph book. Instead, Ray actually signed a will naming Barnabus as the sole beneficiary of Ray's huge estate. May a court set aside this will on the basis of fraud?

Explanation

Barnabus made a false representation to Ray that Barnabus was seeking an autograph. Barnabus knew that he was actually attempting to obtain Ray's signature on a will. Because of the circumstances surrounding these events, that is, a request for an autograph after a concert, Ray's belief of the misrepresentation was reasonable. This then caused Ray to execute a will he would not have executed but for the misrepresentation. Consequently, Ray's will is invalid. Note that this will could also be attacked on the ground that Ray lacked testamentary intent when he signed the instrument. See §5.3, above.

Example 10-15. Fraud in the Execution—Contents of Instrument

While ill, Testator asked Beneficiary to prepare Testator's will. Testator instructed Beneficiary to name Beneficiary as the sole recipient of Testator's estate and to insert a clause in the will stating that the will would be totally void if Testator survived the illness. Beneficiary did not include the clause in the will but read the will to Testator as if it contained the clause. Testator signed the will without checking to see if the clause was actually printed in the will. Testator survived the illness and died later. Would Testator's heirs be able to set aside this will on the basis of fraud?

Explanation

Beneficiary falsely told Testator that the voiding provision was in the will and read the will to Testator as if the provision were included. Beneficiary knew the provision was not actually in the will because Beneficiary drafted the will. Under the facts, there is no reason to suspect Testator's belief of Beneficiary's misrepresentation was unreasonable. Testator would not have executed this will if Testator knew the automatic voiding provision had been omitted. Thus, Testator's heirs should be able to convince a court to set aside the will on the basis of fraud in the execution.

§10.5.3 *Fraud in the Inducement*

A testator who is subject to *fraud in the inducement* knew that the testator was executing a will and knew the contents of that will. However, the individual perpetrating the fraud deceived the testator with regard to an extrinsic fact that caused the testator to make a will containing provisions the testator would not have included if the testator had known the fact was actually false.

Example 10-16. Fraud in the Inducement

Father had two children, Son and Daughter. Father's original will divided his estate evenly between his two children. Son began a campaign to impugn Daughter's reputation by telling Father that she used illegal drugs, abused her children, and embezzled money from her employer. Son forged letters and had friends make confirming telephone calls to Father to support Son's allegations. Son also intercepted letters and telephone calls between Father and Daughter. Upset at his Daughter's evil ways, Father changed his will to leave his entire estate to Son and then died without ever realizing the truth. May Daughter overturn this will on the basis of fraud?

Explanation

Son made many false representations to Father and knew that they were false. Son went to great lengths to make sure Father believed these misrepresentations and thus it appears that Father was reasonable in so believing. As a result of Son's fabrications, Father made a will he would not otherwise have executed. Thus, Father's will can be set aside for fraud in the inducement even though Father knew he was executing a will and what it contained because the will was impliedly conditioned on the truth of Son's representations.

§10.6   Mistake

§10.6.1   Defined

A testator may execute a will under a mistake of law or fact. Unlike with fraud as discussed in §10.5, above, a mistake is not the result of someone's fraudulent conduct. Instead, a mistake arises because the testator believes something to be true when it is not and this belief either is (1) not induced by another person (the testator's belief arises unilaterally) or (2) induced by another person's innocent misrepresentation (this other person is mistaken as well).

§10.6.2   Mistake in the Execution

Mistake in the execution, also called *mistake in the factum,* arises when the testator is in error regarding the identity or contents of the instrument.

Example 10-17.   Mistake in the Execution — Identity of Instrument

Testator had many documents on Testator's desk ready for signature. In a hurry, Testator signed her will believing the document to be a credit application. May this document be probated as Testator's will?

Explanation

Assuming Testator's heirs or the beneficiaries of a prior will can prove that Testator thought Testator was signing a credit application instead of a will, the will may be successfully contested. The mistake regarding the true nature of the instrument prevented Testator from having the requisite testamentary intent and thus the will fails. See the discussion of testamentary intent in §5.3, above.

Example 10-18. Mistake in the Execution — Contents of Instrument — Inadvertently Included Provision

Testator originally intended to make a specific bequest of a car to Friend and made a deliberate effort to tell Attorney about the gift. Attorney dutifully included the gift in the first draft of the will. Testator then made many changes to the will including the removal of this bequest. Attorney made all of the other changes but neglected to delete Friend's gift. Testator did not proofread the will carefully and thus signed it even though it contained the bequest. After Testator's death, may the residual beneficiaries of Testator's will have the court set aside this gift to Friend?

Explanation

Testator did not intend the gift to Friend to be in the will. Accordingly, the court might determine that Testator lacked testamentary intent with regard to Friend's bequest and strike it from the will. See the discussion of testamentary intent in §5.3, above.

Example 10-19. Mistake in the Execution — Contents of Instrument — Missing Provision

Testator intended to make a specific bequest of a car to Friend and made a deliberate effort to tell Attorney about the gift. Attorney inadvertently omitted the gift from the will. Testator did not proofread the will carefully and thus did not notice that Friend's bequest was missing. After Testator's death, may Friend obtain the car?

Explanation

Courts are normally unwilling to add missing provisions to a will that were allegedly omitted because of a testator's mistake. The risk of fraud is too high to permit this type of change. In addition, courts normally lack authority to permit property to pass under provisions which do not meet the requirements of a valid will. Friend may, however, have a remedy for malpractice against Attorney. See §26.1, below.

§10.6.3 *Mistake in the Inducement*

Mistake in the inducement arises when the testator falsely believes a fact to be true and makes the will based on that erroneous fact. The mistake may be caused by the representations of another person or by the testator's unilateral error.

Example 10-20. Mistake in the Inducement

Father has two children, Son and Daughter. Father's original will divided his estate evenly between his two children. Daughter is in the military and is stationed in a dangerous area in Europe. The United States government erroneously informed Father that Daughter was killed during recent hostilities. Father then changed his will to leave everything to Son. Father died before finding out Daughter was still alive. Is a court likely to deny probate to this new will because of Father's mistake?

Explanation

Most courts would not fix this mistake and thus Son would receive Father's entire estate. In the absence of fraud or undue influence, courts do not permit mistakes to defeat the probate of a will, even though it is likely that the testator would have made a different will had the testator known about the mistake. Some courts will grant relief, however, if both the mistake and what the testator would have done but for the mistake are stated in the will. Thus, a court might be sympathetic to Daughter if the will provided, "Because Daughter is dead, I am now changing my will to leave everything to Son rather than dividing my estate equally between Son and Daughter." The court could decide that this provision is actually a conditional revocation based on Daughter's death and because the condition was not met, the revocation did not occur. See §8.6, above.

§10.7 Remedies

If the reason for contesting a will affects the validity of the entire will, the court will hold that the will is ineffective. Examples of these types of grounds include lack of legal capacity, lack of testamentary capacity, and noncompliance with formalities. The decedent's property then passes by intestacy or under a prior will. However, if the will contest ground goes only to an identifiable portion of the will, the court may set aside just that portion and give effect to the balance of the will. For example, a person may exert undue influence on a testator to convince the testator to make a specific bequest to that person but not interfere with how the testator disposed of the balance of the estate. In reality, however, it is very difficult to show that the rest of the will was not affected by the undue influence, duress, or fraud. In addition, most people who engage in such evil conduct attempt to impact the disposition of most or all of the testator's property, not merely identifiable separate items.

If a testator is prevented from executing a will because of undue influence, duress, or fraud, the court may impose a constructive trust on the heirs (or beneficiaries of prior wills) to prevent unjust enrichment. Constructive trusts are covered in detail in Chapter 23, below.

§10.8   Preventing Will Contests[3]

This section discusses a wide range of techniques that may be used to prevent a will contest or to reduce the likelihood of its success. These techniques vary widely in both cost and predictability of results. There is no uniform approach to use for all testators. You need to examine each case on its own merits before deciding which, if any, of the techniques to use. In addition, you must study state law to determine the validity and effectiveness of each technique. Note that several will contest prevention techniques are covered elsewhere in this book; for example, enhancing the will execution ceremony (§5.4.2.5, above) and careful selection of witnesses (§5.4.2.3.14, above).

§10.8.1   No-Contest Provision

A *no-contest provision*, also called an *in terrorem* or *forfeiture* clause, provides that a beneficiary who contests the will loses at least some, and typically all, of the benefits given under the will.[4] In terrorem provisions are one of the most frequently used contest prevention techniques. This widespread use is due to the technique's low cost (a few extra lines in the will), low risk (no penalty incurred if the clause is declared unenforceable), and the potential for effectuating the testator's intent (property passing via the will rather than through intestacy or under a prior will).

---

3. This section is adapted from Gerry W. Beyer, *Drafting in Contemplation of Will Contests*, Prac. Law., Jan. 1992, at 61.

4. In early English law, these terms were not used interchangeably. An in terrorem clause was considered to be an empty threat; that is, the beneficiary still received the gift even if the beneficiary contested the will and lost. A true no-contest or forfeiture clause went beyond a mere threat and actually delivered the punishment; that is, the unsuccessful contesting beneficiary sacrificed the gift under the will. In modern practice, the terms are synonymous.

Sample In Terrorem Provision

If any beneficiary under this will [or the trust created herein] contests or challenges this will [or trust] or any of its [their] provisions in any manner, be it directly or indirectly (including the filing of a will contest action), all benefits given to the contesting or challenging beneficiary are revoked and those benefits pass under the terms of this will as if the contesting beneficiary predeceased me without descendants.

Most jurisdictions uphold forfeiture provisions although several deem them invalid. Even if in terrorem provisions are valid and enforceable, they are unpopular with the courts and are strictly construed. Courts avoid forfeiture unless the beneficiary's conduct comes squarely within the conduct the testator prohibited in the will. Courts frequently treat the beneficiary's suit as one to construe or interpret the will, rather than as one to contest the will, to avoid triggering a forfeiture.

No-contest provisions are often justified on the basis that "they allow the intent of the testator to be given full effect and avoid vexatious litigation, often among members of the same family. Such contests often result in considerable waste of the estates and hard feelings that can never be repaired."[5] On the other hand, the enforcement of an in terrorem provision may be against public policy under certain circumstances. For example, a no-contest provision would be a powerful tool in the hands of a person who fraudulently or through undue influence procured the execution of a will naming the person as one of the beneficiaries of the estate. The clause may give the evil-doer an increased chance of success by terrorizing potential contestants who are also given substantial benefits under the will.

Many jurisdictions have cases or statutes limiting the scope of in terrorem provisions so that forfeiture does not occur if the beneficiary contests the will in good faith and with probable cause. See UPC §§2-517 & 3-905. Courts support the good faith/probable cause exception on several grounds. First, the testator would not have intended to preclude a contest under such circumstances; and second, enforcing the clause would be contrary to public policy if the beneficiary had a legitimate basis for bringing the contest. Nonetheless, a few courts hold that a general condition against contest is enforceable regardless of the contestant's good faith or the existence of probable cause.

Example 10-21. In Terrorem Provision

Testator, a married person with two children from a former marriage, anticipates a distributable estate of $300,000. Assume that Spouse and each child

---

5. Gunter v. Pogue, 672 S.W.2d 840, 842-843 (Tex. Ct. App. 1984).

would receive $100,000 under the applicable state intestacy statute if Testator dies without a valid will. Also assume that Testator's estate is not subject to a forced share statute. Testator's wishes are, however, considerably different; Testator desires to leave the bulk of the estate to the children. How much property, if any, should Testator consider leaving to Spouse?

Explanation

For a no-contest provision to deter a will contest effectively, it must be carefully drafted to place the disgruntled beneficiary at significant risk. If Testator leaves nothing to Spouse, or only a relatively small amount, e.g., $5,000, an in terrorem provision will have little impact on Spouse because Spouse gains tremendously if the will is invalid and loses little if the will and accompanying no-contest provision are upheld. In other words, Spouse is likely to risk a sure $5,000 for a potential $100,000. However, if Testator leaves Spouse a substantial sum, e.g., $50,000, Spouse will hesitate to forfeit a guaranteed $50,000 for fear of taking nothing if the will is upheld, even though the spouse would receive a $100,000 intestate share if the will is invalidated. And, of course, Spouse would not really receive $100,000 because most attorneys take will contest cases on a contingency basis so Spouse is likely to net only about $65,000. Most people in Spouse's position would think long and hard before risking $50,000 for $65,000.

The in terrorem clause should indicate the conduct triggering forfeiture. Does the testator wish to prevent only a will contest or is the testator's intent to prohibit a broader range of conduct? Does forfeiture occur upon the filing of a contest action or must actual judicial proceedings first occur? Is an indirect attack (e.g., where a beneficiary assists another person's contest) punishable the same as a direct attack? Will a contest by one beneficiary cause other beneficiaries to forfeit their gifts (e.g., five beneficiaries/heirs are left a significant sum but less than intestacy, one of them agrees to take the risk of contest because the other four secretly agree to make up the loss if the contest fails)? Will a beneficiary's challenge to the appointment of the designated executor trigger forfeiture?

The testator should name an alternate recipient of the property that is subject to forfeiture under a no-contest provision. This provides someone with a strong interest in upholding the will and the forfeiture provision. This contingent beneficiary, especially if it is a large charity able to elicit the support of the state's attorney general, may be able to place significant resources into fighting the contest. In addition, the law of some states require a gift over for an enforceable no-contest provision.

Although the enforceability of an in terrorem provision that provides that it operates despite the contestant's good faith and probable cause may be uncertain under local law, the clause should contain an express statement of the testator's intent in this regard. The beneficiaries and the court will then have better evidence of the testator's intent, and the court can focus on the clause's legal effect rather than on a determination of the testator's wishes.

§10.8.2   Statement of Reasons for Disposition

The testator may include in the will an explanation of the reasons motivating particular dispositions. For example, a parent could indicate that a larger portion of the estate is being left to a certain child because that child is mentally challenged, requires expensive medical care, supports many children, or is still in school. If the testator makes a large charitable donation, the reasons for benefiting that particular charity may be set forth along with an explanation that family members have sufficient assets of their own. The effectiveness of this technique is based on the assumption that disgruntled heirs are less likely to contest if they realize the reasons for receiving less than their fair (intestate) share.

It is possible, however, for this technique to backfire. The explanation may upset some heirs, especially if they disagree with the facts or reasons given, and thus spur them to contest the will. Likewise, the explanation may provide the heirs with material to bolster claims of lack of capacity or undue influence.

Example 10-22.   Statement of Reasons for Disposition

Testator had two children, Son and Daughter. Testator's will states, "I leave 80% of my estate to Son because Son has frequently visited me in my old age and I am very appreciative of his kindness and consideration. I leave 20% of my estate to Daughter." How might this explanation actually serve to encourage a will contest?

Explanation

If the statement is true, Daughter may use it as evidence that the visiting child unduly influenced the parent into making the lopsided disposition. In addition, if the explanation is factually incorrect because Daughter also visited Testator on a regular basis, Daughter may contest on grounds ranging from insane delusion to mistake or assert that the will was conditioned on the truth of the stated facts.

§10.8.3 Mean-Spirited Language

Example 10-23. Mean-Spirited Language

Testator's will contained the following provision.

> To my grandson . . . I give and bequeath the sum of ten Dollars ($10.00). I have already given my said grandson the sum of One Thousand Dollars ($1,000.00) which he squandered. This provision is no different than that I have made for my said grandson in preceding wills over a number of years and expresses the regard in which I hold my said grandson, who deserted his mother and myself by taking sides against me in a lawsuit, and because he is a slacker, having shirked his duty in World War II.[6]

How might this language encourage Grandson to contest the will?

Explanation

An heir who feels slighted both emotionally and monetarily may be more likely to contest than one who is hurt only financially. Testator's language is filled with bitterness and spite and even if it is factually correct, it is likely to cause a contest so Grandson can receive a bigger share of estate and remove the aspersions cast on his reputation. In addition, Testator's estate may be liable for *testamentary libel* once the will is probated and made part of the public record. Courts addressing the issue of testamentary libel have reached varying conclusions. Some courts simply delete the offensive material from the probated will, while others hold the estate liable for the damages caused by the libelous material. Other courts, however, rule that there is no cause of action for testamentary libel because statements relating to judicial proceedings are privileged or because actions for personal injuries against the testator died along with the testator.

§10.8.4 Holographic Will

A will entirely in the testator's own handwriting often benefits from an aura of validity because it shows that the testator was sufficiently competent to choose the testator's own words and to write them down without outside assistance. You may use the courts' somewhat liberal attitude toward holographic wills to good advantage if you anticipate a will contest. Before

---

6. Kleinschmidt v. Matthieu, 266 P.2d 686, 687 (Or. 1954).

executing a detailed formal will, the testator could handwrite a will which, although not as comprehensive as the formal will, contains a disposition plan preferred to intestacy. Depending on the applicable state law, this will may or may not need attesting witnesses. If the formal will is invalidated, the holographic will could serve as an unrevoked prior will. See §5.4.3, above.

§10.8.5   *Affidavit Acquisition*

One of the most convincing types of evidence of a testator's capacity is testimony from individuals who observed the testator at or around the time the testator executed the will. Frequently, however, this testimony is unavailable at the time of the will contest action; the witnesses to the will may be dead, difficult to locate, or lack a good recollection of the testator. The same may be true of other individuals who had personal, business, or professional contacts with the testator. One way of preserving this valuable evidence is to obtain affidavits from these people detailing the testator's conduct, physical and mental condition, and related matters. Affidavits of attesting witnesses, individuals who spoke with the testator on a regular basis, or health care providers (e.g., doctors, psychiatrists, nurses) who examined the testator close to the time of will execution, will protect this potentially valuable testimony for use should a will contest arise. Even if applicable evidentiary rules would not permit these affidavits to be used as evidence, they would still be helpful for other purposes such as to locate witnesses and refresh recollections.

§10.8.6   *Transaction Documentation*

Under normal circumstances, the testator orally explains the desired disposition plan along with the reasons, you explain the testator's options, and then you prepare a draft of the will. After reviewing the will, the testator makes oral corrections, and you prepare the final version. This procedure supplies little in the way of documentation that can be admitted into evidence in a will contest action. If a contest is anticipated, all of these steps should be documented in writing, on videotape, or both. For example, the testator could write you a letter explaining the disposition scheme and motivating factors behind it. Your written reply would warn that a contest may occur because of the disinheritance of prospective heirs, unequal treatment of children, excessive restrictions on gifts, etc. The testator would respond in writing that the testator has considered these factors but prefers to have property pass as originally indicated. You would then carefully preserve these documents for use should a contest arise.

§10.8.7 Evidence Preservation

Gathering evidence to rebut a will contest is always easier while the testator is alive. For example, the testator may have letters from a child showing family discord supporting the testator's reasons for disinheriting the child. The testator's medical records, which you may collect after the testator signs a release, may also help provide additional proof of the testator's capacity.

§10.8.8 Videotape Will Execution Ceremony

Modern videotape technology provides an inexpensive, convenient, and reliable method of preserving evidence of the will execution ceremony and its important components. A properly prepared videotape can be used to establish testamentary capacity, testamentary intent, compliance with will formalities, the contents of the will, lack of undue influence or fraud, and even the correct interpretation or construction of the will if the tape recorded the testator explaining the provisions. This technique is gaining in popularity as states, either by case law or statute, begin to formulate guidelines for the use of these tapes as evidence in a will contest action.

A videotape of the will execution ceremony has many potential advantages. It is highly accurate, unlike witnesses whose memories and impressions fade with the passage of time. The tape improves the ability of the court or jury to evaluate the testator's condition by preserving valuable nonverbal evidence such as demeanor, voice tone and inflection, facial expressions, and gestures. The tape may also have psychological benefits for both the testator and the survivors. The testator may feel more confident that the intended dispositive plan will take effect and the survivors may gain solace from viewing the testator delivering a final message.

Despite the significant benefits of a will execution videotape, there are several potential problems. In some cases, you can take steps to reduce or eliminate these problems, while in other situations the prudent decision would be to forgo taping the ceremony. Although a situation may otherwise seem appropriate for videotaping, you may be hesitant to expose the testator to the court. An accurate picture of the testator may lead a judge or jury to conclude that the testator was incompetent or unduly influenced. Similarly, bias against the testator may exist because of the testator's outward appearance: the testator's age, sex, race, disability, or annoying habits may prejudice some individuals. There is also a possibility that someone might alter the videotape. The alteration could be accidental through inadvertent erasure or exposure to a strong magnetic field. Careful storage procedures, however, greatly reduce these risks. Intentional alteration through skillful editing and dubbing may also occur, although a videotape is more difficult to alter than a written document.

§10.8.9 Preservation of Prior Will

When a testator executes a new will, it is common practice to physically destroy prior wills. If the testator's capacity is in doubt, however, and the testator indicates a preference for the prior will compared to intestacy, it is a good idea to retain the prior will. If a court holds that the new will is invalid, the old will may be offered for probate much to the chagrin of the contestant.

§10.8.10 Repeated Wills

If a will contest is successful, the estate passes under a prior will, or if none, via intestacy. You may want to preserve a prior will if the testator prefers its dispositive scheme to intestacy. Of course, the testator clearly prefers the new will to both the old will and intestacy. Thus, you may have the testator execute a new will containing the same provisions on a regular basis, for example, once every six months. At the time of the testator's death, the most recent will would be offered for probate. If a contest is successful, then the will executed six months prior would be introduced. If that one is likewise set aside, the will executed one year prior would be introduced, and so on until all wills are exhausted. A potential contestant might forgo a contest when the contestant realizes that sufficient reasons for contest would have to be proved for many different points in time.

§10.8.11 Traditional Disposition

Unusual dispositions, such as those disinheriting close family members, treating like-situated children differently, and imposing excessive restrictions on gifts, are apt to trigger contests. Therefore, you may wish to suggest that the testator consider toning down the disposition plan to bring it closer to conforming to a traditional arrangement. Of course, the client may balk at this recommendation. You would need to explain that although this may cause the testator to deal with property in an undesired way, it may reduce the motives for a contest and thus increase the chances of the will being uncontested. (Or stated another way, half a loaf is better than no loaf at all.) Alternatively, other estate planning techniques may be used to make unconventional dispositions.

§10.8.12 Nonprobate Transfers

A testator who anticipates a will contest should consider using other estate planning techniques to supplement the will. Inter vivos gifts, either outright or in trust, multiple-party accounts, and life insurance, annuities, and other death benefit plans are just some of the alternative techniques available. See Chapters 13-17, below. Although these arrangements may be set aside on grounds similar to those for contesting a will, such as lack of capacity or undue influence, they may be more difficult for a contestant to undo. More people may be involved with the creation or administration of these nonprobate arrangements, thereby providing a greater number of individuals competent to testify about the testator's mental condition. In addition, the contestant may be estopped from contesting certain arrangements if the contestant has already accepted benefits as, for example, a beneficiary of a trust.

§10.8.13 Simultaneous Gift to Heir

The testator may wish to make an inter vivos gift, either outright or in trust, to a disinherited heir apparent at the same time the will is executed (i.e., minutes after will execution). This gift should be substantial but, of course, far less than the amount the heir apparent would take via intestacy. After the testator's death, the heir is less likely to contest the will on the basis of lack of testamentary capacity. If the contestant asserted lack of capacity, the contestant would be forced to concede that the contestant accepted property from a person who lacked the capacity to make a gift or establish a trust. In addition, should the contest succeed, the heir would be required to return any property already received to the estate or use it to offset the intestate share.

§10.8.14 Contract Not to Contest

The testator and the potential contestant may enter into a contract in which the contestant contractually relinquishes all rights to contest, take under a will, take under intestacy, claim homestead or other exempt property in exchange for an immediate cash payment or other consideration. This contract should then prevent the potential contestant from interfering with the probate of the will or the administration of the estate.

§10.8.15 Ante-Mortem Probate

The post-mortem probate model prevalently used in the United States contains a glaring deficiency. The key witness — the testator — is deceased, leaving the courts with only indirect evidence of the testator's capacity and freedom from undue influence. The relative ease with which individuals dissatisfied with the testator's choice of beneficiaries may manipulate this indirect evidence encourages spurious will contests. Though the methods already discussed in this section are helpful, these techniques continue to fall short of the optimal solution — having the testator physically present for observation and examination at the probate proceeding. Ante-mortem probate offers this solution.

Only three states, Arkansas, North Dakota, and Ohio, permit a testator to reap the benefits of offering the will for probate while the testator is still alive. The statutes in these states are based on the *contest model* of ante-mortem probate and operate basically as follows. The testator executes a will and then asks for a declaratory judgment ruling the will valid, that all technical formalities were satisfied, that the testator had the required testamentary capacity to execute a will, and was not under undue influence. The beneficiaries of the will and the heirs apparent are given notice so they may contest the probate of the will. If the court finds that the new will is valid, it will be effective to dispose of the testator's property when the testator dies unless the testator makes a new will or otherwise revokes the will.

Commentators have suggested two other models of ante-mortem probate. Like the contest model, the *conservatorship model* is built on a declaratory judgment base. The testator would petition the court for a declaration of the will's validity, and notice would be given to all the beneficiaries and heirs apparent. In addition, a guardian ad litem would be appointed to represent these interested parties as well as unborn and unascertained beneficiaries and heirs. Thus, there would be no opportunity for an heir apparent or beneficiary to contest the ante-mortem probate; the guardian ad litem would represent these individuals. In ascertaining whether the testator had the required mental capacity to make a will, the judge would evaluate the results of a medical examination of the testator and other relevant evidence prior to rendering a decision.

Departing from both the contest and conservatorship models, the *administrative model* is based on an ex parte proceeding rather than an adversarial action. The ante-mortem probate would begin in the same manner; that is, the testator would petition the court for a declaration that the will complies with all necessary formalities, that the testator had the requisite capacity, and there was no undue influence. The court would then appoint a guardian ad litem. Unlike proceedings under the conservatorship model, however, the guardian would act for the court to determine facts, rather than represent the individual interests of the heirs apparent or beneficiaries. The guardian would interview the testator and others to ascertain the testator's capacity and freedom from undue influence. Because of this arrangement, notice to the heirs apparent or to others would not be required; the court would examine the evidence brought forth by the guardian ad litem in deciding whether the will is entitled to ante-mortem probate.

§10.8.16 Family Settlement Agreement

Regardless of how many will contest techniques the testator uses, a will contest may nonetheless be filed. Instead of litigating the controversy, the heirs and beneficiaries may enter into a family settlement agreement. Under this contractual arrangement, each party gives up all other claims to the decedent's estate in exchange for a portion of the estate as provided in the agreement. Even though this agreement may result in a property distribution that is considerably different from the one the testator anticipated, courts are very prone to approve them because they avoid costly and time-consuming litigation which is disruptive to family harmony. See UPC §§3-1101 & 3-1102. For a discussion of the analogous situation of using settlements to resolve trust litigation, see §20.10.2.4, below.

11

Other Will Issues

In this final chapter of the wills portion of the book, we discuss a variety of other issues that arise in the context of wills and testate succession. These issues are important and some, such as disclaimers, arise with some frequency even though they do not fit into any of our previous discussions.

§11.1 Conditional Wills

A testator may condition the effectiveness of a will on the occurrence or nonoccurrence of a stated event or the truth of a given statement; for example, the cause of the testator's death, the date of the testator's death, the testator's marital status at the time of death, the identity of the United States president when the testator dies, and so on. If the condition is not satisfied, the will has no effect and the testator's property passes under the provisions of a prior unrevoked will or via intestate succession.

If there is doubt regarding the testator's intent, courts typically construe wills as unconditional to prevent the testator from dying intestate. Thus, courts interpret a declaration of the reason the testator made a will as a mere statement of the inducement or motive for writing the will, not as a condition to its effectiveness.

Example 11-1.   Conditional Wills—Actual Condition

The introductory clause of Diane's will provides, "This will is effective only if I die due to injuries suffered in an airplane accident." Diane died in a car accident. Is Diane's will effective?

Explanation

Diane's will is not effective because her death did not result from an airplane accident. The quoted language clearly imposes a condition, that is, the will is effective "only if" her death occurs in the specified manner.

Example 11-2. Conditional Wills — Statement of Inducement

The introductory clause of Joe's will provides, "I am going into the hospital for heart bypass surgery. I am afraid I might die as a result of this operation and thus I make this my last will and testament." The operation is a complete success and Joe dies twenty years later from lung cancer. Is Joe's will effective?

Explanation

Joe's will is effective because the quoted language is a statement of inducement. The language merely states the reason that triggered Joe to make a will at that particular time. Joe's statement of inducement does not condition the effectiveness of his will upon his dying from the heart surgery. The same analysis would apply if Joe's will had said, "I am going to spend three months on space station Mir and I am afraid I may not make it back alive," and Joe returns in good shape and dies later from some other cause.

§11.2 Conditional Gifts

The testator may condition a specified gift (rather than the entire will) on the occurrence or nonoccurrence of a stated event, the conduct of the beneficiary, or the truth of a given statement.[1] There are two basic types of conditions. The first is a *condition precedent*, which means the event must occur before the beneficiary may claim the gift. For example, "I leave $40,000 to Elizabeth Young if she is at least twenty-five years old at the time of my death." The second is a *condition subsequent*, where the beneficiary keeps the gift until the condition is violated. The violation then operates to divest the beneficiary of the property. For example, "I leave my house to Elizabeth Young, but if she is convicted of any crime, then the house passes to Sam Underwood." Courts favor vested interests and thus ambiguous conditions are usually construed as subsequent. Courts will carry out the testator's intent as reflected by both types of conditions unless to do so would be illegal or against public policy.

---

1. Gifts conditioned on a beneficiary not contesting a will are discussed in §10.8.1, above.

Example 11-3. Conditional Gifts — Statement of Use

One of the provisions of Tim's will reads, "I leave my house and land in the Rocky Mountains to Nancy Karns, it being understood that Nancy will use it as a home for her family." After Tim's death, Nancy does not use the property as her home although she does spend some time there skiing in the winter and hiking in the summer. May Nancy retain the property?

Explanation

Most courts would not consider Tim's devise to Nancy to be a conditional gift. Merely stating that the property is to be used for a particular purpose does not impose a condition on the gift. Instead, the statement reflects Tim's motive for making the devise and thus is precatory in nature. See §9.7, above. However, if Tim had continued with language making a gift over, for example, "If Nancy does not use the property as her home, I leave the property to David Anderson," the likelihood of a court deeming the devise to be conditional is substantially increased.

Example 11-4. Conditional Gifts — Personal Habits of Beneficiary[2]

Marin Cemenescu's will left his house and $30,000 estate to his wife, Aneta, on the condition that she smoke five cigarettes per day for the rest of her life. Marin's will went on to say that his wife "could not stand to see me with a cigarette in my mouth and I ended up smoking in the bathroom like a schoolboy. . . . My life was hell." Aneta does not want to smoke. Will the court enforce the condition in Marin's will?

Explanation

Courts are prone to uphold conditions based on personal habits. For example, if Marin had conditioned the gift on Aneta quitting smoking, there is a good chance a court would enforce the condition. However, forcing a beneficiary to do something dangerous to her health as a condition to receiving the property is a different matter. A court could easily decide that it would not enforce this condition. If a court so held, it would then need to decide on the appropriate remedy. Would it allow Aneta to take the property in direct opposition to Marin's intent or would the court merely void the gift and let the property pass under the remaining provisions of the will or, if none, via intestacy? Some courts make this determination based on

---

2. See *Widow Fumes at Order to Start Smoking,* San-Antonio Express-News, Sept. 10, 1993, at 6A.

how they classify the condition. If the condition is treated as subsequent, that is, Aneta has the property unless she fails to smoke, the condition is disregarded and Aneta retains the property. However, if the condition is deemed precedent, that is, Aneta must smoke before being entitled to the property, the gift fails because the condition is not met. On the other hand, many courts sidestep this type of technical analysis and simply make the decision they feel best comports with public policy on a case-by-case basis.

Example 11-5. Conditional Gifts — Marriage

Betty's will left her home and $50,000 to Donald on the condition that he remain single after her death. Donald has just married. Does Donald forfeit his gifts?

Explanation

The court decisions, from early common law to the present, do not provide a clear resolution to this problem. Originally, different rules existed for personal and real property. The common law judges deemed marriage conditions valid for real property but the ecclesiastical decisions considered the restraints invalid for personal property. Later English decisions distinguished conditions that limited the gift until marriage, which were valid, from those that terminated an interest upon marriage, which were invalid.

Modern courts seldom apply these types of mechanical rules but rather look at the policies involved. Is Betty's gift designed to provide extra support for Donald until he is married, at which time he and his spouse are on their own? Or, is the gift designed to restrain marriage and punish Donald for getting married? Courts examine a wide variety of facts in making their decisions. A key fact is the relationship between Betty and Donald. If Betty is actually Donald's wife, the condition has a greater chance of being upheld. Another relevant concern is whether Betty's will contained a gift over upon Donald's marriage. If it did, courts are more likely to enforce the condition. If the condition were narrower, that is, not terminating the gift upon all marriages but only upon certain marriages (e.g., before a stated number of years after Betty's death or to a person of a certain religion), the condition is again more likely to be valid.

Example 11-6. Conditional Gifts — Divorce

Father's will contained the following provision: "I leave Wayne, my son, $250,000 if he divorces his wife within six months of my death." Can Wayne receive this legacy without divorcing his wife?

Explanation

Many courts would invalidate the condition deeming it against public policy for Father to encourage Wayne's divorce. A slight change of wording, however, could increase the chances of courts enforcing the condition. Assume that the will read, "I leave Wayne, my son, $250,000 if his wife divorces him within six months of my death." A court might uphold this provision arguing that it reflects Father's intent of providing financial support in the stressful situation that often follows a divorce, rather than for the gift to be a reward for getting divorced.

§11.3 Combination Wills

Combination wills involve more than one person in their making. This section discusses the three common types of combination wills: (1) joint wills, (2) reciprocal wills, and (3) contractual wills.

§11.3.1 Joint Wills

A *joint will* is a single testamentary instrument that contains the wills of two or more persons, such as a husband and wife.

Example 11-7. Joint Wills

Husband and Wife consult you for their estate plan. Each spouse wishes to leave the entire estate to the other. Upon the death of the survivor, all property is to be divided equally among the children. Should you use a joint will to save the time and expense of preparing two wills?

Explanation

In modern practice, joint wills are rarely, if ever, appropriate. The inconvenience of preparing two documents is minimal due to the widespread use of computers. The expense, delay, and opportunity for error that existed when each will had to be individually typed or handwritten are no longer significant factors.

Problems with joint wills include (1) the difficulty of one party revoking the will by physical act if the other party does not agree, (2) the dilemma of filing the original will for probate when the second party dies because the original was previously turned over to a court, perhaps in a different county, state, or country, when the first party died, and (3) an increased likelihood of claims that the will is contractual in nature. See §11.3.3, below.

§11.3.2 Reciprocal or Mutual Wills

Reciprocal or *mutual wills* are separate wills that contain parallel dispositive provisions. For example, Wife's will leaves all her property to Husband, but if Husband predeceases, to the children equally; Husband's will leaves all his property to Wife, but if Wife predeceases, to the children equally. Reciprocal wills, often called *sweetheart wills,* are very common, especially in "traditional" families where the spouses have been married only to each other and there are no children from other partners. Under modern law, there are no significant problems with reciprocal wills except for the concern that beneficiaries of the first to die's will may claim that the wills were contractual in nature if the survivor attempts to change the survivor's will. See §11.3.3, below.

§11.3.3 Contractual Wills

The term *contractual will* refers to a will that is either (a) executed in whole or in part as the consideration for a contract, or (b) not revoked as the consideration for a contract. The contract must meet all the requirements for a valid contract under applicable state law. Some courts even add additional elements such as requiring the contract to be fair and reasonable.

The threshold issue is how to establish whether the will is contractual. At common law, litigants could use a wide array of evidence in addition to the will itself to establish that the testator executed (or did not revoke) the will pursuant to a contract. Courts commonly admitted extrinsic evidence, both written and oral, in their attempt to determine the contractual nature of a will. This led to considerable litigation as well as claims that joint wills and reciprocal wills were contractual merely because they were joint or reciprocal.

To ensure that only the wills of testators who actually intend to be bound are deemed contractual, the modern trend is to require a writing to prove the contract. Some states and UPC §2-514 permit this evidence to be in the will itself or in a separate writing. Other states adopt a stricter view and require the will to state that a contract exists along with the material terms of the contract. Many states also provide that joint wills and reciprocal wills are not presumably contractual.

Sample Contractual Will Provision[3]

So that no contention may arise concerning the same, when we or either of us be dead, we do hereby each mutually in consideration of

---

3. Adapted from Coffman v. Woods, 696 S.W.2d 386 (Tex. App. — Houston [14th Dist.] 1985, writ ref'd n.r.e.).

the other making this will, and of the provisions made herein in each other's behalf, make this our last will and testament and agree that the same cannot be changed or varied by either without the consent in writing of the other.

To avoid the unintended creation of a contractual will, especially in states that permit extrinsic evidence to establish the contract, it is common practice to include an anticontract provision in reciprocal wills.

Sample Anticontractual Will Provision

At approximately the same time, [Spouse] and I are executing similar wills. The wills are not, however, the result of any contract or agreement between us and either will may be revoked at the sole discretion of its maker.

Example 11-8.   Contractual Wills — Revocation of Contract

Brother agreed to execute a will leaving his house to Sister if Sister wrote a will leaving Brother $100,000. The contingent beneficiary for each gift was that sibling's children. The siblings properly documented the contract under state law and executed their respective wills. Brother then got married and now wants to leave the house to his new bride. May Brother revoke the contract?

Explanation

The majority view is that the contract is unilaterally revocable while all contracting parties are alive. However, the law in many states would require Brother to give notice to Sister in a timely fashion so she has the opportunity to change her will once she realizes she will not be receiving the house. If Sister predeceased Brother, the contract would be irrevocable. It would be unfair for Brother to receive the legacy and then leave the house to his wife.

Example 11-9.   Contractual Wills — Disposition of Subject Property

Assume that Brother from the above example simply made an inter vivos gift of the house to his wife. Brother died with a will leaving the house to Sister but the gift adeemed because it was not in the estate. Does Sister have a remedy?

Explanation

Courts have addressed this situation in various ways. Some courts consider Brother as a constructive life tenant without power to transfer the property.

Other courts look at the entirety of the facts to see what Brother and Sister intended. Alternatively, perhaps Sister could breach her part of the contract and change her will without liability to Brother's children.

Example 11-10.   Contractual Wills — Revocation of Will

Assume that Brother from the above examples did not concern himself with the contract or the property and simply changed his will without telling Sister. What result if Brother dies first?

Explanation

Brother's revocation of the will is effective. As long as Brother is alive and competent, he can revoke his will. However, the revocation would be a breach of the contract. In this type of situation where the subject of the contract is a specified item, the most common remedy would be a constructive trust to prevent the unjust enrichment of his wife. See Chapter 23, below.

Example 11-11.   Contractual Wills — Service Contracts

Burgess and Nicole entered into a contract valid under state law. The contract provided that Nicole would take care of Burgess in his declining years. In exchange for these home care services, Nicole would not be paid but instead would receive his house and $100,000 under Burgess's will. Nicole took excellent care of Burgess for over ten years but he neglected to execute the will. Consequently, Nicole received no compensation, other than room and board, for her services, either while Burgess was alive or under his will. What remedy is available to Nicole?

Explanation

Nicole's most likely remedy would be for *quantum meruit* for the reasonable value of her services. Some courts will presume that the value of the services is the amount of the gift she was supposed to receive. Home care contracts are gaining in popularity. Older individuals find these types of arrangements desirable because they do not have to part with any property while alive. However, there have been many reports of physical and emotional abuse by the caregivers in these situations. Whether abuse is anecdotal or widespread is unknown because of the lack of empirical data. Persons in Burgess's position should take precautions such as completing a background investigation of the prospective care provider and designating a third party to check on the quality of care on a regular basis. Many practitioners advise against contractual wills in this situation. They recommend that Burgess make an inter vivos conveyance of the property to a trustee who would transfer the property to Nicole upon Burgess's death only if her level of care were adequate. In this way, both Nicole and Burgess are protected.

§11.4 Election Will[4]

An *election will* is a will that attempts to give away property the testator does not own but is instead owned by a beneficiary of the will. The beneficiary must make an election between two alternatives. First, the beneficiary could *elect against the will*. The testator cannot give away the beneficiary's property without the beneficiary's consent. Thus, the beneficiary could retain the property that the testator attempted to give away. However, the beneficiary is then precluded from accepting any of the benefits under the will. Second, the beneficiary could *elect to take under the will*. The beneficiary may now receive the benefits under the will but must renounce every right inconsistent with the will. In other words, the beneficiary must consent to the will's disposition of the beneficiary's property as a condition of enjoying any benefits under that will.

Example 11-12. Election Will — Non-Spouse

Testator had been upset for years that Testator's father gave a family heirloom to Testator's brother. In one last attempt for "justice," Testator included in the will the following dispositive provision, "I give the Fawn statue sculpted in Venice, Italy, by Columbo, which my father gave to Bob, my brother, to Son. I leave $100,000 to my brother, Bob. I leave the rest of my estate to Daughter." What is the proper distribution of Testator's estate?

Explanation

This will triggers an election because it attempts to give away property belonging to a beneficiary. Thus, Bob has a choice. Bob may either transfer the statue to Son and then take the legacy or retain the statue and forfeit the legacy. If Bob elects this latter option, the legacy would fail and the money would pass to Daughter under the residuary clause. Son would get nothing.

Although election wills may occur with any property owner/will beneficiary, the most common use of an election will is between spouses who live in a community property marital property jurisdiction. In the typical case, the wage-earning spouse does not approve of the non-wage-earning spouse owning half of the community. In addition, the wage-earning spouse wants

---

4. Compare this type of will with the election that a surviving spouse may need to make between taking the gifts under the deceased spouse's will or a forced share determined according to a statutory formula. See §7.1.1.2, above.

to control how the entire community passes upon the death of the surviving spouse, especially if the wage-earning spouse has children from a prior relationship. Thus, this spouse attempts to control the entire community by coercing the non-wage-earning spouse into agreeing to the wage-earning spouse's disposition plan. The wage-earning spouse's will would not merely dispose of that spouse's separate property and share of community, but instead would purport to dispose of all of the community property. The surviving spouse might consent to this if the will gives that spouse a significant interest in the deceased spouse's community or separate property.

Example 11-13. Election Wills — Community Property Jurisdiction

Testator's will provides the following, "I leave all the community property and all my separate property in trust for the benefit of Spouse during Spouse's lifetime. Upon Spouse's death, all remaining property passes to Albert, my son." Albert is Testator's son from a prior relationship. What is the property distribution of Testator's estate?

Explanation

The first step in the analysis of this example is to determine whether Testator's will actually creates an election situation. Most courts hold that a will requires an election only if the will is open to no other construction. If there is another way to interpret the will, that way is preferred. The key language in Testator's will is "all the community property." Although not as clear as a statement such as, "I leave both my share and my spouse's share of the community property," many courts would hold that Testator's will describes the surviving spouse's share of community because of the reference to "all the" community property. Note that phrases such as "all my estate" or "all my property" are easily interpreted as referring only to property owned by Testator. Assuming this is an election will, Spouse must decide what Spouse would prefer. Does Spouse want to retain Spouse's half of the community, have the unrestricted right to use that property and determine the new owner upon Spouse's death? Or, does Spouse want the lifetime benefits from a huge conglomeration of property (all the community property and all Testator's separate property) and be willing to forgo the right to determine where Spouse's share of community property passes upon Spouse's death? A person in Spouse's position is apt to select the option that provides the most lifetime benefits.

A testator who wishes to trigger an election is advised to state that desire expressly in the will. This prevents the testator's wishes from going unfulfilled because of the reluctance of courts to find that a will triggers an election. On the other hand, the testator must be certain not to create an election where none was intended. This may happen if the testator describes an item of community property in precise terms and then disposes of that item. For example, "I leave the house at 357 Main Street to Friend" may be treated as devising the entire house, not just the testator's community share. If this will also made a gift to the surviving spouse, that spouse would be put to an election. To prevent a will from inadvertently triggering an election, an anti-election provision may be inserted in the will.

Sample Anti-Election Provision

No provision in this will shall cause any beneficiary to elect between taking property under this will and consenting to this will disposing of the beneficiary's own property. No provision of this will shall be interpreted as disposing of any property over which I do not have the right to transfer.

§11.5 Disclaimer

The beneficiary of a will may disclaim the property because a beneficiary is not obligated to accept any testamentary gift. The reasons a beneficiary may decide to disclaim and the requirements of a disclaimer are fundamentally the same as for an heir who disclaims an inheritance. See §4.4, above. If the beneficiary properly disclaims, the disclaimed property passes under the terms of the will just as if the beneficiary had predeceased the testator. The lapse discussion in §7.4, above, would then apply.

Part Three

ESTATE ADMINISTRATION

12

Estate Administration

When a person dies, some type of formal process is required for two main reasons. First, successors in interest need proof that they are indeed the new owners of the decedent's property by virtue of being heirs under the state's intestacy law or by being beneficiaries under the decedent's valid will. Procedures to establish title are relatively simple and often do not require a full estate administration. Second, the decedent's creditors need to be paid. In a sense, death is like going bankrupt. Estate administration ensures that creditors get paid to the fullest extent possible. However, state statutes often shield a portion of the decedent's estate from the claims of creditors to protect the decedent's surviving spouse and minor children.

An estate administration begins with the personal representative collecting all of the decedent's probate assets. The personal representative preserves this property and manages it in a fiduciary capacity. The personal representative then pays the creditors and if property still remains, distributes it to the appropriate heirs or beneficiaries. The details of estate administration vary tremendously among the states. This chapter reviews the basic structure of the administration process.

§12.1 Proper Applicant

Neither the probate of the decedent's will nor an administration of the decedent's estate occurs automatically upon a person's death. Someone must start the process. Normally, this person needs a pecuniary interest by being an heir, beneficiary, or creditor. In some situations, however, a person without an interest may be able to request a temporary arrangement to protect the decedent's property from being dissipated because no one is managing or safeguarding the property.

§12.2   Locate Will

The applicant needs to determine whether the decedent died with a valid will. A careful search is needed to either (1) locate the will, or (2) conclude that the decedent is unlikely to have died testate because a reasonable search did not turn up a will. There are four basic categories of locations where the decedent's will might be found.

(1) Decedent's Home or Office.   The decedent may have retained the will and kept it at home or at the decedent's office. Thus, the applicant should search common storage locations such as filing cabinets, desk drawers, and spiritual books (e.g., Bible, Koran, or Torah). Some testators carefully hide their wills and thus it may take some ingenuity to find them.

(2) Safe Deposit Box.   Instead of keeping the will at home, the testator may have placed the will in a safe deposit box at a bank or other financial institution. Many states have statutes allowing relatively rapid access to the decedent's safe deposit box to locate the decedent's will as well as other documents that need to be found quickly such as a burial plot deed and life insurance policies.

(3) Significant Individuals.   The testator may have transferred possession of the will to someone whom the testator trusted to bring the will forth upon the testator's death. Common repositories for the will include the testator's family members, close friends, the person named as the executor, and the attorney who drafted the will. State law usually requires anyone in possession of a decedent's will to turn that will over to the court or to someone who intends to probate the will. See UPC §2-516.

(4) Clerk of the Court.   Many states permit a testator to deposit the will with the clerk of the court for safekeeping. The clerk files the will in a secure location and then turns the will over to an authorized person or the court upon the testator's death. See UPC §2-515.

§12.3   Prepare Application

The person who desires to initiate the probate or administration process must prepare an application meeting state law requirements. The application may be lengthy and may require the applicant to recite assorted information about the decedent, the decedent's property, the applicant, and the heirs or beneficiaries.

§12.4 File in Appropriate Court

The applicant takes the application, the original will (if any), and the appropriate filing fee (typically between $50 and $150) to the appropriate court. The applicant must make certain the court has both jurisdiction and venue over probate matters. Specialized courts may deal with probate matters. These courts are often called *probate courts, orphans' courts,* or *surrogate's courts.* In other states, courts of more general jurisdiction preside over probate matters such as county courts or district courts. Proper jurisdiction may depend on the population of the county—large urban counties are more likely to have specialized probate courts than small rural counties.

The applicant must also be sure to file in the court that has venue over the decedent's estate. Typically, venue is based on the county of the decedent's domicile at the time of the decedent's death. If the decedent owned real property in another state or country, venue for proceedings affecting title to that land will be in the other jurisdiction. These proceedings are often referred to as *ancillary administration.*

§12.5 Citation

The probate statutes of many states require the clerk of the court to give some type of notice that an administration has been requested or that a will has been filed for probate. This notice alerts interested persons to the pending action so they can contest the will or bring forth the decedent's will when an intestate administration is requested. Jurisdictions vary considerably regarding the method of citation. Some states permit a very broad type of citation such as by posting a notice on the front door of the courthouse or a nearby bulletin board. Other states require more specific notice to heirs and beneficiaries by methods such as personal service or registered or certified mail. Several states even require the beneficiaries named in the most recent will that the decedent revoked be given notice. In some states, parties who receive notice are precluded from contesting the will at a later time while in other states parties who had notice may still contest the will for a statutorily specified period. Common terms for this adversarial process of beginning estate administration after giving notice to interested persons include *solemn form probate* and *formal probate.*

Some states permit probate without the necessity of giving notice to interested persons. Accordingly, the probate process begins with an ex parte proceeding. Because potential contestants did not receive notice, they are not precluded from later bringing a will contest action unless the statute of limitations to do so has expired. Common terms for this type of proceeding include *common form probate* and *informal probate.*

Some states authorize both notice and non-notice types of probate. See UPC Article III. Thus, the applicant needs to decide which method best suits the applicant's needs in terms of expense, time commitment, finality, and resistance to later attack.

§12.6   Probate of Will or Determination of Heirs

The court conducts a hearing to decide whether the will is valid and whether an administration is necessary. As discussed in §12.5, above, this hearing may either be adversarial or ex parte depending on the type of probate. In adversarial situations, this hearing cannot occur too quickly after notice is given. Typically, one to two weeks must elapse after the notice before the court may conduct the hearing to be sure persons who want to oppose or intervene in the action have sufficient time to do so.

If the applicant is attempting to probate a will, the court must determine whether the will is valid. In the usual case where the will is accompanied by a self-proving affidavit and no one is contesting the probate, the hearing is quite brief, perhaps five minutes or less. If there is no self-proving affidavit, the hearing will take longer because the testimony of the subscribing witnesses or of individuals familiar with the testator's or witnesses' handwriting is often required. If the court finds the will valid, it is admitted to probate. The applicant may not need to ask the court to open an administration if one is not necessary. For example, there may be no unpaid debts or all the unpaid debts may be secured by real property. Simply admitting the will to probate as a *muniment of title* may be all that is necessary to document title transfer from the decedent to the beneficiaries.

If the decedent died intestate, the court will make a determination of the identity of the heirs. If there is no need for an estate administration, this *determination of heirship* may be all that is required to prove that title to property passed from the decedent to the heirs. The court will open an administration if one is necessary to pay debts or to partition property among the heirs.

A few states have adopted the civil law concept of *universal succession*. Under this procedure, property passes directly from the decedent to the heirs and beneficiaries. No formal administration is required even if the decedent had creditors. Instead, the creditors must seek payment directly from the heirs and beneficiaries.

§12.7   Type of Administration

There are many different types of estate administration and many states authorize several methods. See UPC Article III. The testator, the court, or the personal representative may have the ability to select or recommend the type of administration used for the decedent's estate.

The traditional type of administration, often called *dependent adminis-tration,* is strictly supervised by the court every step of the way from start to finish. The personal representative must get permission before taking most actions, such as selling estate assets and paying creditors, and then get those acts approved by the court after doing them. Dependent administration is cumbersome, inconvenient, costly, and time-consuming.

A more modern type of administration, *independent, informal,* or *non-intervention administration* as it is often called, allows the representative to work without court supervision unless an issue requires court involvement or an interested person, such as an heir, beneficiary, or creditor, complains about the way the representative is conducting the administration.

If the estate is small or if there are few debts, many states have short-form, summary, or abbreviated administration methods that reduce the procedures necessary to resolve creditor issues and to determine title matters.

§12.8 Appointment of Personal Representative[1]

If an administration is needed, usually because the decedent died with unpaid debts, the court will appoint a personal representative to take charge of and manage the decedent's probate assets, pay creditors, and distribute any remaining property to the heirs and beneficiaries. If the decedent died intestate, the personal representative is usually called an *administrator.* State statutes provide a list of individuals, in priority order, who are entitled to the position. This list usually begins with the intestate's surviving spouse, adult children, parents, and siblings and ends with creditors and other reputable people in the community.

If the decedent died with a valid will, the testator may have named the personal representative, called the *executor,* in the will. If the will did not name an executor, the court will appoint an *administrator with the will annexed,* also called an *administrator c.t.a. (cum testamento annexo),* to carry out the terms of the will and administer the estate.

Example 12-1. Selection of Executor — Legal Capacity and Desirable Characteristics

Shortly after receiving your law license, Client hires you to prepare a will. After carefully questioning Client about how Client wishes to dispose of

---

1. Portions of this section are adapted from Gerry W. Beyer, *Selecting Executors and Trustees,* Est. Plan. Dev. (Dec. 1994).

property, you ask Client, "Who do you want to name as your executor?" Client gives you one of those deer-in-the-headlight looks and says, "I don't know. How do I decide?" What factors do you recommend that Client consider in making this important decision?

Explanation

To start with, the executor must have legal capacity under local law to serve. The basic requirements are relatively uniform although the criteria vary among the states. For example, an individual executor must typically be (1) an adult (usually at least eighteen years of age unless the court has removed a younger person's disabilities of minority or the person is married), (2) not incompetent or incapacitated, (3) not a convicted felon, and (4) not found to be otherwise unsuitable by the court. In some states, a nonresident may not serve as an executor unless the nonresident takes special steps such as appointing a resident agent to accept service of process. If the executor is a corporation, it must comply with applicable state law. States may impose relatively few requirements on a bank or savings and loan association (e.g., merely having a corporate charter authorizing the corporation to act as a fiduciary may be sufficient) while imposing additional requirements on other types of corporations and nondomestic corporations.

The executor should have characteristics that will enhance the likelihood that the person will do a good job of administering Client's estate. The following traits are desirable:

(1) Honesty. The executor must be someone in whom Client has complete trust. If Client has any doubt regarding the potential designee's honesty or integrity, you should urge Client to select a different person.

(2) Common Sense and Good Judgment. The executor must make many discretionary decisions. Accordingly, it is important for the executor to have a good measure of common sense. The executor must act prudently and reasonably at all times.

(3) Financially Responsible. Individuals and corporations who have experienced success in their own financial matters are more likely to be able to do the same for assets managed in a fiduciary capacity. In addition, financially stable persons are usually not as motivated to embezzle estate property as are persons with fiscal troubles. Client should seek an executor who is financially solid and not involved in litigation which could lead to the individual's or corporation's bankruptcy.

(4) Investment Experience and Skill. The level of experience, skill, and knowledge needed to serve as an executor depends on the type, amount, and value of property that the executor will manage. Vastly different expertise is needed to manage diverse investments such as high-rise apartment buildings in a large city, farms, portfolios of stocks, bonds, commodity futures, derivatives, and other securities, retail businesses, and oil and gas properties.

(5) Awareness of Legal Issues. Although an executor need not be an attorney, the executor must be aware of potential legal issues or at least know that consultation with an attorney or other expert is essential.

(6) Fiduciary Personality. An individual needs to possess a special type of personality to successfully serve as an executor. For example, the executor must be calm and patient in dealing with beneficiaries, professional in working with the court, and astute at determining which creditors to pay.

(7) Longevity. An executor may need to serve for several years and perhaps decades if the estate is complex or subject to protracted litigation. Thus, the age and health of an individual executor are often important considerations. The prospect of a corporate fiduciary being in business in the future must also be taken into account.

(8) Proximity. The executor should be someone who would be geographically available to serve. For example, it is difficult for an executor living in Alaska to handle the estate of a Maine decedent.

(9) Lack of Distractions. Just like passengers who sit in airplane exit rows, an executor must be able to perform the required duties without being occupied by other concerns. If Client selects an individual, the individual (or a close member of the individual's family) should not be suffering personal problems such as an illness, a change in job, or a divorce, which could prevent the person from giving the estate the attention it requires. In a corporate setting, Client should avoid fiduciaries in the midst of mergers, takeovers, bankruptcy proceedings, or significant litigation.

(10) Prior Approval. Before naming anyone as an executor, the person should be shown a copy of the will and asked if the person would be willing to serve. It is costly, both in terms of time and money, if the named executor refuses to accept the position.

(11) Successors. Client should name at least one alternate executor in case Client's first choice is unable or unwilling to serve. Client may also specify a method for selecting a successor executor. If there are no alternates and no selection method, court action will be necessary to fill the vacancy. Client may wish to include a provision specifying under what circumstances the executor may be removed from office. This type of provision may reduce delay and court costs if a currently serving executor can no longer serve due to illness, incompetency, or dishonesty.

Example 12-2.   Selection of Executor — Individual or Corporation

Client from Example 12-1, above, listened intently as you explained the legal requirements and desirable characteristics of an executor. Client then told you that Client either wants to name Son or Bank as the executor. Client now seeks your advice as to which of these would be the better choice. What factors should Client consider in making this decision?

Explanation

Client may be motivated to select Son believing that Client is bestowing some sort of honor or privilege. This is not the case. An executor's position is tough, demanding, and filled with potentially overwhelming responsibilities, duties, and exposure to personal liability. The appointment of an executor should be a business decision, not an emotional one.

Client may obtain some important benefits by selecting an individual, such as Son, to serve as the executor. Son may be willing to serve for free unlike corporate executors who expect reasonable compensation for their services. Because Son is well-acquainted with Client, Son is likely to have knowledge of the family situation, Client's goals, and the needs and personalities of the beneficiaries. As a result, Son may be in a good position to exercise the substituted judgment which Client desires. Son may have an appreciation for certain types of estate property which Client would like to see preserved and kept in the family such as heirlooms and collectable items. Likewise, Son may be familiar with the operation of family and closely held businesses.

Client must also evaluate the potential problems that may flow from appointing Son as the executor. Son has probably never served as an executor in the past and thus is unaccustomed to carrying out the fiduciary obligations associated with estate administration. Son may lack experience in making prudent investment decisions and in managing estate assets and is less likely to be as financially solvent as Bank. In addition, Son may lack significant assets that the beneficiaries could reach to remedy a breach of fiduciary duty. Appointing Son could increase family strife if the will places Son in the position of playing favorites among Client's children (Son's siblings).

On the other hand, naming Bank as executor may be advantageous to Client. Probably the foremost advantage of naming Bank as the executor is the skill and experience the corporate fiduciary would bring to the job. Bank handles fiduciary matters on a regular basis and is well-equipped to handle the day-to-day affairs of an estate (e.g., accounting services, record keeping, allocation of receipts and expenditures between principal and income, determining the tax basis of property, filing tax returns, etc.). In addition, Bank has the ability to provide certain services without additional cost to the estate, e.g., protecting valuables in Bank's vault, providing routine administration services, rendering advice on investment and tax matters, etc. Bank also has vast experience with making prudent investments and will have investment opportunities available to it that Son would not. Client's estate would also benefit from having Bank as the executor because of Bank's continuous existence — Bank does not get sick, take vacations, have family emergencies, or die. If Bank does breach its fiduciary duties, the aggrieved beneficiaries may have a greater chance of recovery against Bank than Son. Most individuals lack sufficient nonexempt property to permit a full recovery while corporate executors typically have significant assets against which the beneficiaries may proceed.

Client must also consider the disadvantages of naming Bank as the executor. Bank will charge a fee for its services unlike Son who may be willing to serve without charge. However, the fee may be a small price to pay for the expertise Bank would bring to the job. Of course, if the value of Client's estate is relatively low, the fee may be prohibitive. Another concern may be Bank's lack of a rich history with Client, Client's property, and the beneficiaries, which Son would bring to the job. However, Client may be seeking a neutral or balanced approach. Bank can make unbiased decisions because it is unencumbered by the emotions and feelings of family loyalty and sympathy, which could prevent Son from making objective decisions.

Example 12-3. Selection of Executor — Co-Executors

Client from Example 12-2, above, listened to your critique of the pros and cons of naming Son and Bank as executors. Realizing the benefits of having each of these persons serving, Client asked you, "What about if I name both Son and Bank to serve as co-executors?" How would you advise Client about this alternative?

Explanation

If the court appoints more than one executor, Client's estate benefits from the experience and expertise of both Son and Bank. Better decisions may result because of the deliberation which occurs when the co-executors present and discuss multiple viewpoints. Multiple executors also provide greater protection to the estate and beneficiaries. There are built-in checks and balances because each executor should evaluate the conduct of the other executor. An evil executor will have a harder time carrying out any untoward schemes because there will be another executor watching.

Client must also consider the problems that arise upon the appointment of co-executors. For example, both executors usually must agree before they can take any action. Requiring the consent of Son and Bank may slow down the administration process even if they are in agreement simply because of the extra time and effort needed to obtain and document the consent. Another disadvantage of naming both Son and Bank is the potential of a deadlock and the paralysis that follows upon a tie vote. A costly judicial resolution of this standoff would then be needed. Client could avoid this problem by either (1) appointing an odd number of fiduciaries, or (2) providing a method for resolving tie votes. If Client appoints both Bank and Son, there is a significant likelihood of additional administrative fees because of the extra conferences, telephone calls, and paperwork that is required. Bank may even charge a higher fee if Son is a co-executor because of the additional time it usually takes to deal with an individual. Bank may also be reluctant to serve with Son for fear of liability for Son's improper acts. Normally, each co-executor is jointly and severally liable for the acts of all executors.

§12.9 Qualification of Personal Representative

Once the court appoints the personal representative, the person must take the necessary steps to formally assume office. See UPC §3-601. The personal representative must qualify before the clerk of the court can issue letters. See §12.10, below.

§12.9.1 Oath of Office

The personal representative is usually required to take an oath swearing that the representative will faithfully carry out the duties of the position. In some states, a mere statement of acceptance of the duties of office is sufficient. See UPC §3-601.

§12.9.2 Bond

The personal representative may need to post bond conditioned on the faithful performance of the representative's duties. The court sets the amount of the bond based on the value of the decedent's estate. The personal representative may deliver that amount in cash to the court; however, the personal representative typically obtains the bond from a surety company. In exchange for the payment of premiums, the surety company agrees to pay the amount of the bond to the creditors and beneficiaries if the personal representative breaches the applicable fiduciary duties. Of course, if the surety is required to pay, the surety will seek reimbursement from the personal representative.

States are divided on the bonding requirement. Some state statutes require a bond unless the will expressly waives the bond. On the other hand, some statutes do not require a bond unless the testator expressly requires it in the will or the court deems it necessary. See UPC §3-603. In addition, some states exempt corporate fiduciaries from the bonding requirement.

Example 12-4. Bond

Client from Example 12-3, above, decided to name Son as the executor. You now need to determine whether Client wants Son to post bond before Son can serve. What concerns would you bring to Client's attention to assist Client in making an informed decision?

Explanation

Bond premiums are expensive as is the court proceeding that is necessary to set the amount. Client may save these expenses by waiving the bond. The costs of the hearing and the annual bond premiums are proper estate expenses and thus reduce the amount the beneficiaries eventually receive. However, bonds do protect the beneficiaries from evil executors. Of course, if Client truly believes Son will act improperly, Client should rethink the decision to name Son in the first place.

§12.10   Issuance of Letters

After qualifying by taking the oath of office or filing a statement of acceptance and posting any necessary bond, the personal representative is entitled to letters, either *letters testamentary,* if there is a will, or *letters of administration,* in the case of an intestate decedent. Letters are typically one-page documents issued under the seal of the court that indicate the personal representative has been appointed by the court and has qualified. The personal representative may then show these as evidence of the representative's authority when dealing with estate matters or collecting estate property. Third parties who deal with a person who has letters are usually protected from liability to the heirs or beneficiaries if the executor mismanages the property. Consequently, third parties often want to retain an original letter for their files. Because the cost of letters is nominal, often under $10.00 a copy, the personal representative should estimate the number of letters needed before qualifying and obtain all the necessary letters at the same time to prevent multiple trips to the courthouse and the associated time and monetary cost.

§12.11   Collect and Protect Decedent's Probate Assets

The personal representative must collect and preserve all of the decedent's probate assets for the benefit of the creditors and the heirs or beneficiaries. The personal representative does not have title to these assets but does have a right to possess the assets that is superior to the anticipated distributees. In practice, it may require considerable effort to gain possession of estate property because family members often raid the decedent's home and remove items to which they feel they are entitled. The personal representative does not have authority over nonprobate assets such as life insurance proceeds, joint tenancy property with the survivorship feature, and pay on death bank accounts. See Chapters 13-17, below.

§12.12   Manage Decedent's Probate Assets

The personal representative must manage the decedent's probate assets. For example, the representative may need to sell or rent estate property, decide on issues regarding the management of stock portfolios, run businesses, etc. In all aspects of this management, the representative is a fiduciary and held to a high standard of care and the utmost degree of loyalty. The duties of a personal representative are very similar to those of a trustee as discussed in Chapter 20, below.

§12.13   Inventory and Appraisement

One of the typical duties of the personal representative is to prepare an inventory of all of the decedent's probate assets and indicate the fair market value of each as of the date of the decedent's death. Traditionally, the court is involved in the process of selecting professional appraisers to value the decedent's property for the personal representative. Many modern statutes, however, permit the representative to value the assets without assistance and, if necessary, to select and hire appraisers. See UPC §3-706. The inventory and appraisement helps the creditors to determine which assets are available to pay their claims and thus provides them with valuable insight into how they should proceed to have the best chance of getting paid. Additionally, the inventory helps the heirs and beneficiaries to determine the property to which they may be entitled.

Example 12-5.   Inventory

Assume that you are serving as the executor of Testator's will. You enter the Testator's house with a yellow pad and pen in hand ready to begin the inventory. You look around and see huge bookcases containing thousands of books and magazines, kitchen cabinets filled with dishes, silverware, and pots and pans, and dressers and closets brimming with clothes. How detailed should you make the inventory, that is, do you need to list each book, magazine, utensil, sock, and shirt separately?

Explanation

Inventories need to be in reasonable detail. State statutes usually permit similar items to be grouped together. Thus, it would probably be permissible to list these items by category. However, if there is an item in a particular category that is of significant value, it should be listed separately. For example, you could list all books together but if Testator owned a first edition Blackstone, that should be listed separately. Likewise, costume jewelry could be lumped together but an expensive diamond ring should be specifically listed.

§12.14 Protect Certain Property from Creditors

The surviving spouse, minor children, and, in a few states, unmarried adult children who still live at home may be able to retain some of the decedent's property free from the claims of certain creditors. This property is often in addition to the property they receive by way of intestacy or under the testator's will. State legislatures have made public policy decisions that these individuals deserve protection and that their needs outweigh the rights of the decedent's creditors to be paid and the rights of heirs and beneficiaries to receive the decedent's property. Because this property is unavailable to creditors, the personal representative is usually required to set aside the property for the benefit of the protected individuals early in the administration process.

§12.14.1 Homestead

Many jurisdictions protect the decedent's homestead, that is, the residence used by the decedent and the decedent's family. Jurisdictions vary with regard to limitations placed on the physical size of the homestead. Some states have different rules depending on whether the homestead is in an urban or rural area. In addition, some states extend homestead protection to land used in a family business or farm. State law may accord the homestead two types of special treatment. First, it may be protected from creditors and second, close family members may have a superior right to occupy the homestead.

§12.14.1.1 Creditor Protection

The surviving spouse, minor children, and dependent children may receive a portion of the homestead free from the claims of most creditors. Jurisdictions vary tremendously with regard to the amount of protection accorded the homestead. Some states protect small amounts such as $5,000 or $15,000 as under UPC §2-402. On the other hand, some states protect the entire homestead regardless of its value. If the decedent lived in rental accommodations, some states permit a statutorily specified amount of other property, such as cash, to be protected from creditors in lieu of the homestead.

§12.14.1.2 Occupancy Rights

Some states grant the surviving spouse and minor children the right to live in the homestead even if they do not receive title to it as heirs or will beneficiaries. This right, based on the ancient concept of *quarantine,* may be quite limited or extremely valuable. In some states, the occupancy right of the family members exists for a relatively short period of time such as forty days. Other states, however, give the surviving spouse the right to live in the homestead for the rest of the surviving spouse's life unless the surviving spouse voluntarily abandons the homestead. Minor children may obtain the right to remain until they reach majority.

In states with lengthy homestead occupancy rights, the decedent's heirs and beneficiaries may never actually get to enjoy the property. For example, assume that Husband and Wife married when both were eighteen years old. Wife inherited a house from her parents who died a year later. Shortly after moving into this home, Wife died. Wife's will left the house to Sister. Under the law of some states, Husband could live in the home for the rest of his life, which could easily be more than one-half of a century. Husband could even remarry and bring the new spouse into the home. During this time, which could be the rest of Sister's lifetime, Sister would be unable to benefit from her ownership of this property.

§12.14.2 *Exempt Personal Property*

The surviving spouse and minor children are often granted the right to retain certain personal property free from the claims of creditors. Jurisdictions vary considerably with regard to the type of items that are exempt. Usually, exempt personal property is tangible in nature such as home furnishings, food, clothes, jewelry, firearms, sporting equipment, cars not used for income, certain quantities of farm animals, and household pets. In some states, certain types of intangible personal property may also be exempt such as the cash surrender value of life insurance policies and current wages for personal services.

The maximum value of the exemption varies widely among the states. For example, UPC §2-403 imposes a limit of $10,000 while some states protect $50,000 or more of exempt personal property.

§12.14.3 Family Allowance

The court may have the authority to grant an allowance for the support of the surviving spouse and minor children for some statutorily provided period of time. Typically, it is the amount necessary to keep them in the style of living to which they were accustomed while the decedent was alive for one year after the decedent's death although some states authorize family allowances to be made until the administration is closed. Some states impose an upper limit on the family allowance. See UPC §2-405 (limit of $18,000 for one year).

§12.14.4 Waiver of Protections

States vary as to whether the spouse may waive rights to the homestead, exempt personal property, and the family allowance. For example, UPC §2-213 allows a waiver by a written agreement executed either before or during the marriage. Unimpeded, the rights of the surviving spouse may tremendously disrupt the deceased spouse's estate plan. Accordingly, careful consideration of homestead, exempt personal property, and the family allowance is needed every time an estate plan is prepared.

§12.15 Notice to Creditors

The personal representative must alert the decedent's creditors that the decedent has died and that the court has appointed a personal representative. This information permits the creditors to take the proper steps to present their claims so they can get paid. Jurisdictions vary with regard to how the representative gives this notice, that is, by publication, by mail, or in person. Many states require the personal representative to give the notice in a relatively timely fashion such as within one to four months of receiving letters. Some states have different procedures for different types of creditors, e.g., secured, unsecured, and government claimants such as taxing authorities.

Many states restrict the ability of a creditor to recover on a claim once the creditor receives notice. These provisions are called *nonclaim statutes*. A typical nonclaim statute provides that if a creditor does not present the creditor's claim for payment within four months after receiving notice, the creditor's claim is forever barred even if the statute of limitations on that claim has not yet expired.

In *Tulsa Professional Collection Services, Inc. v. Pope,*[2] the United States Supreme Court indicated that a creditor must receive realistic notice, such as mail service or personal service, before a nonclaim statute can constitutionally deprive a creditor of the creditor's property right to be paid. Thus, it is unlikely that publication notice to known creditors (or those who are reasonably ascertainable) is sufficient. Most state legislatures have revised their nonclaim statutes to comply with this mandate.

§12.16   Pay Creditors

After receiving the notice discussed in §12.15, above, the creditor should present the claim in a timely fashion. Typically, the creditor can present the claim either to the personal representative or the court. The representative then evaluates the claim. If the claim is valid, the representative accepts the claim. Acceptance does not mean the claim will actually be paid. Instead, it merely means that the claim is in the stack of claims to be paid if the estate ends up with sufficient property to do so. If the representative thinks the claim is bogus, the representative will reject the claim. Many states require the creditor to file suit within a relatively short period of time after rejection to preserve the creditor's ability to recover on the claim.

At the appropriate time specified by state law, such as after a certain period of time from the opening of the administration or at the end of the administration, the personal representative pays the accepted claims. Statutes provide a priority order for paying the claims if the estate is insufficient to satisfy all creditors and other claims such as the homestead, exempt personal property, and family allowance. Statutes often favor creditors who provided funeral services or medical care, the property set aside for the surviving spouse and minor children, and administration expenses.

§12.17   Provide Reports and Accountings

Many states require the personal representative, especially in court-supervised administrations, to make annual reports and accountings of all actions taken that involved estate property. These accountings may be extremely detailed and require the representative to justify every expenditure and report all

---

2. 485 U.S. 478 (1988).

income. Accountings are often under oath and must be supported by receipts documenting each reported item. The court may then conduct a hearing to determine if the report or account should be approved.

§12.18 Distribution and Closing Estate

If estate property remains after paying the creditors and other claimants, the personal representative distributes the balance to the appropriate heirs or beneficiaries. If there is insufficient estate property to satisfy all of a testator's devises and bequests, the representative determines which beneficiaries are preferred by following the abatement order. See §6.6, above. Once the representative distributes all of the decedent's property, the estate may be closed and the representative relieved of further responsibilities.

Part Four

NONPROBATE TRANSFERS

Intestacy statutes and the decedent's will can control only property included in the decedent's *probate estate*. Before distributing property under intestacy or a will, you must first determine which property is part of the probate estate and which property has its new owner determined in some other way. The law provides a vast array of property disposition methodologies that prevent property from being included in the probate estate. Typical nonprobate arrangements include joint tenancies with rights of survivorship and contracts that provide for the payment of benefits upon death to designated persons such as life insurance, retirement plans, and accounts with financial institutions (e.g., joint accounts with survivorship rights and pay on death accounts). Some of these transfers are effective during a person's lifetime while others do not result in a transfer of property ownership until the person dies.[1]

Part Four of this book focuses on nonprobate gratuitous methods of transferring property that are either effective while the decedent is alive or do not take effect until the decedent dies. Note that one of the most popular nonprobate transfers, the revocable trust, is separately covered in great detail in Part Five.

---

1. UPC §6-101 considers a wide variety of contractual arrangements as being nontestamentary in nature.

13

Reasons People Use Nonprobate Transfers

This chapter reviews the top ten reasons a person may wish to use nonprobate methods of property transfer. Please note that no particular nonprobate transfer technique can achieve all of the enumerated benefits. The list contains potential benefits that are associated with nonprobate methods in general. A particular benefit may or may not attach to the specific method in question.

Please refer to the diagram in §1.4 as you work through this chapter. This diagram places the techniques under examination into perspective.

§13.1 Provide Non-Estate Planning Benefits

Every day, people make nonprobate property transfers for a variety of reasons unrelated to estate planning. Nonprobate transfers fall generally into one of two categories: nongratuitous and gratuitous. Examples of nongratuitous transfers include to buy groceries, go out for dinner, rent videos, pay tuition, repay loans, make rent or mortgage payments, and take vacations. These types of nongratuitous transfers lack significant estate planning components, other than the fact that they change the composition of the estate, and thus are outside the scope of our discussion.

People make gratuitous nonprobate transfers on a fairly regular basis as well. For example, you may buy a relative or friend a birthday present, take a significant other out on a date, or make a contribution to your favorite charity. Each of these transfers has an estate planning component because, at a minimum, gratuitous nonprobate transfers lessen the value of your estate. Even when a person makes a nonprobate transfer as part of a comprehensive estate plan, a side benefit of the transfer may be unrelated to estate planning.

Example 13-1. Non-Estate Planning Benefits

Husband and Wife are considering opening a joint bank account that provides that upon the death of either spouse, the surviving spouse will own all of the funds remaining in the account. Why might Husband and Wife want to open this account other than to effectuate a quick and simple transfer of the balance in the account upon the death of the first spouse to die?

Explanation

The account makes it easier for the spouses to manage their funds on a day-to-day basis. The account can serve as a common receptacle for the spouses' paychecks and provide a shared fund from which to make purchases and pay bills.

§13.2 Accelerate Asset Distribution

The probate process creates a gap between the time when a decedent dies and the heirs or beneficiaries physically receive the decedent's property. This delay may range from months, to years, and even to decades, especially if the decedent's will is contested. This delay is potentially damaging from three perspectives.

First, the heirs and beneficiaries are unable to use the property. During the delay period, the educational, medical, or other needs of the survivors may go unmet because they cannot reach the decedent's property.

Example 13-2. Accelerate Asset Distribution

Friend has limited finances and insurance and needs an expensive organ transplant procedure to survive. Client can afford to pay for the operation. Client intends to pay but realizes that Client may die before the operation and thus comes to your office for a will. Client wants to leave Friend sufficient funds in Client's will to cover the surgery. How do you advise Client?

Explanation

Client's plan may not work to provide Friend with the money needed for the life-saving transplant. Client may die before Friend has the operation. Client's family may be upset that Client left so much of Client's property to a nonrelative and contest the will. While the contest action is in full swing, Friend could be in dire need of the operation but unable to reach the legacy. Thus, Friend may die. If Client uses a nonprobate method of property transfer (such as a pay on death account or life insurance policy), Friend will be able to get the funds within days of Client's death and consequently Friend will be able to receive the operation.

Second, the decedent's property may not be able to withstand a gap in management. Some types of property require constant monitoring to maintain value. Corporate securities need to be traded as the market dictates, crops need to be timely harvested and then processed or sold, and foreign investments must be evaluated in light of the constantly changing world political scene. The gap between the decedent's death and the beginning of an administration depends on how quickly the decedent's survivors take the appropriate steps to open the estate. Even if they act quickly, there is still a gap during which substantial losses may occur. Some of the nonprobate techniques allow the decedent to appoint a property manager who will be able to take over immediately upon the decedent's death.

Third, the decedent's survivors may have to endure the emotional impact of a prolonged administration. The constant reminder of a loved one's death that results from a drawn-out administration may prevent closure and keep the survivors from moving on with their lives.

§13.3 Reduce Estate Planning and Administration Expenses

Estate planning and administration are relatively expensive procedures. The costs are based on a variety of factors such as the size of the decedent's estate and its composition. For example, planning for cash, bank deposits, and other relatively liquid assets is usually inexpensive while family businesses often require more complex and sophisticated planning. Another key factor is the law of the state in which the estate is administered. Some states have expensive, cumbersome, and lengthy probate procedures while others have procedures that are relatively inexpensive and efficient. Expenses incurred in both planning and administration include attorney's fees, personal representative fees, and court costs. On the other hand, some of the nonprobate transfer techniques are free or very inexpensive to use and some may even be done without legal assistance. Of course, legal counsel may be needed to maximize the benefits of a particular technique and to avoid intent-defeating traps.

§13.4 Enhance Confidentiality

Most people like to keep their financial and family matters private. During life, it is relatively easy to keep these matters confidential, unless the person is a celebrity or politician. A person needs only to be careful with whom the person shares intimate details. However, an entirely different situation exists when the person dies. All estate proceedings are on the public record. Typical documents filed in an administration include inventories of all of the decedent's assets, the appraised value of each asset, and the names of the new owners, be they intestate heirs or will beneficiaries. Of course, the will itself is public record. A curious person needs no excuse to view, copy, distribute, or publish the documents. Used properly, however, many of the nonprobate transfer methods can escape conspicuous notation on the public record or in other readily available sources.

§13.5 Minimize Taxes

Some nonprobate transfer techniques have the potential of saving the decedent a considerable amount of income, gift, and estate taxes. An overview of the basics of wealth transfer taxation is found in Chapter 24, below. It is important to note that many nonprobate transfers may have no tax effect or an unanticipated effect and thus must be used with caution in estates large or complex enough to make tax planning an issue. You should also note that the *taxable estate*, that is, the property that is subject to federal or state death taxes, may include many assets that are not part of the decedent's probate estate. For example, life insurance proceeds on a policy owned by the decedent and payable to a named beneficiary are not part of the decedent's probate estate, but are usually part of the taxable estate. Be careful when you use the terms "probate estate" and "taxable estate"; do not use them interchangeably.

§13.6 Retain Flexibility

Intestate succession is inflexible; property passes without regard to the decedent's intent. A will provides many opportunities for the testator to control the transfer of property, but there are limits on what a testator can do in the will, either from a legal or practical perspective, and, of course, the disposition is not effective until the testator dies and the will is properly probated. Many nonprobate transfers, however, allow their users to exert greater control and individualization over the use and distribution of assets. In addition, nonprobate transfers may be able to provide the testator with immediate benefits such as tax savings and disability protection.

§13.7 Change with Less Difficulty

As discussed in §5.4, above, many formalities are required to execute a valid will as well as to amend an already existing will. Changing an existing will is a hassle and may require as much effort as making the will in the first place. On the other hand, a person may update and revise many of the nonprobate techniques with a minimum of effort thus avoiding extended procedures and technicalities. For example, to make a change to a payable on death bank account (see §16.4, below), the depositor only needs to fill out a new signature card; some banks may even permit this to be done by mail so the depositor does not even need to go to the bank.

§13.8 Protect from Creditors

Most property that passes through a decedent's probate estate is subject to the claims of the decedent's creditors. The primary reason for having an estate administration is to make certain the decedent does not escape the decedent's obligations merely by dying before paying them in full (see Chapter 12, above). If the property does not pass through the probate estate, however, it may escape liability for the decedent's debts.

The use of some nonprobate transfers to avoid creditors is very controversial. Creditors generally accept that they cannot reach certain nonprobate assets such as the proceeds of a life insurance policy payable to a named beneficiary. This makes sense because the creditors did not have the ability to reach the proceeds while the insured was alive. At most, they may have been able to reach the policy's cash value, if any, assuming the policy was not exempt from creditors under state law. However, creditors are reluctant to agree that they cannot pursue other nonprobate transfers to satisfy their claims, such as property passing via a trust the decedent could have revoked while alive. The creditors do not think that the death of a debtor should protect assets that were not protected during the debtor's life. Courts, legislatures, and legal writers are currently debating whether the debtor's death should be deemed a "transfer" of the asset under statutes prohibiting fraudulent conveyances if the asset was subject to the creditor during the decedent's life but passes upon death outside of the probate estate.

§13.9 Isolate from Contest

Nonprobate transfers are often more resilient to contest than wills, although individuals dissatisfied with nonprobate transfers may attack them on many of the same grounds used to contest a will, such as the transferor's lack of mental capacity or that the transfer was the result of undue influence or fraud. The decedent may make arrangements for nonprobate transfers long before the decedent's death. The nonprobate techniques may require the decedent to engage in ongoing transactions with people who can testify to the decedent's capacity, such as bank officials, insurance agents, business associates, and trust officers. Thus, individuals who wish to sustain a nonprobate transfer have a greater likelihood of locating evidence to rebut a contestant's claims.

§13.10 Increase Understandability

A will may be a complex instrument, especially if the testator has complicated distribution desires or a desire to minimize taxes. Some, but by no means all, of the nonprobate transfer methods are effective at handling distribution wishes and tax reduction without as much confusion. Use of transfer methods that the client may more readily understand increases the likelihood that you are carrying out the client's intent.

14

Inter Vivos Transfers

A person may reduce the size of the probate estate by transferring property while the person is still alive. This chapter details a variety of methods a person may use to make these inter vivos transfers of property.

§14.1 Outright Inter Vivos Gifts

§14.1.1 Elements

The simplest of the nonprobate transfer techniques is the outright inter vivos gift. If you complete a gratuitous transfer of property to another person while you are alive, you obviously do not own that property when you die. Thus, the property is unaffected by intestacy or your will.

A transfer must meet three main requirements to qualify as an outright inter vivos gift.

(1) Present Donative Intent. The donor must have the present intent to make a gratuitous transfer.

(2) Delivery. The property must be delivered to the donee.

(3) Acceptance. The donee must accept the property.

Example 14-1. Donative Intent — Voluntary

Donor was walking in a parking lot when Donor was confronted by Donee, who was menacingly waving a gun. Donee demanded, "Gimme all your money or I will hurt you real bad." Filled with fear, Donor handed over $238 in cash. Has Donor made an outright inter vivos gift?

Explanation

Donor's transfer was not voluntary and thus the transfer was not an outright inter vivos gift. A gift arises only when a transferor actually desires to part with the property. The transfer cannot be coerced under threats of violence nor be the result of undue influence or fraud.

Example 14-2.   Donative Intent — No Consideration

Donor and Donee agree that if Donor purchases Donee's car, Donor will give Donor $4,500. Will this transfer be an outright inter vivos gift? Would your answer change if the fair market value of the car was $10,000 and Donee is Donor's child?

Explanation

Donor's transfer is the consideration for a purchase and sale contract and thus will not be an outright inter vivos gift. Gifts must be gratuitous, that is, no quid pro quo. A donor should receive nothing tangible in return for a gift. Any reciprocity is limited to intangible things such as appreciation, gratitude, and affection. However, if the fair market value of the car significantly exceeds the consideration paid and the parties are so closely related that it would be expected that the donor would make a gift to the donee, it is likely that the transfer will be considered part contractual and part gratuitous.

Example 14-3.   Donative Intent — Effective Immediately

Donor makes the following statement to Donee, "I promise to give you $10,000 on your next birthday." Donee replies, "Sounds great! I sure can use the money." Has an outright inter vivos gift occurred? What if Donor actually delivers the money on Donee's birthday? What if instead of cash, Donor delivers a personal check drawn on Donor's account?

Explanation

A transfer must be immediately effective to qualify as an outright inter vivos gift. Donor merely made an unenforceable promise to make a gift in the future. If, however, Donor lives up to Donor's word, an outright inter vivos gift will occur when Donor actually delivers the money. The transfer of the personal check would not qualify as a gift because Donor could stop payment on the check and, since Donor issued the check gratuitously, Donee could not enforce payment. A gift of money made by a personal check is not complete until the check is paid, certified, or transferred for value to a third person.

Example 14-4. Donative Intent—Irrevocable and Unconditional—Generally

Donor made an outright inter vivos gift of a television to Donee because Donor had just purchased a new set and had no further use for the old one. After several months elapsed, Donor's new television broke and the repair technician told Donor that it would take at least a month to obtain the needed parts. Not knowing what to do without a television, Donor called Donee on the telephone and said, "Things have changed. I need my television back. I revoke the gift. When can I come over to pick up the TV?" How would you advise Donee?

Explanation

Donee has no legal obligation to return the television. Outright inter vivos gifts are permanent, unconditional, and irrevocable. Once Donor completes the gift, the gift cannot be legally undone.

Example 14-5. Donative Intent—Irrevocable and Unconditional—Engagement Gifts

Donor and Donee dated for two years. During this time, Donor gave Donee a VCR as a birthday present. Donor eventually proposed to Donee and gave Donee a diamond ring. Several months later, the engagement ended. May Donor regain possession of either the VCR or the ring? Would it matter who broke off the engagement?

Explanation

Despite the irrevocability of gifts generally, courts may permit the donor of an *engagement gift*, typically a ring, to retrieve the gift if the marriage does not occur. The courts imply a condition on the gift even if the donor did not expressly state it. In some states, the donor's rights depend on who breaks off the engagement. If the donor is at fault, the donor may not be able to revoke the gift. If the donee breaks off the engagement without a legal justification or if the break-up is mutual, the donor may seek return of the engagement gifts. Thus, Donor has a good chance of regaining possession of the ring. It is unlikely, however, that Donor could revoke the gift of the VCR. Although courts are willing to imply a condition on gifts predicated on the engagement, they are not willing to do so with *courtship gifts*. Donor gave Donee the VCR as a birthday present. Because this gift was unrelated to the engagement, the gift is irrevocable.

Example 14-6.   Delivery — Generally

Donor called Donee on the telephone and stated, "Happy Birthday, my good friend. I have your present, a new camera, at my apartment. Please come over and pick it up." Has Donor made an outright inter vivos gift?

Explanation

Donor has not made an outright inter vivos gift because Donor has not given up dominion and control of the camera. A gift is not complete until the property has left the donor's sphere of authority such that the donor cannot stop the transfer.

Example 14-7.   Delivery — Real Property

Donor prepared three deeds of real property naming Donee as the grantee. Donor delivered the deed for Parcel A to Donee. Donor placed the deed for Parcel B in Donor's safe deposit box. Donor gave the deed for Parcel C to Escrow Agent with instructions for Escrow Agent to deliver the deed to Donee upon Donor's death. Donor has now died. What are Donee's rights to the three parcels?

Explanation

Donee received an outright inter vivos gift of Parcel A. Real property is transferred by the donor delivering a deed to the donee naming the donee as the grantee as was done here.

Donee's rights to Parcel B are problematic. On one hand, Donor has given up nothing; Donor could enter the safe deposit box at any time, remove the deed, and destroy it without anyone being the wiser. Thus, most courts would hold that no gift occurred. On the other hand, Donor's clear intent was to have Donee own Parcel B. If the deed does not operate as an inter vivos gift, it is unlikely that Donee will receive the property because the deed would not satisfy the requirements of a will. Thus, Parcel B would pass via intestacy or under Donor's will.

Donee's rights to Parcel C are also problematic. It is important to know whether Donor had the right to retrieve the deed from Escrow Agent. If Donor could not regain possession of the deed, most courts would deem the gift complete. However, if Donor could revoke the escrow arrangement and retrieve the deed, courts generally would hold that the gift was incomplete because Donor did not place the deed beyond Donor's control.

Example 14-8. Delivery — Personal Property — Constructive

Donor gave Donee the only key to Donor's safe deposit box. Donor told Donee, "Everything in the box is now yours." Has delivery occurred? Would your answer change if Donor also has a key to the safe deposit box?

Explanation

This example demonstrates the concept of *constructive delivery*. Constructive delivery occurs when the donor transfers to the donee the means of obtaining possession or control of the property rather than the actual property. The most common example of constructive delivery is the delivery of a key to a locked item as a means of making a gift of the item's contents. If Donor gave Donee the only key to the safe deposit box, it is likely that an outright inter vivos gift occurred because Donor relinquished power and dominion over the box and its contents. However, if Donor retains a key, the gift is not complete until Donee actually removes the property from the safe deposit box.

Example 14-9. Delivery — Personal Property — Symbolic

Donor wants to give two items to Donee: Donor's watch, currently located around Donor's left wrist, and Donor's stereo system, currently located in Donor's summer home approximately 1,000 miles away. Donor takes out a sheet of paper and writes, "I, Donor, hereby make an irrevocable outright inter vivos gift of my watch and my stereo system to Donee." After describing these items in great detail, Donor signs the paper and immediately hands it over to Donee. Has an outright inter vivos gift occurred of the watch or the stereo?

Explanation

This example demonstrates the concept of *symbolic delivery*. Symbolic delivery occurs when the donor gives the donee something that represents the property instead of the property itself. The most common symbolic delivery method is the *deed of gift*, a written instrument that evidences the donative intent, names the donee, and describes the property. Jurisdictions vary regarding the effect given to deeds of gift. In some states, deeds of gift are effective for transferring ownership of most types of personal property provided they meet statutory formalities. In many states, however, a deed of gift is effective only if physical delivery of the item is impractical under the circumstances. Thus, it is more likely that a court would uphold the symbolic delivery of the stereo than the watch. Donor could not easily deliver the stereo because it was located many miles away but it would have been easy for the Donor to slip off the watch and hand it to Donee.

Example 14-10.   Delivery—Personal Property—Corporate Stock

Donor owns corporate stock. Donor endorses the stock certificate and delivers it to Donee. What are Donee's rights to these securities? Does it matter whether or not the corporate books have been changed to reflect Donee's ownership?

Explanation

Courts have used at least two approaches to determine whether a donor has satisfied the requirement of delivery with regard to corporate stock. The first view focuses on the gift being the certificate itself. Thus, as long as the certificate is properly endorsed and physically delivered, the gift is complete even if the corporate books have not yet been updated to show the new owner. The second view treats the stock certificate as only a symbol of ownership of an undivided fractional interest in the corporation. Thus, no actual transfer occurs until the corporate books reflect the new owner. The first view reflects the majority approach. Even in these jurisdictions, the fact of re-registration is important because it provides additional evidence of donative intent.

Example 14-11.   Acceptance

Donor prepares a deed of real property, places it in an envelope, and mails it to Donee. Donee opens the envelope, reads the deed, and throws it on Donee's desk. Donee says nothing to Donor and does not record the deed. Has Donee accepted the gift? What additional information about the property would be helpful to your answer?

Explanation

Acceptance is normally presumed because outright inter vivos gifts usually bestow benefits on the donee. This presumption may be rebutted if the property would impose onerous burdens on the donee. Thus, it would appear that Donee accepted the gift of real property. It would be, of course, important to ascertain the nature of the property. The acceptance presumption could be rebutted by evidence showing that the property was a toxic waste site, subject to liens or taxes exceeding the value of the property, or was burdensome in some other way.

§14.1.2 *Potential Benefits*

For a variety of reasons, outright inter vivos gifts play a very important role in the estate plans of most people. The potential benefits include the following:

(1) Donee's Immediate Enjoyment. The donee receives immediate enjoyment of the transferred property.

(2) Donor Satisfaction. The donor is able to watch the donee benefiting from the property and thus will experience the "joy of giving."

(3) Donor Relieved of Responsibility. The donor is relieved of the responsibilities of managing the transferred property.

(4) Tax Reduction. For donors who have estates large enough to have federal gift or estate tax concerns, outright inter vivos gifts may be used to reduce transfer tax liability. Currently, the first $10,000 worth of property a donor gives to a donee each year falls within the *annual exclusion* and escapes taxation. There is no limit as to the total amount of property given nor the number of donees. In addition, all payments for a donee's tuition and health care are not taxed because of the *education and medical expense exclusion.* See Chapter 24 for more information about wealth transfer taxation.

(5) Creditor Protection. The transferred property will not be subject to the donor's creditors unless the transfer violates the applicable fraudulent conveyances statute.

(6) Reduce Elective Share of Surviving Spouse. As discussed in §7.1, above, many states have statutes which permit a surviving spouse to claim a certain portion of the deceased spouse's estate regardless of the terms of the deceased spouse's will. A spouse may use outright inter vivos gifts to transfer a greater portion of the estate to the spouse's desired beneficiaries (e.g., children from a prior marriage) and reduce the size of the estate against which the surviving spouse may claim.

§14.1.3 *Potential Disadvantages*

Despite the benefits of outright inter vivos gifts, they must be used with caution to avoid various complications. Below is a list of some of the potential problems with gift transfers.

(1) Irrevocability. Outright inter vivos gifts are irrevocable. Thus, if the donor falls on hard times and needs the property back, the donor will not have any right to reclaim the transferred property. The donor will be forced to rely on the good will of the donee, relatives, friends, and charitable organizations or may even need to resort to federal, state, or local welfare programs for assistance.

(2) Lack of Control. The donor may not exercise any control over property transferred by way of an outright inter vivos gift. Many donors wish to dictate the use of donated property and the conduct of the donee. These donors will find other techniques, especially trusts, more desirable. See §18.2 for a discussion of the benefits a donor may obtain by transferring property into a trust.

(3) Leverage Reduction. Property ownership is a source of deference and respect. The prospect of being a donee inspires some people to treat grandparents, parents, and other potential donors better than they would if they did not anticipate a windfall. If the donor transfers the property during life, this source of power is gone and the donor may no longer enjoy these considerations.

(4) Jealousy. Outright inter vivos gifts may cause family problems. If the donor makes gifts to children unequally, the children who receive lesser shares may resent the donor and their donee siblings. In addition, family members may be upset if the donor makes gifts to nonfamily members or charity. Although the same disharmony would occur with testamentary gifts, at least the donor would not have to deal personally with the situation.

(5) Minors and Incompetents Lack Legal Capacity. Minors and incompetents are legally unable to manage property. Thus, if the donor elects to transfer property to a minor or incompetent, additional steps are often needed. For example, the donee may need a court appointed guardian or conservator to manage the property. If the donee is a minor, the donor may transfer the property to a custodian for the minor under the state's version of the Uniform Transfers (Gifts) to Minors Act. See §14.6, below.

(6) Transfer Taxation. If the gift does not qualify as a tax-free gift as discussed in §14.1.2(4), above, the donor may be liable for transfer taxes, such as the gift and generation-skipping transfer tax.

§14.2 Gifts Causa Mortis

A *gift causa mortis* is a gift made in contemplation of death. The donor must fear that death is impending or imminent; that is, the donor must be looking the grim reaper in the eye. The donor cannot merely have a general apprehension of an upcoming death.

Gifts causa mortis require donative intent, delivery, and acceptance just like outright inter vivos gifts. Unlike outright inter vivos gifts, however, a gift causa mortis is both conditional and revocable. The gift is either automatically revoked (majority view) or revocable at the donor's discretion (minority view) if the donor survives the peril that induced the donor to make the gift. The gift is also revocable by the donor at any time for any reason.

Attorneys rarely, if ever, use gifts causa mortis in planning a client's estate. A client who wishes to make a revocable transfer would be better served with a trust or some other formal arrangement.

Example 14-12. Gifts Causa Mortis — Basic Operation

Donor suffered a heart attack after eating Thanksgiving dinner. As the ambulance crew was wheeling Donor out of Donor's home, Donor took off Donor's watch and handed it to Donee while stating, "Donee, please take my watch. You can keep it unless I come back from the hospital." Donor died in the hospital. Donor's valid will left the watch to Beneficiary. Who has the superior claim to the watch?

Explanation

Donee is the new owner of the watch. Donor had donative intent while delivering the watch. Donee accepted the watch. Donor made a gift causa mortis because Donor stated that the gift was conditional on the Donor not returning from the hospital. Donor was in fear of an impending death because Donor had just suffered a heart attack. The watch was not in Donor's estate and thus Beneficiary is out of luck. (This principle is called *ademption*. See §6.2, above.)

Example 14-13. Gifts Causa Mortis — Immediacy of Impending Death

Donee and his three police officer friends were playing cards one night when the following events transpired. Donor A received a radio call that a gang war was in progress and he was summoned to help quell the unrest. Before leaving, Donor A went out to his truck and brought in his new notebook computer. Donor A handed it to Donee and stated, "I have a bad feeling about tonight. Please take my computer. Of course, if everything goes well, I want it back." Donor B handed Donee $1,000 in cash and said, "Police work is very dangerous. I just have a gut feeling that something might happen to me when I go on duty tomorrow morning. Please take this money. You can keep it unless I make it through the day." Donor C gave Donee a small envelope containing old United States gold coins. Donor C said, "I'd like you to have these. I don't think I'll be alive tomorrow." Donor A died in the gang war that night, Donor B was killed in a car crash the following morning, and Donor C committed suicide after returning home from the card game. To what property is Donee entitled?

Explanation

This example focuses on the gift causa mortis requirement that the donor be in contemplation of death at the time the donor makes the gift. Donor A was in immediate fear of being killed in the gang war. This is the type of immediacy that is likely to support a gift causa mortis. On the other hand, Donor B was merely apprehensive about going to work the next day. It is unlikely that Donee may retain the money because the transfer is neither an outright inter vivos gift (because it was conditional and revocable) nor a gift causa mortis (because of an insufficient fear of impending death). Donee's rights to the coin collection are uncertain. Donor C was in fear of an impending death but the peril was self-imposed. Courts are divided on whether a self-generated fear of death triggered by anticipated suicide is enough to support a gift causa mortis.

§14.3   Gifts in Trust

Instead of giving the donee outright control of gifted property, the donor may impose restrictions, limitations, and conditions on the gift by transferring it to an *inter vivos* or *living* trust. A trust is a method of dividing title to property so that the legal interest is held by a *trustee* and the equitable interest by the *beneficiary*. The donor in a trust context is called the *settlor*. The trustee is a fiduciary who must deal with the property with reasonable care and must maintain the utmost degree of loyalty (i.e., must avoid self-dealing and conflicts of interest). The trustee is personally liable if the trustee's conduct falls beneath the applicable standards. The beneficiary receives the benefits from the trust property according to the terms of the trust.

Inter vivos trusts are one of the most useful, advantageous, and powerful of the nonprobate transfer techniques. A detailed discussion of trusts is found in Chapters 18-21, below.

§14.4 Transfers of Future Interests[1]

The donor may retain a life estate in property and transfer only a future interest. The donee of a future interest owns an interest in the property but does not have the right to enjoy that ownership until some future time such as the donor's death. Thus, the donor can continue to possess and enjoy the property up to the moment of death but the property will not be in the donor's probate estate because the donor had already transferred the future interest to that property.

The most common type of future interest a donee may receive is the *remainder*. There are two basic types of remainders. First, the *vested remainder* gives the donee the right to obtain possession of the property as soon as the preceding estate terminates. Second, the *contingent remainder* permits the donee to obtain possession of the property only if a condition precedent is satisfied.

The donee may also receive a future interest called an *executory interest*. An executory interest is any type of future interest in a donee that cannot qualify as a remainder. For example, the donee's interest may shift or spring from a preceding estate that has been cut short by a condition subsequent.

Although life estates in personal property are relatively rare, there is a growing trend for donors to use life estates in real property as an estate planning technique. The most frequent use is in a parent-child situation where the parent retains a life estate in the residence and transfers the remainder to the children. The children have no immediate possessory rights and no obligations with respect to the property but will receive an outright fee simple interest upon the parent's death without the need for probate. The use of the life estate/remainder technique may be cheaper than using a trust. Note that this arrangement will not remove the property from the parent's estate for federal estate tax purposes unless special planning techniques are used such as transferring the house to a *grantor retained interest*

---

1. The discussion of future interests in this section is limited to situations where the donor is using the future interest as a probate avoidance technique. For an excellent presentation of this complex subject, see John Makdisi, *Estates in Land and Future Interests* (2d ed. 1995).

trust (*GRIT*). The complex requirements of these arrangements are beyond the scope of this book.

Example 14-14.   Future Interest — Vested Remainder

Donor executed a deed for Donor's farm containing the following language: "To Donor for life, then to Donee." What is the effect of this deed after Donor dies? Does it matter whether Donee outlives Donor?

Explanation

Donor retained a life estate in the farm and transferred a future interest to Donee. Donee's future interest is a remainder because it follows the natural termination of a life estate and it is vested because it is not subject to a condition precedent. When Donor dies, Donee will have full ownership of the farm. The grant does not require Donee to outlive Donor. If Donee fails to outlive Donor, the remainder interest will pass under intestacy to Donee's heirs or under Donee's will to the beneficiaries.

Example 14-15.   Future Interest — Contingent Remainder

Donor executed a deed to a ranch containing the following language: "To Donor for life, then to Donee if Donee survives Donor, otherwise to Charity." What is the effect of this deed after Donor dies?

Explanation

Donor retained a life estate in the ranch and transferred alternative contingent remainders to Donee and Charity. Both Donee and Charity have remainders because they follow the natural termination of Donor's life estate. However, they are contingent because a condition must occur before the holder of either remainder can claim the property; that is, Donee must outlive Donor to take and Donee must predecease Donor for Charity to take.

Example 14-16.   Future Interest — Executory Interest

Donor executed a deed to a home containing the following language: "To Donee One for life, then three years later to Donee Two in fee." What is the effect of this deed after Donee One dies?

Explanation

Donee One originally received a life estate. Donor retained a reversion subject to an executory limitation; that is, Donor's right to the property for the period of time between the date of Donee One's death and the passage of three years. After Donee One died, Donee One's life estate ended and Donor (or, if Donor had already died, Donor's heirs or the beneficiaries of Donor's will) has the right to possess the property for three years. Donee Two has an executory interest rather than a remainder. More is necessary for Donee Two to obtain possession other than the natural termination of Donee One's life estate (that is, the passage of three additional years). Donee Two's interest springs from Donor. Three years after Donee One's death, Donee Two or Donee Two's successors in interest will own the home in fee simple.

§14.5 Powers of Appointment

A *power of appointment* is the right to designate the new owner of property. You have this power with respect to the property you own because you may give anything you own to another person. The power to name a new owner of your property is one of the things you take for granted as accompanying property ownership.

You may sever this power of appointment from the ownership of the property itself. When this happens, the following relationships are created. The owner of property (the person who is severing) is the *donor* of the power, the person with the power to appoint the property is the *donee,* and the prospective new owners are the *objects of the power.* When the donee actually exercises the power, the new owners are called the *appointees.* If the donee fails to exercise the power, the property passes to the *default takers.* If the donor failed to name default takers, the property reverts to the donor or the donor's estate.

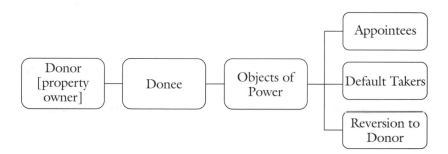

The donor can create a power of appointment in an inter vivos document, such as a deed or trust, or in a separate power of appointment instrument. The donor can also create a power of appointment by will.

Powers of appointment are generally categorized in one of two ways. First, the power of appointment may be *general,* meaning that there are no restrictions or conditions on the donee's exercise of the power. Thus, the donee could even appoint the donee's own self as the new owner. In many aspects, the donee of a general power of appointment is like the actual owner of the property. Second, the power may be *specific, special,* or *limited,* i.e., the donor may specify certain individuals or groups as the objects of the power that do not include the donee, the donee's creditors, the donee's estate, or the creditors of the donee's estate. In addition, the donor may make the donee's exercise of the power conditional on whatever factors, within legal bounds, the donor desires, for example, only for the appointees' health-related and educational expenses.

The donee of a power of appointment does not have title, either legal or equitable, to the subject property. Instead, the donee only has a power to appoint. The appointees take title from the donor, not the donee.

The donee has no duty to exercise the power of appointment in favor of the hopeful appointees. Unlike a trustee, a donee is not a fiduciary and has no duty to manage the property or to distribute the property. A power of appointment is also not an agency relationship; the donee is not the donor's agent.

The donor may dictate the method the donee must use to exercise the power of appointment. For example, the power may be an *inter vivos power,* indicating that the donee must exercise it while alive. Alternatively, it may be a *testamentary power,* which the donee may only exercise by will. The donor may also permit the donee to exercise the power in both ways.

Although the donor may create a power of appointment in anyone, powers of appointment are typically used with trusts. Trustees often have the power to decide which beneficiaries will receive distributions and in what amounts. See §19.8.9, below, for a discussion of discretionary trusts. Settlors of trusts may also give powers of appointment over trust property to the beneficiaries.

Example 14-17. Power of Appointment—Exercise by Will

Donor gave Donee a general power of appointment over Donor's vacation home. The instrument that created the power provided that it may be exercised inter vivosly or by will. Donee died with a valid will that did not make specific reference either to the power of appointment or the underlying property. The will did contain a residuary clause leaving the remainder of Donee's estate to Beneficiary. Who is entitled to the vacation home? Does it matter whether the Donor provided for default takers?

Explanation

The resolution of this problem depends on whether state law provides that a residuary clause is presumed to express Donee's intent to exercise the power. The courts will examine the details of the case searching for evidence of the parties' intent. If a power did not require an express reference to be exercised, is general, and the donor did not provide for default takers, it is likely that the residuary clause will be sufficient to exercise the power. However, if the power expressly provides for default takers, the silent residuary clause will probably be insufficient and thus the property will pass to the default takers. See UPC §2-608.

Example 14-18. Power of Appointment — Creditors

Donee received a general power of appointment over property valued at $100,000. Donee is behind on payments on several personal loans and Donee's creditors want to levy on the property that is the subject of the power of appointment. Can the creditors reach the property even though Donee has not exercised the power?

Explanation

There is a split among the states regarding the resolution of this issue. Some states rely on the fact that a power of appointment is merely a power and not an estate in property and thus hold that the creditors may not reach the property. On the other hand, many states provide that any property to which a donee could acquire ownership is subject to the claims of creditors.

§14.6 Transfers to Minors

Minors lack the legal capacity to manage property. Thus, donors who wish to make inter vivos gratuitous transfers to benefit minors need to select an appropriate method to transfer the property. Donors have several techniques available to them.

First, the donor could simply make the transfer directly to the minor. If the property is of relatively low value, for example, traditional holiday gifts such as toys, clothes, and pocket money, this method works well. However, if the property requires management, a direct transfer will require the court to appoint a guardian or conservator of the minor's estate. An estate guardianship typically requires extensive court involvement and thus is costly and time-consuming. In addition, the minor will receive the property outright at age eighteen, possibly before the young adult has acquired the maturity to handle the property prudently.

Second, the donor could place the property in trust for the benefit of the minor. A trust will avoid the necessity of a guardianship and will give the donor the ability to designate how the property is to be managed and distributed. Significant transaction costs may be incurred, however, such as attorney's fees to draft the trust and trustee's fees to manage the trust.

Third, the donor may transfer the property to a *custodian* for the minor. All states have adopted either the Uniform Gifts to Minors Act or its successor uniform law, the Uniform Transfers to Minors Act. Under these statutes, the donor may make a gift to the minor donee and either retain management powers as the custodian or name another person to serve in that role. The custodian manages the property for the benefit of the minor and then distributes the remaining property to the minor when the minor reaches majority (either age eighteen or twenty-one depending on the type of transfer and the applicable version of the uniform act). Although not achieving all the benefits of a trust, transfers to a custodian are cost-effective, relatively simple to make, and significantly less complex because most of the terms of the arrangement, including the custodian's powers, duties, and responsibilities, are set out in the statute. Custodianships are often used when the value of the transferred property is too low to justify the costs of a trust.

15

Co-Ownership of Property

More than one person may simultaneously have interests in the same item of property. What happens to a co-owner's share when one of the co-owners dies? Either the deceased co-owner's share passes through the decedent's estate to the decedent's heirs or will beneficiaries, or the surviving co-owners divide the decedent's share. The method the concurrent owners use to hold title determines which of these results occurs. This chapter discusses the ramifications of the common types of property co-ownership.

§15.1 Tenancy in Common

Tenancy in common is the fundamental type of concurrent property ownership. A typical granting clause reads, "To Owner One and Owner Two as tenants in common." Tenancy in common is also the default type of concurrent ownership in most jurisdictions. Consequently, a grant reading "To Owner One and Owner Two" is normally presumed to be a tenancy in common.

Upon the death of a tenant in common, the deceased tenant's share passes through the tenant's estate to the appropriate heirs or will beneficiaries. The deceased tenant's share does not belong to the surviving co-owners. Thus, a tenancy in common is not a probate avoidance technique.

Example 15-1. Tenancy in Common — No Survivorship Rights

Parent and Child purchased a farm as tenants in common. Parent supplied 75 percent of the purchase price and Child supplied 25 percent. Parent died

271

with a valid will leaving all of Parent's property to Spouse. Who now owns the farm and in what proportions?

Explanation

Because Parent and Child held title to the farm as tenants in common, Child does not have survivorship rights. Thus, Parent's share passes under Parent's will. Spouse now owns 75 percent and Child still owns 25 percent.

§15.2   Joint Tenancy

A *joint tenancy* is a sophisticated type of concurrent property ownership. At common law, co-owners held as joint tenants if four requirements were satisfied. These requirements are called the *four unities*. Note that many jurisdictions have relaxed some of these technical requirements.

(1) Unity of Time.   All joint tenants had to take their interests at the same time. Thus, a conveyance from "Owner One" to "Owner One and Owner Two as joint tenants" would not create a joint tenancy because Owner One received Owner One's interest at a prior time. To meet the unity of time requirement, Owner One could convey to a third party, a *straw person*, who would then convey the property to Owner One and Owner Two.

(2) Unity of Title.   All joint tenants were required to obtain their interests from the same instrument, that is, through one deed or under the same will.

(3) Unity of Interest.   Each joint tenant must have an equivalent share in the property. Thus, each joint tenant must own the same proportion of the property (e.g., one-half or one-quarter) and each tenant's estate must be of the same duration (e.g., a fee simple interest or a life estate).

(4) Unity of Possession.   Each joint tenant must have the right to occupy the entire property. Likewise, each joint tenant has a duty not to interfere with the rights of other joint tenants to occupy the property.

The key characteristic of a joint tenancy for our purpose is the survivorship feature. A joint tenant's rights end at death in favor of the surviving joint tenants. Thus, when a joint tenant dies, the deceased tenant's share is divided equally among the surviving joint tenants. The rights of these surviving joint tenants are superior to the deceased tenant's heirs or beneficiaries. Thus, a joint tenancy is an effective probate avoidance technique.

At common law, the survivorship feature attached automatically to a joint tenancy. The presumption of survivorship often led to unanticipated property distributions as co-owners held as joint tenants when they intended to hold as tenants in common. Non-legally trained individuals did not appreciate the significant difference between these two types of concurrent ownership. Consequently, many states now provide that the survivorship feature does not attach to a joint tenancy unless it is expressly stated in the instrument.

Example 15-2. Joint Tenancy—Survivorship Rights

Brother and Sister own three parcels of property. The granting language of the deeds reads as follows:

> *Parcel One* — "To Brother and Sister as joint tenants."
> *Parcel Two*— "To Brother and Sister as joint tenants with rights of survivorship."
> *Parcel Three*— "To Brother and Sister as joint tenants, not as tenants in common, with rights of survivorship."

Brother died with a valid will leaving all of his property to Child. Who is entitled to these parcels of property?

Explanation

At common law, all three grants created joint tenancies and thus Sister would own the properties upon Brother's death. Under modern law, however, a mere recital of "joint tenants" is often insufficient to imbue the property with the survivorship feature. Thus, Brother's share of Parcel One is likely to pass to Child. The grants for Parcels Two and Three are adequate to create survivorship rights in Sister in most jurisdictions.

Example 15-3. Joint Tenancy—Irrevocable Gift

Mother owned a valuable parcel of beachfront property. To avoid probate of this asset, Mother created a joint tenancy with Daughter, her only child. What is the effect of Mother's action? May Mother undo the joint tenancy and regain full ownership of the property at a later time?

Explanation

Mother has made a gift of an undivided one-half interest of the beachfront property to Daughter. Accordingly, the property will be subject to federal gift tax to the extent that the value of one-half of the property exceeds the annual exclusion. See §24.1.4.1, below. Whenever the contributions of joint tenants are unequal, the gift portion of the transfer may trigger tax consequences, many of which may not have been anticipated by the co-owners.

Mother may not undo the joint tenancy and revest the entire property in her name alone. Mother made an inter vivos gift of an undivided one-half interest in the property and thus the transfer is irrevocable. An individual contemplating funding more than the individual's own share of a joint tenancy must be aware of the irrevocability of the transfer. This concern is especially important if the prospective joint tenants are spouses because approximately 50 percent of marriages end in divorce.

Example 15-4. Joint Tenancy—Income Entitlement

Parent and Child own a ranch as joint tenants. Parent supplied all of the funds to purchase the property and conducts all of the ranch business. Who is entitled to the income received from grazing leases?

Explanation

Parent and Child own equal shares in the ranch. Thus, each is entitled to one-half of the income. Parent will be entitled to offsets for any expenses Parent incurred and for Parent's labor. Child's right is to one-half of the *net* profits. The co-owner who supplies the bulk of the funds to purchase an asset or who manages that asset may not realize that holding as joint tenants causes each co-owner to be entitled to an equal share of the net income generated by the co-owned property.

Example 15-5. Joint Tenancy—Liability of Noncontributing Joint Tenant

Sister purchased a duplex with her own funds and had title placed in her and Brother's names as joint tenants. With Brother's full consent, Sister lived in one of the units, rented the other, and retained all of the rent. After a disastrous visit to the casinos of Las Vegas, Sister ignored her property tax bill and did not repair a broken sidewalk in front of the duplex causing Mrs. Palsgraf to fall and break her leg. Unable to recover from Sister, County Tax Assessor and Mrs. Palsgraf brought suit against Brother. Is Brother responsible for these obligations?

Explanation

Because Sister and Brother are co-owners of the property, each is responsible for the property taxes and Mrs. Palsgraf's injuries caused by the negligent maintenance. Brother does not escape liability merely because none of Brother's funds were used to purchase the duplex nor because Brother was not actively participating in the management of the property. If Brother pays more than half of these items, Brother will be entitled to contribution from Sister. Use of a joint tenancy to avoid probate must be carefully considered because the co-owner who is not actually going to use the property may not want to be exposed to these types of liabilities.

Example 15-6. Joint Tenancy — Liability of Contributing Joint Tenant

Mother placed her farm in a joint tenancy with Son. Son is a spendthrift and has incurred many debts. May Son's creditors recover against his interest in the farm?

Explanation

The joint tenancy gave Son ownership of an undivided one-half interest in the farm. Thus, Son's creditors may reach his interest despite the fact that Son did not contribute to the purchase of the farm. Many contributing joint tenants fail to recognize that the property may be liable for a noncontributing joint tenant's obligations.

Example 15-7. Joint Tenancy — Sale

Parent and Child owned a mountain cabin as joint tenants with rights of survivorship. Parent needed money for retirement expenses and thus sold Parent's interest to Purchaser. Purchaser died with a valid will leaving the cabin to Charity. Who is entitled to the cabin?

Explanation

Parent's unilateral act of selling the cabin to Purchaser severed the joint tenancy. The unities of time and title no longer exist; that is, Parent and Purchaser did not receive title from the same instrument at the same time. Thus, Purchaser and Child are tenants in common. Upon Purchaser's death, Purchaser's one-half interest will pass to Charity under Purchaser's will. Charity and Child will then hold the cabin as tenants in common.

Example 15-8. Joint Tenancy — Partition

Friend One and Friend Two owned a vacation home as joint tenants. Their relationship deteriorated and they no longer wished to hold as joint tenants for many reasons, with the main one being that neither wanted the other to have survivorship rights. What should they do?

Explanation

Friend One and Friend Two may dissolve the joint tenancy either by a voluntary or court-ordered partition. Each tenant will then have full ownership of a divided share rather than an equal interest with the right to undivided possession of the whole. From a practical standpoint, a physical division of the property into two equally valued parcels may not be possible because the land on which the home sits is likely to be more valuable than the surrounding acreage. To resolve the situation, one tenant could buy the other tenant's portion or they could sell the home and divide the proceeds.

§15.3   Tenancy by the Entirety

At common law, a *tenancy by the entirety* was a special type of joint tenancy between spouses. Instead of four unities like a standard joint tenancy, the tenancy by the entirety included a fifth unity, the unity of marriage. Tenancies by the entirety included the survivorship feature. Unlike joint tenancies, a tenancy by the entirety could not be severed by one of the spouses conveying to a third party. Most states no longer make a distinction between joint tenancies and tenancies by the entirety.

§15.4   Community Property

Nine states use a community property marital property system — Arizona, California, Idaho, Louisiana, New Mexico, Nevada, Texas, Washington, and Wisconsin. Under a community property system, each spouse owns only one-half of his or her income. The remaining half of the income vests in the other spouse. If a spouse uses community income to purchase an asset, that asset is also community property. A spouse may transfer only that spouse's one-half interest in a community asset to that spouse's heirs or will beneficiaries.

Example 15-9.   Community Property

Husband and Wife live in a community property marital property jurisdiction and own several rental houses. Wife purchased the houses solely from her income earned during marriage. Wife's will devises the houses to Child. Upon Wife's death, who owns the houses and in what proportions?

Explanation

The houses are community property because they were purchased with income earned during the marriage. Thus, each spouse owned an undivided one-half interest in the houses regardless of which spouse earned the money that was used to purchase the properties. After Wife dies, Husband still owns his one-half interest in the houses. Child receives only Wife's one-half interest.

16

Multiple-Party Accounts

Multiple-party accounts, such as checking accounts, savings accounts, and certificates of deposit, are contractual arrangements for the deposit of money with financial institutions, such as state or national banks, savings and loan associations, and credit unions. The disposition of the funds remaining in these accounts upon the death of one of the depositors depends on the type of account, the account contract, and the applicable state law.

Multiple-party accounts are important nonprobate transfer mechanisms because these accounts are widely used, easy to understand, and inexpensive to obtain. This chapter discusses the four commonly recognized types of multiple-party accounts: (1) the *joint account,* which may transfer ownership rights to the account's balance to the surviving party; (2) the *agency* or *convenience account,* which does not transfer the balance upon the death of one of the parties; (3) the *payable on death account,* which causes the balance to belong to the surviving pay on death payees upon the death of the depositors; and (4) the *trust account,* under which the beneficiaries receive the account balance upon outliving all trustees.

§16.1 Joint Accounts

A *joint account* is an account payable on the request of one of two or more parties. A typical designation would read, "Payable to Party One or Party Two." Joint accounts are most commonly used by spouses and are frequently used by parents and their children.

277

§16.1.1 Rights during Lifetime of All Parties

§16.1.1.1 Ownership Rights

During the lifetime of all parties, a joint account belongs to the parties in proportion to the net contributions by each party to the amount on deposit unless there is clear and convincing evidence of a contrary intent. A party's net contributions are determined by adding all of the party's deposits, subtracting all of the party's withdrawals, and then adding a proportionate share of the interest earned on the deposit. See UPC §6-211.

A joint account does not operate to transfer current ownership of deposited funds to the other joint parties. Contrast this result with the consequence of creating a joint tenancy; that is, the contributing joint tenant is treated as making an immediate gift to the noncontributing joint tenant. See §15.2, below. The contributing depositor to a joint account does not make a gift to another party until that party withdraws more than that party's net contributions.

§16.1.1.2 Withdrawal Rights

Although ownership of the funds in a joint account is in proportion to net contributions, each party has the virtually unlimited right to withdraw any or all of the money in the account. See UPC §6-222. Consequently, it is extremely important that parties to a joint account trust each other.

Example 16-1.   Joint Account — Rights during Lifetime

Fiancé and Fiancée opened a joint noninterest-bearing checking account. Fiancé deposited $2,500 and Fiancée deposited $7,500. No other deposit has been made. Fiancée withdrew $2,500 to make a payment on her law school tuition. After a big fight, Fiancé withdrew the remaining balance of $7,500 and left town. What are the rights and obligations of the parties and the financial institution?

Explanation

Fiancée had the right to withdraw the $2,500 used to pay law school tuition. At the time of the withdrawal, Fiancée's net contributions were $7,500 and thus Fiancée had ownership rights over that money and could use it in any way she desired. Fiancé had the right to withdraw the $7,500 from the account and thus Fiancée does not have a claim against the bank, even though Fiancé withdrew more than his net contributions. Financial institutions are typically protected from liability for paying contrary to the parties' ownership rights unless they have received written notice prior to the withdrawal. See UPC §6-226. Fiancée has a claim for conversion against Fiancé for the amount withdrawn that exceeds Fiancé's net contributions. Thus, Fiancé is responsible for $5,000, the amount withdrawn in excess of his $2,500 net contribution.

§16.1.2 Rights after Death of a Depositor

§16.1.2.1 Ownership Rights

Two results are possible when one of the parties to a joint account dies: the deceased party's net contributions pass either (1) through the deceased party's estate to the party's heirs or will beneficiaries, or (2) to the surviving joint parties. To resolve this issue, you must determine whether the joint account includes the survivorship feature.

A three-part analysis is used to determine whether a surviving party has survivorship rights. First, examine state law to ascertain the state's presumption regarding survivorship. Some states presume the account has no survivorship rights so that survivorship rights only exist when the parties expressly create them in the account contract. Other states provide that survivorship rights are an automatic characteristic of joint accounts. See UPC §6-212. Second, examine the account contract to see if it rebuts the state law presumption. If the contract expressly states that the account does or does not have survivorship rights, the contract's characterization prevails over the default presumption. Third, determine whether state law permits the use of extrinsic evidence to vary the terms of the account contract. Courts are strongly divided on this issue.

§16.1.2.2 Withdrawal Rights

Any party to a joint account has the right to withdraw any and all of the funds on deposit, before or after the death of another party, even if the withdrawing party does not have ownership rights to the withdrawn funds. If a surviving party to a nonsurvivorship joint account withdraws an amount in excess of the party's net contributions, the party will be liable to the estate of the deceased party for conversion.

Example 16-2. Joint Account — Rights after Death — Language Necessary to Create Survivorship Rights

Depositor One and Depositor Two opened a joint account that provided "upon the death of either of us any balance in said account or any part thereof may be withdrawn by, or upon the order of, the survivor." Depositor One died with a valid will leaving everything to Spouse. Who is entitled to the funds remaining in the joint account?

Explanation

If the applicable state law presumes survivorship, it is likely that Depositor Two is entitled to the funds. The account contract language does not appear inconsistent with survivorship rights. On the other hand, if applicable state law does not presume survivorship rights, Depositor Two must show that the quoted language is sufficient to imbue the account with the survivorship feature. Courts often struggle with this issue with some courts finding that the account language is not strong enough because it only authorizes the survivor to make withdrawals and does not directly transfer ownership to the survivor.

Example 16-3. Joint Account—Rights after Death— Challenging Account Contract

Depositor One and Depositor Two opened a joint account that unambiguously stated that the surviving joint party is to be the owner of all remaining funds in the account. Depositor One died with a valid will leaving everything to Spouse. Spouse has strong evidence showing that Depositor One did not intend to create survivorship rights in Depositor Two. Who is entitled to the funds remaining in the account?

Explanation

Jurisdictions are divided on the issue of whether extrinsic evidence may be used to alter the terms of the deposit contract. Some courts will allow the evidence while other courts hold that absent incapacity, duress, fraud, or undue influence, the contract is conclusive. Otherwise, disgruntled heirs or will beneficiaries would always assert that the deceased depositor did not intend to create survivorship rights.

§16.2 Agency or Convenience Accounts

A joint account without survivorship rights is often termed an *agency* or a *convenience account*. In some states, these accounts are governed by a separate set of statutory provisions to make a clear distinction between accounts that do and do not have the survivorship feature. When an agency account is opened, the depositing party does not intend the other party to obtain the remaining funds when the party dies. Instead, the depositor plans for the other party to serve as a limited agent to transact account business for the depositor's convenience. For example, the depositor may anticipate an extended stay outside of the country and thus needs someone to pay bills in the depositor's absence, or perhaps the depositor has difficulty writing and wants someone to handle the mechanics of check preparation. The depositor could accomplish the same result with a formal power of attorney, but agency accounts are usually simpler and more efficient unless comprehensive management of the depositor's financial affairs is needed.

Example 16-4. Agency or Convenience Accounts — Rights after Death

Party and Agent were named on an agency account. When Party died, the account contained $3,200. Party's valid will left everything to Child. Who is entitled to the remaining balance?

Explanation

Both during and after the Party's death, Agent has the authority to make withdrawals. However, Agent has no survivorship rights. Unless Agent made deposits of Agent's own funds into the account, all remaining funds pass under Party's will to Child.

§16.3 Payable on Death Accounts

A *payable on death* (P.O.D.) account becomes payable to designated persons, the P.O.D. payees, only after the death of all original depositors. See UPC §6-212(b). The funds in the account belong to the original depositors during their lifetimes in proportion to each depositor's net contribution. The original depositors have the unrestricted right to withdraw any or all funds at any time and for any reason. See UPC §6-211(c). The P.O.D. payees are not entitled to notice of withdrawals and their consent or approval is not required.

Although P.O.D. accounts are recognized in most states, this recognition is of relatively recent origin. Unlike a joint account, which is based on property law concepts of joint tenancy, and trust accounts, which are based on trust law principles, P.O.D. accounts developed purely as deposit contracts. The use of a contract to transfer property at death was often considered to be an impermissible sidestepping of the formalities necessary for a will. Consequently, courts would deem the contract testamentary in nature and thus ineffective to make an at-death transfer of the account balance unless, by unlikely coincidence, the contract satisfied the requirements of a will. See Chapter 17, below, for a discussion of contracts as nonprobate transfer mechanisms.

Example 16-5.   Payable on Death Accounts

Who would be entitled to the balances in the following situations involving P.O.D. accounts?

Example 16-5a.   "Depositor payable on death to Payee." Depositor dies.

Explanation

Payee is entitled to the balance because Payee survived Depositor.

Example 16-5b.   "Depositor payable on death to Payee One and Payee Two." Depositor dies.

Explanation

Payee One and Payee Two receive equal shares (50 percent each) of the account balance.

Example 16-5c.   "Depositor payable on death to Payee One and Payee Two." Payee One dies.

Explanation

Depositor still has full rights to all sums on deposit. Payee One's heirs or will beneficiaries have no claim to any of the funds because Payee One did not outlive Depositor.

Example 16-5d.   "Depositor payable on death to Payee One and Payee Two." Payee One dies and then Depositor dies.

Explanation

Payee Two is entitled to the entire account balance because Payee Two was the only payee to outlive Depositor.

Example 16-5e.   "Depositor One or Depositor Two payable on death to Payee." Depositor One dies.

Explanation

As between Depositor One and Depositor Two, the account is a joint account. Thus, you need to determine whether survivorship rights exist between these depositors. See §16.1.2.1, above. If survivorship rights exist, Depositor Two is entitled to the balance. If there are no survivorship rights, Depositor One's net contributions pass to Depositor One's heirs or will beneficiaries. Depositor Two's net contributions would remain in the account. Regardless of the existence of survivorship rights, Payee has no rights because Payee has not yet survived both depositors. This combination of a joint account, usually with survivorship rights, and a P.O.D. account is relatively common. The depositors are typically parents or grandparents with the P.O.D. payee being a child or grandchild.

Example 16-5f. "Depositor pay on death to Payee." Payee dies.

Explanation

The balance belongs to Depositor. If Depositor dies without changing the account designation, any remaining balance will pass to Depositor's heirs or will beneficiaries. Payee's successors in interest have no claim to the funds because Payee did not outlive Depositor.

§16.4 Trust Accounts

A *trust account* is an account in a form such as, "Depositor in trust for Beneficiary" or "Depositor, trustee for Beneficiary." Trust accounts, also called *savings account trusts* or *tentative trusts,* operate in much the same way as P.O.D. accounts; that is, upon the death of all trustees, the surviving beneficiaries divide the balance remaining in the account. See §16.3, above.

Despite their resemblance to P.O.D. accounts, trust accounts have a totally different history because they evolved from trust law rather than contract law. Courts have taken several approaches to cope with trust accounts, most of which prevented the account from operating as the depositor intended. Some common examples include: (1) the depositor lacked the intent to create a real inter vivos trust and thus the court did not recognize the existence of a trust; (2) the depositor intended to create a trust, but the trust was invalid because the depositor retained complete control over the account and did not assume the fiduciary duties required of a trustee; and (3) the true purpose of the arrangement was to effectuate an at-death transfer of property and thus the account would not operate to do so because it did not comply with the formalities of a valid will.

On the other hand, some courts held that the depositor created a valid revocable trust. Thus, the depositor could make withdrawals at any time but, upon death, the balance would pass to the beneficiary. The landmark New York case of *In re Totten*[1] adopted this latter approach and thus trust accounts are often referred to as *Totten trusts.*

Modern law has stripped trust accounts of their trust law components. Trust accounts are generally treated as contractual arrangements providing for payment of the balance upon the death of all trustees to the surviving beneficiaries. Because of this tremendous similarity to P.O.D. accounts, many states and the UPC have abandoned the distinction and now treat trust accounts just like P.O.D. accounts. See UPC §6-201(8).

---

1. 179 N.Y. 112, 71 N.E. 748 (1904).

§16.5   Other Multiple-Party Account Issues

§16.5.1   *Ability to Alter Contract by Will*

It is unlikely that a will provision expressly gifting the account or account funds would be sufficient to alter the terms of an account contract providing for survivorship rights or for payment to a P.O.D. payee or trust account beneficiary. See UPC §6-213(b). Wills control the disposition of property in a decedent's probate estate; the proceeds of a joint account with survivorship rights, P.O.D. account, or trust account never reach the estate but instead pass directly to the surviving joint parties, P.O.D. payees, or beneficiaries.

§16.5.2   *Creditors*

Multiple-party accounts are generally not an effective method of avoiding creditors. While the depositor is alive, the depositor's creditors may reach the account to the extent of the depositor's net contributions. Generally, creditors of an agent, P.O.D. payee, or trust account beneficiary have no right to reach the funds. Upon the depositor's death, the balance passes to a party with survivorship rights, a P.O.D. payee, or a beneficiary. Many states, however, provide that the depositor's creditors may still reach these funds although this right is often restricted to situations where other assets of the estate are insufficient. See UPC §6-215.

§16.5.3   *Divorce*

What is the effect of a divorce on the individuals involved in a multiple-party account? Will ex-Husband still take as the surviving party of a joint account with ex-Wife? Will ex-Wife take as a beneficiary on a P.O.D. account created by ex-Husband? Some jurisdictions allow the ex-spouse to take while others revoke the provisions automatically as a matter of law and then dispose of the property as if the ex-spouse had predeceased the depositor. See UPC §2-804.

§16.5.4   *Survival*

Joint tenants with survivorship rights, P.O.D. payees, and trust account beneficiaries must outlive the depositor to claim account funds. How long must the claimant survive? Many jurisdictions require that a person making a claim to account funds outlive the depositor by a certain length of time, such as 120 hours. See UPC §2-702.

§16.5.5 *Effect of Depositor's Incapacity*

When a depositor becomes incompetent, the depositor no longer has the ability to manage the depositor's property, including multiple-party accounts. Management duties may then pass to a court-appointed guardian of the estate or conservator. Assume that Depositor has two accounts: Account One in Depositor's name alone, and Account Two, which has a P.O.D. provision in favor of Payee. Guardian needs money to pay Depositor's expenses and thus starts spending the money in Account Two. What right, if any, does Payee have to complain and to force Guardian to use the funds in Account One first? There is no clear resolution of this issue.

§16.5.6 *Practical Note*

Depositors usually open multiple-party accounts without consulting an attorney. The depositor visits a financial institution and opens the account after speaking with a new accounts officer. This person, who is rarely legally trained, explains the alleged effect of the account; for example, that the balance will belong to the surviving party. The officer's advice could be incorrect and may even be the practice of law without a license. Thus, it is essential that you personally inspect all of your client's multiple-party account contracts to make sure they comply with the applicable law and carry out your client's intent.

17

Contracts

Contracts may contain provisions directing the payment of money or delivery of other property upon an individual's death. This property will not pass through probate provided that the payee is not the decedent's estate. Instead, the property passes directly to the designated person.

Some types of contractually based at-death transfers, such as life insurance, have been widely accepted for centuries. Other types of contracts, especially those that exist primarily to provide at-death transfers of property the decedent owned at the time of death, have faced difficulty in gaining recognition. In years past, many courts deemed these contracts testamentary in nature and thus ineffective to transfer property for failure to comply with the requirements of a valid will.

Under modern law, these arrangements have achieved broad approval as effective methods of providing for at-death transfers. For example, UPC §6-101 provides that

> [a] provision for a nonprobate transfer on death in an insurance policy, contract of employment, bond, mortgage, promissory note, certificated or uncertificated security, account agreement, custodial agreement, deposit agreement, compensation plan, pension plan, individual retirement plan, employee benefit plan, trust, conveyance, deed of gift, marital property agreement, or other written instrument of a similar nature is nontestamentary.

As UPC §6-101 indicates, the variety of these types of contracts is virtually endless. This chapter discusses some of the contractual arrangements in common use.

§17.1 Life Insurance

§17.1.1 Basic Operation of Life Insurance Policy

A life insurance policy is a contract between the *owner* of the policy and an *insurer*. In exchange for the owner's payment of *premiums,* the insurer promises to pay a stated amount, the *proceeds* or *face value,* to the *beneficiary* when a designated person, the *insured,* dies. In many policies, the owner and the insured are the same individual. The diagram below shows this relationship.

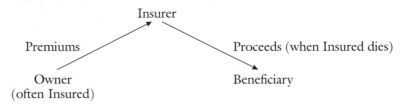

The contract may impose conditions on the insurer's obligation to pay the proceeds in addition to the insured's death. For example, the insurer may not have to pay if the insured commits suicide shortly after the policy was issued or if the insured misstated the insured's medical condition on the insurance application.

To obtain life insurance on a person's life, you must have an *insurable interest* in that person's life. Simply stated, you need to have a strong reason to keep the insured alive other than the fear of criminal or spiritual penalties for murder. Thus, you have an insurable interest in your own life as well as the life of your close family members such as a spouse, children, and parents. In a business setting, a company may have an insurable interest in the life of a key employee. Once the person with an insurable interest obtains the policy, this person may transfer ownership to anyone the person desires, even if the new owner lacks an insurable interest in the insured.

§17.1.2 Use of Life Insurance

Life insurance is an important and powerful estate planning tool. For a younger client, life insurance may be the individual's most valuable asset. The client may literally be worth more dead than alive. This is especially the case because state law typically protects life insurance proceeds from claims of the insured's creditors.

Life insurance can create an "instant estate" for the insured and the insured's family. Insurance proceeds serve as substitute income, replacing the wages of a deceased insured. In addition, the beneficiary is not required to pay income tax on the receipt of life insurance proceeds. The proceeds also serve as a source of liquidity enabling heirs and beneficiaries to pay estate taxes and other expenses. Without ready cash, the insured's survivors may need to sell estate property (such as the home, heirlooms, or a family business or farm) to raise the money needed to pay estate taxes.

§17.1.3 Types of Life Insurance

§17.1.3.1 Term Life Insurance

Term life insurance is the basic type of life insurance. If the insured dies during a specified term, such as one year, the insurer will pay the proceeds to the beneficiary. The insurer will not pay if the insured outlives the term. Term life insurance is the most economical type of insurance, especially for young and healthy individuals, because the premiums cover only the cost of the insurance during the current term. (Insurance agents might not promote term policies because agents typically receive the lowest commissions on these policies.) However, premiums on term insurance increase as the insured ages, there is no build up of cash value (defined in §17.1.3.2, below), and there may be renewability problems if the insured's health deteriorates.

§17.1.3.2 Whole Life Insurance

Whole life insurance is designed to provide insurance protection for the insured's entire life, not just a specified term. With whole life, the amount of the premiums remains constant from the time the insurer issues the policy until the insured dies or reaches an advanced age, such as ninety or 100, at which time premiums will no longer be needed to keep the policy in force.

When the insured is young, the premiums far exceed the amount necessary to pay for insurance coverage, that is, the amount needed to pay for a term policy. These excess premiums accumulate in a reserve called the policy's *cash value* or *cash surrender value*. This build-up in value permits the owner to use the policy as collateral for a loan or to borrow the cash value from the insurer, often at a favorable interest rate. (Note, however, that the owner is actually paying interest to borrow the owner's own money.) If the owner elects to stop making premium payments, the owner can receive the cash value in a lump sum, use the cash value to purchase a *paid up* policy for a lesser face value on which no future premiums need be paid, or use the cash value as premium payments to continue the policy in full effect until the cash value runs out. Traditional whole life insurance is generally considered an unwise choice because the insured overpays for insurance in the early years and does not receive a competitive rate of return on the cash value.

§17.1.3.3 Universal Life Insurance

Universal life insurance works like whole life insurance with one important difference — the cash value receives a competitive rate of return. Instead of the cash value earning income at a below-market rate, the cash value yields a return more like the rate the owner would receive if the owner had made other types of investments. Depending on how the insurance policy is written, the owner may be able to alter the amount and frequency of premium payments, change the face value, and make decisions on how the insurer invests the cash value.

§17.1.3.4 Endowment Life Insurance

Endowment life insurance is similar to whole life and universal life but the premiums stop at a younger age, such as sixty-two or sixty-five. In addition, the cash value will equal the face value at that time. If the insured survives to the stated age, the owner is entitled to receive a lump sum that equals the face value. Because the insurer has an increased likelihood of paying the face value of the policy at a relatively early time, the premiums on endowment polices are quite high.

§17.1.3.5 Split Dollar Life Insurance

The key feature of *split dollar life insurance* is who pays the premiums. With split dollar insurance, the insured and the insured's employer contribute to the premiums. When the insured dies, the insurer pays part of the proceeds to the employer, usually the amount necessary to reimburse the employer for the premium contributions, and then distributes the balance of the proceeds to the beneficiaries. This type of arrangement has the potential of considerable tax savings.

§17.1.4 *Payment of Proceeds*

Insurance policies usually give the owner many options regarding how the insurer will pay the proceeds when the insured dies. The most common method is the *lump sum* payment where the beneficiary simply receives a check for the face value of the policy. Under the *installment* option, the insurer makes periodic payments of the proceeds to the beneficiary. With an *interest* or *deposit* option, the insurer retains the proceeds, makes payments of interest to the beneficiaries, and then transfers the proceeds to the beneficiary at a specified later time.

Many life insurance policy owners have the proceeds paid to trusts, rather than directly to the beneficiaries. This technique is advisable when the beneficiaries are minors, incompetents, or individuals who lack the ability to manage property. In this way, the owner can obtain the benefits of a trust such as control over the use of the proceeds as well as ensure that the proceeds are professionally invested and managed. In addition, a court will not be required to appoint a guardian or conservator to manage the proceeds. See Chapter 18 for a discussion of the benefits of placing property in a trust and §19.8.12 for coverage of life insurance trusts.

Example 17-1. Life Insurance — Beneficiary Murdering Insured

Insured named Beneficiary as the sole beneficiary of Insured's life insurance policy. Beneficiary murdered Insured. Who is entitled to the proceeds? Would it matter if the death were accidental rather than intentional?

Explanation

Beneficiary should not profit from wrongfully and intentionally killing Insured. The way in which the law reaches this result varies among the states. Some states have statutes directly on point that would prevent Beneficiary from receiving the proceeds. The proceeds would then pass to the contingent beneficiaries Insured named in the policy or, if none, to Insured's heirs or will beneficiaries, exclusive of Beneficiary. See UPC §2-803 (applicable to a "felonious and intentional killing"). Other states apply constructive trust theory to prevent Beneficiary from being unjustly enriched. See Chapter 23. However, if Insured's death were accidental, the courts are more likely to permit Beneficiary to claim the proceeds.

Example 17-2. Life Insurance — Survival of Beneficiary

Insured and Beneficiary were in an automobile accident while traveling together. Insured died at the scene. Beneficiary was mortally wounded and died a short time later at the hospital. Who is entitled to the proceeds of the life insurance policy?

Explanation

Absent a contractual or statutory provision on point, Beneficiary or Beneficiary's estate would be entitled to the proceeds because Beneficiary was the owner of a contract right to the proceeds. Accordingly, the proceeds would pass through Beneficiary's estate to the appropriate heirs or will beneficiaries. Most states, however, have statutes that require that Beneficiary outlive Insured by a stated period of time to be entitled to the proceeds. See UPC §2-702 (120 hours). If Beneficiary did not survive to that time,

Beneficiary will be treated as predeceasing Insured and thus the proceeds would pass to the contingent beneficiary or, if none, through the Insured's estate if Insured was the owner of the policy.

Example 17-3. Life Insurance — Divorce of Beneficiary from Insured

Insured named Spouse as the beneficiary of a life insurance policy. Insured designated Spouse's children from a prior relationship as the contingent beneficiaries. Insured and Spouse divorced. Insured died several years later without changing the beneficiary designations. Who is entitled to the proceeds of the life insurance policy?

Explanation

Under traditional common law, a divorce has no effect on the life insurance beneficiary designation and thus Spouse would still take the proceeds. Because of the unlikelihood of an insured intending to benefit a former spouse, several states have enacted statutes automatically revoking beneficiary designations in favor of ex-spouses. If such a law governed the facts in this question, the proceeds would pass to the contingent beneficiaries. But these contingent beneficiaries are also relatives of the former spouse. Only a few jurisdictions have statutes that also avoid beneficiary designations in favor of other ex-relatives. See UPC §2-804.

§17.1.5   Policies Insuring Two Lives

Two types of policies that insure two lives simultaneously, typically spouses, are in common use because the cost of one policy insuring the two lives is cheaper than one policy for each person. In many cases, there is no need to insure both lives. For example, if the spouses are concerned about providing for children, a *second-to-die* or *survivorship* policy is appropriate. A second-to-die policy pays proceeds only when the second of the two insureds die. On the other hand, if the spouses are more concerned about providing for the surviving spouse, a *first-to-die* policy, which pays proceeds only when the first of the two insureds dies, is suitable.

§17.2   Annuities

An *annuity* is a contract between the purchaser of the contract and an annuity provider. In exchange for a lump sum payment, the annuity provider promises to make periodic payments for the life of the *annuitant* or some other specified period of time. The diagram below shows the basic operation of an annuity.

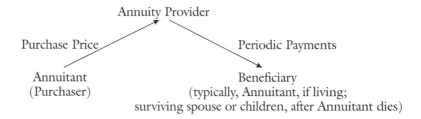

An annuity protects a person from exhausting the person's estate by living longer than anticipated. The purpose of annuities is, in effect, the opposite of life insurance, which protects the insured's family against the risk of the insured dying earlier than anticipated and before accumulating sufficient assets to sustain the family in the manner in which its members were accustomed. Annuities may provide for payments to continue after the annuitant's death and thus annuity contracts often operate to make non-probate transfers.

Annuities are classified from several perspectives. First, they are categorized based on the type of annuity provider, that is, the entity that will make the periodic payments. A *commercial annuity* is one purchased from a company in the business of selling annuities (e.g., an insurance company). A *private annuity* is purchased from someone not in the annuity business (e.g., a family member).

Second, annuities are distinguished by the duration of the periodic payments. Under a *straight life annuity,* the provider makes payments only while the annuitant is alive. If the annuitant outlives his or her life expectancy, the provider loses money. But if the annuitant dies quickly, the provider makes a sizable profit. Straight life annuities lack a nonprobate transfer component. With a *refund annuity,* the provider makes payments for the annuitant's life but if the annuitant dies before receiving at least the amount paid for the annuity, the provider pays the difference between the purchase price and the amount already distributed to the annuitant to a designated beneficiary. A *life annuity with a term certain* provides payments for the annuitant's life but if the annuitant dies before the term expires, the provider continues to make annuity payments to a designated beneficiary until the end of the term. The provider makes payments under a *joint life annuity* until the first of the annuitants dies at which time the payments cease. With a *joint and survivorship annuity,* however, the provider continues payments until both annuitants die.

Third, annuities are characterized by how the periodic payments are determined. In a *straight* annuity, each payment is of the same amount, while in a *variable* annuity, the amount of the payment changes based on the investment success of the annuity provider. Variable annuities are thus useful to offset the deflated buying power that inflation causes when all payments are of the same amount.

§17.3   Employee Benefit and Retirement Plans

An individual may die before exhausting the property accumulated in an employee benefit plan or other retirement arrangement. Most benefit contracts provide that the remaining property or some other type of death benefit will then be payable to the beneficiary named by the employee. Assuming the beneficiary is not the employee's estate, the death benefit is not subject to probate.

A carefully constructed plan gives the employee tremendous benefits in addition to a nonprobate transfer of the death benefit. For example, the amounts the employee contributes to the plan within statutorily established limits are not currently subject to income tax. In addition, the income the property generates while in the plan is tax-deferred. The initial contributions and subsequent income are not subject to income tax until the employee makes withdrawals. Since most employees will be in a lower income tax bracket after they retire than they were when the contributions were made and the income accrued, substantial income tax savings result. Benefit plans are also advantageous for employers because they can usually deduct the contributions on their income tax returns. An employee benefit plan that meets the requirements for this favorable income tax treatment is called a *qualified plan* and is governed by the *Employee Retirement Income Security Act of 1974 (ERISA)* and various provisions of the Internal Revenue Code.

§17.3.1   Types of Employee Benefit Plans

A *defined benefit plan* is a basic plan that provides the employee with a determinable amount of benefits payable for a certain number of years or until the employee dies. The amount of the payments are based on a variety of factors such as how long the employee worked for the employer and the employee's salary.

A *defined contribution plan* is a more sophisticated arrangement. The employer contributes to the plan on the employee's behalf. The contributions may be fixed amounts or they may be computed by a formula, such as a certain percentage of the employer's profits. The amount the employee receives upon retirement is based upon the amount contributed plus the success of the plan's management in investing the contributions.

In a *cash or deferred arrangement*, also called a *CODA* or *401(k) plan*, the employee authorizes the employer to place a percentage of the employee's salary into the benefit plan. The amount invested and the plan's earnings determine the amount the employee eventually receives upon retirement.

If the employee works for a corporation, the employer may create a special type of benefit plan called an *employee stock ownership plan* or *ESOP*. The employer forms a special type of trust and then makes contributions to the trust on behalf of the employee. The trustee purchases the corporate employer's stock with the contributions and holds the stock as the trust corpus. The specific rules of the plan determine the amount of stock the employee will later receive.

A major shortcoming of the qualified plans already discussed is that they require the individual to be an employee. Self-employed persons can use *Keogh plans.* Keogh plans, also called *H.R.-10 plans,* permit sole proprietors, partners, and other noncommon law employees to create retirement plans under basically the same rules as employee plans and receive similar tax benefits.

Both self-employed individuals and employees may use *individual retirement accounts* or *IRAs.* The amounts individuals may contribute are limited and the initial income tax benefit is restricted to individuals who have relatively low incomes. In the standard or *classic IRA,* the contributor does not pay income tax on qualifying contributions nor on the earnings (income and appreciation) of those contributions as they accrue but must pay tax when the contributor makes withdrawals upon retirement. An opposite approach is taken by the *Roth IRA* in which the contributor must pay income tax on qualifying contributions but all distributions of both original contributions and earnings are free of income tax.

Small businesses may not be able to afford to establish traditional qualified retirement plans because of the administrative overhead costs. These employers may make contributions directly to their employees' IRAs using the *simplified employee pension plan* or *SEP* technique.

§17.3.2 *Protection of Surviving Spouse*

Federal law requires that qualified employee benefit plans give the employee's spouse the right to demand that the retirement benefit be paid as a joint and survivor annuity. If the employee spouse dies before the employee spouse retires, the surviving spouse is still entitled to a death benefit payable as an annuity. Congress imposed these conditions on obtaining the tax benefits of qualified plans in the *Retirement Equity Act of 1984 (REA).*

A married employee may regain the ability to control payment of the qualified plan's death benefit by procuring spousal consent. The spouse's waiver must (1) be in writing, (2) indicate that spousal consent is required to change the beneficiary or form of benefits at a later time unless the spouse's current waiver expressly permits redesignations without further consent, and (3) contain the spouse's acknowledgment of the effect of the waiver, witnessed by a plan representative or a notary public.

§17.4 Transfer on Death Arrangements

State and federal law may permit the owners of certain property to specify the person who is entitled to ownership rights upon the owner's death. These types of arrangements have had the toughest time gaining acceptance as nonprobate transfers because they do not have a clear purpose other than acting as will substitutes. There is no transfer of current ownership as with joint tenancies and no bargained-for consideration as with life insurance, annuities, and employee benefit plans. Nonetheless, transfer on death arrangements are rapidly gaining in popularity and approval in the United States.

Owners of United States savings bonds may register them in beneficiary form so that the bond is payable to the named beneficiary upon the death of the owner. The vast majority of states recognize pay on death designations on accounts at financial institutions. See §16.3, above. Many states have enacted the Uniform Transfer on Death Security Registration Act, which permits P.O.D. designations on corporate securities such as stocks and bonds. Other states expand P.O.D. designations to cover other tangible assets such as motor vehicles. Further, some community property marital property jurisdictions permit the spouses to agree to hold community property with survivorship rights.

Part Five

TRUSTS

Part Five of this book focuses on trusts. A person creates a trust by transferring property in such a manner that title is split into legal and equitable interests and fiduciary duties are imposed on the holder of the legal title to manage that property for the benefit of the holder of the equitable title. Chapter 18 introduces trusts by exploring basic principles, terminology, the purposes and uses of trusts, and related matters. The following chapters detail trust creation, administration, and enforcement. Part Five concludes with a discussion of two types of legal relationships, resulting trusts and constructive trusts which, although labeled trusts, are not trusts in the traditional sense.

18

Introduction to Trusts

§18.1 Overview and Terminology

§18.1.1 *Basic Trust Operation*

The owner of property may create a trust by transferring that property in a unique fashion. First, the owner must divide the title to the property into legal and equitable interests; second, the owner must impose fiduciary duties on the holder of the legal title to deal with the property for the benefit of the holder of the equitable title. Once the owner transfers property in this manner, the property is usually referred to as the trust *principal, corpus, estate,* or *res.*

In general, a trust scenario arises when a property owner wants to bestow benefits on a worthy individual or charity but does not want to make an unrestricted outright gift. Thus, the owner transfers legal title to a reliable individual or financial institution and equitable title to the individual or charity deserving the windfall. The holder of legal title manages that property following state law requirements and the original owner's instructions as specified in the trust instrument. The trustee then makes payments to or for the benefit of the individual or charity according to the original owner's instructions. When the property is exhausted or the instructions are completed, the trust ends and, once again, title to any remaining property is unified in the hands of the individual or charity the property owner specified.

§18.1.2 *Parties Involved in Trust Relationship*

The person who creates a trust by splitting title and imposing fiduciary duties is called the *settlor*. You may see the settlor referred to by other terms. In old cases and statutes, the settlor may be dubbed by the archaic term *trustor*. In tax-related discussions, the settlor is frequently designated as the *grantor* because the settlor is making a grant of the property by splitting the title. The settlor may also be called a *donor* because most transfers of beneficial title are actually gifts.

The person who holds the legal interest to the property is the *trustee*. The trustee has all of the duties, responsibilities, and liabilities associated with property ownership but the trustee receives none of the benefits of that ownership. The best the trustee can hope for is a fee for serving as the trustee. Thus, if I told you I am giving you legal title to $1 million, you would not be very happy. In fact, you would be quite upset unless you were going to get paid because I would have imposed upon you all the burdens of owning $1 million. And, it actually gets worse, because you would be holding that legal title as a fiduciary. This means that you would be required to manage the property with reasonable care, avoid any type of self-dealing with the property, and be certain not to be in a position where your own personal interests could be in conflict with those of the beneficiaries. If your conduct would ever fall beneath these standards, even if the lapse were merely negligent, you could be personally responsible in a civil action for damages and could even face a criminal prosecution.

The equitable title to the trust property is held by the *beneficiary*. The beneficiary is entitled to enjoy the trust property but, unlike the donee of an outright gift as discussed in §14.1, above, not in an unrestricted manner. The beneficiary may receive only the benefits from the property as the settlor specified in the trust instrument. Typically, the beneficiary has no control over the trustee or how the trustee manages the legal title to the property. However, the beneficiary has the right to sue the trustee if the trustee's conduct breaches the fiduciary duties or if the trustee does not follow the settlor's instructions as set forth in the trust instrument. You may see the beneficiary referred to by other terms. The French term *cestui que trust* is often used in older cases. When the emphasis is on the tax consequences of equitable title ownership, the beneficiary is typically called the *grantee* and when the gift element of the transfer is most important, the term *donee* may be used.

§18.2 Purposes and Uses of Trusts[1]

Trusts are an extremely powerful, useful, and advantageous estate planning technique. This section discusses some of the reasons a property owner may want to convey property in trust.

§18.2.1 *Provide for and Protect Beneficiaries*

The settlor's desire to provide for and protect someone is probably the most common reason for creating a trust. Although a donor could make a quick, convenient, and uncomplicated outright gift, there are many situations in which such outright gifts would not effectuate the donor's true intent.

§18.2.1.1 Minors

Minors lack legal capacity to manage property and usually have insufficient maturity to do so as well. A trust permits the settlor to make a gift for the benefit of a minor without giving the minor control over the property or triggering the necessity for the minor to have a court-appointed guardian to manage that property. A trust is also more flexible and allows a settlor to have greater control over how the property is used when contrasted with other methods such as a transfer to a guardian or conservator of the minor's estate or to a custodian under the Uniform Transfers to Minors Act (see §14.6, above).

§18.2.1.2 Individuals Who Lack Management Skills

An individual may lack the skills necessary to properly manage the trust property. This deficiency could be the result of mental or physical incompetence or a lack of experience in the rigors of making prudent investment decisions. For example, persons who suddenly obtain large amounts of money, such as performers, professional athletes, lottery winners, or personal injury plaintiffs, tend to deplete these windfalls rapidly because they have never learned how to manage their money wisely. By putting the money under the control of a trustee with investment experience, the settlor increases the likelihood that the beneficiary's interests are served for a longer period of time.

---

1. This section is adapted from Gerry W. Beyer, *Texas Wills and Estates: Cases and Materials* 8-9 (1995) & Gerry W. Beyer, *Teaching Materials on Estate Planning* 54-56 (1995).

§18.2.1.3 Spendthrifts

Some individuals may be competent to manage property but are prone to use it in an excessive or frivolous manner. By using a carefully drafted trust, a settlor can protect the trust property from the beneficiary's own excesses as well as the beneficiary's creditors. Spendthrift trust provisions are analyzed in §19.8.8, below.

§18.2.1.4 Persons Susceptible to Influence

When a person suddenly acquires a significant amount of property, that person may be under pressure from family, friends, charities, investment advisors, and opportunistic scam artists who wish to share in the windfall. A trust can make it virtually impossible for the beneficiary to transfer trust property to these people.

§18.2.2 *Flexible Distribution of Assets*

An outright gift, either inter vivos or testamentary, gives the donee total control over the way the property is used. With a trust, the settlor can restrict the beneficiary's control over the property in any manner the settlor desires as long as the restrictions are not illegal or in violation of public policy. This flexibility allows the settlor to determine how the trustee distributes trust benefits, such as by spreading the benefits over time, giving the trustee discretion to select who receives distributions and in what amounts, requiring the beneficiary to meet certain criteria to receive or continue receiving benefits, or limiting the purposes for which trust property may be used such as health care or education.

§18.2.3 *Protection against Settlor's Incompetence*

Once an individual is incompetent due to illness, injury, or other cause, the person cannot manage the person's own property. The court then needs to appoint a guardian of the estate or a conservator to manage the property. The process of judicially determining a person's incompetency may cause the person considerable private and public embarrassment, and there is no guarantee the incompetent person will be happy with the guardian's decisions. Guardianships are also inconvenient and costly because guardians act under court supervision and are required to submit detailed reports on a regular basis.

A trust can be used to avoid this need for a guardian. The settlor may create a trust and maintain considerable control over the trust property by, for example, serving as the trustee, retaining the power to revoke the trust, and keeping a beneficial life interest. However, upon incompetency, the settlor's designated successor trustee would take over the administration of the trust property in accordance with the directions the settlor expressed in the trust instrument. This type of arrangement is often called a *stand-by trust*.

An alternative method to protect property and avoid the need for a guardian in the event of incompetency is to have the client execute a durable power of attorney for property management. See §25.1.1, below.

§18.2.4 *Professional Management of Property*

The settlor may create a trust to obtain the services of a professional asset manager, either for the benefit of third-party beneficiaries or for the settlor as the beneficiary. Professional trustees, such as banks and trust companies, have more expertise and experience with various types of investments than most individuals. Assume that you have just inherited a wheat farm in Kansas, an office building in New York City, an apartment building in San Francisco, United States government savings bonds, corporate stock in a dozen domestic corporations, oil and gas property in Texas, and an import-export business in Italy. Would you have the skill to handle all of these different types of assets? If not, placing the assets in trust would be one way of obtaining professional management. In addition, there is another advantage to making a trust conveyance. If you negligently manage your own property and suffer financially as a result, there is not much you can do about it — you cannot successfully bring a law suit against yourself. However, if a trustee is negligent, you can bring suit for breach of fiduciary duties; if successful, you have a strong chance of recovery, because most financial institutions and trust companies have money or other assets that can be reached to satisfy a damage award.

Professional trustees also have greater investment opportunities. For example, a bank may combine funds from several trusts into one common trust fund to take advantage of opportunities that require a large investment and to diversify, thus reducing the damage to the value of the trust when one investment turns sour.

§18.2.5 *Probate Avoidance*

Property in a trust created during the settlor's lifetime is not part of the probate estate upon the settlor's death. The property remaining in the trust when the settlor dies is administered and distributed according to the terms of the trust; it does not pass under the settlor's will or by intestate succession. Advantages to avoiding probate include getting the property into the hands of the beneficiaries quickly, avoiding gaps in management, and evading probate publicity. See Chapter 13, above. These advantages, however, do not apply to a trust created in the settlor's will because the property must first pass through the probate process.

§18.2.6 *Tax Benefits*

Another popular reason for utilizing trusts is tax avoidance. Income taxes can be saved by transferring income-producing property to a trust that has a beneficiary in a lower tax bracket than the settlor. Additionally, gift taxes may be avoided by structuring the transfers to a trust to fall within the annual exclusion from the federal gift tax which, as of 1998, is $10,000 per year per donee. See §24.1.4.1, below. Likewise, if a trust is properly constructed, the trust property will not be included in the settlor's taxable estate.

§18.3 Warning about Inter Vivos Trust Over-Promotion

Despite the tremendous potential benefits of a trust discussed in §18.2, above, a trust may not be the best tool to accomplish a client's intent. Some attorneys heavily promote inter vivos trusts as an estate planning panacea. They are not. Although a trust is an extremely useful technique, a person should not create a trust until the person carefully balances the benefits against the trust's creation, administration, and transfer costs. For example, assume that the client's main goal is to plan for disability. Although a properly drafted trust would do the job, it will entail additional time and money to establish the trust and transfer title to the property to the trust. Perhaps a durable power of attorney for property management that can be quickly and economically prepared is all the client needs.

To protect the public from exaggerated claims of the benefits of a trust, some states have taken steps to regulate trust advertisement and trust services. For example, in November 1997, Texas prohibited attorneys from making the following statements about trusts created during the settlor's lifetime because they are potentially misleading and may create unjustified expectations:

1. Living trusts will always save the client money.
2. The use of a living trust in and of itself will reduce or eliminate estate taxes otherwise payable as a result of the client's death.
3. Estate tax savings can be achieved only by use of a living trust.
4. The use of a living trust will achieve estate tax savings that cannot be achieved using a will.

5. The probate process is always lengthy and complicated.
6. The probate process should always be avoided.
7. The use of a living trust will reduce the total expenses incurred compared to expenses incurred using other estate planning devices intended to address the same basic function.
8. The use of a living trust avoids lengthy delays experienced in the use of other estate planning devices intended to address the same basic function.
9. Lawyers use will-writing as a loss leader.[2]

Several states are also attempting to stop the sale of trust services by non-lawyers. Illinois Attorney General Roland Burris stated, "Living trusts in the hands of unscrupulous con artists are one of the fastest growing areas of fraud against senior citizens."[3]

---

2. Interpretive Comment No. 22: Advertisement of Living Trusts, as reported in 61 Tex. B.J. 71 (1998).

3. David N. Anderson, *Living Trust Fraud Bill Is Approved,* ISBA Bar News, June 21, 1993, at 1.

19

Trust Creation

This chapter analyzes the requirements for a valid *express trust;* that is, a trust created based on the expressed intent of the settlor. It is important to make a distinction between two categories of express trusts. First, the *private trust,* which is a trust created for noncharitable beneficiaries, and second, the *charitable trust,* which is a trust the settlor establishes for charitable purposes. The requirements are basically the same for both private and charitable trusts. However, some of the validity requirements are different for charitable trusts. Consequently, §19.10, below, details the special rules applicable to charitable trusts.

Other types of trusts are discussed elsewhere. For example, *resulting trusts* which arise by operation of law when the facts and circumstances show that a person had the intent to hold equitable title to property although legal title is in the hands of another, are explained in Chapter 22, below. The equitable remedy of a *constructive trust,* which courts impose to prevent unjust enrichment, is covered in Chapter 23, below.

The fundamental requirements for a valid express trust are summarized below:

(1) **Trust Intent.** The settlor must intend to split legal and equitable title and impose fiduciary duties on the holder of legal title (trustee) for the benefit of the holder of equitable title (beneficiary).

(2) **Capacity.** The settlor must have the capacity to make a conveyance of property in trust form.

(3) **Statute of Frauds Compliance.** In certain situations, the settlor's trust intent must be documented by a written instrument.

(4) **Purpose.** The purpose of the trust must not be illegal or against public policy.

(5) **Property.** The settlor must place property into the trust and the trust must continue to hold property.

(6) **Trustee.** A trustee must ultimately hold legal title and be obligated to deal with the property for the benefit of the beneficiaries. However, the court will appoint a trustee if necessary to ensure the trust's creation or continued existence.

(7) **Beneficiary.** The trust needs a beneficiary to hold the equitable title to the property. The settlor may either retain equitable title and become a beneficiary or transfer it to a third party.

(8) **Rule against Perpetuities.** Under the law of most, but not all, states, the duration of a private trust cannot exceed the period permitted by the Rule against Perpetuities.

§19.1   Trust Intent

Trust intent is the threshold factor in determining whether a conveyance of property is sufficient to create an express trust. If the transferor does not manifest trust intent, no trust is created and the court will not intervene to create a trust.

§19.1.1   Ascertaining Settlor's Intent

A transferor of property has trust intent if the transferor (1) divides title to the property into legal and equitable components, and (2) imposes enforceable fiduciary duties on the holder of legal title to deal with the property for the benefit of the equitable title holder.

Example 19-1.   Trust Intent — Settlor Lacks Understanding of Trust Terminology

Steve transferred $10,000 to Thomas, stating, "Invest this money for my Son, Brad. Give Brad the income every year on his birthday until he reaches age thirty. Then give him the $10,000." If asked, Steve would define "trust" as having confidence in someone who is honest, "legal title" as the official name of a book in the Library of Congress records, "equitable title" as the formal name of horses used at professional racing tracks, and "trustee" as a special type of tea served at upscale restaurants. Did Steve have the intent necessary to create a trust?

Explanation

Yes, Steve demonstrated trust intent. Steve transferred the money to Thomas, told Thomas to use the money for Brad, and made this use mandatory. It is immaterial that Steve did not understand the legal jargon associated with what he was doing. "No particular form of words or conduct is necessary for the manifestation of intention to create a trust."[1]

Example 19-2. Trust Intent—Settlor's Use of Trust Terminology

Susan transferred $10,000 to Teresa stating, "I am creating a trust of this money. You are the trustee and thus have full power to use any and all of this money for any purpose that you wish." Did Susan have the intent necessary to create a trust?

Explanation

No, Susan lacked trust intent. Although Susan used trust language such as "trust" and "trustee," there is no evidence that the transfer was anything less than an outright gift. The mere use of trust terminology is insufficient to show trust intent.

Example 19-3. Trust Intent—Precatory Language

Steve included the following dispositive language in his valid will, "I give Thomas $10,000 with the hope that he will use this money for the educational expenses of his son, Brad." Did Steve have the intent necessary to create a trust?

Explanation

No, Steve did not have trust intent because he did not impose legally enforceable duties on Steve. To create a trust, a settlor's instructions regarding any limitations on the use of the property must be mandatory. Courts normally consider precatory language such as "I wish," "I recommend," or "I suggest" as merely suggestive and not binding on the beneficiary. Although Thomas may have a moral responsibility to comply with Steve's wishes, precatory requests are not enough to impose the legally enforceable responsibilities associated with being a trustee. Courts will, however, examine extrinsic evidence as well as the alleged settlor's language in making their determinations. As a result, even though Steve used precatory language, the court may give effect to the limitation if it is clear from the context that Steve intended to impose a mandatory restriction. See Example 9-23, above.

---

1. Restatement (Second) of Trusts §24(2) (1957).

Example 19-4. Trust Intent — Future Intent

Susan told Teresa, "Tomorrow morning, I am going to give you $10,000 in trust for you to use for the benefit of your children. In addition, if I ever buy stock in Acme Corporation, I will give that to you in trust for your children as well." Does Susan have the intent which is necessary to create a trust?

Explanation

No, Susan did not have the present intent required to create a trust. Her future intent to create a trust is insufficient. A trust would arise only if Susan either (1) actually gave Teresa the $10,000, or (2) acquired Acme Corporation stock and thereafter transferred it to Teresa.

Example 19-5. Trust Intent — Communication to Beneficiary

Steve transferred his vacation home and surrounding land to Thomas and signed a written instrument instructing Thomas to hold the land in trust for Brad and to deed the land to Brad on his twenty-fifth birthday. Brad was eighteen years old when this happened. Brad is now twenty-four years old and has no knowledge that Thomas is supposed to be holding the property for his benefit. Did Steve have the intent to create a trust?

Explanation

Yes, Steve had trust intent. He clearly split title to the property and imposed enforceable duties on Thomas. Steve is not required to tell Thomas that he is the beneficiary of a trust. Even though there is no requirement that a person be informed of his or her status as a trust beneficiary, this type of notification would be good evidence of trust intent.

§19.1.2 Statute of Uses

The historical origin of the two components of trust intent, the split of title and the imposition of duties, is derived from the common law history of trusts. The common law precursor to a trust was called a *use*. Before the fifteenth century, uses were not enforceable and thus a "beneficiary" had no rights and had to hope that the "trustee" would fulfill a merely honorary obligation. This situation changed in the 1400s as uses started to be enforceable as equitable estates in property. By the 1500s, uses were common and were, from the government's point of view, often abused. Property owners were employing uses to avoid their duties of property ownership under the feudal land ownership system, especially financial obligations such as paying money (today called taxes) to the monarch (now the Internal Revenue Service), to hinder creditors and others with claims against the property, and to provide benefits for various religious organizations contrary to the Crown's wishes.

The English Parliament enacted the Statute of Uses[2] in 1536 to end these abuses. The statute *executed the use,* which meant that the beneficiary's equitable interest in real property was turned into a legal interest as well. Because this had the effect of eliminating the legal interest that the trustee formerly held, the beneficiary was now the owner of all title, both legal and equitable, and was fully responsible for all of the burdens of property ownership. Had the Statute of Uses been carried out exactly as written, trusts as we know them would not exist.

An important exception to the Statute of Uses developed for the *active trust.* An active trust is an arrangement where the trustee's holding of property is not merely nominal in an attempt to gain some untoward benefit, but where the trustee actually needs legal title to the property to perform a power or duty relating to the property for the beneficiary's benefit. This exception provides the basis for modern trust law and the two-pronged trust intent requirement.

Note that most states have a version of the Statute of Uses that still operates to terminate a *passive trust,* that is, an attempted split of title where the trustee is merely holding legal title without any powers or duties with respect to the property. In addition, although the original Statute of Uses applied only to real property, most states typically apply a similar rule for personal property.

§19.1.3 *Split of Title and Merger*

Any separation of legal and equitable title coupled with the imposition of fiduciary duties on the holder of the legal title is sufficient to satisfy the split of title requirement for a valid trust. This section explores the permissible combinations of parties that will achieve this separation of title, both when the settlor initially creates the trust and upon the occurrence of various subsequent events.

§19.1.3.1 Initial Trust Creation

The settlor must split title to trust property so that the same person does not own all legal and equitable interests in that property.

---

2. 27 Hen. 8, ch. 10 (1536).

Example 19-6.   Split of Title — Initial Trust Creation

Examine each of the following situations and determine whether there is a sufficient split of title to create a trust.

Example 19-6a.

Steven transfers legal title to Thomas and equitable title to Brenda.

Explanation

Yes, Steven made a complete division of legal and equitable title between Thomas and Brenda.

Example 19-6b.

Steven retains legal title and transfers equitable title to Brenda.

Explanation

Yes, legal and equitable title are not united in one person. A settlor may serve as the trustee of the property by retaining legal title and conveying only the equitable title.

Example 19-6c.

Steven transfers legal title to Thomas and retains equitable title.

Explanation

Yes, legal and equitable title are not united in one person. A settlor may retain the equitable interest in the settlor's property and transfer just the legal title.

Example 19-6d.

Steven transfers both legal and equitable title to Thomas.

Explanation

No, Thomas now holds all legal and equitable title. Thus, Steven did not create a trust and Thomas owns the property outright.

Example 19-6e.

Steven transfers legal title to Thomas and equitable title to both Thomas and Brenda.

Explanation

Yes, legal and equitable title are not united in one person. A co-beneficiary may also serve as the trustee of a trust.

Example 19-6f.

Steven transfers legal title to both Thomas and Brenda and equitable title to Brenda.

Explanation

Yes, legal and equitable title are not united in one person. A co-trustee may also be the beneficiary of a trust.

Example 19-6g.

Steven transfers legal title to both Thomas and Brenda and equitable title to both Thomas and Brenda as well.

Explanation

Yes, legal and equitable title are not united in one person. The split of title exists despite the same two people holding all the legal and equitable title. In fact, Thomas and Brenda may actually hold the legal and equitable title differently. As co-trustees, they may hold the legal title as joint tenants while as co-beneficiaries, they may hold the equitable title as tenants in common.

§19.1.3.2 Subsequent Events

If all legal and equitable title becomes reunited in one person, *merger* occurs and the trust will cease to exist. In the normal course of events, this is what happens when the trust terminates and the trustee distributes the property to the remainder beneficiaries. However, merger could occur earlier either because of circumstances the settlor did not anticipate or because the trustee and beneficiary are working together to terminate the trust. Some states have statutes that prevent certain types of trusts, such as trusts containing spendthrift provisions (see §19.8.8, below), from ending in this manner by providing for legal title to vest in another person. Legislatures create these exceptions to prevent the trustee and beneficiary from circumventing the settlor's intent by triggering a merger.

Example 19-7. Merger — Trustee Conveys to Beneficiary

Settlor created a valid trust naming Tom and Teresa as trustees. On January 10, 2000, Tom and Teresa conveyed all of their legal title to Bruce, the only beneficiary of the trust. What are the ramifications of the trustees' conduct?

Explanation

Unless state law provides to the contrary, the trust terminated on January 10, 2000, because Bruce now holds all legal and equitable title. This termination could be exactly what Settlor intended. For example, the trust may provide that the trust ends when Bruce, who was born on January 10, 1975, reaches age twenty-five. On the other hand, Tom and Teresa may be acting in derogation of Settlor's intent by terminating the trust through merger because, for example, the trust instrument provides that the trust continues until Bruce's thirtieth birthday. A trustee is unlikely to convey legal title to the beneficiary prior to the time the settlor specified because such conduct would give the trustee a bad reputation and jeopardize future trust business. In addition, the trustee may be liable to other remainder or contingent beneficiaries who are deprived of their interests because of the premature transfer.

Example 19-8. Merger — Beneficiary Conveys to Trustee

Settlor created a valid trust naming Bruce and Brenda as beneficiaries. On January 10, 2000, they conveyed all of their equitable interests to Tom, the trustee. What are the ramifications of the beneficiaries' conduct?

Explanation

The trust terminated on January 10, 2000, because Tom now holds all legal and equitable title. Bruce and Brenda will probably not make these transfers, however, because they would lose all interests in the trust property unless they had some type of agreement with Tom to reconvey the property to them. Of course, courts are likely to determine that this type of agreement is against public policy and Tom may be exposed to liability to remainder or contingent beneficiaries for breach of fiduciary duty. This scenario is also unlikely to occur because practically every trust includes a spendthrift provision preventing beneficiaries from transferring their equitable interests. See §19.8.8, below.

Example 19-9. Merger — Trustee and Beneficiary Convey to Third Party

Settlor created a valid trust naming Tom as the trustee and Bruce as the beneficiary. On January 10, 2000, both Tom and Bruce conveyed their interests to Sarah. What are the ramifications of their conduct?

Explanation

The trust terminated on January 10, 2000, because Sarah now owns all legal and equitable title to the property. For the reasons discussed in Examples 19-7 and 19-8, this type of situation is unlikely to occur.

§19.1.4 *Distinguishing Trusts from Other Legal Relationships*

You must be able to distinguish trusts from other legal relationships that may, at first glance, appear trust-like in nature either because they involve a split of legal and equitable title or because a person is subject to fiduciary duties in favor of another. Correctly making this distinction is of utmost importance because the law governing trusts is often considerably different from the law controlling other relationships. For example, a plaintiff may find the statute of limitations for bringing an action based on breach of trust to be longer than the limitations period for an action grounded in contract or tort.

§19.1.4.1 Agency

Example 19-10. Agency Distinguished from Trust

Paul gave Arthur written authority to sell some of Paul's property located in another state and to remit the proceeds back to Paul. Did Paul create a trust?

Explanation

No, Paul created an agency relationship by naming Arthur as his agent under a power of attorney. Although Paul did impose fiduciary duties on Arthur, Paul did not give Arthur any title to his out-of-state property, much less split that title into legal and equitable portions.

§19.1.4.2 Bailment

Example 19-11. Agency Distinguished from Bailment

Adam and Brooke were neighbors. Adam borrowed a stepladder from Brooke to install a ceiling fan in Adam's living room. Brooke gave Adam her dog to feed and care for while Brooke went on vacation. Brooke lent Adam her notebook computer for one month in exchange for Adam's promise to buy her a new battery for the computer. Did any of these transactions create a trust?

Explanation

No, each of these property transfers created a bailment. When Adam borrowed the ladder, a bailment for the benefit of the bailee (Adam) arose. When Adam took possession of Brooke's dog, a bailment for the benefit of the bailor (Brooke) was created. Adam's borrowing of the computer in exchange for a new battery gave rise to a mutual benefit bailment. All of these transfers involved only a change of possession. Brooke did not transfer any title to the ladder, her dog, or the computer. Although Adam, as the bailee, does owe duties to Brooke with regard to the bailed property, those duties are not fiduciary duties. Rather, they are legal duties with a basis in contract law.

§19.1.4.3   Condition Subsequent

Example 19-12.   Trust Distinguished from Condition Subsequent

Oscar conveyed real property to George as follows, "To George and his heirs but if tobacco products are sold on the premises, then I or my heirs may reenter and terminate the estate." Did Oscar create a trust?

Explanation

No, Oscar's conveyance transferred a fee simple subject to a condition subsequent to George and Oscar retained a right of reentry (also called a power of termination). Oscar did not split title into legal and equitable interests and did not impose fiduciary duties on George. Oscar cannot prevent George from using the property for the sale of tobacco products. But, if George does so, Oscar or his heirs may divest George of his interest.

§19.1.4.4   Custodianship

Example 19-13.   Trust Distinguished from Custodianship

Aunt transferred $10,000 to Sister as custodian for Niece (Sister's daughter) naming Sister as custodian under the state's version of the Uniform Transfers to Minors Act (see §14.6, above). Did Aunt create a trust?

Explanation

No, a conveyance to a custodian under these circumstances does not give rise to a trust. Sister is indeed a fiduciary with respect to the funds and has a duty to manage the money until Niece reaches age twenty-one. However, Sister has no title to the property. Niece, as the donee of an irrevocable gift, owns full legal and equitable title to the property.

§19.1.4.5 Debt

Example 19-14. Trust Distinguished from Debt

David agreed to transfer $5,000 to Cindy in exchange for Cindy's promise to repay the money with interest at a specified future date. Did David create a trust?

Explanation

No, David lent money to Cindy thereby creating a debtor-creditor relationship. David did not split title to the money. Instead, Cindy has full legal and equitable title and may do whatever she wants with the money. Cindy also has no duties with respect to the $5,000. Cindy may spend the money on frivolous items and may commingle the money with other funds. Cindy's only obligation is based on her promise to repay the money, with interest, by the date specified in the agreement.

§19.1.4.6 Equitable Charge

Example 19-15. Trust Distinguished from Equitable Charge

Terry's valid will contained the following devise, "I leave all my real property located in Ottawa County, Michigan to Juanita Gomez provided she pays $25,000 to Sean Edwards." Did this provision of Terry's will create a trust?

Explanation

No, this provision created an equitable charge. An equitable charge on property arises when a donor makes a transfer to a donee subject to the donee paying a certain amount of money to a third person or performing a particular duty. An equitable charge does involve a split of title because Sean has an equitable right to obtain the $25,000. Nonetheless, the relationship is not a trust because Juanita is not a fiduciary. She has no duty to use the property in any particular manner; her only obligation is to pay the specified sum to Sean.

§19.1.4.7 Guardianship

Example 19-16. Trust Distinguished from Guardianship

For an undiagnosed reason, Eve became reality challenged and was no longer able to manage her property. Eve's mother petitioned the local probate court and was appointed as the guardian (conservator) of Eve's vast holdings. Has a trust relationship been established?

Explanation

No, a guardianship does not create a trust relationship. While there is a similarity between a guardianship and a trust because both are fiduciary relationships, a guardian does not have title to the ward's property. Instead, the guardian merely has the right to possess and manage that property.

§19.1.4.8 Personal Representative of Decedent's Estate

Example 19-17. Trust Distinguished from Estate Administration

Erwin was appointed by the probate court as the personal representative of his father's estate. Has a trust relationship been established?

Explanation

No, the administration of a decedent's estate does not give rise to a trust relationship. Although administrators and executors stand in a fiduciary relationship to the heirs and beneficiaries which is extremely similar to the fiduciary relationship between trustees and beneficiaries, the relationships are readily distinguishable because personal representatives have no title to the property. Both legal and equitable title to the decedent's property vests immediately in the heirs and beneficiaries upon the decedent's death. Personal representatives merely have the right to possess and manage that property during the administration process.

§19.1.4.9 Power of Appointment

Example 19-18. Trust Distinguished from Power of Appointment

Father gave Son the power to appoint particular items of Father's property to Grandson. Did Father create a trust?

Explanation

No, Father gave Son a power of appointment over the property. See §14.5, above. The authority Father gave Son does not vest in Son any title to property that is subject to the power. Additionally, Son is not in a fiduciary relationship with either Father or Grandson. Son has no obligation to exercise the power and has no exposure to liability for either exercising or not exercising the power.

§19.1.4.10 Security Arrangements

Example 19-19. Trust Distinguished from Security Arrangements

Pauline could not afford to purchase her dream house and thus she obtained a loan from Bank. Bank, however, was not satisfied with Pauline's mere promise to repay the loan and thus demanded collateral for the loan. She granted Bank a mortgage in her dream house as well as a security interest in her expensive sport utility vehicle. Did any of Pauline's transactions create a trust?

Explanation

No, security arrangements such as mortgages, deeds of trust, and security interests in personal property under Article 9 of the Uniform Commercial Code do not create trust relationships. In most states, security arrangements are contractual liens on property and do not involve a split of title. In some states, however, the mortgagee (Bank) is treated as having a title interest in the mortgaged property. Nonetheless, the relationship is not a trust because the duties between the parties are based on contract law, not fiduciary law.

§19.2 Methods of Trust Creation

The settlor may create a trust while the settlor is alive or delay the time of creation until the settlor's death by including trust gifts in the settlor's will. This section begins with a discussion of how the settlor may create a trust at different points in time and ends with a look at the relevance of consideration to trust creation.

§19.2.1 During the Settlor's Lifetime

A trust that the settlor creates to take effect while the settlor is still alive is referred to as an *inter vivos trust* or a *living trust*. The two basic methods a settlor may use to create an inter vivos trust are distinguished by the identity of the person who holds legal title to the trust property.

§19.2.1.1 Declaration of Trust

In a *declaration* (or *self-declaration*) of trust, the settlor declares him- or herself to be the trustee of specific property and then transfers some or all of that property's equitable title to one or more beneficiaries. The settlor retains the legal title and is subject to self-imposed fiduciary duties.

§19.2.1.2 Transfer in Trust

In a *transfer* or *conveyance* in trust, the settlor transfers legal title to another person as trustee and imposes fiduciary duties on that person. The settlor may retain some or all of the equitable title or transfer all of the equitable title to other persons.

§19.2.2 Upon the Settlor's Death

A settlor can create a trust to take effect upon the settlor's death by including a gift in trust in the settlor's will. The split of title and the imposition of duties does not occur until the settlor dies. This type of trust is called a *testamentary trust*. A precondition to the validity of a testamentary trust is for the will itself to be valid (see Chapter 5, above). If the will fails, any testamentary trust contained in that will is also ineffective. After the will is established, the trust is examined to determine its validity. The trust is not automatically valid just because the will is valid.

§19.2.3 Consideration

§19.2.3.1 Trust Already Created

Because a trust is a type of gratuitous property transfer, rather than a contractual arrangement, the beneficiary does not need to give consideration to the settlor for the transfer. Do not be confused when a written document creating a trust is carelessly referred to as a "trust agreement" rather than a "trust instrument." The term "agreement" in this context does not connote an agreement of any kind, contractual or otherwise, between the settlor and the beneficiary.

Example 19-20. Consideration — Created Trust

Settlor established a valid irrevocable trust for Daughter on September 10, 1999. The trust property consisted of $250,000 worth of investment securities. Settlor served as the trustee of this trust. The trust provided for payments of trust income to Daughter on the first of every month. Daughter never thanked Settlor for the October, November, and December payments. During the holiday season, Daughter did not call or visit Settlor and did not even send Settlor a holiday card. Settlor was furious at Daughter for her ungrateful conduct. Settlor then made a New Year's resolution never to be taken advantage of again and did not make the January 1, 2000 payment to Daughter. May Settlor invalidate the trust on the basis that Daughter did not give any consideration for the creation of the trust?

Explanation

No, consideration is not needed to support a validly created trust. Thus, Daughter is entitled to the monthly payments and Settlor is powerless to do anything about it because the trust is irrevocable.

§19.2.3.2 Promise to Create a Trust

A promise to create a trust in the future, just like any other promise to make a gift, is not enforceable unless the promise qualifies as a contract under local law.

Example 19-21. Promise to Create a Trust

On July 1, 1999, Settlor told Son, "You have been a good son to me and I love you very much. Tomorrow, I am going to create a trust for your benefit containing $500,000 in Orlando airport municipal bonds and my ski lodge in Aspen." Son gave Settlor a big hug and stated, "Thank you Dad. You're the greatest. I love you, too." July 2 came and went without Settlor creating the trust. May Son force Settlor to create this trust?

Explanation

No, Settlor's mere promise to create a trust in the future is not enforceable. If the promise met all the requirements of a valid contract under local law, such as being supported by consideration, then Son would be able to enforce the promise. Thus, if Settlor had agreed to put the property in trust if Son promised to care for Settlor in his old age, Son would have a good chance of convincing a court to enforce Settlor's promise. Of course, Son would have to perform his end of the bargain as well.

§19.2.3.3 Promise as Trust Property

If the settlor transfers only promises to a trust, those promises need to be enforceable contracts to give the promises value as trust property. If the trust consists merely of unenforceable promises, the trust fails for lack of property.

Example 19-22. Promise as Trust Property

Settlor attempted to create two trusts. The first trust was for the benefit of Daughter and consisted of a $100,000 certificate of deposit. The second trust was for the benefit of Son containing a signed document from Settlor's Friend stating, "Settlor, you have been a good friend to me and I promise to pay you $100,000 within the next six months." Which of these arrangements, if any, are enforceable?

Explanation

Both attempted trusts consist of promises to pay $100,000. The first promise, documented by the certificate of deposit, is a binding obligation of a financial institution to repay money that it borrowed from Settlor. Thus, this promise is a valuable contract and will serve nicely as trust property. However, the second promise, absent additional facts, is a mere promise by Friend to pay money in the future. It does not meet the requirements of a contract and thus is not enforceable. Friend's promise does not provide the trust with a corpus and thus the second arrangement is inadequate to create a trust.

§19.3   The Settlor

The settlor creates a trust by splitting the title of property into legal and equitable interests and by imposing fiduciary duties on the holder of legal title. As discussed in §18.1.2, above, the settlor is sometimes referred to by other terms such as the "trustor," "grantor," or "donor." This section focuses on the capacity a person must have to be the settlor of a trust and the extent of control over trust property the settlor may retain.

§19.3.1 Capacity

The settlor must have the capacity to convey property to create a trust. Generally, this requirement does not impose any different standard on the settlor as the settlor would face in an outright, nontrust, transfer of the same property. If the settlor can convey property, the settlor can elect to convey that property by splitting the legal and equitable title and creating a trust. Thus, the capacity required to create an inter vivos trust is the same as the capacity to make an outright gift (see §14.1, above). Similarly, the capacity necessary to create a testamentary trust is the same as the capacity to execute a will (see §§5.1 & 5.2, above). A few states, however, require the settlor to satisfy a higher standard, such as having the capacity to create a contract.

§19.3.2 *Retention of Powers*

The settlor may want to create a trust but may also desire to retain considerable interests in and powers over the trust property. May a settlor do so and still create a valid trust? If the settlor conveys the property in trust so that the settlor and trustee are different persons, there is a clear split of title and imposition of duties. However, if the settlor makes a declaration of trust so the settlor is also the trustee, the reality of the split of title and duty imposition is less clear.

Example 19-23. Settlor's Retention of Powers

Settlor declared herself as the trustee of a farm for the benefit of her children. She executed a deed transferring the farm from herself as an individual to herself as the trustee of the trust. Settlor retained the right to all the income from the farm, the power to modify or revoke the trust at any time for any reason or even for no reason at all, the power to remove her children as the remainder beneficiaries and to substitute anyone Settlor desires, the power to control the administration of the trust, the power to add property to the trust, and the right to remove property from the trust. Is Settlor's trust valid despite the retention of all of these rights and powers?

Explanation

In the past, and in only a few jurisdictions today, Settlor's arrangement would not create a valid trust. The court would hold that the arrangement is an *illusory trust* because Settlor did not really have trust intent. The beneficial title Settlor gave to the children was de minimus because Settlor could retract their interests on a mere whim. Thus, Settlor actually had all the legal and equitable title. Likewise, Settlor did not actually impose fiduciary duties on herself because she could act in whatever manner she wished with regard to the property merely by claiming she revoked the trust prior to the inappropriate conduct. In addition, a court may conclude that Settlor's arrangement is too testamentary in nature because Settlor did not intend to relinquish any rights to the property while alive. Settlor merely wanted to dispose of the property upon death without complying with the requirements of a valid will.

Under the law of most states today, Settlor's plan would create a valid and enforceable trust. Settlor did split the title to the property even though the children's interest as the successor beneficiaries is subject to complete defeasance if Settlor revokes the trust. In other words, just because the children's contingent interests are weak and would not sell for much on the open market, does not mean the interests are not valid equitable interests in property. Settlor also imposed fiduciary duties on herself and, until the moment she revokes the trust, could be liable to the remainder beneficiaries for breaching those duties.

Revocable trusts under which the settlor, trustee, and lifetime beneficiary are the same person are sometimes called *Dacey trusts*, based on a book entitled "How to Avoid Probate" authored by Norman Dacey. This book touted the advantages of this type of trust, which permits a person to retain total control over the property while alive and then have the property pass to the designated remainder beneficiary upon the person's death. Mr. Dacey argued that most people would be better served by placing their property in these trusts, rather than having their property pass under a will which would necessitate a potentially time-consuming and expensive probate process. The book, originally published in 1966, contained approximately 55 pages of text and 310 pages of forms and instructions. Because Mr. Dacey was not an attorney, he got in trouble for allegedly practicing law without a license. However, a New York court later found in Mr. Dacey's favor.[3] In 1983, he penned a sequel, "How to Avoid Probate II."

§19.4 Statute of Frauds

Under certain circumstances, a trust must be evidenced by a writing before the beneficiary has the right to enforce the trust. This section discusses the Statute of Frauds as it applies to trusts.

§19.4.1 *When Writing Required*

English law did not require trusts to be supported by a writing until Parliament enacted the Statute of Frauds in 1677.[4] Section seven of the Statute of Frauds provided that all trusts of real property must be "manifested and proved" by a writing signed by the settlor. This writing could be either inter vivos or testamentary. Most states base their Statute of Frauds on this statute. Thus, the general rule in the United States is that trusts of real property

---

3. New York County Lawyers' Ass'n v. Dacey, 21 N.Y.2d 694, 234 N.E.2d 459 (1967).
4. 29 Chas. II, ch. 3 (1677).

must be evidenced by a written instrument. The precise details of this requirement vary among the states.

Example 19-24. Contents of Writing

Settlor hires you to prepare a trust instrument. Settlor is extremely frugal and thus wants the shortest possible trust instrument. What must the trust instrument contain to satisfy the Statute of Frauds?

Explanation

The precise requirements of the writing may be mandated by local law. In general, the writing only needs to evidence the trust's basic terms such as the identity of the beneficiaries, the property, and how that property is to be used. The writing can be considerably less than a formal trust instrument; a few scratchings on a note pad may be sufficient documentation. In addition, several documents may be used together to form the necessary writing. If the required writing no longer exists, most courts will admit oral evidence of the contents of the original writing and why it was lost or destroyed.

Example 19-25. Writing Signed by Trustee

Settlor transferred a home in Champaign, Illinois, to Thomas instructing Thomas to hold the home in trust for Settlor's grandchildren. Settlor did not place these instructions in writing and did not indicate the trust nature of the transfer in the deed. However, Thomas wrote and signed the following statement, "I am holding the home Settlor transferred to me in trust for his grandchildren." Is this writing sufficient to satisfy the Statute of Frauds?

Explanation

In many states, the writing used to satisfy the Statute of Frauds may be one signed by the trustee, rather than the settlor. Thomas's writing is, in effect, an admission against interest. Why would Thomas sign such a document if he were actually the recipient of an outright gift? This document could act as the writing and estop Thomas from claiming that he holds the house free of trust.

Example 19-26. Time of Writing

Settlor transferred a vacation home located in a desert region of Arizona to Nephew. One month later, Settlor signed a comprehensive trust instrument covering that home. Did Settlor create a valid trust?

Explanation

No, Nephew owns the home outright. Although the writing satisfied the Statute of Frauds, the writing came too late. Settlor cannot undo an outright gift by creating an instrument at a later time stating that the property is actually held in trust.

§19.4.2 Common Exceptions to Writing Requirement

§19.4.2.1 Personal Property

At common law and under the law of most jurisdictions today, a trust of personal property is enforceable even in the absence of a writing. Some states restrict oral trusts of personal property to particular situations such as where the trustee is a third party (that is, neither a settlor nor a beneficiary) and there is evidence that the settlor expressed trust intent either before or contemporaneously with the transfer.

Example 19-27. Oral Trust of Personal Property

Simon delivered to one of his daughters, Teresa, a certificate of deposit in bearer form earning 6 percent interest with a face value of $100,000 and a deed to a 100-acre ranch near Lubbock, Texas. At the same time, Simon said, "I appoint you as trustee of a trust for your brothers Ben and Bert. Use the money and the ranch for their education. When the youngest graduates from college, or if both die prior to graduating, give the remainder of the money and ranch, if any, to Ralph Rogers." Teresa agreed. Did Simon create a legally enforceable trust?

Explanation

Under general principles of trust law, Simon created a valid trust with regard to the certificate of deposit. Despite the fact that Simon failed to document his intent in a writing, the delivery of the CD in bearer form to a third party, coupled with a clear expression of trust intent, would be sufficient to establish the trust. However, the trust of the ranch would fail because trusts of real property must be evidenced by a writing.

§19.4.2.2 Part Performance

Courts typically enforce oral trusts of real property if the trustees partially perform. In other words, if the alleged trustee acts, at least temporarily, as if a trust exists, the trustee is estopped from denying the existence of a trust at a later time and claiming the property as the donee of an outright gift. For example, if the trustee permits the beneficiary to possess the land or make valuable improvements to that land, the trustee cannot later claim that a trust did not exist.

Example 19-28. Part Performance

In 1995, Susan conveyed an apartment building in New York City to Tony. Susan told Tony to hold the building in trust for her children and to use the rent to pay for their education. For the next five years, Tony permitted Susan's children to live in the building, managed the rest of the apartments, collected the rent, and used the rent as Susan had instructed. Tony then met with Larry, a lawyer, about an unrelated case. In the course of their conversation, Tony explained the arrangement with Susan. Larry told Tony he could just keep the rent for himself and evict Susan's children because the arrangement between Susan and Tony was not in writing. Is Larry right?

Explanation

No, Susan created a valid trust of the apartment building even though the trust in not evidenced by a writing. It is too late for Tony to claim that he is the recipient of an outright gift. For five years, Tony acted as if he were a trustee and inconsistently with being the donee of an outright gift of the building. Why would Tony permit Susan's children to live in the building and why would Tony use the rent to pay for the education of Susan's children if he were actually the beneficial owner of the apartments? Courts will not permit transferees who really received trust conveyances to use the Statute of Frauds as a means of perpetrating a fraud.

§19.4.2.3 Conveyance Induced by Evil Conduct

If the trustee's evil conduct induces the settlor to make a conveyance of land without documenting the terms of the trust in a writing, no express trust will arise. However, the court will impose a constructive trust on the property in the trustee's hands for the benefit of the intended beneficiaries to prevent the trustee from being unjustly enriched by the trustee's inappropriate conduct. Examples of this type of improper conduct include (1) preventing the settlor from creating the necessary writing by fraud, duress, or undue influence, (2) abusing a confidential relationship between the settlor and the trustee, or (3) taking advantage of a transfer the settlor made in contemplation of death. Constructive trusts are discussed in detail in Chapter 23, below.

§19.4.3 Standing to Raise Statute of Frauds Defense

The policy underlying the requirement that certain trusts be evidenced by a writing is to protect a transferee who actually received an outright conveyance from having those rights infringed upon by someone claiming that the transfer was actually one in trust. Thus, an alleged trustee will use the lack of a writing to raise the Statute of Frauds as a defense to a plaintiff who is trying to deprive the alleged trustee of that person's rights as the donee of an outright gift.

Example 19-29. Raising Statute of Frauds Defense

George conveyed his house in Boston to Donna. The conveyance was outright, not in trust, and there is no other written instrument involved with this transaction. Several months later, George wanted Donna to deed the house back to him. Donna refused. George then sued Donna alleging that Donna was the trustee of a trust containing that house for George's benefit. What is the likelihood that George will prevail?

Explanation

George is unlikely to prevail because Donna has a good defense based on the Statute of Frauds. No written evidence of the trust exists. Thus, in the absence of facts showing that Donna acted in an inappropriate manner regarding the initial conveyance, Donna can raise the Statute of Frauds defense. Donna should then prevail and thereby retain her status as a donee of the gift.

§19.4.4 Effect of Statute of Frauds Violation

Violating the Statute of Frauds merely makes the trust unenforceable (voidable) rather than void. Although this result may seem inconsistent with the language of the English Statute of Frauds which provided that oral trusts of real property were "utterly void," most modern courts hold that the word "void" as used in this context actually means "voidable." Accordingly, the trustee can carry out the terms of the oral trust of land although no one could have forced the trustee to do so. Of course, once the trustee begins performing the duties associated with the oral trust, those acts become the part performance needed to move the trust outside of the Statute of Frauds. See §19.4.2.2, above.

Example 19-30. Trustee Voluntarily Carrying Out Oral Trust of Real Property

Sean transferred his farmland located in Ohio to Brother. Sean told Brother that he was to hold the land in trust for Sean's children and to use the income for their education and health care expenses. The deed was silent about the trust nature of the transfer and Sean did not sign a separate trust instrument. May Brother carry out Sean's wishes despite Sean's failure to evidence the trust with a writing? May Collin, a creditor of Brother, raise the defense on Brother's behalf and thus reach the land to satisfy Collin's claim?

Explanation

Although the trust is unenforceable because it violates the Statute of Frauds, Brother may voluntarily elect to carry out the trust. Collin, the creditor, is unlikely to have standing to force Brother to raise the defense even though Collin would be able to reach the property if Brother held the property free from trust. However, if Brother filed for bankruptcy, his bankruptcy trustee (a person appointed to represent Brother's unsecured creditors; not a trustee of an express trust) has "the benefit of any defense available to the debtor [Brother] as against any entity [Sean's children] . . . including statutes of limitation, statutes of frauds, usury, and other personal defenses."[5] Thus, the bankruptcy trustee could raise the Statute of Frauds defense even over Brother's objection. This statute makes sense from a policy perspective. If the bankruptcy trustee did not have this authority, everyone who files for bankruptcy would claim that they hold their real property subject to oral trusts for the benefit of others thereby keeping the property out of the hands of their creditors.

§19.4.5 Acknowledgment

An *acknowledgment* is a notarized statement that the settlor willingly executed the trust as an act of the settlor's own free will. Although an acknowledgment is not a prerequisite to a valid trust, many states require instruments to be acknowledged before they can be filed in the public records. Trust instruments that involve real property often must be filed in the deed records to establish the chain of title to the property. Thus, prudent practice is to have the settlor acknowledge all inter vivos trust instruments.

Sample Inter Vivos Trust Acknowledgment

Before me, the undersigned authority, on this day personally appeared [Settlor], known to me to be the person whose name is sub-

---

5. 11 U.S.C. §558 (1998).

scribed to the foregoing instrument, and acknowledged to me that [he] [she] executed the same for the purposes and consideration therein expressed.

Given under my hand and seal of office, this the _____ day of _____, ____.

§19.5   Trust Purposes

The settlor may create a trust for any purpose as long as that purpose is not illegal. In addition, the terms of the trust may not require the trustee to commit an act that is criminal, tortious, or contrary to public policy. This section reviews how courts determine the validity of a trust's purpose and what happens if the court concludes that a trust has an improper purpose.

§19.5.1   Determination of Validity of Purpose

Example 19-31.   Trust Purpose — Conditional Benefits

Settlor created a trust containing the following provision:

> The income of this trust is to be used for the care, comfort, support, medical attention, education, sustenance, and maintenance of children whose parent(s) have been incarcerated, imprisoned, detained or committed in any federal, state, county or local prison or penitentiary, as a result of the conviction of a crime or misdemeanor of a political nature. Should this trust fail for any reason, the trustee shall deliver all trust property to Randy Ramos.[6]

Randy consults you regarding the possibility of Settlor's trust being illegal so that he could demand that the trustee turn over the property to him. What advice would you give Randy and why?

Explanation

Courts have used two main approaches in evaluating the legality of a trust purpose. The first analysis concentrates on the settlor's intent and the effect of the trust's existence on the behavior of other persons. Under the *intent approach*, a trust is illegal if the existence of the trust could induce another person to commit a crime even if the trustee does not have to perform an illegal act. In this case, a court may see the trust as removing one of the deterrents from committing a crime, that is, no longer being able to provide

---

6. Adapted from In re Robbins' Estate, 371 P.2d 573 (Cal. 1962).

support for family members if caught. Thus, the trust would be illegal because it encourages people to break the law and rewards their families for the criminal behavior. The intent view is the majority view in the United States.

The second approach focuses on how the trust property is actually used, rather than on the motives of the settlor. Under the *use approach,* the trust would be valid because of the unquestionable appropriateness of providing for the health, education, and support of children who are deprived of their parents' support. A minority of jurisdictions have adopted the use analysis.

The fact that the crime on which benefits are based in this case is one of a "political nature" may influence the court's view of the trust's validity. A court could conclude that Settlor was limiting benefits to the families of individuals who were wrongfully incarcerated for engaging in controversial but nonetheless legal conduct. Thus, a court may be more willing to adopt the use approach than if the trust provided these same benefits only for the families of individuals convicted of morally repugnant crimes such as murder or rape.

Example 19-32. Trust Purpose — Defrauding Creditors

Settlor, a physician, established an irrevocable trust containing corporate securities valued at approximately $500,000. Shortly thereafter, Patient recovered a $750,000 judgment against Settlor for damages sustained as the result of a botched cosmetic surgery that occurred months prior to Settlor establishing the trust. Assuming Patient prevails, may Patient reach the stocks and bonds in Settlor's trust if Settlor's other assets are inadequate to pay the claim? Would it make a difference if Settlor had actually performed the surgery after Settlor created the trust?

Explanation

Settlor's purpose for establishing this trust appears to be to protect Settlor's stocks and bonds from Patient's claim. Defrauding creditors is an illegal trust purpose. Most states have enacted either the Uniform Fraudulent Conveyance Act of 1918 or the Uniform Fraudulent Transfer Act of 1984 to deal with this type of situation. For example, §4(a) of the 1984 Act provides that a

> transfer made . . . by a debtor is fraudulent . . . whether the creditor's claim arose before or after the transfer was made . . . if the debtor made the transfer or incurred the obligation: (1) with actual intent to hinder, delay, or defraud any creditor . . . , or (2) without receiving a reasonably equivalent value in exchange for the transfer . . . and the debtor: (i) was engaged or was about to engage in a business or transaction for which the remaining assets of the debtor were unreasonably small in relation to the business or transaction; or (ii) intended to incur, or reasonably

should have believed that [debtor] would incur, debts beyond [debtor's] ability to pay as they became due.

In addition, §5(a) states that a transfer

is fraudulent as to a creditor whose claim arose before the transfer was made . . . if the debtor made the transfer . . . without receiving a reasonably equivalent value in exchange for the transfer . . . and the debtor was insolvent at that time or the debtor became insolvent as a result of the transfer.

Under these statutes, it is highly likely that Settlor's conveyance of the securities to the trust is fraudulent as to Patient if Settlor's malpractice occurred prior to the transfer. There is also a significant chance that Patient may prevail if the surgery had not yet occurred. Fortunately for Settlor, however, the 1984 Act requires a creditor to bring a cause of action within four years after the transfer. Consequently, once four years elapse after the trust transfer, Settlor's trust will be safe from attack by disgruntled patients under most circumstances.

Example 19-33. Trust Purpose — Discrimination

Settlor established a trust providing college scholarships to students who can demonstrate that they belong to a Christian church. You are hired by three students of different faiths, a Moslem, a Jew, and a Buddhist, who would like the opportunity to compete for scholarships granted by Settlor's trust. Will you be successful in having the discriminatory provisions of Settlor's trust invalidated?

Explanation

The validity and enforceability of any discriminatory trust provision such as Settlor's is problematic. Settlors often desire to create trusts that limit benefits to persons of a particular religion, sex, race, or national origin. These provisions are contrary to modern law, which prohibits discrimination on these and other grounds. Under traditional analysis, a private person may discriminate as he or she wishes but a court cannot lend its power and authority to the enforcement of discriminatory provisions. The equal protection clause of the Fourteenth Amendment to the United States Constitution prohibits the use of state action to carry out an individual's desire to discriminate. Settlor's trust is charitable in nature because it does not have clearly ascertainable beneficiaries and the purpose of promoting education is in the public interest. See §19.10, below, for a detailed discussion of charitable trusts.

In recent years, there has been a tremendous increase in litigation regarding this type of provision. The decisions reflect that the law is still in a state of flux regarding the enforcement of provisions such as Settlor's. Some courts refuse to enforce the discriminatory restrictions, treating the trust as essentially public because of the special benefits the law grants to charitable trusts and the enforcement assistance the state attorney general's office provides. After the court concludes that a restriction is illegal, the court may either eliminate that restriction or declare the entire trust invalid. In making this decision, the courts attempt to determine what the settlor would have wanted; that is, if the settlor knew the discriminatory provision would not be enforced, would the settlor have expanded the class of beneficiaries or permitted the trust to fail. On the other hand, some courts treat the judicial involvement in such trusts as relatively de minimus, cite the public benefit of providing benefits to members of certain classes, especially if that class had been previously subject to discrimination, and hold that these provisions are valid.

§19.5.2 Remedies for Illegal Trusts

Courts have several options available to them when they decide that a settlor created a trust for an illegal purpose. The appropriate remedy depends on the reason for the illegality. If the complaining party is a defrauded creditor, the usual remedy, and the one provided for in §7 of the 1984 version of the Uniform Fraudulent Transfer Act, is simply to allow the creditor to set aside the conveyance to the trust to the extent of the creditor's claim. The trust remains effective with regard to property in excess of the creditor's claim.

In other situations, courts have the choice of two remedies. First, the court could undo the transfer and permit the settlor to regain the legal and equitable title to the property by application of resulting trust principles (see Chapter 22, below). If the settlor is deceased, the settlor's successors in interest (heirs, if intestate; beneficiaries, if testate) could claim the property. Second, the court could refuse to enforce the rights of the purported holder of equitable title which consequently permits the trustee to be treated as the outright owner of the property (the trustee already had legal title and now no one can enforce the trust). How does a court decide between these two options?

Example 19-34. Trust Purpose—Remedy for Illegal Trust

Settlor created two trusts, both of which the court has determined are invalid because of improper trust purposes. Settlor transferred $100,000 to Tom as trustee of Trust One. Settlor specified that this money was to be used to purchase recreational pharmaceuticals for Settlor's children and grandchildren. Settlor transferred $200,000 to Teresa as trustee of Trust Two. This money was to be used to build and run a nightclub in Settlor's hometown. Due to recent changes to the applicable zoning laws, as well as the enactment of legislation making the sale of alcoholic beverages in Settlor's hometown illegal, the nightclub may no longer legally operate. Assuming neither of these trust instruments have relevant provisions, who is entitled to the property remaining in these trusts?

Explanation

Settlor's purpose of providing illegal drugs to Settlor's descendants is immoral and unethical, in addition to being illegal. Thus, a court is likely to permit Tom to retain the property free of trust. Settlor did not have clean hands and thus is unlikely to convince a court of equity that Settlor is entitled to a return of the property. Although Tom is unjustly enriched from this windfall, the court would want to deter improper conduct on the part of this settlor and other settlors in the future. If the court permitted Settlor to regain the property, Settlor and others would have no reason not to try to create trusts with improper purposes.

On the other hand, a court is likely to declare a resulting trust with regard to Trust Two. Settlor had no moral culpability. Settlor established a legitimate and legal business. Subsequent events, the changing in zoning and the city becoming dry, transformed a legal purpose into an illegal one. Settlor has clean hands and should be able to successfully recoup the remaining trust property.

§19.6 Trust Property

A trust is a method of holding title to property. Consequently, the existence of property is essential for the initial creation and continued existence of a trust. No trust exists until it has property and a trust terminates when no property remains. This section discusses the types of property that may be held in trust and how that property actually gets into the trust.

§19.6.1 Types of Trust Property

Any type of property may be held in trust as long as the settlor can transfer title to that property. Trust property can consist of present and future interests in real property and both tangible and intangible personal property. If a person cannot transfer the property, such as property belonging to another person or property that has valid restrictions on its transfer, then that property cannot support a trust.

Example 19-35. Trust Property — Contract Rights

Settlor owned a life insurance policy on Settlor's life. Settlor changed the beneficiary designation to read, "To Terry Thane, in trust, under the terms of the Settlor's Children's Support Trust." Does this provide sufficient property to create a trust?

Explanation

Yes, choses in action, such as Terry's contract right to receive the proceeds of the life insurance policy upon Settlor's death, are sufficient property to support trusts. Likewise, any right to receive benefits under a retirement plan, pension plan, annuity, or other contract can serve as property.

Example 19-36. Trust Property — Expectancies

Settlor attempted to create a trust consisting of the property Settlor will inherit when Settlor's Father dies and the profit Settlor anticipates earning next year from the sale of Settlor's collection of sports memorabilia. Has Settlor been successful in creating a trust?

Explanation

No, a trust requires property that is in existence and clearly ascertainable. Settlor merely hopes and expects to inherit from Settlor's Father and to make a profit selling the collection. At this point in time, Settlor does not have an interest in the inheritance or profit that rises to the level of property. Settlor cannot place into trust what Settlor does not yet own or have an enforceable right to obtain.

Example 19-37. Trust Property — Debts

Settlor attempted to create a trust with the following two items. First, Settlor owed $5,000 to Bank on a personal loan. Settlor signed a piece of paper stating the Settlor was transferring "the $5,000 debt that I owe Bank" to the trust. Second, Settlor owned a certificate of deposit for $7,500 from Savings & Loan. Settlor endorsed the CD to the trustee of the trust indicating the transfer was for trust purposes. What are the results of Settlor's actions?

Explanation

Settlor could not transfer to the trust the debt Settlor owes to Bank. The debt is a general claim against Settlor's property and thus there is no specific property that can be the subject of the trust. However, the contract right of Settlor as a creditor of Savings & Loan will constitute trust property. Simply stated, the duty of a debtor to pay is not property but the right of a creditor to be paid can be trust property.

§19.6.2 Transfer of Property to Trust

Legal title to the trust property must reach the hands of the trustee. It is not enough for the settlor to sign a trust instrument, own assets that would make good trust property, and intend for that property to be in the trust. The settlor must consummate this intent by actually transferring the property.

Example 19-38. Transfer of Property to Trust — Declaration of Trust

Settlor wants to declare that Settlor holds Settlor's farm and collection of antique toys in trust. What steps should Settlor take to be certain this property becomes part of the corpus of the trust?

Explanation

Settlor should execute a deed for the real property. The grantor of the farm would be Settlor in Settlor's individual capacity and the grantee would be Settlor in the Settlor's capacity as the trustee of the trust. The personal property should be separated from all of Settlor's other property and then be marked in such a way that the trust property can be easily distinguished from Settlor's other property. A formal deed of gift of the toys from Settlor as an individual to Settlor as a trustee would be highly advisable. See §14.1, above.

Example 19-39. Transfer of Property to Trust — Conveyance in Trust

Settlor wants to transfer Settlor's farm and collection of antique toys to a trust. What steps should Settlor take to be certain this property becomes part of the corpus of the trust?

Explanation

As with the declaration of trust example, Settlor should execute a deed for the real property. The grantor of the farm would be Settlor in Settlor's individual capacity and the grantee would be the trustee of the trust in that person's fiduciary capacity. Settlor should transfer physical possession of the toy collection to the trustee. A deed of gift confirming the conveyance would provide additional evidence of the transfer but it is not as imperative that Settlor execute one as where the settlor and the trustee are the same person.

§19.7 The Trustee

The trustee holds legal title to trust property and is bound by a plethora of fiduciary duties to deal with that property for the benefit of the beneficiaries. This section examines what types of persons can serve as trustees, the formal steps to become a trustee, and related matters. The trustee's fiduciary duties are examined in Chapter 20, below.

§19.7.1 Capacity

A person must have the capacity to serve as a trustee. An individual trustee needs the ability to take, hold, and transfer title to the trust property. Thus, an individual must be of legal age (typically age eighteen or have had the disabilities of minority removed) and competent. A corporation or other business entity must have the authority under local law to act as a trustee. The authority is usually found in the corporation's charter. States may have different rules for entities that traditionally serve as trustees, such as banks, specialized trust companies, and other corporations. An entity that is organized under the laws of a different state or nation may need to meet additional requirements to act as a trustee.

Although the trustee may be a person unconnected with the rest of the trust arrangement, such detachment is not necessary. In a declaration of trust, the settlor serves as the trustee. See §19.2.1.1, above. The trustee may also be a beneficiary of the same trust as long as the sole trustee is not also the sole beneficiary. If the same person is the only trustee and the only beneficiary, merger occurs and a trust will not exist. See §19.1.3, above.

§19.7.2 Acceptance

A person does not become a trustee merely because the settlor names that person as the trustee of a trust. The settlor cannot force legal title and the accompanying fiduciary duties on an unwilling person. Thus, a person must take some affirmative step to accept the position. Once acceptance occurs, the person is responsible for complying with the terms of the trust as well as applicable law. Failure to comply would lead to the trustee being liable for breach of trust.

The trustee's acceptance of the trust may be established in two main ways. First, the trustee could sign a written acceptance. This acceptance may be on the trust instrument itself or it may be a separate acceptance document. When creating an inter vivos trust, it is common practice for attorneys to have the trustee sign the trust instrument at the same time as the settlor. In some states, the signature of the trustee is conclusive evidence of acceptance. Second, the trustee's acceptance may be implied from the fact that the trustee has started to act like a trustee by exercising trust powers or performing trust duties. This part performance type conduct raises a presumption of acceptance in some states.

Example 19-40. Acceptance of Trustee Position

Client has just informed you that Client has been named the trustee of a trust. Client is uncertain about whether to serve as the trustee. What factors should Client consider in making this decision?

Explanation

Although many people feel honored at being named as a trustee, the position is quite burdensome. The trustee must comply with a host of requirements and technical rules in carrying out this fiduciary position. Coupled with the responsibility of dealing with the property using a high standard of care and the duty of maintaining the utmost degree of loyalty, there are many traps for the unwary that could lead to significant personal liability. A person named as a trustee must evaluate whether the burden and liability exposure is worth the potential benefits such as monetary compensation (if the trustee is a professional trustee) or emotional satisfaction (if the trust was created by a family member or friend).

Example 19-41. Failure of Trustee to Accept Position

Trevor, the named trustee of a trust, refused to accept the position. How is the position filled? Or, does the trust simply fail?

Explanation

A trust will not fail merely because the named trustee does not accept. The first step to solve the problem arising when a trustee refuses to serve or cannot serve (e.g., has already died or is incompetent) is to look at the trust instrument. The instrument, especially if it was well drafted, should resolve the situation by either expressly naming one or more alternates or by describing a method for selecting a new trustee (e.g., by majority vote of the beneficiaries). If the instrument is silent or otherwise does not provide a solution, the beneficiaries can petition the court for the appointment of a replacement trustee. The court will appoint a replacement unless the trustee's duties are so specialized that only the named trustee could perform them. In these extremely rare cases of a *personal trustee,* the court would be unable to save the trust by appointing someone else to serve as the trustee and the trust would fail.

§19.7.3 *Qualification*

§19.7.3.1 Oath of Office

In some states, the trustee needs to take an oath of office swearing that the trustee will faithfully carry out the duties of the position.

§19.7.3.2 Bond

The trustee may need to post bond conditioned on the faithful performance of the trustee's duties. The court sets the amount of the bond based on the value of the trust property. The trustee may deliver that amount in cash to the court. However, the trustee typically obtains the bond from a surety company. In exchange for the payment of premiums, the surety company agrees to pay the amount of the bond to the beneficiaries if the trustee breaches the applicable fiduciary duties. Of course, if the surety is required to pay, the surety will seek reimbursement from the trustee.

States are divided on the bonding requirement. Some state statutes require bond unless the trust expressly waives bond. On the other hand, some statutes do not require bond unless the settlor expressly requires it under the terms of the trust or if the court deems it necessary. In addition, some states exempt corporate fiduciaries from the bonding requirement.

Example 19-42. Bond

Settlor needs to decide whether to require bond or waive bond for the trustee. What concerns would you bring to Settlor's attention to assist Settlor in making an informed decision?

Explanation

Bond premiums are expensive and the cost increases with the value of the trust property. A court proceeding is typically needed to set the amount of the bond. Settlor may save these expenses by waiving bond. The costs of the hearing and the annual bond premiums are proper trust expenses and thus reduce the amount the beneficiaries eventually receive. Bond does, however, protect the beneficiaries from an evil trustee. But, if Settlor thinks the trustee will act improperly, Settlor should probably name a more trustworthy person to that position.

§19.7.4 *Multiple Trustees*

Example 19-43. Multiple Trustees

Settlor has suggested naming both Daughter and Bank as co-trustees. Is this a good idea? Why or why not?

Explanation

Settlor probably wants to gain the investment expertise of Bank and temper Bank's perceived "coldness" with Daughter's human touch. Better decisions may result because of the deliberation that occurs when the co-trustees present and discuss multiple viewpoints. Multiple trustees also provide greater protection to the trust and the beneficiaries. There are built-in checks and balances because each trustee can evaluate the conduct of the other trustee. An evil trustee will have a harder time carrying out any untoward schemes because there will be another trustee watching. However, having two trustees means that both must agree before any action can be taken. Requiring the consent of Daughter and Bank may slow down the administration process even if they are in agreement simply because of the extra time and effort needed to obtain and document the consent.

One of the biggest disadvantages of naming both Daughter and Bank is the potential of a deadlock and the paralysis that follows. A costly judicial resolution of this standoff would then be needed. In addition, if Settlor appoints both Bank and Daughter, there is a significant likelihood of additional administrative fees because of the extra conferences, telephone calls, and paperwork that would be required. Bank may even charge a higher fee if Daughter is a co-trustee because of the additional time it usually takes to deal with an individual. Because each co-trustee is normally jointly and severally liable for the acts of all trustees, Bank may also be reluctant to serve with Daughter for fear of liability for Daughter's improper acts.

§19.7.5 *Successor Trustees*

A trustee may need to be replaced. The current trustee could die, become incompetent, resign, or be removed by the court. In these circumstances, the settlor's directions as stated in the trust instrument would have first priority. The settlor may have specified successors or provided for a method of selecting the successors. If the instrument does not fill the vacancy, the local trust statutes would be examined. If the statute also does not supply a replacement, the court will appoint a successor to ensure that the trust continues.

§19.7.6 *Effect of Holding Legal Title*

A trustee has only legal title to the trust property. Accordingly, the trustee and those claiming through the trustee have no claim to this property.

Example 19-44. Effect of Holding Legal Title

Trustee, while on business unrelated to the trust, was at fault for causing an automobile accident that caused $25,000 in damage. Before Trustee had the chance to pay this claim, Trustee died. At the time of Trustee's death, Trustee's estate was worth approximately $10,000. The trust property, however, was valued at over $500,000. May Trustee's creditor reach the trust property? May Trustee's successors in interest (heirs or beneficiaries) make a claim to the trust property?

Explanation

Trustee only had legal title to the trust property. Accordingly, Trustee's personal creditor cannot look to the trust property to satisfy the claim. Likewise, the trust property does not pass through intestacy or under Trustee's will. Instead, the legal title to trust property now vests in a successor trustee as discussed in §19.7.5, above.

§19.8 The Beneficiary

Trust beneficiaries hold equitable title to trust property and have standing to enforce the trust. A trust cannot exist without a beneficiary. This section examines a wide variety of issues pertaining to trust beneficiaries and the extent and nature of their trust interests.

§19.8.1 *Capacity*

A person needs the capacity to take and hold title to property to be a trust beneficiary. A beneficiary does not need the ability to transfer or manage the property. Thus, any human who is alive can be a beneficiary. Remember, settlors frequently establish trusts for individuals who cannot manage property themselves. A legal entity, such as a corporation, partnership, association, or governmental unit, may also be a trust beneficiary provided the entity is otherwise empowered to take and hold title to property.

The settlor may be a beneficiary of his or her own trust. A trustee may also be the beneficiary of a trust as long as the sole beneficiary is not the sole trustee. See §19.1.3, above.

The settlor may divide the equitable title among multiple beneficiaries. This division can occur along two lines. First, several beneficiaries may hold concurrent interests so that each is presently eligible for trust distributions. Second, the beneficiaries may hold successive interests. For example, one beneficiary may be entitled to the income from the trust until death with any remaining trust property passing to a remainder beneficiary.

§19.8.2 Adequacy of Beneficiary Designation

The settlor must designate the beneficiaries of a private trust so that their identity is definitively stated or clearly ascertainable. The trust will fail if the settlor fails to describe the beneficiaries with sufficient certainty. See §19.10.1, below, for the special rules applicable to charitable trusts.

Example 19-45. Beneficiary Designation — Vague

Settlor transferred $100,000 to Timothy, in trust, "to distribute to those individuals whom my trustee so desires." Is this a sufficient beneficiary designation?

Explanation

No, the description is too vague. A court could not determine the identity of the individuals who would own the equitable title to the trust property. If this beneficiary designation were found in a power of appointment, however, it may be adequate because the potential appointees of a power of appointment do not need to be specified with the exactness required for beneficiaries of a private trust. See §14.5, above.

Example 19-46. Beneficiary Designation — Class Gift — Certain Membership

Settlor transferred $100,000 to Timothy, in trust, "to distribute to those of my children whom my trustee so desires." Is this a sufficient beneficiary designation?

Explanation

Yes, class designations, such as Settlor's gift to "my children," are adequate beneficiary descriptions as long as the individual members of the specified class are readily ascertainable. The term "children" has a uniformly recognized meaning as direct descendants of the first degree, that is, sons and daughters. See §9.8, above, for a discussion of class gifts in the will context.

Example 19-47. Beneficiary Designation — Class Gift — Uncertain Membership

Settlor transferred $100,000 to Timothy, in trust, "to distribute to those of my friends whom my trustee so desires." Is this a sufficient beneficiary designation?

Explanation

No, the identity of the actual individuals who would fall within Settlor's class gift to "friends" cannot be ascertained with certainty. The term "friends" does not have an established meaning. Some people use this term to refer to mere acquaintances while others reserve the term for individuals with whom they share a very close personal relationship. The court may be willing to consider extrinsic evidence to determine whether Settlor used the term in a restricted manner so that the identity of Settlor's friends could be determined. For example, perhaps Settlor is a recluse who for the past twenty years has always referred to the same three people as "my friends."

§19.8.3 Honorary Trusts

An *honorary trust* is a gift which the donor intends to benefit a nonhuman, noncharitable purpose. Because equitable title is held neither by a human nor by a charity, no one can enforce the arrangement and thus the trustee is on the trustee's "honor" to carry out the settlor's instructions. Common examples of honorary trusts are to care for pet animals, maintain specified items of property in good condition (e.g., a car or a grandfather clock), and to erect monuments. In the past, providing donations for the saying of Masses to honor deceased individuals in a Catholic church ceremony was also a common type of honorary trust. (Under modern law, such arrangements are deemed charitable in nature.)

Most American jurisdictions do not recognize honorary trusts. Instead, an attempted honorary trust fails and the property reverts to the "settlor," or, if the settlor has already died, to the settlor's successors in interest (heirs, if intestate; beneficiaries, if testate) under resulting trust principles. See

Chapter 22, below. However, there is a growing trend to permit trustees to carry out these arrangements as long as the purpose is not unlawful or capricious and the duration does not exceed the Rule Against Perpetuities period. See §19.9, below. Restatement (Second) of Trusts provides in §124 that honorary trusts are unenforceable but that the "trustee" may use the property for the designated purpose. UPC §2-907 goes even further setting up special provisions for both pet and non-pet honorary trusts and providing that "[t]he intended use of the principal or income can be enforced by an individual designated for that purpose in the trust instrument or, if none, by an individual appointed by a court upon application to it by an individual."

Example 19-48.   Honorary Trusts

Client wants to make arrangements for the care of Rover, Client's pet dog, after Client's death. Assuming your jurisdiction does not authorize honorary trusts, what steps could you take to carry out Client's intent?

Explanation

Client could bequeath Rover, along with some investment property, to a testamentary trust naming an individual, preferably someone who likes Rover and would enjoy caring for him, as the beneficiary. As a condition to the beneficiary's receipt of trust distributions, the beneficiary must provide Rover with a good home. The trustee of the trust would be directed to personally visit Rover and inspect his living conditions on a periodic basis. If everything was in order, the beneficiary would receive a trust distribution. This amount could simply be a reimbursement of the beneficiary's expenses such as food and veterinarian care, or it could also be a monetary reward for Rover's new caretaker.

§19.8.4 Incidental Beneficiaries

The term *incidental beneficiary* refers to someone who benefits from the trust but whom the settlor did not name as a beneficiary. Because incidental beneficiaries do not have equitable title to trust property, they usually do not have standing to enforce the trust.

Example 19-49.   Incidental Beneficiary

Settlor transferred a house located in an upscale area of town along with $250,000 to Teresa, in trust, for the benefit of Settlor's child, Brenda. The trust requires Teresa to invest the $250,000 and to pay all the income to Teresa except for amounts used to keep the house in good condition as long as Brenda lives there. Brenda is living in the house but she is not doing a good job of maintaining it. The lawn is frequently uncut and weeds are proliferating. In addition, the bright orange house paint is not only ugly but it is peeling. Brenda does not object to Teresa's failure to fix up the house because her payments of income are larger if Teresa does not pay for upkeep expenses. Nancy, Brenda's neighbor, sues Teresa for breach of her duties as trustee. Nancy claims that the unkempt house lowers her property value and is an eyesore. Will Nancy be successful with her suit?

Explanation

Nancy's likelihood of success on a breach of fiduciary duty suit against Teresa is quite low. Because Nancy is not a beneficiary of the trust, she has no equitable title. Thus, it is unlikely that she has standing to enforce the trust although she could indirectly benefit from the trust if the trust maintained the house in good condition. In some states, however, the standing requirement may be broad enough to cover an "interested person" even if that person does not own equitable title. In this type of state, Nancy may be able to convince a judge that her interest is strong enough to give her standing. Of course, Nancy may have better success with other causes of action such as nuisance, breach of restrictive covenants, or violation of homeowner association rules.

§19.8.5 Disclaimer

Just as heirs may disclaim inheritances and beneficiaries may disclaim testamentary gifts, potential trust beneficiaries are not required to accept the proffered equitable title. The reasons a beneficiary may decide to disclaim and the requirements of the disclaimer are fundamentally the same as for an heir who disclaims an inheritance. See §4.4, above. If the beneficiary properly disclaims, the disclaimed property passes under the terms of the trust as if the beneficiary had predeceased the settlor.

§19.8.6 Transfers and Assignments of Beneficial Interests

The beneficiary of a trust has the power to transfer the beneficiary's interest to the same extent the beneficiary could transfer a nontrust interest. Thus, if the beneficiary has the capacity to transfer property generally, the beneficiary would also have the capacity to transfer the beneficial interest. While the beneficiary is alive, the beneficiary could give away the interest or could sell the interest. If the beneficiary's interest survives death, the beneficiary's interest would pass either to the beneficiary's heirs or to the takers under the beneficiary's will.

Despite the broad powers a beneficiary may have to make inter vivos and at-death transfers of the beneficial interest, settlors rarely permit beneficiaries to exercise these powers. Instead, it is extremely common for settlors to limit the transferability of beneficial interests. First, settlors require beneficiaries to be alive to benefit from the trust. For example, beneficiaries who receive periodic payments only have life interests and remainder beneficiaries must be alive when the trust ends to receive the property. Second, settlors usually include spendthrift provisions that prohibit beneficiaries from transferring or assigning their interests. See §19.8.8, below.

Example 19-50. Priority of Assignment of Beneficial Interest

Settlor created a trust that provides that the trust terminates in the year 2005 and the trustee is then to distribute all remaining trust property to Randy. Randy's interest indefeasibly vested when Settlor created the trust because Settlor did not place any condition on Randy taking the property; he does not even need to be alive in 2005. Additionally, Settlor did not include a spendthrift provision. In 2000, Randy sold his remainder interest to Florence. In 2001, Randy sold the same interest to Sam. To whom should the trustee distribute the remaining trust property when the trust ends in 2005?

Explanation

Courts have developed two basic approaches for resolving the priority of conflicting assignments of the same beneficial interest in a trust. The first approach, often called the *English view,* gives priority to the first assignee who notifies the trustee of the assignment. Under this race of diligence view, notice to the trustee is necessary to complete a beneficiary's assignment vis-à-vis later assignees. Thus, the trustee would distribute the trust property to the first assignee who gave notice. The second approach, often called the *American view,* gives priority to the first assignee unless the trust instrument provides otherwise. The first assignee prevails because the beneficiary did not own any interest in the trust after making the first assignment. Thus, the beneficiary did not transfer anything to the second assignee. If the court applied this view, Florence would prevail because Florence was the first person to receive an assignment. However, if Florence misled Sam into believing Randy could make an effective transfer of the trust interest to him, the court will estop Florence from asserting her priority position. Jurisdictions in the United States are almost evenly divided between these two approaches with the Restatement (Second) of Trusts adopting the American view in §136.

§19.8.7 Availability of Beneficiary's Interest to Creditors

The equitable interest of the beneficiary may be subject to attack from the beneficiary's creditors. Typical state law procedures that a creditor could use to reach this interest include a creditor's bill, a bill for equitable execution, levy, attachment, execution, and garnishment. Once the creditor obtains the interest, the creditor may elect to sell the interest or require the trustee to make distributions directly to the creditor as they come due.

The beneficiary's creditors, however, rarely have the ability to reach the beneficiary's interest in the trust. Almost all trusts contain spendthrift provisions that prevent the creditors from obtaining the equitable interest. See §19.8.8, below. In addition, some states have statutes restricting a creditor's ability to pursue trust interests.

§19.8.8 Spendthrift Restrictions

A *spendthrift clause* is a provision of a trust that does two things. First, it prohibits the beneficiary from selling, giving away, or otherwise transferring the beneficiary's interest. Second, a spendthrift clause prevents the beneficiary's creditors from reaching the beneficiary's interest in the trust. The provision permits the settlor to carry out the settlor's intent of benefiting the designated beneficiary but not the beneficiary's assignees or creditors.

Unless prohibited by state law, settlors include spendthrift restrictions in practically every trust because they protect beneficiaries from their own improvidence and their personal creditors. As one law student wrote on an exam, they "protect people who may not have the good sense that God gave to hamsters." Note, however, that neither the settlor nor the beneficiary must show that a beneficiary is actually incapable of prudently managing property to obtain spendthrift protection.

Example 19-51. Spendthrift Restrictions — Effect After Trustee Distributes to Beneficiary

Settlor created a valid spendthrift trust for Bill. The trust provided that Bill is entitled to all trust income payable on the first of each month. Bill has a gaggle of creditors who are anxious for payment. How should these creditors proceed?

Explanation

The valid spendthrift clause prevents Bill's creditors from reaching the trust. However, once the trustee distributes the income to Bill, the protection of the spendthrift provision ends. Thus, the creditors need to position themselves so they can reach the money under proper state law procedures. Creditors are unlikely to succeed unless Bill is very careless. Normally, Bill receives a check in the mail or goes directly to the trustee's office for payment. Bill can then take the check to the bank and cash it. Bill can spend the money or hide it. Because the creditors are unlikely to be following Bill's every move, Bill can easily keep the money away from the creditors unless Bill does something "dumb" like depositing the money in an account subject to garnishment or keeping the cash where the creditor can directly take it.

Spendthrift restrictions are easy to create. The settlor does not need to use any particular language as long as the settlor's intent is clear. In some states, it is adequate for the settlor to simply write, "This is a spendthrift trust."

Sample Spendthrift Provision

This is a spendthrift trust, that is, to the fullest extent permitted by law, no interest in the income or principal of this trust may be voluntarily or involuntarily transferred by any beneficiary before payment or delivery of the interest by the trustee.

The vast majority of states enforce spendthrift provisions, either through legislative recognition or judicial approval. Three basic policies support the validity of spendthrift provisions. First, the settlor has the right to dispose of property as the settlor wishes. Second, granting this spendthrift protection to beneficiaries prevents them from becoming public burdens should the trust property be exhausted paying the claims of creditors. Third, creditors have the responsibility to investigate the debtor and the wisdom to know that they should not use the trust as a basis for granting credit if it contains a spendthrift provision. A few states, however, refuse to give effect to these provisions because they take away the rights of legitimate creditors and thus are deemed against public policy. Spendthrift provisions can also be viewed as encouraging irresponsible spending because the beneficiary can incur debt with impunity knowing that the creditors cannot reach the beneficiary's source of income. Note that settlors may still insulate the beneficiary's interest by using other techniques such as discretionary or support provisions. See §§19.8.9 and 19.8.10, below.

Even in states that authorize spendthrift provisions, many exceptions to their enforceability have developed as demonstrated by the following examples.

Example 19-52.   Spendthrift Restrictions — Settlor as Beneficiary

Settlor created an irrevocable trust naming Settlor as the sole beneficiary during Settlor's lifetime with the remaining property to pass to Children upon Settlor's death. Settlor has several unpaid creditors who would like to reach the property in the trust. Will they be successful?

Explanation

The creditors have several options. First, they could try to set aside the trust by proving that Settlor funded it with a fraudulent conveyance. Showing the elements necessary to get a trust invalidated as a fraudulent transfer can be a daunting task for creditors. Thus, creditors will prefer the second option of relying on state law, which generally refuses to enforce spendthrift provisions when the beneficiary is also the settlor of the trust. It is against public policy for a person to shield the person's own property from creditors with a spendthrift restriction. Note, however, that some states, such as Alaska, enforce spendthrift provisions even if the trust is self-settled.

Example 19-53.   Spendthrift Restrictions — Necessaries

Settlor created a valid spendthrift trust that provides for annual payments of income to Beneficiary. Beneficiary has two unpaid and consequently angry creditors. One creditor is a cruise line company that granted Beneficiary credit for a European vacation on board a luxury ship. The other creditor is the owner of a local grocery store who, being a nice person, granted Beneficiary credit to buy groceries. What is the likelihood that these creditors can reach the income of the trust despite the spendthrift provision?

Explanation

Creditors with claims for necessaries, such as food, clothing, shelter, and medical care, stand a good chance of reaching trust income despite the spendthrift shield. This exception to the enforceability of spendthrift provisions is based on the public policy of encouraging creditors to supply the basic necessities of life without fear of not getting paid. In contracts class you probably learned an analogous concept for the enforceability of contracts for necessaries made by minors and incompetent persons. Therefore, the grocer is likely to recover and the cruise line will probably go home empty handed.

Example 19-54.   Spendthrift Restrictions — Spousal and Child Support

Settlor established a valid spendthrift trust for Child. Child married, had several children, and then obtained a divorce. Child is now behind on court ordered spousal and child support. May Child's ex-spouse and children reach Child's interest in the trust despite the spendthrift provision?

Explanation

Child's ex-spouse and children stand a good chance of reaching Child's interest. The enforceability of spendthrift restraints is often subject to a legislatively mandated or judicially imposed exception for spousal and child support claimants. This exception is based on the public policy rationale that a beneficiary of a trust should not be able to evade support obligations by hiding behind a spendthrift clause. The needs of the beneficiary's ex-spouse and children are deemed to outweigh the rights of the settlor to control the use of trust property.

Example 19-55.   Spendthrift Restrictions — Federal Tax Claims

Settlor created a valid spendthrift trust for Beneficiary. Beneficiary neglected to pay income tax and thus the Internal Revenue Service obtained a valid tax lien on "all property and rights to property, whether real or personal, belonging to" Beneficiary. I.R.C. §6321. Will the IRS be successful in its attempts to reach Beneficiary's interest in the trust despite the spendthrift clause?

Explanation

Yes. The federal tax lien is the most powerful lien known to our legal system. The lien covers all of the delinquent taxpayer's property and there are no exceptions. State law protections, such as spendthrift clauses, exempt property, and homestead, are ineffective against the tax lien because federal law is superior to state law under the Supremacy Clause of Article VI of the United States Constitution.

Example 19-56.   Spendthrift Restraints — Tort Claimants

Settlor created a valid spendthrift trust for Beneficiary. Beneficiary consumed an excessive quantity of intoxicating beverages and caused a severe car accident. May the injured parties recover against the property of the trust despite the spendthrift clause?

Explanation

A small but increasing number of states permit tort claimants to recover against spendthrift trusts. These jurisdictions balance the public interest of providing a recovery for a tort claimant against carrying out the settlor's desire to protect the beneficiary. The tort claimant did not have any opportunity to investigate the beneficiary as do traditional creditors. Failure to permit recovery may cause financial hardship to tort plaintiffs but providing recovery may cause the same for the beneficiary. Between the two, however, the equities are in favor of the tort plaintiffs because they were innocent of any wrongdoing. Their argument in this case is strengthened by the nature of Beneficiary's conduct, that is, drinking and driving.

Example 19-57. Spendthrift Restraints — Settlement Agreement

Settlor created a valid inter vivos spendthrift trust. After several years elapsed, controversy erupted among the settlor, the trustees, and the beneficiaries. To avoid expensive and time-consuming litigation, all the parties entered into a settlement agreement. Part of the agreement required one of the beneficiaries to transfer part of the beneficiary's interest. May the beneficiary do so despite the spendthrift provision?

Explanation

Although this situation is not very common, courts usually permit the beneficiary to make this type of transfer even though the trust contains a spendthrift clause. Courts view settlement agreements with considerable deference because they help relieve court congestion and permit parties to resolve differences in a more amicable manner than litigation. In this case, a court is even more likely to permit the transfer because the settlor, the person who imposed the spendthrift restriction in the first place, was a party to the agreement.

§19.8.9 *Discretionary Provisions*

Settlors often create trusts for beneficiaries, such as children or grandchildren, whose future needs cannot be predicted with accuracy. For example, if the settlor's children are two and five years old when the settlor creates the trust, the settlor does not know whether one child will need extensive medical care because of a future accident or disease or whether one child will need additional funds to attend college (or, alternatively, will receive a scholarship and thus not need as much assistance). The settlor wants the trustee to make trust distributions in accordance with the beneficiary's needs just as the settlor would if the settlor were still in control of the property. In other words, the settlor is substituting the trustee's judgment for the settlor's judgment typically because the settlor will be deceased at the time the trust distributions are made. The settlor does not want to create a *mandatory trust,* which requires the trustee to make predesignated distributions (e.g., "$1,000 per month for each beneficiary" or "50% of the trust's income in quarterly installments").

To accomplish this objective, settlors frequently give their trustees the discretion to determine which beneficiaries to pay and how much to pay each. A trust containing this type of provision is called a *discretionary trust*. You may also hear these types of trusts called *spray* or *sprinkle* trusts because of the trustee's power to spread the benefits among the beneficiaries.

The trustee's discretion may be very broad ("distribute to my children in your absolute discretion), very narrow ("distribute to my children at your discretion for their dental expenses"), or anywhere in between ("distribute to my children at your discretion for expenses relating to their health, education, maintenance, and support").

Despite broad language in a trust indicating that the trustee has uncontrolled or unbridled discretion, courts require trustees to act in good faith, honestly, and for the purposes the settlor stated in the trust. If a trustee actually could have uncontrolled discretion, no trust would exist because no one could enforce the trustee's duties. In addition, it would be against public policy to permit a trustee to have free rein over the property and to use it contrary to the settlor's intent but yet provide no remedy to the injured parties, the beneficiaries. Likewise, the trustee must exercise the discretion to pay or not to pay; the trustee cannot sit idly by doing nothing.

Courts are divided regarding whether a trustee's exercise of discretion must be reasonable. Most jurisdictions impose an objective reasonableness standard on the trustee's exercise of discretion. However, other courts do not unless the trust instrument expressly burdens the trustee with this additional standard.

Example 19-58. Discretionary Trust — Extent of Discretion

Settlor created a valid discretionary trust in Settlor's will that contained the following provision: "Trustee shall use the income and principal of this trust in the trustee's full, absolute, and uncontrolled discretion for the educational expenses of my children." Settlor had two children, Son and Daughter. Trustee is paying all of Son's expenses at a small state college. However, Trustee refuses to pay any of Daughter's expenses at a prestigious Ivy League college. Daughter brings an action against Trustee to force Trustee to pay for her expenses. Trustee defends by claiming that under the terms of the trust, Trustee has complete discretion and thus Trustee's decision may not be questioned. Who will prevail and why?

Explanation

The court may review Trustee's decisions despite Settlor's broad grant of discretion. Thus, we need to know Trustee's reason for failing to pay Daughter's expenses. If Trustee shows that the trust cannot afford to pay the high fees at the Ivy League school without jeopardizing the trust's ability to continue paying for both children's expenses, Trustee is likely to prevail. Daughter needs to resign herself to the fact that her free ride will take her only to a state-supported school. If Trustee refuses to pay because Trustee believes this school's curriculum is not as good as that of another similar school and that Daughter should attend that school instead, the decision is a close call. Most courts require a trustee's discretion to be exercised reasonably and thus the success of Daughter's action will depend on whether the grounds for Trustee's decision are supported by objective means. In addition, courts are reluctant to overrule a trustee's honest exercise of discretion unless the beneficiary has extremely strong evidence of the trustee's unreasonableness. Courts do not want to get into the business of administering trusts and second-guessing trustees.

Example 19-59. Discretionary Trust—Remedy for Abuse of Discretion

Assume in the above example that Trustee's real reason for refusing to pay Daughter was Daughter's rejection of Trustee's romantic advances. If Daughter can prove that her failure to get distributions is because she broke Trustee's heart, what remedy will she receive?

Explanation

Courts have at least three ways to handle Daughter's situation. First, if the court believed that Trustee's conduct was so outrageous that it demonstrated that Trustee could not carry out the trust, the court would remove Trustee from office and appoint a new trustee who could then evaluate the situation and exercise the discretion. Second, the court may think that Trustee is capable of doing a competent job but is unable to make a completely fair evaluation of the situation. The court could exercise the discretion for Trustee and order Trustee to make specified payments. The third option, and the one most frequently used if Trustee remains in office, is to instruct (scold) Trustee on the trustee's duties and how to bring Trustee's decisions within the permissible bounds of the discretion. Trustee then would make Trustee's own decision on how much to pay Daughter for her educational expenses. If Daughter was still unhappy, she could bring another lawsuit and ask the court either to exercise the discretion or remove Trustee from office. See §21.2.2, below.

Example 19-60. Discretionary Trust—Assignment and Attachment of Beneficiary's "Interest"—General Rules

Settlor created a valid trust for Beneficiary that gave Trustee the discretion to make payments from trust income and principal for Beneficiary's health, education, maintenance, and support. Beneficiary wanted some extra funds for a vacation and thus sold Beneficiary's next year's benefits to Purchaser for $5,000. Beneficiary also got in financial trouble and Creditor attached Beneficiary's interest in the trust for $10,000. Trustee refuses to pay both Purchaser and Creditor and thus they sue. What are the likely results of their suits and why?

Explanation

Beneficiary has no property interest in the income or principal of the trust until Trustee decides to exercise the discretion to make a payment. In effect, Beneficiary merely has an expectancy to receive property under a power of appointment which Settlor placed into the trust. Thus, Beneficiary owned nothing Purchaser could buy and Trustee is not obligated to make payments to Purchaser. Likewise, Creditor's attachment of the trust has little value because Beneficiary has no property interest in the trust for Creditor to reach until Trustee makes the decision to make a discretionary distribution. Although the court cannot force Trustee to make payments to Creditor, the court may require any payments from the trust to go first to Creditor. A deadlock would then result and neither Beneficiary nor Creditor would get paid. However, if the trust permits Trustee to make payments directly for Beneficiary's health, education, maintenance, and support, Trustee may be able to make these payments without interference by Creditor because Beneficiary is still not receiving a distribution.

Example 19-61. Discretionary Trust—Assignment and Attachment of Beneficiary's "Interest"—Exceptions

Settlor placed the bulk of Settlor's property into a discretionary trust naming Settlor as the life beneficiary. Trustee had the discretion to make whatever payments of income and principal to Trustee that Trustee decides. Creditor attempts to reach the trust property. Will Creditor succeed?

Explanation

Most states recognize exceptions to the nonattachability of interests in discretionary trusts in the same type of situations as for spendthrift trusts such as where the settlor and beneficiary are the same person, the creditor's claim is for necessaries, and the claimant is the spouse or child of the beneficiary who is seeking support. See §19.8.8, above. Thus, Creditor is likely to prevail. Most states permit creditors to reach the maximum amount that the trustee, under the terms of the trust, could pay to (or apply for the benefit of) a person who is both the settlor and beneficiary of a discretionary trust. In this case, Trustee could use all the income and principal for Settlor and thus Creditor may be able to reach the entire trust up to the amount of Creditor's claim.

§19.8.10 Support Provisions

The settlor may restrict the use of trust income, principal, or both to the beneficiary's basic needs such as food, clothing, medical care, and educational expenses. A trust containing this type of provision is called a *support trust*. A support trust may either be mandatory or discretionary in nature. If mandatory, the trustee must make distributions to support the beneficiary. However, if the support trust is discretionary, the trustee may, but is not required, to pay for the beneficiary's support and may not, under any circumstances, make distributions for other reasons such as a vacation or second home.

Many courts treat support trusts as being spendthrift in nature even if they lack express spendthrift clauses. As a general rule, the beneficiary of a support trust may not convey the beneficiary's interest. If the beneficiary could alienate the beneficiary's interest, the settlor's purpose of providing for the beneficiary would be circumvented. For the same reason, the beneficiary's creditors may not reach the beneficiary's interest. This creditor protection is usually unavailable, however, in the same types of situations in which a spendthrift clause is ineffective such as where the settlor and the beneficiary are the same person or the creditor's claim is for necessaries. See §19.8.8, above.

Example 19-62. Support Trust—Determination of Level of Support

Settlor was a stereotypical suburban parent living in a middle-class home. Settlor created a valid support trust for the benefit of Son and Daughter in Settlor's will. When Settlor died, Son was unemployed living in a filthy rat-infested SRO. On the other hand, Daughter had recently won the lottery and was enjoying a luxurious lifestyle in an uptown condominium. What type of distributions should Trustee make?

Explanation

Trustee must address several issues in determining how to make distributions. One task is to ascertain the level of support Settlor wanted to provide for the Son and Daughter. What does "support" actually mean? Is it the lifestyle of Settlor, Son, or Daughter? Generally, in the absence of a definition of "support" in the trust instrument, support means the standard of living to which the beneficiary was accustomed at the time of trust creation. Does this mean that Son just gets enough to maintain his meager existence while Daughter gets to raid the trust to finance her extravagant lifestyle? Another question is whether Trustee may consider a beneficiary's other income or resources. Is the trust to provide a minimum level of support and anything the beneficiary has or acquires is irrelevant, or is the trust to provide a safety net if the beneficiary's other resources and income are inadequate? Said another way, did Settlor intend the trust to supply the first or last dollars of the beneficiary's support expenses? A well-drafted trust instrument could resolve most of these problems by defining the level of support or by leaving it up to the trustee's discretion. Likewise, the trust should state whether the trustee may, must, or cannot consider the beneficiary's other property and income. Without an express statement of Settlor's intent, the court will attempt to do what it thinks Settlor would have done if Settlor were still alive. Settlor probably meant for Son and Daughter to have a lifestyle similar to that of Settlor. Thus, Trustee may be authorized to give extra funds to Son to improve his living conditions and withhold distributions from Daughter because she is doing just fine on her own.

Sample Discretionary Support Provision

The trustee shall pay to or apply for the benefit of my children under [age] years old so much of the net income and so much of the principal, up to the whole thereof, of the trust property as the trustee in the trustee's sole discretion deems advisable for the beneficiary's health, education, maintenance, and support. The trustee [is] [is not] required to treat each child equally. The trustee [may] [must] [need not] consider the beneficiary's other resources and income in making distribution decisions.

Example 19-63. Support Trust—Support of Beneficiary's Dependents

Settlor created a valid support trust for Daughter with the remainder to Son when Daughter reaches age thirty. Daughter is twenty-eight years old, married, and has two children. Trustee has recently purchased Daughter a new house to replace the one she was living in prior to being married and giving birth to her children. Trustee is also paying for all of the children's pediatric expenses. Son is outraged about these payments because they are actually benefiting Daughter's husband and children rather than Daughter. Son realizes that these payments are rapidly depleting the amount he will receive in two years. Accordingly, Son sues Trustee for making distributions in breach of Trustee's duties. How should a court resolve this dispute?

Explanation

In the absence of language in the trust instrument to the contrary, most courts hold that support includes not just the support of the beneficiary, but also support of the individuals whom the beneficiary is legally obligated to support. Because Daughter has a legal obligation to support her husband and her minor children, Trustee's disbursements are allowed even though the medical care is only for the children and the house benefits three people other than Daughter, the named beneficiary.

§19.8.11 Pour-Over Provisions

A *pour-over provision* is a clause in a will that makes a gift to an inter vivos trust. Pour-over provisions are very common because many testators wish to obtain the benefits of trusts but do not want to create them in their wills. Section 9.6, above, contains a detailed discussion of these provisions.

§19.8.12 Life Insurance Trusts

The owner of a life insurance policy may name a trust as the beneficiary of the policy. In addition, the owner may transfer the policy itself to the trust. The trust property will then consist of the contract right to receive proceeds upon the insured's death or the life insurance contract itself. As discussed in §19.6.1, above, these contract rights are sufficient property to constitute trust corpus. For a discussion of life insurance generally, see §17.1, above.

For a variety of reasons, the owner of a life insurance policy may wish to name a trust as the beneficiary instead of the person the owner wishes to ultimately benefit from the proceeds. Ultimate Beneficiary (UB) may not have the legal capacity to handle the proceeds. For example, UB could be a minor or incompetent. If the proceeds were payable to UB directly, an expensive and inconvenient guardianship may be needed. Thus, anyone with life insurance and a desire to benefit their minor or incompetent children or grandchildren should seriously consider using a life insurance trust.

Even if legally competent, UB may be unable or unwilling to manage property in a prudent fashion. If UB were to receive the proceeds outright, they may disappear quickly. In addition, the insured may want to exercise control over how the proceeds are used after the insured's death, even if UB has both the legal and functional capacity to manage the property. Another benefit of life insurance trusts is their ability to help an individual create a unified plan for the insured's estate. The person may create one trust and have many different assets pour over into the trust, e.g., life insurance proceeds, pension and retirement plan death benefits, and the person's probate estate via a pour-over provision in the will. See §9.6, above, for a discussion of pour-over provisions.

Example 19-64. Life Insurance Trust—Inter Vivos or Testamentary?

Insured owns a life insurance policy with a face value of $500,000. Currently, Insured has named Spouse as the primary beneficiary and Children as the alternate beneficiaries. Insured realizes that it is not a good idea for the minor children to be named and has thus decided to create a life insurance trust. Should Insured create this trust immediately or would provisions in the Insured's will be sufficient?

Explanation

Most states permit both inter vivos and testamentary trusts to be named as the beneficiaries of life insurance policies. In these states, the question is not a legal one but rather a practical one. Here are some of the ramifications Insured needs to consider. The creation of an inter vivos trust may have additional start-up costs and administration costs. If this trust has no property other than the contract right to receive proceeds, administration costs should be relatively low. However, the trustee still has the responsibility to review the policy and, in some instances, may even have a duty to cash in the policy and reinvest the cash surrender value to gain a better rate of return. Having the policy payable to a testamentary trust avoids these problems but results in greater uncertainty and less protection for UB. For example, the will might not be found upon Insured's death or may be successfully contested. Testamentary trusts also make it harder for Insured to revise the trust as circumstances change because Insured would need to execute a new will. If the life insurance trust were created inter vivos, Insured could make changes rapidly with minimal cost.

Example 19-65. Life Insurance Trust—Funded or Unfunded?

Insured created a valid inter vivos trust and has properly named the trust as the beneficiary of a life insurance policy. Should Insured add additional property to this trust; that is, should the trust be *funded*?

Explanation

Insured does not need to add more property. As in Example 19-64, above, the question is a practical one, not a legal one. The unfunded life insurance trust is the simplest arrangement. Insured does not have to part with additional property and the trustee is not under an obligation to manage other assets. However, the trustee does not have any property with which to pay the premiums. Thus, if Insured forgets to pay them, the policy will lapse and Insured's entire plan will crash. If Insured funds the trust, the trustee would have property available to pay the premiums to make sure the policy stays in force. Of course, the trustee would then have the additional duties of managing the property used to fund the trust.

Example 19-66. Life Insurance Trust — Revocable or Irrevocable?

Insured created a valid inter vivos trust and has properly named the trust as the beneficiary of a life insurance policy. Should this trust be revocable or irrevocable?

Explanation

Insured must weigh a variety of factors in making this decision. A revocable life insurance trust would provide Insured with considerable flexibility. Insured could revise or terminate the trust at any time. However, the amount of protection for UB is reduced because UB's interest could end without a moment's notice. If Insured was also seeking tax benefits, they would not be available with a revocable arrangement. An irrevocable life insurance trust is a stronger and more secure arrangement for UB, especially if Insured also transfers the policy itself to the trust along with property to pay future premiums. On the other hand, Insured is now stuck with a plan that may not be appropriate in later years as circumstances change.

§19.9 Rule against Perpetuities

Under the law of most states, the Rule against Perpetuities prohibits trusts in which the ability to ascertain the identity of the beneficiaries in whom equitable title will vest is delayed beyond a specified period of time. At common law, and still in many states today, this time is twenty-one years after the death of some life in being at the time of the creation of the interest, plus a period of gestation. For irrevocable inter vivos trusts the time period starts to run when the settlor declares the trust or conveys the property to the trust. If the settlor can revoke the inter vivos trust, the period begins to run when the trust is no longer revocable, which is usually when the settlor dies. If the trust is testamentary, the clock begins to run when the settlor dies.

The application of the Rule against Perpetuities is restricted in many cases. Most, if not all, jurisdictions limit the application of the Rule to private trusts; certainty in vesting is not required for trusts in which all beneficial interests are charitable. Some states reject the common law approach of voiding the beneficiary's interest if there is any possibility, no matter how unlikely it may be, that a contingency could occur that would delay vesting beyond the perpetuities period. Instead, they adopted a *wait-and-see* approach and look at how vesting actually occurs instead of how it could occur.

Other jurisdictions lengthen the period or permit the courts to reform the trust using *cy pres;* that is, the court may modify the trust to make it fit within the Rule while still carrying out the settlor's intent as closely as possible. Many states have enacted the Uniform Statutory Rule against Perpetuities Act (also found in UPC §§2-901 to 2-905), which combines many of these reforms such as a ninety-year time period plus wait-and-see and deferred-reformation components.

A growing number of states, such as Alaska, Delaware, Idaho, South Dakota, and Wisconsin, have completely abolished the Rule. In these states, settlors may create *dynasty trusts,* which last indefinitely and restrict benefits to remote descendants of the settlor. The decision to abolish the Rule in these states was, at least in part, an economic decision to encourage wealthy settlors to bring their property into these states, establish trusts, employ local trustees and attorneys, and pay local taxes.

To lessen the impact of a Rule against Perpetuities violation, a trust should include a savings clause that specifies exactly what is to happen to the trust property if a court determines that the settlor violated the Rule.

Sample Rule against Perpetuities Savings Provision

If a court of proper jurisdiction finds that this trust violates the Rule against Perpetuities, the remaining trust property shall be distributed to [Beneficiary].

The following examples demonstrate the basic application of the Rule against Perpetuities to trusts. However, the inner workings of the Rule are beyond the scope of this book. If you would like this complicated yet intriguing doctrine explained in detail, consider consulting the following two books: (1) John Makdisi, Estates in Land and Future Interests (2d ed. 1995) and (2) Mark Reutlinger, Wills, Trusts, and Estates — Essential Terms and Concepts (2d ed. 1998).

Example 19-67.   Rule against Perpetuities — Time of Trust Creation

Settlor indicated that the trust is to begin when "the first person walks on Mars." Assuming the rest of this trust is valid, will this provision cause the trust to violate the Rule against Perpetuities?

Explanation

Yes, Settlor's trust violates the Rule. A trust to begin upon a contingent event must start within the period specified by the Rule against Perpetuities. At this point in time, we cannot determine with certainty whether someone will, or will not, walk on the surface of Mars within the perpetuities period. Accordingly, both the vesting of the legal interest in the trustee and the equitable interest in the beneficiary are contingent on an event that is not certain to occur, or not occur, by the expiration of the perpetuities period and thus, at common law, both interests would fail.

Example 19-68. Rule against Perpetuities — Beneficiaries during Existence of Trust

Settlor created a trust containing the following provision, "The trustee shall pay the income of the trust to Brenda for twenty-five years. At the end of twenty-five years, the trustee shall pay the income to my then-living descendants. Upon the death of the last of these descendants, the trustee shall deliver all remaining trust property to Ralph." Assuming the rest of this trust is valid, will this provision cause the trust to violate the Rule against Perpetuities?

Explanation

Yes, Settlor's trust violates the Rule. All beneficial interests during the existence of a trust must vest within the perpetuities period. If Brenda were to die within the first four years of the trust, we could not ascertain in whom the beneficial interest would vest until after the expiration of the twenty-one year period. Remember, the trust gave Brenda the income interest for twenty-five years. Her interest does not end upon her death. Instead, her right to the income for the balance of the twenty-five years would pass to her heirs or beneficiaries. We cannot determine the identity of Settlor's "then-living" descendants until this period expires. At common law, this delay is beyond the permitted twenty-one years and thus the trust violates the Rule against Perpetuities.

Settlor could have avoided this problem by limiting Brenda's interest to her life. For example, Settlor could have provided that: "The trustee shall pay the income of the trust to Brenda for twenty-five years or life, whichever period is shorter. The trustee shall then pay the income to my then-living descendants. Upon the death of the last of these descendants, the trustee shall deliver all remaining trust property to Ralph." In this case, the interests in Settlor's descendants can be ascertained immediately upon Brenda's death. Vesting is always certain to occur within the period because the interests in Settlor's descendants vest immediately upon the death of Brenda, the life in being. In fact, none of the "extra" twenty-one years is even touched in this arrangement.

Example 19-69. Rule against Perpetuities — Remainder Beneficiaries upon Trust Termination

Settlor created a trust containing the following provision: "The trustee shall pay the income of this trust for twenty-five years to Brenda or, if she dies before the end of twenty-five years, to her closest family members by consanguinity. At the end of the twenty-five years, the trust terminates and the trustee shall pay all remaining trust property to my then-living descendants." Assuming the rest of this trust is valid, will this provision cause the trust to violate the Rule against Perpetuities?

Explanation

Yes, Settlor's trust violates the Rule. All remainder interests in a trust must vest within the perpetuities period. Under this trust, the identity of the recipients of the remainder interest cannot be ascertained until the expiration of the twenty-five year period thus exceeding the twenty-one years allowed by the Rule against Perpetuities. Remember, if any possible fact pattern violates the Rule, the Rule is violated. In this case, all lives in being could die within the first four years of the trust thus causing the remainder interests to vest beyond the perpetuities period.

§19.10   Charitable Trusts

A *charitable trust*, also called a *public trust*, is a trust established for the benefit of the community as a whole or for a relatively large segment of the community. Charitable trusts were originally enforced in England by chancery courts and were statutorily recognized by Parliament when they enacted the Statute of Charitable Uses[7] in 1601. This statute enumerated the purposes regarded as charitable, which have remained relatively unchanged over the past 400 years. The five widely recognized categories of charitable purposes include (1) relief of poverty, (2) advancement of education, (3) advancement of religion, (4) promotion of health, and (5) governmental or municipal purposes (e.g., parks and museums). Courts retain considerable power to decide whether a particular purpose is or is not beneficial to the community.

For the most part, the law governing charitable trusts is substantially the same as the law for private trusts. There are, however, some very important differences and special concerns when the settlor creates a charitable trust. This section reviews these issues, which include the size of the charitable class and the determination of whether a particular purpose is charitable.

§19.10.1   Size of Charitable Class

Unlike private trusts (see §19.8.2, above), charitable trusts require a sufficiently large or indefinite class of beneficiaries so that the actual

---

7. 43 Eliz. ch. 4.

beneficiary of the trust is the public, not a particular person or small group of readily ascertainable people. If the trust fails as a charitable trust, it may nonetheless still be valid as a private trust. However, there are often advantages for the trust to be charitable such as not being constrained by the Rule against Perpetuities and being eligible for significant tax breaks.

Example 19-70. Charitable Trust—Size of Charitable Class—Benefits Limited to One Individual

Settlor established a trust to pay the educational expenses of "some deserving student who wishes to pursue an acting career." Is this a charitable trust?

Explanation

Courts have gone both ways with cases similar to this example. Some courts would hold that Settlor's language created a trust for one person and thus is not charitable. On the other hand, other courts view the language as charitable because the identity of the recipient is uncertain. The amount of property in the trust may play a pivotal role in the court's decision. If the corpus is relatively small, it is more likely only one person could benefit and thus the chances of the court deeming the trust charitable decrease. However, if the corpus is large, the court will have an easier time holding the trust charitable because Settlor must have intended to benefit a series of deserving students over a period of time.

Another important factor is the type of education the student is required to pursue. Some people may argue that there is little social value in adding one more skilled actor or actress to the population of the United States. However, if the education restriction was for a more socially important skill, such as a medical doctor, the court would have an easier time deeming the trust charitable, especially if the person who receives the benefits must agree to practice in an area of the country where there is a shortage of doctors. In these types of cases, the court would view the individual who actually receives the distributions as a mere conduit through which the citizens of that area are benefited.

Example 19-71. Charitable Trust—Size of Charitable Class—Benefits Limited to Family Members

Settlor established a trust for the education and medical expenses of Settlor's children. Is this trust charitable?

Explanation

No, a court will not deem the trust charitable merely because Settlor required trust funds to be spent for purposes that are charitable. Settlor must create a trust that benefits the community. The settlor of a charitable trust needs to be altruistic. Here, Settlor only had Settlor's close family members in mind and thus acted too selfishly to create a charitable trust. The potential of the trust helping to keep Settlor's family members off of the welfare rolls is insufficient to be a public purpose. However, some courts would hold a trust that benefits a settlor's family to be charitable, even if the trustee were required to give preference to family members, if nonfamily members could also benefit.

Example 19-72. Charitable Trust—Size of Charitable Class—Awards and Prizes

Settlor established a trust to provide a $1,000 scholarship to each student who receives an "A" in any law school course that spends at least six weeks on trust law. Is this trust charitable?

Explanation

Most courts would deem Settlor's trust charitable. Although the recipients can be ascertained with certainty each semester, they are not stated with specificity in the trust. Instead, a large number of individuals are potential recipients (students in courses that spend at least six weeks on trusts) and Settlor provided objective criteria (students who receive "A" grades) for selecting the ultimate recipients. Likewise, courts sustain the validity of trusts that award prizes to people who make substantial contributions to medicine, the arts, world peace, and the like. The true beneficiary of these trusts is the public because the awards and prizes encourage and reward socially valuable achievements.

Example 19-73. Charitable Trust—Size of Charitable Class—Disaster Victims

Settlor created a trust to pay for the medical care and housing expenses of victims of the floods and mudslides that occurred in California during 1998. Is this trust charitable?

Explanation

Yes, most courts would hold this trust charitable. Even though the recipients of the trust distributions are ascertainable, society is the ultimate beneficiary. Courts treat trusts as charitable if they provide benefits for groups of people who are linked together by some type of disaster such as a fire, hurricane, tornado, flood, earthquake, plane crash, or anthrax outbreak.

§19.10.2 Description of Charitable Class

The settlor may specify the charitable class in extremely broad terms. Courts have held trusts charitable with language such as "for medical research," "to assist economically challenged families," and "for charity." The trustee has the discretion to select the means for carrying out the settlor's charitable purposes. Broad designations are not, however, necessarily charitable. For example, a trust for "such objects of liberality that the trustee selects" would not be charitable because the recipients are not limited to those of a charitable nature.

§19.10.3 Determination of Charitable Purpose

The court makes the determination of whether the settlor's purpose is charitable. The settlor's opinion that his or her purpose is charitable is irrelevant. As one judge stated, "If a [settlor] by stating or indicating [the settlor's] view that a trust is beneficial to the public can establish that fact beyond question, trusts might be established in perpetuity for the promotion of all kinds of fantastic (though not unlawful) objects, of which the training of poodles to dance might be a mild example."[8]

How, then, do courts determine whether the settlor's purpose is charitable? Courts do not apply a bright-line rule. Instead, the resolution of any particular case depends on the exact facts and the philosophy of the judge. Courts frequently apply some version of a "generally accepted" standard. Thus, if the judge believes that the consensus of the community would be that the settlor's purpose is charitable, then the court will treat that purpose as being charitable. This test, however, is somewhat harsh because its application could prevent trusts from achieving charitable status if they are created for purposes not widely deemed charitable or if they involve new or controversial matters.

Example 19-74. Charitable Purpose — Advancement of Ideas

Settlor created two trusts, each with a different purpose. Settlor directed the trustee of the first trust to expend trust income and principal to advance the idea that the United States should become a communistic country run by one person who is not answerable to any court or legislative body. The trustee of the second trust was to use trust assets to fund the dissemination of Settlor's essays regarding Settlor's belief that operatives from a foreign gov-

---

8. In re Hummeltenberg, 1 Ch. 237, 242 (1923).

ernment are conspiring with extraterrestrial forces to take over the earth. Are either or both of these trusts charitable?

Explanation

Examining these two trusts under the generally accepted test, a court could easily determine that neither of them is charitable. Most people in the United States are unlikely to think advocating dictatorship and spreading one person's far-fetched conspiracy theories are charitable purposes. However, courts are more tolerant of trusts that advance ideas held by a sizeable number of people, even if not a majority. On the other hand, courts are reluctant to treat trusts that disseminate a settlor's own ideas as charitable. Thus, Settlor's first trust may stand a better chance of being held charitable than his second trust.

Example 19-75. Charitable Purpose — Accomplishment of Whims

Settlor's testamentary trust required the trustee to use trust property to build a small office at the entrance to the cemetery in which Settlor was buried. The trustee was then to pay a person to be stationed in this office for ten hours per day, 365 days per year, to greet individuals visiting Settlor's grave and guide them to the appropriate plot while relating stories about Settlor's life experiences. Is this trust charitable?

Explanation

Courts are unlikely to treat trusts established to accomplish mere whims of the settlor as being charitable. The court would view the spending of money in this fashion as being wasteful and against public policy and thus not proper for a charitable trust.

Example 19-76. Charitable Purpose — Religion

Settlor established a trust for the promotion of Santeria, a religion that includes animal sacrifice in its ceremonies. Is this trust charitable?

Explanation

The sacrificing of animals in a religious ceremony is unlikely to be generally accepted as charitable by people in the United States. Nonetheless, this trust has a good chance of being deemed charitable. Courts are much more tolerant of trusts that are religiously based than those based on other categories of charitable purposes such as education or health care. Instead of using the generally accepted test, many courts adopt a "not criminal" or "not against public policy" standard. Killing animals is generally not against the law or public policy. Thus, the trust may stand as charitable. Of course, if the religion advocated human sacrifice, it would not be charitable because the killing of humans is against both the law and public policy unless the government sanctions such conduct (e.g., capital punishment and military actions during times of war).

§19.10.4 *Other Charitable Trust Issues*

§19.10.4.1 Mortmain Statutes

A *mortmain statute* limits or restricts charitable gifts, especially testamentary ones, be they outright or in trust. Only a few states still have mortmain statutes and their constitutional validity is problematic. For a more detailed discussion of these statutes, see §10.3.4, above.

§19.10.4.2 *Rule against Perpetuities*

Charitable trusts are typically not restricted by the Rule Against Perpetuities. Accordingly, charitable trusts may theoretically continue indefinitely. See §19.9, above, for an overview of Rule Against Perpetuities issues in the private trust context.

§19.10.4.3 Enforcement

The state's attorney general is charged with the duty of enforcing charitable trusts for the benefit of the community. Other individuals, such as the settlors, lack standing to enforce charitable trusts unless they can demonstrate a special interest not shared by the general public. Some states require the party initiating an action involving a charitable trust to give notice to the attorney general's office. The attorney general can then decide whether to intervene in the action to protect the charity's interests. If the attorney general does not receive notice, some states permit the attorney general to set aside any judgment or settlement at any time for any reason.

§19.10.4.4 Tax Benefits

A charitable trust that meets the detailed and technical requirements of the Internal Revenue Code can qualify for significant income, gift, and estate tax benefits. Some states even have savings statutes that provide for charitable trusts to automatically be treated as if they include the appropriate language, restrictions, and limitations to achieve these tax benefits unless the settlor expressly provides to the contrary in the instrument.

§19.10.4.5 *Cy Pres*

Under certain circumstances, courts can apply the cy pres doctrine to supply missing charitable trust beneficiaries to prevent a charitable trust from failing. Cy pres applies to a charitable gift in trust just like it does to a testamentary one. See §7.5, above, for a discussion of this concept in the context of a charitable gift in a will.

§19.10.4.6 Split Interest Trusts

A trust can be both private and charitable at the same time. This type of trust is called a *split interest* or *mixed trust*. Assuming the court can separate the charitable from noncharitable purposes, each part must meet the appropriate requirements. Common types of split interest trusts include the *charitable remainder trust,* where the settlor or the settlor's family retains the benefits until a specified time after which the remainder passes to charity, and the *charitable lead trust,* in which the charity obtains the benefits from the trust property for a set period of time after which they return to the settlor or the settlor's family. Split interest trusts are often an effective method of reducing the settlor's estate and gift taxes because they allow the settlor to take advantage of the charitable deduction while still permitting the settlor or the settlor's family to obtain some of the benefits of the property.

20

Trust Administration

The settlor's instructions with regard to the management of trust property and distribution to beneficiaries must be turned from mere words into action. The trustee is in charge of this process. This chapter provides an overview of the administration process, analyzes the fiduciary duties, responsibilities, and powers of the trustee, and concludes with a discussion of the ability of a court and the parties to alter or terminate existing trusts.

§20.1 Overview of Trust Administration

A person who is considering the possibility of serving as a trustee must have a full appreciation of the burdens associated with the position to make an informed decision. This section provides an overview of the trust administration process.

§20.1.1 Accept Trusteeship

A person must make a conscious decision to accept the office of trustee. No duties are imposed and no liability attaches until a trustee accepts the position. A person may be unwilling or unable to accept for many reasons. For example, the person may not want the responsibility or the potential liability of being a trustee. Lack of expertise, incompetence, or an insufficient trustee fee are other reasons a person may decline a trustee position. See §19.7.2, above, for a detailed discussion of acceptance issues and concerns.

§20.1.2 Post Bond

Unless the settlor waived bond in the trust instrument or applicable state law provides otherwise, a trustee must post a bond to protect the beneficiaries from evil trustee conduct. If bond is required, the trustee must follow the applicable state law procedures to have the court determine the amount of the bond and approve any sureties. Issues regarding the trustee's bond are examined in §19.7.3.2, above.

§20.1.3 Register Trust

Under the law of a few states and under UPC §7-101, the trustee has a duty to register the trust with the court. Registration is usually a simple process. The trustee files a statement with the appropriate court acknowledging the trustee's acceptance and identifying the trust. The main purpose behind trust registration is to make it clear to the beneficiaries and other individuals which court has jurisdiction over the trust so they know where they should pursue legal action involving the trust.

§20.1.4 Possess and Safeguard Trust Property

As the holder of legal title, the trustee has the right to possess trust property. As soon as possible after accepting the position, the trustee needs to locate the trust property, assume control over it, and protect it. For example, the trustee should record deeds, buy insurance, keep the property repaired, place valuable personal property in a safe deposit box, and register corporate securities.

§20.1.4.1 Earmark Trust Property

The trustee must *earmark* the trust property, that is, label the property as belonging to the trust. Earmarking prevents trust property from being confused with the trustee's own property so that the trustee's personal creditors, heirs, beneficiaries, and other claimants do not take trust property under the mistaken belief that it belongs to the trustee.

Example 20-1. Earmarking — Effect of Failure to Earmark

Settlor placed two items of property into a valid trust — a collection of gold coins and 100 shares of Omnipotent Corporation stock. Trustee took possession of the coins and the stock certificates but took no steps to label them as belonging to the trust. Trustee's finances suffered and one of Trustee's creditors successfully levied on the coins. When the United States Justice Department began an investigation of the top management of Omnipotent Corporation, the value of the stock dropped precipitously. Is Trustee liable for the lost coins and the decrease in value of the stock?

Explanation

At common law, Trustee would be liable for both the lost coins and the decrease in the value of the stock. Trustees were liable for all losses that occurred to unlabeled trust property, even if those losses would have occurred had the property been properly marked. The rule was very strict, actually punitive, to encourage earmarking. Under modern law, however, trustees are usually liable only if the loss resulted from the failure to earmark. Thus, Trustee would be liable for the coins because the creditor would not have been able to touch them if they had been placed in a safe deposit box labeled to show that its contents were trust property. On the other hand, Trustee would not be liable for the decrease in value to Omnipotent Corporation stock because the loss was not caused by the failure to earmark. Even if the stock had been properly registered in the name of the trust, the value still would have gone down because of the DOJ's investigation.

Example 20-2. Earmarking — Holding as Nominee

Settlor transferred an extensive stock portfolio to a valid trust. Trustee needs to buy and sell securities on a daily basis. Accordingly, it is not practical for Trustee to obtain stock certificates registered in the name of the trust. Instead, Trustee wants the stock to be held in *nominee* or *street name* form by a reputable and fully licensed stockbroker. May Trustee do so?

Explanation

Holding stock in the name of a third party would technically violate Trustee's duty to earmark trust property. However, most states permit some types of property, especially corporate securities, to be held in nominee form as long as the arrangement is properly documented. Thus, the account at the brokerage would be in the name of the trust but the stock itself can be in the broker's name. Trustee can then make rapid stock trades that may enhance the profitability of the trust.

§20.1.4.2 Avoid Commingling

In addition to labeling property as belonging to the trust, the trustee must also keep trust property separate from the trustee's own assets and the property of others.

Example 20-3. Commingling — With Trustee's Own Property

Settlor transferred a coin collection to Trustee. Trustee, also a collector, carefully placed the coins in Trustee's personal coin books. Trustee conspicuously noted the trust's ownership underneath each coin Trustee received from Settlor. A tornado struck Trustee's home and destroyed the collection. Is Trustee personally liable for the value of the coins?

Explanation

Most courts hold a trustee absolutely liable for all losses that occur to commingled trust property, even if those losses are not due to the commingling. This harsh rule prevents the easy misapplication of property that could occur if commingling were permitted. Note that Trustee may have breached other duties by not placing the coins in a safe deposit box and purchasing insurance.

Example 20-4. Commingling — With Property from Other Trusts

Trustee is serving as the trustee of two trusts. Trustee would like to commingle the property from these trusts. Trustee would then have a larger amount to invest and be able to secure higher rates of return with lower transaction costs. In addition, Trustee could diversify the investments to lessen the impact of one investment going bad. Will this conduct violate Trustee's duty not to commingle?

Explanation

Trustee's conduct would violate the basic commingling prohibition. However, most states permit corporate trustees to commingle the property from several trusts into a *common trust fund*. These funds permit trustees to diversify, lower transaction costs, and better leverage the trust property. State legislation typically governs these funds and requires the trustee to keep detailed records so that income and profits can be properly allocated. Some statutes impose requirements geared to protecting the funds from catastrophic losses. Individual trustees do not typically have the option of commingling the property of different trusts. However, they can secure the same benefits by investing in regular commercial mutual funds.

§20.1.5 Identify and Locate Beneficiaries

The trustee must ascertain the identity and location of the beneficiaries of the trust. The beneficiaries' names and addresses are needed so the trustee knows who receives the trust benefits and where to send them. The trustee may have some difficulty doing this if the trust instrument does not contain sufficient identifying information such as the beneficiaries' complete names, addresses, and relationships to the settlor. In such cases, the trustee may need to hire a professional search service.

§20.1.6 Follow Settlor's Instructions

Unless prohibited by state law or public policy, the trustee must follow the settlor's wishes with regard to the trust property as stated in the trust instrument. The settlor inevitably provides instructions regarding the distribution of trust property. In addition, many settlors include directions regarding the investment and management of the trust property.

§20.1.7 Act as Fiduciary

The trustee is subject to a broad range of fiduciary duties. For example, the trustee must exercise a high standard of care when investing trust property and otherwise managing the trust. See §20.2, below. The trustee is also bound by a duty of loyalty and thus must avoid self-dealing and being in any position in which the trustee has interests to serve other than those of the trust. See §20.5, below. If a trustee fails to comply with the requirements and duties of trust administration, the trustee can be held personally liable. A breach of duty may result in both civil and criminal penalties. See Chapter 21, below.

§20.1.8 Support and Defend Trust

The trustee is responsible for defending attacks on the validity of the trust and its administration unless the advice of a competent attorney indicates that there is no reasonable defense. Likewise, the trustee has a duty to appeal an unfavorable verdict unless there is no reasonable ground for seeking a reversal.

Example 20-5. Duty of Trustee to Support and Defend Trust

Settlor attempted to create an inter vivos trust in favor of Son. After Settlor died, Daughter attacked the trust claiming that Settlor executed the trust only after Son exerted undue influence and duress upon Settlor. Trustee put up a valiant defense of the trust, but it failed. May Trustee seek reimbursement for Trustee's court costs and legal fees from the property allegedly the subject of the trust?

Explanation

Many states would permit Trustee to recover reasonable attorney's fees and court costs from the property even if Trustee loses the defense and no trust actually exists. The policy supporting this seemingly inconsistent rule is that no trustee would attempt to uphold a trust if the trustee knew that the trustee had to bear all of the expenses of an unsuccessful defense. Of course, the trustee's defense must be reasonable and in good faith to claim reimbursement.

§20.2   Trust Investments and Standard of Care

The trustee is responsible for investing trust property to make it productive while simultaneously protecting that property from undue risk. Courts and legislatures have developed various standards to judge the propriety of a trustee's conduct. A trustee is not an insurer of the trust's success and consequently is personally liable for loses only if the trustee's conduct falls beneath the applicable standard of care. This section reviews the investment-related duties of the trustee and different ways to evaluate the trustee's conduct.

§20.2.1   *Selection of Investments*

§20.2.1.1   Statutory "Legal" List

At one time, most states had a list of categories of property in which it was proper for trustees to invest. These *statutory* or *legal lists* typically were composed of relatively safe investments such as obligations backed by the United States government (e.g., Treasury bills, savings bonds, or insured certificates of deposit) and first mortgages on real property.[1] Due to the

---

1. As an investment, a first mortgage is safer than the real property itself because the debtor, barring a no deficiency provision, still owes the money even if the value

Great Depression, which began with the stock market crash of October 29, 1929, stocks and corporate securities were usually omitted from these lists. Over time, however, the types of legal investments have been expanded and many legal lists now include corporate securities, mutual funds, and similar investments.

The legal list approach to trust investment has been abandoned by almost all states. Many states that retain the lists expand them to such an extent that they bear little resemblance to true legal list statutes and look more like the prudent person approach discussed in §20.2.1.2, below.

Example 20-6. Legal List Investments

State law permits a trustee to invest in government-backed obligations and first mortgages on real property. Trustee used trust property to purchase a first mortgage on a parcel of land and 100 shares of Omnipotent Corporation stock. Are Trustee's investments proper?

Explanation

Legal lists can be either "mandatory" or "permissive." If the list is mandatory, Trustee must restrict investments to those specified on the list. Thus, the stock investment would be improper. Note, however, that merely because first mortgages are listed, does not mean that all investments in first mortgages are proper; Trustee would still need to make sure that the specific first mortgage is reasonable (e.g., the debtor has the ability to repay the loan and the land is valuable enough to adequately secure the mortgage). If the list is only permissive, the stock investment may be appropriate if Trustee can demonstrate that it was prudent to depart from the list.

§20.2.1.2 Prudent Person Standard

In most states, the propriety of the trustee's investments are judged with the *prudent person standard*. Under the traditional formulation of this rule, a trustee must exercise the degree of care and level of skill that a person of ordinary prudence would exercise in dealing with that person's own property. Many states and UPC §7-302 have modified this standard to focus on how a reasonable person would deal with the property of another. This toughens the test because a reasonable person is more careful with the property of others than with the person's own property.

The trustee must consider three main factors in selecting an investment.

---

of the property goes down or the property is subject to liability for taxes, judgment liens, etc.

First, the trustee must examine the safety of the investment. Risky or speculative investments are not allowed. Second, the trustee must determine the investment's potential to appreciate in value. Third, the trustee is required to evaluate the income the investment is expected to generate.

Example 20-7. Investments — Prudent Person Standard — Generally

Trustee made three investments: (1) 1,000 shares of stock in a fledgling company, Alchemy Corporation, whose scientists claim to be on the verge of perfecting a process of turning lead into gold; (2) an FDIC-insured five-year certificate of deposit for $50,000 paying 7 percent interest; and (3) a collection of antique furniture. What is the propriety of these investments under the prudent person standard?

Explanation

Under the prudent person standard, these investments must be evaluated separately, each on its own merit rather than as a group. The trustee cannot offset a loss (or failure to earn income) from one investment with a gain from another. Each of the investments is suspect after applying the prudent person standard. Stock is a proper type of investment because it can be relatively safe and can both appreciate and earn income (dividends). However, this corporation is engaged in finding a way to turn lead into gold, a business that a reasonable person would consider too speculative. The certificate of deposit is certainly safe and is paying a respectable rate of return. However, it is not appreciating in value. In five years, the trustee will only get back the trustee's original investment of $50,000 which, once inflation is considered, is actually a loss. The antique furniture, like most collectibles such as stamps, coins, comic books, and sports memorabilia, has a considerable amount of risk associated with it although there is a potential for significant appreciation. In addition, collectible items are not earning income for the trust.

Example 20-8. Prudent Person Standard — When Investment Judged

Trustee invested $100,000 in the stock of Oprah's Burger Place. For many years, the stock paid good dividends and appreciated in value. After the publicity following outbreaks of mad cow disease and reports of *E. coli* contamination, the value of the stock dropped in half. Is Trustee liable for making an improper investment?

Explanation

Courts judge the appropriateness of an investment based on the circumstances prevailing at the time of the investment. Because the investment was reasonable when made, the court will not second guess Trustee's decision. Of course, Trustee now has the burden of deciding whether to retain the stock and weather the crisis or to sell before the price drops even more. In making this decision, Trustee must continue to follow the prudent person standard and will incur liability only if Trustee's conduct falls beneath that standard.

Example 20-9. Prudent Person Standard—Trustee with Lower Skill

Trustee invested trust property in an expensive computer program that promised to select winning lottery numbers with a 70 percent accuracy rate. Trustee carefully used the program and then bet trust property on the numbers it suggested. To date, Trustee has gambled away over $50,000 and has won $38.00. When the beneficiaries sued Trustee for breach of duty, Trustee convincingly demonstrated that Trustee is extremely honest and was always acting in good faith. Trustee also proved that Trustee has a long history of being susceptible to get-rich-quick schemes. Has Trustee breached the prudent person standard of care?

Explanation

Trustee is liable even though Trustee exercised the same degree of care with regard to trust matters that Trustee uses in everyday life. Trustee will not be excused by proving Trustee possesses and exercises subnormal skill in handling Trustee's own personal and business affairs.

Example 20-10. Prudent Person Standard—Trustee with Higher Skill

Trustee is a licensed stockbroker. Trustee bought 400 shares of Gates Incorporated stock for the trust. In making this investment, Trustee relied on sources of information generally available to the public. However, Trustee did not bother to check out other sources of information legally available to Trustee. Had Trustee read this information, Trustee would have realized that the investment was risky. The value of the stock has now dropped by 30 percent. Has Trustee breached the prudent person standard of care?

Explanation

Yes. A trustee who has special skills, that is, a higher degree of skill than a reasonable person, has a duty to exercise that higher level of skill. See UPC §7-302. Thus, professional trustees such as banks, trust companies, and attorneys may be held to a higher standard than nonprofessional trustees.

Example 20-11. Prudent Person Standard — Trustee Who Claims Higher Skill

Trustee told Settlor that Trustee is an expert financial planner and thus would be the perfect choice to serve as the trustee of Settlor's trust. Settlor agreed and named Trustee. Trustee made several investments that have gone bad. The reasons for the downturn would not have been apparent to a reasonable person but would have been discovered by an expert financial planner. Has Trustee breached the prudent person standard of care?

Explanation

Yes. A person who is appointed as a trustee because the person represents that the person has special skills or expertise is bound by that level of skill regardless of whether the person actually possesses those abilities. See UPC §7-302. Thus, Trustee breached the standard of care even though Trustee's conduct was otherwise prudent.

§20.2.1.3 Prudent Investor or Portfolio Standard

The modern trend is for trust investments to be judged with a *prudent investor* or *portfolio standard*. Under this "total asset management" approach, the appropriateness of investments is based on the performance of the entire trust portfolio, instead of by examining each investment individually. A prudent investor could decide that the best investment strategy is to select some assets that appreciate and others that earn income, as well as some investments that are rock-solid balanced with some that have a reasonable degree of risk. In selecting investments, the trustee should incorporate risk and return objectives that are reasonably suited to the trust. Different trusts may call for different investment approaches depending on the trustee's abilities, the trust's purposes, the beneficiary's needs, and other circumstances. This approach is adopted by the Uniform Prudent Investor Act and the Restatement (Third) of Trusts.

§20.2.1.4 Noneconomic Considerations

Example 20-12. Trust Investments — Noneconomic Considerations

Trustee does not use tobacco products and does not drink alcoholic beverages. Trustee believes that companies that produce or sell these items are contributing to the delinquency of Americans and the downfall of modern civilization. Accordingly, Trustee dismisses all investment opportunities involving these companies without any consideration of the possible economic advantages of such investments. Is Trustee's conduct proper?

Explanation

The propriety of Trustee's conduct is uncertain because the law regarding *social investment* is still developing. Social investment refers to the consideration of factors other than the monetary safety of the investments and their potential to earn income and appreciate. Other examples of these types of factors include a company's handling of environmental matters, whether a company does business with countries with policies that do not protect human rights, whether a company employs and pays substandard wages to workers in foreign countries, and the political party affiliation of the company's leadership. Generally, if Trustee can continue to make good investments for the trust while doing what the Trustee believes is being socially responsible, Trustee should have no difficulty. However, if Trustee takes social responsibility to an extreme, the result may be different. For example, Trustee could refuse to invest in any company that employs individuals who admit to having used tobacco or alcoholic products any time within the past ten years. This criteria may restrict the available field of investments so dramatically that a court would consider Trustee's conduct improper.

§20.2.2 *Duty to Diversify*

A trustee has a duty to diversify trust investments. To use a rather "fowl" adage, the trustee should not put "all the eggs in one basket." The settlor's entire plan should not fail merely because one investment goes bad.

Example 20-13. Diversification — Small Trust

The fair market value of trust property is $10,000. How should Trustee diversify Trustee's investments?

Explanation

Diversification of trust investments may be difficult if the size of the corpus is modest. The expense and inconvenience of dividing a relatively small amount may exceed the benefits of spreading trust property among several investments. Trustee may want to consider investing in a mutual fund so Trustee can take advantage of the diversification achieved by the fund manager.

Example 20-14.   Diversification — Key Assets

Settlor created a trust containing Settlor's heirloom jewelry and a 20,000 acre farm that has been in Settlor's family for almost 200 years. At the termination of the trust, all remaining trust property passes to Settlor's children. Trustee consults you for advice regarding the diversification of this property. Should Trustee sell some of this property to create a balanced portfolio of investments?

Explanation

Retaining all trust property in two assets of this type is certainly not a proper diversification. On the other hand, it is reasonable to conclude that Settlor wanted the heirloom jewelry and the farm to remain in the trust so they would pass to Settlor's children. Hopefully, Settlor included a provision in the trust instrument permitting Trustee to retain these assets without regard to diversification. Some states have statutes permitting trustees to retain property the settlor transfers to the trust even if doing so restricts diversification. If state law and the instrument are silent, Trustee is in a difficult position. If Trustee does not diversify and the value of the farm or jewelry plummets, the beneficiaries may sue for damages alleging that a prudent person would have diversified to prevent such a loss from occurring. If Trustee sells the property, the beneficiaries may claim that Trustee frustrated Settlor's intent to keep the jewelry and farm in the family. Before proceeding, Trustee should seek guidance either from the court (e.g., request a declaratory judgment) or the beneficiaries (e.g., obtain written consent not to diversify).

§20.2.3 Exculpatory Clauses

The settlor may alter the rules regarding trust investments, either expanding or restricting the types of allowable investments, by providing express instructions in the trust instrument. For example, the settlor could authorize the trustee to invest up to 20 percent of the trust corpus in aggressive growth stocks even if substantial risk is involved.

Instead of expressly authorizing otherwise improper conduct, many settlors decide to reduce the applicable standard of care with a broadly phrased *exculpatory clause*. Settlors who appoint family members or friends as trustees often want this type of clause because they do not want to impose the usual standard on trustees who are serving out of love or affection rather than for a fee.

Sample Exculpatory Clause

The trustee shall not be liable for any loss, cost, damage, or expense sustained through any error of judgment or in any other manner except for and as a result of a trustee's own bad faith or gross negligence.

Example 20-15. Exculpatory Clause — Extent of Enforcement

Settlor created a valid trust transferring an antique chair and $40,000 cash to Trustee. Trustee invested the $40,000 in a mutual fund. The fund performed poorly. Although Trustee did some investigation, it was not very thorough. Had Trustee investigated the fund with reasonable care, Trustee would have discovered the fund was likely to have problems. While drunk, Trustee chopped up the antique chair and used it as fuel for Trustee's fireplace. May Trustee defend the suit on the basis of an exculpatory clause that states: "The trustee shall not be liable for any loss in value to any investment?"

Explanation

Jurisdictions vary as to the validity and enforceability of exculpatory clauses. Under the law of most states, an exculpatory clause, although strictly construed, will protect the trustee from liability for ordinary negligence. However, the clause will not excuse the trustee's reckless, intentional, or bad faith conduct because the enforcement of an exculpatory provision in these circumstances would violate public policy. Thus, it is possible that Trustee can escape liability for the mutual fund investment because Trustee's failure to thoroughly investigate is arguably merely negligent conduct. However, destroying the chair while inebriated is reckless, if not worse, behavior and thus Trustee would not be protected by the exculpatory clause.

§20.2.4 Directory Provision

A *directory provision* requires the trustee to exercise certain trust powers, especially those relating to investments, as directed by another person or group. For example, the settlor may require the trustee to follow the advice of the settlor's stockbroker in making securities trades and of an investment committee in making other investments. A settlor may find this preferable to naming a professional investor as the trustee to the exclusion of the settlor's spouse or children. Many states, either through statute or court decision, restrict the liability of the trustee for complying with instructions given by people whose directions the trustee is required to follow.

§20.2.5 Duty to Review Investments

The trustee must periodically review investments to determine if they are still appropriate for the trust. The trustee cannot assume that just because an investment was prudent when made that it remains so. The type of investment determines how often the trustee should conduct this review. For example, some real property investments may need only occasional reevaluation while active stock portfolios may need the trustee's daily attention. The timing for the review may also be statutorily determined. For example, national banks must conduct a review of all assets of each fiduciary account at least once every calendar year to make sure the investments are appropriate, both individually and collectively.[2]

Example 20-16. Review of Investments

Trustee has just been appointed as the trustee of a trust created in 1990. Trustee promptly began a review of all trust investments and discovered several inappropriate investments made while the predecessor trustee was in office. What steps should Trustee now take?

Explanation

Trustee should take two steps with regard to each inappropriate investment. First, Trustee needs to dump the bad investment as soon as possible while attempting to recoup as much value as possible. Second, Trustee needs to determine if the investment was also imprudent during the time the predecessor trustee was in office. If so, Trustee has a duty to seek redress from the former trustee, who breached trust duties by retaining the investment.

§20.3 Trustee Powers

To carry out the trustee's duties relating to the management of trust property, the trustee needs a wide array of powers such as to buy, sell, rent, lease,

---

2. 12 C.F.R. §9.6(c).

lend, borrow, mortgage, settle claims, and manage corporate securities. This section discusses the sources of a trustee's powers and the ability of a trustee to delegate those powers.

§20.3.1 Sources of Powers

§20.3.1.1 Trust Instrument

The first place a trustee looks for authority to act is the trust instrument. In the past, settlors typically included comprehensive lists of trustee powers that sometimes extended for many pages. Due to many states enacting statutory trustee powers, as discussed in the next section, settlors may have the option of keeping their express grants of powers relatively short. Settlors in these jurisdictions who need to grant additional powers or limit the statutory powers must be certain to include their specific wishes in the trust.

Example 20-17. Trustee Powers — Instrument

State law grants trustees the power to "sell real or personal property at public auction or private sale for cash or for credit or part cash and part credit, with or without security." Settlor included the following provision in the trust, "Any sale of trust property on credit where the amount of credit given exceeds $1,000 must be secured by a mortgage, deed of trust, security agreement, or other security instrument." Trustee has entered into a contract to sell a parcel of trust property for $45,000, taking a $5,000 down payment and the purchaser's unsecured promissory note for the balance. Is Trustee's conduct proper?

Explanation

No. Settlor's restriction in the trust instrument against unsecured sales in excess of $1,000 prevails over the statute that permits such a sale. The settlor has the ability to limit or expand statutory powers in the trust instrument and those directions trump inconsistent powers supplied by state statute.

§20.3.1.2 State Statutes

States often assist settlors in preparing trust instruments by providing trustees with default powers by statute. States have adopted several different approaches to supply these powers. First, some states enact an extensive list of statutory powers that the settlor may incorporate by reference into the trust. The trustee will have the statutory powers only if the settlor expressly mentions the powers in the trust instrument with a provision such as: "My trustees shall have all the powers provided by [description of statute] and I hereby incorporate those powers into this trust instrument as if they were written out in full."

Second, some states enact statutory lists of powers trustees automatically possess unless the settlor expressly restricts them. The Uniform Trustees' Powers Act adopts this approach. In states with these types of statutes, settlors do not have to make any mention of trustee powers unless they need to expand or limit the statutory powers.

Third, some states do not list trustee powers by statute but instead simply provide that trustees have whatever powers are necessary to deal with trust property in the same manner as a prudent person. This approach permits short enabling legislation and provides trustees with broad authority.

§20.3.1.3 Implied by Circumstances

Trustees also have powers that are implied by the circumstances. These powers are also referred to as powers implied by equity. Regardless of whether the settlor or a state statute grants a particular power, the trustee is deemed to possess that power if the settlor must have intended the trustee to have it to accomplish trust objectives. Implied trustee powers are analogous to the necessary and proper powers provided to Congress by the Constitution.[3]

Example 20-18. Implied Trustee Powers

Settlor created a valid trust requiring Trustee to distribute trust income to Son in semiannual installments until Son's twenty-fifth birthday at which time the trust will end and Trustee must distribute the property to Daughter. Settlor transferred several parcels of real property to the trust. Trustee would like to lease the property but Settlor did not provide any express powers and there is no state statute on point. How would you advise Trustee?

Explanation

Trustee has the implied power to lease the property. The trust instrument requires Trustee to make payments of income. Trustee cannot earn income from the trust property without renting it. Thus, Settlor must have intended Trustee to have the power to lease the property even though Settlor did not expressly grant that power. Trustee must now consider the length of the lease, that is, can Trustee enter into a *long-term lease*? A long term lease is one that lasts beyond the term of the trust, which in this case is Son's twenty-fifth birthday. Various policies come into play with regard to these

---

3. U.S. Const. art. I, §8, ¶18.

leases. Long-term leases restrict the ability of the remainder beneficiary, in this case Daughter, to enjoy the property because it is encumbered by the lease. On the other hand, long-term leases permit the trustee to earn more income from the property. For example, a company would not be willing to construct a large building on the property unless the company is assured of being able to use it for a long time. In the absence of permission in the trust instrument or by state statute, Trustee should seek court permission before entering into a long-term lease.

§20.3.1.4 Court Order

A court with proper jurisdiction may render a judgment affecting the trustee's powers. The court may grant additional powers beyond those the settlor or state statute provides. Likewise, the court may limit powers granted by the settlor or state statute.

§20.3.2 *Delegation of Powers*

A settlor expects the trustee to administer the trust. The settlor selected the trustee because the settlor had confidence in that person's judgment and ability to carry out the settlor's instructions. The settlor did not want someone else to be managing the trust property. However, it would be too burdensome to force a trustee to personally perform all acts necessary in the administration of the trust.

Example 20-19. Delegation of Powers — Standard

Settlor created a valid discretionary support trust for settlor's children. Settlor transferred an apartment building into the trust. Trustee is very busy and cannot handle all trust business. Accordingly, Trustee hired a professional management company to run the apartments. The company staffs the office, leases apartments, collects rents, and arranges for repairs. Trustee also gave Trustee's spouse the job of figuring out how much support each of settlor's children needs. Are these delegations of Trustee's powers proper?

Explanation

The traditional rule regarding delegation of powers is that the trustee may delegate mere ministerial duties but may not delegate discretionary acts. Although easy to state, the application of the rule is not always easy. The extreme situations are relatively clear. The trustee can delegate ministerial acts such as secretarial and janitorial duties, record keeping, and the collection of income. But, discretionary acts such as selecting investments, deciding which beneficiary of a discretionary trust to pay and how much, and settling claims against the trust cannot be delegated. Applying this rule, Trustee can delegate the day-to-day management of the apartment building to the management company but could not properly delegate to Trustee's spouse the determination of the amount of benefits each beneficiary should receive.

The difference between ministerial and discretionary acts is, in many cases, difficult to ascertain because all acts involve some degree of judgment or discretion. For example, the management company may make decisions regarding the type of outside lighting to install around the apartment building, which may have an affect on the likelihood of criminal activity. If the company does not install sufficient lighting and tenants are robbed or assaulted, they may sue for failure to maintain a safe environment. Problems can also arise with even trivial decisions. For example, assume a janitor decides to start cleaning at the north end of the building. A tenant could slip on trash in the hallway at the south end that would have been cleaned up before tenant arrived on the scene had the janitor starting cleaning at the south end.

To avoid the problems with the traditional rule, some states apply a prudent person standard. The trustee may delegate responsibilities to agents if a reasonably prudent owner of that type of property holding that property for similar reasons as those of the trust, would employ outside assistance. Of course, arguments can still erupt over the reasonableness of a particular delegation under the circumstances.

Example 20-20. Delegation of Powers — Methods to Delegate Properly

Settlor created a valid trust with an extensive stock portfolio. Trustee no longer wants to manage these stocks because of the volatility of the stock market. However, Trustee is still willing to do everything else related to trust administration such as determining the needs of the beneficiaries and making discretionary distributions according to the instructions in the trust instrument. How should Trustee proceed?

Explanation

Trustee should first look to the trust instrument. Perhaps Settlor provided for delegation via a directory provision. See §20.2.4, above. If Settlor did not do so but Settlor is still alive and has the power to modify the trust, Trustee may try to convince Settlor to amend the trust to permit the delegation. Trustee may also seek approval of all of the beneficiaries (see §21.6.2, below) or obtain a court order authorizing the delegation.

Example 20-21. Delegation of Duties — Effect of Improper Delegation

Trustee hired Secretary to prepare various documents relating to the administration of the trust. Because of Secretary's negligence in failing to timely bill Debtor, the trust failed to collect $15,000. By the time Secretary discovered the mistake, Debtor went bankrupt. Trustee also hired Investor to decide what property Trustee should purchase. Investor recommended stock in TransGlobal Airlines and Trustee purchased 250 shares valued at $10,000. The stock dropped precipitously in price because of TransGlobal's financial problems, which were readily discoverable had Investor done even a cursory investigation. Is Trustee personally liable to the trust for the negligence of Secretary and Investor?

Explanation

No respondeat superior type of liability exists between Trustee and the trust for the acts of agents. Trustee must have done something wrong before the beneficiaries, on behalf of the trust, can hold Trustee liable for the negligence of Secretary and Investor. Trustee's delegation of duties to Secretary appears proper, both under the traditional rule (sending out bills is a ministerial act) and the prudent person rule (prudent people delegate secretarial work). Thus, Trustee is not personally liable for the inability to collect from Debtor unless the beneficiaries can show that Trustee was somehow negligent. For example, Trustee may have been negligent in selecting, supervising, or retaining Secretary. Trustee should not have delegated investment responsibilities to Investor; investing is a discretionary duty and prudent trustees would not delegate such an important act. Thus, Trustee will be personally liable for Investor's negligence because of the improper delegation.

§20.4 Trust Distributions

This section reviews the trustee's responsibilities related to distributions from the trust either because the instrument requires the distribution or because the trustee decided to make a distribution by exercising the discretion granted by the settlor. Coverage includes the trustee's standard of care and the identity of the person or entity to receive the distributions. You may find it helpful to review §19.8.9, above, which discusses the trustee's duties when making the decision to distribute in a discretionary trust context and §19.8.10, above, relating to support trusts.

§20.4.1 Standard of Care

Trustees are generally under an absolute and unqualified duty to make trust distributions to the correct persons. A trustee who makes an improper distribution is liable even though the trustee exercised reasonable care and made the mistake in good faith. This duty is stricter than the standard applicable to other aspects of trust management, as discussed in §20.2, above, because the beneficiary is the owner of the equitable title and is thus entitled to the trust distributions according to the terms of the trust.

Example 20-22. Trust Distributions — Standard of Care

Settlor created a trust providing for payments of $1,000 per month to "Mary Smith until Mary graduates from law school at which time the trust terminates and the trustee shall deliver all remaining property to the American Red Cross." Trustee mailed the May payment to a person named Mary Smith but that person was not the Mary Smith whom Settlor named in the trust. Trustee mailed the June payment to the correct Mary Smith but Trustee was unaware that Mary had graduated from law school on May 15. Is Trustee personally liable for these improper distributions?

Explanation

Trustee is likely to be personally liable for both of these mistaken payments. In effect, Trustee converted property belonging to the correct Mary Smith when the Trustee sent the May payment to the incorrect Mary Smith and property belonging to the American Red Cross when Trustee sent the June payment to Mary. Trustee can obtain a court order to compel both improperly paid persons to return the distributions. But, of course, it may be difficult to get collectible judgments because many people are prone to spend distributions rapidly and own little, if any, property that is not exempt from the claims of creditors. Thus, Trustee may be stuck with liability. A few states, however, have statutes protecting trustees from personal liability for improper distributions in a limited set of circumstances. For example, Texas law exempts a trustee from liability for "a mistake of fact made before the trustee has actual knowledge or receives written notice of the happening of any event that determines or affects the distribution of the income or principal of the trust."[4]

---

4. Tex. Prop. Code Ann. §114.004 (Vernon 1995).

§20.4.2 Competent Adult Beneficiary

The trustee should make trust distributions directly to the beneficiary if the beneficiary is a competent adult unless the settlor requires or authorizes the trustee in the trust instrument to make distributions in another manner. For example, the trust may permit the trustee to pay the beneficiary's college tuition by sending payments directly to the school.

§20.4.3 Minor or Incapacitated Beneficiary

As a general rule, distributions for a minor or incapacitated beneficiary should be made to the beneficiary's guardian of the person or conservator. If the beneficiary is a minor, the trustee may have authority to distribute to a custodian under the Uniform Transfers to Minors Act. See §14.6, above. To eliminate the necessity of creating a guardianship, conservatorship, or custodianship merely to permit someone to receive trust distributions, a settlor may include a trust provision authorizing the trustee to make payments for "the benefit of" or "on behalf of" the beneficiary. The trustee can then pay appropriate entities directly for the beneficiary's expenses such as medical care, tuition, and room and board.

Several states have enacted statutes that give guidance to a trustee when a beneficiary is a minor or incompetent person. These statutes may permit the trustee to make payments to someone other than the beneficiary on the beneficiary's behalf even if the trust instrument does not expressly authorize this type of payment. Some states even permit the trustee to make the determination whether the beneficiary is incapacitated so that expensive and time-consuming court proceedings to determine legal incapacity are not required unless the beneficiary objects to the trustee's conduct.

§20.5 Duty of Loyalty

A trustee owes the beneficiaries duties of undivided loyalty and utmost good faith with regard to all trust matters. In other words, the trustee must avoid self-dealing and all other conflict of interest situations. The trustee owes these duties to all beneficiaries and consequently the trustee cannot favor one beneficiary over another unless the settlor expressly permits favoritism in the trust instrument. In addition, the trustee cannot profit from being a trustee even if the trustee is not otherwise in breach of the trust. There is, of course, an exception for the trustee's compensation as discussed in §20.9, below.

Loyalty duties are based on the common law. In some states, these duties are codified. These statutes range from general statements of the duty to very detailed treatments that carefully spell out both permitted and prohibited conduct. In some states, the duty is measured differently depending on whether the trustee is an individual or a corporation. This section explores the different types of loyalty duties and the ramifications of a breach.

§20.5.1 Buying and Selling Trust Property

A trustee may not purchase trust assets for the trustee's personal use. Likewise, a trustee cannot sell the trustee's personal assets to the trust. A trustee cannot be expected to act fairly in these situations because as a purchaser, the trustee wants to pay as little as possible and as a seller, the trustee wants to receive a favorable price.

Example 20-23. Duty of Loyalty — Selling Trust Property

One of the assets in the trust estate is a beautiful quilt handmade by the founders of Settlor's hometown 150 years ago. Trustee's Child collects quilts and wants to purchase the quilt from the trust paying the quilt's appraised value. May Trustee sell the quilt to Child?

Explanation

No. Trustee's duty to avoid self-dealing extends to sales to close relatives such as Child. A wide range of individuals are usually included within the group of people to whom a trustee cannot sell trust property. These people may include close relatives, employees, employers, partners, business associates, and affiliated entities. Jurisdictions vary regarding the extent of the prohibition. For example, a sale to an aunt or uncle is permitted in some states but not in others. Indirect transfers are also prohibited. Thus, Trustee cannot sell the quilt to a third party with the understanding that the third party would then sell it to Child.

§20.5.2 Borrowing Trust Property

A trustee may not self-deal by borrowing property from the trust either for the trustee's personal use or for the use of closely related or connected persons. However, the settlor may expressly authorize these loans in the trust instrument. For example, Grandparent may establish a trust for Grandchildren naming Child as the trustee and permit Child to make educational loans to Grandchildren from trust property. See §20.5.8, below.

Example 20-24. Duty of Loyalty — Borrowing Trust Property

Octopus National Bank (ONB) is serving as the trustee of a trust. ONB keeps $80,000 in one of its certificates of deposit which is earning a competitive rate of interest. In addition, ONB maintains a checking account for the trust which it uses to pay expenses and make distributions to beneficiaries. Both accounts are fully insured by the federal government. May ONB properly maintain these accounts?

Explanation

Technically, both of these accounts violate ONB's duty of loyalty. In ONB's capacity as a trustee, it is a lender, while in its capacity as a bank, it is a borrower. Thus, ONB has actually lent funds to itself. Because it would be inefficient to force ONB to use another financial institution for banking services, many states have statutes permitting certain self-deposits. Jurisdictions may view these two accounts differently, however. The certificate of deposit is a long-term investment and thus the transaction has a significant self-dealing aspect and it would not be a great burden on ONB to search elsewhere for this type of investment. Retaining funds pending investment, distribution, or debt payment is, however, another matter. The benefit to the trust of having fast and convenient access to trust funds may outweigh the self-dealing nature of the deposit.

§20.5.3 Purchase of Common Investments

A conflict of interest arises if a trustee invests in the same asset as both a trustee and an individual. For example, the trustee and the trust should not each contribute to the purchase of a parcel of real property. This would place the trustee in a position of making decisions for both the trustee as an individual and the trust. The best choice for the trustee, e.g., whether to make improvements, enter into a lease, or sell the property, may not be the best option for the beneficiaries of the trust.

Example 20-25. Duty of Loyalty — Common Investments

Teresa has just been appointed trustee of a trust containing 1,000 shares of IBM stock. Teresa's personal stock portfolio consists of ten shares of IBM and twenty-five shares of AT&T. Teresa wants to diversify the trust by selling 500 shares of IBM stock and buying AT&T stock with the proceeds. She also wants to retain all the stock in her personal portfolio. May Teresa take these actions without violating her loyalty duties?

Explanation

With regard to the IBM stock, Teresa is already in a conflict of interest situation. She could make decisions with regard to the stock that may be to her benefit but not in the trust's best interest. Does Teresa have to divest herself or the trust of the IBM stock? In many states, Teresa may retain stock already owned by the trust at the time the trustee takes office if it is reasonable for the trustee to do so. Note that the type of stock may also influence the outcome of this case. It is unlikely that personal ownership of such a small amount of stock in a huge corporation could have any real impact on the stock held in trust. The situation would be very different if the shares represented a controlling block or a significant minority interest.

With regard to the proposed purchase of AT&T stock, the situation is somewhat different. At the moment, Teresa is not in a potential conflict of interest situation because the trust owns no AT&T stock. Teresa should not purposely put herself into such a predicament by buying AT&T stock for the trust. Of course, Teresa could argue that her ownership in AT&T is so small that the potential conflict is de minimus.

§20.5.4   Transfers between Trusts

A trustee may not sell property to another trust for which the trustee is also serving as the trustee. A conflict of interest arises because as the trustee of the selling trust, the trustee has a duty to get the highest price possible for the asset. However, as the trustee of the purchasing trust, the trustee has the duty to secure the most economical price. Some states permit this type of transfer if there is no negotiation possible regarding the price of the asset, such as where a government obligation is transferred at its current market price.

§20.5.5   Dealings with Beneficiaries

A trustee owes a duty of fairness when dealing with beneficiaries even with regard to nontrust related business. The beneficiary should not be placed in a position where at times the trustee owes high fiduciary duties while at other times they deal at arm's length or are in an adversial context. If a trustee wishes to deal with a beneficiary about nontrust matters, the trustee should make a full disclosure of all applicable law and facts to prevent the beneficiary from claiming that the beneficiary either relied on the trustee being a fiduciary or was subject to overreaching.

§20.5.6 Self-Employment

A trustee with special skills may be tempted to employ him- or herself to provide those services to the trust. For example, the trustee may be an attorney, accountant, stockbroker, or real estate agent. If the trustee succumbs to the temptation, the trustee will create a conflict of interest situation. As a fiduciary, the trustee should seek the best specialist possible within the trust's budget. However, as a specialist, the trustee wants to get the job and secure favorable compensation. Dual roles permit the trustee to engage in schizophrenic conversations such as, "This is too complicated for my trustee mind so I need to consult myself using my attorney brain." Courts typically presume that self-employment is a conflict of interest and thus do not permit trustees to recover extra compensation for the special services. However, the court may permit the trustee to receive compensation in dual capacities if the trustee can prove that the trustee acted in good faith for the benefit of the trust and charged a reasonable fee for the special services.

§20.5.7 Ramifications of Breach of Loyalty Duties

The ramifications of a breach may depend on whether the disputed act was actual self-dealing where the trustee had a motive to favor the trustee, or only a conflict of interest where the trustee had a reason to prefer some other person (but not the trustee) instead of the beneficiaries.

§20.5.7.1 Self-Dealing

Example 20-26. Ramifications of Self-Dealing

Trustee needed to sell a trust asset to raise money to make distributions to the beneficiaries. Coincidentally, Trustee had ready cash and wanted to make some personal investments. Trustee purchased the asset from the trust and paid fair market value plus an extra five percent just to prevent a later claim that Trustee took advantage of Trustee's position. As time passed, this asset appreciated in value and is now worth three times the amount Trustee paid for it. May the beneficiaries recover the profit Trustee has earned?

Explanation

Yes. Trustee is personally liable for breaching the loyalty duty by purchasing a trust asset. Most courts will not consider a trustee's good faith or the fairness of the transaction. Accordingly, it is irrelevant that Trustee was acting honestly, reasonably, and paid more than market value for the asset. Courts adopt this harsh *no-further-inquiry rule* for several reasons. First, the strict rule guards against the trustee having any possible selfish interest in trust transactions because the trustee has nothing to gain and everything to lose by self-dealing. Second, the rule deters the trustees of other trusts from self-dealing. Third, because our legal system does not allow the use of truth-inducing drugs or torture to ascertain the truthfulness of testimony about trust matters, the court cannot determine if a self-dealing trustee was acting in good faith or was really acting in a fraudulent manner to take advantage of the trustee's position. For this reason, a breach of self-dealing duties is often referred to as *constructive fraud*.

§20.5.7.2 Conflict of Interest

Example 20-27. Ramifications of Conflict of Interest

Tom is the trustee of Trust A and Trust B. Trust A needed cash to make trust distributions and Trust B needed a good investment. Tom thus sold an asset from Trust A to Trust B at fair market value. This asset has now tripled in value. May the beneficiaries of Trust A recover this increase in value from Tom?

Explanation

Trustee's conduct is not self-dealing because Trustee did not personally benefit. Instead, Trustee had a conflict of interest as both the seller and buyer of the asset. Many courts take a more relaxed approach in conflict of interest situations than in self-dealing cases by permitting the trustee to justify the conduct. In this case, Trustee appeared to be acting in good faith and, at the time of the sale, the transaction was fair to the beneficiaries of both trusts. If, however, additional facts show that Trustee could reasonably have anticipated the tremendous jump in value of the asset and had close friendships with the beneficiaries of Trust B, the court would probably hold that Tom is liable for the profits.

§20.5.8 *Permitted Self-Dealing*

Self-dealing is not necessarily a bad thing. Assume that Settlor places all of Settlor's property in a testamentary trust for Charity and names Settlor's child as the trustee. Child and Child's siblings may be the only individuals who would pay a fair price for some of Settlor's assets such as photograph albums, videotapes of family gatherings, jewelry, home furnishings, clothes, and interests in family businesses. A settlor who wants to permit self-dealing should include a trust provision giving the trustee permission to self-deal.

Because courts construe waivers of fiduciary duties strictly, the clause must be clearly drafted and the permitted self-dealing should be expressly stated.

Sample Self-Dealing Provision

If Child is serving as the trustee of this trust, Child and Child's relatives may purchase trust property provided they pay full market value as ascertained by averaging the appraisals of three independent appraisers selected by Beneficiaries.

If the settlor did not authorize self-dealing, the trustee has two additional ways to obtain authority to do so. First, the trustee could obtain the consent of all the beneficiaries after making a full disclosure of the applicable law and facts. See §21.6.2, below. Second, the trustee could seek court permission to self-deal after proving that such a transaction would be for the benefit of the trust. See §21.6.3, below.

§20.6 Liability of Trustee to Third Parties

As the legal title holder to property, the trustee may be liable to persons other than beneficiaries and co-trustees. This section reviews the various situations where the trustee may be liable to third parties.

§20.6.1 *Contract Liability*

A trustee frequently enters into contracts in the performance of the trustee's investment and managerial duties. For example, the trustee may contract with an attorney to provide legal services or with a janitorial service to maintain an office building that is part of the trust corpus. Unless the trustee takes special steps to avoid liability as discussed below, the trustee is personally liable for any breach of contract. To recoup damages paid to a contract claimant, the trustee must prove that the trustee properly entered into the contract for the benefit of the trust and then seek reimbursement from the trust property. The trustee would be stuck with any loss that results if the trust does not have adequate property to make a complete reimbursement.

At common law, a contract plaintiff could not sue the trustee in the trustee's representative capacity and could not recover directly against trust property. The common law courts did not take notice of the trust relationship and thus did not recognize the trustee as an individual as being a separate entity from the trustee in a representative capacity. Modern law, however, permits contract plaintiffs to reach the trust property directly by proceeding against the trustee in the trustee's fiduciary capacity. See UPC §7-306(c).

A trustee will usually want to take steps to prevent the trustee's exposure to personal liability on contracts entered into for the benefit of the trust. The following examples demonstrate different techniques for limiting liability and their relative effectiveness. Note, however, that some contracting parties may not allow the trustee to limit liability in the contract because they want an additional party to hold liable and may be entering into the contract on the basis of the trustee's personal credit and reputation.

Example 20-28. Contract Liability of Trustee — Using Provision in Trust Instrument to Limit Liability

Trustee entered into a valid contract with Contractor to build a house on trust property. The contract did not refer to the trust. Contractor was not paid and therefore has a valid claim for $100,000 for labor and materials. Contractor sued Trustee personally. Trustee's defense centers on a provision in the trust instrument signed by the settlor, Scott McCoy, that states: "No trustee of this trust shall be personally liable on any contract properly entered into for this trust." Will Trustee escape personal liability?

Explanation

Trustee is unlikely to escape personal liability. Contractor is not bound by the terms of the trust because those terms were not part of the contract.

Example 20-29. Contract Liability of Trustee — Contract Refers to Trust Instrument That Limits Liability

Using the same facts as Example 20-28, assume the contract contained this provision: "The terms of this contract are subject to and governed by the provisions of the McCoy Family Trust created by Scott McCoy on August 15, 1999." Will Trustee now escape liability?

Explanation

The chances are good that Trustee will escape liability. Contractor is now on notice that another instrument, the trust, must be consulted to determine if the contract is thereby affected. Of course, the contract must sufficiently describe and reference the trust so that Contractor can ascertain which document Contractor needs to inspect.

Example 20-30. Contract Liability of Trustee — Trustee Signing in Representative Capacity

Trustee entered into a valid contract with Accountant to prepare tax returns for the trust. Trustee signed the contract and added the words "as trustee" after Trustee's signature. Accountant has a valid claim for $7,000 for services rendered. Is Trustee personally liable on this contract?

Explanation

Jurisdictions vary regarding whether the mere indication of Trustee's representative capacity is sufficient to avoid personal liability on a contract. In some states, a representative signature does not limit liability. In other states, signing as a trustee is prima facie evidence of an intent to exclude the trustee from personal liability. Under UPC §7-306(a), the trustee must not only reveal the representative capacity but must also identify the trust estate in the contract to escape personal liability. If the contract is a negotiable instrument, such as a promissory note or a check, the special rules of UCC §3-402 will apply.

Example 20-31. Contract Liability of Trustee—Express Contract Provision Excluding Personal Liability

Using the same facts as Example 20-30, assume that the contract also contained a provision that reads: "Trustee is not individually liable on this contract and recourse is limited solely to the property of the Stuart Smalley Support Trust." Is Trustee personally liable on this contract?

Explanation

Trustee is not personally liable. This contract clearly and unequivocally states that Trustee is not personally liable and that Accountant must look only to trust property for any recovery. This example demonstrates the most reliable method of excluding a trustee's personal liability on a contract.

Example 20-32. Contract Liability of Trustee— Reimbursement

Trustee was personally liable on a contract properly entered into for the trust. After paying, Trustee sought reimbursement from the trust. However, the trust did not contain sufficient property to repay Trustee. May Trustee pursue Beneficiaries for this unreimbursed amount?

Explanation

The general rule is that Trustee may not recover from Beneficiaries unless they had previously entered into a binding agreement to indemnify Trustee. Likewise, a contract claimant may not force Beneficiaries to pay if the claimant cannot fully recover from Trustee and the trust property.

§20.6.2 *Tort Liability*

A trustee may commit a tort during the administration of the trust. For example, the trustee may negligently injure someone or may convert the property of another believing it belongs to the trust. The trustee may also be liable for the tortious acts of the trustee's employees and agents committed in the scope of their work for the trust under normal respondeat superior rules. At common law, a tort plaintiff was required to sue the trustee personally and could not reach the trust property directly by suing the trustee in the trustee's representative capacity. The trustee could seek indemnification or reimbursement from the trust only if the trustee had not engaged in willful misconduct. If the trust property was inadequate, the trustee was stuck with the loss. Courts justified this strict rule on the grounds that it encouraged trustees to exercise a high level of care for fear of being personally liable and protected trust property from tort claimants.

Many states now permit tort plaintiffs to sue the trustee in the trustee's representative capacity and to recover directly against trust property. See UPC §7-306(c). States also expand the situations in which the trustee may seek reimbursement or exoneration from the trust property. For example, the trustee may be able to recover from the trust not only when the trustee is not personally at fault, such as a strict liability tort, but also if the tort is a common incident of the business activity in which the trust was properly engaged (e.g., the trust owns a grocery store in which a customer slips, falls, and is injured because an employee negligently failed to clean up a spill), or if the tort actually increased the value of trust property, such as conversion. Some states go even further in their protection of a trustee by absolving a trustee of personal liability to the injured party unless the trustee was personally at fault. See UPC §7-306(b).

Example 20-33. Tort Liability — Protection

Settlor transferred a business, the Love the Law Bookstore, into a trust. Trustee was working in the store one day and negligently stacked about 100 books into a pile. When a city bus rumbled by the store, the pile collapsed injuring Plaintiff. Plaintiff sued Trustee personally. Trustee points to a clause in the trust which states: "Trustee is not personally liable for any torts committed in the scope of Trustee's work for this trust." Is Trustee liable for Plaintiff's injuries?

Explanation

Trustee was personally at fault and thus will be personally liable for Plaintiff's damages. The attempted exculpation in the trust instrument is ineffective because Plaintiff is not bound by a waiver to which Plaintiff did not consent. Trustee should purchase adequate insurance to protect against such eventualities. The cost of this insurance would be a legitimate trust expense.

Example 20-34. Tort Liability — Charitable Immunity

A trust owns a small hospital that provides services to the uninsured citizens of the city. One of the doctors practicing at this hospital committed malpractice and Patient sued the doctor, the trust, and Trustee personally. Against which of these entities may Patient recover?

Explanation

At common law, entities run as charitable trusts, such as hospitals, churches, and private schools, were protected from tort liability under the doctrine of charitable immunity. Most states have abolished charitable immunity leaving the doctor, the trust, and Trustee potentially liable. In some states, tort reform has led to a resurgence of partial charitable immunity for these parties. In addition, as already discussed, some states will protect Trustee from liability because Trustee was not personally at fault for the doctor's carelessness.

§20.6.3 *Liability as Property Owner*

Example 20-35. Liability as Property Owner

The trust corpus consists of a parcel of land near the outside of town. Currently, Trustee rents this land under a long-term contract to a farmer to graze cattle. The value of the land has risen dramatically over recent years due to the town's expansion and the new Mega-Mall built nearby. Consequently, the taxes on the property have increased significantly. Trustee has not been able to pay these taxes because the rent the farmer pays is inadequate to cover them. Is Trustee personally liable for the overdue property taxes?

Explanation

At common law, Trustee would be personally liable for the taxes because Trustee is the holder of the legal title to the property. Some modern courts may deem Trustee responsible but limit liability to the amount which the trust can reimburse Trustee. Under UPC §7-306(b), Trustee lacks personal liability for obligations arising from ownership or control of property of the trust unless Trustee is personally at fault.

§20.7 Allocation of Receipts and Expenses

The settlor may grant certain beneficiaries the right to trust income (income beneficiaries) and other beneficiaries the right to the principal when the trust terminates (remainder beneficiaries). This arrangement places these two types of beneficiaries in conflict. The income beneficiaries want the trust corpus invested in property that generates high rates of return such as corporate bonds and mutual funds. On the other hand, remainder beneficiaries want the trustee to invest in property that appreciates in value such as real property and growth stocks. Many investments that are good for one type of beneficiary will not benefit another. For example, assume that the trustee invested in a government insured certificate of deposit earning 7 percent interest. The income beneficiaries will be elated because the rate of return is relatively high and the investment is extremely safe. However, the remainder beneficiaries will be furious. The CD will not grow in value because the trustee will get back the same amount the trustee invested when the CD matures. In addition, because of inflation, the buying power of the proceeds will shrink to less than the amount invested so the remainder beneficiaries actually incurred a loss. To resolve this problem, a trustee either selects investments that earn both income and appreciate in value, such as rental real property and certain types of stock, or diversifies trust investments to balance investments that earn income and investments that increase in value. See §20.2.2, above.

A trustee needs to know how to categorize property received from the trust assets to carry out the trustee's duty to be fair and impartial to both the income and remainder beneficiaries. Likewise, the trustee must determine whether to reduce income or principal when the trustee pays trust expenses. The trustee has three ways to determine how to allocate receipts and expenses between income and principal. First, the settlor may have provided instructions in the trust instrument. These instructions may state specific allocation rules or may merely give the trustee discretion to make the allocation. Second, if the instrument is silent, the trustee must follow any relevant state statute. Over forty states have enacted either the Uniform Principal and Income Act of 1931 or its 1962 revision. (The UPIA was revised in 1997 to adjust allocation rules to mesh with modern trust investment practices such as the prudent investor rule. As of August 1998, only Oklahoma had adopted the 1997 revision.) Third, if neither the instrument nor state statute specifies the proper method of allocation, the trustee must allocate in a reasonable and equitable manner taking into account the interests of both income and principal beneficiaries.

This section reviews some of the widely accepted principles for allocating receipts and expenses between principal and income. In practice, many trustees and their attorneys hire accountants and CPAs to assist in this often complicated and technical process.

§20.7.1 General Allocation Rules

Example 20-36. General Allocation Rules

Trustee received the following amounts of money with respect to trust property. How should these receipts be allocated between principal and income?

Example 20-36a. Appreciation

Trustee sold Gates Incorporated stock for $50,000. Trustee paid $1,000 for the stock in 1980.

Explanation

A receipt from the sale of trust property is principal and thus all of the stock proceeds are principal. Appreciation inures to the benefit of the remainder beneficiaries. Note that for tax purposes, this type of profit is called a *capital gain* and is taxed as income.

Example 20-36b. Rent

Trustee received $20,000 in rent from the tenants of an apartment building held by the trust.

Explanation

Rent on real or personal property is income. The trustee should allocate the $20,000 rent to income.

Example 20-36c. Interest

Trustee received an interest check for $7,000 from a certificate of deposit held by the trust.

Explanation

Interest on money the trustee has lent is income. Accordingly, the interest check from the CD is income.

Example 20-36d. Eminent Domain Award

Trustee received $250,000 from the local government as compensation because the government condemned some trust real property to build a sports stadium.

Explanation

Eminent domain awards compensate for the loss of principal and thus the $250,000 is principal.

Example 20-36e. Insurance Proceeds

Trustee received $300,000 from an insurance company as compensation for a building on trust property which was destroyed by fire.

Explanation

The proceeds of property insurance compensate for lost principal and are allocated to principal.

§20.7.2 *Corporate Distributions*

Example 20-37. Allocation of Corporate Distributions

Trustee received the following distributions from corporate stock owned by the trust. How should these distributions be allocated between principal and income?

Example 20-37a. Cash Dividend

A cash dividend of $1,000.

Explanation

Cash dividends are allocated to income.

Example 20-37b. Stock Dividend

A stock dividend of fifty shares of the declaring corporation's stock.

Explanation

Most states and the Uniform Acts follow the *Massachusetts rule*, which provides that stock dividends of shares of the declaring corporation's own stock are principal. The logic behind this rule is that the trust owns the same proportion of the corporation both before and after the dividend. The trust may own a greater number of shares but because all other stock holders also own proportionately the same number of additional shares, the stock dividend did not improve the trust's position. Consequently, it would be unfair to allocate the stock dividends to income. However, if the dividend consists of shares in another corporation, or if the trustee has the choice of receiving a stock or cash dividend and elects to take the stock dividend, the stock dividend will be treated as income. (Antiquated allocation rules include the *Kentucky rule*, under which all corporate distributions were income and the technically complicated *Pennsylvania rule*, which required the trustee to allocate the dividend between principal and income based on when the corporation earned the surplus used to fund the dividend.)

Example 20-37c. Stock Split

100 shares of stock because the corporation declared a stock split.

Explanation

Stock splits are also principal for the same reason that stock dividends of shares of the declaring corporation's stock are principal; that is, there is no change in the percentage of the corporation owned by the trust.

Example 20-37d. Merger

Seventy-five shares of stock in Megalon Corporation in exchange for 500 shares of Lilliputian Corporation, which had just merged with Megalon.

Explanation

Shares that result from a merger, consolidation, reorganization, or similar transactions merely reflect a change of form, not substance. Accordingly, Trustee should allocate these new shares to principal.

§20.7.3 *Wasting Assets*

A *wasting asset* is one that goes down in value as it is used to produce income beyond what would be considered mere depreciation from normal use and age. The trustee needs to allocate a portion of the proceeds from wasting assets to principal to compensate for the depletion of the principal which occurs as the proceeds are generated. Different types of wasting assets raise different concerns.

§20.7.3.1 Mineral Property

Example 20-38. Allocation — Wasting Assets — Mineral Property

Settlor placed into trust a parcel of property on which there was one copper mine. Trustee negotiated an arrangement with Kryptonite Mining Corporation that permitted the corporation to operate the mine and keep the ore that it removed in exchange for a 12.5 percent royalty. After several years elapsed, Trustee granted Kryptonite permission to dig a new mine with the same royalty arrangement. How should Trustee allocate these royalties?

Explanation

The key fact needed to resolve this question is whether governing state law still includes the common law *open mine doctrine*. Under this rule, the income beneficiary is entitled to all proceeds from the mine if the settlor had begun to exploit the mineral interest before transferring the property to the trust. However, if the exploitation began after the transfer, all proceeds are allocated to principal. Applying the open mine doctrine to this example, Trustee would allocate the royalties from the old mine to income and the royalties from the new mine to principal. Many states have abrogated this doctrine and require the trustee to allocate the royalties between income and principal regardless of whether any natural resources were being taken from the land when the settlor established the trust. Statutes often contain a formula for making this allocation. For example, the 1962 Uniform Act provides that 27.5 percent of the royalties are allocated to principal and the remaining 72.5 percent to income.

§20.7.3.2   Timber

Example 20-39.   Allocation — Wasting Assets — Timber

Trustee contracts with Bunyan Logging Company for the removal of trees from forest land the trust owns. The contract provides that the trust will receive 20 percent of the net proceeds of the timber. How should these receipts be allocated?

Explanation

Timber is unlike other natural resources because it is renewable; the trees will grow back. The time it will take the trees to regrow, however, depends on the type of trees. For example, some varieties of pine trees may be ready to harvest in twenty years while other trees such as redwoods take over a century. Consequently, it is difficult to create a precise allocation rule so most states permit Trustee to make the allocation in accordance with what is reasonable and equitable to both the principal and income beneficiaries under the circumstances.

§20.7.3.3   Intangibles

Intangible property, such as patents, copyrights, and artistic royalties, is also subject to depletion. For example, the patent on the eight-track tape was very valuable in the 1970s but has little value today. Likewise, a royalty interest in today's blockbuster motion picture may have little value fifty years from now. Accordingly, the trustee must allocate a portion of the receipts from this type of property to principal to compensate for the loss in value. The 1962 Uniform Act provides that any receipts in excess of 5 percent of the asset's inventory value must be allocated to principal. For example, if the inventory value of a patent is $1,000 and it earned $75.00 in one year, the trustee would allocate $50.00 to income (5 percent of $1,000) and the remaining $25.00 to principal.

§20.7.4 Business and Farming Operations

The income of businesses and farms is typically computed in accordance with *generally accepted accounting principles (GAAP)*. These extensive rules known to accountants and CPAs describe how business and farm income is determined. The trustee then allocates these amounts to the income of the trust.

Example 20-40. Allocation — Business Loss

A trust business had a bad year and sustained a net loss. How should Trustee allocate this loss?

Explanation

In the year of the loss, Trustee has nothing to allocate to income or principal. The loss operates to decrease the value of the principal. But, what happens if the business earns a profit in the following year? Under tax rules, the loss in the prior year may be used to offset profit in a subsequent year. However, for trust purposes, most states provide that a loss cannot be carried into future years to reduce the amount of net income to which the income beneficiaries are entitled.

§20.7.5 Bond Premiums and Discounts

The trustee may lend trust funds to a corporation or governmental entity and receive in exchange an instrument representing that loan called a bond. (If the trustee lends money to a bank or other financial institution, the trustee receives a certificate of deposit.) The price the trustee pays for the bond may be different from the face value of the bond (the amount the trust will receive when the bond is due). Various factors cause this price differential such as the interest rate of the bond compared to the market rate and the financial status of the debtor which provides an indication of the likelihood that the debtor will be able to repay the loan.

The trustee may be willing to pay more for a bond than its face value, that is, a *premium*, if the interest rate on the bond is higher than the market rate. Income beneficiaries will be thrilled by this investment but principal beneficiaries will be very upset because the trustee will not get back the amount of principal expended for the bond when the bond matures. The trustee may also purchase a bond for less than its face value, that is, at a *discount*, if the interest rate on the bond is below the market rate. This time, the income beneficiaries are unhappy because they are not even receiving the market rate but the remainder beneficiaries are elated because the trustee will make a nice profit when the bond matures.

To be fair, the trustee may want to make adjustments when bonds are purchased at prices other than their face value. The trustee could amortize the bond premium by allocating part of the interest each year to the principal to prevent loss to the principal when the bond matures. The trustee could accumulate for the discount by allocating some of the principal each year to the income to make sure the income beneficiaries receive an appropriate yield.

The record keeping necessary to perform these allocations could be extensive if the trust's bond portfolio is large or if the trustee frequently trades the bonds. Thus, many states follow the 1962 Uniform Act by providing that the trustee shall neither amortize bond premiums nor accumulate for discount unless the bond pays no interest but appreciates in value according to a fixed schedule such as a United States Savings Bond. The logic behind this rule is that over time the discounts and premiums will balance out and thus it is not worth the time and expense to compute the amortizations and accumulations. Other states adopt a more flexible rule by granting the trustee the discretion to amortize and accumulate if the trustee so desires. Some states retain the traditional approach of requiring the trustee to amortize bond premiums to protect the remainder beneficiaries but not requiring the trustee to accumulate for discount.

§20.7.6 *Underproductive Property*

The trustee should not retain property that does not earn income absent express permission in the trust instrument. Although some nonproductive assets, such as collectible items and unleased land, may have the potential of significantly appreciating in value, the retention of the property would violate the trustee's duty of fairness to the income beneficiaries. The trustee should promptly sell underproductive property which, under the 1962 Uniform Act, means property that does not earn at least 1 percent of its value per year. Once the trustee sells the underproductive property, the trustee may be required to allocate a portion of the sale proceeds to income as *delayed income* to make up for the income the trust should have earned had this portion of the trust been placed in income-producing investments. State statutes often include formulas for the trustee to use to compute the amount of delayed income. If the trustee is at fault for acquiring or retaining underproductive property for too long of a period, the trustee is likely to be liable for breach of the trustee's investment standard of care. See §20.2.1, above.

§20.7.7 *Rights of Income Beneficiaries*

An income beneficiary's right to income arises on the date specified in the trust or, if no date is stated, the date the asset becomes subject to the trust. An asset becomes subject to an inter vivos trust on the date the settlor transfers the asset to the trust. An asset becomes subject to a testamentary trust on the date of the testator's death regardless of the intervening period of administration.

Example 20-41. Rights of Income Beneficiaries — Inter Vivos Trust

Settlor created an inter vivos trust on May 15. One of the items Settlor transferred to the trust was a certificate of deposit which pays interest once a year on June 1. How should Trustee allocate the June 1 payment of interest?

Explanation

Under the law of most states, Trustee should allocate the entire June 1 payment to the income of the trust even though most of the income accrued during the time Settlor held the CD. Trustee does not need to apportion the income between Settlor and the trust because Settlor knew the certificate had unpaid interest at the time Settlor transferred it to the trust. Presumably, Settlor intended to transfer the entire CD to the trust, including the accrued interest.

Example 20-42. Rights of Income Beneficiaries — Testamentary Trust

Testator died on March 15 leaving Testator's entire estate to a testamentary trust. All estate expenses have been paid. How should Trustee allocate the following items?

Example 20-42a.

A check dated March 20 for the February rent of real property that is now part of the trust.

Explanation

Generally, receipts due but not paid at the date of a testator's death are principal. Thus, the March 20 check augments trust principal even though it is for rent and was paid after the property was subject to the trust.

Example 20-42b.

A check dated April 1 for the March interest earned on a certificate of deposit now belonging to the trust.

Explanation

Receipts in the form of periodic payments such as rent and interest that are not due on the date of the testator's death are usually treated as accruing from day to day. Thus, Trustee should apportion the April 1 interest check by allocating the portion that accrued before Testator's death (March 15) to the principal and the amount which accrued after Testator's death to income.

Example 20-42c.

A check dated April 15 representing cash dividends on corporate stock which is now part of the trust.

Explanation

The correct distribution of the cash dividends depends on the *record date* for the dividends, that is, the date that a person needed to be the owner of the stock on the corporation's books to be entitled to the dividends. The dividends will not be apportioned. If the record date was before March 15 the dividends belong to the principal even though the check is dated after Testator's death. If the record date was after March 15, the trustee should allocate the dividends to income.

§20.7.8 *Apportionment of Income among Beneficiaries*

Example 20-43. Apportionment of Income among Beneficiaries

Settlor created a trust giving Son the right to all trust income until Son's thirtieth birthday. Trustee is then required to deliver all remaining property to Daughter. Trustee had a practice of making distributions of income to Son on the first of every month. After receiving his September 1 payment, Son turned thirty on September 12. To what property, if any, is Son entitled?

Explanation

Under the law of most states, Son is entitled to the following types of property.

    1.   Income Settlor collected prior to September 12 but had not yet given to Son.

2. Income that was owed to the trust prior to September 12 but which Trustee had not yet collected.

3. Periodic payments, such as rent and interest, that accrued prior to September 12 even though not paid until thereafter.

4. Corporate distributions that had a record date before September 12.

§20.7.9 Allocation of Expenses

Examples of the types of expenses usually allocated to income include property taxes, insurance premiums, interest on loans, ordinary repairs, reasonable allowances for depreciation, legal expenses that concern primarily the interests of income beneficiaries, and taxes on receipts that are considered income. Principal expenses typically include the costs of investing the principal, capital improvements, legal expenses that concern primarily the interests of remainder beneficiaries, and taxes on profits such as the income tax on capital gains. In addition, some expenses benefit both income and principal beneficiaries and are allocated between them. Examples of these types of expenses include the trustee's compensation and expenses associated with accountings such as court costs and attorney's fees.

§20.7.10 Unitrust Approach

To avoid the accounting hassle of allocating receipts and expenses between the income and remainder interests, as well as to reduce the inherent conflict of interest between current and future beneficiaries, some settlors adopt a *unitrust* approach. The current beneficiary of a unitrust is entitled to receive a fixed percentage of the value of the trust property annually. The current beneficiary may or may not also be entitled to additional distributions. For example, the trust could provide: "Trustee shall distribute 5 percent of the value of the trust property to Current Beneficiary on the first of every month. Trustee has the discretion to make additional distributions to Current Beneficiary for Current Beneficiary's health, education, and support. Upon Current Beneficiary's death, Trustee shall deliver all remaining trust property to Remainder Beneficiary." Under a unitrust, both beneficiaries have the same goal — they want the value of the property in the trust to increase. It does not matter to them whether the increase in value is due to receipts traditionally nominated income (e.g., interest or rent) or principal (i.e., appreciation). All increases inure to the benefit of all beneficiaries. Likewise, all beneficiaries share in the expenses regardless of their usual characterization.

§20.8   Accountings

The trustee has a duty to keep accurate records of all transactions involving trust property and to provide accountings to the beneficiaries. This information helps the beneficiaries to determine whether the trustee is doing an acceptable job of administering the trust.

Example 20-44.   Accountings — When Required

Trustee hired you to provide legal services for the trust. One of the first questions Trustee asks you is, "When do I need to provide an accounting to the beneficiaries?" How would you answer Trustee's question?

Explanation

State statutes vary significantly regarding the timing of trust accountings. Some states require the trustee to provide an accounting on an annual basis. On the other hand, some states and UPC §7-303 simply impose on the trustee a general duty to "keep the beneficiaries of the trust reasonably informed of the trust and its administration" but do not require periodic accountings. Most states permit the beneficiary to ask the trustee for an accounting. For example, UPC §7-303(c) gives the beneficiary the right to make a reasonable request for an accounting once per year as well as when the trust terminates or there is a change in the trustee. The reason behind the limitation to one accounting per year is to prevent unhappy beneficiaries from making demands for accountings merely to harass the trustee. A beneficiary can also petition the court for an order requiring the trustee to account.

Example 20-45.   Accountings — Contents

Your knowledge of trust law impressed Trustee from Example 20-44. Trustee decided to hire you to address additional concerns about accountings. Trustee's next question dealt with the proper contents of the accounting. How would you advise Trustee?

Explanation

An accounting should generally contain a comprehensive list of (1) trust property, (2) all receipts and disbursements along with an indication of which ones the trustee allocated to income and which to principal, and (3) the liabilities of the trust. Some state statutes enumerate the precise contents of the accountings while others do not. In a comment to UPC §7-303, the drafters stated that the "preparation of an accounting in conformity with the Uniform Principles and Model Account Formats promulgated by the National Fiduciary Accounting Project shall be considered as an appropriate manner of presenting a fiduciary accounting." To ease Trustee's burden of rendering an account, Trustee should keep trust records in a form that will allow Trustee to produce an accounting with little effort and upon short notice.

Example 20-46. Accountings—Voluntarily Providing

Trustee from Example 20-44 continued to be pleased with your work and has one last question. Trustee wants to know if Trustee should render accountings on an annual basis even though the applicable state statute does not require them and even if no beneficiary makes a request. How would you advise Trustee?

Explanation

Many good reasons exist for Trustee to render an annual accounting even though not required to do so by law or under the trust. Trustee will have an easier time preparing the accounting when the transactions are fresh in Trustee's mind. Trustee may have a difficult time recalling trust events years or decades later. Accountings also have a good psychological impact on the beneficiaries. Beneficiaries like to know what is going on and voluntarily submitted annual accountings may reflect highly on Trustee's conscientiousness and candor. In addition, some states prevent beneficiaries from challenging facts that are fully disclosed in an accounting after a stated limitations period. See UPC §7-307.

Example 20-47. Accountings—Waiver by Settlor

Settlor realized that the process of preparing an accounting may be costly and time-consuming. Because Settlor had full confidence in Trustee, Settlor included a provision in the trust stating that Trustee does not need to render accountings. Is this provision enforceable?

Explanation

Courts are divided regarding whether a settlor may waive the trustee's accounting obligations. Some courts hold that the waiver is against public policy. Beneficiaries need the information which the accounting would contain to determine whether the trustee is administering the trust in accordance with the trustee's duties. On the other hand, some courts indicate that the settlor can waive the requirement of statutorily mandated accountings. Even these courts, however, are unlikely to uphold a total bar on accountings because the settlor cannot deprive the court of jurisdiction to order an accounting.

§20.9 Compensation

At common law, a trustee was presumed to serve without compensation unless the trust instrument expressly provided otherwise. The policy behind this rule was that a trustee should not earn a profit by serving in a fiduciary capacity. Otherwise, the trustee might take certain actions that were not necessary or not in the best interest of the trust merely to increase the compensation.

Most states now permit a trustee to receive compensation from the trust unless the trust expressly provides that the trustee is not to be paid. If the settlor indicated in the trust instrument the method by which the fee is to be determined, that method is used. If the instrument is silent, compensation may be computed by using a statutorily provided fee schedule based on the value of the trust or the amount of trust transactions, or may be whatever compensation is reasonable under the circumstances. Jurisdictions vary regarding whether a trustee may take the compensation from the trust without first seeking court permission.

Example 20-48. Trustee Compensation — Provision in Trust Instrument

Settlor consults you regarding trustee compensation. Specifically, Settlor wants to know first, whether Settlor should waive compensation in the instrument, and second, if Settlor decides to compensate Trustee, how that compensation should be described. What advice will you give Settlor?

Explanation

Compensation is a proper trust expense, and thus reduces the value of the trust and consequently the property available for the beneficiaries. Settlor may want to require the trustee to serve without compensation to save this expense. A trustee who is a family member or close friend may be willing to serve for free. However, professional and corporate trustees will usually demand a fee for their services. Settlor should avoid stating a fixed fee, such as $1,000 per month, because the amount may not be appropriate based on the actual time the trustee needs to spend administering the trust. Even if the fee is fair in the beginning, as trust assets and the economy change over the years, the fee is likely to become inadequate. The most common method of specifying a fee is for Settlor to indicate that the trustee is entitled to a "reasonable" fee under the circumstances.

Example 20-49. Trustee Compensation — Determination of Reasonable Fee

Terrance is serving as the trustee of two trusts. Under the terms of one trust, Terrance is entitled to "a reasonable fee." The second trust is silent about compensation but the applicable statute provides that a trustee may receive "reasonable compensation." How should Terrance determine his compensation for serving as the trustee of these two trusts?

Explanation

Terrance should arrive at the amount of his compensation after considering a variety of relevant factors such as those listed below.

1. The amount of time Terrance spent working on trust matters.
2. Gross income of the trust.
3. Appreciation in value of trust property.
4. Terrance's unusual or special skills or experience (e.g., being an attorney or accountant).
5. Terrance's degree of fidelity or disloyalty to the trust.
6. The amount of risk and responsibility Terrance assumed.
7. The fees charged by other trustees in the local community for similar services.
8. The character of Terrance's work; that is, did it involve skill and judgment, or was it merely routine or ministerial.
9. Terrance's own estimate of the value of his services.

In some states, Terrance may then take this amount from the trust without court approval. If a beneficiary or co-trustee believes the fee is excessive, that person may seek judicial review. In other states, Terrance may need to get court approval of the fee prior to paying himself from the trust.

§20.10   Trust Modifications

The terms of a trust are not frozen as of the date the settlor created the trust. Under proper circumstances, the court and the parties may alter the provisions of a trust. This section discusses the scope of the permitted changes and the conditions imposed thereon.

§20.10.1 By Court

A beneficiary or a trustee may petition the court to modify a trust. The court may grant the request if it believes that doing so would carry out the settlor's intent. Judicial modification of trusts falls into two categories, deviation and cy pres. Although a few states have codified these principles, in most states the doctrines are judicially created and recognized.

§20.10.1.1 Deviation

A court may be willing to permit the trustee to deviate from the settlor's instructions as contained in the trust instrument if the court is convinced that the settlor would have consented to the change had the settlor anticipated the current situation. *Deviation* typically occurs if (1) the purposes of the trust have been fulfilled, (2) the purposes of the trust have become illegal, (3) the purposes of the trust are now impossible to fulfill, or (4) because of circumstances not known to or anticipated by the settlor, compliance with the terms of the trust would defeat or substantially impair the trustee's ability to accomplish the purposes of the trust. This latter situation is the most often asserted ground for a deviation.

Using its deviation powers, the court can authorize a wide array of administrative revisions such as (1) changing the trustee, (2) permitting the trustee to perform acts that are not authorized or are forbidden by the trust instrument, (3) prohibiting the trustee from performing acts that the settlor mandated in the trust instrument, (4) modifying the terms of the trust, and (5) terminating the trust. Courts will not, however, authorize changes to the dispositive provisions of a trust such as the identity of the beneficiary or the nature of the beneficiary's interest.

Example 20-50. Deviation

Settlor created a valid trust in 1930 for Settlor's recently born child. The trust required all income to be paid to Child with the remainder passing to various charities upon Child's death. The trust prohibited the trustee from making investments in corporate stock. The trustee was required to retain a home and surrounding property located in the hills surrounding Los Angeles as Child's permanent residence. The mudslides triggered by an El Niño weather pattern destroyed this luxurious home and eroded away about one-half of the lot. Trustee would like to invest in corporate stock and sell the LA land. In addition, Child's expenses have increased to the point that the trust income does not provide a suitable level of care. Accordingly, Trustee would like to use some of the principal for Child's benefit. How is a court likely to rule on these deviation requests?

Explanation

Settlor, just like many people who created trusts after the 1929 stock market crash and during the ensuing depression, prohibited trustees from investing in corporate stock. Over time, however, stocks have proven to be a relatively safe type of trust investment and thus part of a reasonably prudent trustee's investment portfolio especially because stock may both earn income and appreciate in value. The court may be willing to remove this restriction because failure to do so may prevent the trustee from making prudent investments. On the other hand, a court could decide there are other types of relatively safe assets that both earn income and appreciate and consequently honor Settlor's restriction.

Settlor never anticipated that the house and its supporting property would cease to exist because of disastrous mudslides. The court would likely grant Trustee permission to sell the property because of this change in circumstances that Settlor did not anticipate.

The court may be sympathetic to the plight of Child caused by the trust's income being inadequate to cover Child's expenses. However, the court is extremely unlikely to order a deviation because to do so would change the beneficial interests in the property. The charities own the remainder interest in the trust. If the court permitted Trustee to invade principal on Child's behalf, the court would actually be taking property away from the charities. However, if Child were the sole remainder beneficiary as well as the income beneficiary, the court might be willing to accelerate Child's enjoyment of the principal.

§20.10.1.2   Cy Pres

The court may apply the equitable doctrine of *cy pres* to provide a substitute beneficiary for a charitable trust under proper circumstances. This doctrine applies to a charitable gift in trust just like it does to an outright charitable gift in a will as discussed in §7.5, above. After reviewing this section, consider the following example.

Example 20-51.   Cy Pres[5]

Settlor created a trust to pay for the expenses of law students who attend your law school. Settlor stated that the trust income was to be divided equally among the law students to offset their tuition and living expenses. When the trust was originally created, the trust generated enough income to pay about one credit's worth of tuition per student per year. Due to Trustee's phe-

---

5. This example is loosely based on the 1986 California Superior Court of Marin County case of In re Estate of Buck as found in 21 U.S.F.L. Rev. 691 (1987).

nomenal investing abilities, the trust income is now enough to pay 100 percent of the tuition of all law students and give each a sizeable living allowance as well. The undergraduate students are jealous and petition the court for cy pres. They claim that the money would be better spent subsidizing undergraduate expenses because the trust would then benefit a greater number of students who are pursuing diverse occupations. Should the court grant cy pres?

Explanation

Cy pres is appropriate when Settlor's purpose has already been fulfilled, becomes illegal to perform, impossible to fulfill, or is permanently impracticable of performance. A court is unlikely to exercise cy pres in this case because Settlor's purpose can still be carried out exactly as Settlor intended. Merely because it is arguable that spending money on undergraduates would be a better use of trust income from the perspective of the students, the university, and the community would not be enough to permit the court to alter Settlor's clearly stated intent.

§20.10.2 By Parties

§20.10.2.1 Settlor

The settlor may have the power to modify, amend, or revoke the trust. Under the law of most states, the settlor has these powers only if the trust instrument specifically reserves them to the settlor. In other words, there is a presumption that the settlor may not make changes to the terms of the trust and may not regain title to trust property. In a few states, however, trusts are presumed revocable and are irrevocable only if the settlor expressly so provides. Regardless of the applicable law, the settlor should always state whether or not the settlor may amend or revoke the trust to avoid any confusion.

§20.10.2.2 Trustee

The trustee normally lacks the power to make unilateral changes to the terms of the trust. Under certain circumstances, however, the trust instrument or state law may give trustees the authority to take certain actions that result in a modification or a termination. For example, the settlor may provide that if the value of the trust property drops below a specified amount, the trustee has the discretion to terminate the trust and distribute the remaining property. Many states permit the trustee to divide a trust into two or more trusts with terms identical to the original to reduce taxes by permitting the trustee to make different tax elections with regard to each trust.

§20.10.2.3 Beneficiaries

The beneficiaries may consent to a trust modification. The trustee should not rely on a consent unless all beneficiaries agree. Consent may be difficult to obtain because some beneficiaries may be unborn or unascertainable. The discussion in §21.6.2, below, regarding the consent of a beneficiary to a trustee's breach of trust is also applicable to a beneficiary consenting to a trust modification.

§20.10.2.4 Family Settlement Doctrine

Because of potential or ongoing litigation, trust beneficiaries and trustees often try to reach an amicable resolution of their differences. As a result of these negotiations, the parties may agree to a settlement that includes various changes to the terms of the trust. Courts look favorably at these types of agreements because they seek to preserve property and reduce the amount of trust property wasted on litigation expenses. In addition, nonjudicial settlements encourage harmony among the parties who are in many cases family members. For a discussion of the analogous situation of using settlements to resolve will contests, see §10.8.16, above.

Example 20-52. Family Settlement Doctrine — Genuine Controversy

Settlor created a trust for Settlor's children that provides that the trustee is to use trust income for their medical expenses until the youngest child's twenty-fifth birthday. Despite the crystal clarity of Settlor's instructions, the children bring an action alleging that the terms of the trust are ambiguous. The children then agree that the trust should pay for their educational and support expenses as well. Will the court enforce this agreement?

Explanation

The court may not enforce this "settlement" even though all beneficiaries agree. Courts usually require that the controversy be genuine and not merely trumped up by the beneficiaries who desire terms that are more favorable to them than those the settlor included in the trust. Public policy is not served by the enforcement of settlements that resolve friendly disagreements that the beneficiaries designed merely to circumvent the settlor's intent.

§20.11 Trust Termination

Most trusts eventually terminate unless they are charitable or are permitted to continue indefinitely unfettered by the Rule Against Perpetuities because the state has abolished the Rule. Upon termination, all legal and equitable title to any remaining trust property becomes reunited in the hands of the remainder beneficiaries. This section discusses the various ways in which a trust may terminate.

§20.11.1 Express Terms of Trust

The most common reason a trust terminates is because of the express terms of the trust. The settlor usually ties trust termination to an event or date such as when a beneficiary reaches a certain age, meets specified educational requirements, or dies.

§20.11.2 Revocation by Settlor

The settlor may revoke the trust if the settlor has retained that right or if it is provided by state law. See §20.10.2.1, above. Once the settlor revests legal and equitable title to all the trust property in the settlor, the trust ends.

§20.11.3 Termination by Beneficiaries

Beneficiaries often seek to terminate a trust early because they would prefer to own the property outright and be free from the limitations the settlor imposed. Perhaps they are frustrated at receiving less than they would like because of the settlor's instructions in the trust instrument or because the trustee conservatively exercises discretion to make distributions. Even if all beneficiaries consent, most courts will not allow them to terminate the trust if any *material purpose* remains. Examples of trusts the courts usually deem to have material purposes unsatisfied are those that contain support provisions, spendthrift provisions, or specify payment at a stated date, when the beneficiary reaches a certain age, or upon some event that may still occur. This principle is often called the *Claflin doctrine* because of its enunciation in a famous 1889 Massachusetts case.[6]

A few states still follow the English view that permits the beneficiaries to agree to terminate the trust even if the settlor does not consent and a

---

6. Claflin v. Claflin, 149 Mass. 19, 20 N.E. 454 (1889).

material purpose remains unfulfilled. On the other hand, some American states are more restrictive than the *Claflin* doctrine and do not permit the beneficiaries to agree to an early termination if any trust purpose remains, regardless of how immaterial.

Example 20-53. Trust Termination — Beneficiaries

Settlor created a testamentary trust for Child. Settlor provided that Child was entitled to the income in the trustee's discretion for health, education, and support until Child reached age seventy-five. On Child's seventy-fifth birthday, Trustee shall deliver all trust corpus to Child. If Child dies prior to age seventy-five, the remainder passes to various named individuals. Settlor died when Child was five years old. Child has reached the age of sixty and figures it is about time that Child get all of the property so Child can enjoy life before age-related health complications set in. Child is tired of Child's financial life being manipulated by Settlor's hand that has been dead for over a half a century. Child and the contingent remainder beneficiaries agree that the trust should be terminated and they formulate a plan for the distribution of the trust property. What are the chances that Child will be successful in getting court approval for the termination?

Explanation

Child has only a remote chance of terminating the trust because material purposes still remain. For example, the uses of trust income are limited to support related expenses and the settlor specified a termination age. In addition, the agreement between Child and the other beneficiaries is not a settlement of a bona fide controversy regarding the trust and thus a court is unlikely to approve it as a settlement. See §20.10.2.4, above.

Example 20-54. Trust Termination — Beneficiaries and Settlor

Settlor created an inter vivos irrevocable spendthrift trust for Beneficiary's support to terminate when Beneficiary reached age fifty. Settlor created this trust in 1970 when Beneficiary was two years old. Settlor has been impressed with Beneficiary's maturity and investment prowess and agrees with Beneficiary that it would be great if Beneficiary could obtain the property free of trust immediately. Will the court permit Beneficiary and Settlor to terminate the trust?

Explanation

Although the trust is irrevocable and despite the existence of material purposes (the trust is spendthrift and provided for distribution at a certain age), many courts would allow Settlor and Beneficiary to terminate the trust. This situation is unlike Example 20-53 because Settlor agreed with Beneficiary to terminate the trust. Settlor's intent is the most important factor that the court will consider. Of course, if the trust has other beneficiaries, they must agree to this termination as well. Obtaining the consent of all of the beneficiaries is often difficult especially if some are incompetent, unborn, or unascertainable.

§20.11.4 Merger

By working together, the trustees and the beneficiaries may terminate a trust by uniting all legal and equitable title in one person. This person could be the trustee (assuming that there is no spendthrift clause restricting the ability of the beneficiary to convey the beneficiary's interest to the trustee), a beneficiary, or a third party. See §19.1.3, above, for a detailed discussion of merger. Note that some courts will not permit a trust to terminate because of merger if a material purpose remains. Instead, the court will appoint a new trustee to be sure the legal and equitable titles are split.

§20.11.5 Lack of Property

A trust must have property and thus a trust may terminate because it runs out of property. See §19.6, above. The trustee may expend all the assets of the trust prior to the termination date or event the settlor specified in the trust.

§20.11.6 Court Order

A court may terminate a trust under proper circumstances by using its deviation power. The trust may no longer be necessary because the purposes of the trust have been fulfilled, have become illegal, or are impossible to fulfill. Additionally, continuance of the trust could defeat or substantially impair the settlor's intent because of circumstances not known to or anticipated by the settlor. See §20.10.1.1, above.

§20.11.7 Duties of Trustee upon Termination

Example 20-55. Duties of Trustee upon Termination

The trust corpus consists of a variety of investments including a grocery store, an oil well, an apartment building, bank accounts, and corporate securities. The trust instrument provides that the trust ends today, Beneficiary's twenty-fifth birthday. May Trustee continue to run the grocery store, collect royalties on the oil well and rent on the apartments, and manage the accounts and securities even though the trust is technically no longer in existence? How quickly should Trustee transfer the property to Beneficiary?

Explanation

Trustee's powers do not end immediately upon trust termination. Most courts would permit Trustee to continue to exercise trust powers for the reasonable period of time necessary to wind up the affairs of the trust. The length of this period depends on the circumstances of each case and the type of property involved. More sophisticated investments and businesses may take longer to wrap up and transfer to Beneficiary than other assets that need a mere change in registration or physical delivery.

21

Trust Enforcement

If everything proceeds smoothly, the judicial system is not involved with the administration of a trust. The trustee invests property, makes distributions to beneficiaries, and does everything else necessary to carry out the settlor's wishes without court supervision. The trustee does not need to seek court permission or authorization and is usually not required to make regular reports to the court. However, if a dispute arises that cannot be settled amicably, the aggrieved parties are forced to seek the assistance of the courts to enforce their rights. This chapter begins with an overview of some important procedural matters and then examines the methods that may be used to enforce a trust.

§21.1 Procedural Matters

§21.1.1 Standing

A person must have standing to bring an action to enforce a trust. Beneficiaries and trustees have standing because they hold title to trust property. Normally, other individuals lack the ability to meddle in trust affairs because they have no legally recognized basis to support their actions. Even the settlor usually lacks standing because the settlor has conveyed away all title to the property. The settlor may, however, have standing in some other capacity such as by retaining the power to revoke, serving as a trustee, or being named as a beneficiary.

Some states permit individuals who do not hold title to trust property to enforce a trust. These jurisdictions grant standing to *interested persons* and then define "interested persons" broadly. For example, the Texas definition provides that "whether a person [other than a beneficiary or trustee] is an interested person may vary from time to time and must be determined according to the particular purposes of and matter involved."[1] Review §19.8.4, above, discussing incidental beneficiaries for further information and an example of a situation where a person without title to trust property may wish to have standing to enforce a trust.

The state's attorney general traditionally has standing to enforce a charitable trust. See §19.10.4.3, above, for additional information.

§21.1.2 *Jurisdiction and Venue*

A person attempting to enforce a trust must be certain to bring the action in the proper court. First, the court must have jurisdiction over trust matters. The determination of the proper court may depend on a variety of factors such as whether the trust is inter vivos or testamentary and the court structure of the particular county. For example, counties with large populations may have specialized courts to deal with trusts while courts of general jurisdiction hear trust cases in rural counties. Second, the action must be brought in the court that has venue over the trust. Typically, venue is based on the residence of the trustee. In some states, the venue rules vary depending on whether the trustee is an individual or a corporation.

§21.1.3 *Virtual Representation*

Parties to trust actions often need to be concerned with binding individuals who are not parties to the lawsuit. Trust actions often impact beneficiaries who are minors, incompetent, unborn, or unascertainable.

Example 21-1. Procedural Matters — Virtual Representation

Settlor created a trust with the following dispositive provision: "The income of the trust property is to be paid to Nancy, Janet, and Ellen until the last one dies. The remainder of the trust property shall then be distributed to my then-living descendants, per capita with representation." Settlor is still alive, Nancy is fifteen years old, and Janet is incompetent. Ellen has brought suit claiming that Trustee has made investments in violation of the applicable standard of care. You represent Trustee and believe that you will prevail in the lawsuit. You are afraid, however, that Nancy, Janet, or Settlor's descendants may raise the same arguments at a later time. How could you bind these individuals by the court's decision?

---

1. Tex. Trust Code Ann. §111.004(7) (Vernon Supp. 1998).

Explanation

Trustee needs to bind a minor (Nancy), an incompetent person (Janet), and unborn/unascertainable beneficiaries (Settlor's descendants who are alive when the last income beneficiary dies). Although the exact techniques are highly dependent on state law, here are some common methods to bind these individuals. If Nancy and Janet have court-appointed guardians, it is likely that an order binding the guardians would bind the wards. Thus, you must be certain to include these guardians as parties to the lawsuit. If some of the income beneficiaries do not have guardians, you should request that the judge appoint a guardian ad litem to represent their interests. A guardian ad litem may also be needed to obtain a judgment binding on the unborn or unascertained beneficiaries. Some states permit unborn and unascertained beneficiaries to be bound by an order if their interests are adequately represented by another party to the action who has a substantially identical interest. Thus, if Settlor had an adult descendant who was a party to the lawsuit, a judgment binding on that party may act to bind other parties who are potentially in a similar situation. Some states also allow the trustee to represent unborn or unascertained beneficiaries if the trustee's interest is not adverse.

§21.2 Remedies against the Trustee

§21.2.1 Money Damages

The most often sought remedy against the trustee is money damages. Courts use four basic methods to compute money damages when *surcharging* a trustee, that is, when holding the trustee personally liable for a breach.

(1) Lost Value. The court may award the loss or depreciation in value to the trust property caused by the breach. The plaintiff must be able to demonstrate that the trustee's breach caused the loss but does not need to show that the trustee personally benefited from the breach.

(2) Profit Made by Trustee. The trustee is responsible for any profit the trustee gained by being a trustee, except for the trustee's compensation. The trustee is liable for the profit even if the trust did not suffer a loss because of the breach.

(3) Lost Profits. The court may hold the trustee liable for the profits the trust would have earned had the trustee not breached the trustee's fiduciary duties. These damages are more difficult to prove because of their speculative nature.

(4) Punitive Damages. An intentional breach of duty by the trustee is considered a tort in many states. Consequently, the court may be able to justify an award of punitive damages.

Example 21-2. Money Damages — Generally

Beneficiary brought suit against Trustee to surcharge Trustee. Beneficiary's action is based on two breaches of trust. First, Trustee paid $5,000 for an investment now worth $1,000. Beneficiary can show that had Trustee performed even cursory research, Trustee would have learned that the price drop was widely anticipated in the business community. Second, Trustee purchased corporate stock from the trust to raise money to make required distributions to the beneficiaries. Trustee paid $20,000 for this stock, which was its fair market value on the date of the purchase. The corporation experienced tremendous success and the stock is now worth $50,000. For what amounts may the court hold Trustee personally liable?

Explanation

The first breach involved a negligent investment. Trustee owes a duty to investigate before investing trust funds. Thus, Trustee is liable for the $4,000 loss in value to the trust. In addition, Trustee will also be responsible for the lost profits, that is, the amount the trust would have earned had Trustee invested the $5,000 prudently. This amount may be difficult to determine. The court may base damages on a standard such as the prime rate or some generally accepted percentage which indicates the average return rate on trust investments.

The second breach involved self-dealing. Trustee is responsible for the $30,000 profit Trustee made on the stock even though Trustee paid fair market value. The court may also hold Trustee liable for punitive damages because of the tortious nature of this breach; that is, Trustee intentionally and knowingly bought trust property for Trustee's personal use.

Example 21-3. Money Damages — Liability of Successor Trustee for Breach by Predecessor

Original Trustee embezzled $50,000 from the trust and then resigned before anyone had detected this breach of trust. Successor Trustee assumed the office and has just discovered Original Trustee's misappropriation. Is Successor Trustee personally liable for this breach?

Explanation

Generally, a successor trustee is not liable for a breach committed by a predecessor trustee. Under certain circumstances, however, liability could attach. For example, a successor trustee could have actual knowledge of or have reason to know about the breach and then either permit the breach to continue or fail to make a reasonable effort to rectify it. Thus, Successor Trustee should make a timely and diligent effort to recover the money from Original Trustee either by nonjudicial means or by filing suit if necessary.

§21.2.2 Removal of Trustee

Courts have the ability to remove the trustee from office. Most removal statutes require a showing of cause before the court can remove a trustee. Examples of conduct constituting cause are listed below.

(1) Breach of Trust. If a trustee violates the investment standard of care, self-deals, or places the trustee in a conflict of interest situation regarding the trust, the court may decide to remove the trustee from office.

(2) Trustee Becomes Incompetent. If the trustee is no longer competent to manage trust property, the court will remove the trustee.

(3) Trustee Becomes Insolvent. Once the trustee becomes insolvent, the beneficiaries have no one, in a practical sense, to hold personally liable for a breach. In addition, an insolvent person has a greater incentive to embezzle than someone who is not in financial trouble. Accordingly, the court may remove a trustee who becomes insolvent.

(4) For Other Cause. A court has great leeway to remove a trustee for any reason which the court believes constitutes sufficient grounds for removal.

Some jurisdictions do not require a finding of cause to justify a removal but focus instead on the effectiveness of the trustee's administration of the trust. Thus, if the beneficiaries can show that the trustee is not administering the trust in the best way to meet the needs of the beneficiaries, the court will remove the trustee even if the trustee has not been guilty of any wrongdoing.

Example 21-4. Removal of Trustee—Breach of Trust

Settlor created a trust naming Child as trustee and Grandchildren as the beneficiaries. Child had no prior experience as a trustee and consequently made an investment a prudent person would not have made. Grandchildren now seek to have Child removed from office for breaching the trust. How should the court rule?

Explanation

The court certainly has the power to remove Child from office because Child breached the trust. However, courts are reluctant to remove a trustee for a breach of trust caused by an error of judgment or a mistake when there was no bad faith. Instead, most courts would surcharge Child for the appropriate monetary damages but permit Child to remain in office.

Example 21-5. Removal of Trustee — Conflict between Trustee and Beneficiaries

Settlor established a testamentary trust for Settlor's children. Trustee was given the discretion to decide which children receive distributions and in what amounts until the youngest child reaches age sixty. Trustee has invested well and the trust has grown significantly in value over the years. The trust property is now worth over $10,000,000 and earns over $1,000,000 per year in income. Trustee, however, is very careful about making trust distributions. Trustee requires the children to exhaust their own resources first and then only supplies bare minimums. For example, one child is currently in law school. Trustee has refused to pay tuition because the child qualifies for government loans. Although Trustee supplies adequate funds for food and lodging and pays for comprehensive medical insurance, Trustee will not give this child money to buy a car because the law school is located in a city with an excellent public transportation system. The children are fed up with living meager lifestyles while the trust is brimming with money which they will not be able to reach for many decades. Consequently, they sue to have Trustee removed from office. How should the court rule?

Explanation

Most courts would not remove Trustee. Trustee is not in breach of trust. Instead, Trustee is simply not very generous with trust funds. The children are hoping that a different trustee would loosen the pursestrings and provide more substantial trust distributions. Courts are extremely reluctant to remove a trustee because of dissent between the trustee and the beneficiaries, especially when the settlor appointed the trustee (as compared to a court-appointed trustee). Settlor may have anticipated the children's greed and wanted Trustee to stand firm against their demands. Settlor may have preferred the children to make their own way through life and only receive assistance that is really needed.

§21.2.3 Pre-Breach Remedies

Before a breach of trust actually occurs, concerned parties have several potential remedies, which are discussed in this section.

§21.2.3.1 Decree to Carry Out the Trust

The beneficiaries could sue the trustee to obtain a court order forcing the trustee to carry out the trustee's duties under the terms of the trust instrument or applicable trust law. This remedy is particularly effective if a trustee has not yet breached the trust but appears to be in danger of breaching because of inattention to trust matters.

§21.2.3.2 Injunction

If a breach of trust appears imminent, a beneficiary or co-trustee may obtain an injunction or restraining order to prevent the trustee from performing the improper act. The court can hold the trustee in contempt if the trustee fails to comply.

§21.2.3.3 Appointment of Receiver

A court may appoint a receiver who can quickly swoop in and take possession of the trust property if the court fears that the trustee will not obey an injunction. Generally, a court is reluctant to appoint a receiver unless it is clear that the property would be lost, destroyed, or materially injured unless a receiver is appointed and that recovery by the complaining party is probable. After resolution of the issue, the court will either appoint a new trustee or, if the trustee turns out to have been administering the trust properly, return the property to the trustee.

§21.2.3.4 Increase Bond

The court may require a bond in cases where the settlor waived bond or increase the amount of an existing bond. This remedy is appropriate when the value of the trust property has increased significantly and additional bond is needed to provide beneficiaries with adequate protection.

§21.2.3.5 Declaratory Judgment

The trustee or a beneficiary may ask the court for a declaratory judgment to determine whether a contemplated action would be a breach of trust. In this way, the trustee does not run the risk of having a court later determine that a particular action was in breach. However, courts are leery about granting instructions unless there is an immediate and genuine legal problem. Otherwise, the courts would be flooded with petitions by timid or overcautious trustees who wish to obtain free legal advice.

§21.2.4 Criminal Sanctions

In many states, breaches of trust that result from the trustee's intentional, knowing, or reckless conduct (but not mere negligent conduct) may lead to criminal liability. The severity of the crime, often called *misapplication by fiduciary,* depends on the amount of money put at risk because of the trustee's improper conduct. The trustee could face decades of imprisonment for breaching the trust. Note that a conviction under most of these statutes does not require a finding that the trustee received a benefit from the misapplication. If the trustee does personally benefit, the court may impose punishment for additional crimes such as theft and embezzlement.

§21.3 Remedies Involving Trust Property

§21.3.1 Tracing

Tracing permits the beneficiary to recover the actual trust property or its proceeds from the trustee or a third party for the benefit of the trust. The beneficiary follows the trail of the misappropriated property and once located, can recover that property unless it is in the hands of a bona fide purchaser. See §21.3.4, below. The tremendous benefit of this remedy is that the beneficiary has priority over the asset vis-à-vis the trustee's other creditors. The traced asset actually belongs to the trust and is thus not included among the trustee's personal assets that are subject to the claims of creditors. The beneficiary may have to elect between (1) tracing to the trust property or its proceeds and (2) recovering monetary damages; double recovery is not allowed.

Example 21-6. Tracing — Distinct Items

Settlor's will left all of Settlor's property to a testamentary trust. Trustee took various items of Settlor's estate and appropriated them for Trustee's own purposes. When Beneficiary discovered what Trustee had done, Trustee was wearing some of Settlor's jewelry and had the other items sitting around Trustee's home. Trustee's creditors have levied on all of Trustee's property. Who is entitled to the property Trustee took from the trust?

Explanation

Beneficiary can positively trace the jewelry and other assets from the trust to Trustee's home. Because these are trust assets and do not belong to Trustee, Beneficiary will be able to recover them for the trust to the detriment of Trustee's other creditors.

Example 21-7. Tracing — Commingled Items

Trustee embezzled $300 from the trust and deposited those funds into Trustee's personal bank account which prior to this deposit had a balance of $500. Trustee then withdrew $400 from this account to pay for a weekend at a ski resort. Later, Trustee withdrew an additional $300 to pay for a weekend at a beach resort. Trustee then received Trustee's income tax refund and deposited the $600 check in the account. To how much could Beneficiary trace after each of these transactions?

Explanation

The best way to determine the amount of money Beneficiary can trace into a commingled fund is to construct a chart separating the money based on its source and then evaluate each transaction under the appropriate legal rules that apply.

	Trustee's Personal Funds in Account	Money Embezzled from Trust in Account	Balance in Trustee's Personal Account
Trustee's personal account's opening balance	$500	0	$500
Trustee embezzles $300	$500	$300	$800
Trustee withdraws $400. The court will apply a presumption that Trustee first withdraws money that is not subject to the claims of others. This is an unrealistic presumption of honesty because Trustee probably thinks Trustee is spending the embezzled funds rather than Trustee's own funds. At this point, Beneficiary can trace to the entire $300 because that amount still remains in the account due to the application of the presumption that Trustee is first spending Trustee's own money. This rule preserves the most money as possible for Beneficiary to the detriment of Trustee's other creditors.	$100	$300	$400

	Trustee's Personal Funds in Account	Money Embezzled from Trust in Account	Balance in Trustee's Personal Account
Trustee withdraws an additional $300. Again, the court presumes that Trustee first spends Trustee's own funds. Because the withdrawal exhausts all of Trustee's own funds, Trustee is now spending the money embezzled from the trust so there is less available to Beneficiary. Beneficiary can trace to $100.	0	$100	$100
Trustee deposits income tax refund of $600. Money that Trustee adds to the commingled account is Trustee's own money; it is not the same money that was embezzled. Thus, the deposit inures to the benefit of Trustee and Trustee's other creditors. Beneficiary can only trace to $100. Because $100 is both the amount remaining from the embezzled money as well as the lowest balance of the account, the principle demonstrated by this example is often referred to as the *lowest intermediate balance rule*.	$600	$100	$700

Example 21-8. Tracing — Paying Personal Creditor

Trustee embezzled $1,000 from a trust and used it to pay a credit card bill. Does Trustee have any property to which Beneficiary may trace?

Explanation

Trustee's payment of the credit card debt did not increase the amount of assets Trustee owns and thus Beneficiary cannot trace. Instead, one debt has been substituted for another. Trustee now owes $1,000 to the trust rather than to the credit card company. Nonetheless, a few courts apply the *swollen assets doctrine* and hold that Trustee was actually benefited because Trustee was able to retain property that otherwise would have been used to pay the credit card company. If the court applies this doctrine, Beneficiary would be able to trace using the normal tracing rules for commingled accounts as discussed in Example 21-7.

§21.3.2 Subrogation

Subrogation may be useful if the beneficiary cannot recover the trust property through tracing because the trustee used trust property to pay a personal debt. The court may subrogate the beneficiary to the rights of the creditor who was paid. Thus, the beneficiaries "step into the shoes," that is, have the same position as, the creditor who was paid. If this creditor had a special right, such as a mortgage, Article 9 security interest, or a priority position in bankruptcy, the beneficiaries can use those rights against the trustee and other creditors.

Example 21-9. Subrogation

Trustee embezzled $15,000 from a trust. Trustee used $2,000 to pay a credit card debt and $13,000 to pay off the note on Trustee's car. A personal injury creditor has levied on all of Trustee's property. What rights to Trustee's property may Beneficiary be able to obtain?

Explanation

Under the law of most states, Beneficiary will not be able to trace because Trustee used the trust property to pay off existing debts. However, Beneficiary is not relegated to the position of a mere general creditor. Instead, the court will subrogate Beneficiary to the position of the creditors who were paid. The credit card debt was probably unsecured and thus Beneficiary does not gain anything from being subrogated to that position. Fortunately, it is very likely that the note on the car was secured by a security interest in the car itself. The court can reinstate that debt placing Beneficiary into the creditor's position and thus Beneficiary now has the benefit of a lien on the car. This lien would then be superior to the personal injury creditor's levy.

§21.3.3 Marshalling

A beneficiary who has a claim against the trustee may be able to force the trustee's other creditors to marshal their claims. *Marshalling* is an appropriate remedy when a creditor has a right to recover out of more than one fund or asset and another creditor, such as a trust beneficiary, has recourse to only one of those funds or assets. The creditor must first resort to the fund or asset that will not interfere with the rights of the beneficiary to preserve as much of that fund or asset as possible for the beneficiary. Of course, if both funds are needed for the creditor and the creditor has priority as to both, then the marshalling remedy will not help the beneficiary.

Example 21-10. Marshalling

Creditor has a priority claim to Trustee's only two valuable assets. Asset One is worth $7,000 and Asset Two is worth $3,000. Beneficiary obtained a right to Asset Two through subrogation but that right is junior to Creditor's right. Creditor has a $5,000 claim and Beneficiary has a $2,500 claim. Trustee also has a variety of unsecured creditors with claims totaling $30,000 who are anxious to be paid. How should the claims of these creditors be resolved?

Explanation

Because Creditor has a priority claim in both assets, Creditor could elect to take all of Asset Two and $2,000 from Asset One. Although this completely satisfies Creditor's claim, it leaves Beneficiary without any type of priority and in the pool with all of Trustee's other general creditors. Only $5,000 of Asset One would remain and there would be total claims of $32,500 ($30,000 of unsecured claims plus Beneficiary's claim of $2,500). Beneficiary would receive only $384.62 [$2,500 × ($5,000 ÷ $32,500)] on Beneficiary's $2,500 claim or approximately 15 percent. The unsecured creditors would, under the circumstances, be relatively pleased with this arrangement because they would receive 15 percent of their claims as well.

Beneficiary should request marshalling so Creditor is forced to first use Asset One, which is not subject to Beneficiary's claim. In this manner, Creditor is still paid in full and Asset Two is preserved for Beneficiary's $2,500 claim. Beneficiary's claim is satisfied in full and the remaining $500 of Asset Two would be shared by Trustee's general creditors along with the remaining $2,000 of Asset One. The unsecured creditors will now receive only 8.3 percent ($2,500 ÷ $30,000) of their claims.

§21.3.4 Bona Fide Purchasers

Remedies against trust property end when that property reaches the hands of a *bona fide purchaser* (BFP). Under the common law, a person becomes a BFP of trust property by (1) paying value for the property and (2) being without actual or constructive notice of the existence of the trust and the concomitant equitable interest of the beneficiary. A BFP takes free of the beneficiary's interest and may retain and transfer the property without subsequent question by the beneficiary or someone claiming through the beneficiary. Because BFP status is denied to purchasers who know they are buying trust property or are dealing with a trustee, purchasers are prone to pay less than fair market value for trust property because of the increased risk associated with the purchase. They cannot be sure that the trustee is not breaching the trust by selling the property or that the property is not subject to claims by the beneficiaries. The BFP rule was designed to protect beneficiaries but the rule can operate to their detriment in many instances.

To alleviate this problem, many states have modified the common law rule and permit a purchaser to achieve BFP status even if the purchaser is on notice that the purchaser is dealing with a trustee or buying trust property. This modern approach permits people to deal with trustees with relative safety and permits trustees to negotiate for higher sale prices. Of course, the purchaser will not be a BFP if the purchaser has actual notice of a breach of trust.

§21.4   Remedies against the Beneficiary

A beneficiary is generally not in a position to breach the trust and is not liable for breaches of trust committed by the trustee. Under certain circumstances, however, a beneficiary may be liable to the trust. Situations in which a court may hold a beneficiary liable include (1) misappropriation or wrongful dealing with trust property, (2) consenting to or participating in a breach of trust with the trustee, (3) failure to repay a loan of trust funds that was authorized under the trust instrument, and (4) failure to repay a distribution from the trust that was in excess of the amount to which the beneficiary was entitled.

§21.5   Causes of Action against Third Parties

Third parties may also be liable to the trust. For example, a third party who contracts with the trust and subsequently breaches that contract is liable. Additionally, a person is liable for torts that cause damage or loss to trust property. If the trustee does not bring these actions, the beneficiaries may be able to move forward with them on behalf of the trust. Alternatively, the beneficiaries can seek to have the trustee removed and replaced with a trustee who is willing to pursue these trust claims. Beneficiaries may also recover from third parties who assist a trustee to commit a breach of trust.

§21.6   Barring of Remedies

A beneficiary may be prevented from recovering for a breach of trust for a variety of reasons. This section discusses various situations that restrict or eliminate the beneficiary's ability to win a breach of trust action.

§21.6.1 Settlor's Approval in Trust Instrument

The settlor may have authorized the conduct that allegedly constitutes a breach of trust in the trust instrument. The settlor may expressly approve certain conduct that would otherwise be in breach, such as a direction to retain certain property even though these assets are not earning income and are not appreciating. Likewise, a valid exculpatory clause restricts the situations in which a trustee may be held liable. For example, the clause may lower the standard of care the trustee must use when making investments or permit certain types of self-dealing. See §§20.2.3 and 20.5.8, above.

§21.6.2 Prior Approval or Ratification by Beneficiary

A beneficiary may give prior approval to the trustee for actions that would otherwise be in breach of trust. Likewise, the beneficiary may ratify breaches of trust that have already occurred. The typical requirements for an effective approval or ratification are listed below.

(1) **Breach Waivable under Local Law.** Some states provide that a beneficiary cannot waive statutorily enumerated breaches of trust. This limitation protects a beneficiary from a trustee who is in a superior bargaining position, such as a corporate trustee, from exerting undue pressure on a beneficiary to consent.

(2) **Beneficiary Is Competent.** The beneficiary must have capacity to consent; that is, the beneficiary must be of legal age and competent. Guardians may be able to give consent for a beneficiary who is a minor, incompetent, or unascertainable.

(3) **Trustee Makes Full Disclosure.** The trustee must make a complete disclosure of all relevant facts and applicable law.

(4) **Consent Documented in Writing.** Many jurisdictions require that the approval or ratification be in writing, signed by the beneficiary, and delivered to the trustee.

Example 21-11. Prior Approval or Ratification by Beneficiary — Specificity

Trustee wanted to purchase stock in Alchemy Corporation. This company claimed to be on the verge of being able to turn lead into gold. Trustee recognized the speculative nature of this investment but after diligent research learned that the company's scientists were making economically valuable discoveries even if they were unable to accomplish the transmutation. Because of the tremendous potential for appreciation and income, Trustee gathered the four beneficiaries together and fully explained the situation. After listening carefully, all the beneficiaries signed a letter telling Trustee to "use your own best judgment as to what is best for our trust." Trustee made the investment. The investment lost money and the beneficiaries brought suit against Trustee for breach of trust. Trustee defended on the basis of the letter. How will the court rule?

Explanation

The court is likely to hold that the letter is not an effective release. The letter did not give Trustee permission to buy Alchemy stock but only told Trustee to use Trustee's own judgment. The letter merely stated what the law already required Trustee to do. Trustee cannot turn a statement that basically says "perform your duties as trustee" into a release of a breach of trust. Courts strictly construe waivers and thus they need to be specific.

Example 21-12. Prior Approval or Ratification by Beneficiary — Unanimity

Assume that in Example 21-11, three of the beneficiaries signed a letter that stated: "We hereby release Trustee from all liability associated with purchasing shares of stock in Alchemy Corporation provided that no more than 5 precent of the trust is invested in this corporation." The fourth beneficiary did not sign. Will this letter be an effective defense for Trustee?

Explanation

The letter would be an effective release with regard to the three signing beneficiaries. However, the letter does not bind the nonconsenting beneficiary and thus Trustee will still be liable for making the speculative investment vis-à-vis the fourth beneficiary.

Example 21-13. Prior Approval or Ratification by Beneficiary — Acceptance of Benefits

Assume that in Example 21-12, the Alchemy stock paid excellent cash dividends. Trustee distributed those dividends evenly among the beneficiaries. Does this fact change the outcome of the nonconsenting beneficiary's action against Trustee for breach?

Explanation

An acceptance of benefits from a known breach of trust may act as an implied ratification and thus prevent the nonconsenting beneficiary from complaining about the breach. This beneficiary's act of taking the fruits of the breach with full knowledge of the breach may estop the beneficiary from later objecting.

Example 21-14. Prior Approval or Ratification by Beneficiary — Revocation

Continuing with the facts of Example 21-13, assume now that all four beneficiaries signed the release. After several years elapse, the beneficiaries realize that Alchemy's research is not yielding any commercially valuable results and no longer want Trustee to make additional stock purchases. Can the beneficiaries revoke their consent?

Explanation

The general rule is that a consent is irrevocable with regard to prior acts but may be withdrawn for future acts. Thus, the beneficiaries can revoke their consent as to future purchases of Alchemy stock but remain bound by the permission they gave for the purchases Trustee made while the consent was in force.

§21.6.3   Court Decree

The court has the power to relieve a trustee from any duty, limitation, or restriction that exists under the terms of the trust, trust statutes, or common law. Accordingly, the trustee can beg for the mercy of the court and demonstrate why the trustee should not be liable for a breach of trust.

Example 21-15.   Court Decree

Settlor appointed Child as the trustee of a trust in which Friend was the named beneficiary. One of the items of trust property was a photograph album containing pictures of Settlor and Child. Child bought the album from the trust for $250. Friend sued Child for self-dealing asking for both compensatory and punitive damages for this flagrant breach of trust. What argument would you make to the court in your defense of Child?

Explanation

Despite the clear breach of trust, Child could try to show that the album had no monetary value because only family members would want the pictures; neither Settlor nor Child are famous people. Child paid a significant amount for an item with only sentimental value. A court might be persuaded that this "innocent" although intentional breach of trust is not severe enough to merit damages. Courts are, however, extremely hesitant to exercise their power to excuse trustees for breaching their fiduciary duties unless the circumstances are compelling.

§21.6.4 Statute of Limitations

A beneficiary must bring an action against the trustee for breach before the applicable statute of limitations expires. The time varies among the states with most periods being between two and six years.

When does the cause of action against a trustee accrue? Or, said another way, from what point in time does the statute of limitations begin to run? Most states do not begin the statutory period with the date of the breach. A breach of trust is inherently undiscoverable because the beneficiary is either unable to inquire into the fiduciary's actions or is unaware of the need to do so. A beneficiary does not have a duty to investigate the fiduciary's conduct as long as the trust relationship is ongoing. On the other hand, a beneficiary cannot wait until the trust relationship ends before bringing suit if the beneficiary is already aware of the breach of trust. Accordingly, most courts apply a discovery rule. The statute of limitations begins to run from the date the beneficiary actually knows or should have known by the use of reasonable diligence that the trustee had breached the trust.

§21.6.5 Laches

A beneficiary's right to recover may be barred by laches even if the statute of limitations has not yet run. It is unfair to expect the trustee to defend an action if the beneficiary unreasonably delays in asserting the beneficiary's rights and this delay makes it difficult for the trustee to make an adequate defense. For example, material witnesses could have died or become incompetent or relevant documents may have been lost or destroyed.

22

Resulting Trusts

A *resulting trust* arises by operation of law when the facts and circumstances show that a person had the intent to hold equitable title to property although legal title is in the hands of another. Unlike an express trust where the manifestation of the settlor's trust intent must be shown by written or spoken words, a resulting trust exists when the person's conduct demonstrates that the person anticipated holding a beneficial interest in the property. Accordingly, resulting trusts are sometimes called *implied trusts* because they are implied from a person's conduct and actions rather than arising after the person makes an express statement of intent.

Resulting trusts do not have actual trust terms and do not involve an ongoing fiduciary relationship. Instead, the holder of the legal title ("trustee") simply has the obligation to convey that legal title to the holder of the equitable title ("beneficiary"). The beneficiary of a resulting trust is the person who had the implied intent to hold equitable title and thus the beneficiary and the "settlor" are the same person. If the settlor has already died, the beneficiaries of a resulting trust are the settlor's successors in interest; that is, the settlor's heirs if the settlor died intestate or, if the settlor died testate, the beneficiaries of the settlor's will.

This chapter discusses various scenarios that may give rise to the court declaring the existence of a resulting trust.

§22.1 Failure to Create Express Trust

A resulting trust may arise if the settlor attempts to create an express trust but that attempt fails because, for example, the settlor did not indicate a trust purpose, describe the beneficiaries specifically, or comply with the Rule Against Perpetuities. Although the would-be settlor may have been successful

441

in transferring legal title to the property, the settlor is treated as retaining the equitable title if the would-be settlor's attempt to create a trust fails. In effect, the would-be settlor has an implied reversionary interest in the property.

Example 22-1.   Failure to Create Express Trust — No Remainder Beneficiary

Susan signed a trust instrument that indicated the beneficiaries of the trust would be "her friends as selected by Trustee." Susan then conveyed several items of property to Trustee. The court declared the trust invalid because Susan did not name ascertainable beneficiaries, a key requirement of a valid express trust (see §19.8.2, above). What happens to the property in Trustee's possession?

Explanation

Trustee should first look to the trust instrument to see if it provides a beneficiary who takes if the trust fails. Assuming the instrument is silent, Trustee holds the property as the trustee of a resulting trust in favor of Susan. Susan's attempt to convey beneficial title to the property failed and thus she is deemed to have retained that title. Trustee should convey the legal title to the various items of property back to Susan. Susan would then own the property outright and could try again to create the trust or use the property for whatever purposes Susan desires.

Example 22-2.   Failure to Create Express Trust — The "Semi-Secret Trust"

Testator's will contained the following dispositive provision: "I leave $50,000 to Thomas, in trust. I direct Thomas to distribute this money to the individuals I indicated in my various conversations with Thomas. I leave the residual of my estate to Richard." Thomas is willing to testify that Testator told him on many occasions to distribute the $50,000 to Natalie and Janet. Who is entitled to the $50,000?

Explanation

This example demonstrates what is often referred to as a *semi-secret trust*. In other words, the fact that the gift is in trust is clear; that is, Thomas has no authority to retain a beneficial interest in the money. However, the terms of the trust are secret and known only to Trustee. Most courts will hold that Testator's attempt to create a trust fails because the beneficiaries and terms of the trust are not stated. Consequently, a resulting trust arises for the benefit of Richard, Testator's successor in interest (the remainder beneficiary of Testator's will).

§22.2   Failure of Express Trust to Dispose of All Trust Property

A resulting trust arises if the settlor creates a valid trust but fails to dispose of all of the equitable title to the trust property. This can occur when an unanticipated set of circumstances arises or because the trust instrument was poorly drafted. The settlor's failure to convey all equitable title means that the settlor retained that title and is thus entitled to the return of the legal title to the remaining trust property.

Example 22-3.   Failure of Express Trust to Dispose of All Trust Property

Settlor created a valid trust which had the following dispositive provision: "Trustee shall pay all income from the trust property to Beneficiary so long as Beneficiary is alive." Beneficiary is now wearing a marble hat and taking a dirt nap. What should Trustee do with the remaining trust property?

Explanation

Normally after the death of the life beneficiary, a trustee should deliver the remaining property to the remainder beneficiary of the trust. Settlor, however, failed to name a remainder beneficiary. The most likely outcome is that the court will find a resulting trust in favor of Settlor or, if Settlor has already died, Settlor's successors in interest. Trustee should convey the trust property to Settlor or the proper successors. A different conclusion is possible if Trustee can prove that Trustee paid Settlor to create the trust. Under this unusual scenario, Trustee could argue that the consideration for Trustee's payment was the right to retain the trust property when the trust terminated. Trustee's position would be enhanced by facts such as a close relationship between Settlor and Trustee and Trustee providing valuable fiduciary services without charge.

§22.3   Purchase-Money Resulting Trust

In the typical purchase of property, the seller gives title to the purchased property to the buyer. Even if the buyer intends to use the property as a present for a relative or friend, the buyer first receives the item and then transfers it to the donee on the appropriate occasion. A purchase-money resulting trust (PMRT) may arise if the person who pays the purchase price for property does not receive the title to that property but instead directs the seller to transfer the property to another person. Because of the highly unusual nature of this type of transaction, the court may conclude that the person who paid the purchase-money actually intended to obtain an equitable interest in the property even though the seller conveyed legal title to someone else. Note that a few states do not recognize PMRTs and thus a court may determine that the person who paid the purchase-money has no interest in the property.

If you are confronted with a fact pattern involving the purchase of property by one person with title to that property being taken by another person, the result is not necessarily a PMRT. The transaction could actually be an outright gift or a loan.

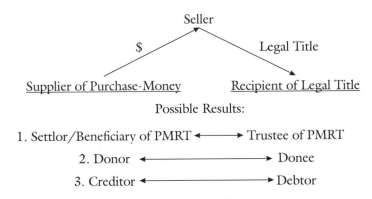

Example 22-4.   Purchase-Money Resulting Trust—Parent-Child

Parent gave $100,000 to Seller for the purchase of a home and had Seller place title to the land in the name of Child who had recently graduated from college and gotten married. Several years later, Parent and Child had a big argument during which many hurtful words were exchanged. Parent then demanded that Child convey the home to Parent. How should a court rule on Parent's request?

Explanation

If the relationship between the supplier of the purchase-money and the recipient of the legal title is close, most courts presume that an outright gift took place and thus do not imply a PMRT. Because the parties are related as parent-child, the court is likely to presume that Parent made a gift of the home to Child. The same result would occur for other close relationships such as transfers between spouses. The buyer may rebut the presumption of gift between closely related individuals and show that a PMRT is the appropriate result. Thus, Parent may be able to come forward with evidence showing that Parent actually intended, at the time of purchase, to acquire an equitable interest in the home. Some states require the person attempting to rebut the gift presumption to do so with clear and convincing evidence rather than a mere preponderance of the evidence.

Example 22-5. Purchase-Money Resulting Trust — Aunt-Nephew

Use the same facts as Example 22-4, except this time assume that the purchaser is Aunt and that Seller placed title in Nephew's name.

Explanation

Jurisdictions vary regarding how far the gift presumption will extend. Courts are reluctant to apply the presumption to individuals who are not the natural objects of the buyer's bounty. Thus, if Aunt has a spouse or children of her own, Nephew is not a natural object of her bounty, that is, he would not inherit if Aunt died intestate. Consequently, most courts would hold that the gift presumption does not apply and that Nephew holds the home as the trustee of a PMRT in favor of Aunt. However, the presumption of PMRT that arises in situations where the parties are not closely related can be rebutted with evidence showing that the buyer actually intended to make an outright gift at the time of the transfer. The fact that Nephew had just graduated from school and was recently married may lend weight to Nephew's argument that the house was a gift, especially if Aunt is wealthy enough to afford to make such a lavish present.

Example 22-6. Purchase-Money Resulting Trust — Debt

Buyer gave $150,000 to Seller and had title to the property placed in Daniel's name. Buyer now wants Daniel to pay back the money. Will Buyer be successful in obtaining a PMRT over this property?

Explanation

A PMRT is not appropriate under these facts because Buyer did not intend to obtain an interest in the property. Instead, Buyer wants the return of $150,000. The transaction was actually a loan; Buyer is the creditor and Daniel is the debtor. A PMRT arises only if the buyer intended to receive an equitable interest in the property the buyer purchased.

23

Constructive Trusts

A *constructive trust* is an equitable remedy a court imposes to prevent unjust enrichment. Constructive trusts do not arise because of the expressed or implied intent of the parties. Instead, the court adapts the split of title attribute of a trust to create a remedy when a person acquired title to property in an unconscionable manner. The court decides that the person with apparent full ownership of the property actually holds only the legal title because it would be unfair for that person to retain the beneficial interest in that property. The judgment of the court then acts to transfer legal title from the evil property owner ("trustee") to the person who would have owned the property but for the property owner's inappropriate conduct ("beneficiary").

Example 23-1. Particular Property

Defendant stole $10,000 from Plaintiff and used the money to take an exotic vacation to Tahiti. Defendant owns a variety of valuable assets such as automobiles, a home, and corporate securities. May Plaintiff obtain a constructive trust over any of this property?

Explanation

To obtain a constructive trust remedy, the plaintiff must be able to identify particular property to which the defendant's improper conduct relates. The property Defendant stole from Plaintiff is gone; it was used to pay expenses relating to Defendant's vacation such as airfare, food, and lodging. None of the stolen money remains and the money cannot be traced into the automobiles, home, or corporate securities. Accordingly, the court may not impose a constructive trust over this property for Plaintiff's benefit.

447

Example 23-2. Equitable Position of Plaintiff

Defendant purchased Plaintiff's home. Shortly thereafter, Defendant paid $80,000 on the mortgage and made valuable improvements by building a three-room addition and a swimming pool. Plaintiff proves to the satisfaction of the court that Defendant's conduct during the sale was fraudulent and convinces the court that a constructive trust remedy is proper. Is Defendant entitled to compensation for the mortgage payment and the improvements?

Explanation

A plaintiff must "do equity" to qualify for a constructive trust remedy. Thus, Plaintiff must reimburse Defendant for the mortgage payment and the improvements if Plaintiff wants to regain title to the home. Plaintiff would be unjustly enriched if Plaintiff received the benefit of the mortgage payment and improvements without paying for them.

Courts are reluctant to enumerate a list of the types of wrongs for which a constructive trust remedy may be appropriate. Judges like to keep this equitable remedy flexible so that they can apply it in as many situations as possible. Nonetheless, the types of conduct giving rise to a constructive trust fall into three basic categories: (1) fraudulent conduct, (2) abuse of confidential relationships, and (3) unperformed promises made in contemplation of death.

§23.1 Fraudulent Conduct

The property a person procures through fraudulent means may be subject to a constructive trust remedy. In this context, the term "fraud" is used broadly to refer to any type of wrongdoing, that is

> all the multifarious means which human ingenuity can devise and are resorted to by one individual to get an advantage over another by false suggestions or by the suppression of the truth. No definite and invariable rule can be laid down as a general proposition defining fraud, as it includes all surprise, trick, cunning, dissembling, and any unfair way by which another is cheated.[1]

Example 23-3. Fraudulent Conduct — Traditional Fraud

Defendant convinced Plaintiff to sell Plaintiff's house to Defendant at a price substantially below market value. In exchange for this good deal, Defendant

---

1. Johnson v. McDonald, 39 P.2d 150, 150 (Okla. 1934) (defining fraud although not in constructive trust situation). See George T. Bogert, Trusts §77, at 287 (6th ed. 1987) (fraud in constructive trust context as referring to "any kind of wrongdoing").

promised to permit Plaintiff to live in the house until Plaintiff's death. Within days after the closing, Defendant had Plaintiff evicted and sued Plaintiff for trespassing. Will Plaintiff's request for a constructive trust be successful?

Explanation

Plaintiff has an excellent chance of obtaining a constructive trust remedy. Defendant's conduct appears fraudulent in the traditional sense. In other words, Defendant knowingly made a false representation to Plaintiff that Plaintiff reasonably relied on to the Plaintiff's detriment. Plaintiff would not have conveyed the house to Defendant had Defendant not promised to permit Plaintiff to live there for the rest of Plaintiff's life. Defendant knew from the beginning that Defendant was making the promise merely to get a lower price and had no intention of permitting Plaintiff to remain in the house.

Example 23-4. Fraudulent Conduct — Generic[2]

On Halloween night, Carrie wanted to execute her will, leaving all her property to Claytonia, a nonfamily member. Several of Carrie's family members were in the room and noticed that the will disinherited them. They then used physical force to prevent Carrie from signing her will. Carrie tried to sign the will but unlike Stephen King's Carrie, this Carrie was weak. She struggled so hard that she suffered a severe hemorrhage and lapsed into a coma from which she never recovered. Accordingly, Carrie died intestate and her entire estate passed to her heirs. How could the court use a constructive trust to rectify this situation? What if Carrie had other heirs who were not present on Halloween night?

Explanation

The court may impose a constructive trust on the property that the heirs inherited from Carrie for the benefit of Claytonia. The heirs' inappropriate actions prevent them from enjoying the fruit of Carrie's intestate death. Had it not been for the nefarious conduct of the heirs, Claytonia would have received all of Carrie's property under the will. The fact that the property eventually goes to a person named in a document that was not executed with the formalities of a will does not matter because the constructive trust is imposed on the property after it passes to the heirs under intestate succession. The court can ascertain the ultimate recipients of the title to property by referring to documents that cannot stand on their own because they would violate the Statute of Frauds or Statute of Wills. Refer to §3.8.4.1, above,

---

2. This example is based on Pope v. Garrett, 211 S.W.2d 559 (Tex. 1948).

which discusses the imposition of a constructive trust on the property a person inherits if that person was responsible for the death of the intestate.

Some courts will even impose a constructive trust remedy on Carrie's innocent heirs who were not involved with the dastardly conduct. The innocent heirs would not have received any property but for the acts of the evil heirs and thus the court may use its equitable power to do complete justice and impose the constructive trust on both evil and innocent heirs alike so that Claytonia receives full title to all of Carrie's property.

§23.2   Abuse of Confidential Relationships

Constructive trusts also arise if a transfer of property occurs because of an abuse of a confidential relationship existing between the parties. The courts treat a wide variety of family, personal, social, and business relationships as being confidential if the complaining party was justified in relying on the other party to the transaction to be fair, honest, and to fully disclose all relevant facts. In other words, the relationship is confidential if the person's guard was down and was not treating the other person as if they were in an arm's-length transaction.

Example 23-5.   Abuse of Confidential Relationship

George and Leo had been good friends for twenty years. Leo decided to open a new business and convinced George to transfer some of his property to the business. Although Leo's conduct did not amount to fraud, he knew that the business was risky and that George would have difficulty regaining his property. George could easily have discovered these facts if he had done even a cursory investigation but due to their long friendship, George did not believe that it was necessary. May George obtain a constructive trust and force Leo to return the property?

Explanation

George has a good chance of securing a constructive trust remedy to recover the property. Although Leo's conduct did not amount to fraud, he abused a long-standing friendship relationship. Many courts will impose a constructive trust if one party to a close relationship takes advantage of the relationship to obtain a conveyance of property which would not have occurred if the parties were dealing with each other at arm's-length.

§23.3 Unperformed Promises Made in Contemplation of Death

A constructive trust may arise if one person induces the transfer of property by promising the transferor to do something with that property at a later time and then reneges on the promise. For example, assume that Donor gave property to Donee based on Donee's oral promise to execute a will leaving that property to Donor's child. If Donee fails to make a will containing the promised bequest, the court may impose a constructive trust on the property in favor of Donor's child regardless of who receives title to the property under Donee's will or, if Donee did not have a will, via intestacy.

Example 23-6. Unperformed Promises Made in Contemplation of Death

Testator executed a will containing the following dispositive provision: "I leave my home to Beneficiary." After Testator died, Victor claims that Testator and Beneficiary had an oral agreement that Beneficiary would hold the home in trust for Victor's benefit. How should a court rule on Victor's claim?

Explanation

This example demonstrates a *secret trust*, that is, a will that purports to make an absolute gift but where there is actually an agreement between the beneficiary and the testator that the beneficiary will hold the property in trust for a person the testator had separately indicated. If Beneficiary retained the property, Beneficiary would be unjustly enriched because Testator would not have made the devise but for Beneficiary's agreement to hold the property in trust for Victor. Even though the will does not contain the terms of the trust, the court may impose a constructive trust on the property for Victor's benefit.

Part Six

OTHER ESTATE PLANNING CONCERNS

24

Wealth Transfer Taxation

For thousands of years, governments have taxed the transfer of property to raise revenue to fund wars and other government activities as well as to restrict the ability of families to accumulate wealth. Death taxes in some form existed under the laws of ancient Greece, Rome, Egypt, and England. These taxes typically take one of two forms. The first type is the *estate tax,* which is a tax on an individual's privilege of transferring property. This excise tax is usually based on the value of the transferred property and is payable out of the decedent's estate. The second type is the *inheritance tax,* which is an excise tax on an heir's or beneficiary's privilege of receiving a gratuitous transfer of property.

Congress imposed the first transfer tax on United States citizens in 1797 in response to political difficulties with France. This tax was repealed shortly thereafter and it was not until 1862, when additional revenue was needed to fund the Civil War, that Congress enacted another transfer tax. This inheritance tax was repealed in 1870 and over the next forty-six years several transfer taxes were enacted but they had little permanence because either (1) the courts found these taxes to be unconstitutional as a type of *direct tax* prohibited under the Constitution because they were not apportioned among the states according to population, or (2) they were repealed by Congress. In 1916, Congress passed a federal estate tax. The United States Supreme Court decided in 1921 that this tax passed constitutional muster in *New York Trust Co. v. Eisner.*[1] The Court held that the tax was an *indirect tax* because it was levied on a transaction rather than the property itself and thus not subject to the apportionment restriction. Since 1916, a federal estate tax has continuously remained in force.

---

1. 256 U.S. 345 (1921).

Estate planners quickly learned to avoid this estate tax by transferring property while the original owner was still alive. Congress became wise to this ploy and enacted a federal gift tax in 1924. This tax, however, was short-lived; it was repealed in 1926. After realizing the folly of its decision, Congress imposed a revamped gift tax in 1932. Many of the basic characteristics of this legislation can still be seen in our modern gift tax. In 1976, Congress combined the gift tax and the estate tax to create a unified system of wealth transfer taxation.

The federal wealth transfer taxation system is in a constant state of change. Almost every year, Congress tinkers with the Internal Revenue Code making changes that range from the trivial to the far-reaching. Many members of Congress support the repeal of the federal gift and estate tax because they bring in less than 2 percent of the federal revenue. In 1995, only 31,500 citizens left taxable estates, which means that 98.6 percent of deaths had no transfer tax consequences.[2]

This chapter reviews the fundamentals of wealth transfer taxation. The material focuses on basic rules and thus there may be special rules and exceptions that are not mentioned. The discussion is designed to give you a working knowledge of the essential concepts. If you need detailed information on wealth transfer taxation, you should consult a text devoted exclusively to the subject. Examples of such materials are cited in the bibliography at the end of this book.

§24.1 Federal Gift Tax

This section outlines the operation of the federal gift tax beginning with an overview of the basic gift tax computation and continuing with discussions of various aspects of this process.

§24.1.1 Overview

The basic computation of the federal gift tax involves the following steps.

(1) Determine All Gifts Made by Donor. The first step in computing the federal gift tax is to prepare a comprehensive list of all gifts of property the donor has made during the donor's entire lifetime. I.R.C. §2501(a)(1). In addition to listing the transferred property, you should list the date of the gift, the identity of the donee, the relationship between the donor and the donee, and how the gift was used. These matters may be significant later in

---

2. Alissa J. Rubin, *Congressmen say cut in estate tax would aid small businesses, farmers,* Dallas Morning News, Mar. 30. 1997, at 6H.

the computation process. See §24.1.2, below, for a discussion of the types of transfers that must be included in this list.

(2) Value Each Gift. You must next determine the value of each gift on the list prepared in step one. I.R.C. §2502. Generally, the value of a gift is its fair market value on the date the donor made the gift. See §24.1.3, below, for further information on the valuation of gifts.

(3) Subtract Excluded Gifts. Several types of gifts are excluded from the federal gift tax and must now be removed from the list of gifts. The two most important excluded gifts are those that qualify for the *annual exclusion* and the *educational and medical expense exclusion*. I.R.C. §2503. These exclusions are discussed in §24.1.4, below.

(4) Subtract Deductions. Two other types of gifts are also subtracted from the list of gifts: gifts to a spouse, which qualify for the *marital deduction*, and gifts for the public benefit, which qualify for the *charitable deduction*. I.R.C. §§2522 and 2523. Section 24.1.5, below, explains how these deductions operate.

(5) Adjust for Certain Pre-1977 Gifts. If the donor made gifts after September 8, 1976, but before January 1, 1977, an amount computed under I.R.C. §2505(b) is subtracted.

(6) Compute Gift Tax. You may now compute the gift tax by (a) figuring the tentative tax on all taxable gifts the donor has made over the donor's entire life, (b) subtracting the tentative tax on all taxable gifts the donor has made in prior years, and (c) subtracting any unused portion of the *applicable credit amount*. I.R.C. §§2010 and 2502. These steps are detailed in §24.1.6, below.

§24.1.2 Transfers Subject to Gift Tax

Three types of property transfers are subject to the federal gift tax. The first type is the irrevocable gift. This gift may be outright or in trust as long as it is complete. In other words, the donor must not have retained the right to reacquire the asset or change the beneficiary. See §14.1, above, for a discussion of inter vivos gifts. The second type of taxable transfer is one that is for less than adequate and full consideration in money or money's worth. The third type occurs when the holder of a general power of appointment exercises the power in favor of someone other than the holder or the holder's creditors. See §14.5, above, for a discussion of powers of appointment.

Example 24-1. Transfers Subject to Gift Tax—Completed Gifts

Donor gave Donee the following items on Donee's birthday: (1) a new sport utility vehicle that Donor had already titled in Donee's name, (2) Donor's promissory note for $50,000 payable to Donee, and (3) Donor's personal check for $30,000 payable to Donee. Which of these transfers are potentially subject to the federal gift tax?

Explanation

Donor's transfer of the sport utility vehicle is a gift subject to gift tax. Donor had present donative intent, irrevocably delivered the vehicle, and Donee accepted it. However, the transfers of the note and the check are not subject to gift tax because the transfers are still incomplete. The promissory note is merely Donor's promise to make a gift in the future. Donee could not force Donor to pay the $50,000 because Donee did not give consideration for the note. Donor will not be treated as making a taxable gift until Donor actually turns over the money. Likewise, the gift of the check is incomplete because Donor could stop payment on the check or could die prior to Donee cashing the check. The gift of the check would not be complete until the drawee (the bank, savings and loan association, credit union, or other financial institution) pays the check, certifies the check, or Donee negotiates the check for value to a third person. The timing of a gift by check has special significance when we discuss the annual exclusion that permits certain tax-free gifts. See §24.1.4.1, below. If Donor delivered a personal check on December 25, 1999 in an amount qualifying for the annual exclusion and Donee did not cash it until on or after January 1, 2000, the gift would be treated as occurring in 2000 and thus Donor would have lost the opportunity to make a tax-saving gift in 1999.

Example 24-2. Transfers Subject to Gift Tax—Gifts of Services

Assume that you are having difficulty with your Wills, Estates, and Trusts course and ask Friend for assistance. Friend took the course last semester and earned an "A." Friend spends many hours helping you master the material. Has Friend made a gift subject to the federal gift tax to you for the value of Friend's tutoring services?

Explanation

No, the federal gift tax is imposed only on a "transfer of property by gift." I.R.C. §2501(a)(1). Consequently, gifts of services are not within the scope of the gift tax.

Example 24-3. Transfers Subject to Gift Tax — Irrevocable Gifts

Donor created a trust in favor of Donee. Donor transferred a certificate of deposit for $50,000 to the trustee of this trust. Is this transfer subject to the federal gift tax?

Explanation

The answer depends on whether Donor has the right to revoke the trust either under the terms of the trust instrument or state law. If the trust is irrevocable, a completed taxable gift has occurred. However, if the trust is revocable, the gift is incomplete and thus not subject to gift tax.

Example 24-4. Transfers Subject to Gift Tax — Uneven Exchanges

Seller owned two parcels of property appraised for $200,000 each. Seller sold the first parcel to Son for $100,000 and the second parcel to Daughter for $185,000. Are these transfers subject to the federal gift tax?

Explanation

A transfer is not subject to gift tax merely because the consideration the transferor gave is not equal to the consideration received. A taxable gift occurs when the transfer is for less than an adequate and full consideration in money or money's worth. I.R.C. §2512(b). Accordingly, there is little doubt that the transfer to Son is subject to gift tax because of the tremendous difference between the appraised value and the price Son paid. In addition, the family relationship between the parties serves as evidence of Seller's donative intent.

The transfer to Daughter is problematic. Daughter paid less than the property's appraised value but Daughter could argue that Daughter did pay adequate and full consideration because of the facts and circumstances surrounding the transfer. If Stranger, rather than Daughter, had purchased this parcel of land for $185,000 as part of an arm's length transaction, the transfer would have no gift component. Likewise, if Stranger paid $225,000 for the land, Stranger would not be considered as making a gift to Seller merely because Stranger paid more than the appraised value.

Example 24-5. Transfers Subject to Gift Tax — Exercise of Power of Appointment

Parent has the right under a valid trust to appoint $60,000 per year to anyone Parent selects, including Parent. Parent appointed $35,000 to Creditor to pay an existing debt and $15,000 to Son as a birthday present. Parent failed to appoint the remaining $10,000. What are the federal gift tax consequences of these events?

Explanation

Parent has a general power of appointment because Parent has the power to exercise the power in favor of Parent and the power is not limited by an ascertainable standard relating to Parent's health, education, support, or maintenance. I.R.C. §2514(c). Accordingly, Parent is treated for the most part as if Parent actually owns the property subject to the power of appointment. Parent did not make a gift when Parent exercised the power in favor of Creditor. The act of paying an existing debt is not a gift. However, Parent's exercise of the power in favor of Son to provide Son with a nice birthday present was a taxable gift.

Parent's failure to exercise the power of appointment over the remaining $10,000 may be a taxable gift. The failure of the holder of a power of appointment to appoint the property is generally treated as a gift. An exception exists for a lapse that does not exceed the greater of (1) $5,000 or (2) 5 percent of the value of the assets out of which the exercise of the power could be satisfied, which in this case is the corpus of the trust. I.R.C. §2514(e). (Donors who create general powers of appointment often limit the amount the donee can appoint with a *five-or-five power* to prevent lapses from being treated as taxable gifts.) Thus, we need to know the value of the trust corpus to see how much, if any, of the $10,000 is subject to gift tax. If the trust corpus exceeds $200,000, none of the lapsed amount is subject to gift tax ($200,000 × .05 = $10,000). If the trust corpus is between $200,000 and $100,000, a portion of the lapse is taxable. For example, if the trust corpus is worth $160,000, $2,000 is subject to tax ($160,000 × .05 = $8,000; $10,000 − $8,000 = $2,000). If the trust is worth $100,000 or less, tax will be owed only on $5,000 because the first $5,000 of property subject to a lapsed power is not susceptible to gift tax regardless of the value of the trust corpus. Note that Parent can use only one five-or-five exemption per calendar year regardless of the number of powers of appointment Parent may hold.[3]

Example 24-6.   Transfers Subject to Gift Tax — Disclaimed Property

Beneficiary under a will disclaimed $100,000 worth of property. This property then passed under the will to Beneficiary's children. Did Beneficiary make a gift subject to the federal gift tax?

---

3. Rev. Rul. 85-88, 1985-2 C.B. 201.

Explanation

Beneficiary's disclaimer will not trigger gift tax liability provided the disclaimer satisfied the requirements of I.R.C. §2518, such as being in writing, irrevocable, and made within nine months of the testator's death. See §4.4, above.

Example 24-7. Transfers Subject to Gift Tax — Interest-Free Loans

Parent lent Child $500,000 to help Child purchase corporate bonds. Under the terms of the loan, Child was not obligated to make interest payments. What are the federal gift tax consequences of this arrangement?

Explanation

Parent will be treated as making a gift each year of the interest Parent could have earned during that year. In addition, Child will be treated as if Child were paying that interest to Parent and thus Parent must pay income tax on this constructive interest, which Child in reality never paid. I.R.C. §7872.

Example 24-8. Transfers Subject to Gift Tax — Consideration Compared to "Money or Money's Worth"

Parent told Child, "If you quit smoking and don't use any tobacco product for one year, I will give you $20,000 toward the down payment on your house." Child immediately accepted this offer and quit cold turkey. Although suffering from nicotine withdrawal at first, Child never used tobacco again. After one year elapsed, Parent made good on Parent's promise and handed Child $20,000 in cash. What are the gift tax ramifications of this transfer?

Explanation

Parent will be treated as making a gift to Child of $20,000 which is subject to gift tax. The exchange necessary to prevent a transfer from being a gift must be "in money or money's worth." I.R.C. §2512(b). Although Child's forbearance from using tobacco products may be consideration sufficient to support an enforceable contract, it was neither money nor money's worth.

Example 24-9. Transfers Subject to Gift Tax — Use of Property

Uncle owns a secluded cabin in the Montana wilderness. Uncle normally rents the cabin to outdoor adventurers during the summer. This year, however, Uncle decides to let you use the cabin at no charge while you are studying for the bar exam. What are the federal gift tax consequences of this situation?

Explanation

Uncle may be treated as making a gift to you for the value of the forgone rent. If this value when combined with other gifts from Uncle during the year exceeds the annual exclusion (see §24.1.4.1, below), Uncle will be responsible for any gift tax due on this amount. On the other hand, Uncle could argue that this type of use is not actually a gift. In any event, in reality taxpayers like Uncle are highly unlikely to report this transaction and the IRS does not aggressively pursue the gift taxation of this type of transfer.

Example 24-10. Transfers Subject to Gift Tax—Joint Tenancies

Parent purchased a parcel of real property using Parent's money and had title to the land placed in the names of Parent and Child as joint tenants with rights of survivorship. Has Parent made a gift that may be subject to the federal gift tax?

Explanation

Yes, by creating a joint tenancy and supplying the entire purchase price, Parent made a gift to Child of one-half of the value of the property. See §15.2, above, for a discussion of joint tenancies. Thus, Parent is responsible for any gift tax due because of this transfer. If Parent and Child had contributed equally towards the purchase of property, no gift would have occurred.

Example 20-11. Transfers Subject to Gift Tax—Joint Bank Accounts

Parent opened a new checking account with $50,000 and named Child as the joint owner with rights of survivorship. Has Parent made a gift that may be subject to federal gift tax?

Explanation

No, Parent will not be treated as making a gift subject to tax until Child makes a withdrawal from the account that is for Child's own benefit and does not incur any obligation to account to Parent for the withdrawn amount. This rule is different from the rule that applies to a true joint tenancy, as discussed in the previous example, because the opening of the joint account did not immediately transfer any ownership rights to Child. Parent retains control over the money because Parent has the right to withdraw the funds without Child's consent. Instead, Child merely has the right to withdraw funds and consequently Parent has not made a gift until Child actually makes a withdrawal. See §16.1, above, for a discussion of joint bank accounts.

§24.1.3 Valuation of Gifts

The value of a gift is "the price at which such property would change hands between a willing buyer and a willing seller, neither being under any compulsion to buy or to sell, and both having reasonable knowledge of relevant facts." Treas. Reg. §25.2512-1. The following examples demonstrate some of the basic valuation principles. Note that there are sophisticated rules for determining the value of annuities, life estates, terms for years, remainders, reversions, and other similar interests which include the consideration of interest rates and the life expectancies of the donor and donee. The valuation of certain types of property, such as collectibles and fractional interests, is often the subject of litigation between the donor and the IRS.

Example 24-12. Valuation of Gifts — Date of Value Determination

On January 10, 1999, Donor transferred two parcels of real property to Donee. Each of these parcels had a fair market value of $100,000 at the time of the gift. On April 15, 2000, the date the federal gift tax return was due, one parcel had appreciated in value to $250,000 because of its location near a new amusement park. The other parcel depreciated in value to $25,000 because of the discovery of toxic waste on nearby property. What is the value of Donor's gifts for federal gift tax purposes?

Explanation

The amount of a gift for gift tax purposes is the value of the property at the date of the gift. I.R.C. §2512(a). Subsequent changes to the value of the property are irrelevant. Thus, each of Donor's gifts will be valued at $100,000. Accordingly, if minimizing gift tax is the motivating factor behind making a gift, a donor should consider transferring property likely to appreciate in value.

Example 24-13. Valuation of Gifts — Retail vs. Wholesale Price

Donor gave Donee a recreation vehicle as a birthday gift. On the date of the gift, Donee could have purchased a similar RV for $25,000 from a local dealer who sells used RVs to the public. However, an RV dealer could purchase this type of vehicle for the wholesale price of $17,500. What is the value of Donor's gift for federal gift tax purposes?

Explanation

The value of an item of property which is generally obtained by the public in the retail market is the retail price, not the wholesale price or some other price from a market other than that in which RVs are most commonly sold to the public. Treas. Reg. §25.2512-1. Consequently, Donor's gift will be valued at $25,000.

Example 24-14. Valuation of Gifts — Amount Donor Paid

Donor inherited a vacation home in Florida from Donor's parent in 1970. Donor has just transferred the home to Child. Does Donor have to pay gift tax on the value of the home even though Donor did not buy or otherwise give consideration for the home?

Explanation

Yes, the amount of the gift is not based on how much Donor paid for the gifted property. The amount of Donor's gift will be the value of the home on the date of the gift.

Example 24-15. Valuation of Gifts — Stock

Donor gave 1,000 shares of Humongous Corporation (HC) stock to Donee on January 30. When trading for HC stock opened that day, the price per share was $20.00. After a rollercoaster ride during which the price fluctuated between $12.00 and $24.00 per share, HC stock closed at $19.00 per share. What is the value of Donor's gift for federal gift tax purposes?

Explanation

The general rule for valuing stock is to use the average of the highest and lowest quoted selling prices on the date of the gift. Treas. Reg. §25.2512-2(b)(1). The average price on January 30 was $18.00 (($12.00 + $24.00) ÷ 2). Accordingly, Donor's gift is valued at $18,000.

Example 24-16. Valuation of Gifts — Gifts Disguised as Sales

Grandchild purchased a car from Grandparent for $1,000. The car was only one year old and similar cars sold for $20,000 at local car dealerships. Has

Grandparent made a gift for federal gift tax purposes and, if so, in what amount?

Explanation

Grandparent has made a gift because Grandparent transferred the car for less than an adequate and full consideration in money or money's worth. The value of the gift is the amount by which the value of the car exceeded the value of the consideration. I.R.C. §2512(b). Consequently, Grandparent's gift is valued at $19,000.

Example 24-17. Valuation of Gifts — Life Insurance Policies

Insured owned two life insurance policies. Insured paid $500 in premiums for the first policy, a one-year term policy with a face value of $50,000. Insured transferred the policy to Donee immediately after making the premium payment. Insured purchased the second policy many years ago and has paid all the necessary premiums. This policy has a $100,000 face value. Insured also gave this policy to Donee. What is the value of Insured's gifts for federal gift tax purposes?

Explanation

The value of the first policy is $500, the amount of premiums Insured paid. If Insured waited to transfer the policy to Donee until days, weeks, or months after Insured purchased it, the value of the gift would be less than $500 because Donee would not own the policy for the entire year term. The longer the delay, the lower the value of the gift. The value of the second policy would be the amount the insurance company would charge for a single premium policy with the same face value on the life of a person who is the same age as Insured. Treas. Reg. §25.2512-6(a).

§24.1.4 Exclusions

Certain gifts are excluded from the gift tax computation process. These transfers are not treated as gifts even though they otherwise satisfy the definition of a gift. Many taxpayers attempt to structure their gifts to fall within these exclusions to minimize their federal transfer tax burdens.

§24.1.4.1 Annual Exclusion

The first $10,000 in value of present interest gifts to each donee per calendar year are not subject to federal gift tax. I.R.C. §2503(b)(1). There is no upper limit on the total amount a donor may exclude. Likewise, there is no limit on the number of donees who may receive gifts that qualify for the annual exclusion. Accordingly, a donor may transfer a considerable amount of wealth each year without incurring gift tax liability.

Beginning in 1999, the amount of the annual exclusion will be indexed for inflation. I.R.C. §2503(b)(2). However, the amount of the exclusion is rounded to the closest multiple of $1,000 below the indexed amount. For example, if the indexed amount is $10,999, the annual exclusion will remain at $10,000. If the rate of inflation continues to be low, it may be after the year 2000 before the annual exclusion reaches $11,000.

Example 24-18.   Annual Exclusion — Offset

Donor made a total of $50,000 in gifts divided among five donees. Are these gifts excluded from Donor's taxable gifts because of the annual exclusion?

Explanation

Donor's gifts would qualify for the annual exclusion only if Donor gave $10,000 to each of the five donees. Donor cannot offset gifts that are over the annual exclusion amount with the unused exclusion from gifts that are under. Assume that Donor gave $30,000 to one donee and $5,000 to each of the other four donees. In this case, Donor would be subject to tax on $20,000; the four $5,000 gifts are covered by the annual exclusion but Donor can exclude only the first $10,000 of the $30,000 gift.

Example 24-19.   Annual Exclusion — Time between Gifts

Donor gave Donee property valued at $10,000 on December 25, 1999. On January 1, 2000, Donor gave Donee $10,000 in cash. Are these gifts covered by the annual exclusion?

Explanation

Both gifts qualify for the annual exclusion. The exclusion is on a calendar year basis and thus the time between the gifts is irrelevant. As discussed in Example 24-1, a donor who wishes to make a gift near the end of the year must make certain the gift is completed within that calendar year. If a donor makes a gift by using a personal check that is not certified, the donor must be certain that the donee cashes or deposits the check prior to the end of the year.[4] To alleviate these concerns, the donor should make year-end gifts by way of certified or cashier's checks.

---

4. Rev. Rul. 96-56, 1996-2 C.B. 161.

Example 24-20. Annual Exclusion — Future Interests — Generally

Donor owned a parcel of real property. Donor retained a life estate in that property and transferred a remainder interest to Donee. Does the first $10,000 in value of the remainder interest qualify for the annual exclusion?

Explanation

Donor's gift will not qualify for the annual exclusion because the remainder is a future interest in property. Except for the minor's trust discussed in Example 24-22, below, the annual exclusion applies only to present interests in property. A present interest is "[a]n unrestricted right to the immediate use, possession, or enjoyment of property or the income from property." Treas. Reg. 25.2503-3(b). Future interests such as "reversions, remainders, and other interests or estates, whether vested or contingent, and whether or not supported by a particular interest or estate, which are limited to commence in use, possession, or enjoyment at some future date or time" do not qualify for the annual exclusion. Treas. Reg. 25.2503-3(a).

Example 24-21. Annual Exclusion — Future Interests — Gifts in Trust

Settlor funded an irrevocable trust with stock valued at $100,000. The trust instrument requires Trustee to pay all income to Beneficiary at least once a year until Beneficiary reaches age thirty at which time the trust ends and Beneficiary becomes entitled to all remaining trust property. May the value of either of these transfers be reduced by the annual exclusion?

Explanation

Settlor made two transfers. The first transfer was of an income interest. This is a present interest and thus its value may be offset by the annual exclusion. The second transfer was of a remainder interest. A remainder is a future interest and thus not eligible for the annual exclusion.

Example 24-22. Annual Exclusion — Future Interests — Minor's Trust

Donor would like to transfer $10,000 to a trust for the benefit of Child. Child is now twelve years old. May Donor structure the trust or the transfer in such a way as to qualify for the annual exclusion?

Explanation

Except for the value of any income interest, a transfer to a trust does not usually qualify for the annual exclusion because the donee/trust beneficiary does not receive a present interest. The donee does not have an unrestricted right to the immediate use, possession, or enjoyment of the property placed into the trust. I.R.C. §2503(c), however, provides an exception for a special type of arrangement often called a *minor's trust*. If these requirements are met, the transfer will not be treated as a gift of a future interest and thus will qualify for the annual exclusion. These requirements are as follows:

(1) Beneficiary Is under Age Twenty-One. The beneficiary of the trust must be under age twenty-one at the time of the transfer. Note that the term "minor's trust" is somewhat of a misnomer because the beneficiary does not have to be under age eighteen; the beneficiary may also be eighteen, nineteen, or twenty years old. The beneficiary does not need to be related to the donor.

(2) Beneficiary Is Sole Life Beneficiary. The only person who may receive the benefit from any distributions from the trust during the beneficiary's lifetime is the beneficiary. All distributions must be to the beneficiary or for the benefit of the beneficiary. The trustee may, however, have the discretion to determine the amount to be distributed and the donor may limit the purposes for which an expenditure may be made as long as there are no substantial restrictions under the terms of the trust on the trustee's exercise of discretion. Treas. Reg. §25.2503-4(b). For example, the trust could limit distributions to those that the trustee deems necessary for the beneficiary's health, education, and support.

(3) Beneficiary Is Sole Remainder Beneficiary at Age Twenty-One. The beneficiary must have the right to obtain all remaining trust income and principal upon reaching age twenty-one.

(4) Beneficiary Controls Remainder If Beneficiary Dies Before Reaching Twenty-One. If the beneficiary dies before reaching age twenty-one, all remaining principal and income must pass either (1) into the beneficiary's estate, or (2) to the person the beneficiary directed if the trust gave the beneficiary a general power of appointment over the balance of the trust estate.

Example 24-23.   Annual Exclusion — *Crummey* Provisions

Settlor would like to make contributions to trusts for Settlor's children and grandchildren which qualify for the annual exclusion. These trusts are irrevocable and give Trustee total discretion regarding when to make payments and the reasons for which they may be made. Upon the death of any beneficiary, Trustee must distribute the remaining property to the trusts established for the beneficiaries who are still alive. May Settlor structure these contributions to qualify for the annual exclusion?

Explanation

Generally, contributions of this type would not qualify for the annual exclusion. The beneficiaries are not receiving present interests nor do the trusts meet I.R.C. §2503(c) requirements. However, courts have long recognized a clever way of permitting Settlor to structure the trust so that these contributions to the principal of the trust will qualify for the annual exclusion. These trusts are usually referred to as *Crummey trusts*, based on the landmark case of *Crummey v. Commissioner*,[5] which first recognized the effectiveness of this technique. Settlor should give each beneficiary the right to withdraw each year the lesser of (1) the annual exclusion or (2) the value of the assets Settlor contributed during the year. Because each beneficiary has the right to demand this property, the right is a present interest and thus can be offset by the annual exclusion. Settlor, of course, intends that the beneficiary will not exercise this withdrawal power. Courts have permitted the beneficiary to be a young minor who cannot from a practical standpoint exercise the right to demand a distribution. However, if the beneficiary is an adult, courts hold that the beneficiary must be notified of the right to withdraw and be given a reasonable time to exercise the right. In other words, the annual exclusion is not available if the withdrawal right is too narrowly drawn. For example, if the beneficiary may exercise the withdrawal right only on December 30 between 3:14 A.M. and 3:16 A.M. by delivering a notice to the trustee in person at the base of the Statue of Liberty, the right to withdraw will not be sufficient to qualify as present interest for annual exclusion purposes.

As mentioned above, the settlor of a *Crummey* trust intends that the beneficiary will not exercise the withdrawal right. The failure of a beneficiary to exercise the right is treated as the lapse of a general power of appointment and thus may trigger gift tax consequences for the beneficiary. As discussed in Example 24-5, above, amounts that do not exceed the greater of (1) $5,000, or (2) 5 percent of the value of the corpus of the trust are not treated as gifts. Thus, Settlor may wish to limit the beneficiary's withdrawal right to the lesser of (1) the annual exclusion or (2) the greater of $5,000 or 5 percent of the principal's value.

---

5. 397 F.2d 82 (9th Cir. 1968).

§24.1.4.2   Educational and Medical Expense Exclusion

All payments that a donor makes for the donee's educational or medical expenses are not subject to the federal gift tax. I.R.C. §2503(e). There is no limit on the amount of these gifts or on the number of donees. The donor and the donee do not need to be related.

Example 24-24.   Educational and Medical Expense Exclusion — Direct vs. Indirect Payment

Maternal Grandmother (MGM) and Paternal Grandfather (PGF) decide to assist you with your tuition expenses. MGM sends you a check for $20,000. You endorse the check to Law School as partial payment of your tuition. PGF pays for the balance of your tuition by sending his check directly to Law School. Are these gifts eligible for the educational and medical expense exclusion?

Explanation

The educational and medical expense exclusion applies only to gifts that are made directly to an educational organization or a person who provides medical care. Thus, MGM's gift would not qualify because the check was payable to you even though you immediately endorsed the check over to Law School. Likewise, the exclusion would not be available if MGM funded a trust on your behalf and required the trustee to pay your tuition expenses. On the other hand, PGF's check was sent directly to Law School on your behalf and thus would qualify for the exclusion.

Example 24-25.   Educational and Medical Expense Exclusion — Educational Expenses

MGM from Example 24-24 realizes the mistake she made in sending you the tuition check directly. Accordingly, she pays Law School directly for your dorm room and meal contract. MGM also establishes a prepaid account for you at the Law School's bookstore. Are these gifts eligible for the educational and medical expense exclusion?

Explanation

Neither of these gifts qualifies for the educational and medical expense exclusion. The only gifts which qualify are those for tuition; gifts for room, board, and books do not qualify.

Example 24-26.   Medical and Educational Expense Exclusion — Medical Insurance

MGM from Example 24-24 decides to try again to make a gift which qualifies for the medical and educational expense exclusion. This time, she pays all the premiums on your health insurance policy. Will this gift be eligible for the exclusion?

Explanation

Yes, the exclusion applies to all amounts paid for medical insurance even though MGM is not making premium payments directly to someone who provides medical care. Treas. Reg. §25.2503-6(b)(3).

§24.1.5 Deductions

§24.1.5.1 Marital Deduction

Gifts to a donee who is the donor's spouse at the time of the gift are generally deductible and thus are not subject to federal gift tax. I.R.C. §2523. Because there is no restriction on the amount of property the donor may transfer to a spouse in this fashion, this deduction is often called the *unlimited marital deduction*. Gifts of life estates and other terminable interests usually do not qualify for the deduction. In addition, special rules apply if the donor's spouse is not a citizen of the United States. See §24.3, below, for a more detailed discussion of the marital deduction.

§24.1.5.2 Charitable Deduction

An unlimited amount of gifts to qualifying religious, educational, governmental, and other charitable organizations are deductible. I.R.C. §2522. See §24.4, below, for a more detailed discussion of the charitable deduction.

§24.1.6 Computation of Gift Tax

The computation of the federal gift tax begins by determining the total amount of *taxable gifts* the donor has made over the course of the donor's entire lifetime. You compute this amount by totaling the value of all of the donor's gifts (see §§24.1.2 and 24.1.3, above) and then subtracting (1) exclusions (see §24.1.4, above), (2) deductions (see §24.1.5, above), and (3) adjustments for pre-1977 gifts (see §24.1.1(5), above).

§24.1.6.1   Tentative Tax

The next step is to compute a tentative tax on all the taxable gifts which the donor has made by using the rate schedule in I.R.C. §2001(c) as reproduced below. In this step, you are computing a tentative tax as if all of the donor's taxable gifts were made in the current year.

If the amount with respect to which the tentative tax to be computed is:	*The tentative tax is:*
Not over $10,000	18 percent of such amount.
Over $10,000 but not over $20,000	$1,800, plus 20 percent of the excess of such amount over $10,000.
Over $20,000 but not over $40,000	$3,800, plus 22 percent of the excess of such amount over $20,000.
Over $40,000 but not over $60,000	$8,200, plus 24 percent of the excess of such amount over $40,000.
Over $60,000 but not over $80,000	$13,000, plus 26 percent of the excess of such amount over $60,000.
Over $80,000 but not over $100,000	$18,200, plus 28 percent of the excess of such amount over $80,000.
Over $100,000 but not over $150,000	$23,800, plus 30 percent of the excess of such amount over $100,000.
Over $150,000 but not over $250,000	$38,800, plus 32 percent of the excess of such amount over $150,000.
Over $250,000 but not over $500,000	$70,800, plus 34 percent of the excess of such amount over $250,000.
Over $500,000 but not over $750,000	$155,800, plus 37 percent of the excess of such amount over $500,000.
Over $750,000 but not over $1,000,000	$248,300, plus 39 percent of the excess of such amount over $750,000.
Over $1,000,000 but not over $1,250,000	$345,800, plus 41 percent of the excess of such amount over $1,000,000.
Over $1,250,000 but not over $1,500,000	$448,300, plus 43 percent of the excess of such amount over $1,250,000.
Over $1,500,000 but not over $2,000,000	$555,800, plus 45 percent of the excess of such amount over $1,500,000.
Over $2,000,000 but not over $2,500,000	$780,800, plus 49 percent of the excess of such amount over $2,000,000.
Over $2,500,000 but not over $3,000,000	$1,025,800, plus 53 percent of the excess over $2,500,000.
Over $3,000,000	$1,290,800, plus 55 percent of the excess over $3,000,000.

Phaseout of graduated rates and unified credit. — The tentative tax determined under paragraph (1) shall be increased by an amount equal to 5 percent of so much of the amount (with respect to which the tentative tax is to be computed) as exceeds $10,000,000 but does not exceed the amount at which the average tax rate under this section is 55 percent.

The next step in the process is to compute a tentative tax on the taxable gifts the donor made in all prior years. In other words, you now compute a tentative tax as if the donor made all of the donor's prior taxable gifts in the current year but did not make any of the current year's gifts.

You now compute the donor's *tentative tax* for the current year by subtracting the tentative tax on all taxable gifts made in prior years from the tentative tax on all taxable gifts the donor has ever made.

§24.1.6.2 Applicable Credit Amount

To determine the amount of tax the donor owes, you subtract any portion of the donor's *applicable credit amount* that the donor has not already used to offset gift tax liability for prior years from the donor's tentative tax. I.R.C. §§2505 and 2010(c). The applicable credit amount, also called the *unified credit*, is a credit against the tentative tax. The amount of this credit will gradually increase over the next several years. The table below shows the amount of the credit and the *applicable exclusion amount*, that is, the total amount of property a donor may give away, either while alive or upon death, without transfer tax liability.

Year of Donor's Gift or Death	Applicable Credit Amount	Applicable Exclusion Amount
1987-1997	$192,800	$600,000
1998	$202,050	$625,000
1999	$211,300	$650,000
2000 2001	$220,550	$675,000
2002 2003	$229,800	$700,000
2004	$287,300	$850,000
2005	$326,300	$950,000
2006 or later	$345,800	$1,000,000

Example 24-27. Gift Tax Computation

Donor made $500,000 of taxable gifts in 1999. Donor had previously made a total of $700,000 of taxable gifts and had used $192,800 of Donor's gift tax credit to offset Donor's gift tax liability on those gifts. How much federal gift tax does Donor owe for Donor's 1999 gifts?

Explanation

Donor owes $179,500 in federal gift tax computed as follows:

Taxable gifts over Donor's entire life:
$700,000 of previous gifts + $500,000 of gifts in 1999 = $1,200,000

Tentative tax as if all taxable gifts made in 1999:
$345,800 + .41($1,200,000 − $1,000,000)
$345,800 + .41($200,000)
$345,800 + $82,000 = $427,800

Tentative tax as if only taxable gifts made prior to 1999 were made in 1999:
$155,800 + .37($700,000 − $500,000)
$155,800 + .37($200,000)
$155,800 + $74,000 = $229,800

Tentative tax for taxable gifts made in 1999:
$427,800 − $229,800 = $198,000

Unused applicable credit amount:
$211,300 − $192,800 = $18,500

Federal estate tax due:
$198,000 − $18,500 = $179,500

§24.1.7 Split Gifts

Spouses may treat gifts made by one spouse to a third person as if each spouse made one-half of the gift. I.R.C. §2513. This *split gift* technique permits spouses to reduce their gift tax liability by lowering their tax brackets, using two annual exclusions per donee, and offsetting tax liability with two applicable credit amounts. Even if the spouses do not owe gift tax, the donor spouse must file a gift tax return and the nondonor spouse must sign the return and agree to split gifts. The nondonor spouse is usually required to file a separate gift tax return as well.

Example 24-28. Split Gifts — Annual Election

Wife made two large taxable gifts in 1999. The first gift was to Son whose father is Wife's former spouse. The second gift was to Daughter, the only child of Wife and Husband. May Husband agree to use the split gift technique with regard to Wife's gift to Daughter but not for the gift to Son, Husband's stepchild?

Explanation

No, the election to split gifts must be made on an annual basis. If spouses decide to split gifts in any particular year, they must elect to split all gifts to all donees during that year.

Example 24-29. Split Gifts — Community Property

Husband and Wife reside in a community property state. Husband gave $100,000 directly traceable to his earnings during the marriage to Daughter. Must Husband and Wife comply with the split gift procedures?

Explanation

Earnings during marriage are community property. See §1.3.2, above. Each spouse owned $50,000 of the money Husband gave to Daughter. Consequently, gift splitting occurs automatically and Husband and Wife need not take any special steps.

Example 24-30. Split Gifts — Divorce

Husband agreed to split gifts with Wife. After five years of marriage and enough split gifts to exhaust Husband's applicable credit amount, Wife divorced Husband. May Husband regain any of his applicable credit amount, either from the IRS or Wife, by showing that all of the split gifts consisted of Wife's property and all the donees were Wife's children from a prior marriage?

Explanation

Husband is unlikely to have a cause of action. Husband should have considered the ramifications of a possible divorce before consenting to split gifts with Wife. There is an outside chance Husband could show fraud on Wife's part if she has a practice of marrying economically challenged men, splitting gifts until their applicable credit amounts are used up, divorcing them, and then starting the process over again.

§24.1.8 Gift Tax Return

The donor must file any required gift tax return by April 15 of the year after the year in which the donor made the gift. I.R.C. §6075(b). The IRS designates the gift tax return as *Form 709*. In most situations, a donor does not need to file a gift tax return if all gifts are below the annual exclusion amount or are made to a spouse. A donor must file a return for taxable gifts such as making a gift worth more than $10,000 to a nonspouse donee or a gift of a future interest that does not qualify for the marital deduction. The return is needed even if no tax is owed because of the application of the applicable credit amount.

Example 24-31. Gift Tax Return

Megalon Corporation gave $200,000 in 1999 to various individuals and noncharitable organizations. Does Megalon need to file a gift tax return?

Explanation

No, corporations do not make gifts. If a corporation, partnership, trust, or estate makes a gift, the true donors are typically the stockholders, partners, or beneficiaries and they are responsible for filing the gift tax return and paying the appropriate tax.

§24.1.9 *Liability for Gift Tax*

The donor of the gift is primarily liable for paying the gift tax. I.R.C. §2502(c). As the following examples demonstrate, however, there are situations where the donee may be responsible for the gift tax.

Example 24-32. Liability for Gift Tax—Donor Fails to Pay

Donor's federal gift tax liability is $35,000 for gifts made in 1999. Donor has not paid. Are the donees liable for this tax?

Explanation

A donee is personally liable for the gift tax to the extent of the value of the gifts the donee received. I.R.C. §6324(b). The donee cannot escape liability by proving that the donee no longer owns the item or has spent the proceeds of the gift. Although the donee's liability is restricted to the value of the gifts the donee received from the donor, it is not limited to the unpaid gift tax on the donee's particular gift. Instead, the liability is for the entire amount of the unpaid gift tax for that year. Thus, a donee will not avoid liability by showing that the donee's gift was exempt from gift tax because of the annual exclusion or the educational and medical expense exclusion. In addition, the government has a lien on the actual property for ten years from the date of the gift.

Example 24-33. Liability for Gift Tax—Donee Agrees to Pay

Donor wants to give Donee a valuable painting as a birthday present. Donor does not, however, want to pay the gift tax. May Donee agree to pay the tax?

Explanation

A *net gift* occurs when Donee agrees to pay the gift tax as a condition of Donor's gift. A net gift is actually two transactions in one. First, Donor is treated as selling the painting to Donee for the amount of the gift tax Donee will pay. If this amount exceeds Donor's adjusted basis in the painting, Donor will realize a capital gain, which is subject to income tax liability. (See §24.6, below.) Second, Donor is treated as making a gift to Donee of the difference between the painting's fair market value and the amount of gift tax Donee will pay. See Rev. Rul. 75-72, 1975-1 C.B. 310 for the formula Donor would use to determine the amount of tax owed on the net gift.

§24.2 Federal Estate Tax

This section outlines the operation of the federal estate tax beginning with an overview of the basic estate tax computation and continuing with discussions of various aspects of this process.

§24.2.1 Overview

The basic computation of the federal estate tax involves the following steps.

(1) Determine Contents of Gross Estate. The first step in computing the federal estate tax is to determine the property in the decedent's *gross estate*. I.R.C. §§2031-2046. This total may include assets that are not included in the decedent's probate estate. In other words, the federal government taxes many items of property that do not pass to the decedent's heirs or will beneficiaries. See §24.2.2, below, for a review of the types of property that are included in the decedent's gross estate.

(2) Value Gross Estate. A value must then be placed on each item of property in the decedent's gross estate. Generally, this amount is the value of the property at the time of the decedent's death. I.R.C. §2031(a). See §24.2.3, below, for further information on the valuation of the gross estate.

(3) Subtract Deductions. The decedent's *taxable estate* may then be determined by subtracting the marital deduction, the charitable deduction, and deductions for expenses, debts, taxes, and losses during the administration process. I.R.C. §§2053-2055. These deductions are reviewed in §24.2.4, below.

(4) Determine Tax Base. All taxable gifts the decedent made after December 31, 1976 are then added to the taxable estate to determine the *tax base*. I.R.C. §2001. This process is detailed in §24.2.5.1, below.

(5) Compute Estate Tax. You may now compute the estate tax by (a) figuring the tentative tax on the decedent's estate and then (b) subtracting credits and related adjustments such as the applicable credit amount, gift tax payable on lifetime transfers, state death tax credit, and the credit for recently paid estate taxes on the same property. I.R.C. §§2010-2016. These steps are detailed in §§24.2.5.2 and 24.2.5.3, below.

§24.2.2   Contents of Gross Estate

The *gross estate* includes all property, real or personal, tangible or intangible, wherever located to the extent of the decedent's interest at the time of the decedent's death. I.R.C. §§2031 and 2033. The I.R.C. defines the gross estate broadly so it encompasses not only property passing by intestacy or will, but also many nonprobate assets as well as a variety of lifetime transfers.

§24.2.2.1   Probate Assets

Example 24-34.   Contents of Gross Estate — Probate Assets Generally

Decedent died in an automobile accident caused by the negligence of Jim Daniels. Which of the following assets are included in Decedent's gross estate for federal estate tax purposes?

1. Decedent's wedding ring.
2. The contents of Decedent's wallet.
3. Decedent's home and personal property exempt from creditors under state law.
4. Decedent's kangaroo ranch located in Australia.
5. Tax-free municipal bonds owned by Decedent.

6. Property in which Decedent received a life estate under Parent's will.

7. Property over which Decedent has a remainder interest and the life tenant is still alive.

8. Property Decedent would have received because Decedent is named as the primary beneficiary under Child's will. Child is still alive.

9. The corpus of a trust for which Decedent served as the trustee. Friend created this trust for the benefit of Friend's children.

10. Decedent's certificate of deposit with a face value of $50,000.

11. Decedent's shares in Goliath Corporation.

12. Decedent's interest in a family-owned business.

Explanation

1. The ring would be part of the gross estate unless Decedent required the ring to be buried with Decedent and it is actually so buried. The estate tax is a tax on the privilege of transferring an asset upon death; if the ring is buried with Decedent, Decedent would not be exercising the privilege and thus would not be taxed. If Decedent had purchased a burial plot, the same logic prevents the value of the portion of the plot in which Decedent is buried from being part of the gross estate.

2. The money, pictures, and other contents of Decedent's wallet would be part of Decedent's gross estate.

3. Decedent's home and personal property are included in the gross estate. Any protection this property may have under state law is irrelevant.

4. The Australian ranch is part of the gross estate. All of Decedent's property is included in the gross estate regardless of where it is physically located.

5. The municipal bonds are also part of the gross estate. Although the bonds are tax-free from an income tax perspective, they are not excluded from transfer tax liability.

6. Decedent's life estate, which Parent granted to Decedent by will, ended upon Decedent's death and thus there is nothing left to include in Decedent's gross estate.

7. Assuming that the remainder interest is not conditioned on Decedent outliving the life tenant, the remainder interest is part of Decedent's gross estate.

8. The expectancy of Decedent to be the beneficiary of a living

person's will is not a property interest and thus is not part of Decedent's gross estate.

9. None of the corpus of the trust is part of Decedent's gross estate because Decedent only held legal title, not equitable title, to the property.

10. The certificate of deposit is part of Decedent's estate as is any interest accrued prior to Decedent's death.

11. The Goliath stock is part of Decedent's gross estate along with any dividend based on a record date that was before Decedent's death regardless of when the dividend was actually paid.

12. The business interest is normally part of Decedent's gross estate. However, a portion of a family-owned business may be excluded from Decedent's gross estate under I.R.C. §2033A. See §24.2.2.11, below.

Decedent's estate would also include the survival action of Decedent against Jim Daniels for negligence for the pain and suffering Decedent endured while still alive as well as for medical expenses. Rev. Rul. 75-127. Valuation of this asset would be difficult because of the uncertainty of the size of the judgment or settlement for Decedent's pain, suffering, and medical expenses. On the other hand, recoveries of family members under wrongful death statutes for Decedent's premature death are not included in the gross estate. Rev. Rul. 75-126.

Example 24-35. Contents of Gross Estate — Rights of Surviving Spouse

Decedent's will left Decedent's entire estate to Child. Under applicable state law, Spouse has the right to elect against the will and receive 40 percent of Decedent's estate. Will this 40 percent be included in Decedent's gross estate?

Explanation

Yes, Decedent's gross estate includes the value of all of Decedent's property in which Spouse obtains a right by dower, curtesy, or by virtue of a statute that creates an estate for a surviving spouse in lieu of dower or curtesy. I.R.C. §2034. Note that if Decedent lived in a community property state, only Decedent's share of the community property would be included in the gross estate because Spouse would already own half of the community property.

Example 24-36. Contents of Gross Estate—Income in Respect of a Decedent

Decedent performed work for Employer and agreed to accept payment on July 1. Decedent died on May 15. Decedent used the cash method of computing income so that Decedent treated income as earned only when received, not when earned. How will the July 1 payment be treated for income and estate tax purposes?

Explanation

Decedent earned the July 1 payment prior to death (obviously) but was not entitled to receive the payment until after death because of Decedent's agreement with Employer. Decedent used the cash basis to figure income tax and thus the July 1 payment will not show up on Decedent's last income tax return. This situation gives rise to *income in respect of a decedent (I.R.D.)* under I.R.C. §691 because Decedent was not entitled to the income prior to death. The right to this income then becomes part of Decedent's gross estate. Depending on the circumstances, the income itself is taxed either to Decedent's estate or to Decedent's successors in interest (heirs or beneficiaries). The payor of the income tax will get an income tax deduction for the estate tax Decedent's estate incurred because the gross estate included the July 1 payment.

§24.2.2.2 Property Held in Joint Tenancy with Rights of Survivorship

Although property the decedent owned with another person as joint tenants with rights of survivorship passes outside of the probate process, some or all of the property may nonetheless be included in the decedent's gross estate. I.R.C. §2040. Special treatment is not needed for property the decedent held with another as tenants in common because the decedent's undivided interest is in the probate estate as well as the gross estate. For a discussion of the differences between a joint tenancy and a tenancy in common, see §§15.1 and 15.2, above.

§24.2.2.2.1 Non-Spousal Joint Tenant

In determining the amount of joint tenancy property to include in the decedent's gross estate when the joint tenants are not spouses, you begin with the presumption that *all* of the property is included. A lesser amount may be included if there is proof that the survivor originally contributed toward the purchase of the property with the survivor's own funds. In this case, the amount attributable to the survivor will not be in the decedent's gross estate.

Example 24-37. Contents of Gross Estate—Joint Tenancy Property—Non-Spousal Joint Tenant

Decedent owned a vacation home and placed it in the name of "Decedent and Child as joint tenants with rights of survivorship." Upon Decedent's death, how much of this property is in Decedent's gross estate?

Explanation

The entire vacation home is in Decedent's gross estate because the property was held in survivorship form and Child did not contribute any funds toward the purchase of the home.

Example 24-38. Contents of Gross Estate—Joint Tenancy Property—Non-Spousal Joint Tenant—Original Contribution

Decedent and Child purchased a vacation home together. Decedent paid $80,000 and Child paid $20,000. Decedent and Child held the home as joint tenants with rights of survivorship. When Decedent died, the home was worth $200,000. How much of the home is included in Decedent's gross estate?

Explanation

Although the general rule is that the entire value of joint tenancy property is included in a decedent's gross estate, amounts attributable to the survivor's contributions are excluded. Child contributed $20,000, which was 20 percent of the original price. Accordingly, 20 percent of the date of death value of $200,000, or $40,000, is excluded and only $160,000 of the home is actually included in Decedent's gross estate.

Example 24-39. Contents of Gross Estate—Joint Tenancy Property—Non-Spousal Joint Tenant—Source of Original Contribution

Decedent gave Child $10,000 in 1999 as an annual exclusion gift. In 2000, Decedent and Child purchased an asset and held it as joint tenants with rights of survivorship. Decedent contributed $40,000 and Child contributed $10,000. When Decedent died, the asset was still worth its original $50,000 purchase price. How much of this property is in Decedent's gross estate?

Explanation

The key fact needed to resolve this question is the source of Child's $10,000 contribution. To qualify for the original contribution exception to the normal rule of including the entire value of the jointly held property in Decedent's gross estate, Decedent's personal representative must prove that Child's contribution did not come from Decedent. If Decedent's personal representative can show that the $10,000 came from a source other than Decedent, then only $40,000 will be in Decedent's gross estate. However, if Decedent's personal representative cannot prove where the $10,000 came from, it will be presumed that it actually came from Decedent and thus the entire $50,000 would be in Decedent's gross estate.

§24.2.2.2.2 Spouses as Joint Tenants

A special rule applies if the only joint tenants with rights of survivorship are spouses or if the spouses hold the property as tenants by the entirety. One-half of the property is in the decedent's gross estate regardless of the contributions of the spouses; that is, it does not matter whether the survivor contributed none of the funds, all of the funds, or a portion of the funds. In all cases, 50 percent of the value of the jointly held property will be in the decedent's gross estate. As discussed in §24.2.4.1, below, the marital deduction will prevent Decedent's estate from owing estate tax because of this inclusion.

§24.2.2.3 Annuities and Other Death Benefits

Various types of contracts, such as annuities, pension plans, and individual retirement accounts, provide for the payment of proceeds upon the decedent's death. Assuming the decedent had the right to receive the benefits from these arrangements, the value of the death benefits that remain when the decedent dies is part of the gross estate. I.R.C. §2039. However, if the decedent did not have the power to name the beneficiary of the death benefits because they are payable by statute to the decedent's spouse or children, none of these benefits are included in the decedent's gross estate. An example of this type of benefit is Social Security.

Example 24-40.   Contents of Gross Estate — Straight Life Annuity

Decedent purchased a straight life annuity (see §17.2, above). Is any portion of this annuity included in Decedent's gross estate?

Explanation

The provider of the straight life annuity made payments only while Decedent was alive. There is no residual value that the provider will pay to death beneficiaries. Accordingly, there is nothing to include in Decedent's gross estate.

Example 24-41. Contents of Gross Estate — Life Annuity with Term Certain

Decedent purchased a life annuity with a 20-year term certain (see §17.2, above) naming Child as the beneficiary if Decedent should die within the twenty years. Decedent died in year seven. Is any portion of this annuity included in Decedent's gross estate?

Explanation

The present value of the thirteen years of remaining benefits will be part of Decedent's gross estate. The exact computation of this value involves a sophisticated process detailed in the I.R.C. and accompanying Treasury Regulations.

§24.2.2.4   Proceeds of Life Insurance

The gross estate contains the value of life insurance proceeds paid by reason of the decedent's death if either (1) the proceeds are payable to the decedent's estate or personal representative, or (2) the decedent owned any *incidents of ownership* in the policy at the time of the decedent's death. I.R.C. §2042. Examples of incidents of ownership include the right to change the beneficiary, surrender or cancel the policy, assign the policy, use the policy as collateral for a loan, borrow the cash value, or change the method for the payment of the proceeds.

Example 24-42. Contents of Gross Estate — Life Insurance

Decedent was the insured on three life insurance policies, each with a face value of $100,000. Decedent started paying premiums on Policy One in 1980 and named Son as the primary beneficiary. Decedent purchased Policy Two in 1990, named Grandchild as the primary beneficiary, and transferred the entire contract to Grandchild. Daughter bought Policy Three on Decedent's life in 1994 and named Decedent's Spouse as the primary beneficiary and Decedent's estate as the secondary beneficiary. Decedent's spouse died in 1995 and Decedent died in 1999. The proceeds of which of these policies will be included in Decedent's gross estate?

Explanation

Decedent appeared to be the owner of Policy One and to have all incidents of ownership over that policy. Accordingly, all the proceeds of Policy One are in Decedent's gross estate. None of the proceeds of Policy Two are in Decedent's gross estate because Decedent did not retain any of the incidents of ownership over the policy. Instead, Grandchild was the owner of the policy and possessed all of those rights. Decedent did not purchase Policy Three and thus normally the proceeds would not be in Decedent's gross estate. In this case, however, the proceeds are payable to Decedent's estate under the terms of the policy because the primary beneficiary, Decedent's spouse, died first. Thus, all of the proceeds of Policy Three are in Decedent's gross estate. See also Example 24-51, below.

§24.2.2.5 Transfers with Retained Life Estate or Control of Beneficial Interests

The gross estate includes property the decedent transferred during life if the decedent retained (1) a life estate, (2) a right to income for any period that does not end prior to the decedent's death, (3) a right to income for any period not ascertainable without reference to the decedent's death, or (4) the right to designate the recipients of that property or the income therefrom. I.R.C. §2036.

Example 24-43. Contents of Gross Estate — Life Estate

Decedent created an irrevocable trust. Under the terms of the trust, Decedent was entitled to all trust income and upon Decedent's death, the remainder passed to Friend. Is any of the trust property included in Decedent's gross estate?

Explanation

The entire trust corpus is included in Decedent's gross estate because Decedent retained a life interest in the trust income.

Example 24-44. Contents of Gross Estate — Unexpired Income Interest

Decedent created an irrevocable trust. Under the terms of the trust, Decedent was entitled to all trust income for ten years after which the remainder passed to Friend. Decedent died in year four. Is any of the trust property included in Decedent's gross estate?

Explanation

The entire corpus of the trust is in Decedent's gross estate because Decedent's retained right to income did not end prior to Decedent's death.

Example 24-45. Contents of Gross Estate—Income Interest Not Ascertainable without Reference to Decedent's Life

Decedent created an irrevocable trust. Under the terms of the trust, Decedent was entitled to all trust income for the year if Decedent was alive on December 31. Upon Decedent's death, Friend received all undistributed income and the corpus. Is any of the trust property included in Decedent's gross estate?

Explanation

The entire trust corpus is in Decedent's gross estate because the duration of Decedent's retained interest could not be ascertained without reference to Decedent's death.

Example 24-46. Contents of Gross Estate—Control of Beneficial Interests

Decedent created an irrevocable trust for Children naming Bank as Trustee. Decedent retained the right to determine which of Decedent's children receive distributions and the amount thereof. Is any of the trust property included in Decedent's gross estate?

Explanation

The entire trust corpus is included in Decedent's gross estate because Decedent had the right to designate the recipients of the income from the property.

§24.2.2.6 Revocable Transfers

If the decedent had the ability to alter, amend, revoke, or terminate a transfer, then that property is included in the decedent's gross estate. I.R.C. §2038. The property is also included if the decedent had one or more of the prohibited powers and relinquished it within three years of the decedent's death.

Example 24-47. Contents of Gross Estate—Revocable Trust

Settlor created a revocable trust for Friend. Is any of the trust property included in Decedent's gross estate?

Explanation

The entire trust corpus is in Decedent's gross estate because Decedent had the right to revoke the trust.

Example 24-48. Contents of Gross Estate—Power to Change Trust Beneficiary

Settlor created an irrevocable trust for Friend. Settlor retained the right to remove Friend as beneficiary and to substitute Grandchild. Is any of the trust property included in Decedent's gross estate?

Explanation

The entire trust corpus is in Decedent's gross estate because Decedent retained the right to alter the trust. It is irrelevant that this alteration may not occur and that it would not benefit Decedent personally.

Example 24-49. Contents of Gross Estate—Relinquishing Revocation Power

Decedent created a revocable trust in 1995 for the benefit of Friend. In 1999, Decedent amended the trust to eliminate all of Decedent's authority to alter, amend, revoke, or terminate the trust. Is any of the trust property included in Decedent's estate?

Explanation

The resolution of this example depends on the date of Decedent's death. If Decedent dies within three years after the 1999 trust amendment, the entire trust corpus will be part of Decedent's gross estate. However, if Decedent lives more than the requisite three years, none of the trust property will be in the gross estate.

§24.2.2.7 Transfers with Retained Reversionary Interest

Property the decedent transferred during life may be part of the gross estate if the decedent retained a reversionary interest. The property is included only if (1) the donee must survive the decedent to receive the property, *and* (2) the decedent retained a reversionary interest that exceeds 5 percent of the value of the transferred property. I.R.C. §2037. This section rarely results in property being included in a decedent's gross estate because trusts and other instruments usually contain a sufficient number of alternate beneficiaries so the property does not revert to the decedent's estate.

§24.2.2.8   Certain Transfers within Three Years of Death

Certain transfers the decedent made within a relatively short time prior to the decedent's death are included in the gross estate. I.R.C. §2035. Examples of these types of transfers include (1) gifts of life insurance policies and similar assets that have the potential of being far more valuable when the decedent dies than when the decedent gave them away, if the gift occurred within three years of death, and (2) gift tax paid on gifts that the decedent made within three years of death.

Example 24-50.   Contents of Gross Estate — Gift of Land within Three Years of Death

Decedent gave Child a parcel of land worth $300,000 two weeks before Decedent's death. Is the land part of Decedent's gross estate?

Explanation

Decedent owned no interest in the land at the time of Decedent's death and thus the land is not part of Decedent's gross estate even though the transfer occurred within a very short period before Decedent died. A different rule formerly applied. If Decedent had died prior to 1982, the land would have been part of Decedent's gross estate merely because the gift was made within three years of Decedent's death.

Example 24-51.   Contents of Gross Estate — Gift of Life Insurance within Three Years of Death

Decedent owned a life insurance policy on Decedent's life with a face value of $100,000. On January 10, 1998, Decedent gave Child this policy. Decedent died on April 1, 2000. Are the proceeds of this policy included in Decedent's gross estate?

Explanation

All of the proceeds are part of Decedent's gross estate. Even though Decedent had no incidents of ownership in the policy at the time of death, Decedent transferred the policy within three years of death and thus it is included. The amount of proceeds in the gross estate is not reduced by the annual gift tax exclusion.

Example 24-52. Contents of Gross Estate—Gift Tax Paid on Gifts Made within Three Years of Death

Decedent was diagnosed with a serious illness and knew that Decedent's death was likely to occur within the next several years. Decedent started to make taxable gifts and pay the applicable gift tax. Decedent figured that the money used to pay the tax would escape both the gift and estate tax. Otherwise, if Decedent made the gifts by will and waited for the personal representative to pay the tax, Decedent's estate would pay estate tax on the money used to pay the estate tax. Will Decedent's ploy work?

Explanation

Decedent's strategy will work only if Decedent lives at least three years after making the gift. If Decedent dies within the three-year period, the amount of the gift tax paid on these gifts is added to the gross estate and thus subject to the estate tax.

§24.2.2.9 Powers of Appointment

The property subject to a general power of appointment that the decedent had at the time of the decedent's death is included in the gross estate. I.R.C. §2041. The property is included regardless of whether the decedent exercised the power by will or failed to exercise the power. A general power of appointment is one that the decedent could exercise in favor of the decedent, the decedent's estate, the decedent's creditors, or the creditors of the decedent's estate. If, however, the decedent's power was limited to an *ascertainable standard* relating to the decedent's health, education, support, or maintenance, the power is not general, and thus the property subject to the power would not be part of the decedent's gross estate. This type of restriction is often referred to as a *HEMS* standard, an acronym for *h*ealth, *e*ducation, *m*aintenance, and *s*upport.

Example 24-53. Contents of Gross Estate—Powers of Appointment

Decedent had four powers of appointment at the time of Decedent's death.

1. Power One: Decedent was the trustee of a discretionary trust created by Friend for the benefit of Friend's children.
2. Power Two: Decedent held a general power of appointment that

Decedent validly exercised by naming Child as the appointee in Decedent's will.

3. Power Three: Decedent held a power of appointment that stated Decedent could appoint the property but only for Decedent's "health, education, support, and maintenance."

4. Power Four: Decedent held a power of appointment that stated Decedent could appoint the property but only for Decedent's "health, education, support, maintenance, comfort, and general happiness."

Is the property subject to these powers of appointment part of Decedent's gross estate?

Explanation

1. Power One: Decedent did not have a general power of appointment over the trust property. Instead, the power was limited to Friend's children. Thus, none of the property is in Decedent's gross estate.

2. Power Two: Decedent had a general power of appointment and thus the property subject to the power is part of Decedent's gross estate.

3. Power Three: Decedent's power is not considered a general power of appointment because the exercise of the power is limited to an ascertainable standard. Accordingly, the property subject to the power is not in Decedent's gross estate.

4. Power Four: Decedent's power is a general power of appointment and thus the property subject to the power is part of Decedent's gross estate. The "comfort and general happiness" language of the power is too vague to qualify as an ascertainable standard, and consequently the exception to includibility does not apply.

§24.2.2.10   Q-TIP Property

A spouse may make unlimited tax free transfers to the other spouse, both during life and at death. However, the transfers must meet the requirements of I.R.C. §2056 (estate tax) or §2523 (gift tax) to qualify for this favorable treatment. One of these requirements is that the surviving spouse cannot receive a terminable interest, that is, an interest the surviving spouse could lose because of a lapse of time or the occurrence or nonoccurrence of some event. Examples of terminable interests include life estates and gifts that end upon remarriage. Terminable interests do not normally qualify for the marital deduction because the property may not be in the surviving spouse's gross estate and thus the property could escape transfer taxation for a second time.

There is an extremely important exception to this rule for *qualified terminable interest property (Q-TIP)*. The deceased spouse can construct a trust to provide lifetime benefits for the surviving spouse, require the remaining corpus to be paid to whomever the deceased spouse desires, and still permit the deceased spouse's estate to claim the marital deduction for this property. To prevent the property from again escaping transfer tax liability, Q-TIP property that remains upon the surviving spouse's death is part of the surviving spouse's gross estate despite the fact that the surviving spouse may have no control over the corpus nor any power to direct its distribution. I.R.C. §2044. Section 24.3, below, discusses the marital deduction and Q-TIP arrangements in more detail.

Example 24-54. Contents of Gross Estate—Q-TIP Property

Husband's will provided that property valued at $300,000 was to be placed in trust with all the income payable to Wife annually. Upon Wife's death, the corpus of the trust was to be distributed to Husband's children from other partners. Husband's estate elected to take the marital deduction treating the entire $300,000 as Q-TIP property. Wife has just died and the value of the trust property is $1,000,000. How much of the trust property is included in Wife's gross estate?

Explanation

Wife's gross estate will include the trust property at its date of death value of $1,000,000. The personal representative is entitled to charge this property with the estate tax triggered by the inclusion of the property in Wife's gross estate at the highest marginal rate. This prevents the beneficiaries of the surviving spouse's estate from shouldering the burden of the taxes on the Q-TIP property.

§24.2.2.11 Family-Owned Business Exclusion

A portion of the value of certain family-owned businesses may be excludable from the decedent's gross estate. See I.R.C. §2033A. The requirements to qualify for this exclusion are exceedingly complex. For example, the business must pass to specified close family members, the value of the business interest must exceed 50 percent of the decedent's adjusted gross estate, and the decedent or members of the decedent's family must have materially participated in the business for at least five of the eight years before the decedent's death. If the heirs fail to materially participate for a sufficiently long enough period of time following the decedent's death, the heirs are subject to a recapture tax. Despite the complexity, the exclusion can save the estate over $100,000 in estate taxes.

§24.2.3 *Valuation of Gross Estate*

§24.2.3.1 General Principles

Property in the gross estate is normally valued as of the date of the decedent's death. I.R.C. §2031. (But see §24.2.3.4, below.) The value of the asset when the estate tax return is due, when the tax is actually paid, or when the property is distributed to the beneficiaries or heirs is irrelevant. The principles discussed in §24.1.3, above, regarding the valuation of gifts are, for the most part, also applicable to valuing the gross estate.

Example 24-55. Valuation of Gross Estate — Specificity of Inventory

Assume that you are in the process of inventorying the items in Decedent's gross estate so you can assign a value and compute the federal estate tax. As you look around Decedent's home, you see shelves full of books, drawers stuffed with dishes, closets brimming with clothes, and knick-knacks everywhere. Must you list each item individually along with its value?

Explanation

Treas. Reg. §20.2031-6(a) provides that

> [a] room by room itemization of household and personal effects is desirable. All the articles should be named specifically, except that a number of articles contained in the same room, none of which has a value in excess of $100, may be grouped. . . . In lieu of an itemized list, the executor may furnish a written statement, containing a declaration that it is made under penalties of perjury, setting forth the aggregate value as appraised by a competent appraiser or appraisers of recognized standing and ability, or by a dealer or dealers in the class of personalty involved.

Treas. Reg. §20.2031-6(b) also provides that the appraisal of an expert under oath is necessary if the gross estate contains items having an artistic or intrinsic value exceeding $3,000 each, such as "jewelry, furs, silverware, paintings, etchings, engravings, antiques, books, statuary, vases, oriental rugs, [or] coin or stamp collections."

§24.2.3.2 Discounts

Certain types of property may be valued at less than the amount that would at first glance seem appropriate. A *fractional interest discount* may be available if the value of owning a certain portion of the property is less than that portion of the item's value. For example, the value of an undivided one-half interest in a parcel of real property worth $200,000 may be less than $100,000 because a buyer may not want to be a tenant in common with another person, especially if the property cannot easily be partitioned. A *marketability discount* may be appropriate for assets that are hard to sell because very few people would be willing to purchase the asset. In one case, the Tax Court allowed a 35 percent discount for shares of stock in a corporation because the stock was not listed on an exchange and could not be valued using traditional means.[6] A *blockage discount* may apply to the sale of stock if the decedent's estate contains a large number of shares so that liquidating the stock within a reasonable time would lower the stock's market price.

§24.2.3.3 Special Use Valuation

Real property used for farming and closely held business real property that passes to a member of the decedent's family may qualify for *special use valuation* under I.R.C. §2032A. If the complex requirements of this section are satisfied, the property may be valued as it is actually being used instead of at its market value. The reduction in value in a decedent's estate because of the special use valuation is, however, limited to $750,000, regardless of the number of properties involved. (Beginning in 1999, this amount will be adjusted for inflation.)

For example, assume that Grandparent owned and operated a farm that had been in the family for several generations. Grandparent's will left the farm to Grandchild along with the rest of Grandparent's estate valued at $100,000. Because the farm is located on the outskirts of a rapidly growing city, the fair market value of the land is $1,000,000. However, as a farm, the property is only worth $500,000. If Grandchild plans to continue operating the farm, this property may be valued at $500,000 (the $500,000 reduction in value is below the $750,000 maximum). The policy supporting the ability to value the property at below its market value is to reduce the likelihood that the decedent's personal representative will have to sell the property to pay the estate taxes and thereby disrupt or destroy a family farm or business merely because the real property used in connection with the farm or business has appreciated in value.

§24.2.3.4 Alternate Valuation Date

Normally, the property in the gross estate is valued as of the date of the decedent's death. The personal representative may, however, elect to value the property at the *alternate valuation date,* which is the date six months

---

6. Jung v. Commissioner, 101 T.C. 412 (1993).

after decedent's death. This option is available if doing so would reduce both (1) the value of the gross estate and (2) the amount of estate tax. I.R.C. §2032. This dual requirement prevents the personal representative from increasing the income tax basis of appreciating assets, and thus reducing the amount of capital gains tax imposed when the heirs or beneficiaries sell the assets, in cases where there is no estate tax liability because of, for example, the applicable credit amount or the marital deduction. If the personal representative elects to use the alternate valuation date, it must be used for all estate assets; the personal representative cannot value some assets using the date of death value and others using the value six months later.

The personal representative must study the overall tax ramifications of valuing property at the alternate date. From an estate tax perspective, a lower value is better because it reduces the estate tax. The beneficiaries and heirs, however, prefer a higher value so that the carry over basis is greater resulting in less capital gains tax when they sell the asset. Because the income tax rates on capital gains are generally lower than the estate tax rates, the personal representative usually elects the alternate valuation date if it would reduce the estate tax. See §24.6, below, for a more detailed discussion of income tax issues.

§24.2.4 Deductions

§24.2.4.1 Marital Deduction

Property passing to the donor's spouse generally is deductible and thus not subject to federal estate tax. I.R.C. §2056. Because there is no restriction on the amount of property which the decedent may transfer to a spouse in this fashion, this deduction is often called the *unlimited marital deduction*. Gifts of life estates and other terminable interests usually do not qualify for the deduction. In addition, special rules apply if the donor's spouse is not a citizen of the United States. See §24.3, below, for a more detailed discussion of the marital deduction.

§24.2.4.2 Charitable Deduction

An unlimited amount of testamentary gifts to qualifying religious, educational, governmental, and other charitable organizations are deductible. I.R.C. §2055. See §24.4, below, for a more detailed discussion of the charitable deduction.

§24.2.4.3 Deduction for Expenses, Debts, and Taxes

Funeral expenses, administration expenses, debts, and taxes are deductible from the gross estate. I.R.C. §2053. The personal representative may have the option of deducting some administration expenses from the decedent's estate income tax return instead. I.R.C. §642. The personal representative will determine which use of these expenses will be most beneficial based on the facts of the situation.

Example 24-56. Deduction for Expenses, Debts, and Taxes

During the administration of Decedent's estate, Personal Representative made the payments listed below. Which of them may Personal Representative deduct from the gross estate?

1. Personal Representative's compensation for services rendered.
2. Legal expenses such as attorney's fees and court costs.
3. Fees charged by appraisers and accountants.
4. Expenses incurred to sell estate property to pay debts and taxes.
5. Utility bills, such as electricity, cable TV, water, telephone, and gas.
6. Balances on credit cards.
7. Taxes, such as local property taxes, unpaid gift tax, income tax on pre-death income, state estate taxes, and the federal estate tax.
8. Principal and interest due on collateralized transactions such as real estate mortgages and security interests in personal property under Article 9 of the Uniform Commercial Code.

Explanation

1. Compensation actually paid to Personal Representative is deductible.
2. Legal expenses are deductible.
3. Fees charged by appraisers and accountants are deductible.
4. Expenses incurred to raise money to pay debts and taxes are deductible.
5. Expenses for utilities that accrued prior to Decedent's death are deductible.
6. Credit card principal and interest owed as of the date of Decedent's death are deductible.
7. The property taxes are deductible as are the federal gift and income taxes owed on pre-death gifts and income. However, both the state and federal estate tax are not deductible. See §24.2.5.3.3, below, for a discussion of the state death tax credit.
8. Assuming the full value of the property is included in the gross estate, the principal as well as the interest accrued as of the date of Decedent's death are deductible.

§24.2.4.4 Deduction for Losses

Losses caused by fires, storms, shipwrecks, or other casualties as well as theft losses are deductible from the gross estate if they are incurred during the settlement of the estate. This deduction is, however, not available if insurance compensates for the losses. I.R.C. §2054. The personal representative may have the option of deducting some losses from the decedent's estate income tax return instead. I.R.C. §642. The personal representative will determine which use of the losses will be most beneficial based on the facts of the situation.

Example 24-57. Deduction for Losses

Personal Representative (PR) was besieged with bad luck while PR was administering Decedent's estate. First, a tornado destroyed Decedent's house. The house was worth $250,000 at the date of Decedent's death but the insurance was only for $200,000. Second, shortly after Decedent delivered a coin collection to Beneficiary, Thief broke into Beneficiary's home and stole the collection. Third, the stock market took a dive and stock worth $100,000 when Decedent died is now worth $5,000. Which of these losses may PR deduct from Decedent's gross estate?

Explanation

PR can deduct $50,000 for the destroyed house. PR cannot deduct the $200,000 covered by insurance. The loss of the coin collection is not deductible because the loss occurred after PR distributed the asset to Beneficiary. Only casualty types of losses are deductible and thus the loss in value of the stock due to market conditions is not deductible. PR may want to consider using the alternate valuation date. See §24.2.3.4, above.

§24.2.5 Computation of Estate Tax

The computation of the federal estate tax begins by determining the *taxable estate*. The taxable estate is the value of the gross estate (§§24.2.2 and 24.2.3, above) reduced by the estate tax deductions (§24.2.4, above).

§24.2.5.1 Tax Base

You must next determine the *tax base* by adding to the taxable estate all taxable gifts (except those already in the gross estate) the decedent made on or after January 1, 1977 at their date of gift values. Only taxable gifts are included in the tax base so gifts covered by the annual exclusion, medical and educational expense exclusion, marital deduction, and charitable deduction are not thrown back into the tax base. The reason the decedent's inter vivos gifts are added to the tax base is to determine the total amount of taxable gratuitous transfers the decedent has ever made. In effect, gift tax payments are nothing more than "estimated payments" of the estate tax.

§24.2.5.2 Tentative Tax

The next step is to compute a tentative tax on the tax base by using the rate schedule in I.R.C. §2001(c) as reproduced in §24.1.6.1, above.

§24.2.5.3 Estate Tax Credits and Related Adjustments

From the tentative tax, you now subtract various estate tax credits and related adjustments as delineated in this section. The sum remaining is the amount of federal estate tax due to the government.

§24.2.5.3.1 Adjustment for Gift Taxes

The gift tax payable on the decedent's inter vivos taxable gifts made after December 31, 1976 is subtracted from the tentative tax. I.R.C. §2001(b)(2). This amount is *not* necessarily the actual amount of gift tax the decedent paid on the inter vivos gifts. Instead, it is the amount of tax the decedent would have paid if the tax were computed by using the rate schedule in effect at the time of the decedent's death, rather than when the gift was made. In doing this calculation, the amount subtracted as the unused unified credit is, however, still based on the credit which was in effect for the year in which the gift was made. Consequently, you must do "mini" gift tax calculations for each year in which the decedent made taxable gifts and then add the results together to determine the total transfer taxes payable. This amount is then subtracted from the tentative tax.

If the decedent made taxable gifts before January 1, 1977, the estate receives a credit for any gift tax the decedent actually paid on those gifts if the gifted property is included in the decedent's gross estate. I.R.C. §2012.

§24.2.5.3.2 Applicable Credit Amount

The tentative tax is reduced by the *applicable credit amount*. I.R.C. §2010(c). The applicable credit amount, also called the *unified credit*, is gradually increasing. The table in §24.1.6.2, above, shows the amount of the credit and the *applicable exclusion amount*, that is, the total amount of property which an individual may give away, either while alive or upon death, without transfer tax liability. This estate tax credit is available even if the decedent exhausted it while making lifetime transfers because those transfers were added back to the gross estate to ascertain the tax base. See §24.2.5.1, above.

§24.2.5.3.3 State Death Tax Credit

The smaller of (1) the actual amount of state death tax paid, or (2) the amount computed according to the tax credit table is subtracted from the tentative tax, provided that the credit does not exceed the tentative tax reduced by the applicable credit amount. I.R.C. §2011. This table is reproduced below.

If the adjusted taxable estate* is:	The maximum tax credit shall be:
Not over $90,000	8/10ths of 1 percent of the amount by which the adjusted taxable estate exceeds $40,000.
Over $90,000 but not over $140,000	$400 plus 1.6 percent of the excess over $90,000.
Over $140,000 but not over $240,000	$1,200 plus 2.4 percent of the excess over $140,000.
Over $240,000 but not over $440,000	$3,600 plus 3.2 percent of the excess over $240,000.
Over $440,000 but not over $640,000	$10,000 plus 4 percent of the excess over $440,000.
Over $640,000 but not over $840,000	$18,000 plus 4.8 percent of the excess over $640,000.
Over $840,000 but not over $1,040,000	$27,600 plus 5.6 percent of the excess over $840,000.
Over $1,040,000 but not over $1,540,000	$38,800 plus 6.4 percent of the excess over $1,040,000.
Over $1,540,000 but not over $2,040,000	$70,800 plus 7.2 percent of the excess over $1,540,000.
Over $2,040,000 but not over $2,540,000	$106,800 plus 8 percent of the excess over $2,040,000.
Over $2,540,000 but not over $3,040,000	$146,800 plus 8.8 percent of the excess over $2,540,000.
Over $3,040,000 but not over $3,540,000	$190,800 plus 9.6 percent of the excess over $3,040,000.
Over $3,540,000 but not over $4,040,000	$238,800 plus 10.4 percent of the excess over $3,540,000.
Over $4,040,000 but not over $5,040,000	$290,800 plus 11.2 percent of the excess over $4,040,000.
Over $5,040,000 but not over $6,040,000	$402,800 plus 12 percent of the excess over $5,040,000.
Over $6,040,000 but not over $7,040,000	$522,800 plus 12.8 percent of the excess over $6,040,000.
Over $7,040,000 but not over $8,040,000	$650,800 plus 13.6 percent of the excess over $7,040,000.
Over $8,040,000 but not over $9,040,000	$786,800 plus 14.4 percent of the excess over $8,040,000.
Over $9,040,000 but not over $10,040,000	$930,800 plus 15.2 percent of the excess over $9,040,000.
Over $10,040,000	$1,082,800 plus 16 percent of the excess over $10,040,000.

* For purposes of this section, the term "adjusted taxable estate" means the taxable estate reduced by $60,000.

Example 24-58. State Death Tax Credit

Decedent died leaving a taxable estate of $1,000,000. Personal Representative (PR) has already paid $50,000 in state death taxes. How large a credit may PR claim for these death taxes on the federal estate tax return?

Explanation

PR can claim the smaller of $50,000 or the amount computed by using the state death tax credit table. To use the table, you must first compute the *adjusted taxable estate*. This term refers to the taxable estate (gross estate minus deductions) less $60,000. Thus, the adjusted taxable estate is $940,000. Using the table, the maximum credit is $33,200 as shown below:

$$\$27,600 + .056(\$940,000-\$840,000)$$
$$\$27,600 + .056(\$100,000)$$
$$\$27,600 + \$5,600 = \$33,200$$

Because the amount computed using the table is smaller than the actual amount of state estate taxes PR paid, the credit is limited to the table amount. See §24.7.2, below, for a discussion of the interrelationship between state estate taxes and the federal estate tax which exists in many states.

§24.2.5.3.4 Previously Taxed Property Credit

An estate tax credit exists if property that is taxed in the decedent's estate has recently been taxed in another decedent's estate. I.R.C. §2013. For example, assume that in March, Pat died, leaving Pat's entire estate to Chris. Chris died in August, leaving Chris's entire estate, which now includes all of Pat's property, to Kim. Chris's estate will be entitled to a credit for a portion of the estate tax Pat's estate recently paid.

The computation of the credit involves a complex two-step process. First, you must determine the maximum allowable credit, which is the smaller of (1) the amount of estate tax that was attributable to the property because the property was included in the first-to-die's estate (Pat), and (2) the amount of estate tax that would be attributable to the property because it is included in the second-to-die's estate (Chris). Second, you ascertain the percentage of this maximum allowable credit, which is available to the second-to-die's estate based on how long the second-to-die (Chris) outlived the first-to-die (Pat). During the first two years, the entire amount is usable as a credit. The credit decreases by 20 percent over each subsequent two-year period and thus the credit is not available after ten years.

§24.2.5.3.5 Other Estate Tax Credits

Other estate tax credits may be available, such as the credit for foreign death taxes under I.R.C. §2014 and for death taxes on remainders under I.R.C. §2015. The details of these credits are beyond the scope of this chapter.

§24.2.6 Estate Tax Return

The estate tax return must be filed and the estate tax paid within nine months of the decedent's death. I.R.C. §§6075(a) and 6151. For reasonable cause, the I.R.S. may grant a six-month extension for the filing of the return and under certain circumstances up to ten years of extensions for the payment of the estate tax. However, the estate must pay interest on any unpaid tax liability during the extension periods. The I.R.S. designates the estate tax return as *Form 706*. In most situations, no return is needed if the decedent's gross estate combined with inter vivos taxable gifts does not exceed the applicable exclusion amount.

§24.2.7 Liability for Estate Tax

The personal representative of the decedent's estate is obligated to pay the federal estate tax. I.R.C. §2002. If the court has not appointed a personal representative, "any person in actual or constructive possession of any property of the decedent is required to pay the entire tax to the extent of the value of the property in [the person's] possession." Treas. Reg. §20.2002-1.

The personal representative needs to determine which items of the decedent's property are to be used to pay the estate tax. Issues regarding tax apportionment are addressed in §6.7, above.

§24.3 Marital Deduction and Bypass Planning

Prior to 1948, there was no deduction for inter vivos or at-death gifts to a surviving spouse. From 1948 to 1976, the marital deduction was limited to one-half of the adjusted gross estate. The computation was changed in 1976 so that at least the first $250,000 of gifts to a surviving spouse could be totally deducted — the martial deduction was the greater of $250,000 or one-half of the adjusted gross estate. Congress enacted the unlimited marital deduction in 1981, which applies equally to inter vivos gifts and at death transfers. I.R.C. §§2056 and 2523.

Not all gifts to a surviving spouse qualify for the marital deduction. Generally, the transfer cannot be of a *terminable interest,* that is, an interest that may end or fail because of a lapse of time or the occurrence/nonoccurrence of an event. Thus, interests such as life estates or conditional gifts ending upon remarriage do not qualify for the marital deduction. The government exacts a "price" for granting the deceased spouse's estate an unlimited deduction for gifts to the surviving spouse—any remaining property from the estate of the first spouse to die must be included in the surviving spouse's gross estate. This section reviews the different types of transfers that qualify for marital deduction treatment as well as reasons a married couple may not want to take full advantage of the deduction.

§24.3.1 Transfers Qualifying for the Marital Deduction

A transfer must meet six basic requirements to qualify for the marital deduction. First, the deceased spouse must have been a United States citizen or resident at the time of death. Second, the deceased spouse must actually be survived by a surviving spouse. Third, the surviving spouse must be a citizen of the United States (see §24.3.1.5, below, for an exception to this requirement). Fourth, the deceased spouse's gross estate must include the property. Fifth, the interest must pass from the deceased spouse to the surviving spouse such as by will, through intestacy, or via a nonprobate transfer (e.g., survivorship rights or as the named beneficiary on a life insurance policy or other contract). Sixth, the interest cannot be a nondeductible terminable interest.

§24.3.1.1 Outright Gifts

The most common and straightforward technique to qualify a gift to a spouse for the marital deduction is the basic outright gift. An outright gift is easy for the attorney to draft and simple for the spouses to understand. The surviving spouse has maximum flexibility because there are no restrictions on the use of the transferred property. A spouse, however, may want to impose restrictions on how the surviving spouse uses the property or the surviving spouse may lack the skills necessary to prudently manage the property. Thus, a spouse may want to consider one of the more restrictive techniques discussed in the following sections.

Example 24-59. Marital Deduction—Outright Gift—Survival

Deceased Spouse's will left the entire estate to Surviving Spouse if Surviving Spouse outlives Deceased Spouse by ninety days. Does this outright gift qualify for the marital deduction even though there is a survival condition?

Explanation

An outright gift conditioned on a survival period that is no longer than six months does not violate the terminable interest rule. I.R.C. §2056(b)(3). Thus, this gift, which has only a ninety-day survival requirement, will qualify for the marital deduction.

§24.3.1.2 Qualified Terminable Interest Property Trust

The first spouse to die can impose the greatest number of restrictions on the surviving spouse's use of property that qualifies for the marital deduction by creating a *qualified terminable interest property trust*, often referred to as a *Q-TIP trust*. I.R.C. §2056(b)(7). Property transferred to a Q-TIP trust qualifies for the marital deduction even though the interest is terminable; that is, the interest may end upon the surviving spouse's death and pass under the terms of the trust, rather than through the surviving spouse's probate estate or according to the surviving spouse's directions. Any property remaining in a Q-TIP trust is included in the surviving spouse's gross estate. See §24.2.2.10, above. The surviving spouse's personal representative may charge this property with the estate tax triggered by the inclusion of the property in the surviving spouse's gross estate at the highest marginal rate applicable to the estate. This prevents the beneficiaries of the surviving spouse's estate from shouldering the burden of the taxes on the property in a Q-TIP trust.

Q-TIP trusts are very popular. For example, a spouse may want property to benefit the surviving spouse but may also wish to preserve any remaining property for the spouse's children from a prior partner. The spouse may fear that the surviving spouse will remarry and does not want property passing to a new spouse, their children, or the family of the new spouse.

The following requirements must be met for a transfer of property to qualify for Q-TIP treatment and hence the marital deduction:

1. The surviving spouse must be entitled to all income from the property.
2. The surviving spouse's income interest must last for the surviving spouse's life. The interest cannot terminate after a set number of years or upon a condition such as remarriage.
3. The surviving spouse must be entitled to receive the income at least once per year.
4. The surviving spouse need not have any rights to the property itself either during life or at death. Thus, the entire corpus of the trust can pass to the beneficiary the deceased spouse named in the trust. Of course, the deceased spouse may grant the surviving spouse the

right to withdraw some or all of the corpus or appoint the property by will.

5. No one can have the power to appoint trust property to anyone besides the surviving spouse while the surviving spouse is alive. Accordingly, neither the surviving spouse, the trustee, nor anyone else can have the power to make distributions of trust corpus to anyone other than the surviving spouse.

6. The personal representative of the deceased spouse must timely elect Q-TIP treatment on the deceased spouse's federal estate tax return—a Q-TIP trust does not automatically qualify for marital deduction treatment even if it meets all the requirements.

Example 24-60. Marital Deduction—Q-TIP Trust

Deceased Spouse established a testamentary trust to benefit Surviving Spouse. The trust requires the trustee to pay all income to Surviving Spouse at the first of every month until Surviving Spouse dies. Surviving Spouse also has an inter vivos power to appoint property to Deceased Spouse's children. When Surviving Spouse dies, all remaining property passes to Deceased Spouse's children. May Deceased Spouse's executor elect Q-TIP treatment for this trust?

Explanation

Deceased Spouse's trust does not qualify for Q-TIP treatment because Surviving Spouse has the power to appoint property to Deceased Spouse's children while Surviving Spouse is still alive. No one, not even Surviving Spouse, can have the right to appoint property to anyone other than Surviving Spouse during the lifetime of Surviving Spouse.

§24.3.1.3 Power of Appointment Trust

The deceased spouse may establish a *power of appointment trust* granting the surviving spouse the power to appoint trust property which will qualify for the marital deduction. I.R.C. §2056(b)(5). Prior to the advent of the Q-TIP trust in 1981, this technique was commonly used by spouses who did not want to make an outright gift to the surviving spouse but did want to take advantage of the marital deduction. A power of appointment trust will qualify for the marital deduction only if the following requirements are satisfied. Note that many of these requirements are the same as for a Q-TIP trust.

1. The surviving spouse must be entitled to all income from the property.

2. The surviving spouse's income interest must last for the surviving spouse's life.

3. The surviving spouse must be entitled to receive the income at least once per year.

4. The surviving spouse must have a general power of appointment over the trust corpus. The deceased spouse cannot place any restrictions or limitations on this power of appointment. Consequently, the surviving spouse could elect to appoint all of the property directly to the surviving spouse. However, the deceased spouse may indicate the beneficiary of the remaining trust property if the surviving spouse dies without exercising the power of appointment.

5. The surviving spouse must have the right to exercise the power of appointment without the consent or permission of any other person. The deceased spouse may, however, give the surviving spouse only a testamentary power of appointment. The trust will still qualify for the marital deduction even though the surviving spouse cannot exercise the power of appointment while alive.

6. The surviving spouse's interest cannot be subject to a power in anyone else, such as a trustee, to appoint the property to someone other than the surviving spouse.

§24.3.1.4   Estate Trust

The *estate trust* is a relatively inflexible technique rarely used to qualify a gift for the marital deduction. Instead of leaving the property to the surviving spouse outright, the deceased spouse leaves the property to a trust in which the surviving spouse is named as the exclusive beneficiary. The surviving spouse has the entire beneficial interest during the surviving spouse's lifetime and, upon death, all remaining principal and income is paid to the surviving spouse's estate. However, annual distributions of income to the surviving spouse are not necessary. I.R.C. §2056(b)(1). The estate trust becomes advantageous where property comprising the trust corpus is primarily unproductive, such as raw land being held for appreciation or closely held corporate stock that does not pay dividends. Under both a Q-TIP trust and a power of appointment trust, the surviving spouse would need to have the power to force the trustee to convert the unproductive property into income-producing assets or to invade the principal to make up for the lost income. The deceased spouse can avoid this problem with an estate trust because there is no requirement that the surviving spouse receive annual income payments. The downside is, of course, that the estate trust gives the deceased spouse absolutely no control over where the property goes upon the surviving spouse's death.

§24.3.1.5 Qualified Domestic Trust

If the surviving spouse is not a citizen of the United States, the marital deduction is unavailable unless the property passes into a *qualified domestic trust,* typically called a *QDOT.* I.R.C. §2056(d). This trust, which can be created either before or after the deceased spouse's death, holds the property to make sure the assets do not escape federal estate taxation upon the surviving spouse's death. QDOTs must meet a host of requirements, such as having a United States citizen or domestic corporation as one of the trustees. When the surviving spouse dies, the property is taxed at the deceased spouse's rates rather than those otherwise applicable to the estate of the surviving spouse.

§24.3.2 *Sheltering the Applicable Exclusion Amount*

A married person may pass the entire estate to the surviving spouse totally tax free by using transfers that qualify for the marital deduction. This simple strategy to avoid estate tax in the estate of the first spouse to die may be short-sighted because the surviving spouse's estate is now larger. This property will be taxed upon the surviving spouse's death unless the surviving spouse spends the property, leaves it to a new spouse, or otherwise disposes of it in a tax-free manner. The government's granting of the unlimited marital deduction is viewed by some people as a subterfuge to lure people into leaving property to their surviving spouses so that the government can tax the property at higher rates when the surviving spouses die. In effect, the government "invests" in each surviving spouse because the government obtains greater revenue by collecting more tax on one large estate than two taxes on two smaller estates.

As an estate planner wise to this ploy, you must advise your client not to waste the client's ability to leave property valued at the applicable exclusion amount (see §24.1.6.2, above) to individuals other than the surviving spouse without incurring federal estate tax liability. Failure to do so wastes a spouse's applicable exclusion amount and is costly. The amount that could have been transferred to a nonspouse tax-free may be subject to tax in the surviving spouse's estate at rates as high as 60 percent. If the surviving spouse died in the year 2000, the extra tax burden could exceed $400,000.

The simplest way to use the applicable exclusion amount is to leave property, either outright or in trust, equal in value to the exclusion amount to individuals other than the surviving spouse such as children and grandchildren. This technique works very well if the deceased spouse wants to prefer certain beneficiaries over the surviving spouse, such as children from a prior partner, or if the surviving spouse is so wealthy that the surviving spouse will not need the money.

In many situations, however, the deceased spouse actually wants to leave everything to the surviving spouse but does not like the prospect of a high tax in the surviving spouse's estate. This additional tax reduces the amount available for the surviving spouse's beneficiaries, who are often their children and grandchildren. Accordingly, the deceased spouse wants to give the surviving spouse as many rights in the property as possible without causing the property to qualify for the marital deduction. This arrangement is called a *bypass trust, credit shelter trust,* or *B trust* (as contrasted with an *A trust,* which qualifies for marital deduction treatment).

The deceased spouse can grant the surviving spouse many rights in the bypass trust. As long as the surviving spouse does not have a general power of appointment over the property, the property will not qualify for the marital deduction and thus will be subject to tax in the deceased spouse's estate. Of course, no tax should actually be payable in the deceased spouse's estate because the value of property going into the bypass trust would be the same as the applicable exclusion amount.

Below is a list of rights the deceased spouse may give the surviving spouse in a bypass trust. If the surviving spouse has all of these rights, the trust is often called a *maximum benefit bypass trust.* Remember that this is a list of maximums; the deceased spouse does not need to give the surviving spouse any of these rights.

1. All trust income.
2. The power to invade principal under an ascertainable standard relating to the surviving spouse's health, education, maintenance, and support.
3. Ability to serve as the sole trustee.
4. The right to withdraw the greater of $5,000 or 5 percent of the principal of the trust one time each calendar year for any purpose.
5. A special power of appointment to third parties, that is, anyone except the surviving spouse, the surviving spouse's estate, the surviving spouse's creditors, or the creditors of the surviving spouse's estate.

Example 24-61. Bypass Trust—Ascertainable Standard— Surviving Spouse Controls

Deceased Spouse created a trust funded with property equal to the applicable exclusion amount. Deceased Spouse gave Surviving Spouse the right to demand distributions from corpus for "happiness and comfort." What is the tax treatment of this transfer?

Explanation

The property in this trust will not be taxed in Deceased Spouse's estate because the transfer qualifies for the marital deduction. Surviving Spouse has a right, the ability to demand distributions for "happiness and comfort," which is too broad to permit the property to be in Deceased Spouse's estate. Surviving Spouse's ability to invade principal must be limited by an ascertainable standard for the property to be in Deceased Spouse's estate.

Example 24-62. Bypass Trust—Ascertainable Standard— Trustee Controls

Using the same facts as Example 24-61 except that this time it is not Surviving Spouse who has the right to demand corpus distributions but instead Trustee has the ability to distribute to surviving spouse for "happiness and comfort." What is the tax treatment of this transfer?

Explanation

The trust will now qualify as a bypass trust and be taxed in Deceased Spouse's estate. A trustee, or any other third party, may have the power to make discretionary distributions to the surviving spouse that are not limited by an ascertainable standard.

Example 24-63. Bypass Trust—Disclaimer

Spouses would like to leave their entire estates to each other outright but are hesitant to do so because of the adverse tax consequences of wasting the applicable exclusion amount. However, Spouses are not extremely wealthy so they are reluctant to make outright bypass gifts or create bypass trusts because the surviving spouse may prefer to have full control over all the property and assume the responsibility of planning to reduce estate taxes upon the surviving spouse's death. What can you suggest to help Spouses?

Explanation

It is often difficult to decide how to plan for married individuals who have estates with uncertain estate tax consequences or who have estates large enough to incur tax liability, but not so large that the surviving spouse is comfortable with sacrificing the opportunity to have all of the deceased spouse's property outright. A common solution is to create a *bypass disclaimer trust*. The will first makes an outright gift of all the desired property to the surviving spouse followed by an express provision that any property that the surviving spouse disclaims passes into a bypass trust for the surviving spouse's benefit. Thus, the surviving spouse can examine the actual situation at the time of the deceased spouse's death and make the best decision.

§24.4 Charitable Deduction

All transfers to qualified charities are totally deductible when computing both federal gift and estate taxes. I.R.C. §§2055 and 2522. The transferor must ascertain whether the recipient's use of the property for religious, charitable, scientific, literary, or educational purposes is sufficiently charitable to qualify the gift for charitable deduction treatment. In addition, certain purposes that might seem charitable are excluded, such as providing athletic facilities or equipment to international amateur sports competitions and contributions to organizations that attempt to influence legislation or political campaigns.

§24.4.1 Non-Split Transfers

If the transfers are solely to qualified charities, the deduction is for the entire value of the property computed using the normal gift or estate tax rules. See §§24.1.3 and 24.2.3, above. There is no limit to the value of property that a donor or decedent can pass tax free in this manner. This deduction operates to reduce the tax burden on the person contributing to a charity but increases the tax burden on individuals who elect not to make charitable gifts. In other words, individuals who may not be able to afford to make charitable gifts actually subsidize the tax obligations of individuals who make charitable gifts.

§24.4.2 Split Transfers

Some individuals do not wish to leave their property outright to charity because they want to preserve the property for family members or friends. On the other hand, these individuals also want to reduce their tax burden and benefit society by making charitable gifts. These individuals may accomplish both of these seemingly disparate goals with a *split transfer,* that is, a transfer with both charitable and noncharitable purposes. Split transfers need to be properly structured to obtain the benefit of the charitable deduction.

§24.4.2.1 Remainder Interest to Charity

A remainder interest following a life estate held by a noncharity may qualify for the charitable deduction if the property is a personal residence or a farm. For example, Donor could deed Donor's home to a charity while retaining a life estate for Donor. All other types of charitable remainder interests must meet highly technical special requirements to obtain the charitable deduction. Thus, the charitable deduction would be unavailable for the settlor of a trust that provides "income to A for life, remainder to charity."

Three basic types of remainder interests qualify for the charitable deduction. Note that with all of these interests, the entire remainder must pass to charity and neither the trustee nor the noncharitable beneficiary can have a discretionary power to invade the principal of the trust.

§24.4.2.1.1 Charitable Remainder Annuity Trust

The first technique is the *charitable remainder annuity trust (CRAT)*. Under this arrangement, the noncharitable life beneficiary must be entitled to receive a fixed sum of money from the trust at least one time per year. This sum must be at least 5 percent of the original value of the trust corpus. Thus, if the transferor creates a CRAT, the life beneficiary receives the same amount each year regardless of the current value of the trust property and the amount of income the property earns. Note that the trust instrument must prohibit additional contributions to the trust.

Example 24-64. Charitable Deduction — Charitable Remainder Annuity Trust

Settlor created a testamentary trust by transferring property valued at $500,000. The trust provides that Settlor will receive a fixed amount per year during Settlor's lifetime. When Settlor dies, the remainder passes to a qualified charity. Will this gift qualify for the charitable deduction?

Explanation

The answer to this question depends on the amount of the fixed payment to which Settlor is entitled under this charitable remainder annuity trust. The charitable deduction is available only if this amount is at least 5 percent of the value of the trust corpus at the time the property is placed in the trust. Thus, Settlor can claim a charitable deduction if the fixed payment is at least $25,000. The amount of the charitable deduction is determined actuarially by applying various tables set forth in Treasury regulations.

§24.4.2.1.2 Charitable Remainder Unitrust

The second type of remainder interest that qualifies for the charitable deduction is the *charitable remainder unitrust (CRUT)*. The noncharitable life beneficiary of a CRUT must be entitled to receive a fixed percentage of the value of the trust property annually. This percentage cannot be less than 5 percent of the value of the trust corpus computed once per year. If trust income is less than 5 percent, the settlor may provide that the life beneficiary only receives the actual amount of trust income. Under a CRUT, the life beneficiary receives a different amount each year as the value of the trust changes. If trust property is appreciating in value, the unitrust permits the noncharitable life beneficiary to receive larger distributions, unlike a CRAT where the amount of each payment is always the same regardless of the value of the principal and the income actually earned by the trust property. Note that the trust instrument can permit additional contributions to the trust if the instrument contains certain provisions mandated by statute and Treasury regulations.

Example 24-65. Charitable Deduction — Charitable Remainder Unitrust

Settlor created a testamentary trust by transferring property valued at $500,000. The trust provides that Settlor will receive an annual distribution from the trust determined by applying a fixed percentage to the value of the trust corpus. When Settlor dies, the remainder passes to a qualified charity. Will this gift qualify for the charitable deduction?

Explanation

The answer to this question depends on the size of the fixed percentage to which Settlor is entitled under this charitable remainder unitrust. The charitable deduction is available only if the percentage is 5 percent or greater. Treasury regulations contain instructions for valuing the remainder interest.

§24.4.2.1.3 Pooled Income Fund

The third type of transfer of a remainder interest that will qualify for the charitable deduction is a transfer to a *pooled income fund,* which the charity establishes according to detailed requirements. The donor transfers property to the charity's pooled income fund in exchange for the charity's promise to pay the donor a rate of return on the donor's donation ("investment") that is equal to the rate of return the charity earns on the fund. Upon the donor's death, the charity retains the donated property.

§24.4.2.2 Present Interest to Charity

The donor can give the present interest of property to charity for a certain period of time and retain the remainder interest for the donor or for anyone the donor specifies. The transfer must be in trust form and the trust must either be an annuity trust (the charity receives the same amount each year) or a unitrust (the charity receives the same percentage of the value of the trust property each year). Together, these arrangements are called *charitable lead trusts.*

§24.5 Federal Generation-Skipping Transfer Tax

The federal *generation-skipping transfer (GST)* tax is imposed on certain inter vivos and at-death transfers to donees who are more than one generation younger than the transferor. I.R.C. §§2601-2663. The GST tax is an additional 55 percent flat-rate tax on top of any federal gift or estate tax that the donor or decedent might also owe on the transfer. I.R.C. §2641. The policy behind this tax is to prevent a property owner from manipulating the transfer of property to avoid a taxable event. For example, assume that Grandparent wants to transfer property with as little transfer tax as possible from a family perspective. If Grandparent gave property to Child and then Child later transferred the same property to Grandchild, two taxable transfers will have occurred. However, if Grandparent gave the property directly to Grandchild, only one taxable transfer occurs. The government imposes the GST tax on this latter transfer to compensate for Grandparent's attempt to avoid a second taxable transfer of property.

There is no separate GST tax return form. Instead, the donor reports inter vivos generation-skipping transfers on the gift tax return and the executor of a decedent's estate reports them on the estate tax return.

§24.5.1 Skip Person Defined

A transfer to a *skip person* triggers the GST tax. A skip person is a person who is two or more generations younger than the donor or decedent. I.R.C. §2613(a). Generally, the second generation begins with individuals who are more than thirty-seven and one-half years younger than the transferor unless lineal descendants are involved. I.R.C. §2651(d). A trust can also be a skip person if all present interests in income and corpus (either by mandatory right or through the exercise of the trustee's discretion) belong to skip persons.

Example 24-66. Skip Person Defined—Generally

Your Wills and Estates professor believes you are a professional and intelligent person, especially after your stellar performance on your examination. As a graduation present, Professor makes a generous gift to you. Is this gift potentially subject to GST tax?

Explanation

If you are more than thirty-seven and one-half years younger than Professor, this gift will be potentially subject to GST tax. There is no requirement that the donor and donee of a gift be related for the GST tax to apply.

Example 24-67. Skip Person Defined — Lineal Descendants

Donor had two children, Daughter and Son. Daughter, who was born when Donor was forty years old, gave birth to Granddaughter in 1995. Son died in 1997 survived by Grandson. In 1999, Donor made inter vivos gifts to Daughter, Granddaughter, and Grandson. Which of these transfers are potentially subject to GST tax?

Explanation

When lineal descendants are involved, the actual ages of the donor and donee do not matter. Instead, the number of generations between the donor and donee are counted. I.R.C. §2651(b). However, if a member of the intermediate generation predeceased the transfer, then that generation is ignored. I.R.C. §2651(e). The policy behind this special rule is that the transferor is not actually making a transfer to intentionally skip a taxable event. Instead, the transferor has no choice because the intermediate person is already dead. Accordingly, Donor's gift to Daughter is not subject to GST tax because Daughter is only one generation removed from Donor even though she is more than thirty-seven and one-half years younger than Donor. Donor's gift to Granddaughter is subject to GST tax because Granddaughter is two generations beneath Donor and Daughter is still alive. Donor's gift to Grandson escapes the GST tax because Son died prior to the transfer, which effectively bumps Grandson up one generation.

Example 24-68. Skip Person Defined — Spouse

When Donor was sixty years old, Donor married Donee, who was twenty years old. Several years later, Donor made a gift to Donee. Is this transfer potentially subject to GST tax?

Explanation

Spouses are always treated as being in the same generation regardless of their actual ages. I.R.C. §2651(c). Consequently, Donor's transfer is not subject to GST tax even though Donee is forty years younger than Donor.

Example 24-69. Skip Person Defined — Trusts

Settlor created two trusts. Trust One provided that the trustee could use principal and income for Settlor's children and grandchildren. Trust Two restricted distributions to Settlor's grandchildren. Do any of these trusts qualify as skip persons?

Explanation

Trust One is not a skip person because someone other than a skip person has the ability to receive present distributions from the trust, that is, Settlor's children. Trust Two qualifies as a skip person because all present interests are held by skip persons, namely, the grandchildren.

§24.5.2 Transfers Subject to GST Tax

Three basic types of transfers are subject to GST tax: the direct skip, the taxable termination, and the taxable distribution. This section reviews these three transfers.

§24.5.2.1 Direct Skip

The simplest type of transfer subject to GST tax is the *direct skip*, that is, a transfer directly to a skip person which is also subject to federal gift or estate tax. I.R.C. §2612(c). For example, a gift from Grandparent to Grandchild is a direct skip assuming that the intermediate person is still alive. If the gift is inter vivos, the value of the gift for gift tax purposes is increased by the GST tax. However, the donor does not need to pay GST tax on the money used to pay the gift tax.

Example 24-70. Direct Skip — Generally

Donor's goal is to give $100,000 to Grandchild outright. Donor has already exhausted all applicable exclusions and deductions. Assuming that this gift would be subject to gift tax at a 50 percent rate and that Grandchild's parent (Donor's child) is still alive, how much money does Donor need to make the desired transfer?

Explanation

GST tax is computed on a tax exclusive basis so the GST tax is not treated as part of the transfer. Thus, the value of the gift for GST tax purposes is

$100,000. The GST tax rate is set at the highest estate tax rate, which is 55 percent, and thus the GST tax is $55,000. The value of the gift is increased by the GST tax so that the value of the gift for gift tax purposes is $155,000. Donor is in the 50 percent gift tax bracket, which results in a gift tax of $77,500. Totaling the amount of the gift and the two taxes due, Donor must have $232,500 to make the $100,000 gift to Grandchild.

Example 24-71.   Direct Skip—Multiple Generations

Great-grandparent makes a large inter vivos gift to Great-grandchild. Both the intermediate parties (Grandparent and Parent) are still alive. Does Great-grandparent need to make two GST tax payments because two generations are being skipped?

Explanation

No, only one taxable direct skip occurs even though the property skips two or more generations.

§24.5.2.2   Taxable Termination

The second type of transfer subject to GST tax is the *taxable termination*. A taxable termination occurs when property passes to a skip person because of the termination of a trust. I.R.C. §2612(a). For example, Donor created an irrevocable trust for Child that provided that upon Child's death, the trustee must distribute the remaining property to Grandchild. When Child dies, a taxable termination occurs and GST tax is imposed when the trustee turns over the remainder to Grandchild. However, the transfer will not be treated as a taxable termination if (1) a transfer subject to federal transfer tax occurs because of the termination, (2) a nonskip person has an interest in the trust immediately after the termination, or (3) a skip person has no more than a 5 percent chance of receiving a distribution after the termination. The GST tax is imposed on the entire remainder without reduction for the GST tax, which must be paid from the property.

§24.5.2.3   Taxable Distribution

The third type of transfer subject to GST tax is the *taxable distribution*. A taxable distribution occurs when the trustee of a trust makes a distribution of trust income or principal to a skip person that does not qualify as a direct skip or a taxable termination. I.R.C. §2612(b). For example, Donor created a trust giving the trustee the discretion to make payments to Donor's children and grandchildren. When the trustee makes a payment to a grandchild, a taxable distribution occurs and the trustee owes GST tax. The GST tax is imposed on the entire value of the payment made to the grandchild without adjustment for the GST tax that will be paid from the property. If the trust pays the GST tax, that amount is treated as a taxable distribution and will be subject to GST tax as well.

§24.5.3 Exemptions and Exclusions

The GST tax is not as onerous as it may originally seem because there are significant exclusions and exemptions.

§24.5.3.1 Annual Exclusion

Transfers that are not subject to gift tax because of the annual exclusion (see §24.1.4.1, above) are usually not subject to GST tax. I.R.C. §2642(c)(1). Transfers to a trust must meet certain requirements to be protected from GST tax even if they escape gift tax because of *Crummey* powers.

§24.5.3.2 Educational and Medical Expense Exclusion

Gifts that qualify for the educational and medical expense exclusion (see §24.1.4.2, above) are not subject to GST tax. I.R.C. §2611(b)(1).

§24.5.3.3 $1,000,000 Exemption

Each donor has a $1,000,000 exemption (adjusted for inflation beginning in 1999) from GST tax. I.R.C. §2631. The donor can "spend" this exemption as the donor desires among the donor's transfers to skip persons. By allocating this exemption to trusts containing appreciating property, the $1,000,000 exemption can be leveraged into a much larger exemption over time because the *exclusion ratio* (the percentage of the trust which is covered by the exemption) is based on the value of the property when it is originally transferred even though the GST tax may not be owed until years later and after the property has increased in value.

§24.6 Federal Income Tax Ramifications of Gratuitous Transfers

The recipient of a gratuitous transfer incurs no income tax liability merely by receiving the property because I.R.C. §102(a) provides that "[g]ross income does not include the value of property acquired by gift, bequest, devise, or inheritance." However, if the property is other than money, income tax consequences may flow from the subsequent sale of the property by the recipient. The recipient will owe capital gains tax on the profit, that is, the difference between the *basis* of the property and the selling price. The basis of property is typically the purchase price of the property adjusted for various things, such as amounts spent to improve the property. Luckily, the basis of gratuitously obtained property is not zero even though the recipient did not pay for the property. The determination of the recipient's basis depends on how the recipient obtained the property, that is, whether the property was received as an inter vivos gift or through an at-death transfer. Because tax planning is often done from a "family perspective," you must consider the effect of a gratuitous transfer on the recipient's taxes as well as the transferor's taxes, especially if the parties are closely related. Your goal may be to reduce the total amount of tax rather than the tax imposed on each individual.

§24.6.1 *Inter Vivos Gifts*

The donee's basis of property the donee receives because of an inter vivos gift is the donor's basis. In other words, an inter vivos gift has no effect on the basis; the donor's basis simply passes through to the donee. (See Example 24-73, below, for a discussion of the adjustment to basis that occurs when gift tax is paid on the transfer.) When the donee sells the property, the donee will pay capital gains tax on all of the appreciation, both the appreciation that occurred while the donor owned the asset and the appreciation that occurred after the donee received the gift. I.R.C. §1015(a).

Example 24-72. Income Tax—Inter Vivos Gift—General Rule

Donor bought a coin in 1950 for $10. In 1990, Donor gave the coin to Donee when the coin was worth $7,000. Donee sold the coin in 2000 for $10,000. What are the federal tax ramifications of these transactions?

Explanation

The gift of the coin had no tax consequences. Donor did not incur federal gift tax because the value of the coin at the date of the gift ($7,000) was less than the annual exclusion ($10,000). Donee did not need to pay income tax on the gift because gifts are not included in gross income. Donee is subject to income tax, however, on the profit made from the sale of the coin. Because Donee received the coin as a gift, Donee's basis is the same as Donor's basis, that is, $10. Consequently, Donee will owe capital gains tax on $9,990.

Example 24-73. Income Tax—Inter Vivos Gift—Basis Increase for Gift Tax Paid

Donor made an inter vivos gift of an item of property that had a basis of $100,000 and a fair market value of $200,000. Donor paid $82,000 in federal gift tax. What is Donee's basis in the property?

Explanation

Normally, Donee's basis would be Donor's basis of $100,000. However, because Donor paid federal gift tax on the transfer, Donee's basis is increased by the amount of federal gift tax Donor paid on the gain portion of the transfer. I.R.C. §1015(d). This basis increase is not for the entire gift tax Donor paid but only for the proportional amount of the gift tax paid on the amount of the gift that would have been a gain had the property been sold on the date of the gift for its fair market value. In this case, Donor had a potential gain of $100,000 at the date of the gift which was 50 percent of the value of the gift. Thus, Donee's basis of $100,000 is increased by 50 percent of the gift tax Donor paid or $41,000 (.5 × $82,000). Donee's basis will be $141,000.

Example 24-74. Income Tax—Inter Vivos Gift—Loss

Donor purchased corporate stock in 1995 for $5,000. Donor gave the stock to Donee in 1997 when it was worth $2,000. Donee sold the stock in 1999 for $250. May Donee claim an income tax loss and, if so, in what amount?

Explanation

When computing a loss, Donee's basis is the lower of (1) Donor's basis, or (2) the fair market value of the property at the date of the gift. I.R.C. §1015(a). Thus, Donee's basis is $2,000 rather than $5,000 and Donee's loss is only $1,750. Donor's initial loss of $3,000 is wasted because neither Donor nor Donee can take advantage of it. Donor should have sold the stock, claimed the $3,000 loss, and then given the proceeds of the sale to Donee.

§24.6.2 At-Death Gifts

The basis of property acquired from a decedent is the value of the asset at the date of the decedent's death (or six months thereafter if the personal representative elects to use the alternate valuation date). I.R.C. §1014(a). This *step-up* in basis permits the heir or beneficiary to sell property that has appreciated in the decedent's hands without paying capital gains tax on the increase. Only appreciation that occurs after the decedent's death is subject to tax.

Example 24-75. Income Tax — At-Death Gift — General Rule

Decedent bought a coin in 1950 for $10. In 1990, Decedent died with a will bequeathing the coin, which was then worth $7,000, to Beneficiary. Beneficiary sold the coin in 2000 for $10,000. On what amount must Beneficiary pay capital gains tax?

Explanation

Beneficiary's basis in the coin is $7,000, the value of the coin at the date of Decedent's death. Thus, Beneficiary will only be subject to capital gains tax on the appreciation that occurred after Decedent died ($3,000).

Example 24-76. Income Tax — At-Death Gift — Gifts to Spouse

Decedent purchased a house for $40,000 in 1970. Decedent died in 2000 with a valid will leaving the house to Spouse. At the date of Decedent's death, the house was worth $250,000. What is Spouse's basis in the house?

Explanation

Spouse is entitled to a step-up in basis to $250,000. It does not matter that the house escaped taxation in Decedent's estate because of the marital deduction. In community property states, the surviving spouse even receives the step-up in basis with regard to the half of the community that already belonged to the surviving spouse.

Example 24-77. Income Tax — At-Death Gift — Regifted Assets

The only item of property of value that Client owns is a Picasso painting. The basis of the painting is $50,000 and the painting is now worth $400,000. Client would like to sell the painting but is unhappy about paying capital gains tax on $350,000. Client's Parent is competent but extremely ill. Client would like to give the painting to Parent and file the appropriate federal gift tax return showing no tax due because the gift is well under the applicable exclusion amount. Parent's valid will names Client as the sole beneficiary of Parent's estate which, except for the painting, has a value of under $100,000. Thus, when Parent dies, Client will inherit the painting and obtain a step-up in basis permitting Client to sell the painting and not pay tax on the appreciation. In addition, Parent's estate, even with the addition of the valuable painting, is too low to result in federal estate tax liability. Will Client's plan work?

Explanation

Client's scheme will not work. If a decedent receives property from someone as a gift within one year of death and then leaves that property to the same person or that person's spouse, there is no step-up in basis. I.R.C. §1014(e). Thus, Client cannot run the property through Parent's estate to obtain a step-up in basis unless Parent lives at least one year. Of course, Parent could leave the painting to someone else, such as Client's child, and child would obtain the step-up in basis.

Example 24-78. Income Tax — At-Death Gift — Loss

Decedent purchased corporate stock in 1995 for $5,000. Decedent died in 1997, bequeathing the stock to Beneficiary. The stock was then worth $2,000. Beneficiary sold the stock in 1999 for $250. May Beneficiary claim an income tax loss and, if so, in what amount?

Explanation

Beneficiary's basis is $2,000, the value of the stock at the date of Decedent's death. Thus, Beneficiary's loss is only $1,750. Decedent's initial loss of $3,000 is wasted because neither Decedent nor Beneficiary can take advantage of it.

§24.6.3 Planning Suggestions

If your client anticipates having an estate that will not incur federal estate tax liability, the client should retain appreciating assets. The heirs and beneficiaries will then receive the benefit of the step-up in basis. In this way, the new owners will pay capital gains tax only on appreciation that occurs after your client's death.

On the other hand, if your client anticipates having a taxable estate, the client should generally make inter vivos gifts of appreciating assets. Although it is true that the donee only receives your client's basis and will be responsible for capital gains tax on the appreciation when the donee sells the asset, the capital gains rates are significantly lower than the estate tax rates. Thus, from the family perspective, it is more cost effective to have the donee pay the capital gains tax, which has a maximum rate of 28 percent on the appreciation rather than have that appreciation taxed in the client's estate at between 37 and 60 percent.

If your client has depreciating assets, the client should sell these assets while alive and use these losses to offset income. Losses on depreciating assets that occur pre-gift or pre-death are wasted regardless of whether the gifts occur inter vivos or at death.

§24.7   State Wealth Transfer Taxation

§24.7.1   *Inter Vivos Transfers*

Approximately ten states impose a gift tax on inter vivos transfers. The methods used to compute state gift taxes fall into two main categories. The first is a tax on total taxable gifts in a manner analogous to the federal gift tax. The second is a tax on each gift separately with the rate of tax being based on the relationship between the donor and the donee. Typically, the closer that the donee is related to the donor, the lower the rate of tax and the greater the number and size of exemptions.

§24.7.2   *At-Death Transfers*

Almost all states impose a tax on at-death transfers. These taxes fall into three main categories. The most common type of death tax is the *pick-up* tax, also called the *sponge* or *soak-up* tax. Under this type of tax, the state estate tax is set at the maximum amount of credit the decedent's estate could claim for paying state death taxes. See §24.2.5.3.3, above. A pick-up tax is a cost-free tax. The amount of the state death tax is the same as the amount of the federal credit; if the state did not impose the tax, the decedent's estate would owe more tax to the federal government. The decedent's personal representative simply sends two checks, one to the IRS and one to the state government, totaling the same amount that would be owed to the IRS alone if the state did not have an estate tax.

States impose two other types of taxes on at-death transfers that may be in place of or in addition to the pick-up tax. The first of these is an estate tax imposed on the privilege of transferring property at death. State estate taxes operate in a similar fashion to the federal estate tax although the property included in the gross estate and the types and amounts of deductions and credits may differ significantly. The second type is an inheritance tax imposed on the heir's or beneficiary's privilege of receiving property. Typically, the closer that the heir or beneficiary is related to the decedent, the lower the rate of tax and the greater the number and size of exemptions.

25

Disability and Death Planning

You are statistically more likely to become disabled in the next twelve months than to die if you are under age sixty. When the eventuality of death looms on the immediate horizon, you may no longer be capable of exerting control over this most personal and spiritual event. Until recently, a person could do very little to plan for either disability or the process of dying. Estate planning was originally limited to carrying out a person's intent regarding property disposition, that is, making sure the desired beneficiaries received the person's property with as small a tax burden as possible. Beginning in the last half of the twentieth century, courts and legislatures have made great progress in developing tools to permit people to plan for disability and the death event.

The best way to recognize the benefits of disability and death planning is to consider the alternative. If a disabled person has not made prior arrangements, the person flounders in society until a relative, friend, or governmental entity petitions the court for the appointment of a guardian. The court will then conduct a hearing to determine whether the person is able to manage the individual's own personal and business affairs. Some states permit these proceedings to continue even if the person does not attend and consequently the person may have no opportunity to demonstrate capacity or express a preference for a particular person to serve as the guardian. The person may suffer embarrassment and humiliation during this potentially costly and time-consuming process. If the court determines that the person is unable to manage the person's own affairs, a court-appointed fiduciary will assume that role.

Once the court appoints a guardian, the person's right of self-determination is highly compromised. Decisions regarding personal and business matters are now made by an individual whom the person may not have known or whom the person would never have wanted in charge of these matters. Every aspect of the person's existence is subject to the control and manipulation of others such as what to eat, where to live, what to watch on television, what to wear, what type of medical treatment to have, and the timing and method of death.

This chapter reviews the techniques modern law has made available to persons who wish to plan for disability, with regard to both property management and health care, and for the death event itself.

§25.1   Property Management

The focus of disability planning for property management is to ensure that the individual the disabled person desires is in charge of the person's property upon disability as well as to provide a continuous income stream when the disabled person is no longer able to work. This section reviews the available planning strategies.

§25.1.1   *Durable Power of Attorney for Property Management*

A *power of attorney* is a formal method of creating an agency relationship under which one person has the ability to act in the place of another. The person granting authority is called the *principal* and the person who obtains the authority is the *agent* or *attorney-in-fact*. Note that in this context, the term "attorney" is not synonymous with "lawyer" and thus any competent person may serve as an agent even if the person has no legal training. The discussion in §12.8, above, regarding the desirable traits of the executor of a will is also applicable to the agent selection process.

Under traditional agency law, an agent's authority terminates when the principal becomes incompetent because the principal is no longer able to monitor the agent's conduct. This rule prevented powers of attorney from being used as a disability planning technique. In 1954, Virginia became the first state to authorize a *durable power of attorney,* which provides that the agent retains the authority to act even if the principal is incompetent. All states now have legislation sanctioning durable powers of attorney. Enabling provisions are also contained in the UPC, the freestanding Uniform Durable Power of Attorney Act (1979), and the Uniform Statutory Form Power of Attorney Act (1988), which includes a fill-in-the-blank form.

Example 25-1.   Durable Power of Attorney for Property Management—Validity and Extent of Authority

Principal wanted to appoint Agent to handle Principal's property affairs should Principal become disabled. Principal signed the following statement,

"I, Principal, hereby appoint Agent as my attorney-in-fact. Agent shall have the power and authority to perform or undertake any action I could perform or undertake if I were personally present." Principal is now disabled. May Agent sell Principal's art collection to raise money to pay medical bills and Principal's other expenses?

Explanation

The first step in analyzing this question is to determine whether the power of attorney is valid. Principal and Agent must have had legal capacity, typically by being at least eighteen years old, at the time Principal signed the power of attorney. Principal and Agent also needed to be competent. Assuming that Principal and Agent were both competent, the power of attorney must comply with the requisite formalities. This power of attorney meets the basic formalities of being in writing and signed. However, some states impose additional requirements such as being witnessed, acknowledged by a notary, or filed in the public records.

Assuming Principal satisfied the appropriate formalities, the second step is to determine whether the power of attorney has the durability feature. Under the law of most states, the writing must expressly state the durability feature with language such as, "This power of attorney is not affected by my subsequent disability or incapacity." Powers of attorney are presumed durable in only a few states. Thus, in the majority of states this power of attorney would not be durable and Agent could not sell the art collection.

For the sake of discussion, let's assume that this power of attorney is durable. The third step of the analysis would be to determine whether Agent has the power to sell the art collection. Principal attempted to create a *general* power of attorney granting the agent broad authority to take any actions the principal could take. However, many states narrowly construe powers of attorney so that the agent only has the exact powers enumerated in the document itself. In these states, Agent would not have the authority to sell the art collection because Principal did not grant a power to sell Principal's property. To prevent this type of problem, many states and the Uniform Statutory Form Power of Attorney Act permit principals to incorporate by reference extensive lists of statutorily enumerated powers.

A principal must carefully consider the powers the principal wants to delegate to the agent. Sufficient powers need to be granted so the agent can effectively manage the principal's property. On the other hand, the principal may have reasons to limit the agent's powers. For example, the principal may not want the agent to sell certain assets like the art collection in this case and other property such as a home and family heirlooms. In addition, the law prevents the principal from delegating certain powers such as to serve jail time, vote, and take examinations (e.g., the bar exam). If the principal is in a state with statutory powers, these powers may need to be expanded as well as restricted. For example, the principal may want the agent to be able to make gifts that qualify for the federal gift tax annual exclusion to family members. See §24.1.4.1, above.

Example 25-2. Durable Power of Attorney for Property Management — Termination

Principal created a valid durable power of attorney in 1990. In 1998, Principal became incompetent. In 2000, Guardian was appointed to manage Principal's property. Principal died in 2002. At what point did Agent's authority end?

Explanation

Agent's authority may have terminated before 1998 because under the law of a few states, durable powers of attorney expire a statutorily provided number of years after execution. Depending on local law, Agent's authority may end automatically upon the appointment of Guardian in 2000 or Guardian may have the power to revoke or modify the power of attorney. To prevent the appointment of a guardian from interfering with Principal's plan, Principal should sign a self-designation of guardian document as discussed in §25.1.3, below, naming Agent as the preferred guardian. Under no circumstances would Agent's authority continue beyond 2002 because powers of attorney end upon the death of the principal.

Example 25-3. Durable Power of Attorney for Property Management — When Effective

Principal signed a valid durable power of attorney that gave Agent the authority to sell Principal's property. Although Principal was still competent, Agent sold Principal's art collection because Agent believed Principal needed the money. Principal is angry because Principal would rather have kept the art collection and sold some of Principal's stock portfolio. May Principal retrieve the collection from Purchaser?

Explanation

The answer depends on the terms of the durable power of attorney. If the power of attorney is silent, Agent immediately had the power to sell the collection and thus Principal's only remedy is against Agent. On the other hand, Principal may have created a *springing* power of attorney under which Agent's authority begins upon Principal's disability or incapacity. In this case, Principal could recover the collection from Purchaser because Agent would have had no authority to sell. Springing powers of attorney are common because principals do not like the idea of delegating authority to agents while they are still competent. Springing powers should indicate the method by which the principal's incapacity is to be determined such as with a physician's written certification that based upon the physician's medical examination of the principal, the principal is incapable of managing financial affairs. Springing powers, however, cause delay while the agents seek medical determinations of incapacity. Thus, a principal may permit the power of attorney to be effective immediately but tell the trusted agent not to exercise any authority until the principal is actually incompetent.

Example 25-4. Durable Power of Attorney for Property Management — Third Party's Refusal to Accept

Principal signed a valid durable power of attorney that gave Agent the authority to sell Principal's property. After Principal became incompetent, Agent went to Principal's stockbroker and requested that the broker sell certain stock. Despite the validity of the power of attorney, the broker refused to sell the stock. How should Agent proceed?

Explanation

Under the law of most states, Agent cannot force a third party to accept Agent's authority. To decrease the likelihood of this happening, many powers of attorney contain indemnification language such as the following.

> I agree that any third party who receives a copy of this document may act under it. Revocation of the durable power of attorney is not effective as to a third party until the third party receives actual notice of the revocation. I agree to indemnify the third party for any claims that arise against the third party because of reliance on this power of attorney.

If a third party refuses to deal with Agent, it may be necessary to have the court appoint a guardian for Principal.

Example 25-5. Durable Power of Attorney for Property Management — Spouse as Agent

Principal named Spouse as Principal's agent in a valid durable power of attorney. Principal and Spouse divorce. Principal is now incompetent. If Principal never changed the power of attorney, may Spouse still serve as the agent?

Explanation

Unless state law automatically revokes the designation of an agent who is now the principal's ex-spouse upon divorce, Spouse can still serve as Principal's agent. Accordingly, a principal may wish to include a provision stating that the agent's authority ends upon divorce or even earlier, such as when either spouse files for divorce.

Example 25-6. Durable Power of Attorney for Property Management—Compensation of Agent

You are in the process of preparing a durable power of attorney for Principal. Principal asks you whether Agent should get paid for Agent's services. How do you respond?

Explanation

Principal should state whether Agent is to be paid. Agent may be willing to serve for free if Agent is a family member or close friend. However, if Agent is a professional, such as an attorney or financial planner, Principal's failure to provide for compensation may cause Agent to decline the job. The power of attorney itself or a separate document should detail compensation. Principal may provide for compensation to be determined by a variety of methods such as an hourly rate, by reference to a corporate trustee fee schedule, or based on a percentage of the income Agent earns on the Principal's property.

Example 25-7. Durable Power of Attorney for Property Management—Will Beneficiary Concerns

Principal's valid will provides as follows, "I leave all my stocks, bonds, and corporate securities to Daughter. I leave the rest of my estate to Son." Principal signed a valid durable power of attorney that gave Agent the authority to sell Principal's property. After Principal became incompetent, Agent needed to raise money to pay medical bills and other expenses. Agent would like to sell a portion of Principal's stock portfolio to raise the money because the sale would be quick and relatively inexpensive. May Daughter prevent the sale?

Explanation

Assuming that the power of attorney is silent, it is unlikely that Daughter could prevent the sale of the stock. Just as when a principal is competent, any transfer of property may effect the eventual disposition of property under a will. In this case, Agent's decision to sell stock negatively impacts Daughter and benefits Son. The power of attorney should specifically limit Agent's dispositive powers if Principal wants to preserve certain assets for Principal's estate.

§25.1.2 Custodial Trusts

The Uniform Custodial Trust Act (1987) has been enacted in a few but growing number of states. This act provides an effective, albeit primitive, method for a person to protect property upon disability. The act, modeled after the Uniform Transfers to Minors Act, permits a person to create a statutory custodial trust by delivering property to a custodial trustee under the act. The terms of this simple arrangement are specified in the statute, not by the transferor. Although there are many reasons why an adult may want to use this technique, the drafters anticipated that the primary users would be elderly individuals who want to make arrangements for the future management of their property if they become incompetent.

To create a custodial trust, the owner of property either (1) makes a written transfer directing the transferee to hold the property as a custodial trustee under the Act, or (2) executes a written statement declaring that the owner is now holding the property as a custodial trustee. Any such transfer or declaration cannot be revoked by the transferor or the original owner.

Sample Custodial Trust Transfer

I, [transferor], transfer to [trustee] as custodial trustee for [beneficiary] as beneficiary and [final distributee] as distributee on termination of the trust in absence of direction by the beneficiary under the [state] Uniform Custodial Trust Act, the following property: [property description legally sufficient to identify and transfer each item of property].

As long as the beneficiary is not incapacitated, the custodial trustee must follow the beneficiary's instructions. A competent beneficiary may wisely or capriciously use the property without question by the trustee. In effect, the trustee is actually acting like the beneficiary's agent rather than as a true trustee. Once the beneficiary is incapacitated in the opinion of the custodial trustee, the trustee uses the property as the trustee considers to be reasonably prudent for the beneficiary and the beneficiary's dependents. Distributions are not restricted to the beneficiary's support, maintenance, education, or health care and thus the trustee may even make payments for nonessential items.

Several distribution options are possible if the trust terminates because of the beneficiary's death. First, the beneficiary's directions control distribution provided they were formalized in a writing the beneficiary signed while competent and the trustee received it during the beneficiary's lifetime. If the beneficiary did not leave instructions, the property passes to the final distributee as stated in the custodial trust instrument. In the absence of a designation, the property passes to the deceased beneficiary's estate.

Example 25-8. Custodial Trusts

Pat is quite ill but is still competent. Pat fears that Pat's condition will continue to deteriorate and wants to have someone manage Pat's life savings of $10,000. Pat decides to transfer the money to Grandchild under the Uniform Custodial Trust Act naming Pat as the beneficiary. Pat's condition takes an unexpected upward turn and Pat would like to spend the money on a Las Vegas vacation. How should Pat proceed?

Explanation

Pat cannot revoke the custodial trust arrangement in Pat's capacity as the original transferor. However, in Pat's capacity as the beneficiary, Pat has full control over the property and thus can demand that all the property be turned over to Pat. Alternatively, Pat could submit bills from the vacation and direct Grandchild to pay them. If the transferor and the beneficiary are the same person, as in this example, the transferor gives up no real control over the transferred property. The custodial arrangement just "stands by" until it is needed, that is, when the transferor becomes incompetent.

§25.1.3 Self-Designation of Guardian of Estate or Conservator

Historically, most courts held that they were not required to give weight to an incompetent person's preference for a guardian. An incompetent's opinion was inherently suspect because a person lacking the capacity to handle property may also lack the capacity to select a proper guardian and may also be more susceptible to undue influence. The modern trend is to permit a competent individual to designate the individual the person would like the court to appoint as the person's guardian before the onset of incompetency. Thus, should the need for a guardian arise, the court can follow the person's intent expressed at a time when the person was competent to do so.

State legislatures have developed various methods a person may use to nominate a guardian prior to incompetency or disability. Some jurisdictions may authorize several of these techniques. The most common techniques include a designation in (1) a durable power of attorney (see §25.1.1, above) and (2) a document executed with formalities similar to those for a will. Some states allow designation of guardians in other types of documents. A few states have more unusual methods such as permitting the court to appoint a guardian while the person is still competent or having the prospective ward file a guardianship application while competent and then waiting until incompetency occurs before conducting a hearing.

Example 25-9. Self-Designation of Guardian of Estate — Priority and Disqualification

Ward executed a guardian self-designation document that stated as follows: "I hereby designate Friend as the guardian/conservator of my estate. I expressly disqualify Spouse." Ward has now become incompetent and Friend, Spouse, and Child seek to be appointed guardian. Whom should the court appoint?

Explanation

The court should appoint Friend. The individual designated in a guardian self-designation document usually takes priority over the individuals listed in state statutes such as the person's spouse, adult children, and parents. Thus, Spouse and Child will not be appointed even though they would otherwise have had priority. In some states, an express disqualification of someone prevents the court from ever appointing that person even if the instrument does not provide an alternate. For example, assume that Friend refused to serve so that the court would be forced to use the statutory order. Although Spouse is listed first, Spouse could not serve and Child would become the first choice.

Example 25-10. Self-Designation of Guardian of Estate — Correlation with Durable Power of Attorney

Parent executed a valid durable power of attorney naming Friend as the agent. Parent is now incompetent and Friend is doing an excellent job of managing Parent's property. However, Children are very upset with Friend. Friend is spending Parent's money on allegedly frivolous items for Parent's use. For example, Friend knew that Parent liked to rent and watch movies so Friend bought a big-screen television, a Dolby Digital surround sound system, and a special chair so Parent may enjoy movies at home. Friend also hires professional health care aids to provide Parent with a comfortable and relatively enjoyable time at home. May Children stop Friend from spending their inheritance at such a rapid pace?

Explanation

Assuming Friend is not breaching any of Friend's fiduciary duties, Children cannot change Friend's spending habits by attacking Friend as an agent. However, in many states, a court-appointed guardian trumps the authority of an agent. Children would petition the court to be appointed as guardian and prevail over Friend because children have superior priority, second only to a spouse. Friend would then lose Friend's authority and Parent would be forced to live a meager lifestyle under the selfish rule of Children. However, if Parent had executed a self-designation of guardian document naming Friend as the priority guardian, Children's end run attempt to control Parent's finances would fail. Friend would simply present the court with Parent's document and either stop the proceedings or secure appointment as Parent's guardian. Either way, Parent will have the person in charge of Parent's property that Parent wanted.

§25.1.4 Disability Income Insurance

When disability occurs, a person's expenses usually increase and the ability to earn money decreases. Disability income insurance provides regular payments to substitute for the income a person cannot earn because of a disability.

If a person does not have disability insurance, the person will be stuck with receiving only Social Security benefits. Reliance on Social Security is a bad option for several reasons. First, it is often harder for a person to be considered disabled under Social Security law than under insurance policies. Under Social Security, the person must be unable to "engage in any substantial gainful activity"[1] while insurance definitions of disability are often more liberal such as being unable to perform the job, or a reasonable equivalent thereof, which the person was performing prior to becoming disabled. Second, Social Security pays relatively low benefits compared to disability insurance. This difference is especially important for people who are highly compensated.

Example 25-11. Disability Income Insurance

Client earns $100,000 per year and is attempting to obtain a disability income policy. However, Client does not know where to go and what type of provisions are desirable. What advice would you give Client?

Explanation

There are three main sources of disability income insurance. First, many employers make this type of insurance available to employees at very favorable rates. Second, professional and social organizations often contract with insurance companies to offer disability insurance to its members at competitive rates. Third, and usually the most expensive option, insurance agents sell this type of policy to their customers. Client should expect the policy to pay

---

1. 42 U.S.C. §416(i)(1).

between 60 and 80 percent of Client's current income—the policies will not pay 100 percent of current income because a person would lack a financial incentive to recover and return to work. Of course, Client should look for the lowest premiums consistent with maximum benefits. Policies will differ regarding the degree of disability Client must have to collect benefits, how long Client must wait from the onset of disability to collect benefits (the longer the waiting period, the more economical the premiums), whether the insurer will adjust benefits for inflation, the reliability of the insurer, the requirements to renew, and whether the policy will cover preexisting conditions. In most cases, Client (rather than Client's employer as a fringe benefit) should pay all the premiums so that the proceeds will not be subject to income tax.

§25.2 Health Care

A carefully prepared disability plan should cover health care matters as well as property management issues. Health care matters are of equal, if not greater, importance because of their intensely personal character and the ramifications those decisions may have on the person's length and quality of life. If no planning is done, the most likely result is that the court will appoint a guardian of the person to make the decisions. A growing number of states have recognized the problems caused by a person's failure to plan, the subsequent need for a guardian, and the cumbersome nature of the process. Legislatures in these states have enacted *statutory surrogate* laws, which authorize close family members to make medical decisions for people who are unable to do so and have not planned for this eventuality. Typically, family members are listed in a priority order. States vary as to whether physician consent is needed and what happens if there is disagreement among surrogates who have equal priority such as when two of the person's three children agree to certain medical treatment and the third child objects.

With proper planning, a person can avoid the need for a guardian and prevent statutory surrogates from making health care decisions. This section discusses these planning techniques as well as methods to fund medical care.

§25.2.1 *Durable Power of Attorney for Health Care*

Traditionally, a person could not use a power of attorney to delegate the authority to make health care decisions. These decisions were considered too intimate to delegate. In addition, the existence of the patient's informed consent to any medical treatment was problematic because the agent, not the patient, would be making the decision. However, there are persuasive arguments in favor of this type of delegation. Medical decisions could then be made by a person specified by the patient. This person is likely to have a better understanding of how the patient would like to be treated than a guardian, doctor, or family member.

In 1982, the National Conference of Commissioners on Uniform State Laws approved the Model Health-Care Consent Act, which included a provision permitting a person to transfer health care decision authority to a *health care representative*. The next year, California became the first state to address this issue when it enacted legislation approving a durable power of attorney for health care accompanied by a statutory fill-in-the-blank form. A rapidly growing number of states have followed California's lead and the 1993 Uniform Health Care Decisions Act continued this trend by permitting a person to designate a health care agent.

The principal must have legal capacity and be competent to designate a health care agent. The document must meet the applicable statutory formalities, which may include signing a separate disclosure statement, witnessing, or notarization.

Example 25-12. Durable Power of Attorney for Health Care — Qualities of Agent

Principal has already named Friend as Principal's agent under a valid durable power of attorney for property management. Should Principal name Friend as the health care agent as well?

Explanation

The desirable traits for a property management agent are different from those of a health care agent. A health care agent may be called upon to make life and death decisions but does not need the business acumen that the property agent should possess. Instead, the health care agent needs to be in a good position to exercise substituted judgment for the principal and thus should have a solid grasp of the principal's attitudes, the quality of life the principal would find acceptable, and the principal's religious beliefs and philosophy of life. The principal and agent should have serious conversations about health care matters so the principal is confident in placing these important decisions into the agent's hands.

Example 25-13. Durable Power of Attorney for Health Care — Extent of Authority

Mother and Father named Child as their health care agent in a valid durable power of attorney. Mother and Father were in a terrible automobile accident and both are hospitalized and unconscious. Mother has a good chance for recovery if she has surgery within the next twenty-four hours. Father is on life support equipment and his physicians agree that he has no chance of regaining consciousness. However, he could be kept technically alive by machines for an indefinite period of time. Child would like to use Child's status as the agent to consent to Mother's surgery and to remove life support from Father. Does Child have the authority to make these decisions?

Explanation

The durable powers of attorney for health care must be examined first. Most states permit the principal to include express instructions that may restrict or limit the agent's authority to make health care decisions. Assuming the documents are silent, there is little doubt Child may consent to the Mother's surgery. In most states, Child would also have the authority to consent to disconnecting Father from the machines despite the fact that Father will die as a result and accelerate Child's ability to take under intestacy or under Father's will. The doctor, however, may not be obligated to follow Child's directions. States vary as to the extent of a health care provider's duty to follow the agent's instructions.

Example 25-14. Durable Power of Attorney for Health Care — When Effective

Principal delegated to Agent the authority to make health care decisions in a valid durable power of attorney. Principal is now in the hospital to have elective liposuction treatment. Agent has read about the dangers of the procedure and tells Principal's physician not to proceed with the operation. May the doctor treat Principal over Agent's objection?

Explanation

Durable powers of attorney for health care normally are springing, that is, the agent has no authority until the principal is unable to make health care decisions. Thus, Agent has no authority to stop Principal from having the operation.

Example 25-15. Durable Power of Attorney for Health Care — Revocation

Principal delegated to Agent the authority to make health care decisions in a valid durable power of attorney. Principal is now in the hospital after a severe accident. The doctors have outlined several courses of treatment to Principal and Agent. However, Principal and Agent disagree on which treatment to select, causing Principal to orally state, "I revoke your authority; please go away." Agent argued that because of the accident and the medication Principal is taking, Principal is not competent to revoke the power of attorney. Whose instructions should Principal's doctor follow?

Explanation

Most states permit a principal to revoke the durable power of attorney for health care orally. In addition, many states do not inquire into a principal's capacity with regard to a revocation as they would with other types of documents (e.g., an incompetent person cannot revoke a will). Thus, Principal's doctor cannot follow Agent's instructions. Whether the doctor can abide by Principal's selection of treatment is another issue. If Principal is competent, the doctor should abide by Principal's request. However, if Principal is incompetent, the doctor will need to follow the instructions of a guardian or statutory surrogate.

§25.2.2   Self-Designation of Guardian of Person

Many states allow a person to predesignate the individual the person would like to serve as the guardian of the person. Most of the discussion regarding self-designations of guardians of the estate in §25.1.3, above, is also applicable. For continuity, the same person named as the health care agent should also be named as the guardian of the person.

Example 25-16.   Self-Designation of Guardian of Person — Selection

Client has already named someone to serve as guardian of Client's estate should the need ever arise. Should that person also be designated as the guardian of Client's person?

Explanation

Client may want the same trusted person, such as the spouse or a child, to serve in both capacities. However, different people may be appropriate if the same person would not have the skills necessary for both positions. For example, a corporate fiduciary may be a good choice to serve as the guardian of Client's estate, especially if Client owns assets needing professional management, while a family member may be the best choice as the guardian of Client's person.

§25.2.3 *Funding Long-Term Health Care Expenses*

This section reviews the various sources from which a person may pay the cost of long-term health care.

§25.2.3.1 Patient's Personal Resources

If the patient does not make other arrangements for health care expenses, the patient will be responsible for those expenses unless the patient can qualify for government assistance. Health care expenses can quickly deplete even relatively large estates and disrupt the person's plans for property disposition upon death. Accordingly, it is extremely important to plan for the funding of long-term health care expenses to prevent the depletion of the patient's estate.

§25.2.3.2 Long-Term Care Insurance

Long-term care insurance is designed to pay for a person's care when the person is confined to a nursing home or other facility. Many policies will also pay for home care, a tremendous benefit because most people would rather live in familiar surroundings than in an institutional setting.

Example 25-17. Long-Term Care Insurance — Appropriate Insureds

Client has just learned that statistically a large number of people will have to enter a nursing home because of an accident, illness, or disease. In fact, more than one-third of the individuals who reach age sixty-five will need nursing home care. Statistically, the risk is much higher for women than men. Should Client purchase long-term care insurance?

Explanation

Long-term care insurance has tremendous potential benefits. Client will be able to preserve estate assets and avoid being a burden on family members. However, the premiums for this type of insurance are relatively high. According to United Seniors Health Cooperative, Client should consider long-term care insurance only if Client has more than $75,000 in assets (not counting Client's home and car) for each member of Client's household, has an annual income of $30,000 or more for each member of Client's household, would not spend more than 10 percent of Client's income for premiums, and Client could still afford the policy if premiums increased by 30 percent.[2] If Client does not meet these criteria, from a financial standpoint, Client may wish to consider relying on governmental assistance for long-term care expenses.

Example 25-18. Long-Term Care Insurance — Policy Provisions

Client has a net worth of approximately $500,000 and has decided to purchase a long-term care policy. The thought of spending a lifetime of savings on these expenses and leaving nothing to Client's family is distasteful. In addition, Client does not want to be forced into a facility that accepts governmental assistance should Client's estate eventually be exhausted by paying for these expenses. What considerations should Client examine in selecting a long-term care policy?

Explanation

Client should examine the benefits that the insurance company will pay if Client is admitted to a nursing home. Benefits are typically paid on a per day (e.g., $200 per day) or a percentage of cost (e.g., 75 percent of actual cost) basis. Is there an upper limit on these benefits, either in money or the time during which they can be collected? What is the length of the period of time between the onset of disability and the payment of benefits? The longer the waiting period, the lower the premiums. Does Client have to pay premiums even while Client is receiving benefits? Will the policy cover in-home care as well as nursing home care? For what type of care will the policy pay, that is, will the policy cover only professional care or will the policy pay for other providers as well? Must Client first be admitted to a hospital before being eligible for nursing home care? Are nursing home admissions based on any preexisting conditions of Client covered? How is disability determined? Is disability based on Client not being able to perform a specified number of activities of daily living (e.g., eating, toileting, transferring, bathing, dressing, and continence) or may disability also be shown through a cognitive impairment such as Alzheimer's disease?

§25.2.3.3 Accelerated Life Insurance Payments and Viatical Settlements

Two innovative uses of life insurance can provide valuable benefits to an insured while the insured is still alive but facing a rapidly approaching death.

---

2. Jane Bryant Quinn, *The Ins and Outs of Long-Term Care Insurance*, San Juan Star, Nov. 23, 1997, at B55.

(For a discussion of life insurance, see §17.1, above.) One technique involves a life insurance policy that requires the insurer to prepay all or a portion of the death benefit to the insured when the insured has a disabling or life threatening condition doctors predict will cause death within a relatively short period of time. These provisions are referred to by terms such as *accelerated death benefit*, *living needs benefit*, *acceleration-of-life-insurance benefit*, and *living payout option*. The insured may then use the proceeds to offset health care expenses. Depending on the debilitating extent of the illness, the extra money may also allow the insured to enjoy the remainder of the insured's life to its fullest such as by taking a vacation before the insured becomes too ill to do so. Some policies will also provide benefits to pay for a life-saving organ transplant. State governments have been quick to authorize insurance companies to offer policies that contain accelerated benefits. By the end of 1991, the insurance commissions of all states had authorized accelerated benefits.

The other technique provides basically the same result but through a different means. In a *viatical settlement*, a third party purchases the life insurance policy of an insured (the *viator*) who has a life-threatening disease or illness. The insured either receives a one-time payment that usually ranges from 50 to 80 percent of the policy's face value or can elect to receive periodic payments. Most purchasers require the insured to have two years or less to live. The shorter the insured's life expectancy, the greater the purchase price will be. During 1994, viatical settlement companies paid an average of $76,000 for a $100,000 policy. The purchaser becomes the owner of the policy and typically names itself as the beneficiary. The purchaser continues to pay any required premiums and receives the policy's entire face value when the insured dies. Many states have extensive provisions regulating viatical settlements.

Example 25-19. Accelerated Life Insurance Payments — Non-Tax Ramifications

Insured has been diagnosed with a terminal illness and Insured's doctors anticipate that Insured has less than one year to live. Should Insured exercise an accelerated benefits option?

Explanation

Under most policies, the proceeds of an accelerated benefit can be used in whatever manner the insured desires, be it to pay for medical expenses, spend frivolously, or make gifts to family members and friends. Insured may enjoy having the funds for these purposes. However, accepting accelerated benefits reduces the face amount of Insured's policy thereby reducing or eliminating death benefits payable to the beneficiary when Insured dies. Insured may not wish to sacrifice the future financial security of a spouse or children in exchange for accelerated benefits. In addition, the accelerated proceeds may now be subject to Insured's creditors, both while Insured is alive and after Insured dies. If the proceeds were payable to a designated beneficiary upon Insured's death, they would escape liability for Insured's debts. Another concern is the financial vulnerability of Insured after receiving the accelerated benefits. Insured may be subjected to charlatans claiming that they can cure Insured's ailment or to scam artists who boast they can earn large returns on Insured's newly gained wealth.

Example 25-20. Accelerated Life Insurance Payments — Tax Ramifications

Insured has been diagnosed with a terminal illness and Insured's doctors anticipate that Insured has less than one year to live. Insured has adequate insurance to cover all of Insured's health care expenses. Should Insured exercise an accelerated benefit option for tax reasons even though Insured does not need the money?

Explanation

Insured needs to consider both income and transfer taxes before making a decision. Under the Health Insurance Portability and Accountability Act of 1996, most accelerated payments, as well as viatical settlements, are excluded from an insured's gross income. I.R.C. §101(g). Thus, Insured will not experience any adverse income tax consequences from electing an accelerated payment.

As a general rule, the proceeds of a life insurance policy an insured owns at the time of the insured's death are included as part of the insured's gross estate. I.R.C. §2042 (see §24.2.2.4, above). Consequently, if Insured's policy has a face value of $100,000 and Insured is in the 55 percent estate tax bracket, only $45,000 will actually pass to the beneficiary. On the other hand, if Insured opts for accelerated benefits, Insured will immediately receive a discounted amount of the face value and will not have to pay income tax on that amount. Using the same $100,000 policy and assuming a discount of 25 percent, Insured would receive $75,000 income tax free. Insured could then use this money either to pay expenses or to make gifts to beneficiaries. If Insured elected to make gifts with the money, they could easily be structured to avoid transfer taxation such as by keeping them within the annual exclusion or by using them for the donee's medical expenses or tuition. In this case, Insured can transfer an extra $30,000 ($75,000 − $45,000). The savings would be even greater for lower discount rates.

Accordingly, the potential tax savings of accelerating benefits for insureds with estates large enough to trigger transfer taxes are significant.

§25.2.3.4 Home Care Contracts

The use of a contract in which a person agrees to leave property to a caretaker in the person's will in exchange for home care services is discussed in Example 11-11, above.

§25.2.3.5 Governmental Assistance

A person might not have the resources to provide for the person's long-term care and thus may be forced to rely on *Medicaid*. Medicaid is a jointly funded effort of the federal government and the states to provide medical assistance and institutional care for elderly or disabled individuals who have limited assets. Congress enacted Medicaid in 1965 as a companion to *Medicare*, the federal health insurance program for citizens age sixty-five and over. State agencies administer Medicaid and make payments directly to health care providers rather than the patients.

Medicaid eligibility is based on a variety of factors. Both the person's income and assets must be below specified amounts, which vary among the states. In addition, voluntary transfers by the person or the person's spouse within the *look-back period* of thirty-six months are treated as if the person still owned them. If the transfer was to an irrevocable trust under which the trustee cannot make a principal distribution to the person, the look-back period is extended to sixty months. The person is then disqualified from receiving Medicaid for the period of time those assets could have paid for the person's care.

Because Medicaid is need based, some individuals plan to be poor so they will qualify for Medicaid benefits. These people wonder why they should save money and hold on to their assets only to pay their own medical costs until they exhaust their funds and become eligible for Medicaid. Why not just start off on the Medicaid dole? Of course, people do not like to give up total control of their assets and the federal government is wise to the "let's look poor" ploy and thus a person must use great care in sheltering a person's assets. The person may also strategically invest in property not counted toward Medicaid eligibility such as a car, jewelry, and in some cases, a home.

Is it morally right for a person to do this type of planning, which may prevent funds from reaching the truly needy as well as increasing taxes for everyone? Medicaid was designed for people without other options — not for middle class individuals who want to save money for their heirs and beneficiaries. On the other hand, what is wrong with exploiting loopholes in the rules to save money just like a person may use the annual gift tax exclusion, the unlimited marital deduction, and income tax itemized deductions?

Example 25-21. Medicaid Planning

Client explained Client's financial situation to you and desire to obtain Medicaid benefits. You realize that Client should consider making a few strategic property transfers to protect property and make it easier to qualify for Medicaid. What advice can you give Client?

Explanation

You may not advise Client on how to transfer assets to enhance Medicaid eligibility under the terms of the applicable statute. Federal law imposes a criminal penalty which includes a $10,000 fine and up to a one year prison sentence to anyone who "for a fee knowingly and willfully counsels or assists an individual to dispose of assets (including by any transfer in trust) in order for the individual to become eligible for [Medicaid] if disposing of the assets results in the imposition of a period of ineligibility for such assistance."[3] However, many practitioners and bar associations believe that this rule violates First Amendment free speech rights and prevents attorneys from counseling clients about perfectly legal conduct. In 1998, one United States District Court enjoined the government from "commencing, maintaining, or otherwise taking action to enforce" the statute.[4]

§25.3 The Death Event

Death is inevitable and the process of dying may be physically and emotionally agonizing. Fortunately, an individual may control many aspects of this process such as whether to use heroic means to sustain life, whether to permit others to benefit from the death through organ donation, and the final disposition of the individual's remains. Failure to plan for death may result in the loss of the person's dignity and cause unnecessary pain and suffering while providing nothing medically necessary or beneficial. For example, in *Cruzan v. Director, Missouri Department of Health*,[5] the United States Supreme Court did not allow life-support equipment to be removed from a patient in a persistent vegetative state with virtually no chance of recovery

---

3. 42 U.S.C. §1320a-7b(a)(6).
4. New York State Bar Assoc. v. Reno, 999 F. Supp. 710, 716 (N.D. N.Y. 1998).
5. 497 U.S. 261 (1990).

because there was no clear and convincing evidence that the patient would have wanted the removal. This section reviews the legal techniques an individual may use to plan for the death event.

§25.3.1 Living Wills

A competent individual has the right to refuse medical treatment for any reason even if that refusal will lead to an otherwise preventable death. What happens, though, if the person is in a coma, brain damaged, or for some other reason cannot communicate the person's wishes? Perhaps the person designated an agent in a durable power of attorney for health care. This agent would now have the authority to make medical decisions, including a refusal of treatment. See §25.2.1, above. Alternatively, the person may have signed a *living will,* also called a *directive to physicians, natural death statement,* or *advance directive,* expressing the person's desire not to be kept alive through the use of medical technology when the person is in a terminal condition and unable to communicate the person's wishes to decline further treatment.

California was the first state to statutorily authorize a person to make an advance statement regarding the use of life-sustaining procedures when its legislature enacted living will legislation in 1976. Other states quickly followed suit so that practically all states now have enabling statutes, most of which contain fill-in-the blank forms. The scope of these statutes and the accompanying forms, however, vary tremendously. Some permit a person to make only basic statements regarding the person's intent while others ask for the person's opinion on a variety of issues (e.g., whether nutrition and hydration are included within the scope of life-sustaining procedures) or provide extensive opportunities for the person to indicate the type of treatment and the length of its application under a number of circumstances. Likewise, the formal requirements (e.g., whether the documents must be witnessed or notarized) are not uniform among the states.

Sample Living Will Provision[6]

If I should have an incurable and irreversible condition that, without the administration of life-sustaining treatment, will, in the opinion of my attending physician, cause my death within a relatively short time, and I am no longer able to make decisions regarding my medical treatment, I direct my attending physician, pursuant to [state enabling legislation], to withhold or withdraw treatment that only prolongs the process of dying and is not necessary for my comfort or to alleviate pain.

---

6. Uniform Rights of the Terminally Ill Act §2(b) (1989).

Many of your clients will be extremely interested in obtaining a living will. They are often discussed in the media and gain national attention when they are used to hasten the death of famous people such as former President Richard Nixon and former first lady Jacqueline Kennedy Onassis. In addition, the federal Patient Self-Determination Act[7] requires all hospitals, nursing homes, and other health care providers that participate in Medicare or Medicaid to give all patients at the time of their admission written information regarding their rights to refuse medical treatment under state law.

Example 25-22.   Living Wills — Effectiveness and Warnings

Client consults you regarding a living will. Client is convinced that Client would not want to "take up space" and be a burden on Client's family should Client be in a terminal condition, unconscious, with no chance of recovery, and unable to communicate Client's desire to "pull the plug." What other concerns should Client contemplate before deciding to execute the living will?

Explanation

Client needs to consider both the possibility of the living will (1) being used when it should not be used, and (2) not being used when it should be used. At least three situations could lead to the living will being inappropriately applied. First, heirs and beneficiaries may nudge the doctors into withdrawing support too early because they are anxious for their inheritances and do not want their gifts reduced by the continuously accruing medical expenses. Second, the medical literature is filled with reports of individuals who recover after doctors had pronounced their situations as completely hopeless. Third, the living will may be used to withhold treatment in an inappropriate circumstance. For example, assume that Client has cancer and fears a lingering death and thus signs a living will. Before the cancer has significantly decreased Client's quality of life, Client has a heart attack, which although life-threatening, could be treated with a high degree of success. A fear exists that Client would not get treatment for the heart attack because of the living will.

Several situations could also cause Client's directions in the living will to be ignored. Family members may hide Client's living will because they do not agree with Client's decision to have life-support removed. If Client already had the living will placed in Client's medical records, Client's family may claim that Client revoked the living will. In most states, a family member could easily do this because the formalities of a revocation are minimal, such

---

7. U.S.C. §1395cc(f).

as an oral statement to anyone. In addition, a doctor afraid of malpractice liability may delay carrying out Client's directions.

To avoid these types of problems, Client should consider appointing a trusted person as an agent to make these decisions. Depending on state law, Client may be able to do this in the living will itself or under a durable power of attorney for health care. See §25.2.1, above.

Example 25-23. Living Wills — Financial Ramifications

Client consults you regarding whether Client should sign a living will. Client explains that Client has already considered Client's personal, religious, and philosophical beliefs. Client tells you, "I do not want to spend years in a hospital or nursing home like a piece of broccoli." However, Client is concerned about the financial ramifications of Client's decision to sign a living will. How would you advise Client?

Explanation

Many estate planners believe that a living will is one of the best estate preservation techniques available. Approximately 50 percent of all health care costs in the United States are incurred in the last five days of a person's life. Experts estimate that, on average, a living will saves $60,000 per client. On the other hand, it may be economically advantageous to incur these costs and stay alive for a little longer. For example, assume that it would otherwise be appropriate to remove life-support equipment on December 29. Client may prefer to be kept alive until early January so that Client's property management agent could make many annual exclusion gifts in the new year. The transfer tax savings could easily exceed the health care costs.

Client does not need to worry about the existence of the living will having any financial implications while Client is alive. Most states prevent health insurance companies from lowering rates for individuals who have living wills. Likewise, most states prohibit life insurance companies from raising rates when a person signs a living will that could cause the insurer to have to pay the proceeds days, months, or even years earlier than if the insured had not authorized an accelerated death.

§25.3.2 *Assisted Suicide*

Assisted suicide arises when the person committing suicide needs help in procuring the means to commit the act such as a weapon, drugs, or Dr. Jack Kevorkian's "suicide machine." The person, however, self-administers the lethal agent by pulling the trigger, swallowing the pills, turning on the gas, or the like. If a doctor assists the person in procuring the fatal drugs, the term *physician assisted suicide* is often used. Assisted suicide in general is sometimes called *passive euthanasia* because the euthanatizer merely supplies the means of death rather than directly causing the death. Assisted suicide can be contrasted with *voluntary euthanasia* in which the euthanatizer actually kills the person at that person's request. The term *involuntary euthanasia* is reserved for cases where the euthanatizer kills a person out of reasons of mercy but where the person did not specifically request to be killed.

Most state legislatures have enacted statutes making it a crime to assist someone to commit suicide. These statutes withstood constitutional muster in the United States Supreme Court case of *Vacco v. Quill*.[8] The Court held that the United States Constitution does not guarantee a person the right to die and that states can prohibit assisted suicide. However, the Court indicated that a state may decide to authorize and regulate assisted suicide. As of August 1998, Oregon is the only state to permit its citizens to seek assistance in procuring the means to commit suicide. The key language of this landmark statute reads as follows:

> An adult who is capable, is a resident of Oregon, and has been determined by the attending physician and consulting physician to be suffering from a terminal disease, and who has voluntarily expressed his or her wish to die, may make a written request for medication for the purpose of ending his or her life in a humane and dignified manner in accordance with this Act.[9]

§25.3.3 Anatomical Gifts

Regardless of financial situation, each person has extremely valuable assets that can be transferred at death, namely the person's own body and its parts. Doctors performed over 19,000 organ transplants in the United States in 1996. Despite the media attention given to organ donation, organs are in short supply. As of March 1998, over 50,000 people were waiting for organ transplants.[10] Many people will find organ donation an exciting prospect because a high degree of self-satisfaction can come from the knowledge that donated organs will enhance or save lives. The American Bar Association urges all attorneys to discuss the topic of organ and tissue donations with their clients.[11]

On the other hand, some people consider the use of their dead bodies for transplantation or research to be distasteful or contrary to their religious

---

8. 117 S. Ct. 2293 (1997).

9. Oregon Death with Dignity Act §2.01 (1994).

10. Clinton Colmenares, *The Paradox of Medical Transplants,* San Antonio Express-News, Mar. 16, 1998, at 1F.

11. *Organ Donor Resolution,* Prob. & Prop., Jan.-Feb. 1992, at 6.

beliefs. In a way, organ donation is nothing more than cannibalism by technology. The argument is made that there is little difference between ingesting human flesh and having that flesh surgically inserted into the body; in both situations, part of a deceased person ends up inside a living person. A more widespread reason people refuse to donate organs is the fear that medical personnel may not work as hard to save the lives of organ donors as nondonors. The media are brimming with reports of people who were presumed dead but who were actually alive. For example, in one study of people pronounced dead by physicians at a major metropolitan hospital, researchers discovered upon closer examination that 12 percent were still alive.[12] In another case, a man was declared dead after a traffic accident, taken to a mortuary, and placed in a box. He woke up about two days later, made lots of noise, and was freed from the box. Unfortunately, his fiancée, who was also in the accident, refused to have anything to do with him believing that he had turned into a zombie and had come back to haunt her.[13]

Organ donation has a relatively long history. Bones were first transplanted in 1878 and cornea transplants began in the 1940s. It was not until the kidney transplants of the 1950s, however, that the need for comprehensive organ donation law arose. The failure of then-existing law to govern anatomical gifts uniformly and comprehensively led the National Conference of Commissioners on Uniform State Laws to approve the Uniform Anatomical Gift Act in 1968. Within five years, all fifty states and the District of Columbia substantially adopted the act. Many states have now enacted a revised version of the act promulgated in 1987 to simplify the method of making anatomical gifts and to make it more likely that the donor's intentions will be carried out.

Example 25-24. Anatomical Gifts — Methods

Client is very interested in making arrangements for Client's organs to be donated upon Client's death. What methods could Client use to make anatomical gifts?

Explanation

Client may have several ways of documenting Client's intent to make anatomical gifts depending on the law of Client's residence. First, Client may sign a card indicating Client's wishes. The card should be small enough for

---

12. *Checking for Pulse Misses Some Who Are Still Alive,* Boston Globe, Feb. 3, 1992, at 27.

13. *Man Cheats Death, Loses His Fiancee,* New Orleans Times Picayune, Mar. 22, 1993, at E15.

Client to carry in Client's wallet so it will be spotted in a timely fashion after Client's death. States vary with regard to the requirements of this card. In all states, Client or the Client's authorized proxy must sign the card. In states following the original version of the Uniform Act, two witnesses are also required. Second, Client may include anatomical gifts in Client's will. Such gifts are effective without the necessity of probating the will. This method is not recommended because time is very critical. Many organs need to be removed immediately to be useful and Client's will may not be located or read until it is too late. Third, some states permit Client to make anatomical gifts by an appropriate designation on Client's driver's license.

Example 25-25. Anatomical Gifts — Prevention

Client does not want any anatomical gifts to occur upon Client's death. What steps, if any, should Client take to document Client's intent?

Explanation

Client cannot simply decline to sign a document making anatomical gifts and then believe that anatomical gifts will never occur. Close family members have the right to donate Client's organs even without Client's consent. Anatomical gift statutes enumerate a priority order of these relatives with Client's spouse, adult children, parents, and adult siblings heading the list. Even if these persons did not independently know of their ability to make anatomical gifts for Client, they are likely to find out because state law often requires hospitals to routinely ask family members if they would like to make anatomical gifts. In addition, certain government officials such as the coroner, medical examiner, and justice of the peace, may be authorized to remove organs for transplantation. Individuals on the priority list and government officials are, however, precluded from consenting if Client has documented Client's refusal to make anatomical gifts. Thus, Client should execute an anti-anatomical gift card and carry it in Client's wallet just as an organ donor would carry the donor card.

Example 25-26. Anatomical Gifts — Identity of Donee

Client wants to make anatomical gifts and is completing an anatomical gift card. Who should Client name as the proper recipient of the gift?

Explanation

Client may precisely designate the recipient of the anatomical gift and the purpose for which the gift may be used. For example, if Client's sibling needs a kidney, Client may specify that the only recipient of Client's kidneys is this sibling. If Client wants to donate the entire body for use by a specific medical school, Client may indicate the name of that school. If Client does not have a specific donee in mind, as is usually the case, Client will not name a donee. Instead, any hospital may accept the gift. This is the normal scenario because Client does not know when or where death will occur and which organs may be needed or useable. Client may restrict the use of the gift even if no donee is named. Many people permit any organs to be taken for transplantation but do not want to relinquish their entire body, i.e., they do not want to be used as a cadaver for medical research or training.

Example 25-27. Anatomical Gift—Rights of Donee

Client signed a valid anatomical gift card indicating Client's desire to donate any needed organs for transplantation. As Client is about to die, Client's spouse objects. Will the anatomical gift still take place?

Explanation

The rights of the donee are generally superior to the rights of other persons, such as family members, unless Client's body is needed for an autopsy under state law. Accordingly, Client's spouse has no standing to object and cannot legally prevent the gift from occurring. However, from a practical standpoint, physicians are reluctant to accept anatomical gifts over the objection of close family members for fear of protracted litigation.

Anatomical gifts raise a wide spectrum of other pertinent issues beyond the scope of this book. Examples of these concerns include (1) the determination of priority in the allocation of organs to potential donees, (2) the development of underground organ markets, (3) whether a donor can sell a future interest in the donor's organs that would entitle the purchaser to the organs upon the donor's death, (4) keeping brain-dead donors functioning with machines so that scientists can perform research while the body is, to some extent, still working on its own, (5) the morality of using tissue from miscarriages and abortions, (6) the liability of the donor's estate if donated organs are defective, such as a weak heart, or the person is infected with a disease such as HIV or hepatitis, and (7) whether death row inmates can trade bone marrow or a kidney in exchange for a life sentence without parole.

§25.3.4 Disposition of Body

A significant number of individuals are deeply concerned about how their bodies will be disposed of upon their death. Many people have strong preferences regarding the disposition method, that is, burial or cremation.

Other individuals wish to spell out the particulars of their funeral in great detail such as the location of the burial, whether the viewing is open or closed casket, the type of religious service, the inscription on the headstone, the kind of flowers and music, and the contents of the obituary. The legal systems of the ancient Greeks and Romans gave great weight to the deceased's instructions concerning bodily disposition. However, the common law courts recognized no property rights in a dead body. This view gained widespread acceptance in the United States and thus a person's desires regarding disposition of the body were considered to be only precatory. A growing number of states have rejected this rule and recognize a person's right to determine the final disposition of the body.

Example 25-28.   Disposition of Body — Methods to Carry Out Intent

Client has many specific instructions regarding the disposition of Client's body. How should you proceed in assuring that Client's intent is followed?

Explanation

States vary tremendously with regard to the methods, if any, which a person may use to control body disposition. Most states have a statutory list of individuals who make disposition decisions in a priority order. The list typically begins with the decedent's spouse, adult children, parents, and adult siblings, and continues with more distant relatives. Depending on state law, Client may be able to use one or more of the following methods to document body disposition desires.

(1) Inter Vivos Document. Client may be able to execute a document containing Client's specific requests. Certain formalities may be necessary such as being witnessed or acknowledged by a notary.

(2) Will Provision. Client may be able to provide instructions in Client's will. These directions are valid to the extent they are acted on in good faith even if the will is never probated or if a court declares that the will is invalid. The use of will provisions to give body disposition instructions is not recommended, however, because the will may not be found or read until after the funeral.

(3) Prearranged Funeral. Client may plan ahead for the funeral with the desired funeral home. Funeral homes are willing to make such arrangements, which will help assure that Client's particular requests are followed and relieve Client's family from the heavy burden of making funeral arrangements. Client may also want to consider whether to prepay the funeral costs.

(4) Body Disposition Agent. A few states permit Client to appoint an agent to make body disposition decisions and may provide a statutory form for this purpose.

(5) Conditional Gift in Will. If Client fears that close family members may attempt to interfere with Client's wishes, Client may make gifts to these individuals conditioned upon following Client's disposition directions. The fear of losing a sizable gift may encourage individuals opposed to Client's plans to carry them out or, at least, not object.

Example 25-29. Disposition of Body — Unusual Requests

Several of your clients have unusual disposition requests. For example, one client wants to be buried in his car, another wants to have his skin removed, tanned, and then used to bind a volume of his poetry, and still another wants to be cremated and have the ashes launched into orbit around the earth. Assuming you follow the appropriate state law method for documenting body disposition desires, what are the chances that these wishes will be carried out over the objection of family members?

Explanation

Courts are reluctant to interfere with a person's body disposition desires. However, if a court considers Client's wishes too untraditional or they are deemed against public policy, they may be ignored. All of the examples in this question are based on real cases. George Swanson was buried in his Corvette and the cremated remains of many individuals have already been launched into space. However, the court refused to carry out Donal Russell's hide-tanning request.

26

Malpractice and Professional Responsibility

§26.1 Professional Negligence

The potential malpractice liability of an attorney for negligently preparing an estate plan is great because estate planning requires an especially high degree of competence. The attorney must have a thorough knowledge of many areas of the law including wills, probate, trusts, taxation, insurance, property, government benefits, business associations, and domestic relations. Surprisingly, however, the most common errors do not involve complicated or sophisticated matters. Instead, problems usually arise because of clerical errors in the preparation of wills and the attorney's failure to understand the effect of the language used in dispositive provisions, which results in beneficiaries not receiving what the testator or settlor intended.

When a defect in an estate plan is discovered during the client's lifetime, the client's only loss may be the cost of having the errors corrected; for example, the expense of having a new will prepared and executed. This is not the type of situation where malpractice liability is likely to be litigated. The attorney may be able to avoid becoming a defendant by simply correcting the errors without cost to the client and offering appropriate apologies for the inconvenience. Of course, if the attorney's negligence caused tax or other benefits to be permanently lost, the attorney's potential liability would be much greater.

Errors often do not manifest themselves until after the client has died. At that time, the decedent's estate may be able to sue the negligent attorney.

551

The damages would probably consist only of the fees paid for drafting the estate plan because no other diminution of the decedent's property would have resulted from the error. Consequently, if there is a flaw in the estate plan rendering it invalid or ineffective and that flaw can be traced to the negligent conduct of the attorney in charge, it is the intended beneficiaries who now find themselves short-changed who are likely to bring the malpractice action.

Example 26-1. Malpractice — Privity

Client hired Attorney to prepare a will leaving Client's entire estate to Sibling. Attorney was a slacker in law school and barely passed the bar examination so Attorney did not know that all wills require two witnesses under the applicable state law. Instead, Attorney thought that one witness was sufficient. As a result, Client's will could not be admitted to probate. All of Client's property passed via intestacy to Client's parents. May Sibling recover from Attorney the value of the property Sibling would otherwise have received?

Explanation

Under the traditional common law rule, the lawsuit between Sibling and Attorney would fail. Attorney did not owe a duty to Sibling because there was no *privity of contract* between Attorney and Sibling; the contractual relationship was only between Client and Attorney. Courts consistently rejected arguments that Sibling was a third-party beneficiary of the contract.

However, beginning with the landmark California cases of *Biakanja v. Irving*[1] *and Lucas v. Hamm*,[2] a growing number of courts have rejected this traditional approach because it insulates an entire group of negligent attorneys from accepting the responsibility and the consequences of their careless conduct. As the *Lucas* court wrote,

> [o]ne of the main purposes which the transaction between defendant [attorney] and the testator intended to accomplish was to provide for the transfer of property to plaintiffs; the damage to plaintiffs in the event of invalidity of the bequest was clearly foreseeable; it became certain, upon the death of the testator without change of the will, that plaintiffs would have received the intended benefits but for the asserted negligence of defendant; and if persons such as plaintiffs are not permitted to recover for the loss resulting from negligence of the draftsman, no

1. 320 P.2d 16 (Cal. 1958).
2. 364 P.2d 685 (Cal. 1961), *cert. denied,* 368 U.S. 987 (1962).

one would be able to do so, and the policy of preventing future harm would be impaired.[3]

Courts following this modern rule would permit Sibling to recover from Attorney. Likewise, the first Restatement of the Law Governing Lawyers (1998) adopts the principle that an attorney is liable to a nonclient when the lawyer knows the client intends the representation to benefit a nonclient.

Despite the trend toward removing the requirement of privity for a successful malpractice action against a negligent estate planner, some courts extol the wisdom of the traditional rule. In the 1996 Texas Supreme Court case of *Barcelo v. Elliott*,[4] the court held that "the greater good is served by preserving a bright-line privity rule which denies a cause of action to all beneficiaries whom the attorney did not represent. This will ensure that attorneys may in all cases zealously represent their clients without the threat of suit from third parties compromising that representation."[5] Allowing disappointed will and trust beneficiaries to sue "would subject attorneys to suits by heirs who simply did not receive what they believed to be their due share under the will or trust. This potential tort liability to third parties would create a conflict during the estate planning process, dividing the attorney's loyalty between his or her client and the third-party beneficiaries."[6] The court provided the following example of this type of conflict:

> Suppose . . . that a properly drafted will is simply not executed at the time of the testator's death. The document may express the testator's true intentions, lacking signatures solely because of the attorney's negligent delay. On the other hand, the testator may have postponed execution because of second thoughts regarding the distribution scheme. In the latter situation, the attorney's representation of the testator will likely be affected if he or she knows that the existence of an unexecuted will may create malpractice liability if the testator unexpectedly dies.[7]

Example 26-2. Malpractice — Statute of Limitations

Using the facts of Example 26-1, assume that Client signed the invalid will in 1990 and that Client died in 1999. If the applicable state law does not bar Sibling's action because of lack of privity, may Sibling recover?

---

3. 364 P.2d at 688.
4. 923 S.W.2d 575 (Tex. 1996).
5. Id. at 578-579.
6. Id. at 578.
7. Id.

Explanation

The key issue is when the statute of limitations began to run on Sibling's cause of action for Attorney's negligence. Some courts would permit Sibling to recover by applying a discovery rule so the statute does not begin to run until Sibling knew or should have known about Attorney's negligence. However, other courts would hold that the limitations period began to run when Client executed the will. These courts focus on the employment contract between Attorney and Client. If this contract, as is typically the case, did not impose on Attorney a continuing duty to review and update the will, the court may find no basis to justify delaying the running of limitations until Client's death.

§26.2   Ethical Concerns

Attorneys who prepare wills and trusts and perform other services in the estate planning field must pay attention to facts that raise professional responsibility issues. Most states have enacted a version of the Model Rules of Professional Conduct promulgated by the American Bar Association in 1983. These rules and their comments do not always adequately address estate planning concerns because they are geared to issues that arise in adversarial situations.[8] This section reviews some of the common ethical concerns you may encounter.

§26.2.1   Drafting Attorney as Beneficiary

Concerns that arise when the drafting attorney is also a beneficiary are discussed in §10.3.3, above.

§26.2.2   Drafting Attorney as Fiduciary

Example 26-3.   Drafting Attorney as Fiduciary

You are interviewing Client so you can prepare Client's estate plan. When you ask Client about the persons Client would like to name as fiduciaries, such as the executor of the will, the trustee of the trust, and the agent under

---

8. For a detailed analysis of the interface between estate planning and the Model Rules, see American College of Trust and Estate Counsel, *ACTEC Commentaries on the Model Rules of Professional Conduct* (2d ed. 1995).

a durable power of attorney, Client says that Client would like you to serve. May you ethically designate yourself to serve in these fiduciary capacities?

Explanation

The Model Rules do not prohibit you from agreeing to serve as Client's executor, trustee, or agent. Nonetheless, you should think very carefully before accepting these positions. You must be certain that Client's desire for you to serve is not the result of any importuning on your part. Some courts hold that you may not suggest yourself to fill these fiduciary roles and that Client must make an unprompted request for your services. Before agreeing to serve, you should make a full disclosure of relevant information such as the fact that a nonattorney can serve, the fee you expect to charge for your services, and the fee other individuals or businesses would charge. You also need to watch out for any exculpatory clauses that may be included in the instruments. Courts may consider them as impermissible agreements to limit your liability for malpractice.

§26.2.3 Drafting Attorney as Fiduciary's Attorney

Example 26-4. Drafting Attorney as Fiduciary's Attorney

You and Client have had a long professional and personal relationship. Client wants to name Spouse as the executor of Client's will and make certain that you serve as Spouse's attorney to take care of estate business. May you ethically draft the will and include a provision requiring Spouse to hire you as the attorney for the estate?

Explanation

The Model Rules do not prohibit you from including a provision directing Spouse to retain your services. Most wills, however, do not contain these types of provisions and thus the inclusion of such a clause may raise suspicions that you improperly influenced Client. In addition, many courts will treat this type of provision as merely being precatory and thus not binding on Spouse.

§26.2.4 Drafting Attorney as Will Custodian

The propriety of the drafting attorney retaining custody of a client's will is discussed in §5.4.2.5.3(3), above.

§26.2.5 *Estate Planning for Both Spouses*

Example 26-5. Estate Planning for Both Spouses

Today you are meeting with a new client to discuss estate planning matters. Your secretary has just informed you that this client has arrived. When you enter your reception area, you are surprised to see *two* people waiting for you — the client and the client's spouse. The client explains that the client wants you to prepare estate plans for both of them. How should you proceed?

Explanation

The joint representation of a husband and wife in drafting wills and establishing a coordinated estate plan can have considerable benefits. However, joint representation may cause you to have difficulties with loyalty and confidentiality duties. Accordingly, the decision regarding whether to represent the spouses jointly or to represent only one spouse must be made cautiously.

A conflict of interest between the spouses or between you and the spouses can arise for many reasons.

(1) Family Structure. With the frequency of remarriage and blended families in today's society, it is not surprising that nontraditional families are a ripe source of conflict. For example, a stepparent spouse may not feel the need or desire to provide for stepchildren or other relatives who are not biologically related.

(2) Past Relationship of One Spouse with Attorney. If one of the spouses has a prior relationship with you, regardless of whether that relationship is personal or professional, there is a potential for conflict. The longer, closer, and more financially rewarding the relationship between one of the spouses and you, the less likely you will be free from that spouse's influence.

(3) Differing Testamentary Goals. Spouses may also have different ideas and expectations regarding the forms and limitations of support provided by their estate plan to the survivor of them and their descendants. By including need-based or other restrictions on property, one spouse may believe that the other spouse will be "protected" while that spouse may view the limitations as unjustifiable, punitive, or manipulative.

(4) Power Difference between Spouses. One spouse may dominate the marital relationship and thus the client side of the attorney-client relationship. If one spouse is unfamiliar or uncomfortable with the prospect of working with you or if one spouse is unable, for whatever reason, to make his or her desires known to you and instead simply defers to the other spouse, it will be difficult for you to fairly represent both parties.

(5) Stability of Marriage. If you seriously question the stability of the marriage, it will be practically impossible to create an estate plan that contemplates the couple being separated only by death. In addition, the spouses may not reveal their marital problems to you and thus prevent you from making an informed decision on how to proceed.

(6) Relative Size of Estates. Significant conflict may arise if one spouse's estate is of substantially greater value than that of the other spouse, especially if the wealthier spouse wants to make a distribution that differs from the traditional plan where each spouse leaves everything to the survivor and upon the survivor's death to their descendants. You may generate a great deal of conflict between the spouses if, to act in the best interest of the not-so-wealthy spouse, you explain that spouse's financial standing under the estate plan if the wealthy spouse were to die first.

Joint representation will force the spouses to forgo their normal confidentiality and evidentiary privileges. The fact that there is no confidentiality between the spouses may not be a problem if the spouses have nothing to hide and have common estate planning goals. On the other hand, joint representation can place one or both of the spouses in the compromising position of having to reveal long-held secrets in the presence of his or her spouse, e.g., the existence of a child born out of wedlock. Likewise, if one spouse reveals something to you "privately," you may have the obligation to tell the other spouse.

Despite these problems, joint representation of spouses is very common because of the savings in time and money and ease by which the estate plan of each spouse can be coordinated with the other. If you decide to represent both spouses, you should provide full disclosure of the possible conflicts of interest and confidentiality concerns. Each spouse should sign a consent to the joint representation.

§26.2.6 *Representation of Non-Spousal Relatives*

Example 26-6. Representation of Non-Spousal Relatives

You have recently completed preparing an estate plan for Client. Client was extremely pleased with your services and has referred Parent to you. May you ethically prepare Parent's will?

Explanation

Representation of more than one family member raises a number of ethical concerns such as avoiding conflicts of interest, maintaining confidences, and preserving independent professional judgment. These issues are analogous to those discussed in §26.2.5, above, relating to representation of both spouses. The safest course of action would be to decline to represent Parent. If you nonetheless decide to draft Parent's will, you must exercise caution and be sure both Parent and Client receive a complete disclosure and then sign a document consenting to the joint representation.

§26.2.7   Fiduciary Hiring Self As Attorney

The conflicts of interest which may arise when an attorney who is serving as a fiduciary decides to hire him- or herself as the attorney for the estate are discussed in §20.5.6, above.

§26.2.8   Capacity of Representation

Example 26-7.   Capacity of Representation

Trustee hired you to perform legal services for the trust. Beneficiary filed suit against Trustee alleging that Trustee breached various fiduciary duties. You have just been served with a subpoena to produce all documents relating to your work with this trust. What should you do?

Explanation

The key issue is to determine the person to whom you owe your fiduciary duties, that is, is your client (a) Trustee in an individual capacity, (b) the trust itself, or (c) the beneficiaries? The courts in the United States are divided. Some courts would hold that you actually work for the trust and thus owe a higher duty to the trust and Beneficiary than to Trustee. On the other hand, other courts would hold that you represent Trustee personally. In this latter situation, you would not have to turn over your files because of the attorney-client privilege.

Sample Will with Testamentary Trust Form

The first time you are asked to draft a will, an application for probate, or other estate planning document, you may initially panic wondering where to start. Although you know the legal rules, it is often quite a different experience to actually draft the documents. Do not despair. There are many form books available to start you on the right track. Always remember, of course, that no form should be used blindly and that no form will exactly fit your needs. Use a form as a guideline and be sure to make all appropriate changes. Never leave language in a document from a form without being sure you understand it and intend for it to be included.

Computer programs are being used on an increasingly frequent basis to assist will preparation. Many attorneys prepare and store forms in computer-usable formats. Commercial publishers also market computer programs that assist in form preparation. Some programs supply only the text of forms, much like traditional form books. Other programs prompt the user to enter relevant information and then use that data to select and print a suitable form, inserting individualized information at the appropriate locations. Most of these programs are designed for use by attorneys but others are targeted at the lay community.

The following form may be used as a starting point for drafting a simple will.

Last Will of [Client][1]

I, [Client],[2] a resident of [City], [State], [County], declare that this is my last will and I revoke all prior wills and codicils. My social security number is [social security number].[3]

ARTICLE I
DESCRIPTION OF FAMILY

A. Marital Status

[if never married] I am not married and I have never been married.

[if single but previously married] I am not married. I was formerly married to [Ex-Spouse]. [We were divorced] [[Ex-Spouse] died] on [date].[4]

[if currently married for first time] I am married to [Spouse]. We were married on [date]. This is my only marriage.

[if remarried] I am married to [Spouse]. We were married on [date]. I was formerly married to [Ex-Spouse]. [We were divorced] [[Ex-Spouse] died] on [date].[5]

---

1. This sample will is designed to help you prepare Client's will. Please remember that this form, like any form, is just a guide; do not use it without considering the ramifications of each clause. The provisions must be individualized to fit the particular needs of Client and the requirements of local law.

A will is only one part of an estate plan. You should be sure to plan for Client's potential disability, both with regard to property management and health care, as well as end-of-life decisions such as the use of artificial life sustaining procedures, anatomical gifts, and body disposition instructions.

Please note the following features of this form which are designed to reduce the likelihood of unauthorized page substitution. (1) Spaces on the bottom of each page for the initials of Client and the witnesses. (2) Use of *ex toto* pagination in the header.

2. If Client has been known by other names (e.g., nickname, name prior to marriage, name used during previous marriage, etc.), they should be listed here. For example, "I [Client], also known as. . . . " or "I have also been known as. . . . "

3. The decedent's social security number is often needed to track down assets, obtain other benefits, and complete various forms during the administration process.

4. Continue in a similar manner if Client has been divorced more than once.

5. Continue in a similar manner if Client has been divorced more than once.

B. Descendants

[if no living descendants] I have no living descendants.[6]

[if living descendants] I have [number] child[ren] [and [number] grand-children]. [description][7]

C. Parents

My parents are [Mother] and [Father].[8]

D. Siblings

[if no siblings] I have no siblings.

[if siblings] I have [number] siblings. [description][9]

E. Additional Family Description[10]

ARTICLE II
GENERAL PROVISIONS

A. Definitions[11]

B. Survival

If any beneficiary dies within [number] days of my death, such person shall be deemed to have predeceased me. The phrase "survives me" and similar expressions used in this will refer to this [number] day survival requirement.

---

6. Include a description of deceased descendants, if any.

7. Provide a description of each child and grandchild including identity of the other parent and date of birth. If any child was adopted, indicate this fact and the date of the adoption.

8. Indicate whether living or deceased.

9. Indicate names and whether living or deceased. If the family tree is relatively small, nieces and nephews may also be indicated.

10. Additional description of family members may be necessary if Client has few living relatives.

11. Define any terms used in the will which may cause controversy if left undefined. For example, if Client makes a class gift to "children," you should carefully explain whether Client intends to include adopted children and children born out of wedlock. The same considerations arise if a class gift is made to "grandchildren." In addition, Client should specify the age by which an adopted grandchild needs to be adopted by Client's child to fall within the class.

| _____ | _____ | _____ |
| [Client] | [Witness One] | [Witness Two] |

C. Express Disinheritance[12]

I expressly intend that my [description of relationship], [Name], take no property from my estate either under this will or by intestacy.

D. Pretermitted Children[13]

I intentionally make no provision for any child whom I may have or adopt after execution of this will.

E. Divorce[14]

If I am divorced from [Spouse] or [condition][15] at the time of death, all provisions in this will in favor of [Spouse] are to be given no effect. For purposes of this will, [Spouse] will then be treated as if [Spouse] predeceased me.

F. *In Terrorem* Provision[16]

If any beneficiary under this will [or the trust created herein] contests or challenges this will [or trust] or any of its [their] provisions in any manner, be it directly or indirectly (including the filing of a will contest action), all benefits given to the contesting or challenging beneficiary are revoked and those benefits pass as if the contesting beneficiary predeceased me without descendants.

---

12. If Client wishes to make certain an heir does not take any portion of the estate, even if by chance Client dies partially intestate, an express disinheritance provision is appropriate if local law recognizes negative will provisions. If Client fears that an as yet unknown person may claim paternity (such as occurred when Elvis "died"), you may include a statement such as, "I expressly disinherit any child of mine whom I have not expressly listed by name in Article [ ]."

13. An after-born or after-adopted children may be entitled to a statutory forced share. This provision may preclude the application of the statute. However, this section is not appropriate if Client intends to have or adopt children and wants them to share in the estate. Instead, these after-born and after-adopted children should be included as beneficiaries, such as by the use of a class gift to "children."

14. Provisions in favor of an ex-spouse are automatically revoked unless the will provides otherwise in most states. However, merely filing for divorce is not treated as a divorce and will not revoke any provisions of the will unless the will expressly so states.

15. State any condition Client wishes to trigger a revocation of spousal provisions, e.g., a filed and pending divorce petition.

16. This provision may prevent heirs who are also beneficiaries of the will (but who are not receiving as much as they would under intestacy) from contesting the will. Note that the clause may be unenforceable if the contestant has probable cause for instituting the proceedings and brings them in good faith.

| [Client] | [Witness One] | [Witness Two] |

G. Satisfaction[17]

No gift of any kind that I make under this will shall be considered either fully or partially satisfied by any inter vivos gift that I hereafter make.

H. Not Contractual[18]

At approximately the same time, [Spouse] and I are executing similar wills. The wills are not, however, the result of any contract or agreement between us and either will may be revoked at the sole discretion of its maker.

I. Anatomical Gifts[19]

I hereby confirm my intent to make the following anatomical gifts: [description of gift].[20]

J. Body Disposition Instructions[21]

I request that I be given a simple funeral and that my remains be [buried] [cremated] in an economical manner. It is my desire that the greatest possible portion of my estate pass to the beneficiaries I have named in this will.

ARTICLE III
SETTLEMENT OF ESTATE OBLIGATIONS[22]

A. Exoneration

[if no exoneration desired] All specific gifts made in this will pass subject

---

17. This provision prevents a remainder beneficiary from claiming that inter vivos gifts to the beneficiary of a pecuniary gift reduce the amount to which that beneficiary is entitled from the estate.

18. This provision is appropriate only if Client and Spouse are executing wills with parallel dispositive provisions.

19. Although anatomical gifts may be made by will, it is not prudent because Client's will may not be found and read until long after the time for making usable gifts has passed. Thus, a separate document is recommended. However, confirmation in a will may be helpful if the family is unsure about Client's intent reflected only by a less formal anatomical gift card.

20. Typical gifts include (1) certain specified organs such as the heart, liver, or kidneys; (2) any needed organ; and (3) the entire body.

21. Although body disposition instructions may be stated in a will, they will not be effective unless the will is found immediately after death. Thus, if permitted under state law, it is better practice to use a separate document or appoint an agent to control the disposition.

22. If Client is satisfied with some or all of the state law presumptions on the issues covered in this section, you may omit this Article or integrate the remaining provisions into Article II.

[Client]	[Witness One]	[Witness Two]

Last Will of Client
Page 5 of 13

to any mortgage, security interest, or other lien existing at the date of my death without right of exoneration.

[if exoneration desired] If any specific gift made in this will is subject to a mortgage, security interest, or other lien, I direct that my executor pay the debt from other property of my estate which is not specifically given.

B. Abatement

I direct the gifts made in this will abate in the following order: [order].

C. Apportionment

I direct that any tax payable because of a transfer of property upon my death, such as the federal and state estate tax, be paid from the following property of my estate in the order listed. [list]

ARTICLE IV
DISTRIBUTION OF PROPERTY[23]

[Option 1 — by type of gift]

A. Specific Gifts

I leave my [item[24]] to [Beneficiary]. If [Beneficiary] does not survive me, I leave my [item] to [Alternate Beneficiary].[25] If [item] is not in my estate, [ademption instructions].[26]

B. General Gifts

I leave [amount] to [Beneficiary]. If [Beneficiary] does not survive me, I leave [amount] to [Alternate Beneficiary].[27]

---

23. This form contains three popular distribution options. Do not feel bound by these suggestions; your goal is to provide for the distribution Client desires. You may find it useful to combine portions of each option.

24. Each gift must be precisely described so that there will be no doubt as to the item referred to after Client dies.

25. Naming an alternate beneficiary prevents the application of the anti-lapse statute even in cases where the family relationship is close enough to make the statute otherwise applicable.

26. Express instructions regarding ademption prevents the gift from failing if the Client wants Beneficiary to receive an alternate gift (e.g., another item or money) if the named item is no longer in the estate.

Continue in a similar manner for each specific gift. If several beneficiaries are to receive multiple items, consider drafting subsections titled with each beneficiary's name which list the gifts.

27. See note 25.

| [Client] | [Witness One] | [Witness Two] |

C. Residuary Gift[28]

I leave the residue of my estate to [Beneficiary]. If [Beneficiary] does not survive me, I leave the residue to [Alternate Beneficiary].[29]

[Option 2 — by identity of survivors — spouse and children example]

A. If Survived by [Spouse]

If I am survived by [Spouse], I leave [Spouse] all of my property.

B. If Not Survived by [Spouse][30]

If [Spouse] does not survive me, I leave all my property to [Children]. If any of my children predecease me survived by descendants who survive me, these surviving descendants receive the deceased child's share [description of type of distribution, e.g., per stirpes, per capita with representation, or per capita at each generation].[31]

C. If Not Survived by [Spouse] or Descendants

If I am survived by neither [Spouse] nor descendants, I leave all my property to [Beneficiary]. If [Beneficiary] does not survive me, I leave all my property to [Alternate Beneficiary].[32]

[Option 3 — conditional gifts — spouse and children example]

A. If Survived by [Spouse]

If I am survived by [Spouse], I leave [Spouse] all of my property.

B. If Not Survived by [Spouse] and My Youngest Child Is At Least [Age] Years Old[33]

If I am not survived by [Spouse] and if my youngest surviving child is at least [age] years old, I leave all my property to my surviving children.

---

28. The distributions contained in Option 2 and Option 3 may be used in place of this outright gift.

29. See note 25.

30. If the children are minors, consider using Option 3, which triggers a trust for underage children.

31. Revise this sentence if Client prefers surviving children to grandchildren, e.g., "If any of my children predecease me, the share which that child would have received had that child survived me shall be divided equally among my surviving children."

32. See note 25.

33. If Client desires to provide for children of deceased children (i.e., Client's grandchildren), this section needs to be revised appropriately. See §B of Option 2, above.

| [Client] | [Witness One] | [Witness Two] |

C. If Not Survived by [Spouse] and My Youngest Child Is Under [Age] Years Old[34]

If I am not survived by [Spouse] and if my youngest surviving child is under [age] years old, I leave all my property to the trustee, in trust, of the [Name] Trust created in Article V of this will.[35]

D. If Not Survived by Spouse or Children

If I am survived by neither [Spouse] nor children, I leave all my property to [Beneficiary].[36] If [Beneficiary] does not survive me, I leave all my property to [Alternate Beneficiary].[37]

ARTICLE V
[NAME] TRUST[38]

A. Conditions of Creation

This trust is to be created upon the conditions stated in Article IV.

B. Governing Law

This trust is to be governed by [State] law unless this Article provides to the contrary.

---

34. See note 33.

35. This provision assumes that Client's primary desire is to benefit the younger children. If Client's primary desire is to treat all children equally, this provision needs to be changed to give children over the stated age their shares outright with only shares for the younger children passing into the trust.

36. If Client names grandchildren, consider whether these shares should be held in trust.

37. See note 25.

38. This Article is appropriate if Client desires to create a testamentary trust. The example assumes that Client wishes to create the trust for the benefit of Client's children.

For a coordinated estate plan, consider having Client's life insurance and other death benefit contracts payable to this trust. For example, Client's spouse could be named as the primary beneficiary, the trust as the contingent beneficiary if the children are under the stated age, and the children outright if they are over the stated age or if for some reason this testamentary trust is not created.

This Article may also be used as a basic guide if you are preparing an inter vivos trust provided you address additional concerns such as the property Client wishes to transfer to the trust and whether or not Client may revoke the trust. Unless Client is creating the trust for tax purposes, Client probably wants to retain the power to revoke.

| [Client] | [Witness One] | [Witness Two] |

C. Trustees

I appoint [Trustee] as Trustee of this trust. If [Trustee] is unwilling or unable to serve, I appoint [Alternate Trustee] as trustee.

D. Bond

No bond shall be required of any trustee named in this Article.[39]

E. Trustee Compensation

[trustees to be compensated]

The trustee shall be entitled to reasonable compensation from the trust for serving as trustee.

[trustees to be uncompensated][40]

No trustee shall be entitled to compensation for serving as trustee.

F. Beneficiaries of Trust

The beneficiaries of this trust are [Children].[41]

G. Distribution of Trust Property Until Youngest Beneficiary Is At Least [Age] Years Old[42]

The trustee shall pay to or apply for the benefit of my children under [age] years old so much of the net income and so much of the principal, up to the whole thereof, of the trust property as the trustee in the trustee's sole discretion deems advisable for the beneficiary's proper care, support, education, medical expenses, and maintenance.[43] The trustee [is] [is not] required

---

39. If Client wishes to enhance beneficiary protection by requiring a bond, despite its cost, this provision should expressly state that the trustee must post bond.

40. A waiver of compensation may be appropriate if Client names a family member or close friend as the trustee. However, a corporate or other professional trustee will probably not accept the trust if Client prohibits compensation.

41. Depending on Client's circumstances, you may wish to list the children by name or use a class designation.

42. This provision assumes that Client's primary desire is to provide for the younger children. If Client's desire is to treat all children equally, this provision needs to provide for the trust property to be divided into shares, one for each child. Distributions for each child would then be limited to this share. As soon as a child reaches the stated age, the trustee would then distribute the balance of that child's share, if any, directly to the child.

43. The use of the property should be adjusted, if necessary, to fit Client's wishes. For example, some clients may wish to impose additional conditions, e.g., academic and disciplinary good standing in school.

_____   _____   _____
[Client]   [Witness One]   [Witness Two]

to treat each child equally. The trustee [may] [must] [need not] consider the beneficiary's other resources and income in making distribution decisions.[44]

[if Client also wishes to provide benefits for older children]

If in the trustee's opinion the trust income and corpus will be sufficient to satisfy the needs of my children who are under [age] years old for the duration of this trust, the trustee may pay to or apply for the benefit of my children who are at least [age] years old so much of the income [and principal] as the trustee in the trustee's sole discretion deems advisable for the beneficiary's proper care, support, education, medical expenses, and maintenance. The trustee [is] [is not] required to treat each child equally. The trustee [may] [must] [need not] consider the beneficiary's other resources and income in making distribution decisions.[45]

H. Events Causing Termination of this Trust[46]

This trust terminates when the first of the following events occurs:

1. The death of all the beneficiaries [my children], or
2. My youngest child beneficiary becoming [age] years old.

I. Distribution of Property Upon Termination

1. If this trust terminates because of the death of all the beneficiaries [my children], the trustee shall deliver all remaining trust property to [Beneficiary].[47] If [Beneficiary] is not living at the time of trust termination, the trustee shall deliver all remaining trust property to [Alternate Beneficiary].

2. If this trust terminates because my youngest child reaches [age] years of age, the trustee shall deliver all remaining trust property to my then surviving children in equal shares.[48]

---

44. Adjust this provision to carry out Client's intent, i.e., is the trust to provide a minimum level of support and anything the beneficiary has or acquires is irrelevant or is the trust to provide a safety net if the client's other resources and income are inadequate.

45. See note 44.

46. If Client wishes to provide for grandchildren, this provision needs to be revised accordingly. This is especially the case if any of the grandchildren are minors.

47. Grandchildren, if any, are commonly named as remainder beneficiaries. Client may wish to have the shares of grandchildren held under the terms of the trust until they reach a stated age within the bounds of the Rule against Perpetuities.

48. If Client wishes to provide for grandchildren (i.e., children of deceased children), this provision needs to be revised accordingly; e.g., create one share for each surviving

---

| [Client] | [Witness One] | [Witness Two] |

J. Spendthrift Provision[49]

This is a spendthrift trust, that is, to the fullest extent permitted by law, no interest in the income or principal of this trust may be voluntarily or involuntarily transferred by any beneficiary before payment or delivery of the interest by the trustee.

K. Principal and Income[50]

The trustee shall have the discretion to credit a receipt or charge an expenditure to income or principal or partly to each in any manner which the trustee determines to be reasonable and equitable.

L. Trustee Powers[51]

[if Client is satisfied with default powers]

The trustee shall have all powers granted to trustees under [State] law.

[if Client wishes to alter default powers]

The trustee shall have the following powers in addition to the powers [State] law grants trustees: [description]

The trustee shall not have the following powers which are ordinarily accorded trustees under [State] law: [description]

M. Exculpatory Clause[52]

The trustee shall not be liable for any loss, cost, damage, or expense sustained through any error of judgment or in any other manner except for and as a result of a trustee's own bad faith or gross negligence.

---

child and one share for each deceased child who left surviving descendants who are still alive and then give one share to each surviving child and distribute a share created for a deceased child to that child's descendants.

49. Most clients will be excited about the possibility of preventing the beneficiaries from transferring their interest as well as protecting that interest from the beneficiaries' creditors.

50. To make it easier for noncorporate trustees to administer the trust, it may be advisable to include this provision which grants the trustee discretion. This provision is less likely to be used if Client names a professional or corporate trustee because they have the expertise and bookkeeping systems to make the allocation.

51. Extensive trustee powers may be provided by state statute. If Client wishes the trustee to retain any particular item in the trust (e.g., a family heirloom or the family home) without regard to diversification or its wisdom as an investment, include an express provision permitting the retention.

52. This provision will increase the likelihood that a trustee, especially a noncorporate one, will accept the trust.

<table>
<tr><td>_____</td><td>_____</td><td>_____</td></tr>
<tr><td>[Client]</td><td>[Witness One]</td><td>[Witness Two]</td></tr>
</table>

Last Will of Client
Page 11 of 13

N. Rule Against Perpetuities Savings Clause

If a court of proper jurisdiction finds that this trust violates the Rule Against Perpetuities, the remaining trust property shall be distributed to [Beneficiary].

ARTICLE VI
ESTATE ADMINISTRATION

A. Appointment of Executor

I appoint [Executor] as executor of this will. If [Executor] is unwilling or unable to serve, I appoint [Alternate Executor] as executor.

B. Creation of [ ] Administration[53]

C. Bond[54]

No bond shall be required of any executor named in this will.

D. Executor Compensation[55]

[executor to be compensated]

The executor shall be entitled to reasonable compensation for serving as the executor of my estate.

[executor to be uncompensated][56]

The executor shall not be entitled to compensation for serving as the executor of my estate.

E. Executor Powers[57]

I vest my executor with full power and authority to sell, lease, encumber, or otherwise dispose of or convert any or all of my estate in such a manner

---

53. If state law requires specific language to authorize a desired type of administration, such as an independent administration, include the appropriate language.

54. If Client wishes to enhance beneficiary protection by requiring a bond, despite its cost, this provision should expressly state that the executor must post bond.

55. In the absence of a provision waiving compensation, the executor is usually entitled to compensation as determined by state law.

56. A waiver of compensation may be appropriate if Client names a family member or close friend as the executor. However, a corporate or other professional executor will probably not agree to serve if Client prohibits compensation.

57. This section provides a broad grant of powers. Revise this section as needed if Client wishes to restrict the executor's powers or to provide an unusual power.

[Client]	[Witness One]	[Witness Two]

as my executor may see fit, it being my desire that, subject only to the terms of this will, my executor shall have full power and authority to do all things reasonably necessary for the settlement of my estate.

F. Exculpatory Clause[58]

The executor shall not be liable for any loss, cost, damage, or expense sustained through any error of judgment or in any other manner except for and as a result of the executor's own bad faith or gross negligence.

ARTICLE VII
GUARDIANS AND CONSERVATORS[59]

A. Guardian of Person

I appoint [Guardian] as guardian of the person of [Child]. If [Guardian] is unwilling or unable to serve, I appoint [Alternate Guardian] as guardian of [Child].

B. Guardian [Conservator] of Estate

I request that the guardian of the person named in subsection A above also seek appointment as guardian [conservator] of [Child's] estate.

C. Waiver of Bond[60]

I direct that no bond or other security shall be required of any guardian appointed in my will.

TESTIMONIUM

I hereby sign my name to this my last will [in blue ink],[61] consisting of this and the [number] preceding pages (each of which I am initialing and/or signing for the purpose of identification), all in the presence of the two

---

58. This provision will increase the likelihood that an executor, especially a noncorporate one, will accept the position.

59. This Article is appropriate if Client has a minor child. Guardian appointments are typically effective only upon the death of the surviving parent. Many states permit guardian and conservator appointments by way of a separate document as well as in a will.

60. Some states do not permit Client to waive bond for guardians.

61. Writing on a will should be in a color other than black (most commonly blue) to make an obvious distinction between the original and a photocopy.

_____   _____   _____
        [Client]   [Witness One]   [Witness Two]

persons who have at my request and in my presence acted as witnesses on this the [day] day of [month], [year], at [city], [state].

_____
[Client]

ATTESTATION

The foregoing instrument consisting of this and the [number] preceding pages was signed, published, and declared by [Client] to be [his] [her] last will. We now, at [his] [her] request, in [his] [her] presence, subscribe our names [in blue ink][62] as witnesses this the [day] day of [month], [year]. For identification, we have each initialed or signed the [number] preceding pages of this will.

_____   _____
[Witness One]   [Witness Two]

_____   _____
[Address]   [Address]

_____   _____
Social Security Number[63]   Social Security Number

_____

62. See note 61.

63. Although it is not legally necessary for the witnesses to provide their addresses or social security numbers, this information makes it easier to locate the witnesses if they are needed during the probate of Client's will.

_____   _____   _____
[Client]   [Witness One]   [Witness Two]

SELF-PROVING AFFIDAVIT[64]

THE STATE OF TEXAS   }
                          }
COUNTY OF [County]   }

Before me, the undersigned authority, on this date personally appeared [Client], [Witness One], and [Witness Two], known to me to be the [testator] [testatrix] and the witnesses, respectively, whose names are subscribed to the annexed or foregoing instrument in their respective capacities, and, all of said persons being by me duly sworn, the said [Client], [testator] [testatrix], declared to me and the said witnesses in my presence that said instrument is [his] [her] last will and testament, and that [he] [she] had willingly made and executed it as [his] [her] free act and deed; and the said witnesses, each on his or her oath stated to me, in the presence and hearing of the said [testator] [testatrix], that the said [testator] [testatrix] had declared to them that said instrument is [his] [her] last will and testament, and that [he] [she] executed same as such and wanted each of them to sign it as a witness; and upon their oaths each witness stated further that they did sign the same as witnesses in the presence of the said [testator] [testatrix] and at [his] [her] request; that [he] [she] was at that time eighteen years of age or over (or being under such age, was or had been lawfully married, or was then a member of the armed forces of the United States or of an auxiliary thereof or of the Maritime Service) and was of sound mind; and that each of said witnesses was then at least fourteen years of age.

_____
[Client]

_____   _____
[Witness One]   [Witness Two]

Subscribed and sworn to before me by the said [Client], [testator] [testatrix], and by the said [Witness One] and [Witness Two], witnesses, this [day] day of [month], [year].

[seal]   _____
                                Notary Public

                                My commission expires:

                                _____

---

64. This form is based on the Texas statutory form. Most states have statutes that contain the appropriate form for the self-proving affidavit.

_____   _____   _____
  [Client]   [Witness One]   [Witness Two]

Bibliography

This book is designed to provide you with the information you need to master a law school course in wills, trusts, and estates. However, you may need more information on a particular topic or would benefit from a different approach to the same material. Below is a bibliography of other sources you may wish to consult if the occasion arises.

Thomas E. Atkinson, Law of Wills (2d ed. 1953) (one-volume treatise extensively footnoted; stresses historical development and common law).

Lawrence H. Averill, Jr., Uniform Probate Code in a Nutshell (4th ed. 1996) (detailed coverage of UPC).

Thomas F. Bergin & Paul G. Haskell, Preface to Estates in Land and Future Interests (2d ed. 1984).

George T. Bogert, Trusts (6th ed. 1987) (one-volume treatise extensively footnoted).

Regis W. Campfield, Estate Planning and Drafting (2d ed. 1995).

A. James Casner & Jeffrey N. Pennell, Estate Planning (1980 & most recent supplement) (emphasis on taxation).

Paul G. Haskell, Preface to Wills, Trusts and Administration (2d ed. 1994).

L. Rush Hunt, A Lawyer's Guide to Estate Planning (1995).

Robert J. Lynn, Introduction to Estate Planning (4th ed. 1992).

William M. McGovern, Jr., et al., Wills, Trusts and Estates Including Taxation of Future Interests (1988) (detailed treatise extensively footnoted; stresses modern law).

John Makdisi, Estates in Land and Future Interests (2d ed. 1995) (concise and understandable text with over 400 problems; highly recommended if your course has an estate and future interest component).

Robert L. Mennell, Wills and Trusts in a Nutshell (2d ed. 1994).

W. Leslie Peat & Stephanie J. Willbanks, Federal Estate and Gift Taxation: An Analysis and Critique (1991).

Chris J. Prestopino, Estate Planning and Taxation (most recent ed.) (emphasizes fundamentals).

Mark Reutlinger, Wills, Trusts, and Estates — Essential Terms and Concepts (2d ed. 1998) ("quick reference text geared to specific terms and concepts").

Austin Wakeman Scott, Abridgment of the Law of Trusts (1960) (detailed one-volume treatise with emphasis on common law).

Austin Wakeman Scott, William Franklin Fratcher & Mark L. Ascher, Scott on Trusts (comprehensive 12-volume treatise).

Thomas L. Shaffer & Carol Ann Mooney, The Planning and Drafting of Wills and Trusts (1991) (humanistic approach).

Richard B. Stephens, et al., Federal Estate and Gift Taxation (most recent edition).

Harold Weinstock, Planning An Estate (most recent ed.) (stresses taxation issues).

David Westfall & George P. Mair, Estate Planning Law and Taxation (3d ed. 1994).

Table of Uniform Probate Code (UPC) Provisions

Table of Internal Revenue Code (IRC) Provisions

Index

[References are to sections.]